SATURDAY AM

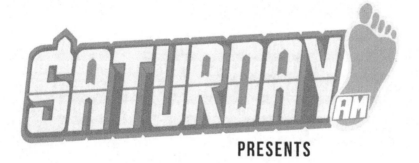

PRESENTS

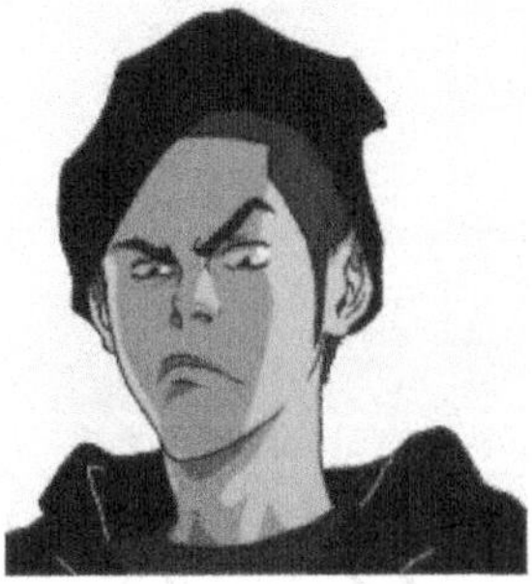

WITH THE RELEASE OF THIS BOOK, ONE OF MY MANY DREAMS HAS BEEN ACCOMPLISHED. THIS COMIC, APPLE BLACK, HAS GONE THROUGH SO MANY CHANGES, DEVELOPMENTS AND IMPROVEMENTS OVER THE YEARS, BOTH STORY AND ART WITH ME GROWING AND LEARNING AS AN ARTIST AND AS A PERSON. I AM PROUD OF THE RESULTS AND I HOPE TO WORK EVEN HARDER AS I GO ON THIS JOURNEY COMPLETING THE STORY AND IN LIFE AS A WHOLE. I WILL BE EVEN HAPPIER IF APPLE BLACK, MY FIRST BOOK, IS ENJOYED BY ALL THOSE WHO READ IT. A LOT OF BLOOD, SWEAT, TEARS AND SACRIFICE WAS PUT IN TO THIS BOOK AND I BELIEVED IT WAS ALL WORTH IT.

-ODUNZE OGUGUO [WHYTMANGA]

AUTHOR | ARTIST ODUNZE OGUGUO, NIGERIAN, WAS BORN IN 1992.
OGUGUO IS THE CREATOR AND OWNER OF THE SERIES "APPLE BLACK".
OGUGUO IS ONE OF THE CO-FOUNDERS OF MYFUTPRINT ENTERTAINMENT LLC.
OGUGUO GRADUATED FROM THE UNIVERSITY OF TEXAS AT ARLINGTON WITH A BACHELORS IN FINE ARTS AND A MINOR IN COMPUTER SCIENCE.
OGUGUO IS ALSO KNOWN ONLINE BY THE NAME "WHYTMANGA".
"APPLE BLACK" WAS ORIGINALLY JUST "BLACK" BUT AFTER OGUGUO TAKING SOME HISTORY CLASSES AND GETTING INSPIRATIONS FROM A LOT OF THINGS INCLUDING MOST RELIGIONS, THE "APPLE" WAS INCLUDED BECAUSE OF IT'S SYMBOLIC MEANING. THE NEW TITLE ALSO TIED IN SEAMLESSLY WITH THE ACTUAL STORY.

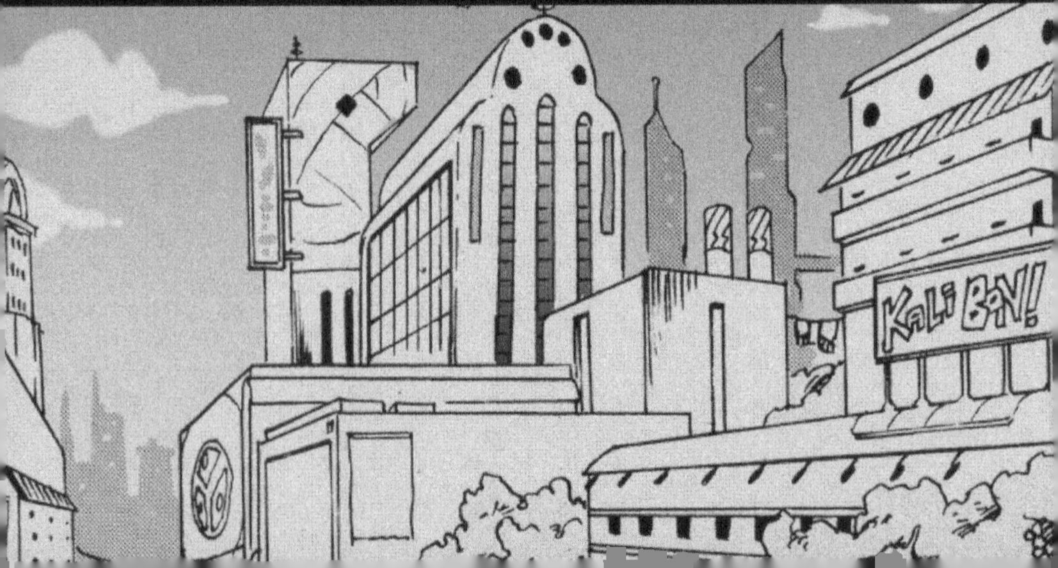
KaLi BaN!

APPLE BLACK

VOL. 1

FREEDOM DAYS

STORY AND ART BY

ODUNZE OGUGUO [WHYTMANGA]

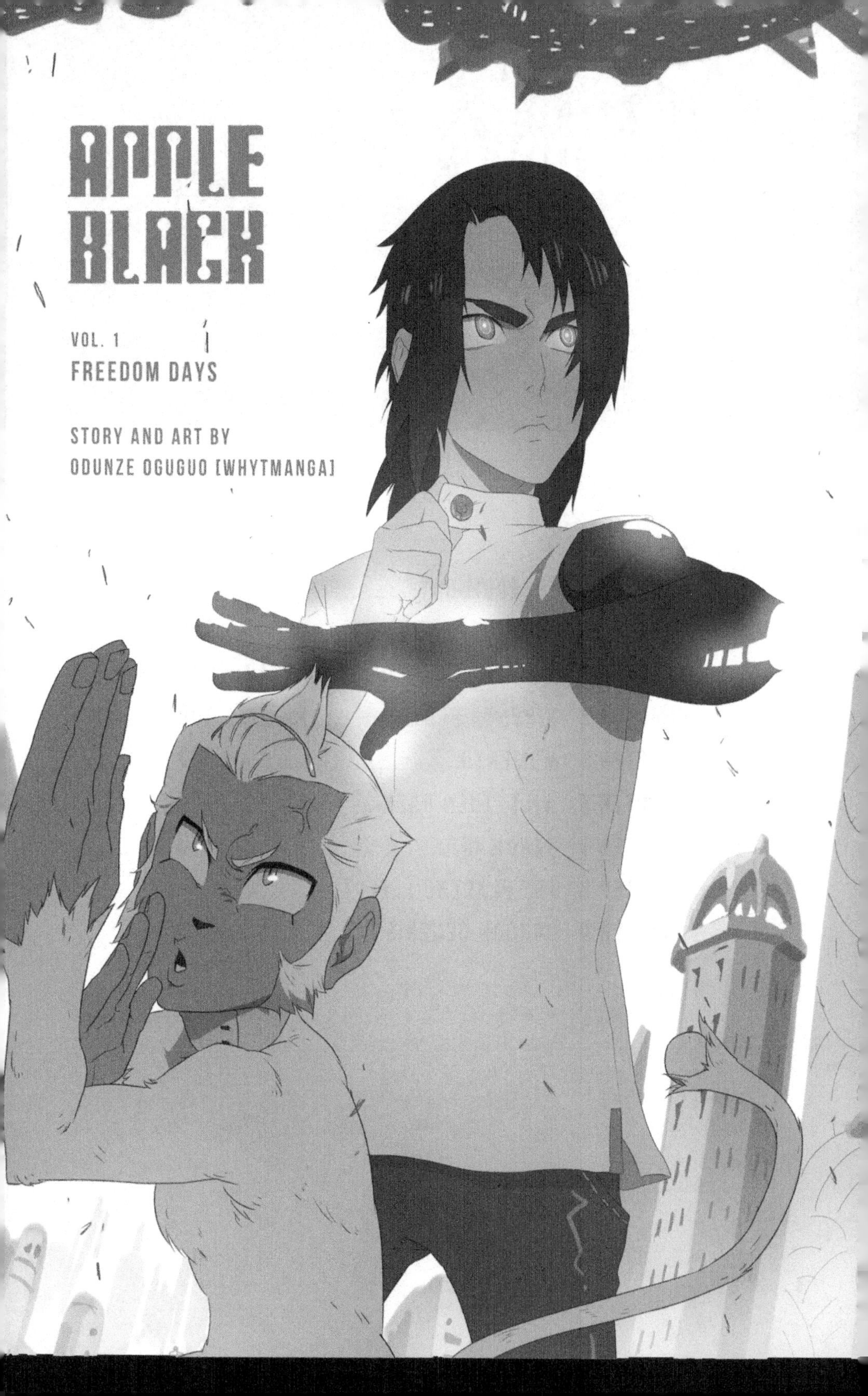

APPLE BLACK

VOL. 1
FREEDOM DAYS

CONTENTS

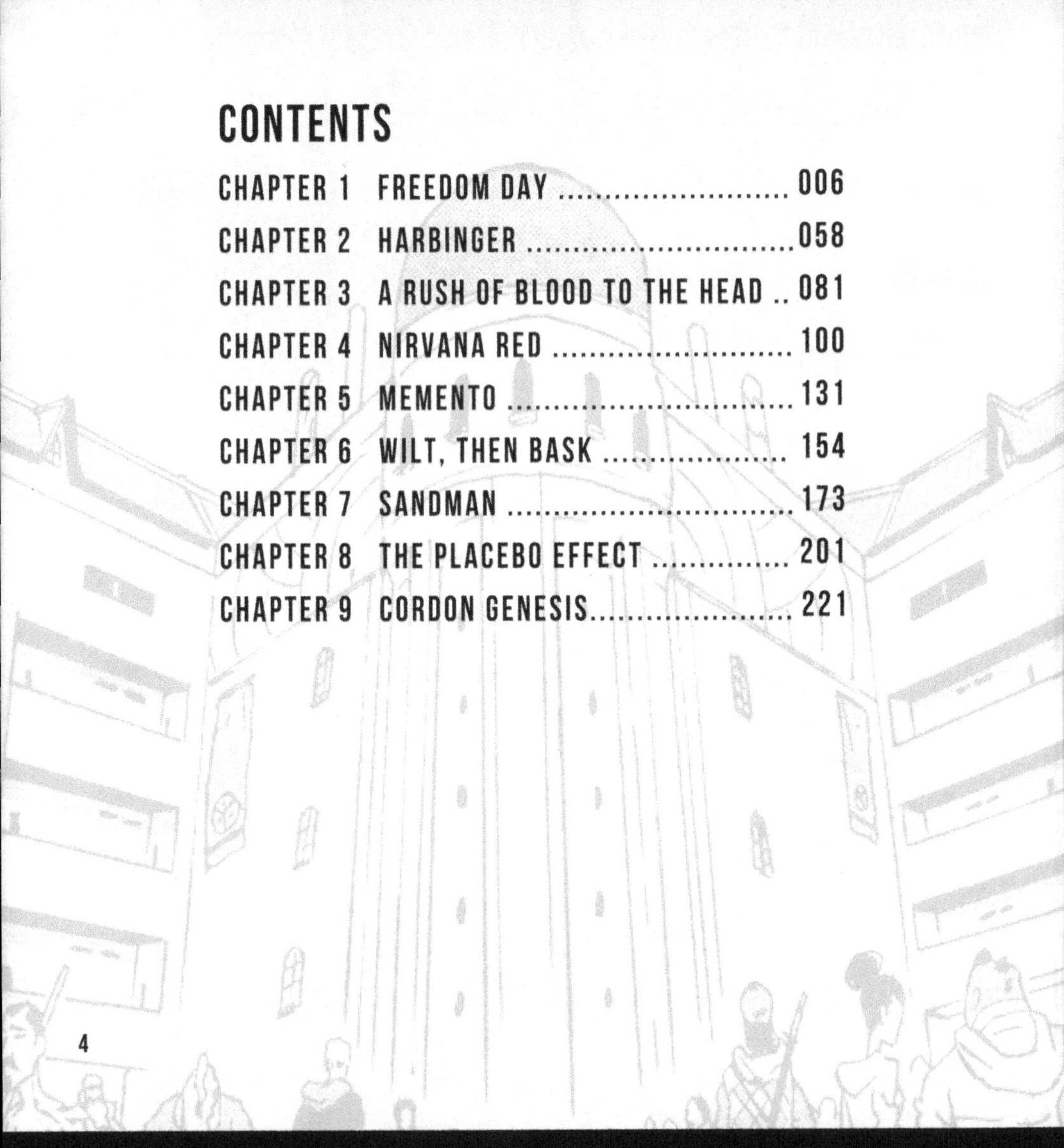

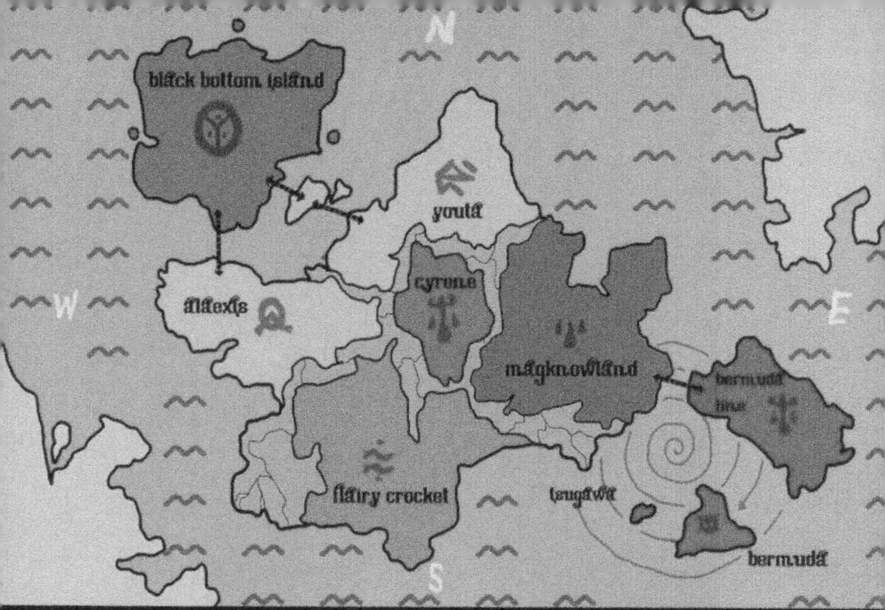
N
black bottom island
youta
W
alaexis
cyrene
E
magknowland
bermuda
flairy crocket
tsugawa
bermuda
S

MAP OF EDEN

THE EDEN CONTINENT CONSISTS OF SIX MAIN COUNTRIES NAMELY, ALAEXIS, BLACK BOTTOM ISLAND, CYRENE, FLAIRY CROCKET, MAGKNOWLAND AND YOUTA. THE COUNTRY "CYRENE" IS THE CAPITAL OF EDEN. THESE COUNTRIES WERE FORMED AS PART OF THE PEACE TREATY BY ALL EXISTING TRIBES AFTER THE EBONY PEAK WAR 15 YEARS AGO, THUS THE NEW EDEN REGIME WAS BORN.

APPLE BLACK
whyt MANGA
1
FREEDOM DAY
Story & Art by
ODUNZE W. OGUGUO
TWITTER.COM/WHYTMANGA
FACEBOOK.COM/WHYTMANGA
ODUNZE.DEVIANTART.COM

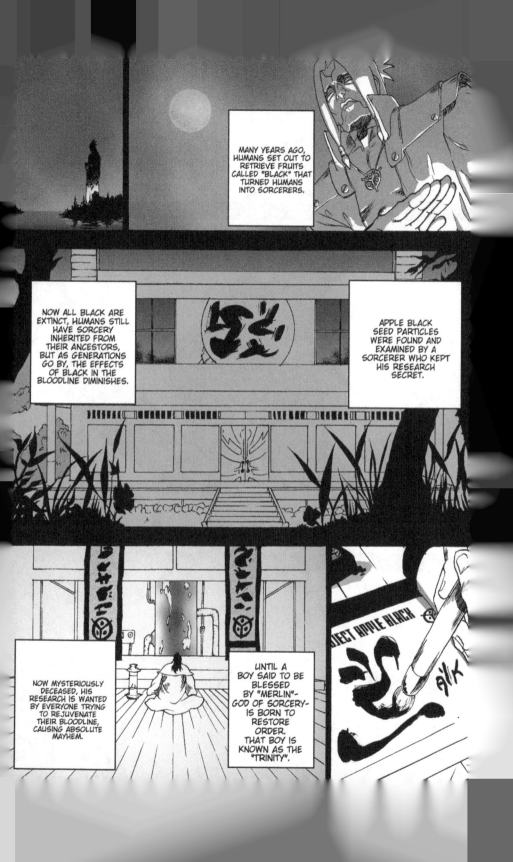

MANY YEARS AGO, HUMANS SET OUT TO RETRIEVE FRUITS CALLED "BLACK" THAT TURNED HUMANS INTO SORCERERS.

NOW ALL BLACK ARE EXTINCT, HUMANS STILL HAVE SORCERY INHERITED FROM THEIR ANCESTORS, BUT AS GENERATIONS GO BY, THE EFFECTS OF BLACK IN THE BLOODLINE DIMINISHES.

APPLE BLACK SEED PARTICLES WERE FOUND AND EXAMINED BY A SORCERER WHO KEPT HIS RESEARCH SECRET.

NOW MYSTERIOUSLY DECEASED, HIS RESEARCH IS WANTED BY EVERYONE TRYING TO REJUVENATE THEIR BLOODLINE, CAUSING ABSOLUTE MAYHEM.

UNTIL A BOY SAID TO BE BLESSED BY "MERLIN"- GOD OF SORCERY- IS BORN TO RESTORE ORDER. THAT BOY IS KNOWN AS THE "TRINITY".

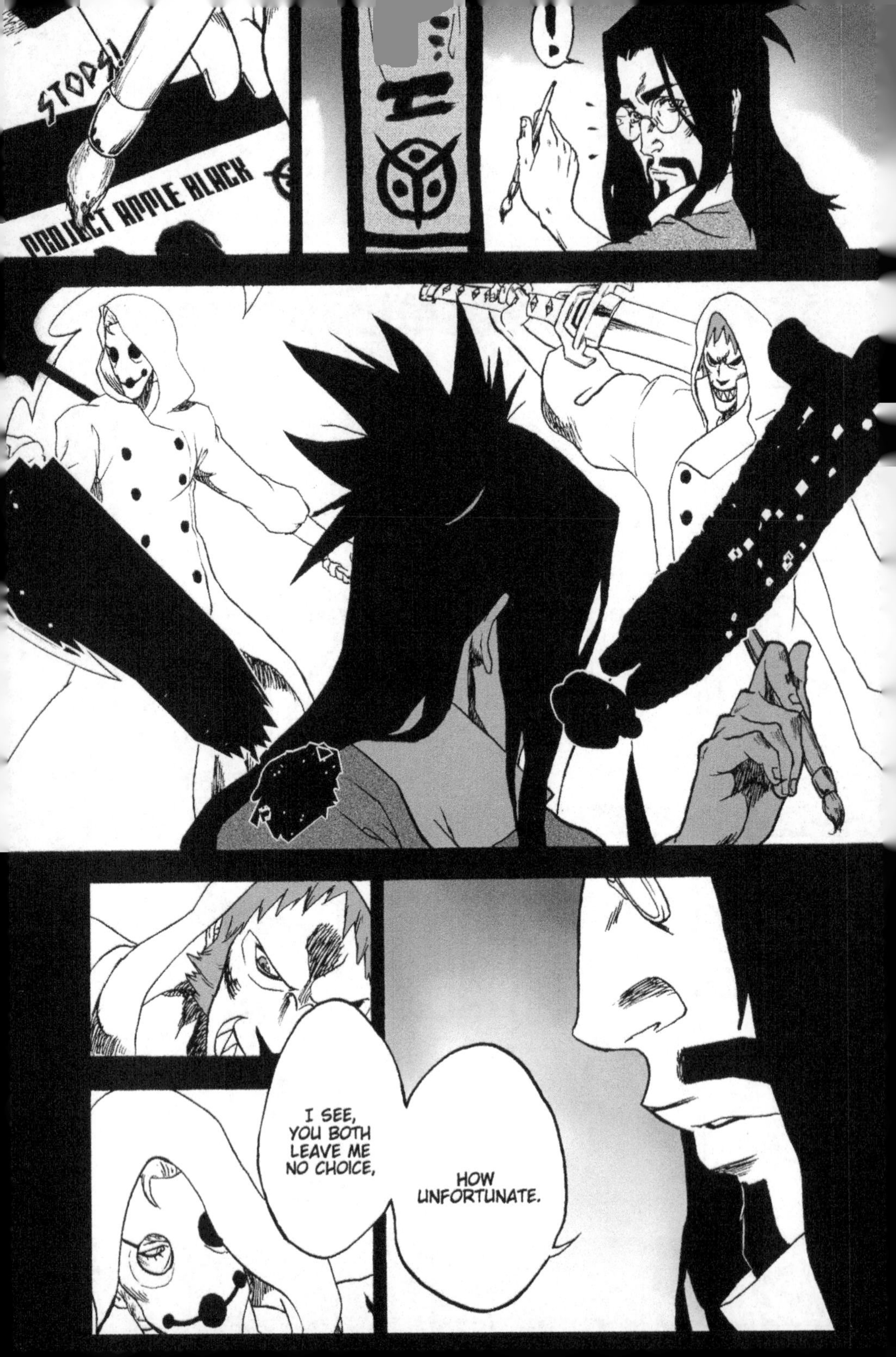
STOPS!
PROJECT APPLE BLACK
!
I SEE, YOU BOTH LEAVE ME NO CHOICE,
HOW UNFORTUNATE.

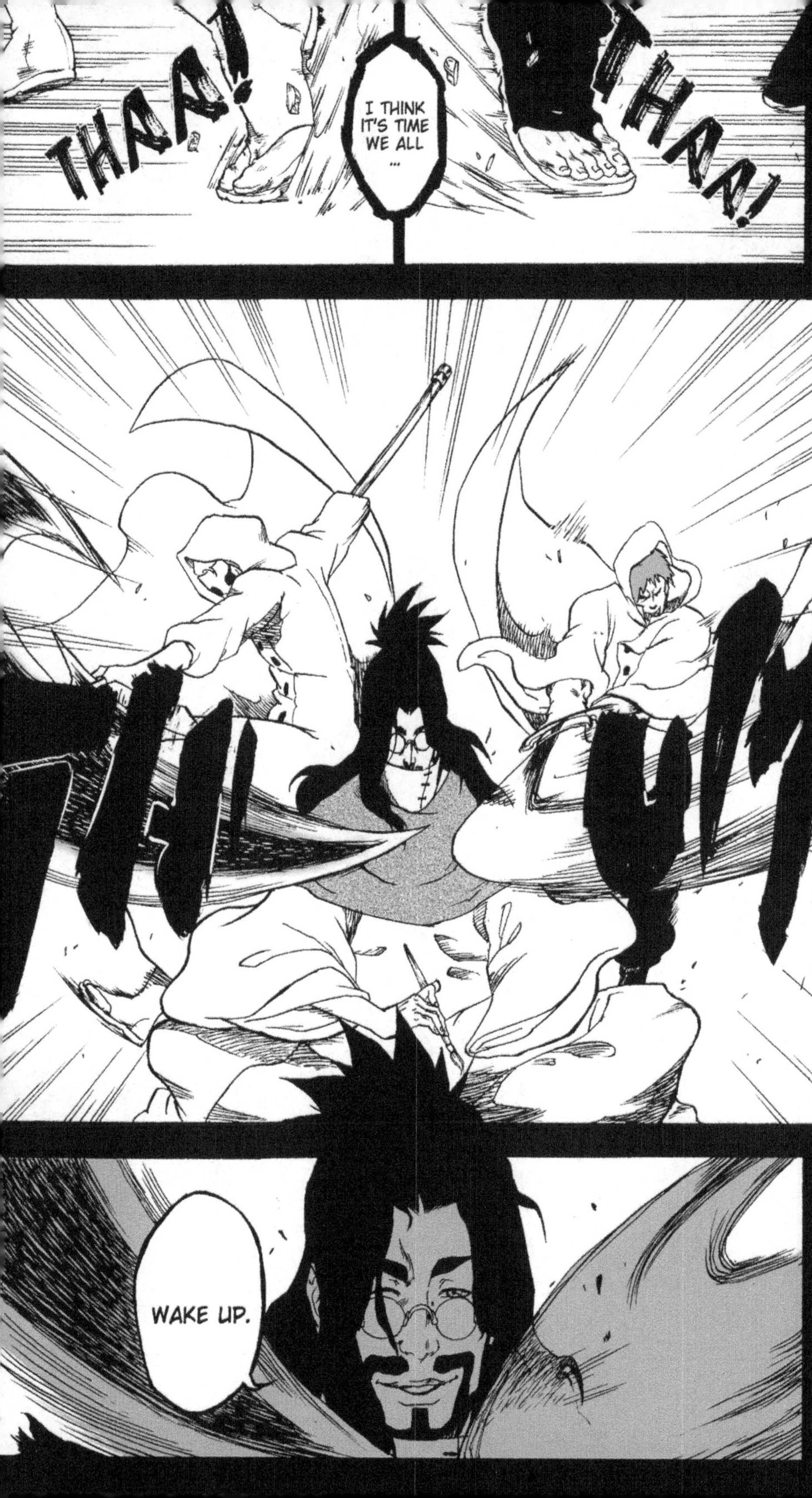
THAA!
I THINK IT'S TIME WE ALL ...
THAA!
WAKE UP.

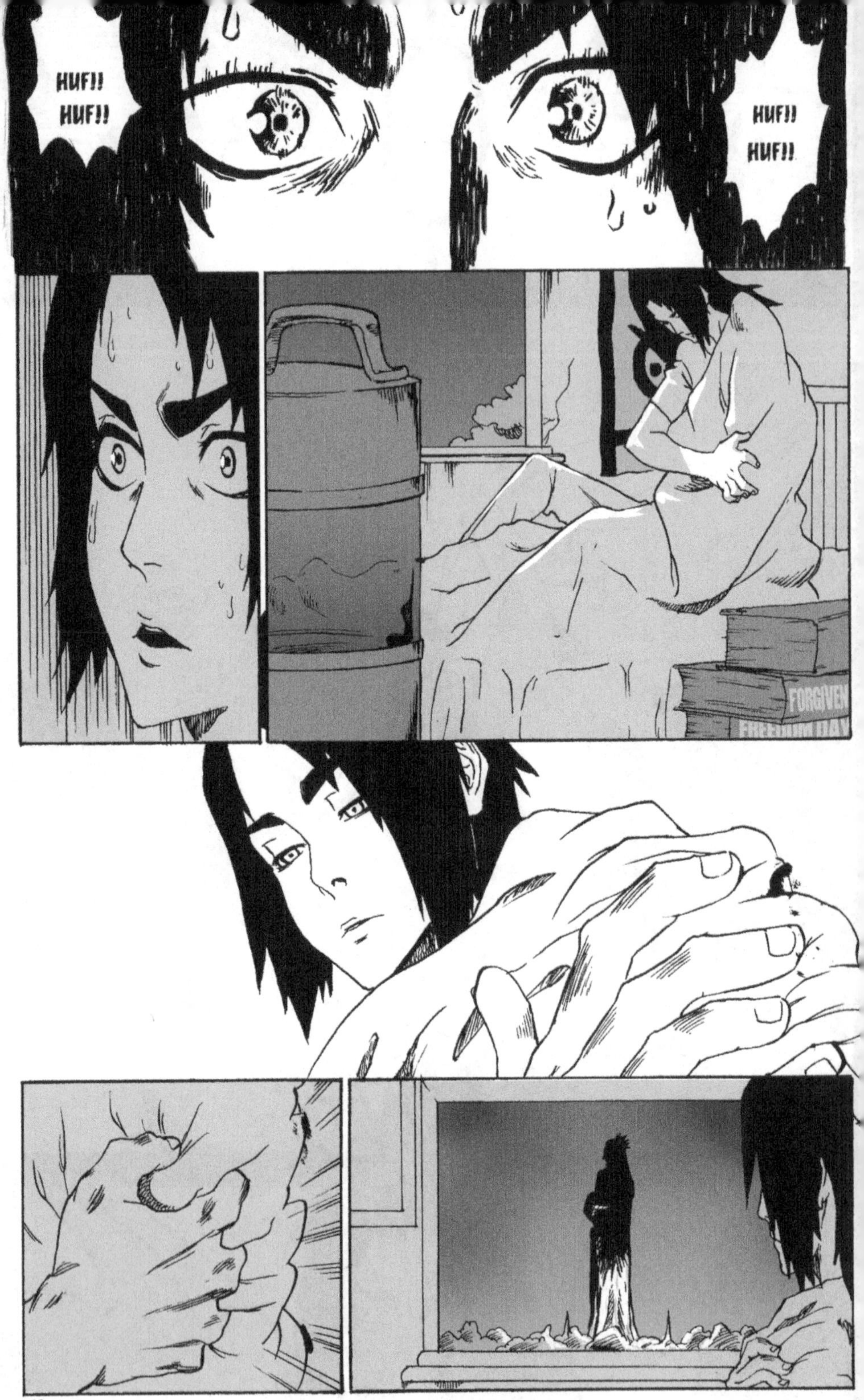
HUF!!
HUF!!
HUF!!
HUF!!
FORGIVEN

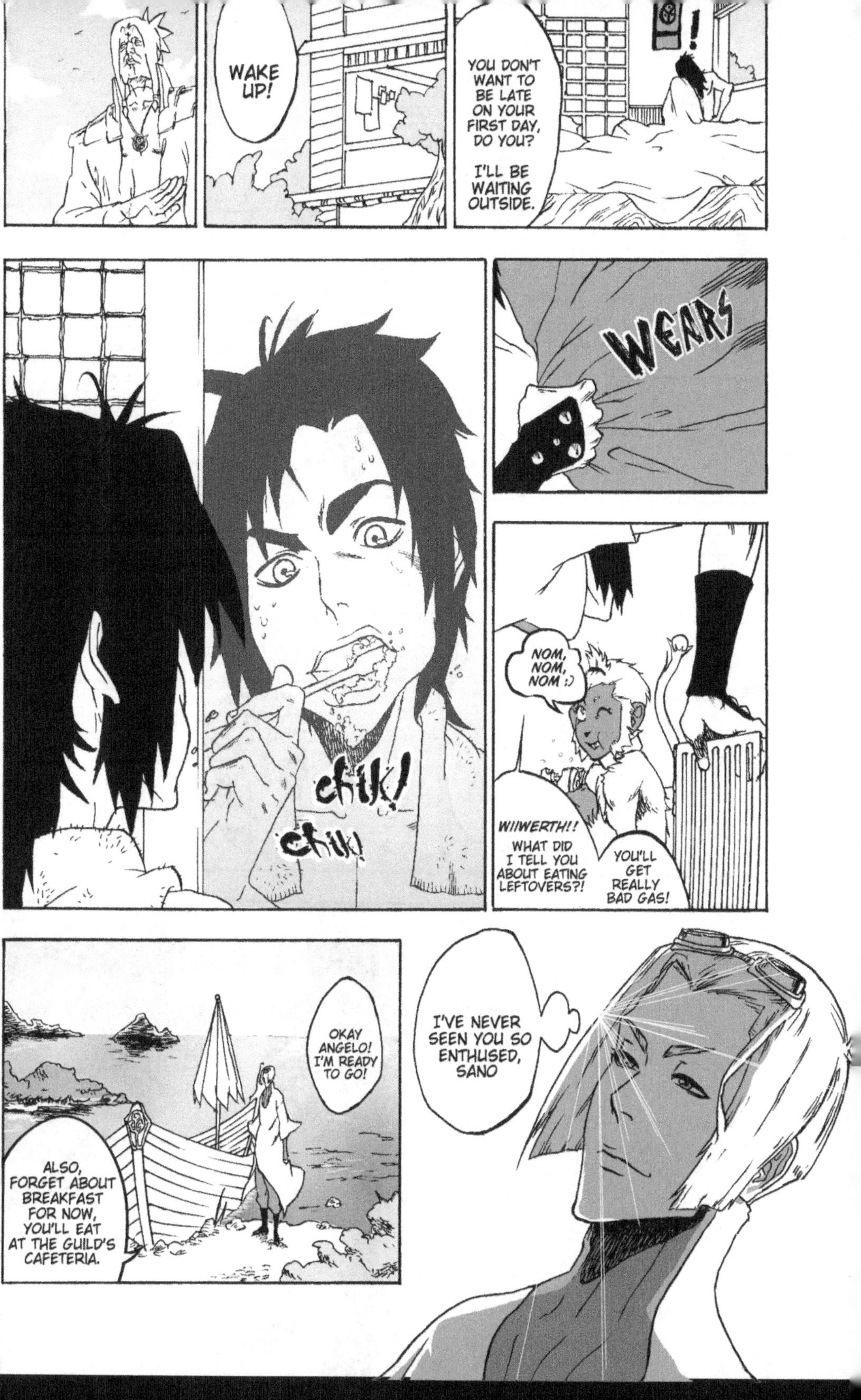
WAKE UP!
YOU DON'T WANT TO BE LATE ON YOUR FIRST DAY, DO YOU?
I'LL BE WAITING OUTSIDE.
!
chik!
chik!
WEARS
NOM, NOM, NOM :)
WIIWERTH!! WHAT DID I TELL YOU ABOUT EATING LEFTOVERS?!
YOU'LL GET REALLY BAD GAS!
OKAY ANGELO! I'M READY TO GO!
ALSO, FORGET ABOUT BREAKFAST FOR NOW, YOU'LL EAT AT THE GUILD'S CAFETERIA.
I'VE NEVER SEEN YOU SO ENTHUSED, SANO

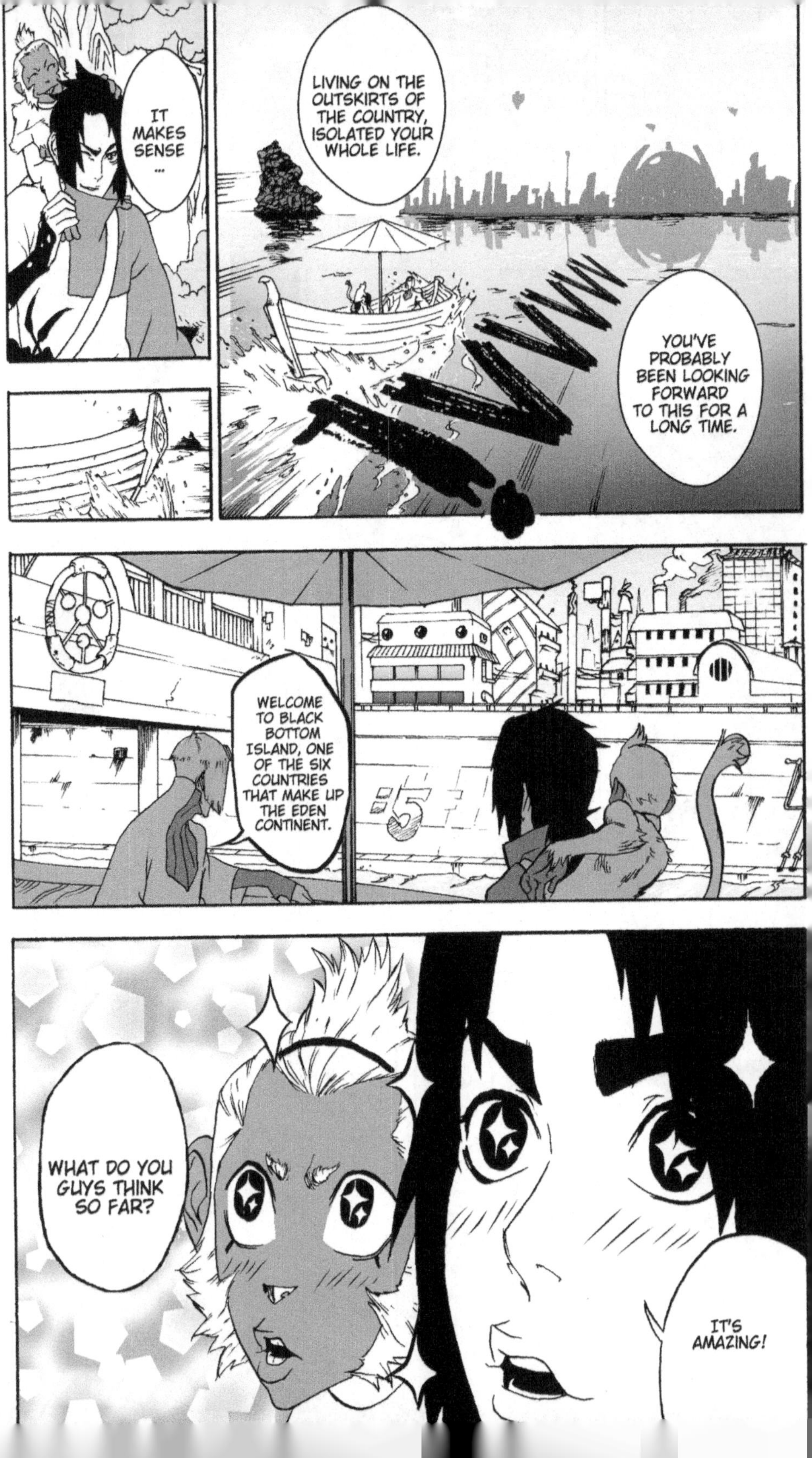
IT MAKES SENSE ...
LIVING ON THE OUTSKIRTS OF THE COUNTRY, ISOLATED YOUR WHOLE LIFE.
YOU'VE PROBABLY BEEN LOOKING FORWARD TO THIS FOR A LONG TIME.
WELCOME TO BLACK BOTTOM ISLAND, ONE OF THE SIX COUNTRIES THAT MAKE UP THE EDEN CONTINENT.
WHAT DO YOU GUYS THINK SO FAR?
IT'S AMAZING!

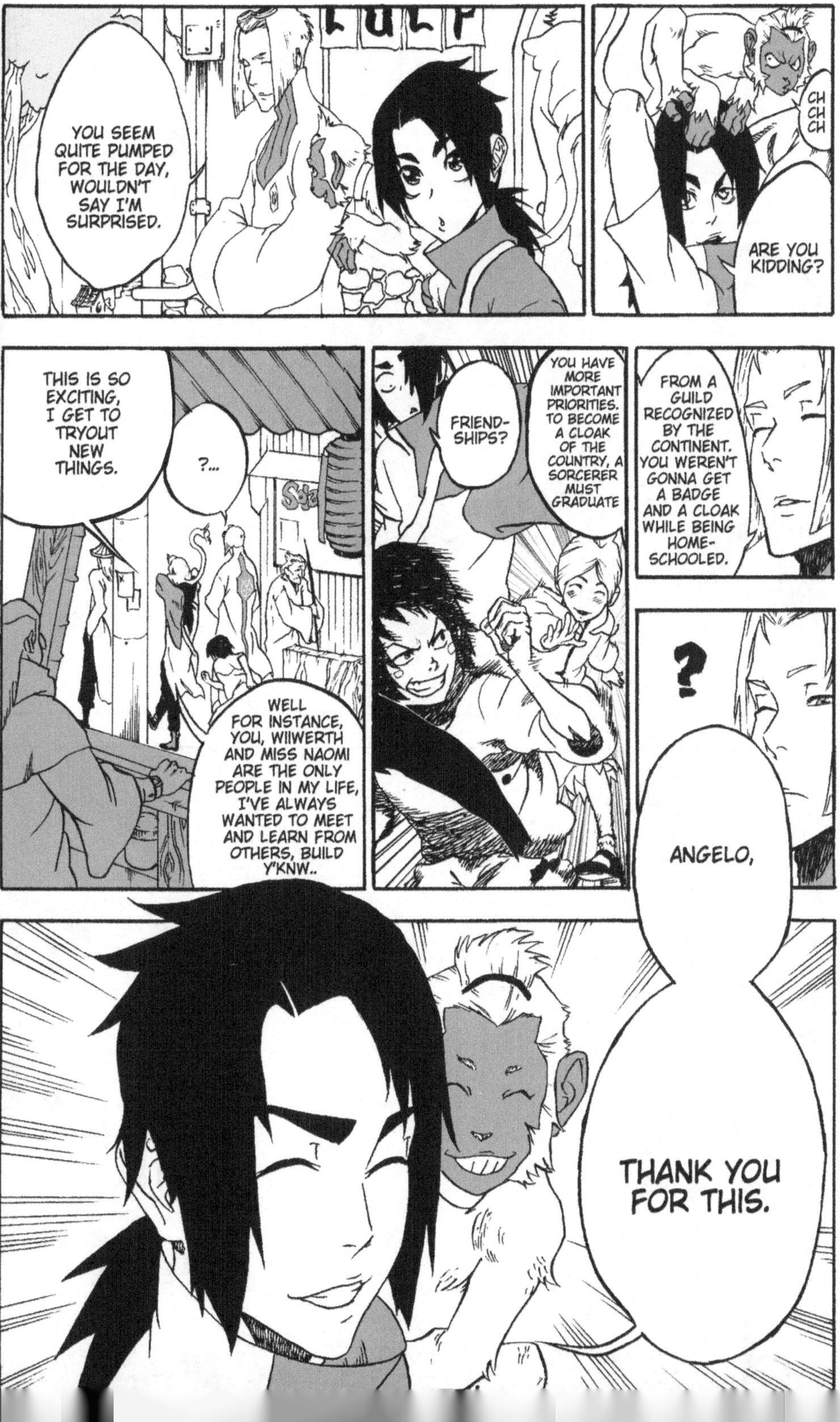
YOU SEEM QUITE PUMPED FOR THE DAY, WOULDN'T SAY I'M SURPRISED.
CH CH CH
ARE YOU KIDDING?
THIS IS SO EXCITING, I GET TO TRYOUT NEW THINGS.
?...
WELL FOR INSTANCE, YOU, WIIWERTH AND MISS NAOMI ARE THE ONLY PEOPLE IN MY LIFE, I'VE ALWAYS WANTED TO MEET AND LEARN FROM OTHERS, BUILD Y'KNW..
FRIEND-SHIPS?
YOU HAVE MORE IMPORTANT PRIORITIES. TO BECOME A CLOAK OF THE COUNTRY, A SORCERER MUST GRADUATE
FROM A GUILD RECOGNIZED BY THE CONTINENT. YOU WEREN'T GONNA GET A BADGE AND A CLOAK WHILE BEING HOME-SCHOOLED.
?
ANGELO,
THANK YOU FOR THIS.

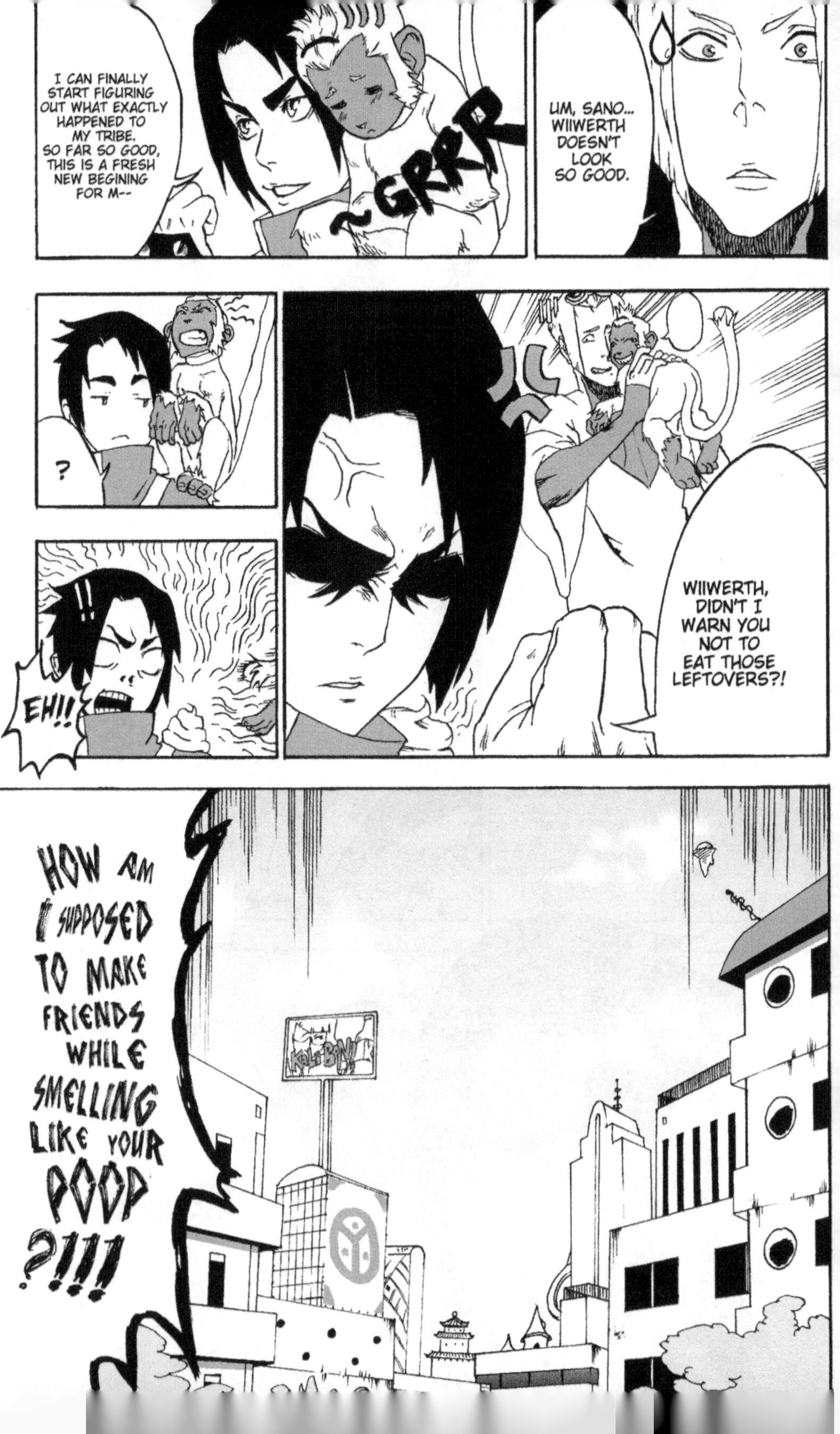
I CAN FINALLY START FIGURING OUT WHAT EXACTLY HAPPENED TO MY TRIBE. SO FAR SO GOOD, THIS IS A FRESH NEW BEGINING FOR M--
~GRRR
UM, SANO... WIIWERTH DOESN'T LOOK SO GOOD.
?
EH!!
WIIWERTH, DIDN'T I WARN YOU NOT TO EAT THOSE LEFTOVERS?!
HOW AM I SUPPOSED TO MAKE FRIENDS WHILE SMELLING LIKE YOUR POOP ?!!!

NOW THIS IS JUST PATHETIC.

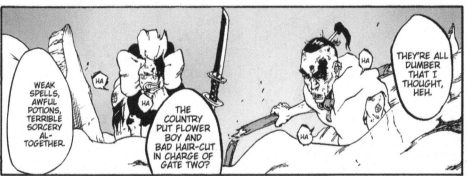

WEAK SPELLS, AWFUL POTIONS, TERRIBLE SORCERY ALTOGETHER.

THE COUNTRY PUT FLOWER BOY AND BAD HAIR-CUT IN CHARGE OF GATE TWO?

THEY'RE ALL DUMBER THAT I THOUGHT, HEH.

HA

HA

HA

HA

HOW POINTLESS.

YOU'RE A FOOL TO THINK YOU COULD GET INTO THE COUNTRY ALONE AND UNNOTICED! OUR DEFENSE SYSTEMS HAVE DETECTED YOU AND ALERTED THE MAIN HEADQUARTERS

EVEN IF YOU DEFEAT US, WE HAVE STRONGER CLOAKED SORCERERS, LORDS AND DARKS LORDS WHOM YOU ARE NO MATCH FOR!

YOU CAN'T HIDE EITHER, YOUR CLOAK AND THE FLAG HANGING FROM YOUR BELT IS A DEAD GIVEAWAY!... *YOU'RE GENERAL GRUDON FATTIMUNGA OF THE BANBURI REBELS!!*

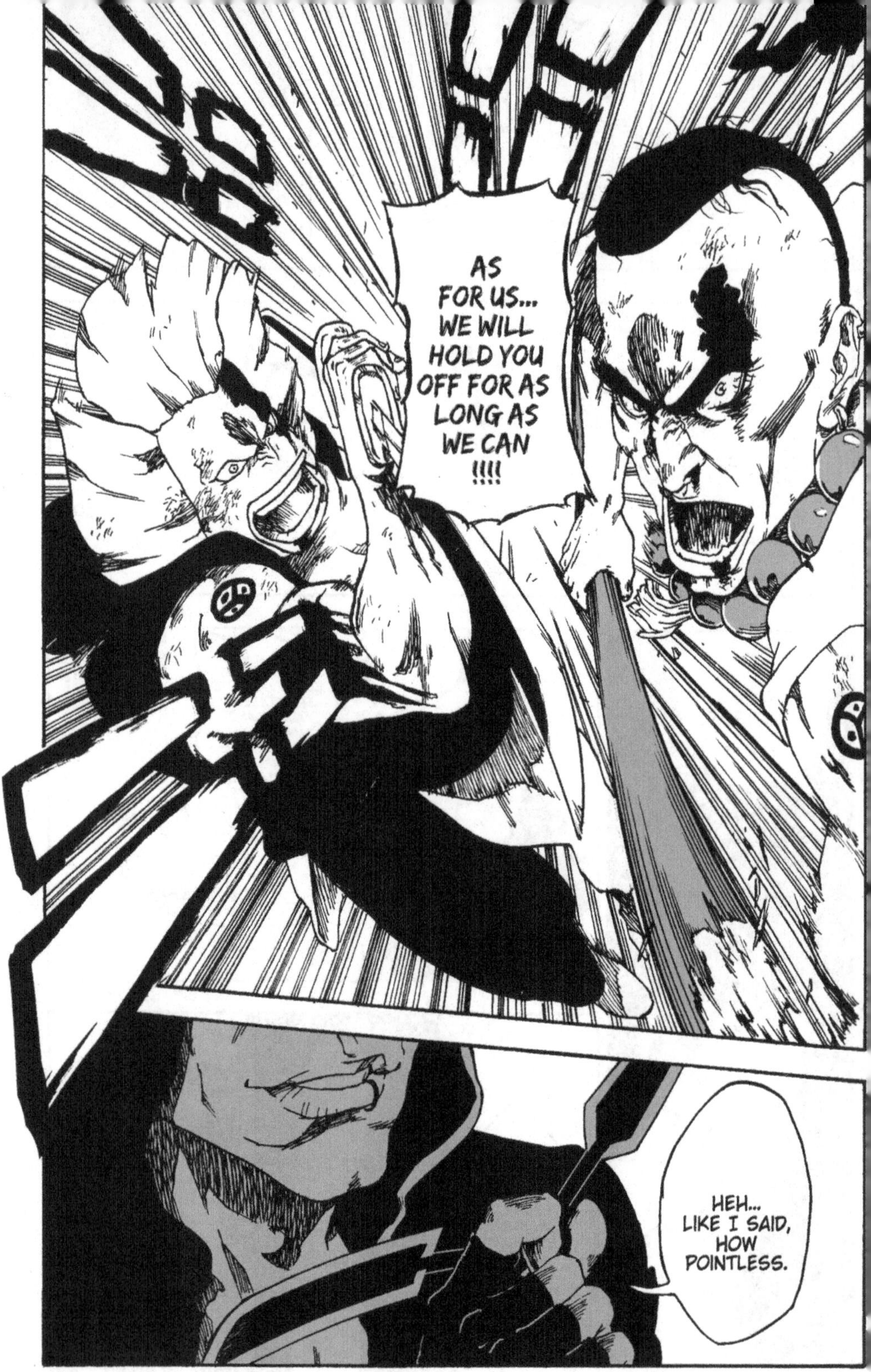
AS FOR US... WE WILL HOLD YOU OFF FOR AS LONG AS WE CAN !!!!
HEH... LIKE I SAID, HOW POINTLESS.

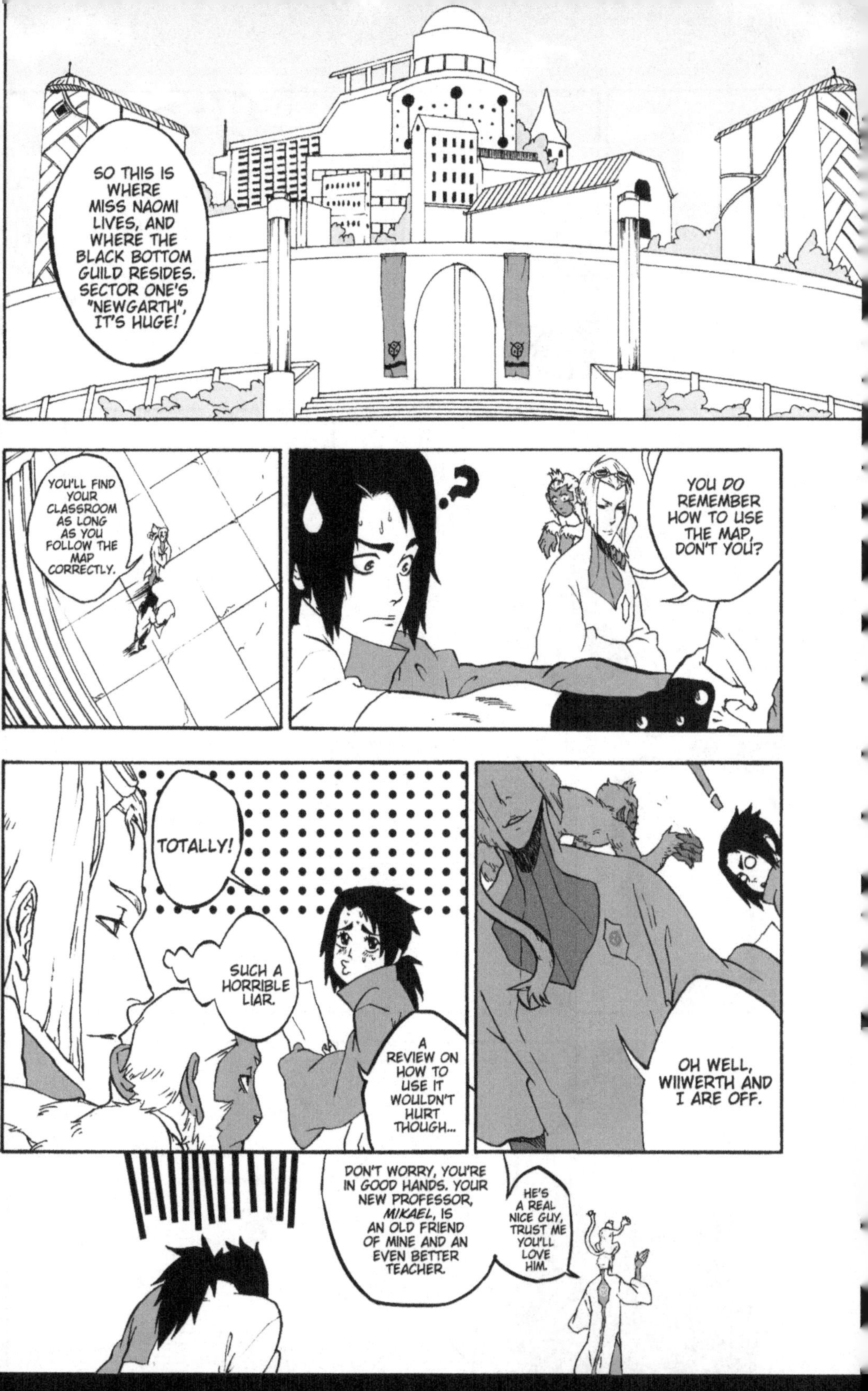
SO THIS IS WHERE MISS NAOMI LIVES, AND WHERE THE BLACK BOTTOM GUILD RESIDES. SECTOR ONE'S "NEWGARTH", IT'S HUGE!
YOU'LL FIND YOUR CLASSROOM AS LONG AS YOU FOLLOW THE MAP CORRECTLY.
YOU DO REMEMBER HOW TO USE THE MAP, DON'T YOU?
TOTALLY!
SUCH A HORRIBLE LIAR.
A REVIEW ON HOW TO USE IT WOULDN'T HURT THOUGH...
OH WELL, WIIWERTH AND I ARE OFF.
DON'T WORRY, YOU'RE IN GOOD HANDS. YOUR NEW PROFESSOR, MIKAEL, IS AN OLD FRIEND OF MINE AND AN EVEN BETTER TEACHER.
HE'S A REAL NICE GUY, TRUST ME YOU'LL LOVE HIM.

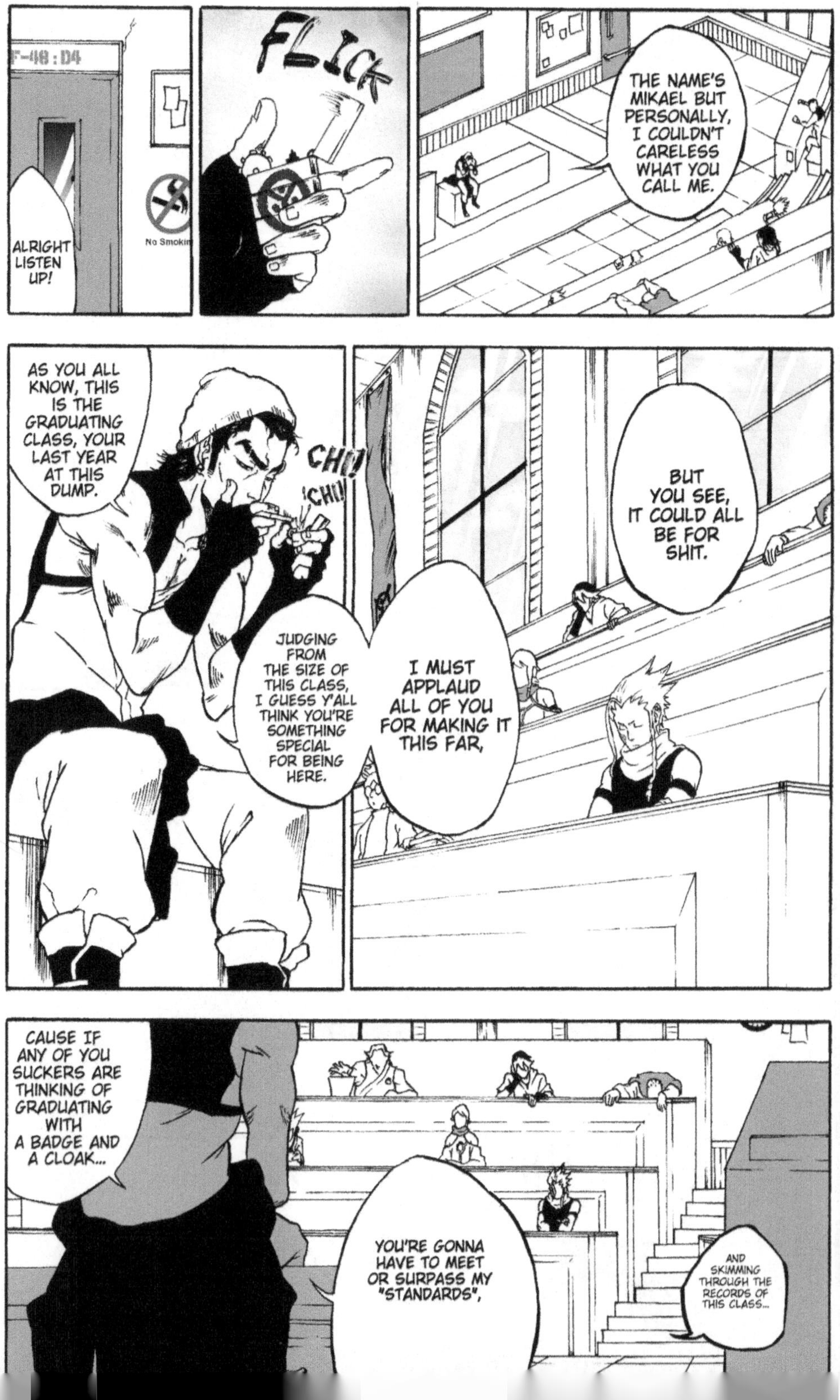
F-48 : D4
ALRIGHT LISTEN UP!
No Smoking
FLICK
THE NAME'S MIKAEL BUT PERSONALLY, I COULDN'T CARELESS WHAT YOU CALL ME.
AS YOU ALL KNOW, THIS IS THE GRADUATING CLASS, YOUR LAST YEAR AT THIS DUMP.
CHI! CHI!
JUDGING FROM THE SIZE OF THIS CLASS, I GUESS Y'ALL THINK YOU'RE SOMETHING SPECIAL FOR BEING HERE.
I MUST APPLAUD ALL OF YOU FOR MAKING IT THIS FAR,
BUT YOU SEE, IT COULD ALL BE FOR SHIT.
CAUSE IF ANY OF YOU SUCKERS ARE THINKING OF GRADUATING WITH A BADGE AND A CLOAK...
YOU'RE GONNA HAVE TO MEET OR SURPASS MY "STANDARDS",
AND SKIMMING THROUGH THE RECORDS OF THIS CLASS...

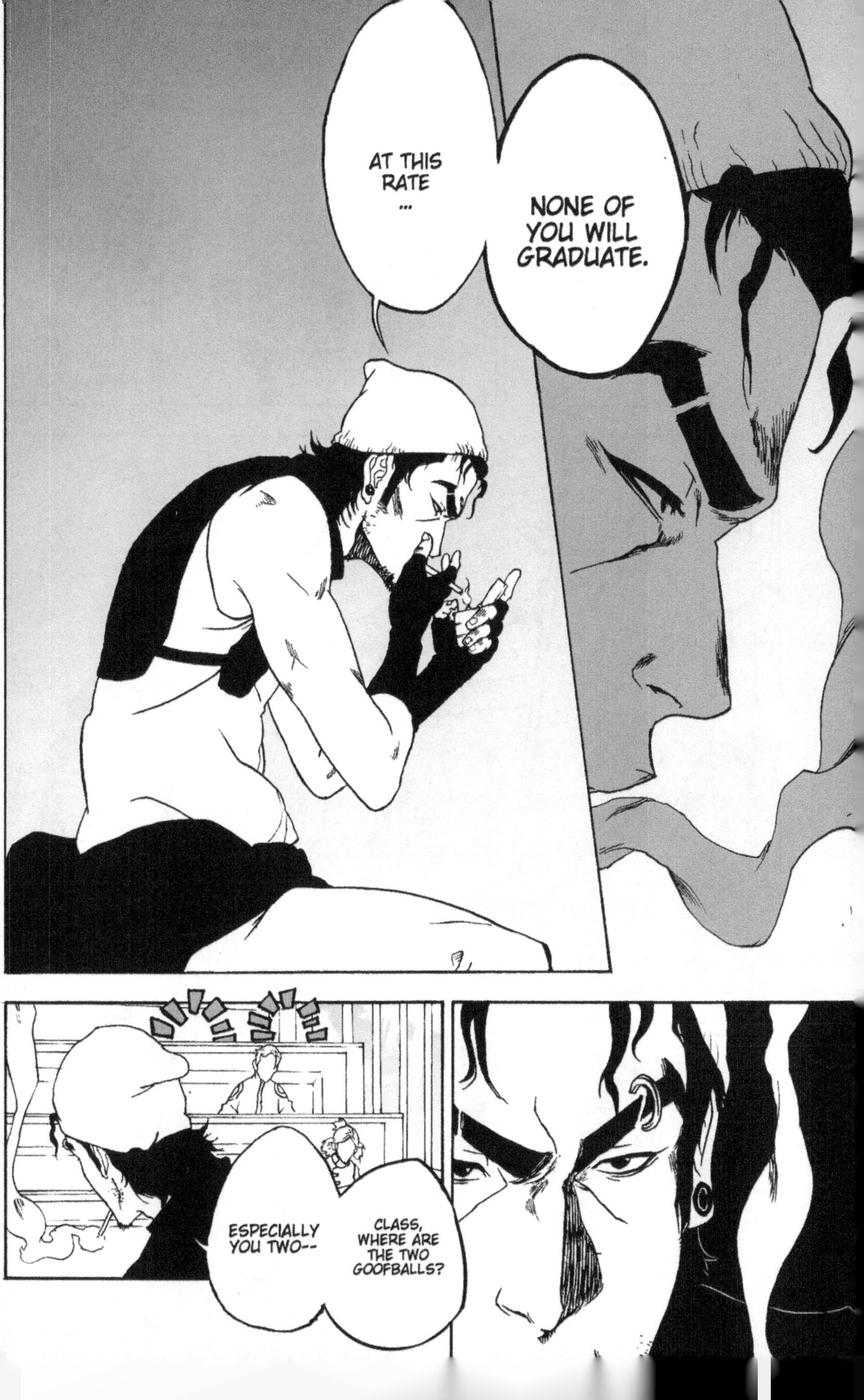
AT THIS RATE ...
NONE OF YOU WILL GRADUATE.
ESPECIALLY YOU TWO--
CLASS, WHERE ARE THE TWO GOOFBALLS?

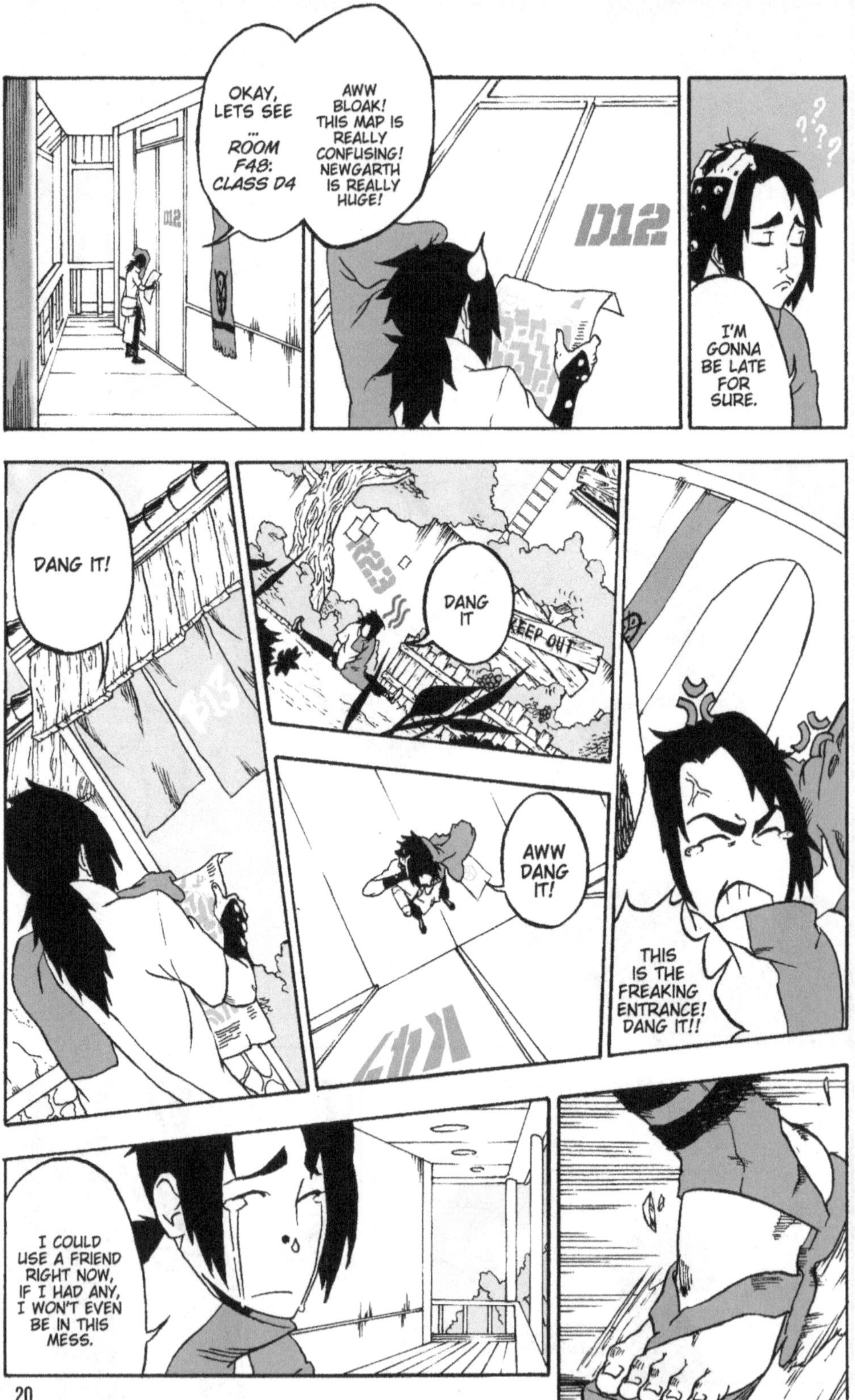
OKAY, LETS SEE ... ROOM F48: CLASS D4
AWW BLOAK! THIS MAP IS REALLY CONFUSING! NEWGARTH IS REALLY HUGE!
D12
I'M GONNA BE LATE FOR SURE.
DANG IT!
DANG IT
KEEP OUT
AWW DANG IT!
THIS IS THE FREAKING ENTRANCE! DANG IT!!
I COULD USE A FRIEND RIGHT NOW, IF I HAD ANY, I WON'T EVEN BE IN THIS MESS.

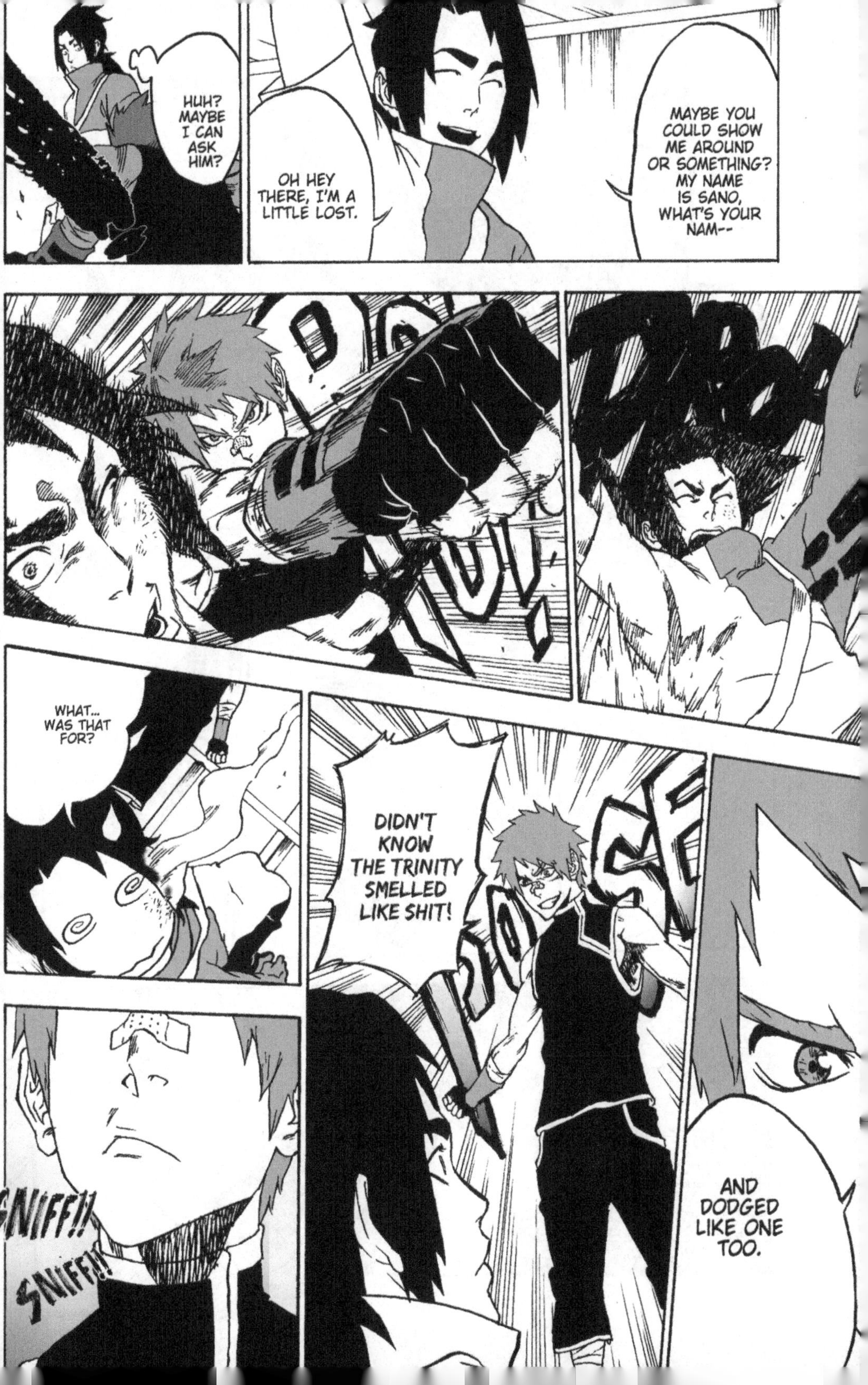
HUH? MAYBE I CAN ASK HIM?
OH HEY THERE, I'M A LITTLE LOST.
MAYBE YOU COULD SHOW ME AROUND OR SOMETHING? MY NAME IS SANO, WHAT'S YOUR NAM--
WHAT... WAS THAT FOR?
SNIFF!!
SNIFF!!
DIDN'T KNOW THE TRINITY SMELLED LIKE SHIT!
AND DODGED LIKE ONE TOO.

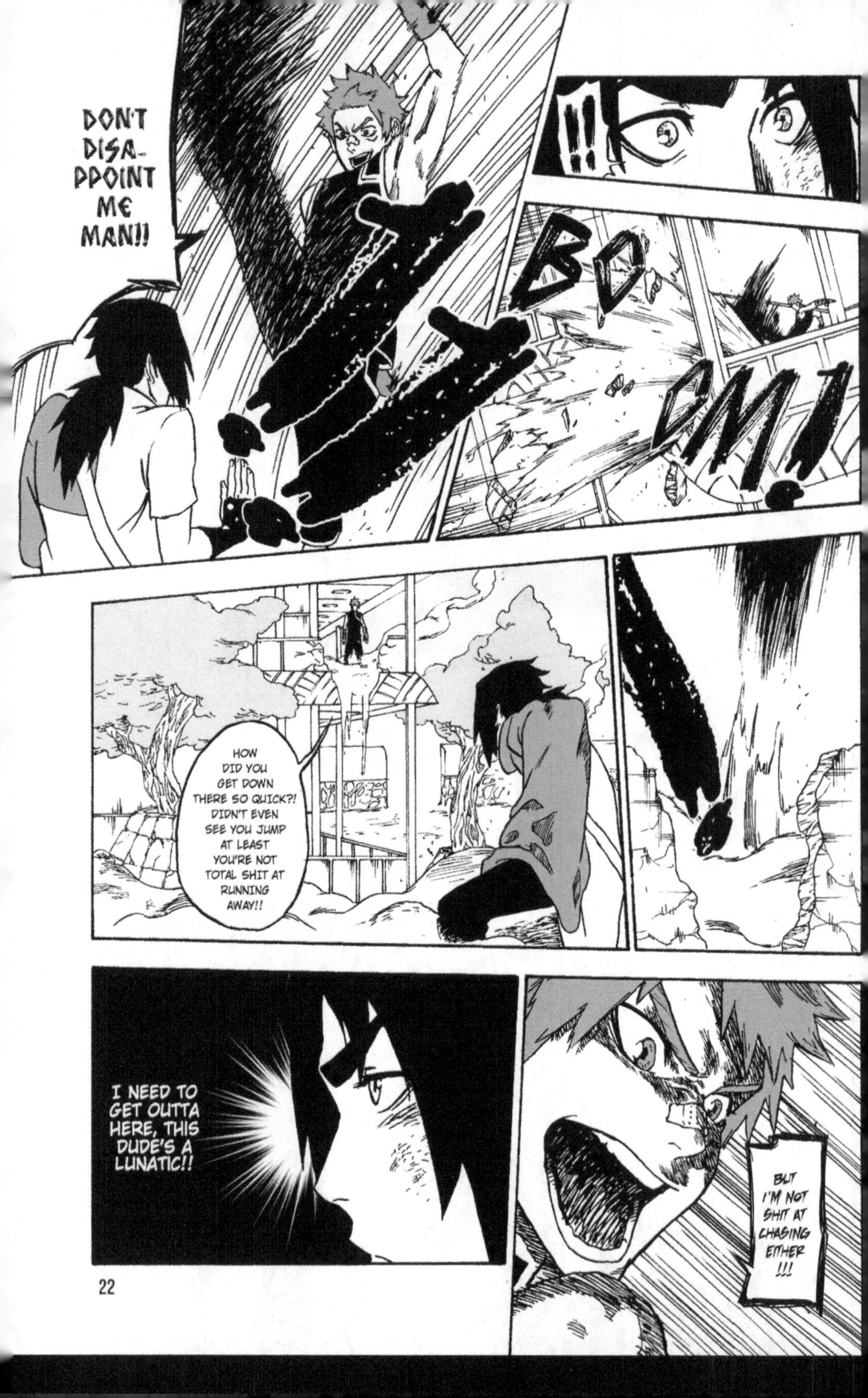
DON'T DISA-PPOINT ME MAN!!
!!!
BOOM!
HOW DID YOU GET DOWN THERE SO QUICK?! DIDN'T EVEN SEE YOU JUMP AT LEAST YOU'RE NOT TOTAL SHIT AT RUNNING AWAY!!
I NEED TO GET OUTTA HERE, THIS DUDE'S A LUNATIC!!
BUT I'M NOT SHIT AT CHASING EITHER !!!

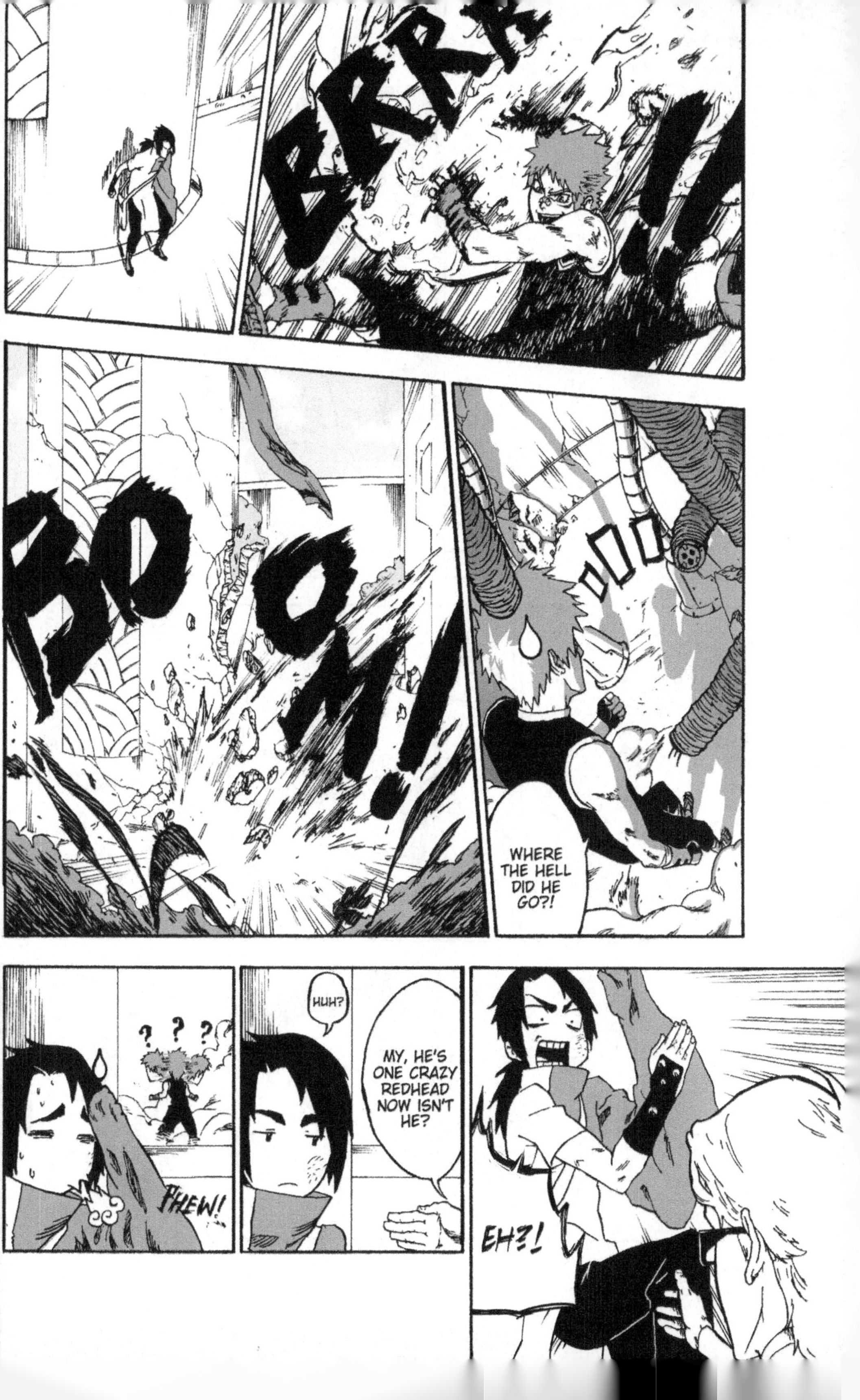
BRRR
BOOM!!
WHERE THE HELL DID HE GO?!
? ? ?
PHEW!
HUH?
MY, HE'S ONE CRAZY REDHEAD NOW ISN'T HE?
EH?!

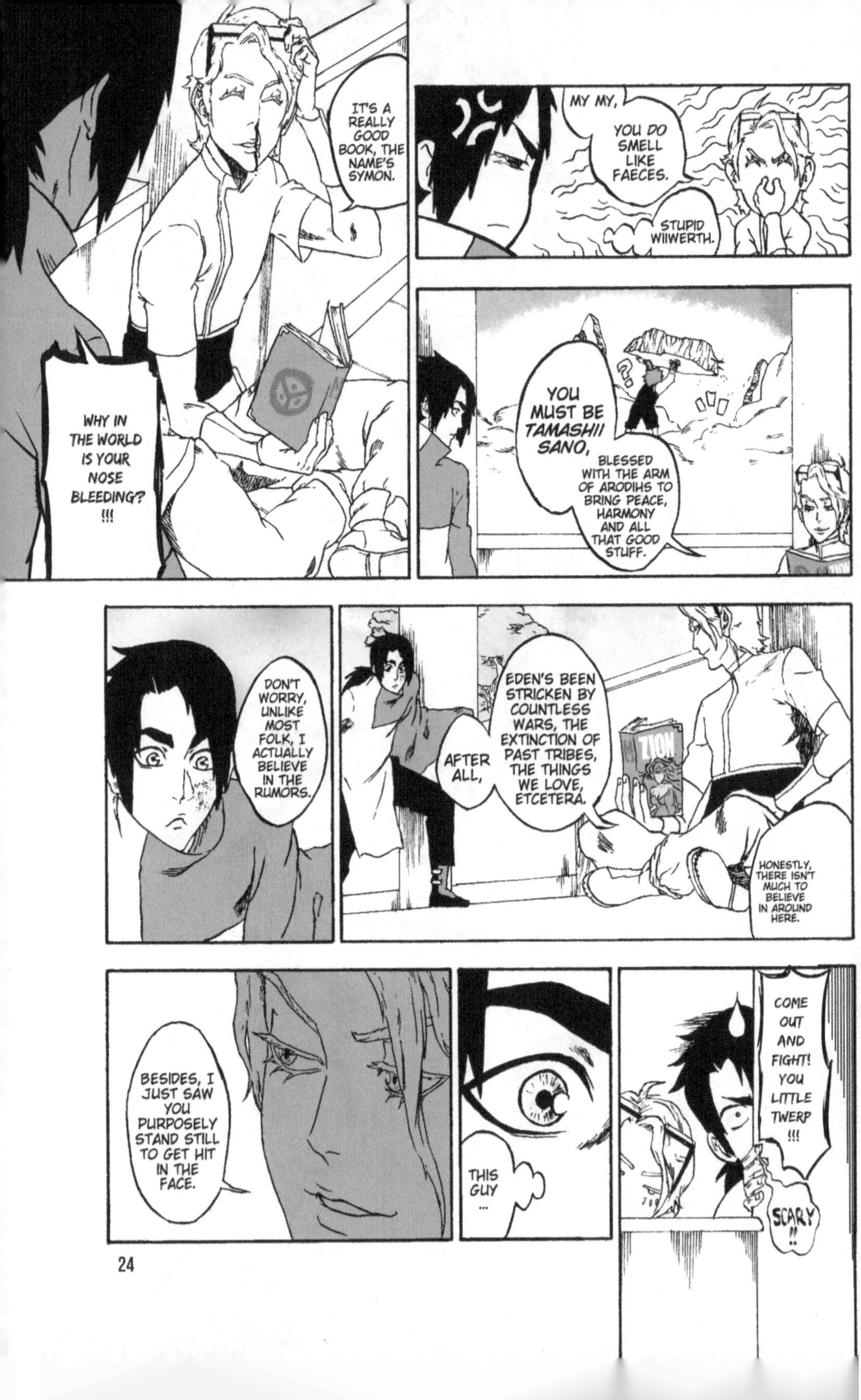

IT'S A REALLY GOOD BOOK, THE NAME'S SYMON.
WHY IN THE WORLD IS YOUR NOSE BLEEDING? !!!
MY MY, YOU DO SMELL LIKE FAECES.
STUPID WIIWERTH.
YOU MUST BE *TAMASHII SANO,*
BLESSED WITH THE ARM OF ARODIHS TO BRING PEACE, HARMONY AND ALL THAT GOOD STUFF.
DON'T WORRY, UNLIKE MOST FOLK, I ACTUALLY BELIEVE IN THE RUMORS.
AFTER ALL,
EDEN'S BEEN STRICKEN BY COUNTLESS WARS, THE EXTINCTION OF PAST TRIBES, THE THINGS WE LOVE, ETCETERA.
ZION
HONESTLY, THERE ISN'T MUCH TO BELIEVE IN AROUND HERE.
BESIDES, I JUST SAW YOU PURPOSELY STAND STILL TO GET HIT IN THE FACE.
THIS GUY ...
COME OUT AND FIGHT! YOU LITTLE TWERP !!!
SCARY !!

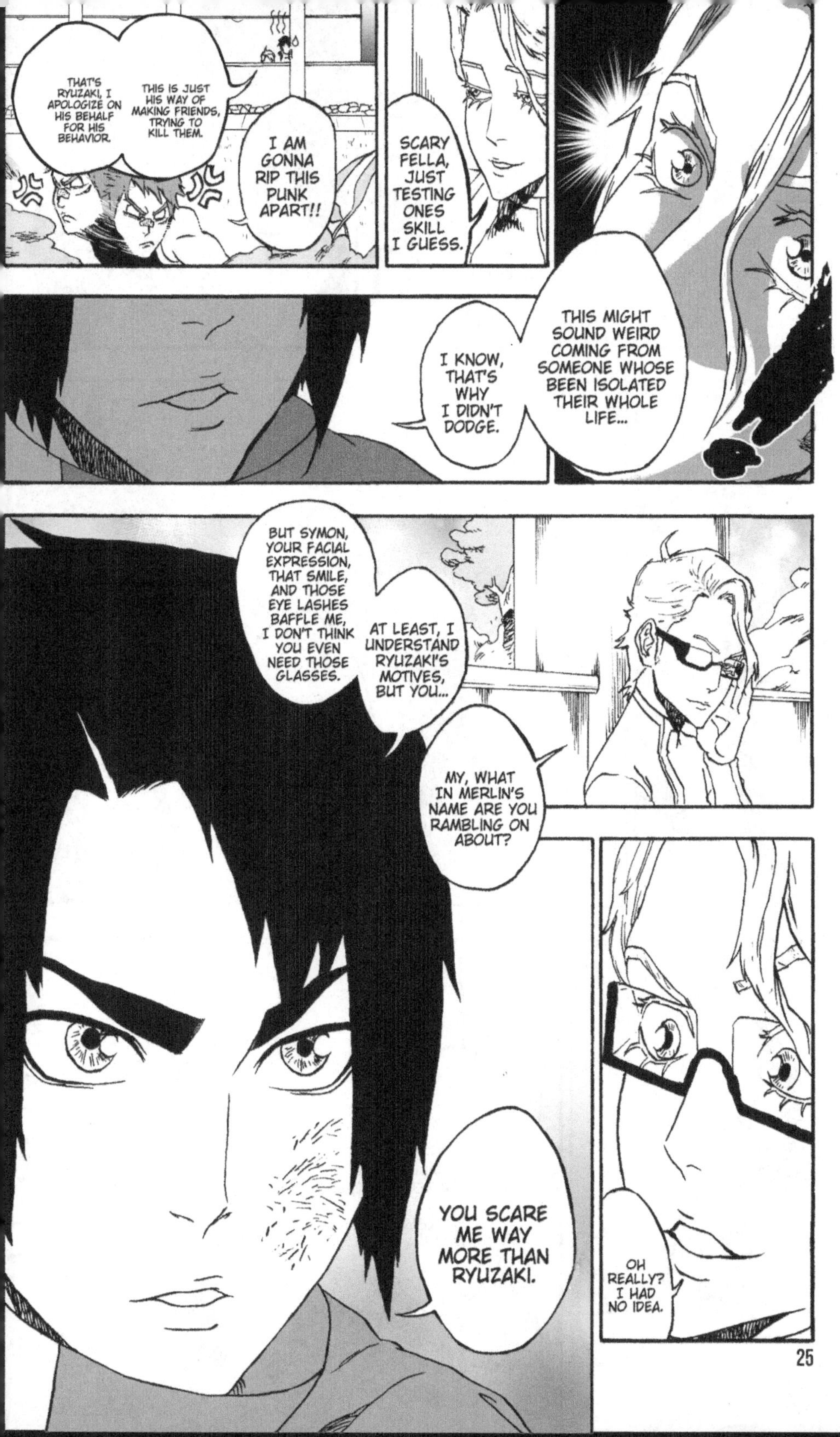
THAT'S RYUZAKI, I APOLOGIZE ON HIS BEHALF FOR HIS BEHAVIOR.
THIS IS JUST HIS WAY OF MAKING FRIENDS, TRYING TO KILL THEM.
I AM GONNA RIP THIS PUNK APART!!
SCARY FELLA, JUST TESTING ONES SKILL I GUESS.
I KNOW, THAT'S WHY I DIDN'T DODGE.
THIS MIGHT SOUND WEIRD COMING FROM SOMEONE WHOSE BEEN ISOLATED THEIR WHOLE LIFE...
BUT SYMON, YOUR FACIAL EXPRESSION, THAT SMILE, AND THOSE EYE LASHES BAFFLE ME, I DON'T THINK YOU EVEN NEED THOSE GLASSES.
AT LEAST, I UNDERSTAND RYUZAKI'S MOTIVES, BUT YOU...
MY, WHAT IN MERLIN'S NAME ARE YOU RAMBLING ON ABOUT?
YOU SCARE ME WAY MORE THAN RYUZAKI.
OH REALLY? I HAD NO IDEA.

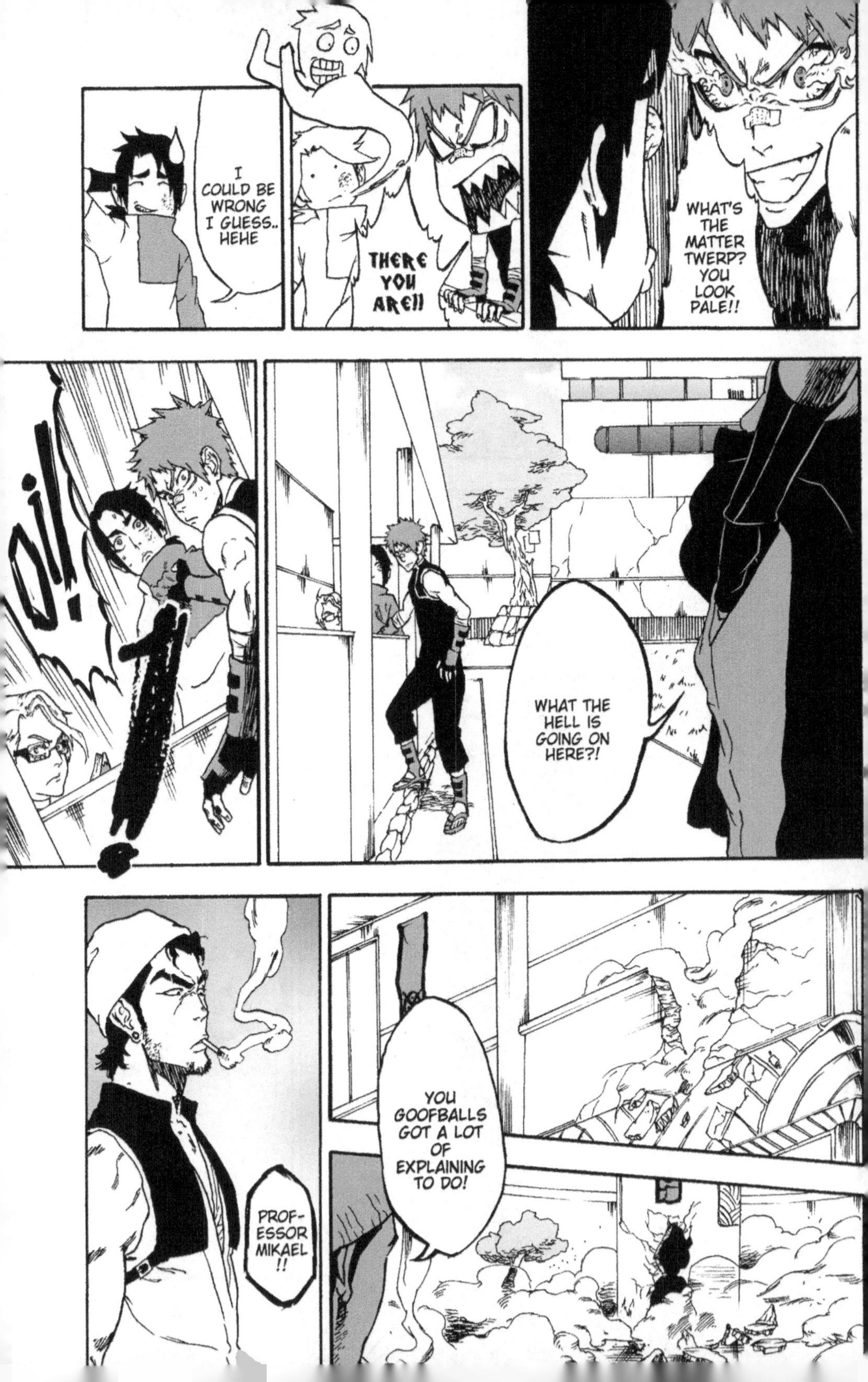
I COULD BE WRONG I GUESS.. HEHE
THERE YOU ARE!!
WHAT'S THE MATTER TWERP? YOU LOOK PALE!!
OI!!
WHAT THE HELL IS GOING ON HERE?!
PROF-ESSOR MIKAEL!!
YOU GOOFBALLS GOT A LOT OF EXPLAINING TO DO!

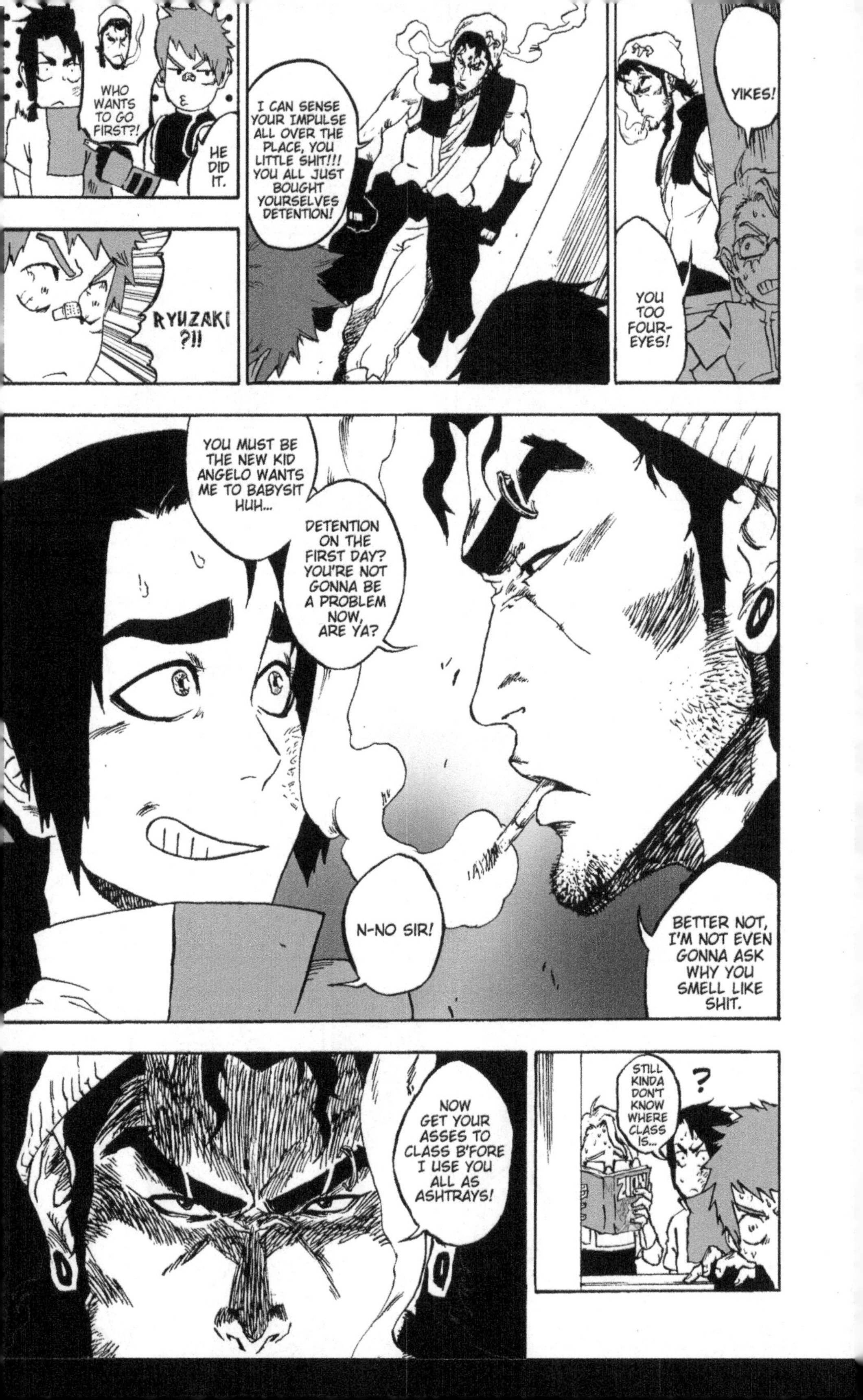
WHO WANTS TO GO FIRST?!
HE DID IT.
I CAN SENSE YOUR IMPULSE ALL OVER THE PLACE, YOU LITTLE SHIT!!! YOU ALL JUST BOUGHT YOURSELVES DETENTION!
YIKES!
RYUZAKI ?!!
YOU TOO FOUR-EYES!
YOU MUST BE THE NEW KID ANGELO WANTS ME TO BABYSIT HUH...
DETENTION ON THE FIRST DAY? YOU'RE NOT GONNA BE A PROBLEM NOW, ARE YA?
N-NO SIR!
BETTER NOT, I'M NOT EVEN GONNA ASK WHY YOU SMELL LIKE SHIT.
NOW GET YOUR ASSES TO CLASS B'FORE I USE YOU ALL AS ASHTRAYS!
STILL KINDA DON'T KNOW WHERE CLASS IS...
?

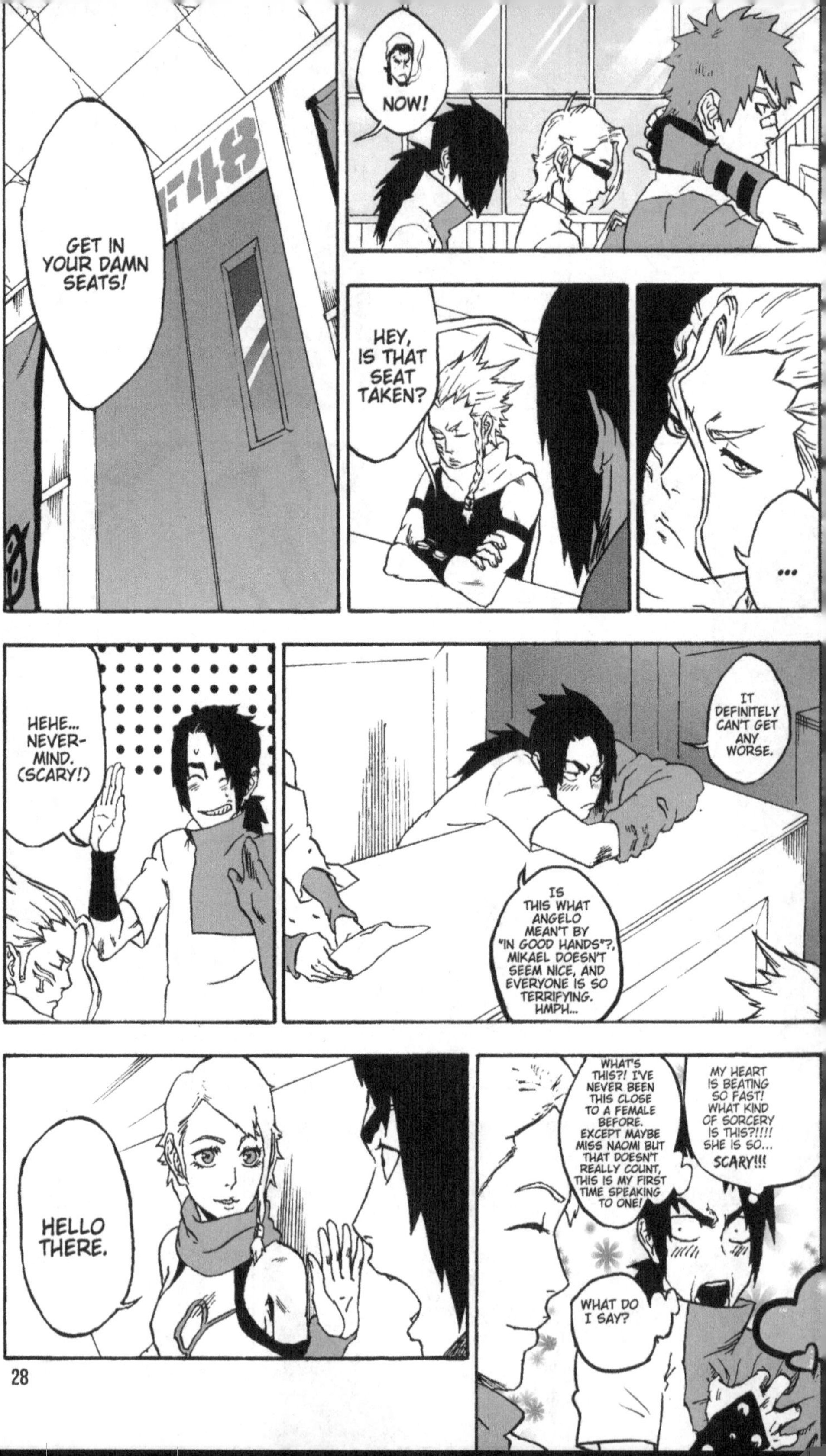
GET IN YOUR DAMN SEATS!
NOW!
HEY, IS THAT SEAT TAKEN?
...
HEHE... NEVER-MIND. (SCARY!)
IT DEFINITELY CAN'T GET ANY WORSE.
IS THIS WHAT ANGELO MEAN'T BY "IN GOOD HANDS"?, MIKAEL DOESN'T SEEM NICE, AND EVERYONE IS SO TERRIFYING. HMPH...
HELLO THERE.
WHAT'S THIS?! I'VE NEVER BEEN THIS CLOSE TO A FEMALE BEFORE. EXCEPT MAYBE MISS NAOMI BUT THAT DOESN'T REALLY COUNT, THIS IS MY FIRST TIME SPEAKING TO ONE!
MY HEART IS BEATING SO FAST! WHAT KIND OF SORCERY IS THIS?!!!! SHE IS SO... SCARY!!!
WHAT DO I SAY?

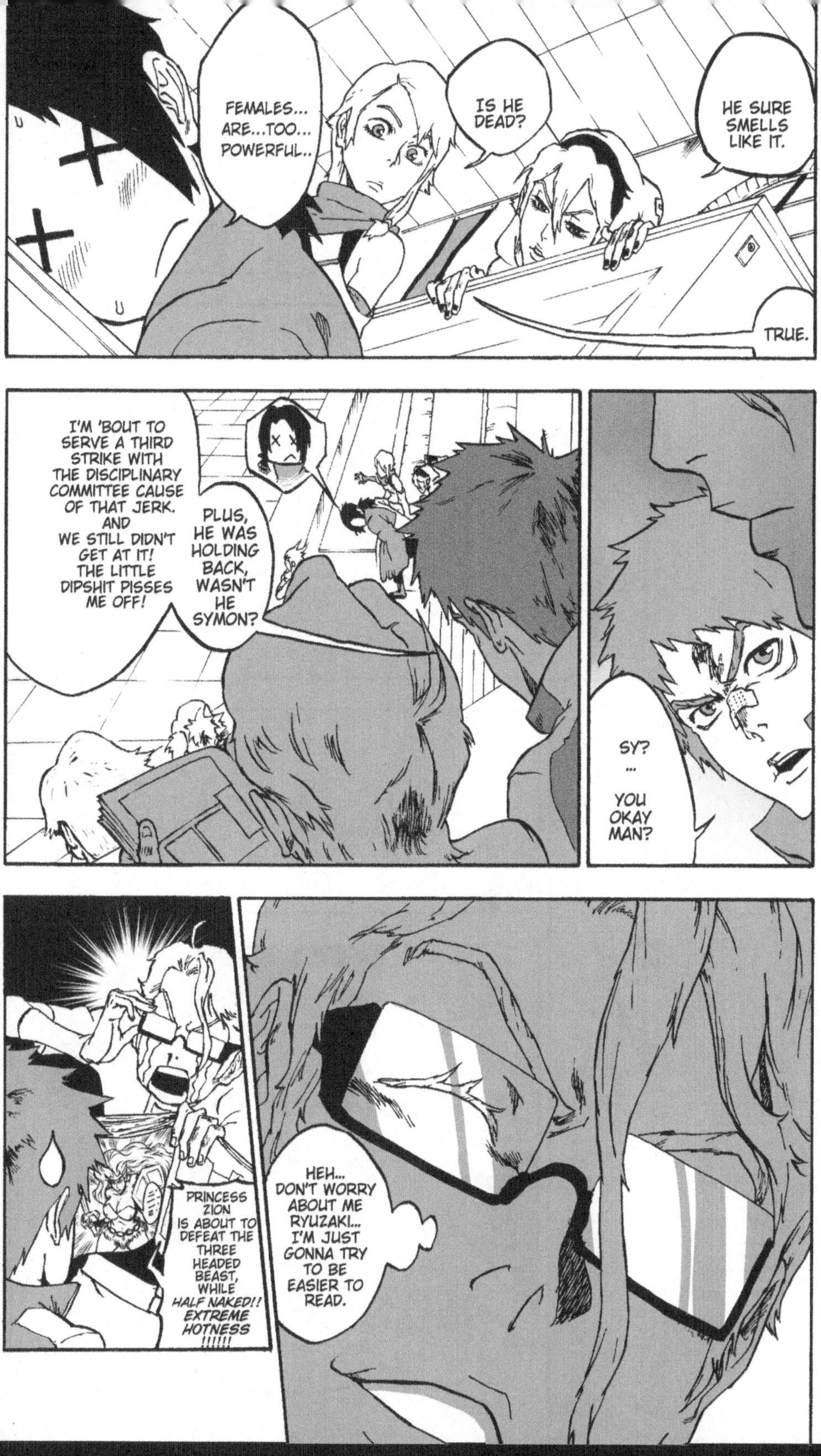

FEMALES... ARE...TOO... POWERFUL...
IS HE DEAD?
HE SURE SMELLS LIKE IT.
TRUE.
I'M 'BOUT TO SERVE A THIRD STRIKE WITH THE DISCIPLINARY COMMITTEE CAUSE OF THAT JERK. AND WE STILL DIDN'T GET AT IT! THE LITTLE DIPSHIT PISSES ME OFF!
PLUS, HE WAS HOLDING BACK, WASN'T HE SYMON?
SY? ... YOU OKAY MAN?
PRINCESS ZION IS ABOUT TO DEFEAT THE THREE HEADED BEAST, WHILE *HALF NAKED!! EXTREME HOTNESS !!!!!!*
HEH... DON'T WORRY ABOUT ME RYUZAKI... I'M JUST GONNA TRY TO BE EASIER TO READ.

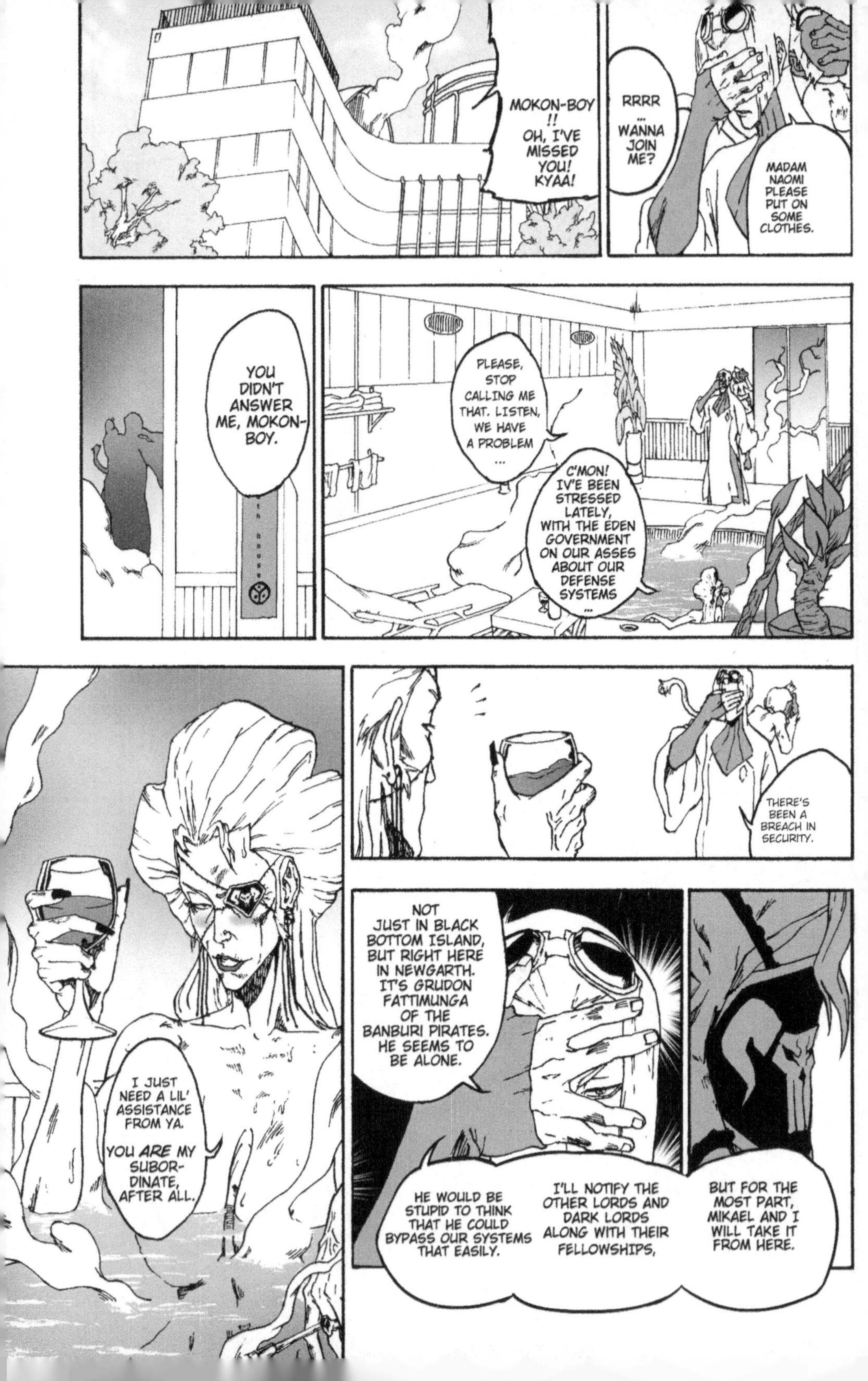
MOKON-BOY !! OH, I'VE MISSED YOU! KYAA!
RRRR ... WANNA JOIN ME?
MADAM NAOMI PLEASE PUT ON SOME CLOTHES.
YOU DIDN'T ANSWER ME, MOKON-BOY.
PLEASE, STOP CALLING ME THAT. LISTEN, WE HAVE A PROBLEM ...
C'MON! IV'E BEEN STRESSED LATELY, WITH THE EDEN GOVERNMENT ON OUR ASSES ABOUT OUR DEFENSE SYSTEMS ...
I JUST NEED A LIL' ASSISTANCE FROM YA.
YOU ARE MY SUBOR-DINATE, AFTER ALL.
THERE'S BEEN A BREACH IN SECURITY.
NOT JUST IN BLACK BOTTOM ISLAND, BUT RIGHT HERE IN NEWGARTH. IT'S GRUDON FATTIMUNGA OF THE BANBURI PIRATES. HE SEEMS TO BE ALONE.
HE WOULD BE STUPID TO THINK THAT HE COULD BYPASS OUR SYSTEMS THAT EASILY.
I'LL NOTIFY THE OTHER LORDS AND DARK LORDS ALONG WITH THEIR FELLOWSHIPS,
BUT FOR THE MOST PART, MIKAEL AND I WILL TAKE IT FROM HERE.

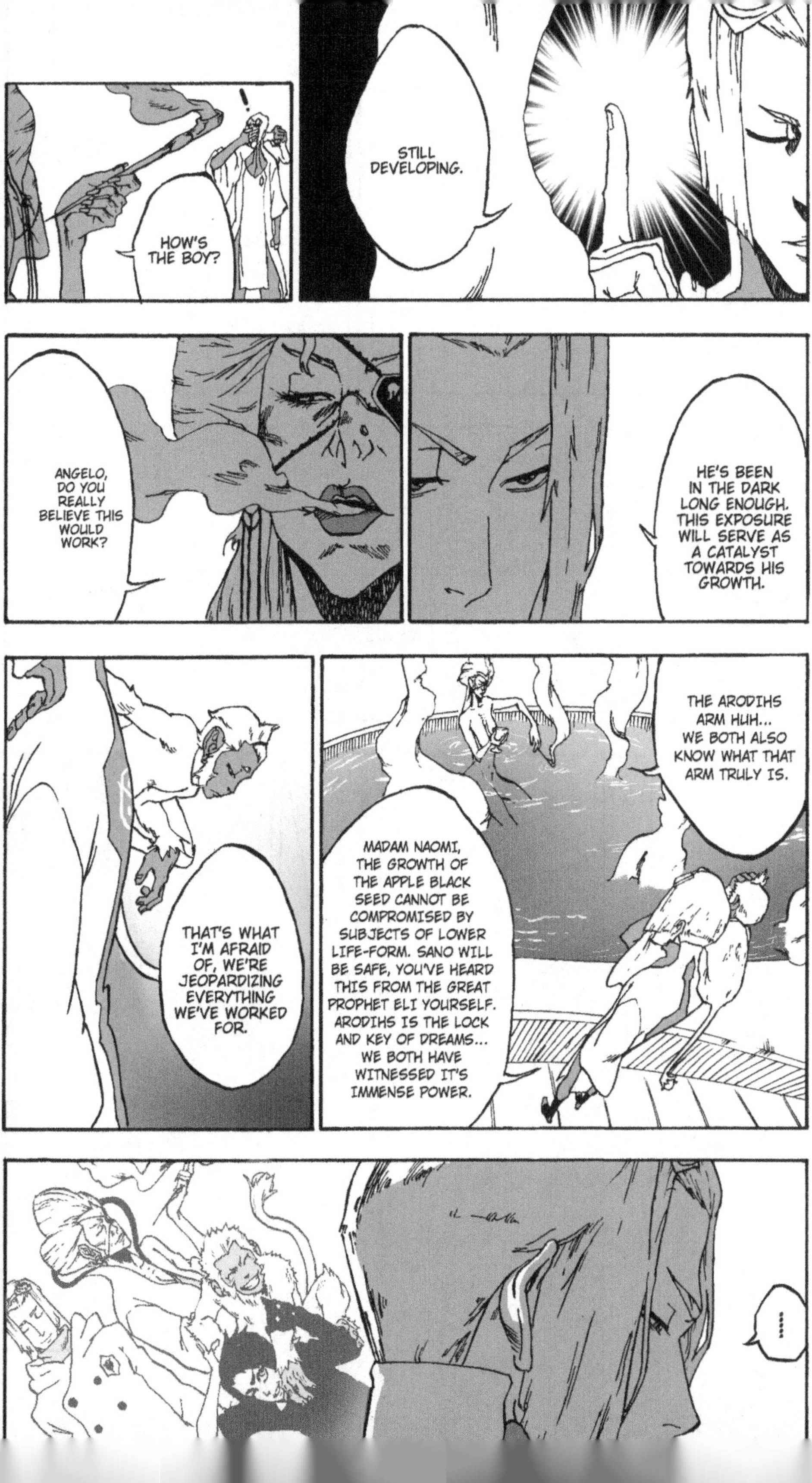
HOW'S THE BOY?
STILL DEVELOPING.
ANGELO, DO YOU REALLY BELIEVE THIS WOULD WORK?
HE'S BEEN IN THE DARK LONG ENOUGH. THIS EXPOSURE WILL SERVE AS A CATALYST TOWARDS HIS GROWTH.
THAT'S WHAT I'M AFRAID OF, WE'RE JEOPARDIZING EVERYTHING WE'VE WORKED FOR.
THE ARODIHS ARM HUH... WE BOTH ALSO KNOW WHAT THAT ARM TRULY IS.
MADAM NAOMI, THE GROWTH OF THE APPLE BLACK SEED CANNOT BE COMPROMISED BY SUBJECTS OF LOWER LIFE-FORM. SANO WILL BE SAFE, YOU'VE HEARD THIS FROM THE GREAT PROPHET ELI YOURSELF. ARODIHS IS THE LOCK AND KEY OF DREAMS... WE BOTH HAVE WITNESSED IT'S IMMENSE POWER.
......

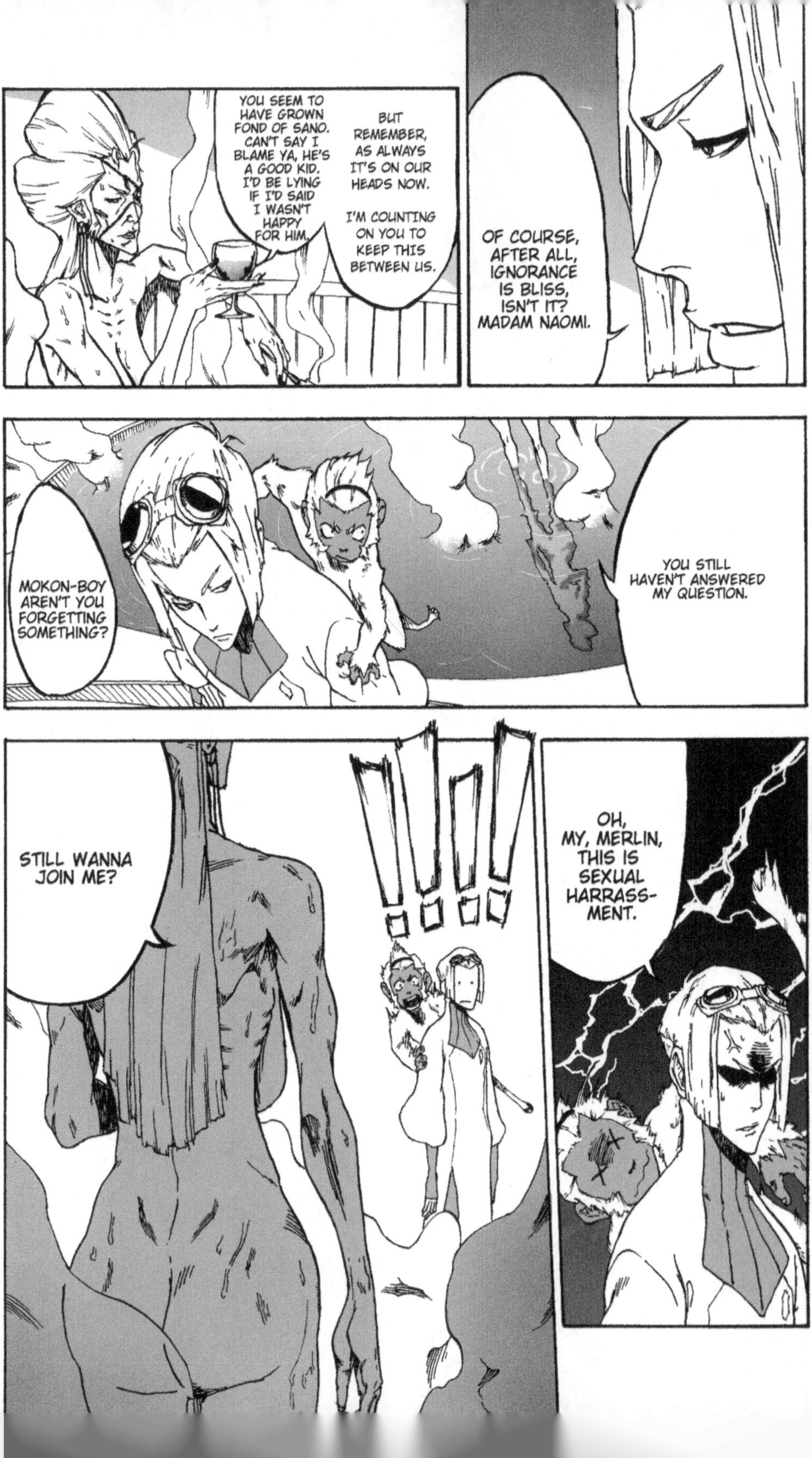
YOU SEEM TO HAVE GROWN FOND OF SANO. CAN'T SAY I BLAME YA, HE'S A GOOD KID. I'D BE LYING IF I'D SAID I WASN'T HAPPY FOR HIM.
BUT REMEMBER, AS ALWAYS IT'S ON OUR HEADS NOW.
I'M COUNTING ON YOU TO KEEP THIS BETWEEN US.
OF COURSE, AFTER ALL, IGNORANCE IS BLISS, ISN'T IT? MADAM NAOMI.
MOKON-BOY AREN'T YOU FORGETTING SOMETHING?
YOU STILL HAVEN'T ANSWERED MY QUESTION.
STILL WANNA JOIN ME?
!!!!
OH, MY, MERLIN, THIS IS SEXUAL HARRASS-MENT.

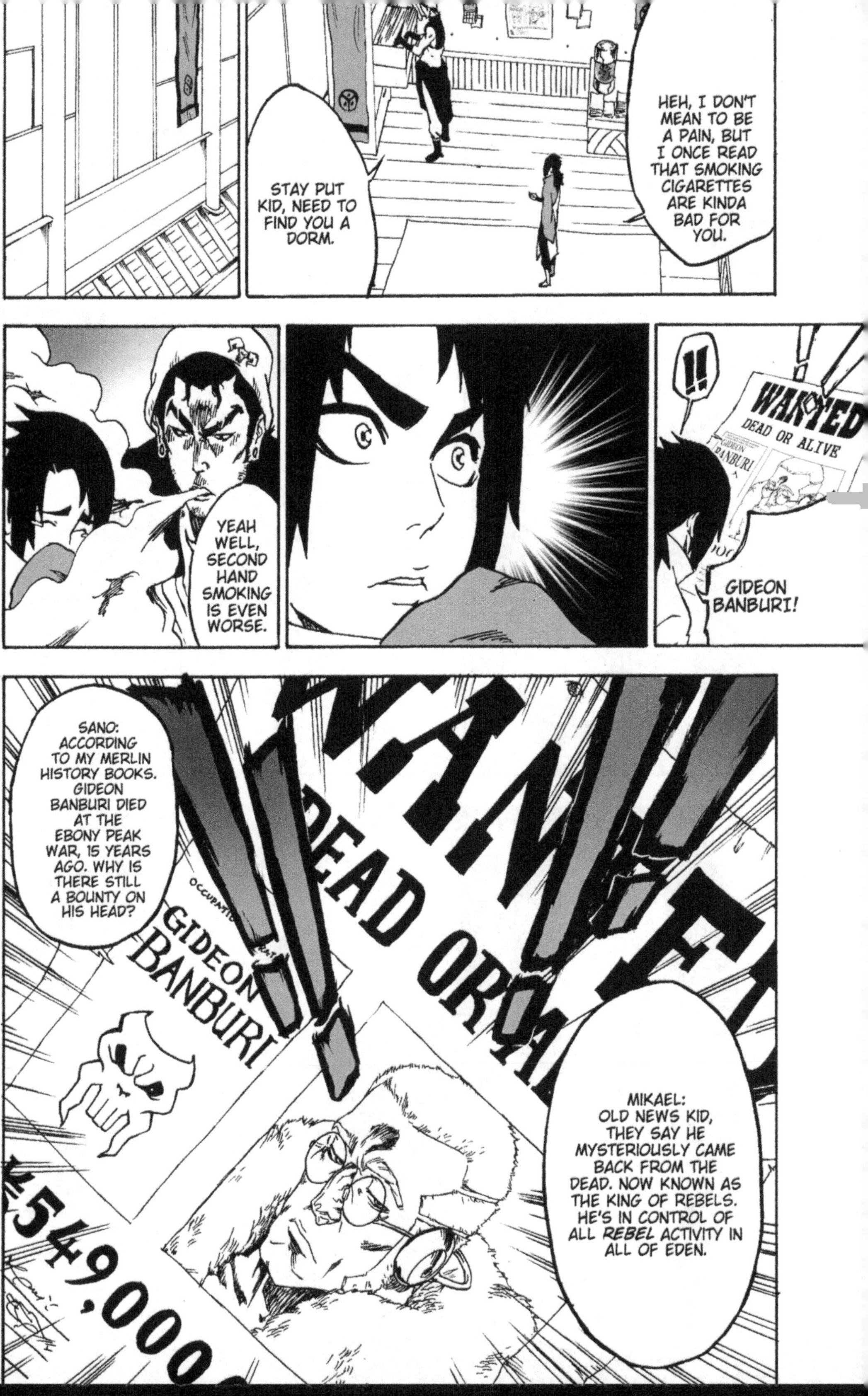
STAY PUT KID, NEED TO FIND YOU A DORM.
HEH, I DON'T MEAN TO BE A PAIN, BUT I ONCE READ THAT SMOKING CIGARETTES ARE KINDA BAD FOR YOU.
YEAH WELL, SECOND HAND SMOKING IS EVEN WORSE.
!!
WANTED
DEAD OR ALIVE
GIDEON BANBURI
GIDEON BANBURI!
SANO: ACCORDING TO MY MERLIN HISTORY BOOKS. GIDEON BANBURI DIED AT THE EBONY PEAK WAR, 15 YEARS AGO. WHY IS THERE STILL A BOUNTY ON HIS HEAD?
GIDEON BANBURI
549,000
MIKAEL: OLD NEWS KID, THEY SAY HE MYSTERIOUSLY CAME BACK FROM THE DEAD. NOW KNOWN AS THE KING OF REBELS. HE'S IN CONTROL OF ALL *REBEL* ACTIVITY IN ALL OF EDEN.

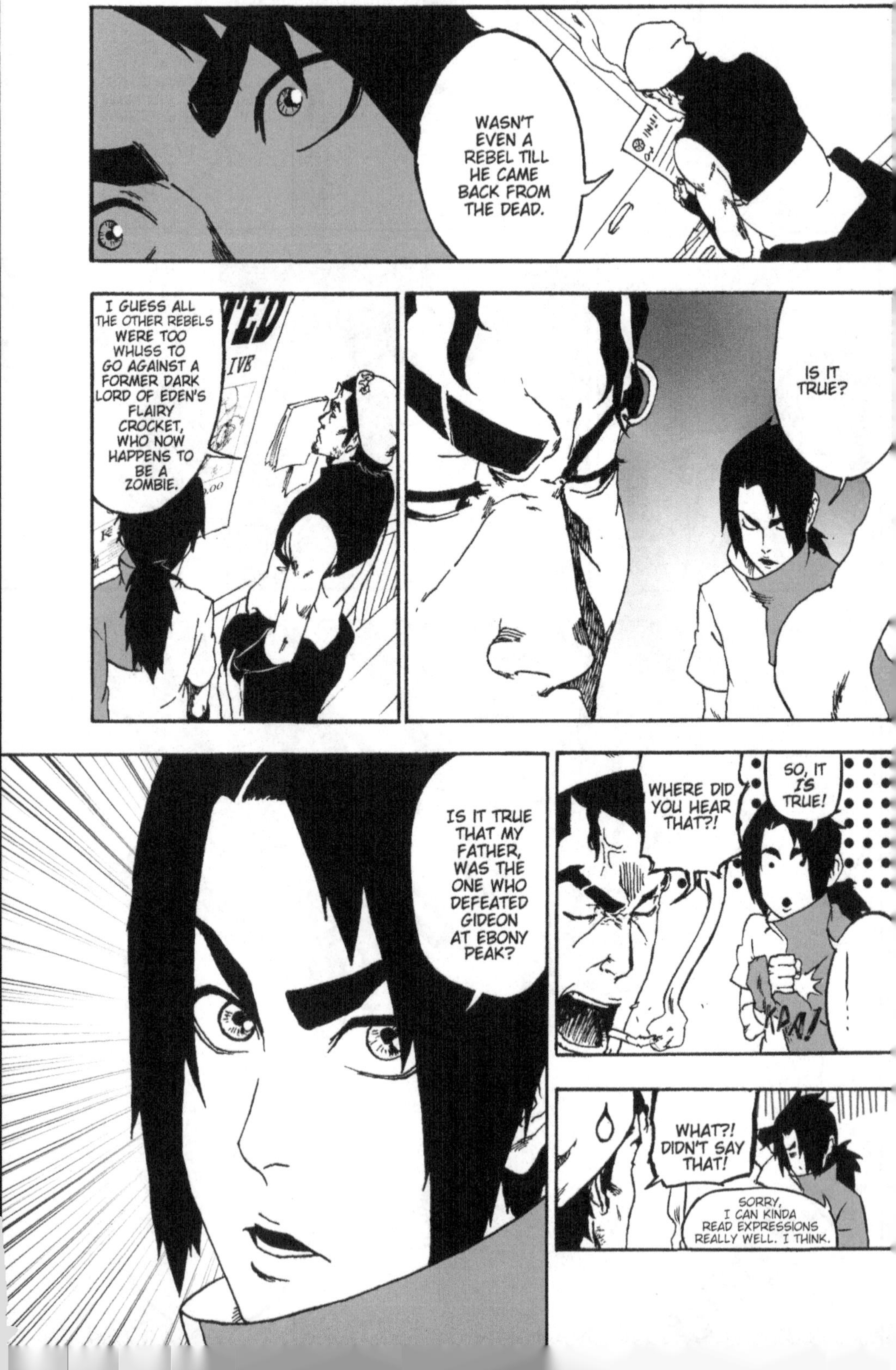
WASN'T EVEN A REBEL TILL HE CAME BACK FROM THE DEAD.
I GUESS ALL THE OTHER REBELS WERE TOO WHUSS TO GO AGAINST A FORMER DARK LORD OF EDEN'S FLAIRY CROCKET, WHO NOW HAPPENS TO BE A ZOMBIE.
IS IT TRUE?
IS IT TRUE THAT MY FATHER, WAS THE ONE WHO DEFEATED GIDEON AT EBONY PEAK?
WHERE DID YOU HEAR THAT?!
SO, IT IS TRUE!
WHAT?! DIDN'T SAY THAT!
SORRY, I CAN KINDA READ EXPRESSIONS REALLY WELL. I THINK.

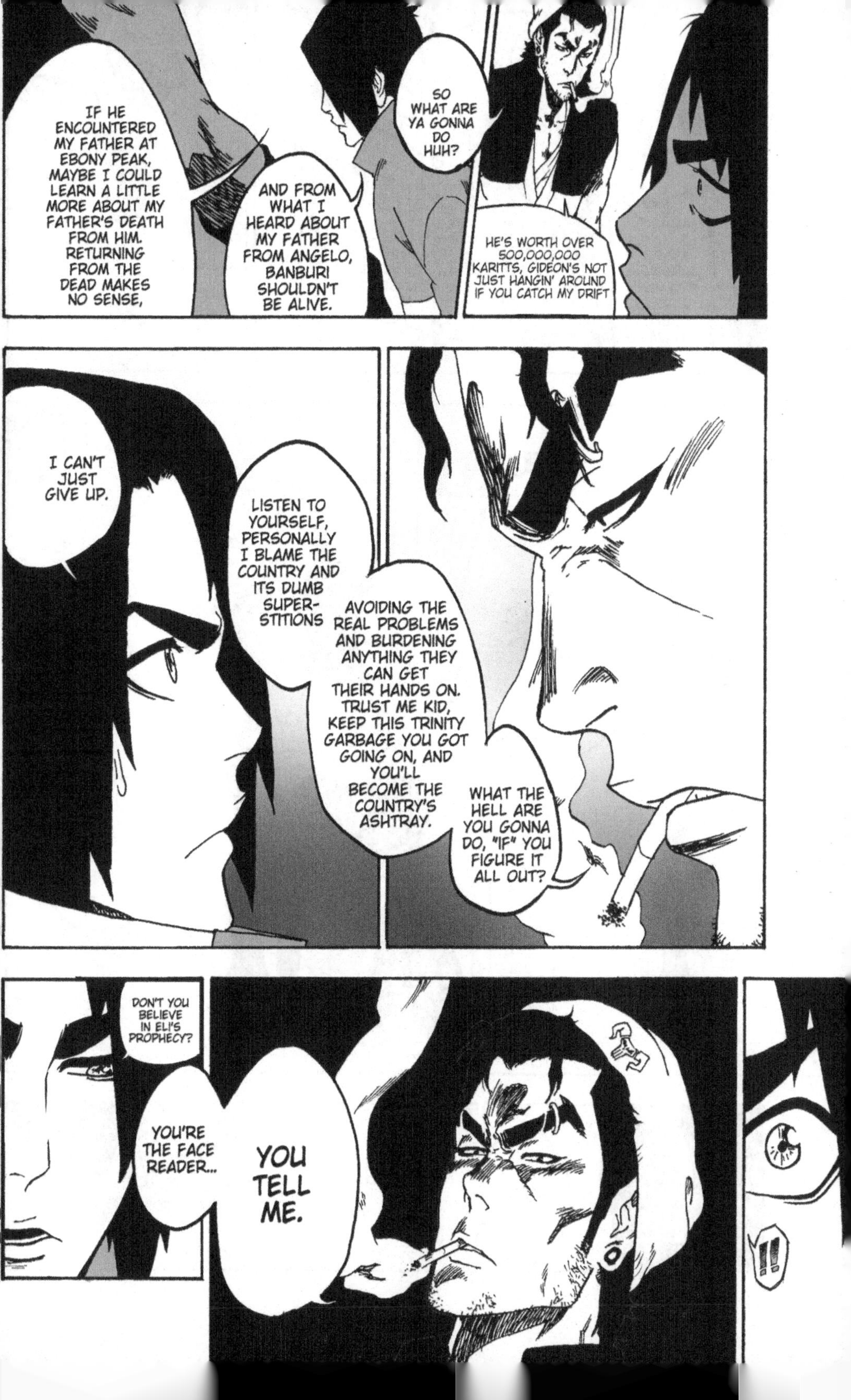
IF HE ENCOUNTERED MY FATHER AT EBONY PEAK, MAYBE I COULD LEARN A LITTLE MORE ABOUT MY FATHER'S DEATH FROM HIM. RETURNING FROM THE DEAD MAKES NO SENSE,
AND FROM WHAT I HEARD ABOUT MY FATHER FROM ANGELO, BANBURI SHOULDN'T BE ALIVE.
SO WHAT ARE YA GONNA DO HUH?
HE'S WORTH OVER 500,000,000 KARITTS, GIDEON'S NOT JUST HANGIN' AROUND IF YOU CATCH MY DRIFT
I CAN'T JUST GIVE UP.
LISTEN TO YOURSELF, PERSONALLY I BLAME THE COUNTRY AND ITS DUMB SUPER-STITIONS
AVOIDING THE REAL PROBLEMS AND BURDENING ANYTHING THEY CAN GET THEIR HANDS ON. TRUST ME KID, KEEP THIS TRINITY GARBAGE YOU GOT GOING ON, AND YOU'LL BECOME THE COUNTRY'S ASHTRAY.
WHAT THE HELL ARE YOU GONNA DO, "IF" YOU FIGURE IT ALL OUT?
DON'T YOU BELIEVE IN ELI'S PROPHECY?
YOU'RE THE FACE READER...
YOU TELL ME.
!!

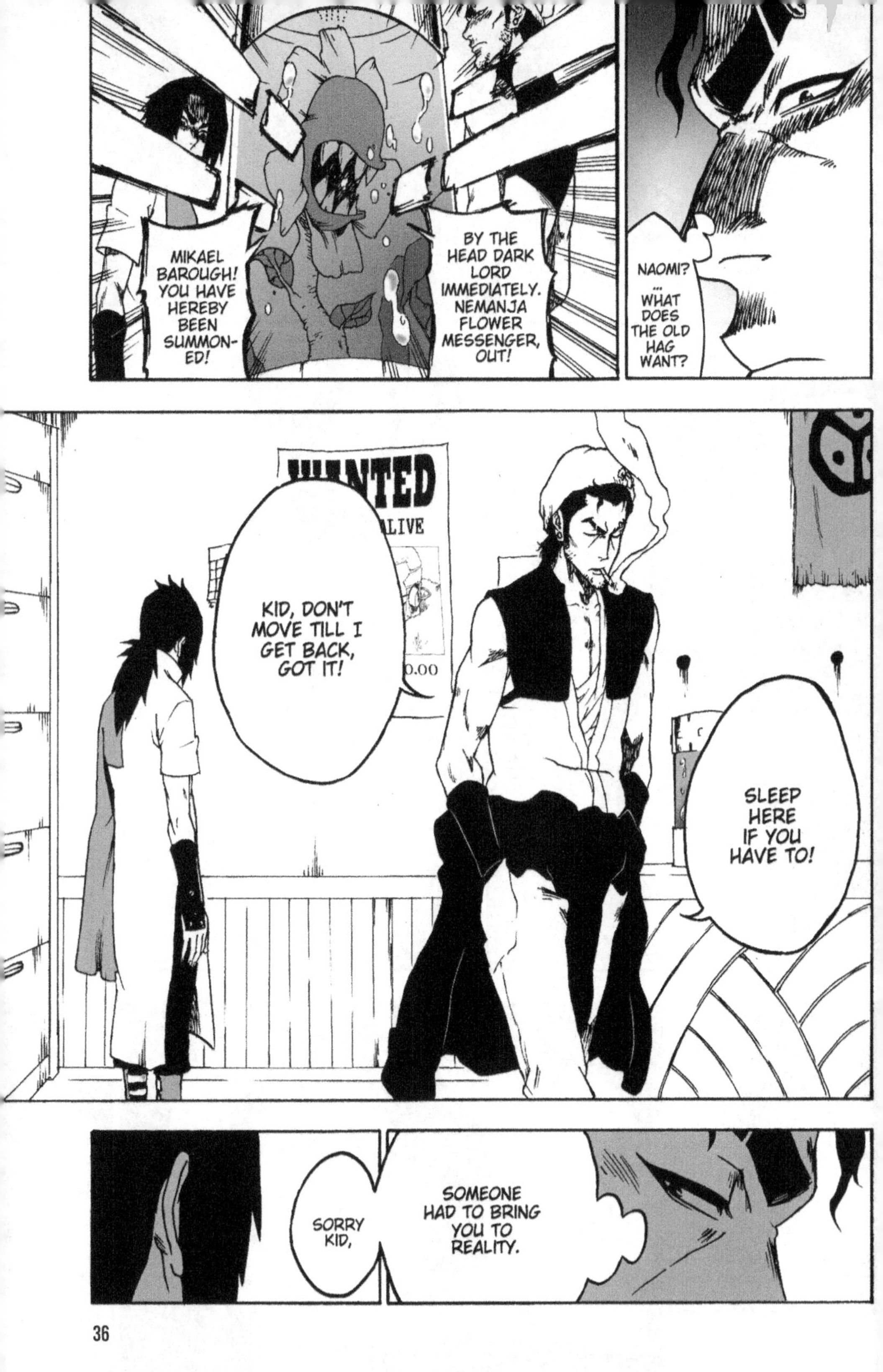
MIKAEL BAROUGH! YOU HAVE HEREBY BEEN SUMMON-ED!
BY THE HEAD DARK LORD IMMEDIATELY. NEMANJA FLOWER MESSENGER, OUT!
NAOMI? ... WHAT DOES THE OLD HAG WANT?
WANTED
ALIVE
0.00
KID, DON'T MOVE TILL I GET BACK, GOT IT!
SLEEP HERE IF YOU HAVE TO!
SORRY KID,
SOMEONE HAD TO BRING YOU TO REALITY.

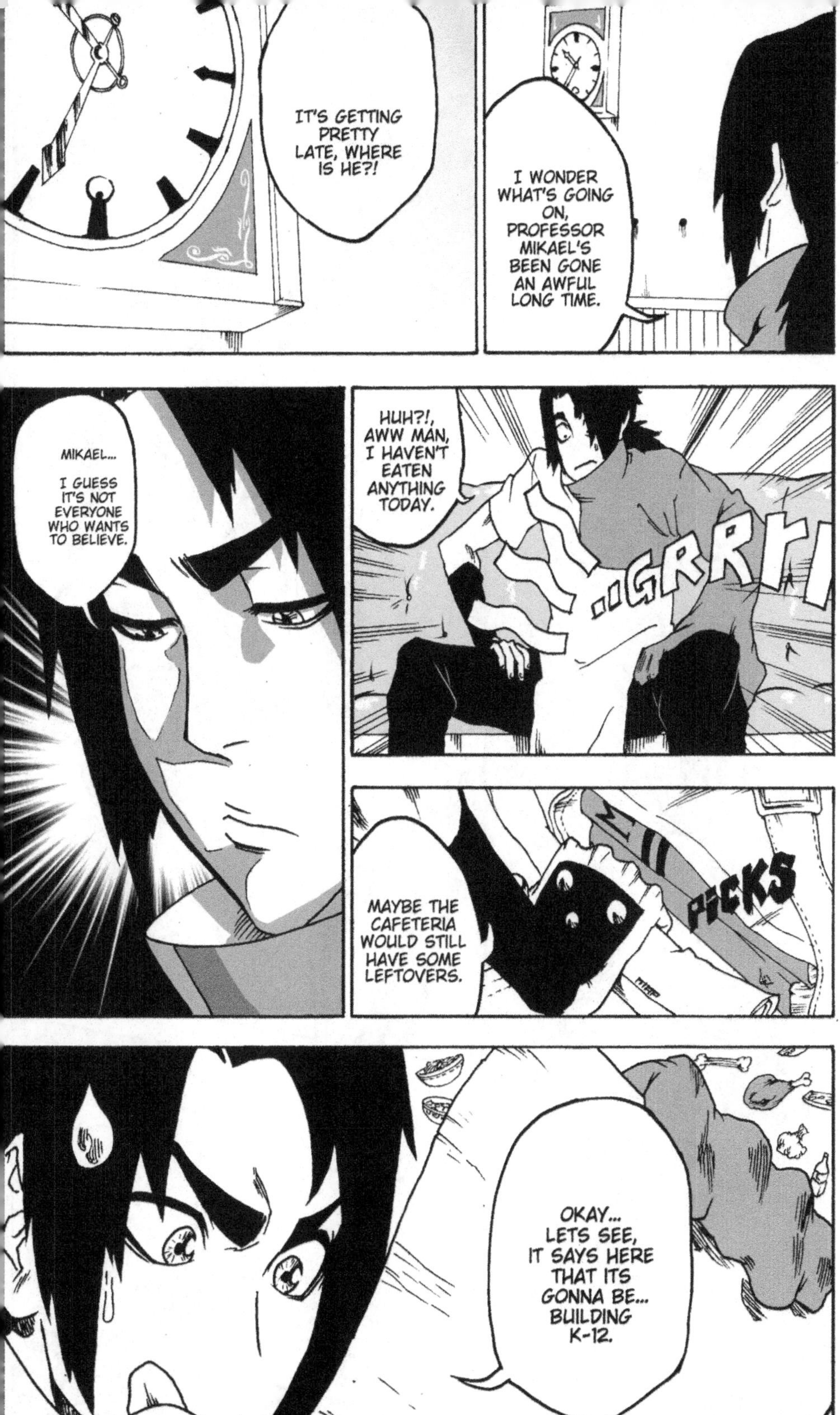
IT'S GETTING PRETTY LATE, WHERE IS HE?!
I WONDER WHAT'S GOING ON, PROFESSOR MIKAEL'S BEEN GONE AN AWFUL LONG TIME.
MIKAEL...
I GUESS IT'S NOT EVERYONE WHO WANTS TO BELIEVE.
HUH?!, AWW MAN, I HAVEN'T EATEN ANYTHING TODAY.
..GRRR
MAYBE THE CAFETERIA WOULD STILL HAVE SOME LEFTOVERS.
PICKS
OKAY... LETS SEE, IT SAYS HERE THAT ITS GONNA BE... BUILDING K-12.

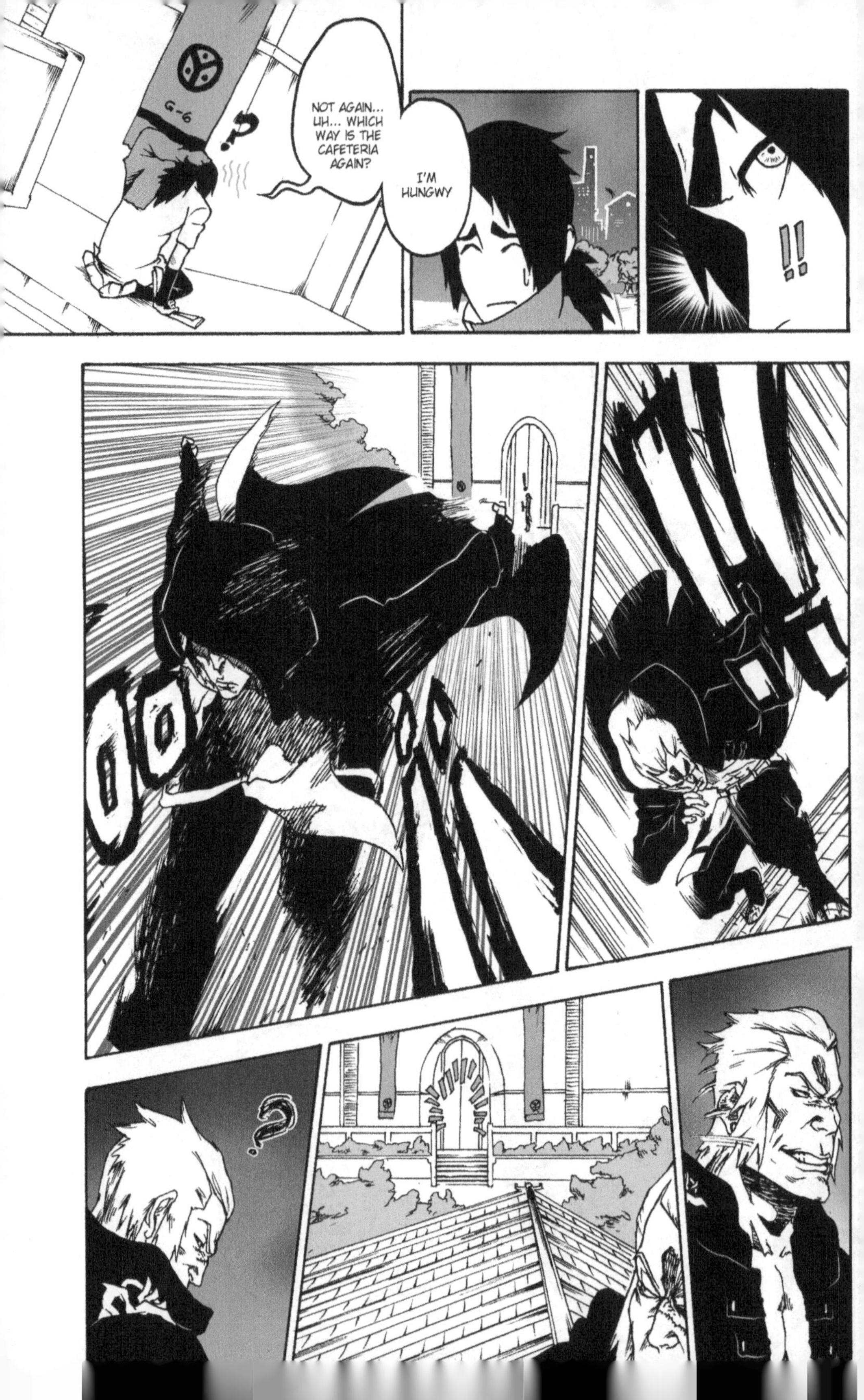
G-6
?
NOT AGAIN... UH... WHICH WAY IS THE CAFETERIA AGAIN?
I'M HUNGWY
!!
?

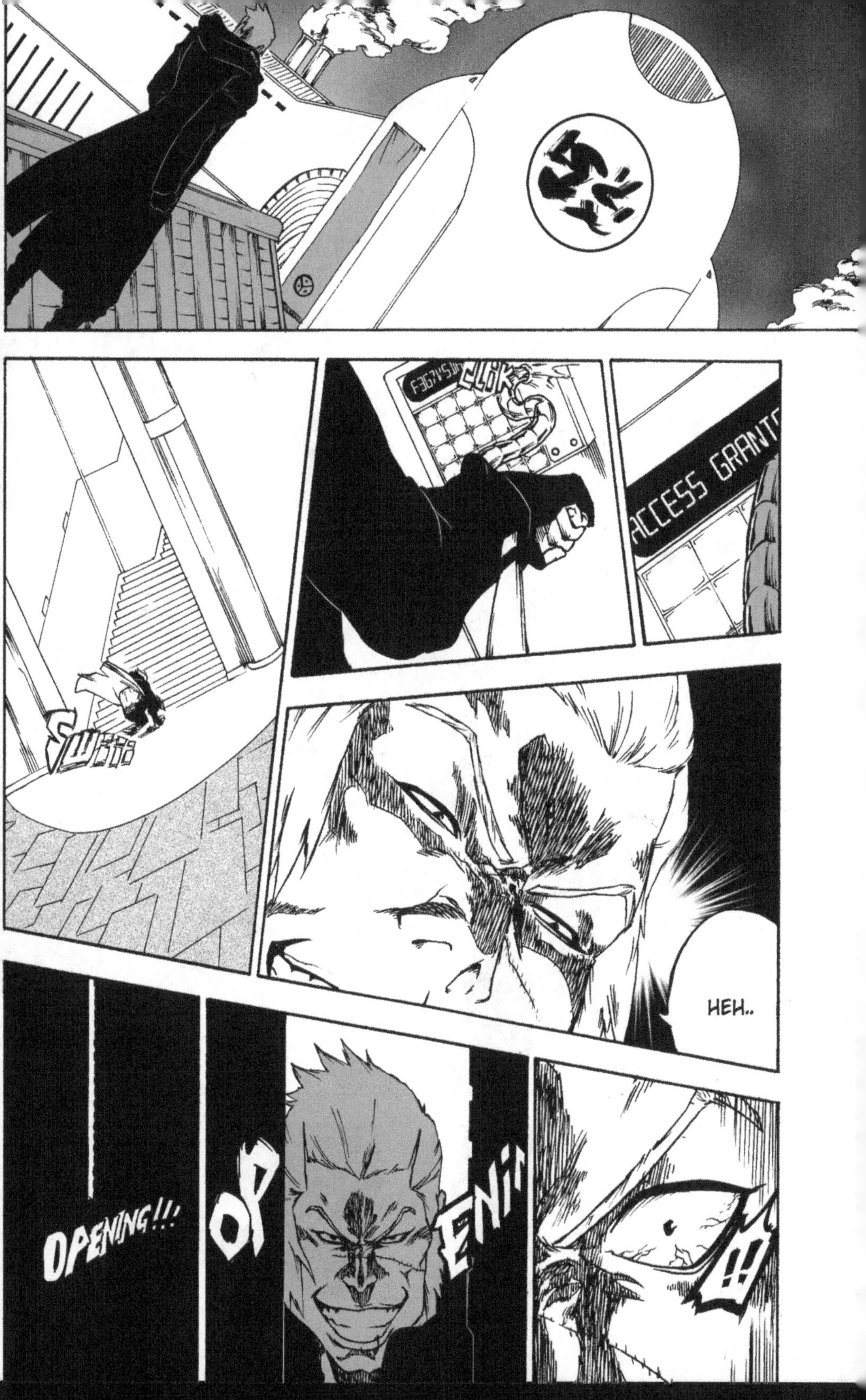
CLIK
ACCESS GRANT
HEH..
OPENING!!!
OP
ENI
!!

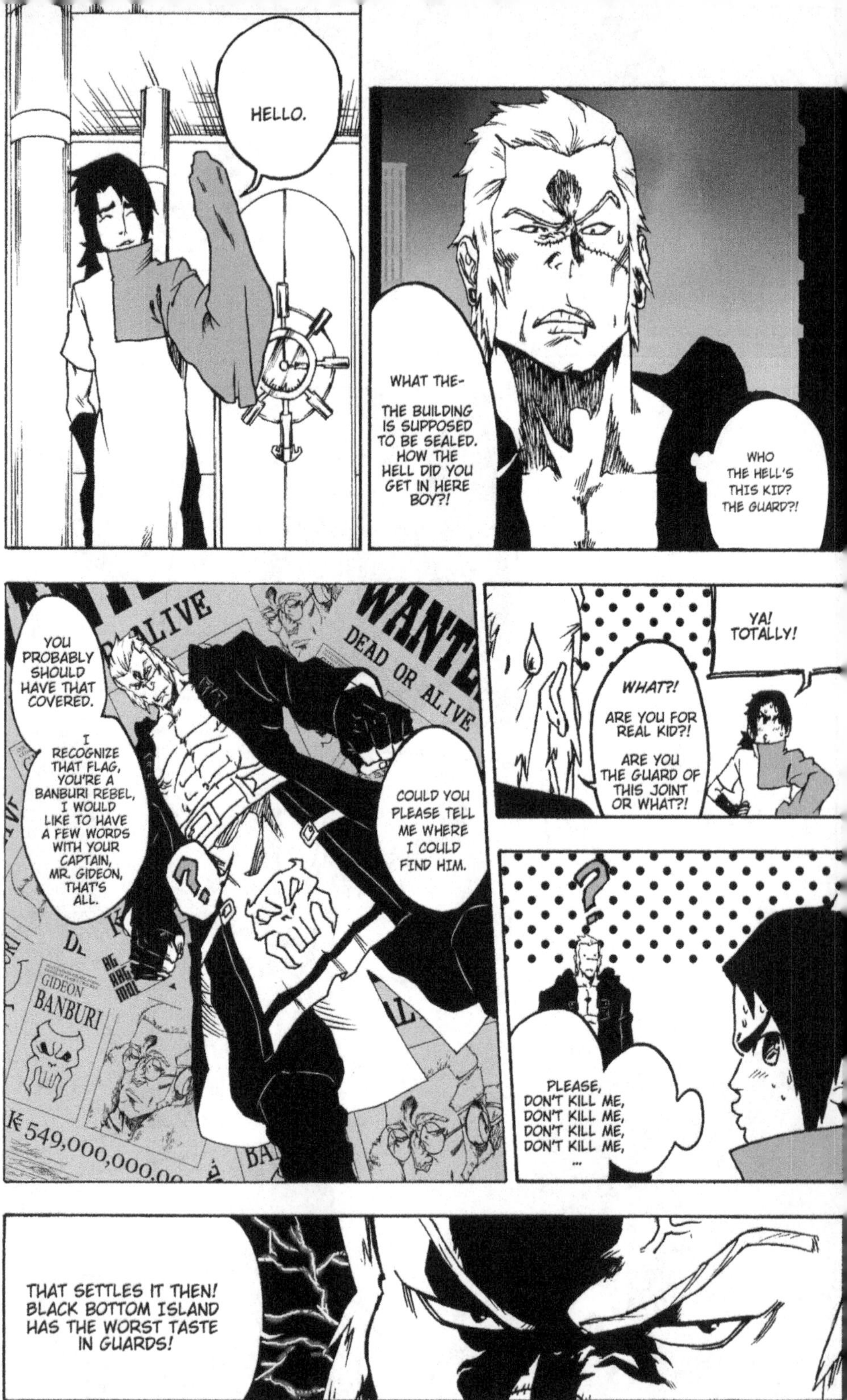
HELLO.
WHAT THE-
THE BUILDING IS SUPPOSED TO BE SEALED. HOW THE HELL DID YOU GET IN HERE BOY?!
WHO THE HELL'S THIS KID? THE GUARD?!
YOU PROBABLY SHOULD HAVE THAT COVERED.
I RECOGNIZE THAT FLAG, YOU'RE A BANBURI REBEL, I WOULD LIKE TO HAVE A FEW WORDS WITH YOUR CAPTAIN, MR. GIDEON, THAT'S ALL.
COULD YOU PLEASE TELL ME WHERE I COULD FIND HIM.
DEAD OR ALIVE
GIDEON BANBURI
WHAT?!
ARE YOU FOR REAL KID?!
ARE YOU THE GUARD OF THIS JOINT OR WHAT?!
YA! TOTALLY!
PLEASE, DON'T KILL ME, DON'T KILL ME, DON'T KILL ME, DON'T KILL ME, ...
THAT SETTLES IT THEN! BLACK BOTTOM ISLAND HAS THE WORST TASTE IN GUARDS!

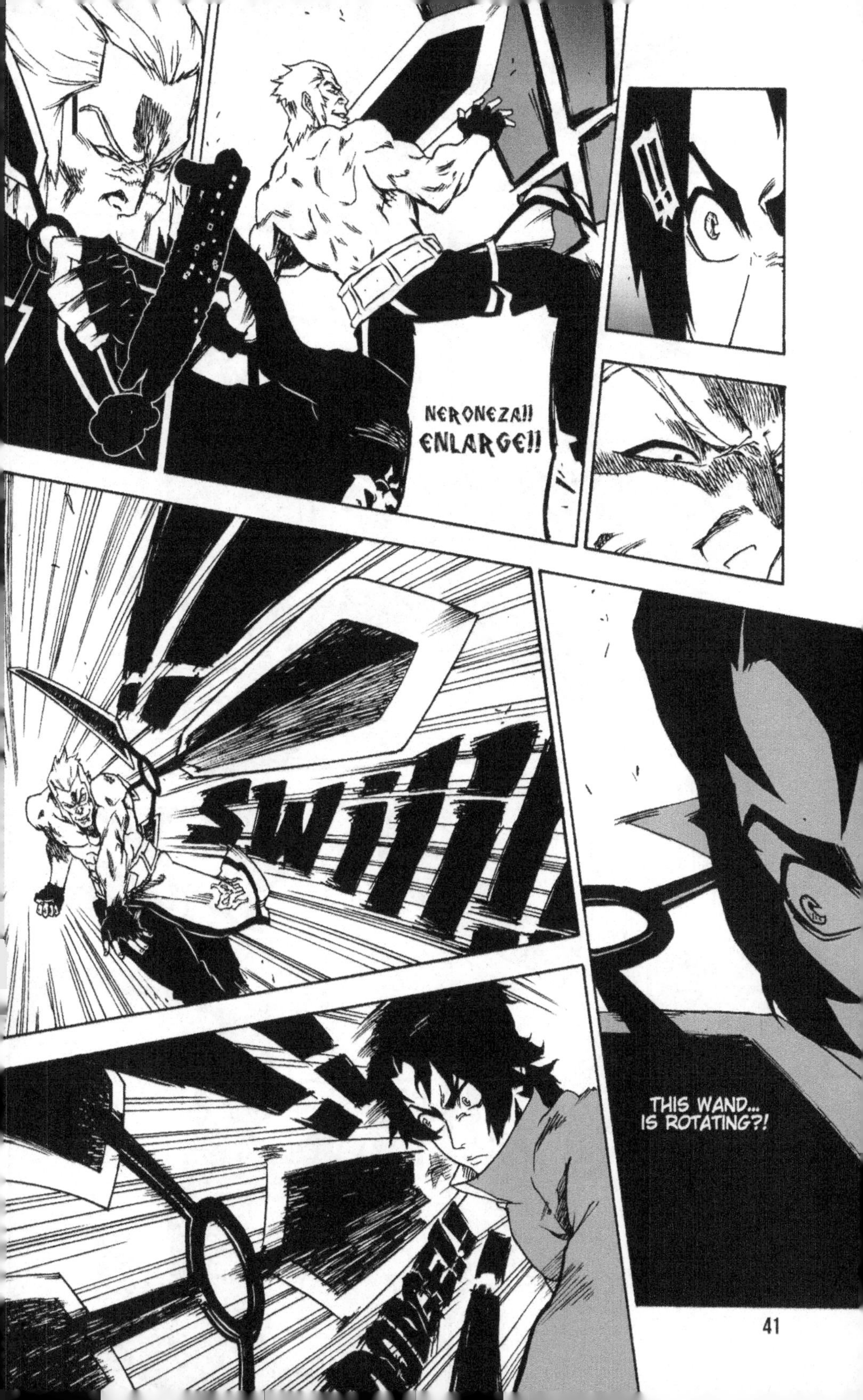
NERONEZA!!
ENLARGE!!
THIS WAND...
IS ROTATING?!

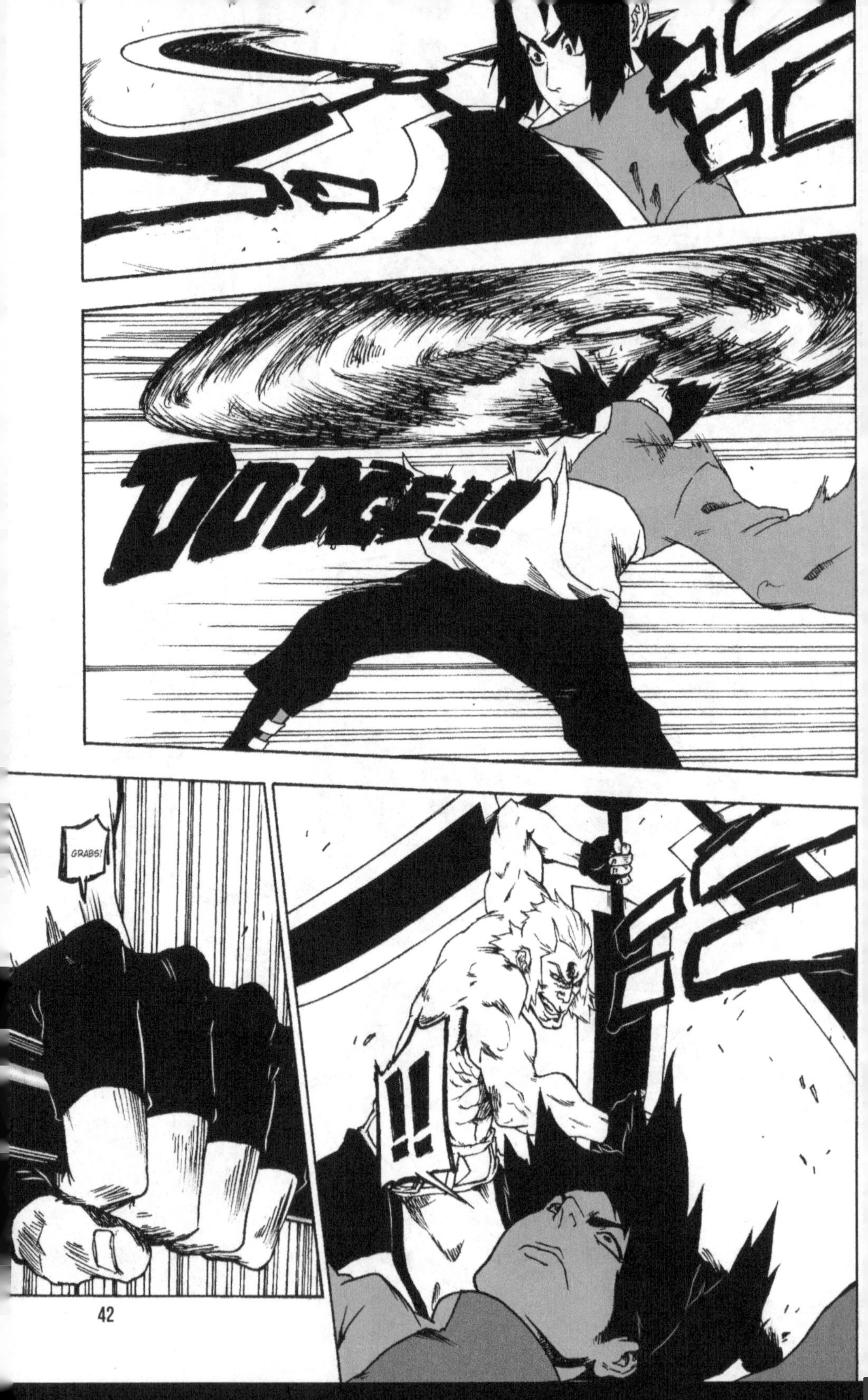
DODGE!!
GRABS!
!!

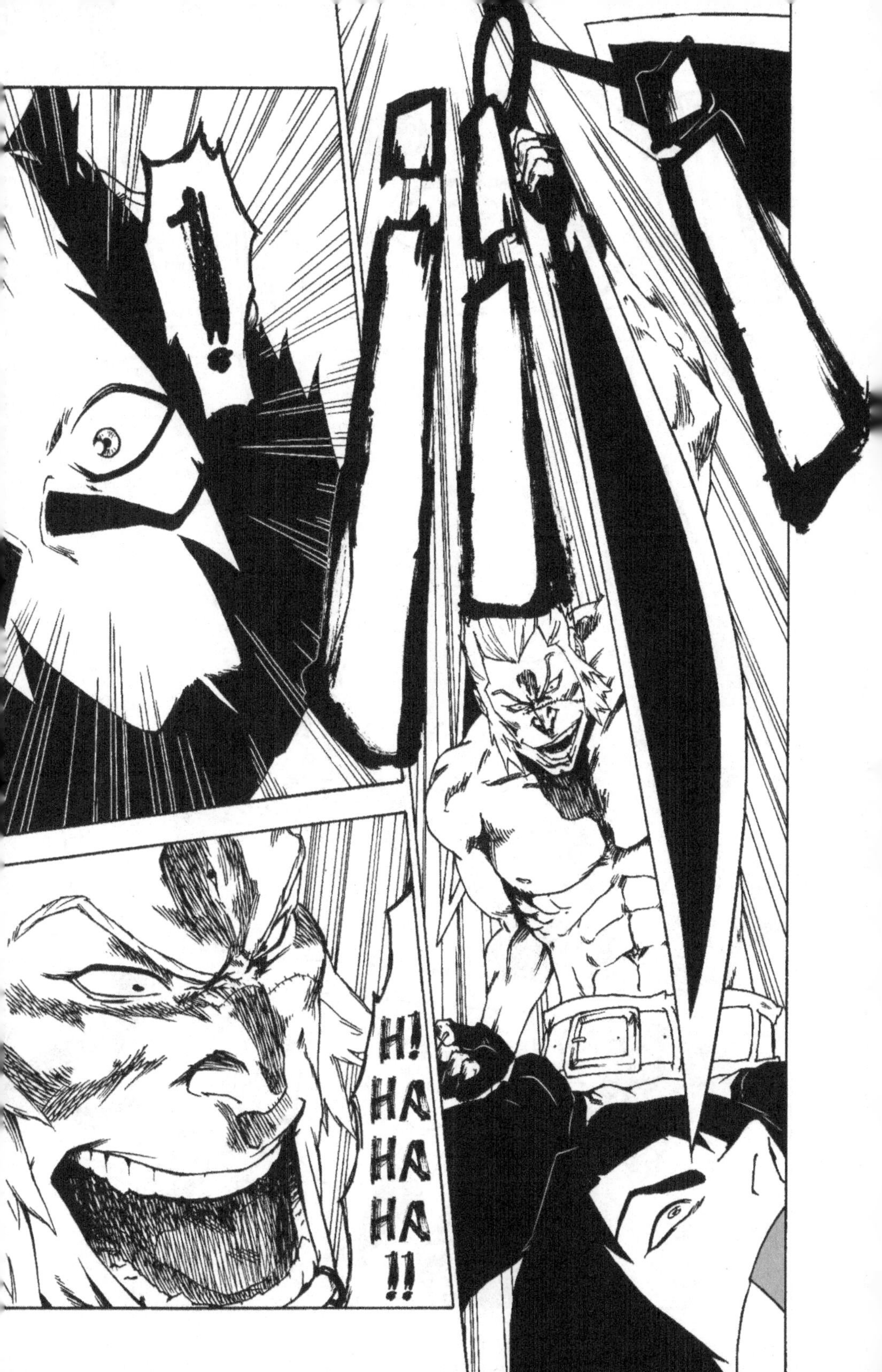
!!
H! HA HA HA HA!!

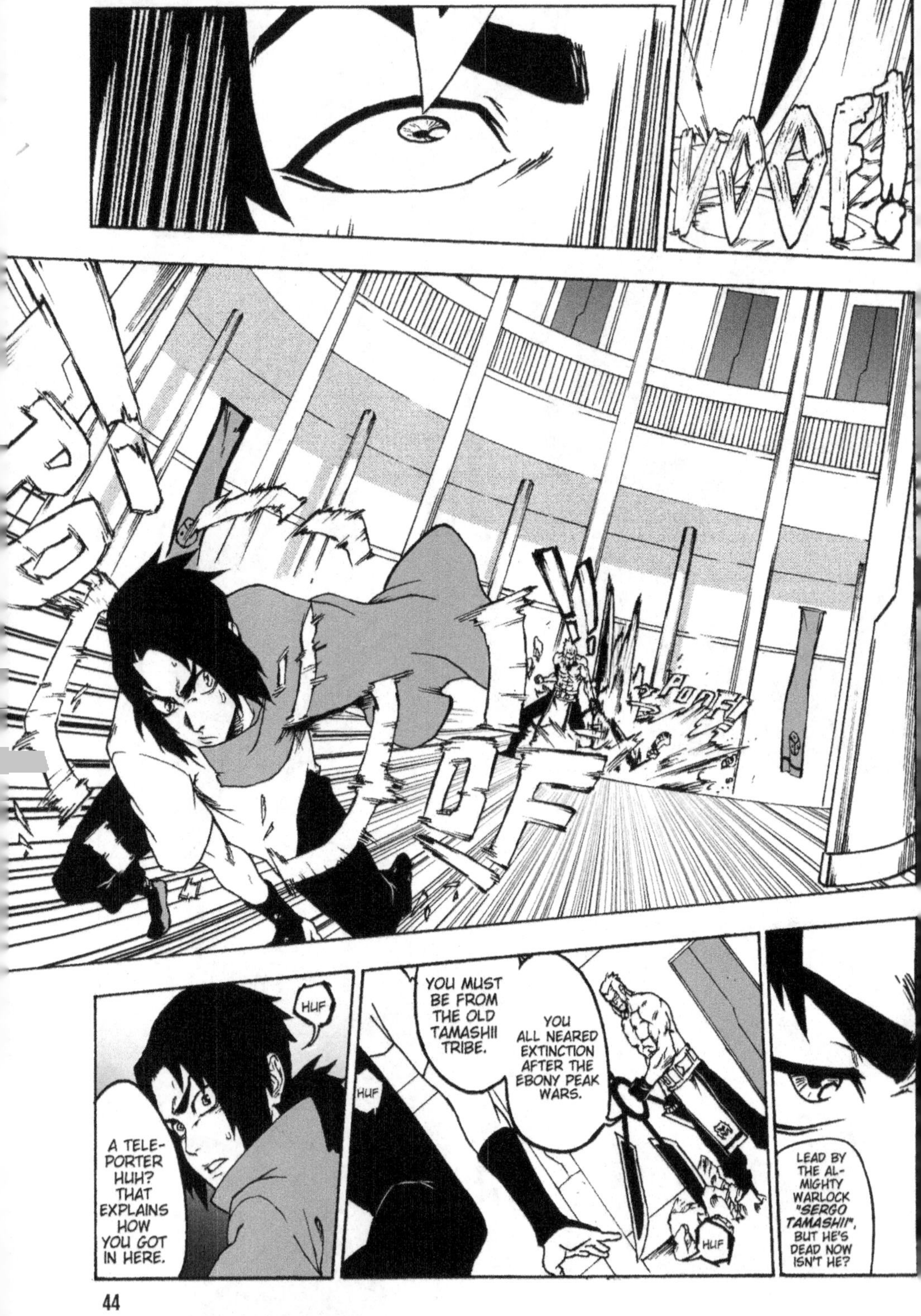
VOOF!
POOF!
HUF
A TELE-PORTER HUH? THAT EXPLAINS HOW YOU GOT IN HERE.
YOU MUST BE FROM THE OLD TAMASHII TRIBE.
YOU ALL NEARED EXTINCTION AFTER THE EBONY PEAK WARS.
HUF
HUF
LEAD BY THE AL-MIGHTY WARLOCK "SERGO TAMASHII", BUT HE'S DEAD NOW ISN'T HE?

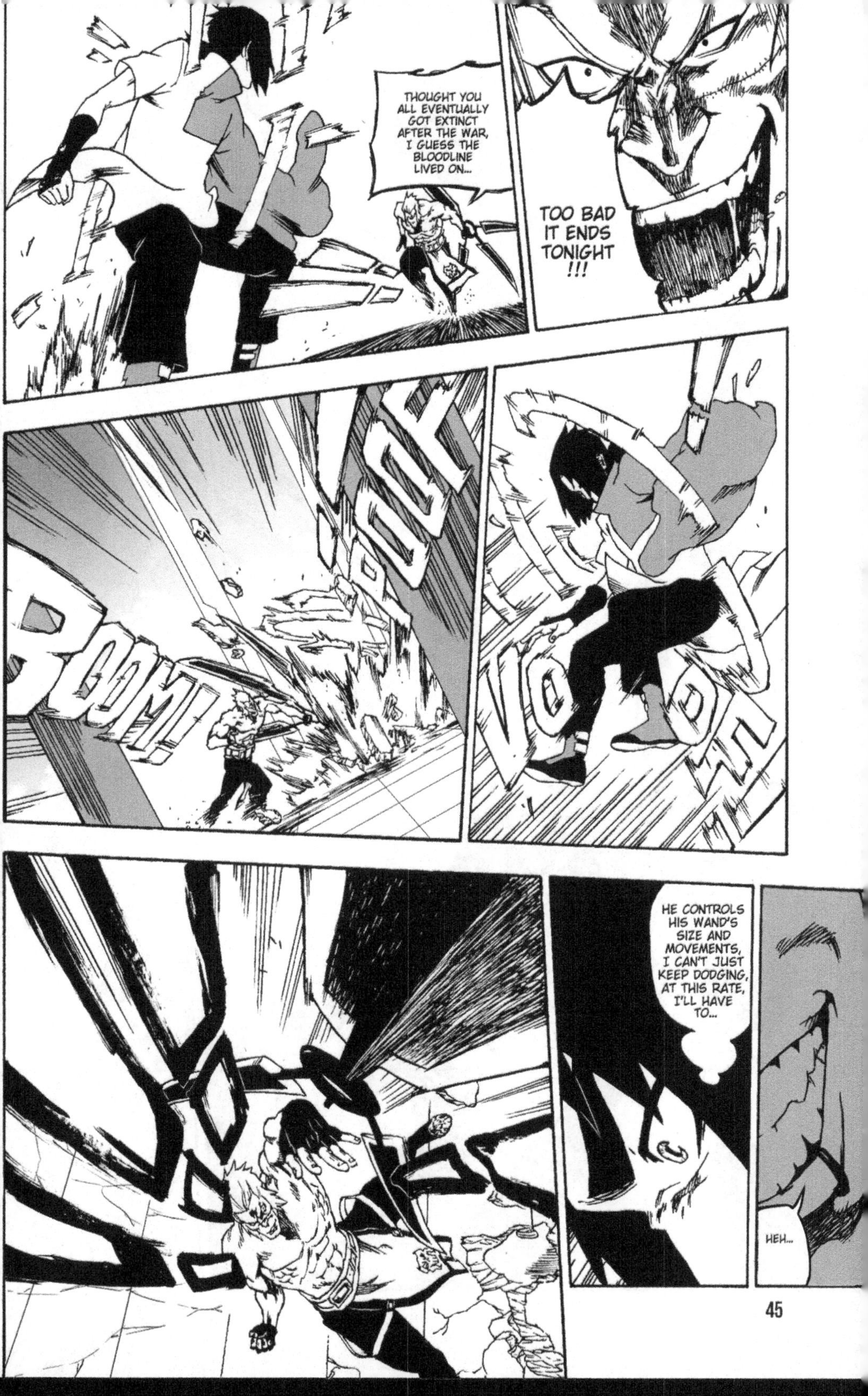
THOUGHT YOU ALL EVENTUALLY GOT EXTINCT AFTER THE WAR, I GUESS THE BLOODLINE LIVED ON...
TOO BAD IT ENDS TONIGHT !!!
BOOM!
HE CONTROLS HIS WAND'S SIZE AND MOVEMENTS, I CAN'T JUST KEEP DODGING, AT THIS RATE, I'LL HAVE TO...
HEH...

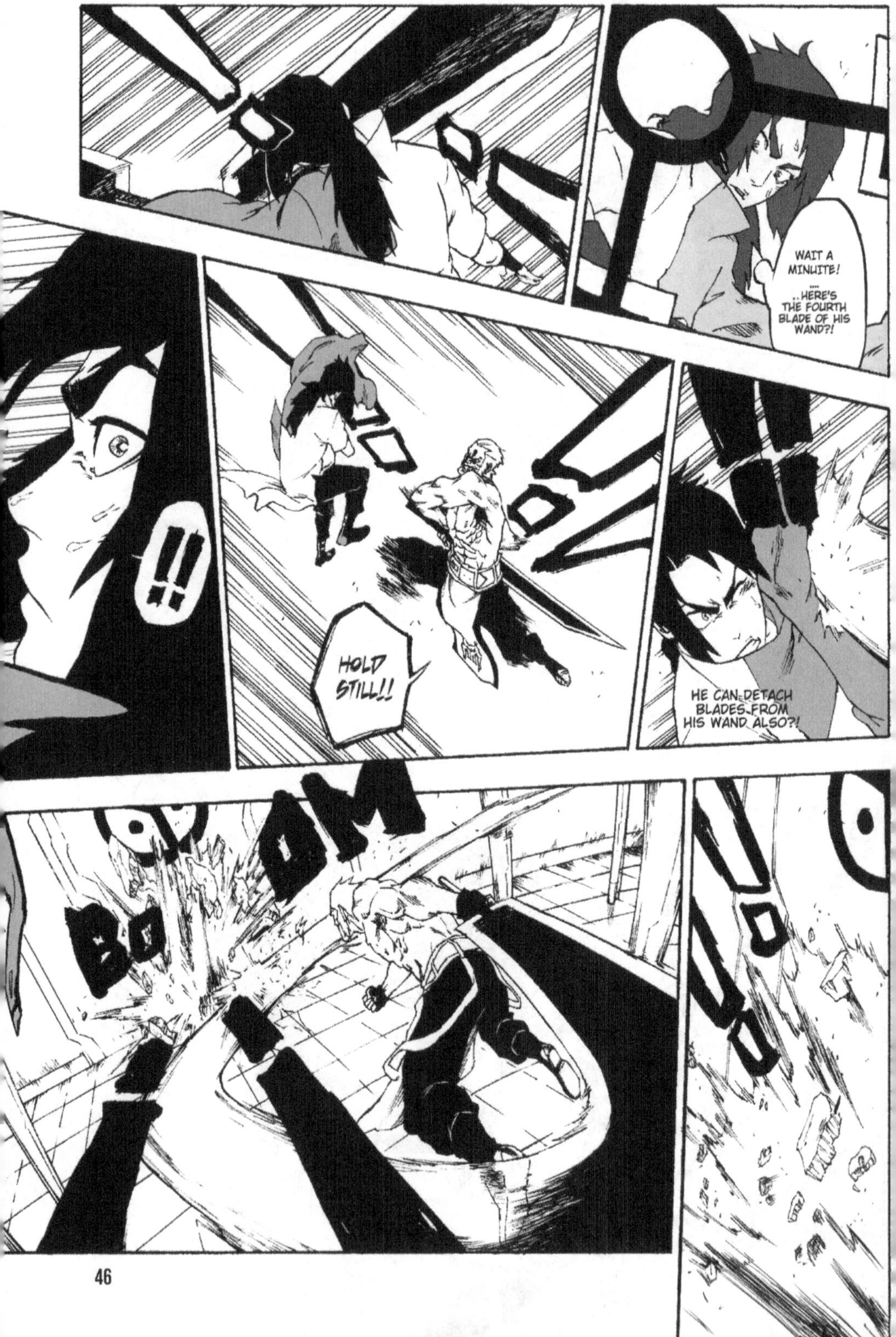
WAIT A MINUITE!
.....
..HERE'S THE FOURTH BLADE OF HIS WAND?!
!!
HOLD STILL!!
HE CAN DETACH BLADES FROM HIS WAND ALSO?!
BOOM

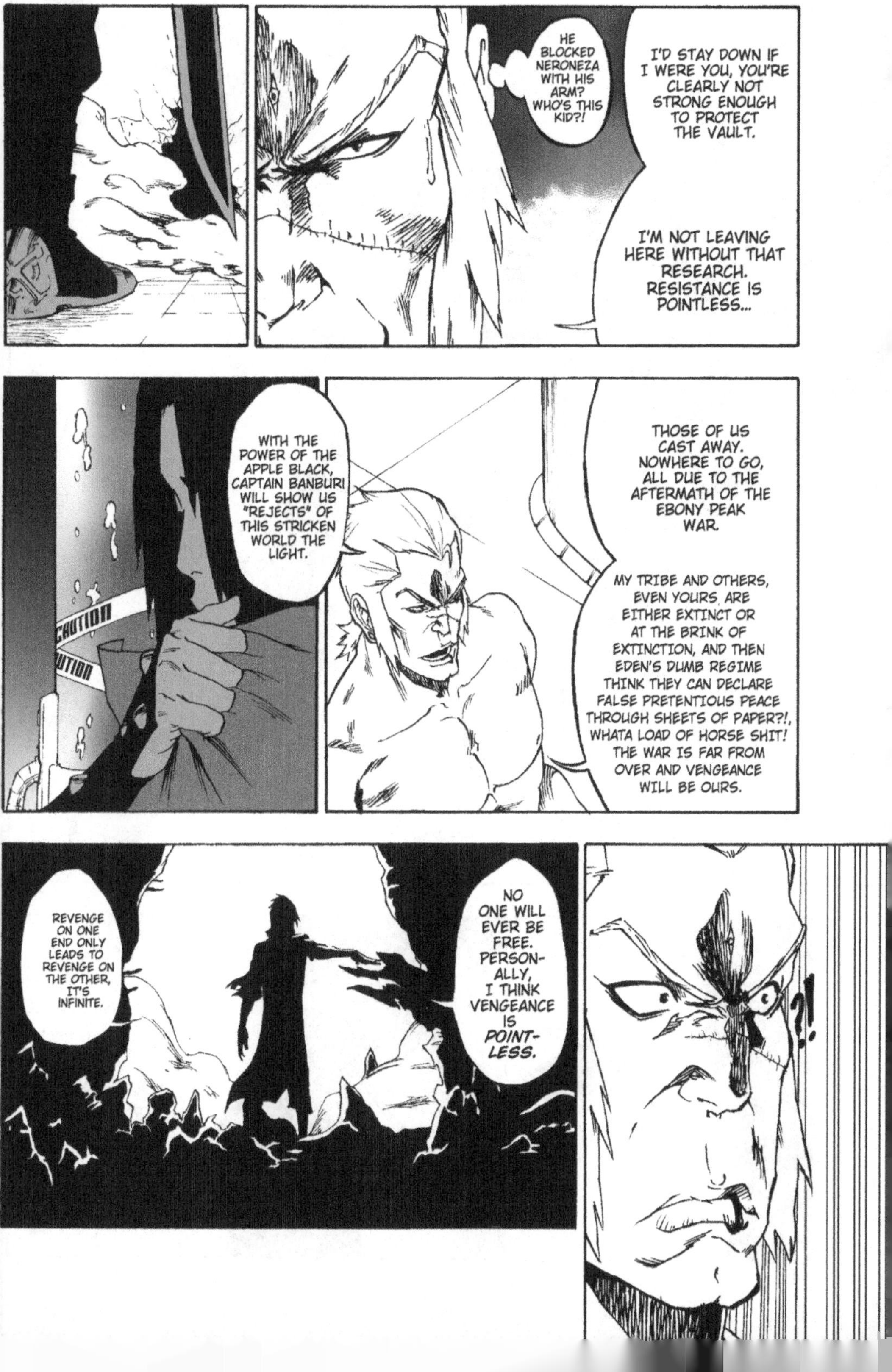
HE BLOCKED NERONEZA WITH HIS ARM? WHO'S THIS KID?!
I'D STAY DOWN IF I WERE YOU, YOU'RE CLEARLY NOT STRONG ENOUGH TO PROTECT THE VAULT.
I'M NOT LEAVING HERE WITHOUT THAT RESEARCH. RESISTANCE IS POINTLESS...
CAUTION
UTION
WITH THE POWER OF THE APPLE BLACK, CAPTAIN BANBURI WILL SHOW US "REJECTS" OF THIS STRICKEN WORLD THE LIGHT.
THOSE OF US CAST AWAY. NOWHERE TO GO, ALL DUE TO THE AFTERMATH OF THE EBONY PEAK WAR.
MY TRIBE AND OTHERS, EVEN YOURS, ARE EITHER EXTINCT OR AT THE BRINK OF EXTINCTION, AND THEN EDEN'S DUMB REGIME THINK THEY CAN DECLARE FALSE PRETENTIOUS PEACE THROUGH SHEETS OF PAPER?!, WHATA LOAD OF HORSE SHIT! THE WAR IS FAR FROM OVER AND VENGEANCE WILL BE OURS.
REVENGE ON ONE END ONLY LEADS TO REVENGE ON THE OTHER, IT'S INFINITE.
NO ONE WILL EVER BE FREE. PERSON-ALLY, I THINK VENGEANCE IS *POINT-LESS.*
?!

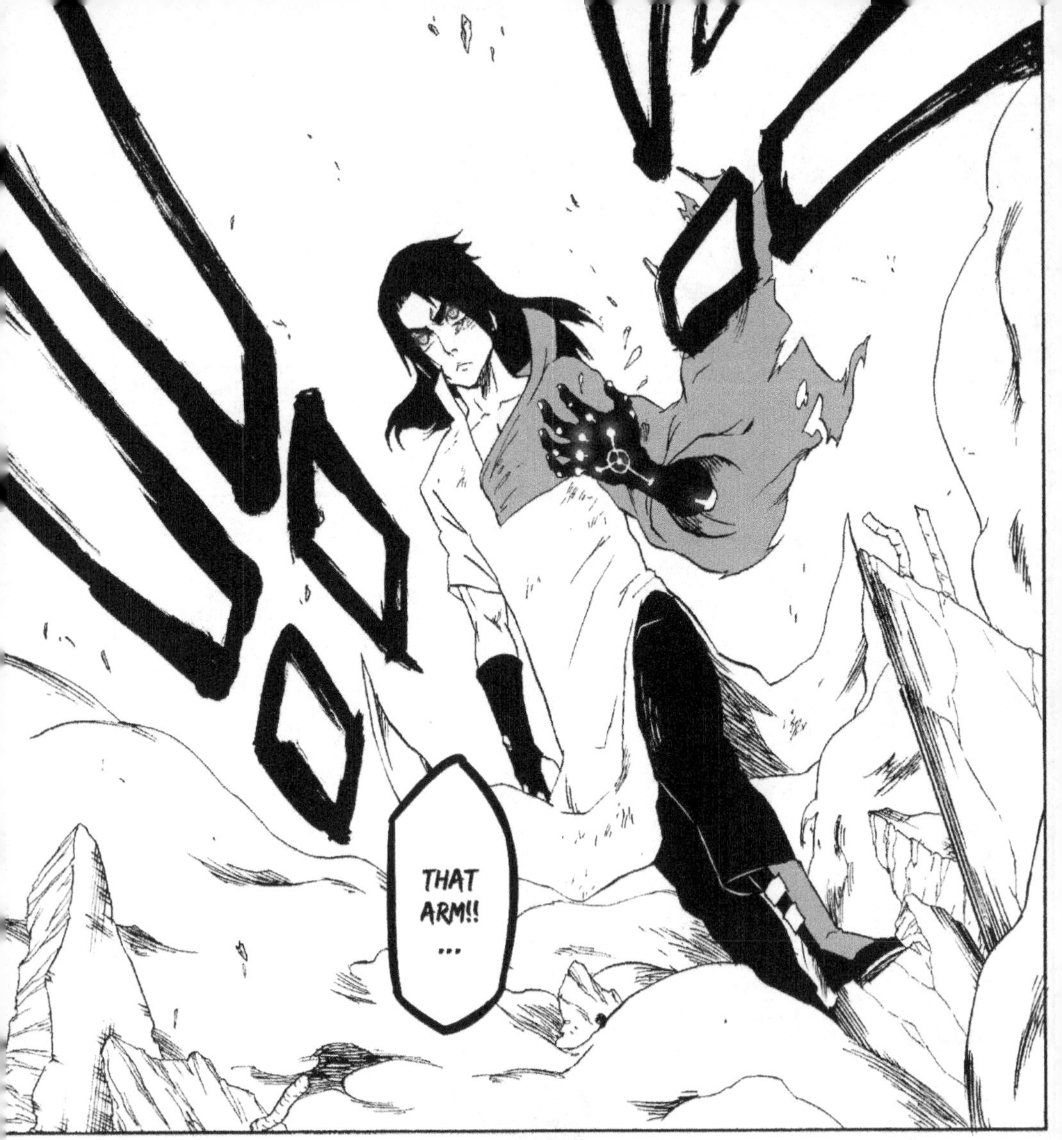
THAT ARM!! ...

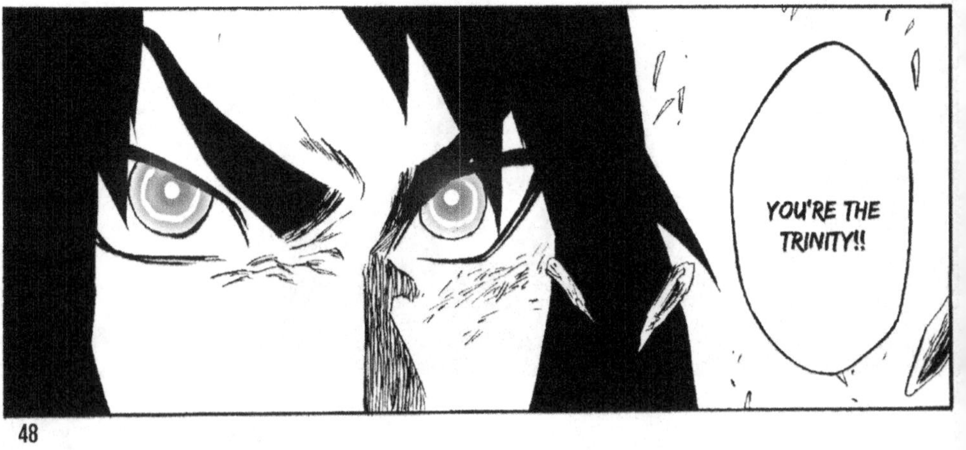
YOU'RE THE TRINITY!!

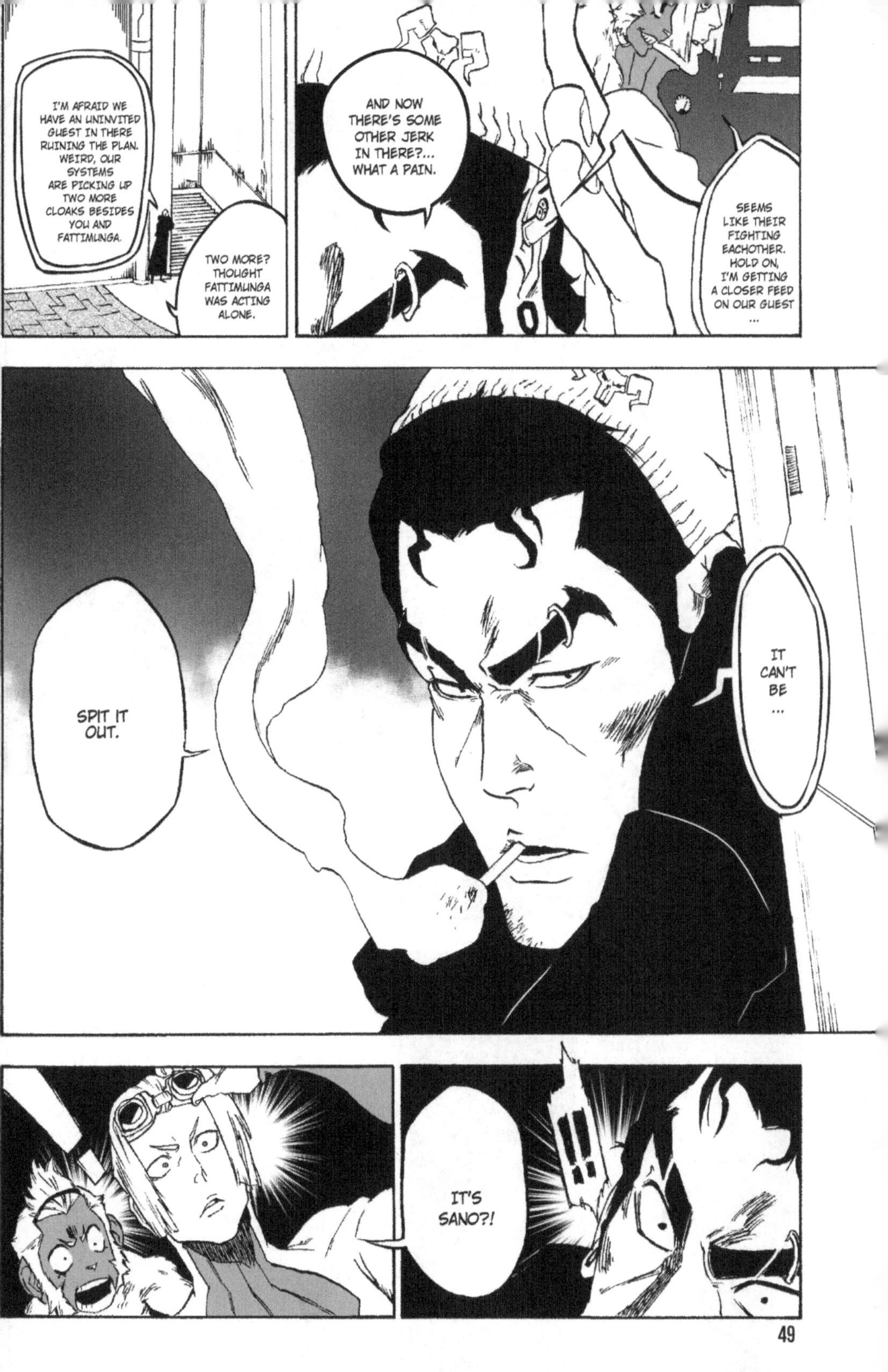
I'M AFRAID WE HAVE AN UNINVITED GUEST IN THERE RUINING THE PLAN. WEIRD, OUR SYSTEMS ARE PICKING UP TWO MORE CLOAKS BESIDES YOU AND FATTIMUNGA.
TWO MORE? THOUGHT FATTIMUNGA WAS ACTING ALONE.
AND NOW THERE'S SOME OTHER JERK IN THERE?... WHAT A PAIN.
SEEMS LIKE THEIR FIGHTING EACHOTHER. HOLD ON, I'M GETTING A CLOSER FEED ON OUR GUEST ...
SPIT IT OUT.
IT CAN'T BE ...
IT'S SANO?!

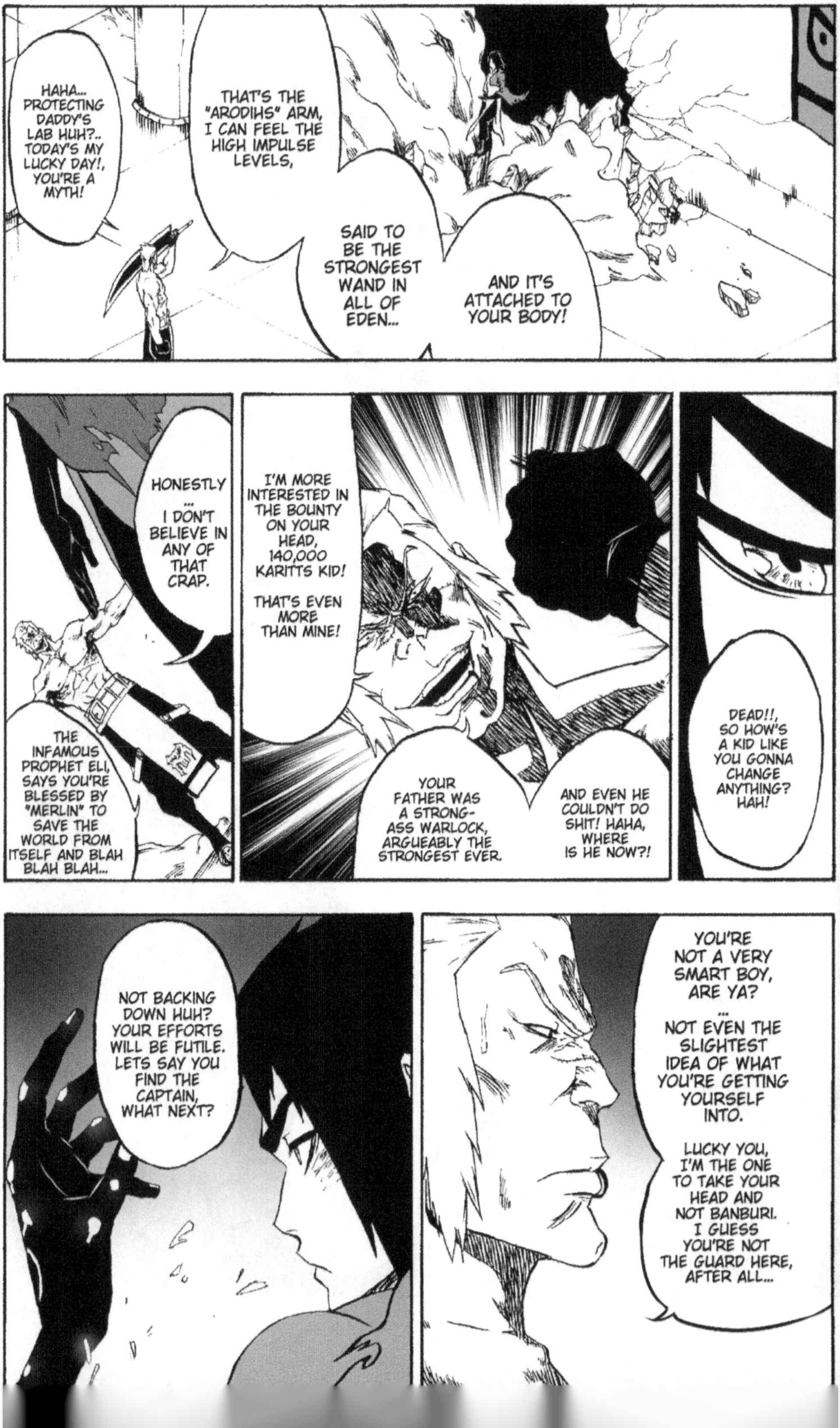
HAHA... PROTECTING DADDY'S LAB HUH?.. TODAY'S MY LUCKY DAY!, YOU'RE A MYTH!
THAT'S THE "ARODIHS" ARM, I CAN FEEL THE HIGH IMPULSE LEVELS,
SAID TO BE THE STRONGEST WAND IN ALL OF EDEN...
AND IT'S ATTACHED TO YOUR BODY!
HONESTLY ... I DON'T BELIEVE IN ANY OF THAT CRAP.
THE INFAMOUS PROPHET ELI, SAYS YOU'RE BLESSED BY "MERLIN" TO SAVE THE WORLD FROM ITSELF AND BLAH BLAH BLAH...
I'M MORE INTERESTED IN THE BOUNTY ON YOUR HEAD, 140,000 KARITTS KID!
THAT'S EVEN MORE THAN MINE!
YOUR FATHER WAS A STRONG-ASS WARLOCK, ARGUEABLY THE STRONGEST EVER.
AND EVEN HE COULDN'T DO SHIT! HAHA, WHERE IS HE NOW?!
DEAD!!, SO HOW'S A KID LIKE YOU GONNA CHANGE ANYTHING? HAH!
NOT BACKING DOWN HUH? YOUR EFFORTS WILL BE FUTILE. LETS SAY YOU FIND THE CAPTAIN, WHAT NEXT?
YOU'RE NOT A VERY SMART BOY, ARE YA? ... NOT EVEN THE SLIGHTEST IDEA OF WHAT YOU'RE GETTING YOURSELF INTO.
LUCKY YOU, I'M THE ONE TO TAKE YOUR HEAD AND NOT BANBURI. I GUESS YOU'RE NOT THE GUARD HERE, AFTER ALL...

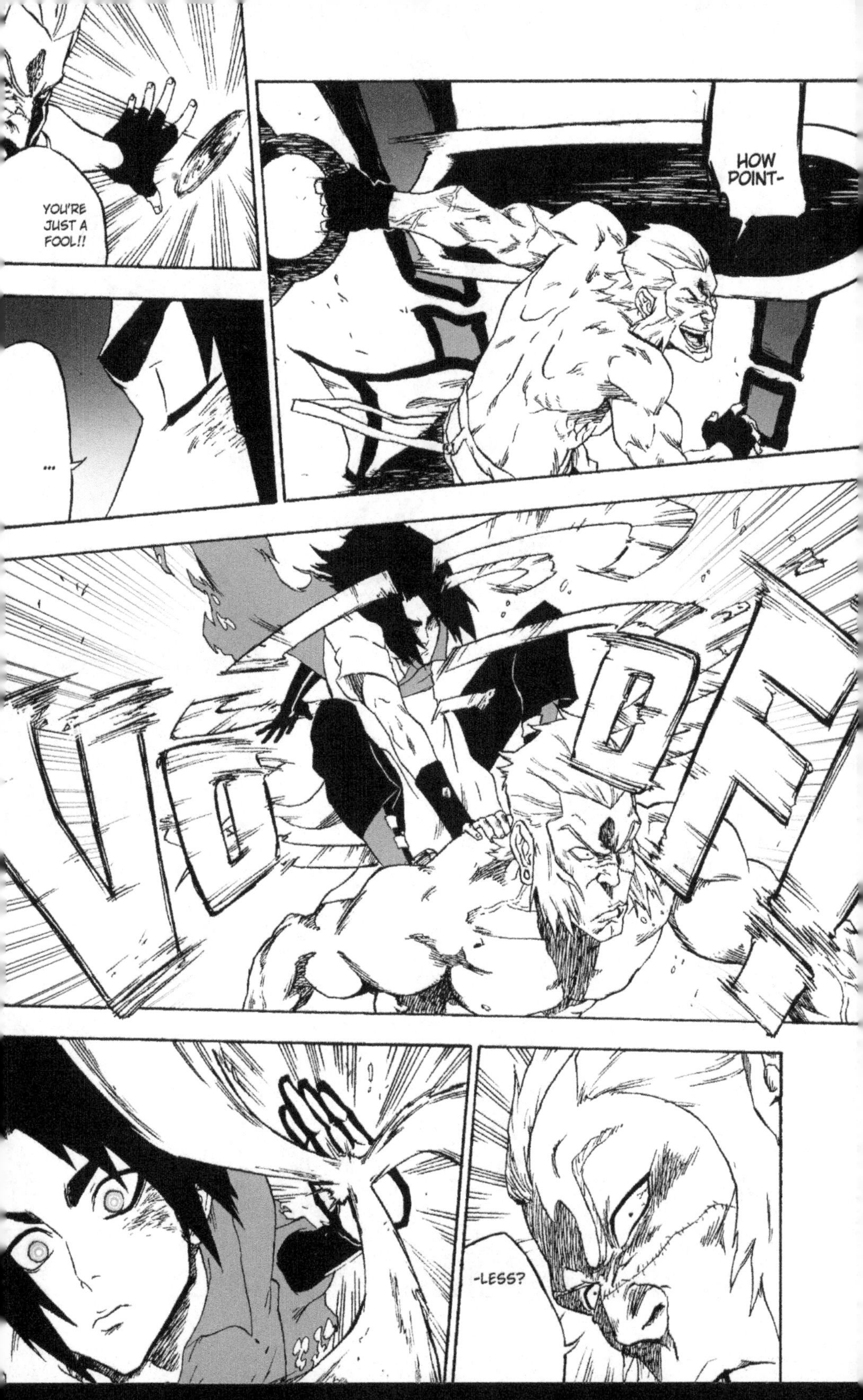
YOU'RE JUST A FOOL!!
HOW POINT-
...
-LESS?

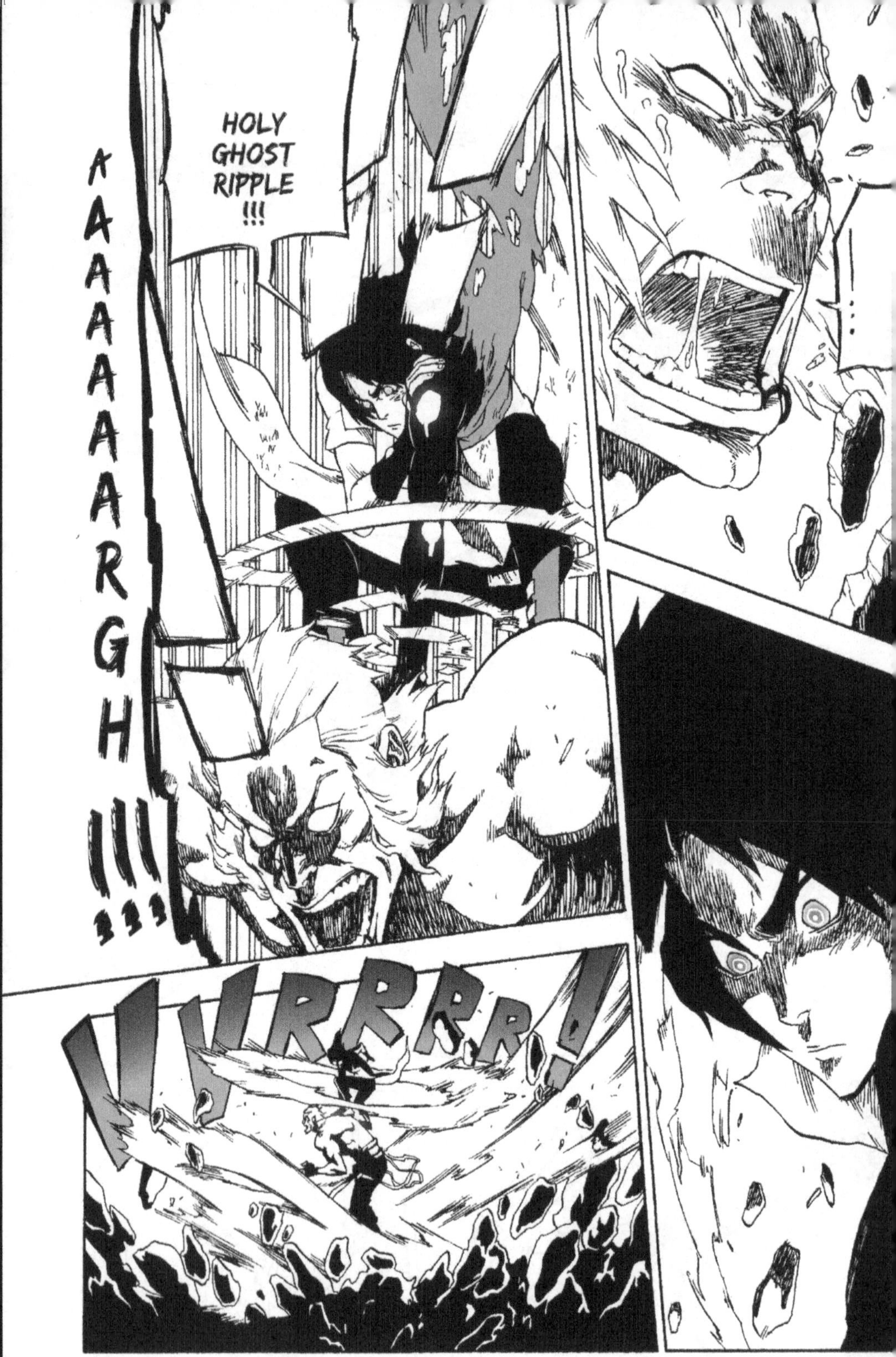
HOLY GHOST RIPPLE !!!
AAAAAAARGH!!!
VRRRR!

SANO!! ARE YOU OKAY?!

A SPELL STRONG ENOUGH TO KNOCK FATTIMUNGA OUT?!

URGH

HOW THE HELL?

YOU JUST MIGHT BE WORSE THAN RYUZAKI AND SYMON!

I THOUGHT I TOLD YOU TO STAY IN THE ROOM!

YOU COULDA GOTTEN YOURSELF KILLED DIPSHIT!!

WE HAVE FORCES FOR SITUATIONS LIKE THIS! WHY THE HELL DID YA COME OUT HERE?!, TO SHOW OFF?! THIS WAS A DECOY OPERATION! WE ALREADY LURED FATTIMUNGA TO THE WRONG VAULT! YOU ALMOST RUINED EVERYTHING!

I KNOW

BECAUSE THE REAL VAULT IS RIGHT IN FRONT OF ME.

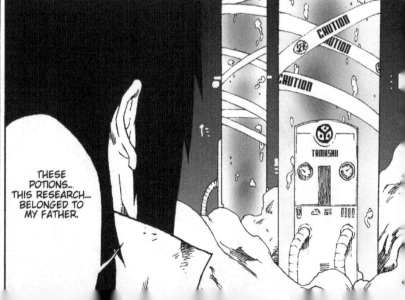

THESE POTIONS... THIS RESEARCH... BELONGED TO MY FATHER.

CAUTION
CAUTION
CAUTION

TAMASHII

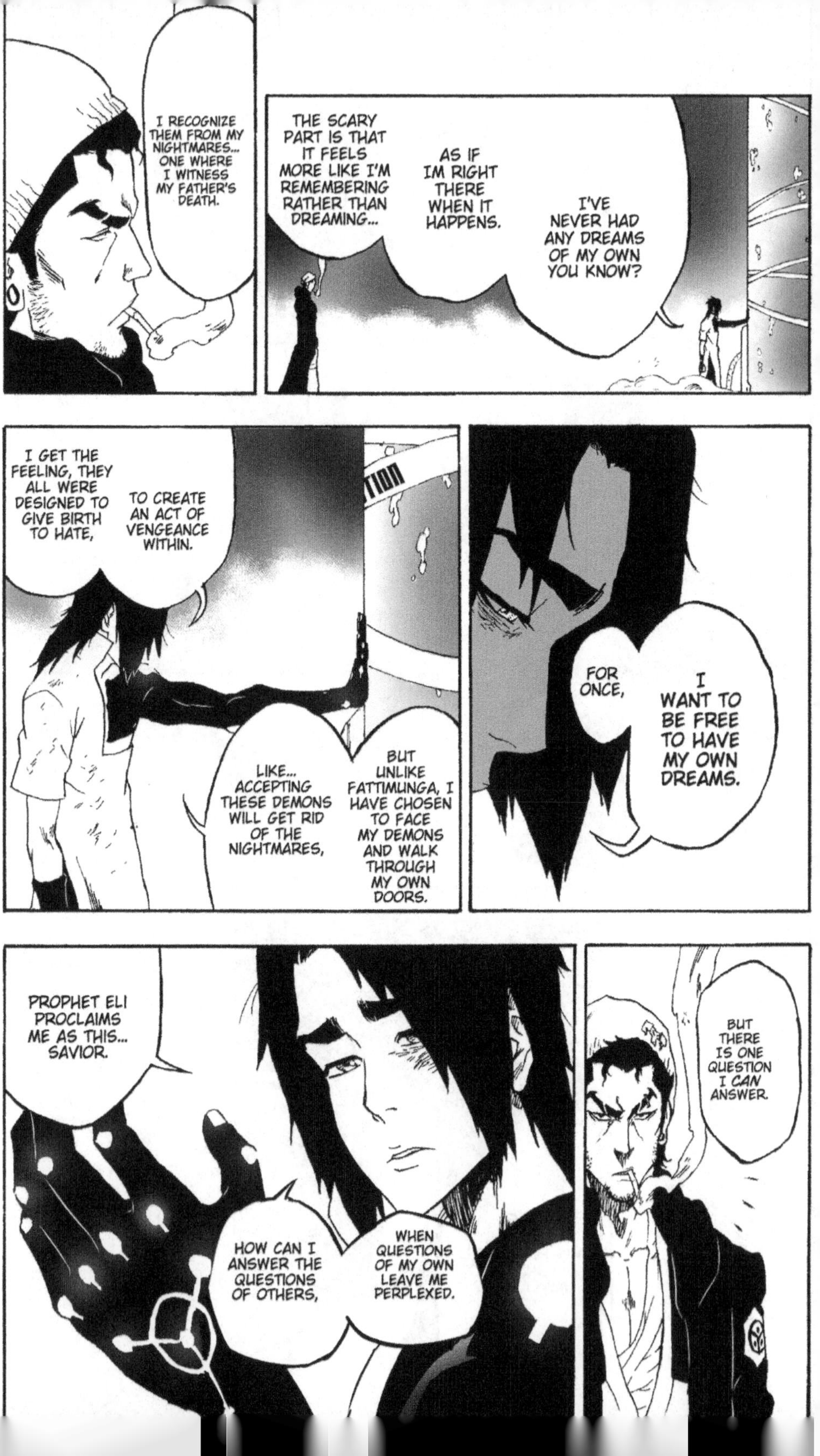
I RECOGNIZE THEM FROM MY NIGHTMARES... ONE WHERE I WITNESS MY FATHER'S DEATH.
THE SCARY PART IS THAT IT FEELS MORE LIKE I'M REMEMBERING RATHER THAN DREAMING...
AS IF I'M RIGHT THERE WHEN IT HAPPENS.
I'VE NEVER HAD ANY DREAMS OF MY OWN YOU KNOW?
I GET THE FEELING, THEY ALL WERE DESIGNED TO GIVE BIRTH TO HATE,
TO CREATE AN ACT OF VENGEANCE WITHIN.
LIKE... ACCEPTING THESE DEMONS WILL GET RID OF THE NIGHTMARES,
BUT UNLIKE FATTIMUNGA, I HAVE CHOSEN TO FACE MY DEMONS AND WALK THROUGH MY OWN DOORS.
FOR ONCE,
I WANT TO BE FREE TO HAVE MY OWN DREAMS.
PROPHET ELI PROCLAIMS ME AS THIS... SAVIOR.
HOW CAN I ANSWER THE QUESTIONS OF OTHERS,
WHEN QUESTIONS OF MY OWN LEAVE ME PERPLEXED.
BUT THERE IS ONE QUESTION I *CAN* ANSWER.

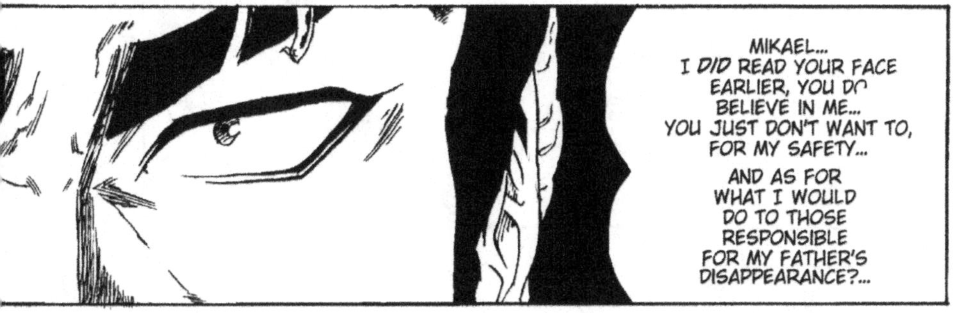
MIKAEL...
I *DID* READ YOUR FACE EARLIER, YOU DO BELIEVE IN ME... YOU JUST DON'T WANT TO, FOR MY SAFETY...
AND AS FOR WHAT I WOULD DO TO THOSE RESPONSIBLE FOR MY FATHER'S DISAPPEARANCE?...

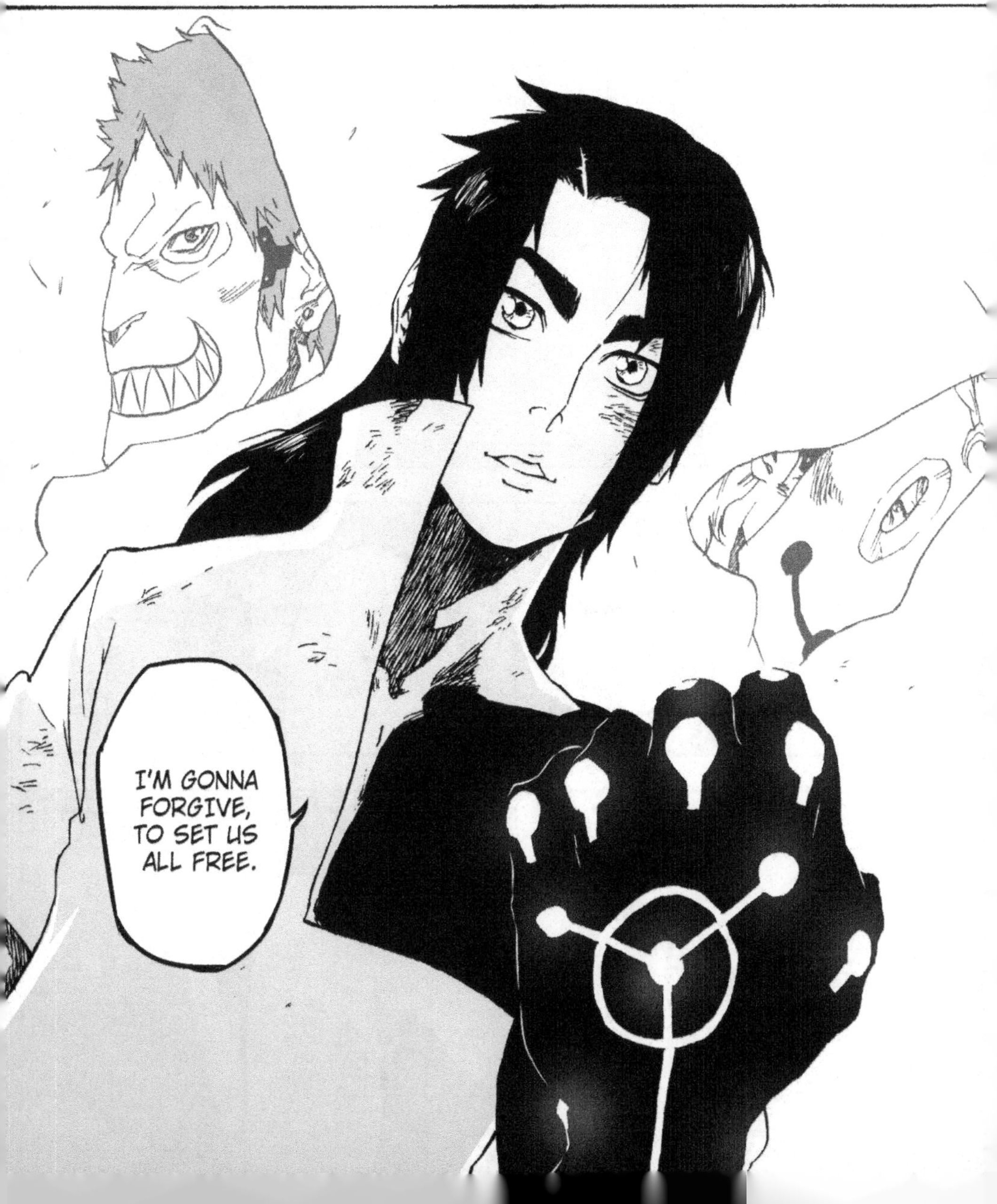
I'M GONNA FORGIVE, TO SET US ALL FREE.

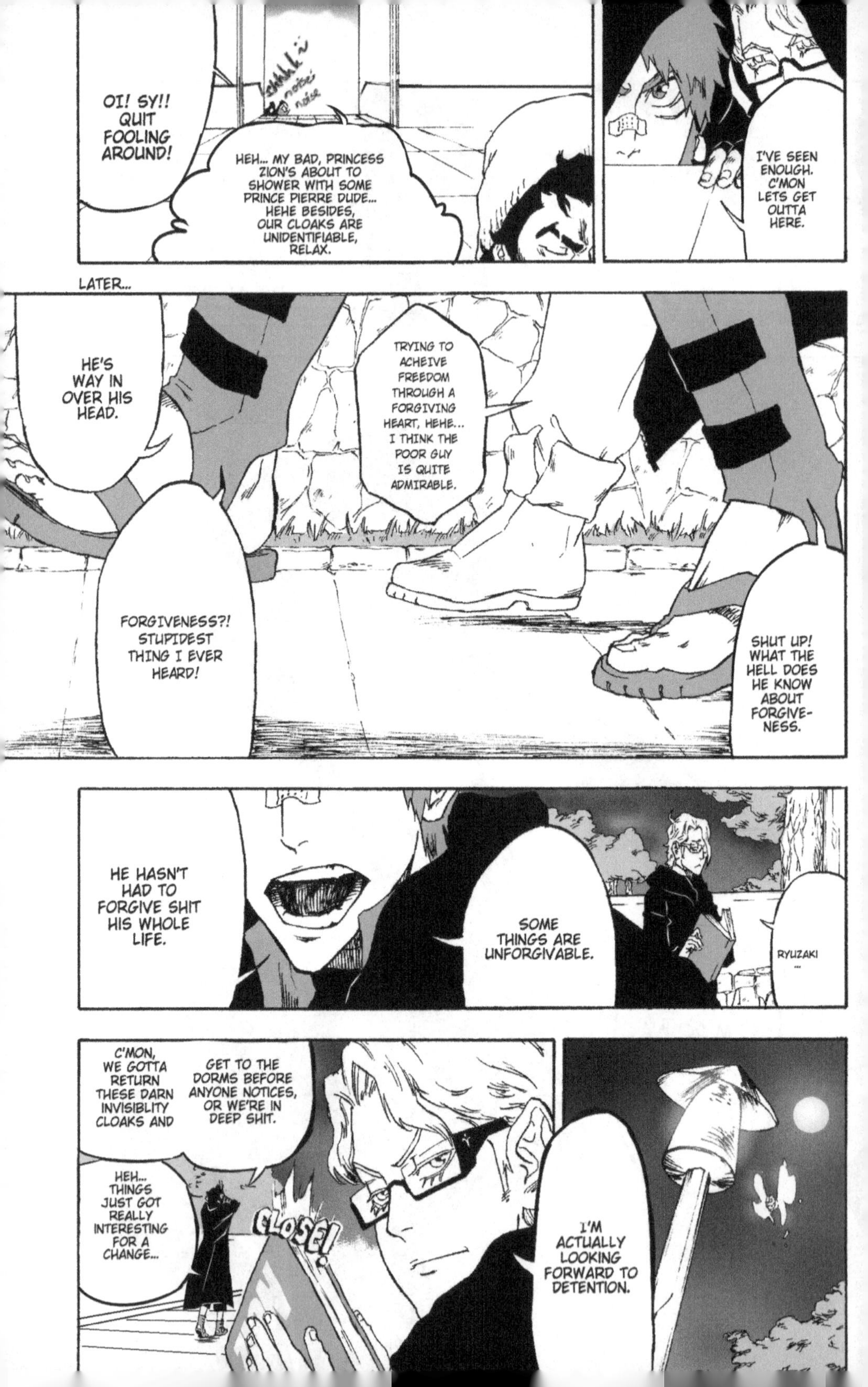
OI! SY!! QUIT FOOLING AROUND!
HEH... MY BAD, PRINCESS ZION'S ABOUT TO SHOWER WITH SOME PRINCE PIERRE DUDE... HEHE BESIDES, OUR CLOAKS ARE UNIDENTIFIABLE, RELAX.
I'VE SEEN ENOUGH. C'MON LETS GET OUTTA HERE.
LATER...
HE'S WAY IN OVER HIS HEAD.
TRYING TO ACHEIVE FREEDOM THROUGH A FORGIVING HEART, HEHE... I THINK THE POOR GUY IS QUITE ADMIRABLE.
FORGIVENESS?! STUPIDEST THING I EVER HEARD!
SHUT UP! WHAT THE HELL DOES HE KNOW ABOUT FORGIVE-NESS.
HE HASN'T HAD TO FORGIVE SHIT HIS WHOLE LIFE.
SOME THINGS ARE UNFORGIVABLE.
RYUZAKI ...
C'MON, WE GOTTA RETURN THESE DARN INVISIBLITY CLOAKS AND
GET TO THE DORMS BEFORE ANYONE NOTICES, OR WE'RE IN DEEP SHIT.
HEH... THINGS JUST GOT REALLY INTERESTING FOR A CHANGE...
CLOSE!
I'M ACTUALLY LOOKING FORWARD TO DETENTION.

GRUDON FATTIMUNGA

APPLE
BLACK

APPLE BLACK
2
HARBINGER
Story & Art by
ODUNZE W. OGUGUO
TWITTER.COM/WHYTMANGA
FACEBOOK.COM/WHYTMANGA
ODUNZE.DEVIANTART.COM

CREST BOREAS

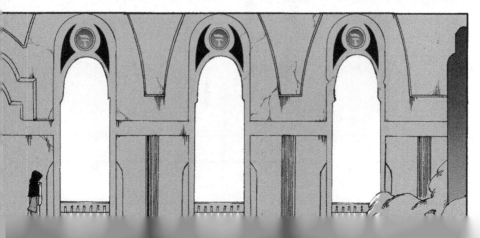

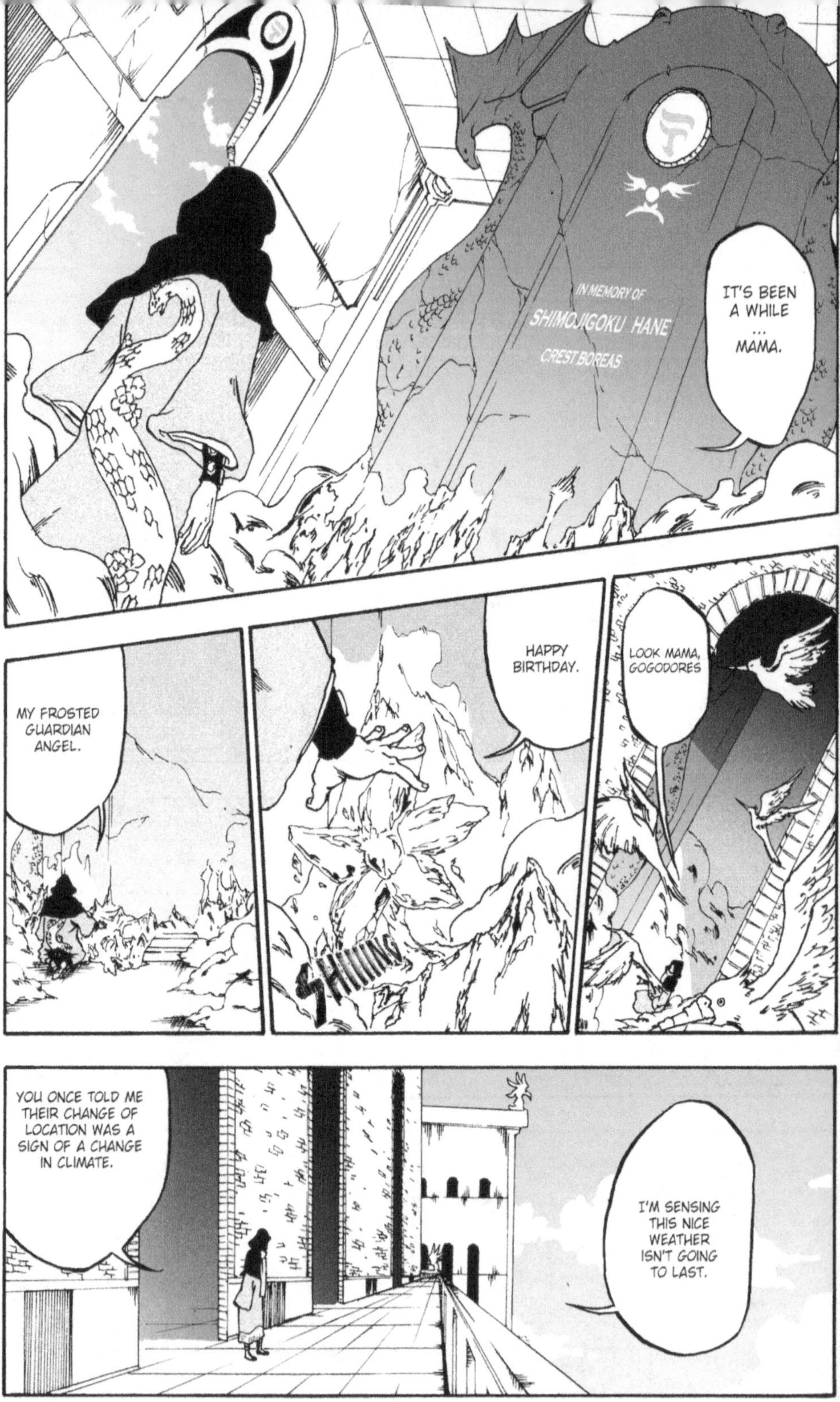
IN MEMORY OF
SHIMOJIGOKU HANE
CREST BOREAS
IT'S BEEN A WHILE ... MAMA.
LOOK MAMA, GOGODORES
HAPPY BIRTHDAY.
SHIIIING
MY FROSTED GUARDIAN ANGEL.
YOU ONCE TOLD ME THEIR CHANGE OF LOCATION WAS A SIGN OF A CHANGE IN CLIMATE.
I'M SENSING THIS NICE WEATHER ISN'T GOING TO LAST.

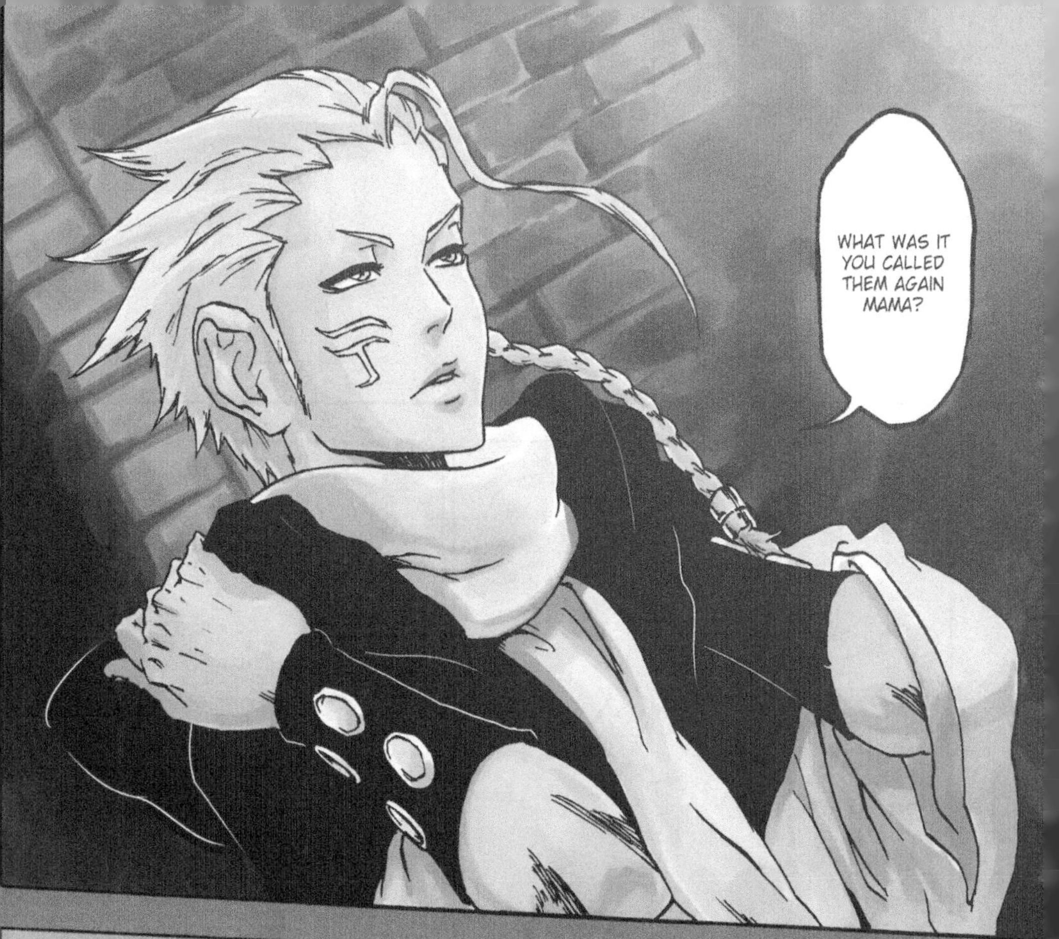
WHAT WAS IT YOU CALLED THEM AGAIN MAMA?

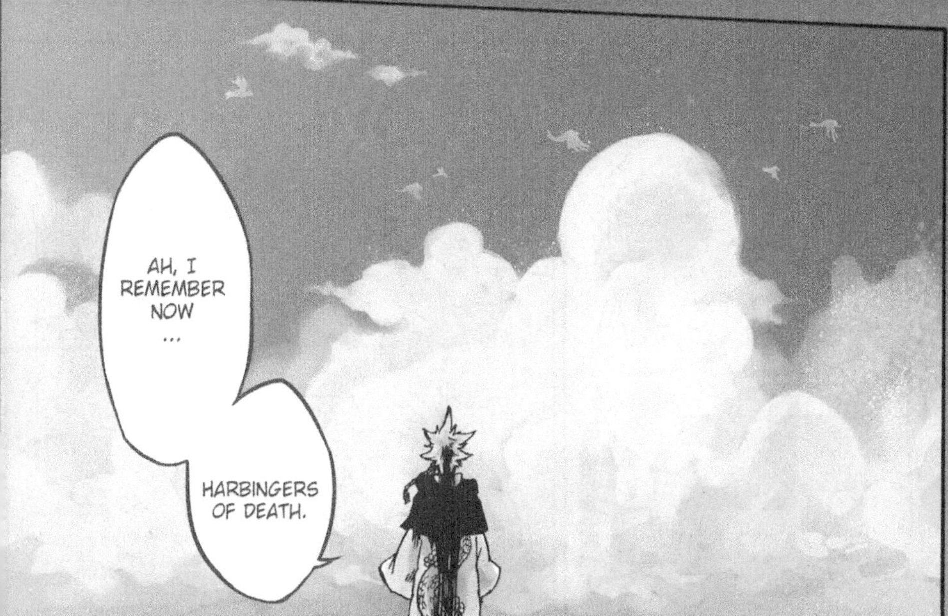
AH, I REMEMBER NOW ...
HARBINGERS OF DEATH.

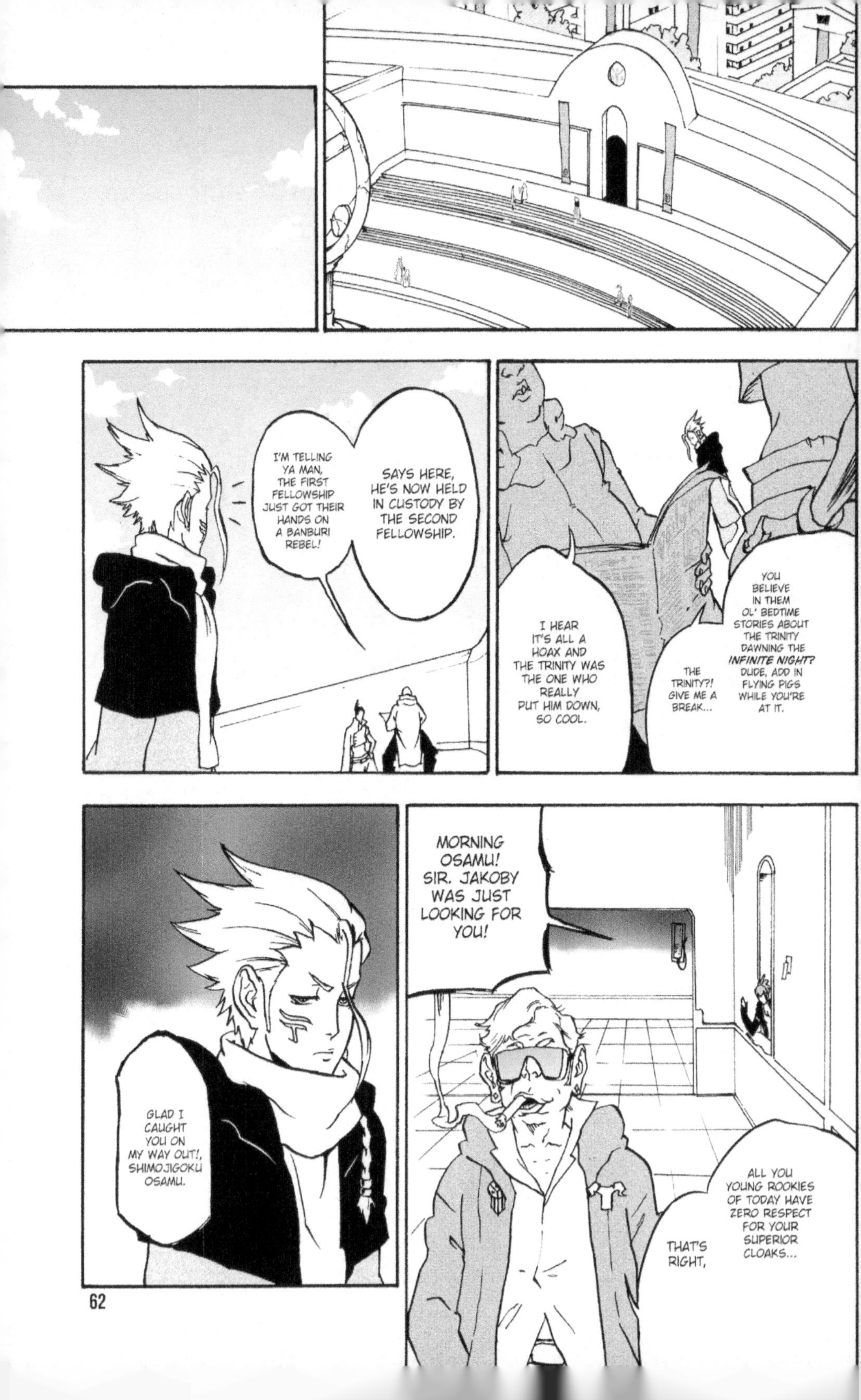

I'M TELLING YA MAN, THE FIRST FELLOWSHIP JUST GOT THEIR HANDS ON A BANBURI REBEL!
SAYS HERE, HE'S NOW HELD IN CUSTODY BY THE SECOND FELLOWSHIP.
I HEAR IT'S ALL A HOAX AND THE TRINITY WAS THE ONE WHO REALLY PUT HIM DOWN, SO COOL.
THE TRINITY?! GIVE ME A BREAK...
YOU BELIEVE IN THEM OL' BEDTIME STORIES ABOUT THE TRINITY DAWNING THE ***INFINITE NIGHT?*** DUDE, ADD IN FLYING PIGS WHILE YOU'RE AT IT.
GLAD I CAUGHT YOU ON MY WAY OUT!, SHIMOJIGOKU OSAMU.
MORNING OSAMU! SIR. JAKOBY WAS JUST LOOKING FOR YOU!
THAT'S RIGHT,
ALL YOU YOUNG ROOKIES OF TODAY HAVE ZERO RESPECT FOR YOUR SUPERIOR CLOAKS...

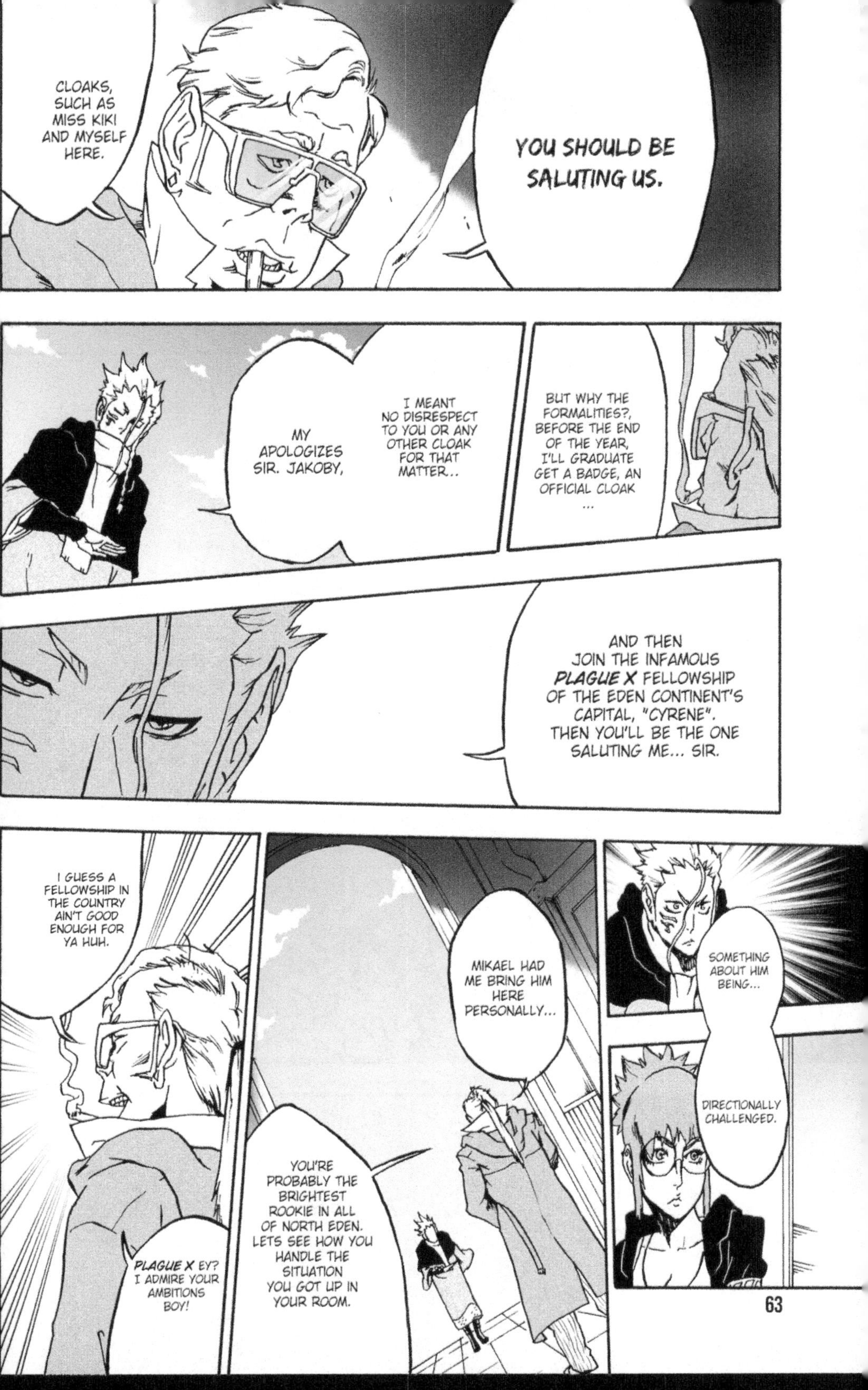

CLOAKS, SUCH AS MISS KIKI AND MYSELF HERE.
YOU SHOULD BE SALUTING US.
MY APOLOGIZES SIR. JAKOBY,
I MEANT NO DISRESPECT TO YOU OR ANY OTHER CLOAK FOR THAT MATTER...
BUT WHY THE FORMALITIES?, BEFORE THE END OF THE YEAR, I'LL GRADUATE GET A BADGE, AN OFFICIAL CLOAK ...
AND THEN JOIN THE INFAMOUS PLAGUE X FELLOWSHIP OF THE EDEN CONTINENT'S CAPITAL, "CYRENE". THEN YOU'LL BE THE ONE SALUTING ME... SIR.
I GUESS A FELLOWSHIP IN THE COUNTRY AIN'T GOOD ENOUGH FOR YA HUH.
PLAGUE X EY? I ADMIRE YOUR AMBITIONS BOY!
MIKAEL HAD ME BRING HIM HERE PERSONALLY...
YOU'RE PROBABLY THE BRIGHTEST ROOKIE IN ALL OF NORTH EDEN. LETS SEE HOW YOU HANDLE THE SITUATION YOU GOT UP IN YOUR ROOM.
SOMETHING ABOUT HIM BEING...
DIRECTIONALLY CHALLENGED.

I GUESS YOU'RE THE NEW BABY-SITTER.

HE'S THE MOST GIFTED STUDENT I'VE SEEN, MAKES SENSE TO PAIR THEM UP.

OSAMU'S NOT HAD A ROOMMATE IN YEARS, ALL HIS PAST ROOMMATES ALWAYS TURN IN TRANSFER REQUESTS. IS THIS REALLY A GOOD IDEA?, HE'S KIND OF A LONER IF YOU ASK ME, I PITY THE NEW GUY.

WHO'S THE NEW GUY ANYWAY?

HEH...

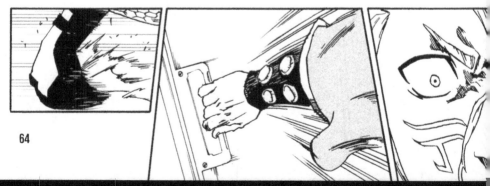

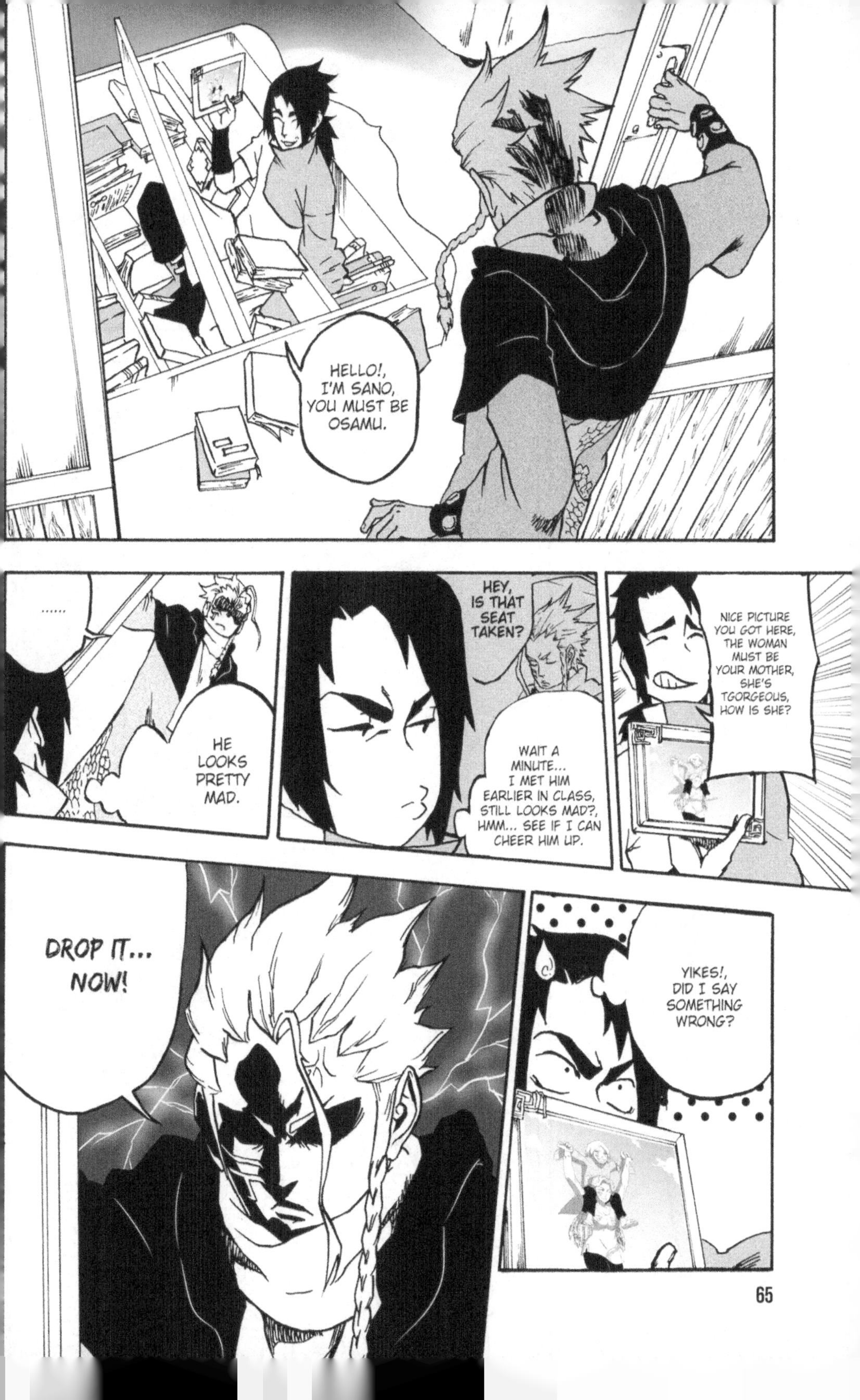

HELLO!, I'M SANO, YOU MUST BE OSAMU.
......
HE LOOKS PRETTY MAD.
HEY, IS THAT SEAT TAKEN?
WAIT A MINUTE... I MET HIM EARLIER IN CLASS, STILL LOOKS MAD?, HMM... SEE IF I CAN CHEER HIM UP.
NICE PICTURE YOU GOT HERE, THE WOMAN MUST BE YOUR MOTHER, SHE'S TGORGEOUS, HOW IS SHE?
DROP IT... NOW!
YIKES!, DID I SAY SOMETHING WRONG?

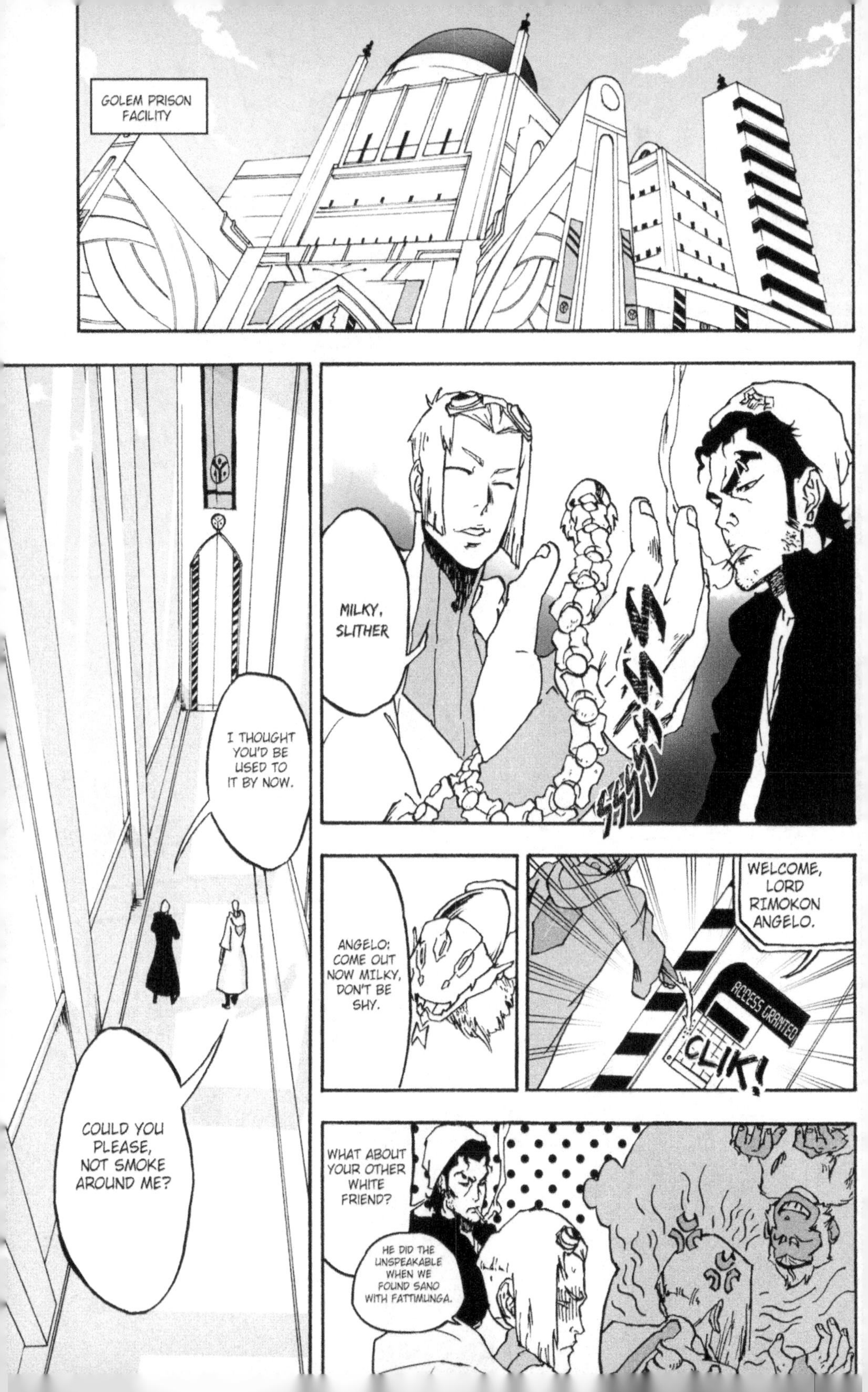
GOLEM PRISON FACILITY
I THOUGHT YOU'D BE USED TO IT BY NOW.
COULD YOU PLEASE, NOT SMOKE AROUND ME?
MILKY, SLITHER
SSSSSSS
ANGELO: COME OUT NOW MILKY, DON'T BE SHY.
WELCOME, LORD RIMOKON ANGELO.
ACCESS GRANTED
CLIK!
WHAT ABOUT YOUR OTHER WHITE FRIEND?
HE DID THE UNSPEAKABLE WHEN WE FOUND SANO WITH FATTIMUNGA.

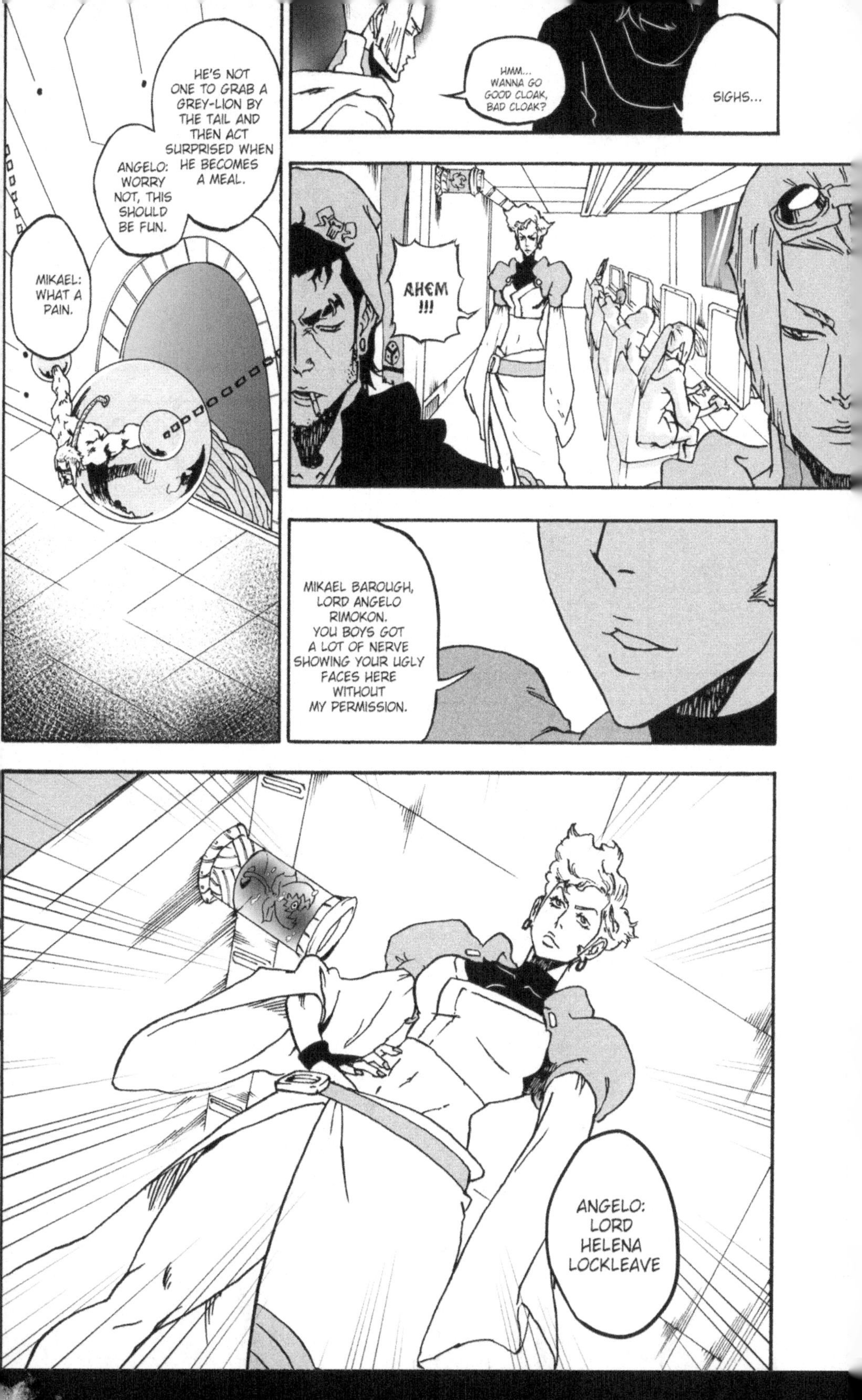
HE'S NOT ONE TO GRAB A GREY-LION BY THE TAIL AND THEN ACT SURPRISED WHEN HE BECOMES A MEAL.
ANGELO: WORRY NOT, THIS SHOULD BE FUN.
MIKAEL: WHAT A PAIN.
HMM... WANNA GO GOOD CLOAK, BAD CLOAK?
SIGHS...
AHEM !!!
MIKAEL BAROUGH, LORD ANGELO RIMOKON. YOU BOYS GOT A LOT OF NERVE SHOWING YOUR UGLY FACES HERE WITHOUT MY PERMISSION.
ANGELO: LORD HELENA LOCKLEAVE

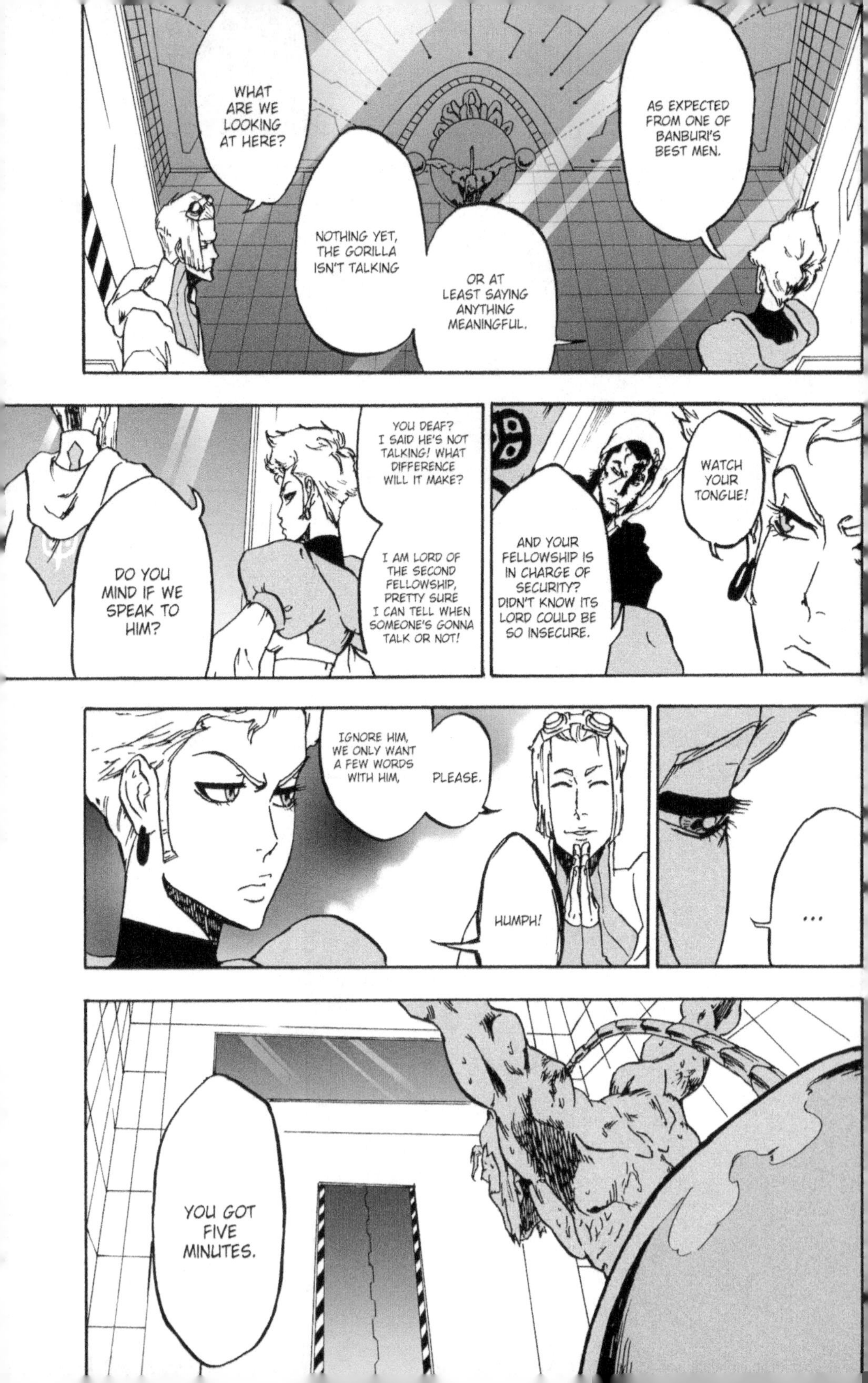
WHAT ARE WE LOOKING AT HERE?
NOTHING YET, THE GORILLA ISN'T TALKING
OR AT LEAST SAYING ANYTHING MEANINGFUL.
AS EXPECTED FROM ONE OF BANBURI'S BEST MEN.
DO YOU MIND IF WE SPEAK TO HIM?
YOU DEAF? I SAID HE'S NOT TALKING! WHAT DIFFERENCE WILL IT MAKE?
I AM LORD OF THE SECOND FELLOWSHIP, PRETTY SURE I CAN TELL WHEN SOMEONE'S GONNA TALK OR NOT!
AND YOUR FELLOWSHIP IS IN CHARGE OF SECURITY? DIDN'T KNOW ITS LORD COULD BE SO INSECURE.
WATCH YOUR TONGUE!
IGNORE HIM, WE ONLY WANT A FEW WORDS WITH HIM,
PLEASE.
HUMPH!
...
YOU GOT FIVE MINUTES.

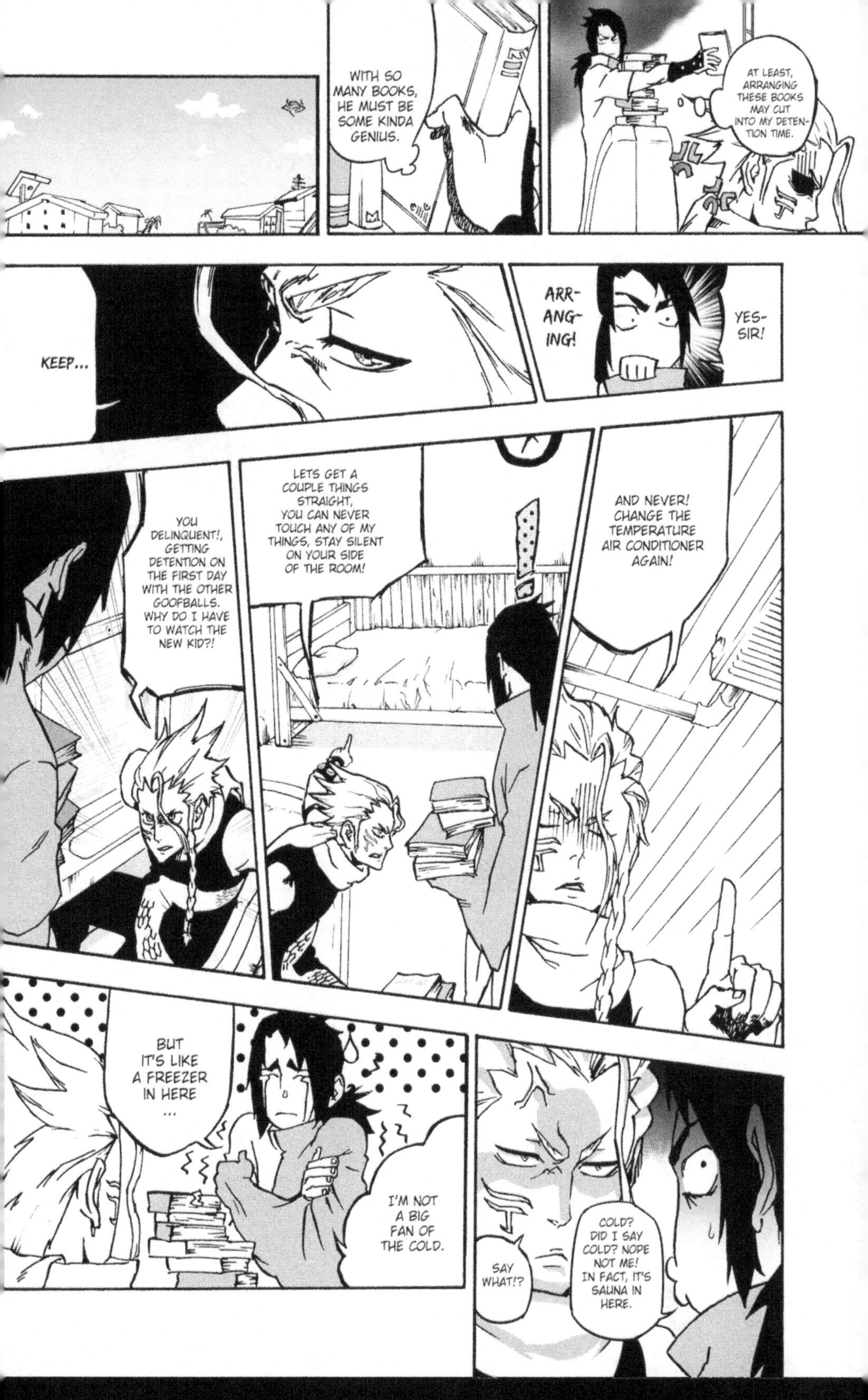
WITH SO MANY BOOKS, HE MUST BE SOME KINDA GENIUS.
AT LEAST, ARRANGING THESE BOOKS MAY CUT INTO MY DETENTION TIME.
KEEP...
ARR-ANG-ING!
YES-SIR!
YOU DELINQUENT!, GETTING DETENTION ON THE FIRST DAY WITH THE OTHER GOOFBALLS. WHY DO I HAVE TO WATCH THE NEW KID?!
LETS GET A COUPLE THINGS STRAIGHT, YOU CAN NEVER TOUCH ANY OF MY THINGS, STAY SILENT ON YOUR SIDE OF THE ROOM!
AND NEVER! CHANGE THE TEMPERATURE AIR CONDITIONER AGAIN!
BUT IT'S LIKE A FREEZER IN HERE ...
I'M NOT A BIG FAN OF THE COLD.
SAY WHAT!?
COLD? DID I SAY COLD? NOPE NOT ME! IN FACT, IT'S SAUNA IN HERE.

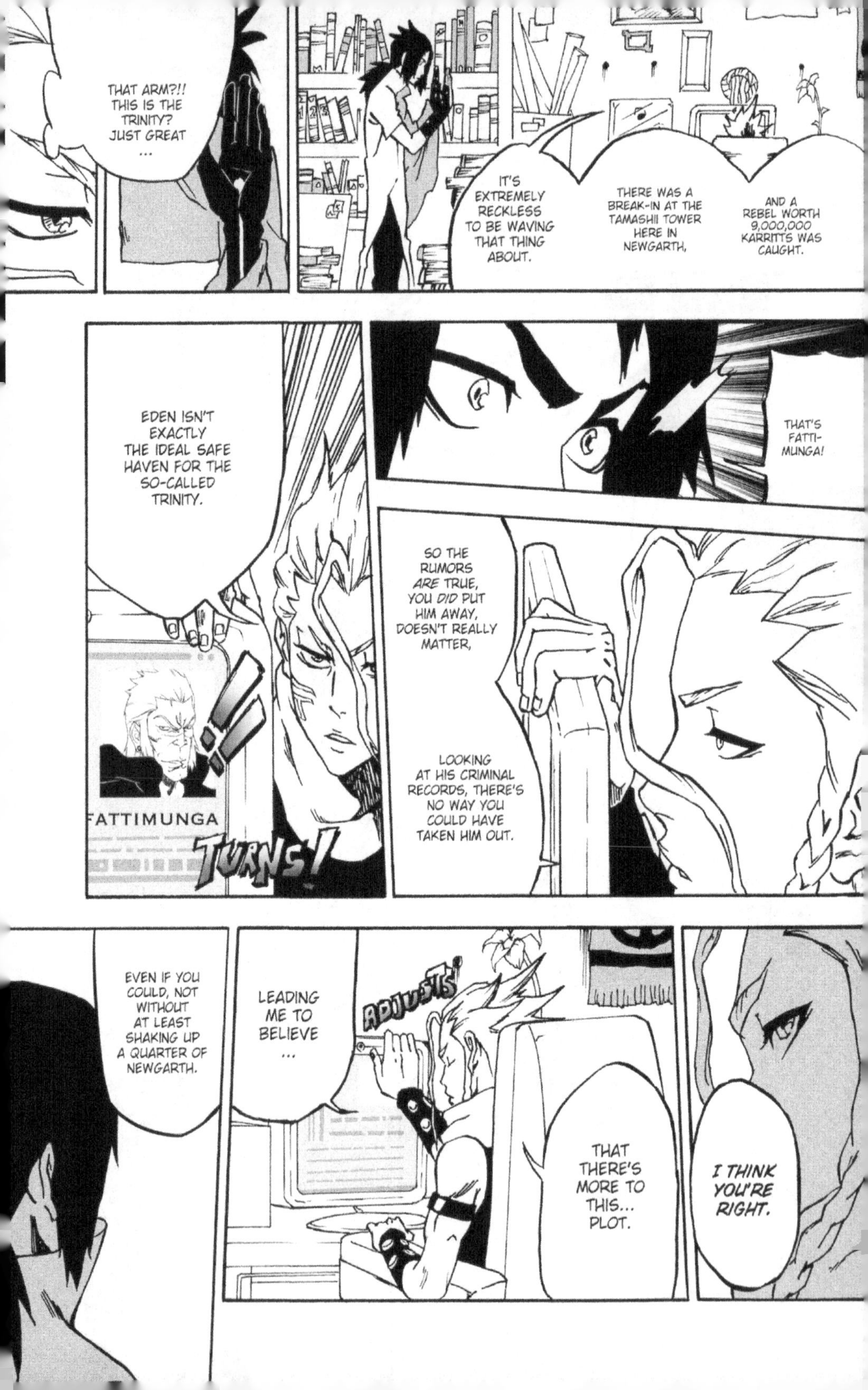
THAT ARM?!! THIS IS THE TRINITY? JUST GREAT ...
IT'S EXTREMELY RECKLESS TO BE WAVING THAT THING ABOUT.
THERE WAS A BREAK-IN AT THE TAMASHII TOWER HERE IN NEWGARTH,
AND A REBEL WORTH 9,000,000 KARRITTS WAS CAUGHT.
EDEN ISN'T EXACTLY THE IDEAL SAFE HAVEN FOR THE SO-CALLED TRINITY.
FATTIMUNGA
TURNS!
THAT'S FATTI-MUNGA!
SO THE RUMORS *ARE* TRUE, YOU *DID* PUT HIM AWAY, DOESN'T REALLY MATTER,
LOOKING AT HIS CRIMINAL RECORDS, THERE'S NO WAY YOU COULD HAVE TAKEN HIM OUT.
EVEN IF YOU COULD, NOT WITHOUT AT LEAST SHAKING UP A QUARTER OF NEWGARTH.
LEADING ME TO BELIEVE ...
ADJUSTS
THAT THERE'S MORE TO THIS... PLOT.
I THINK YOU'RE RIGHT.

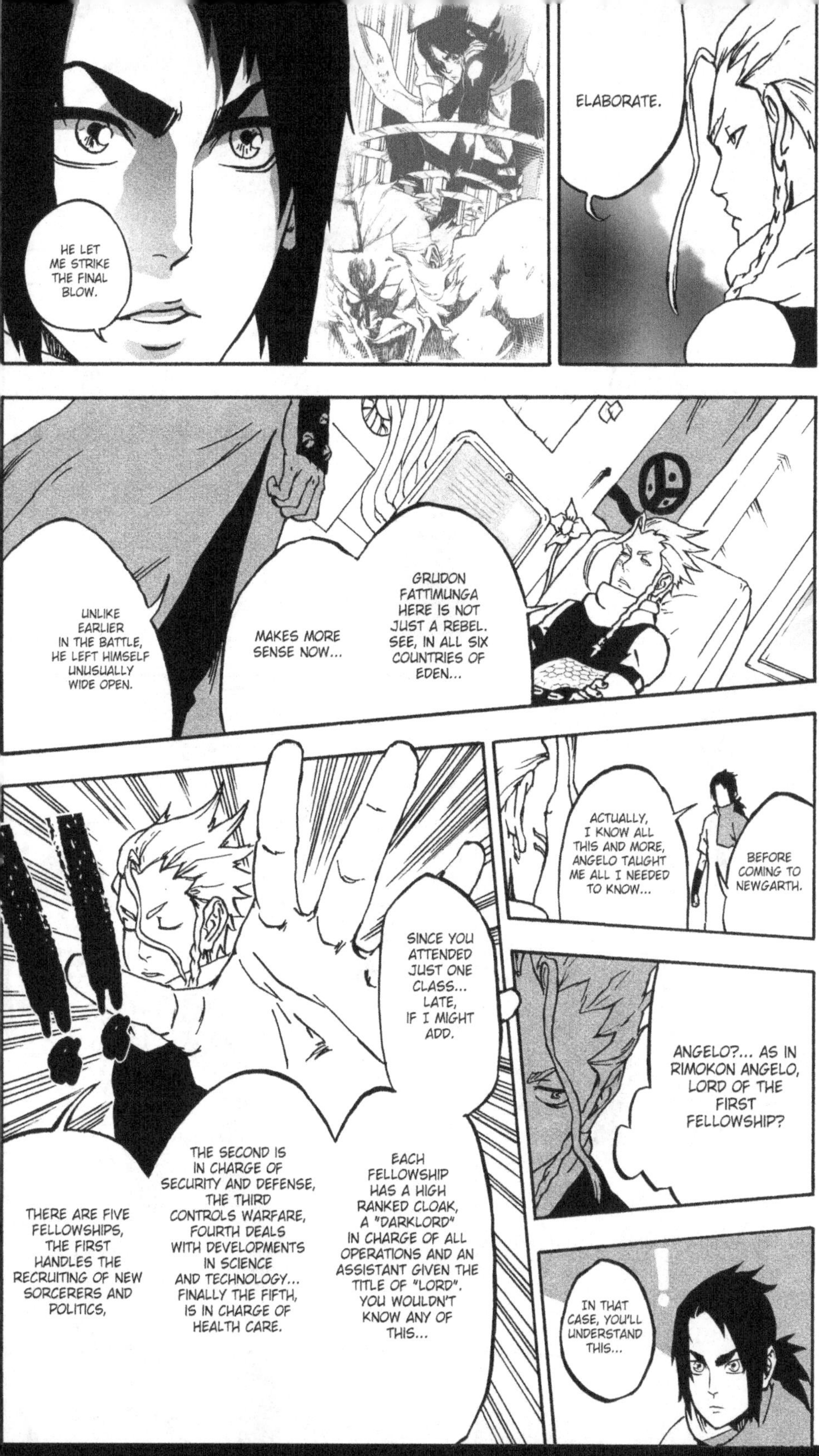
HE LET ME STRIKE THE FINAL BLOW.
ELABORATE.
UNLIKE EARLIER IN THE BATTLE, HE LEFT HIMSELF UNUSUALLY WIDE OPEN.
MAKES MORE SENSE NOW...
GRUDON FATTIMUNGA HERE IS NOT JUST A REBEL. SEE, IN ALL SIX COUNTRIES OF EDEN...
SINCE YOU ATTENDED JUST ONE CLASS... LATE, IF I MIGHT ADD.
THERE ARE FIVE FELLOWSHIPS, THE FIRST HANDLES THE RECRUITING OF NEW SORCERERS AND POLITICS,
THE SECOND IS IN CHARGE OF SECURITY AND DEFENSE, THE THIRD CONTROLS WARFARE, FOURTH DEALS WITH DEVELOPMENTS IN SCIENCE AND TECHNOLOGY... FINALLY THE FIFTH, IS IN CHARGE OF HEALTH CARE.
EACH FELLOWSHIP HAS A HIGH RANKED CLOAK, A "DARKLORD" IN CHARGE OF ALL OPERATIONS AND AN ASSISTANT GIVEN THE TITLE OF "LORD". YOU WOULDN'T KNOW ANY OF THIS...
ACTUALLY, I KNOW ALL THIS AND MORE, ANGELO TAUGHT ME ALL I NEEDED TO KNOW...
BEFORE COMING TO NEWGARTH.
ANGELO?... AS IN RIMOKON ANGELO, LORD OF THE FIRST FELLOWSHIP?
IN THAT CASE, YOU'LL UNDERSTAND THIS...
!

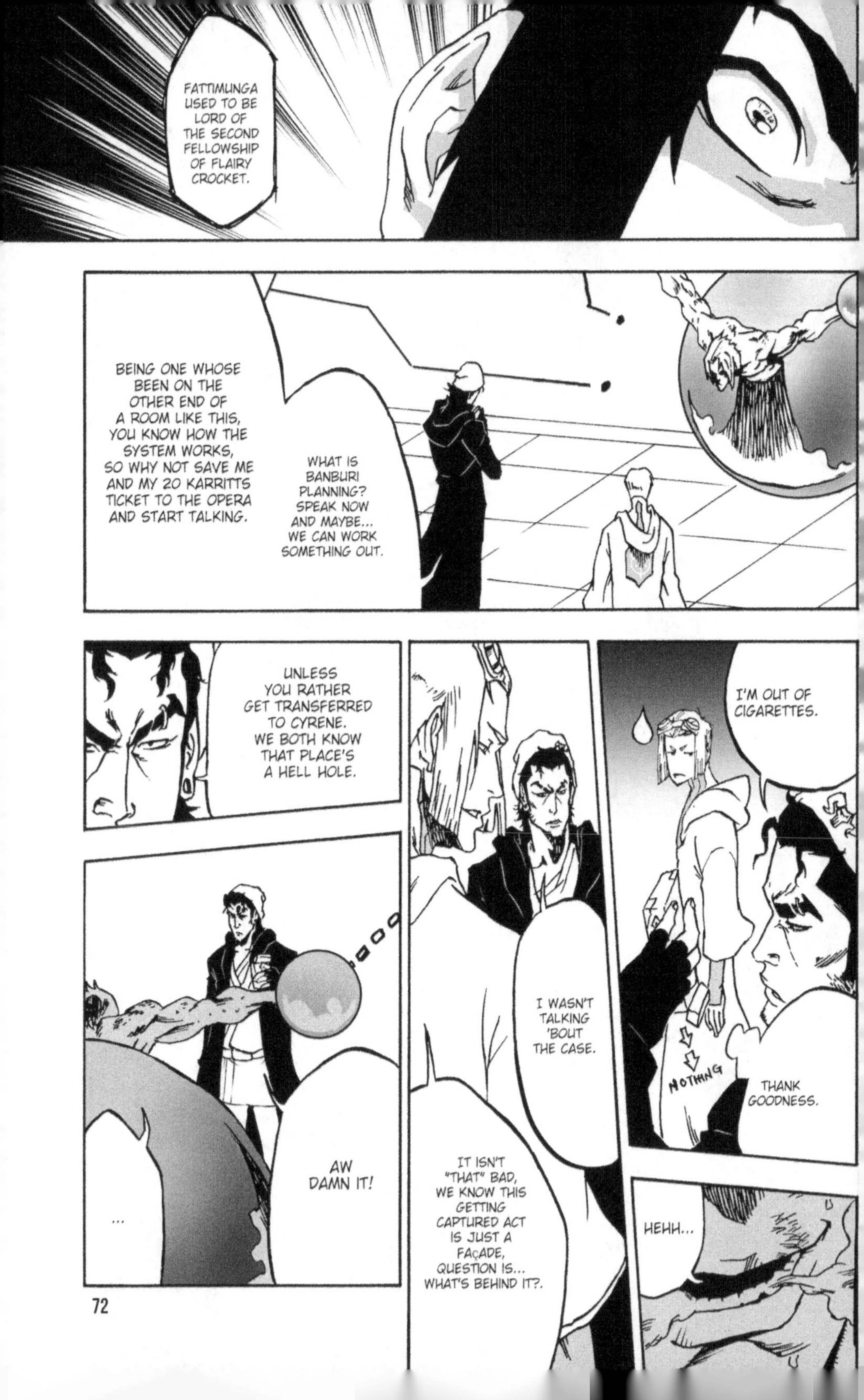
FATTIMUNGA USED TO BE LORD OF THE SECOND FELLOWSHIP OF FLAIRY CROCKET.
BEING ONE WHOSE BEEN ON THE OTHER END OF A ROOM LIKE THIS, YOU KNOW HOW THE SYSTEM WORKS, SO WHY NOT SAVE ME AND MY 20 KARRITTS TICKET TO THE OPERA AND START TALKING.
WHAT IS BANBURI PLANNING? SPEAK NOW AND MAYBE... WE CAN WORK SOMETHING OUT.
UNLESS YOU RATHER GET TRANSFERRED TO CYRENE. WE BOTH KNOW THAT PLACE'S A HELL HOLE.
...
AW DAMN IT!
I WASN'T TALKING 'BOUT THE CASE.
IT ISN'T "THAT" BAD, WE KNOW THIS GETTING CAPTURED ACT IS JUST A FAÇADE, QUESTION IS... WHAT'S BEHIND IT?.
I'M OUT OF CIGARETTES.
NOTHING
THANK GOODNESS.
HEHH...

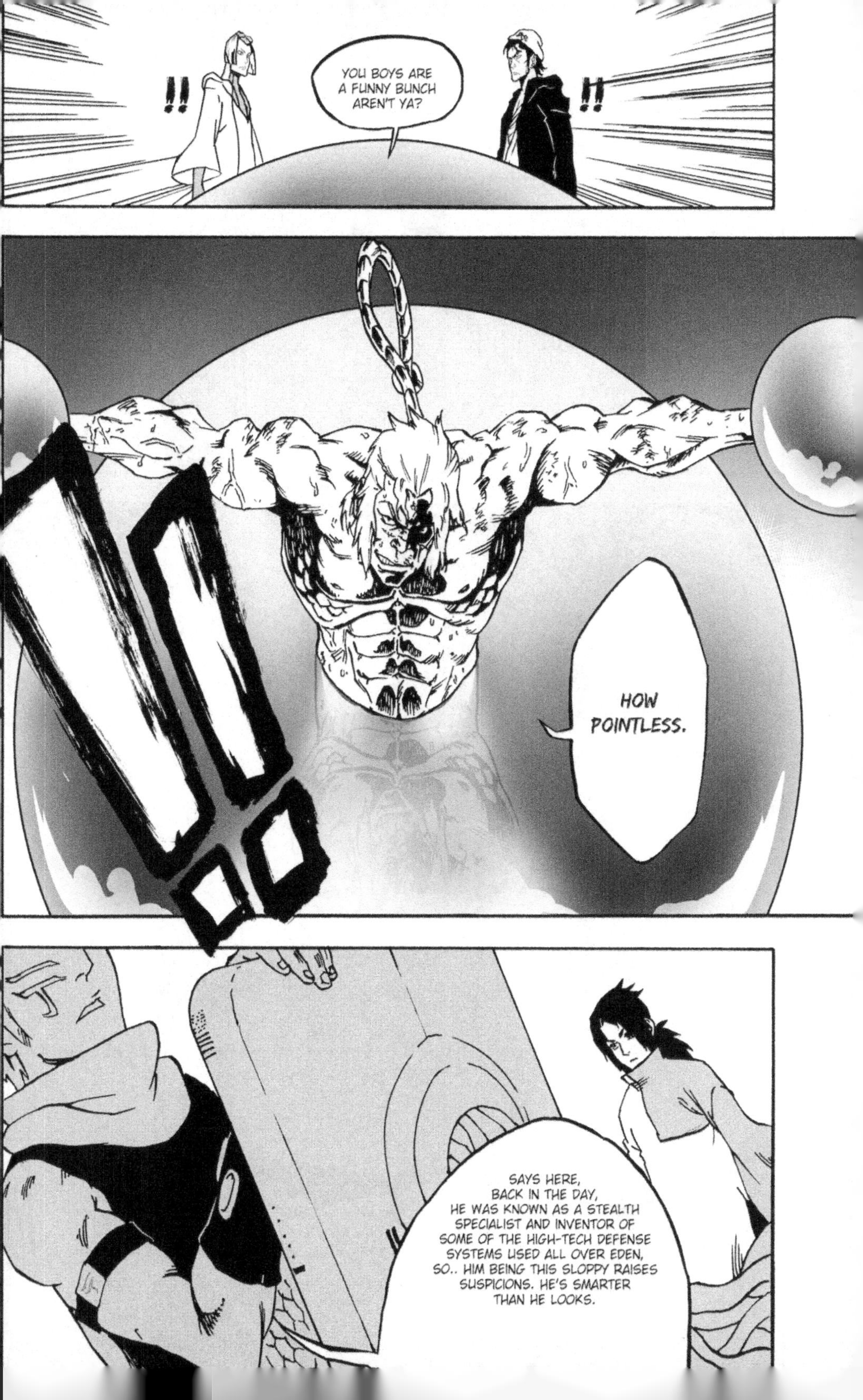
!!
YOU BOYS ARE A FUNNY BUNCH AREN'T YA?
!!
HOW POINTLESS.
SAYS HERE, BACK IN THE DAY, HE WAS KNOWN AS A STEALTH SPECIALIST AND INVENTOR OF SOME OF THE HIGH-TECH DEFENSE SYSTEMS USED ALL OVER EDEN, SO.. HIM BEING THIS SLOPPY RAISES SUSPICIONS. HE'S SMARTER THAN HE LOOKS.

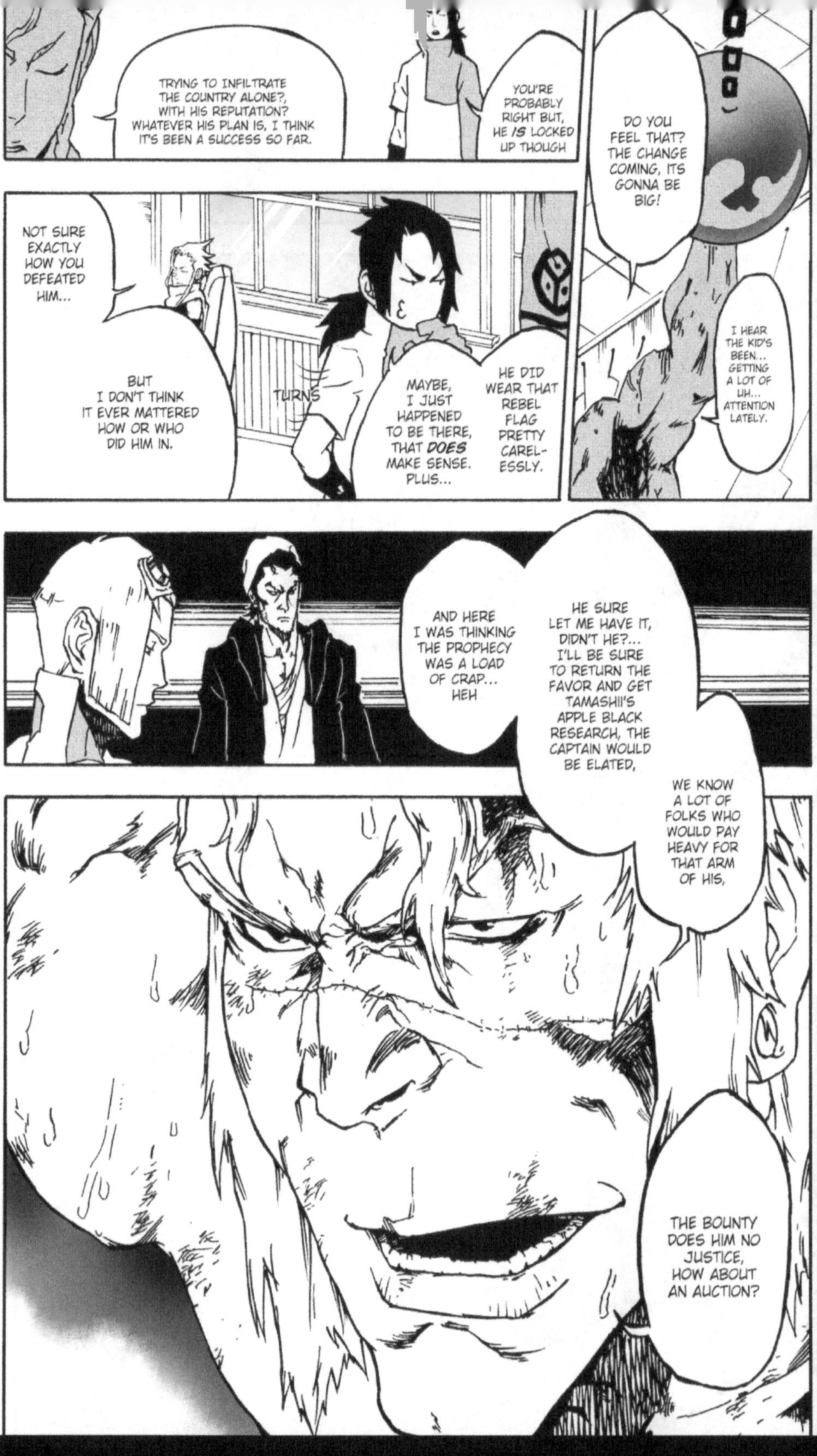
TRYING TO INFILTRATE THE COUNTRY ALONE?, WITH HIS REPUTATION? WHATEVER HIS PLAN IS, I THINK IT'S BEEN A SUCCESS SO FAR.
YOU'RE PROBABLY RIGHT BUT, HE *IS* LOCKED UP THOUGH
NOT SURE EXACTLY HOW YOU DEFEATED HIM...
BUT I DON'T THINK IT EVER MATTERED HOW OR WHO DID HIM IN.
TURNS
MAYBE, I JUST HAPPENED TO BE THERE, THAT ***DOES*** MAKE SENSE. PLUS...
HE DID WEAR THAT REBEL FLAG PRETTY CAREL-ESSLY.
DO YOU FEEL THAT? THE CHANGE COMING, ITS GONNA BE BIG!
I HEAR THE KID'S BEEN... GETTING A LOT OF UH... ATTENTION LATELY.
AND HERE I WAS THINKING THE PROPHECY WAS A LOAD OF CRAP... HEH
HE SURE LET ME HAVE IT, DIDN'T HE?... I'LL BE SURE TO RETURN THE FAVOR AND GET TAMASHII'S APPLE BLACK RESEARCH, THE CAPTAIN WOULD BE ELATED,
WE KNOW A LOT OF FOLKS WHO WOULD PAY HEAVY FOR THAT ARM OF HIS,
THE BOUNTY DOES HIM NO JUSTICE, HOW ABOUT AN AUCTION?

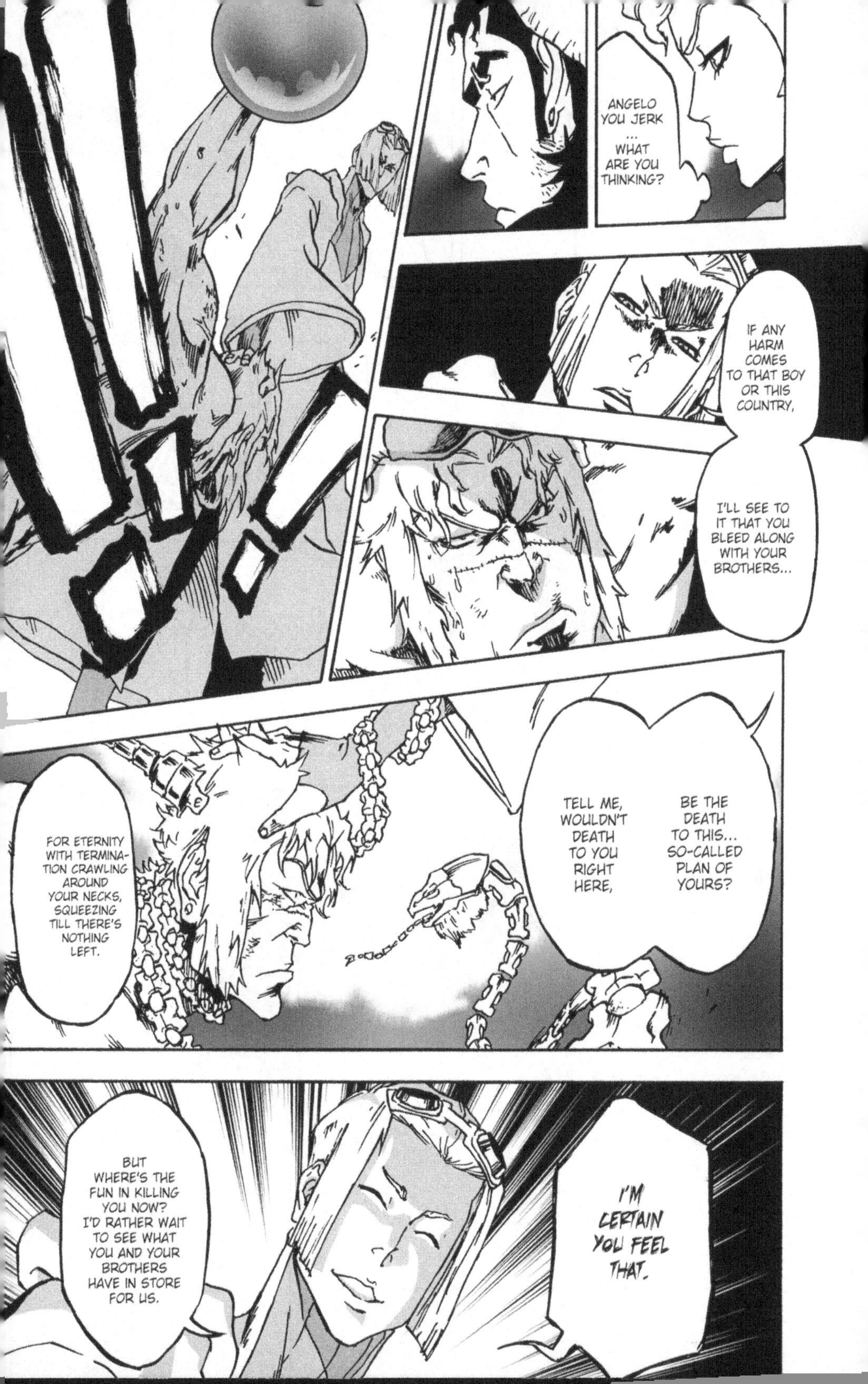

ANGELO YOU JERK ... WHAT ARE YOU THINKING?
IF ANY HARM COMES TO THAT BOY OR THIS COUNTRY,
I'LL SEE TO IT THAT YOU BLEED ALONG WITH YOUR BROTHERS...
FOR ETERNITY WITH TERMINATION CRAWLING AROUND YOUR NECKS, SQUEEZING TILL THERE'S NOTHING LEFT.
TELL ME, WOULDN'T DEATH TO YOU RIGHT HERE, BE THE DEATH TO THIS... SO-CALLED PLAN OF YOURS?
BUT WHERE'S THE FUN IN KILLING YOU NOW? I'D RATHER WAIT TO SEE WHAT YOU AND YOUR BROTHERS HAVE IN STORE FOR US.
I'M CERTAIN YOU FEEL THAT.

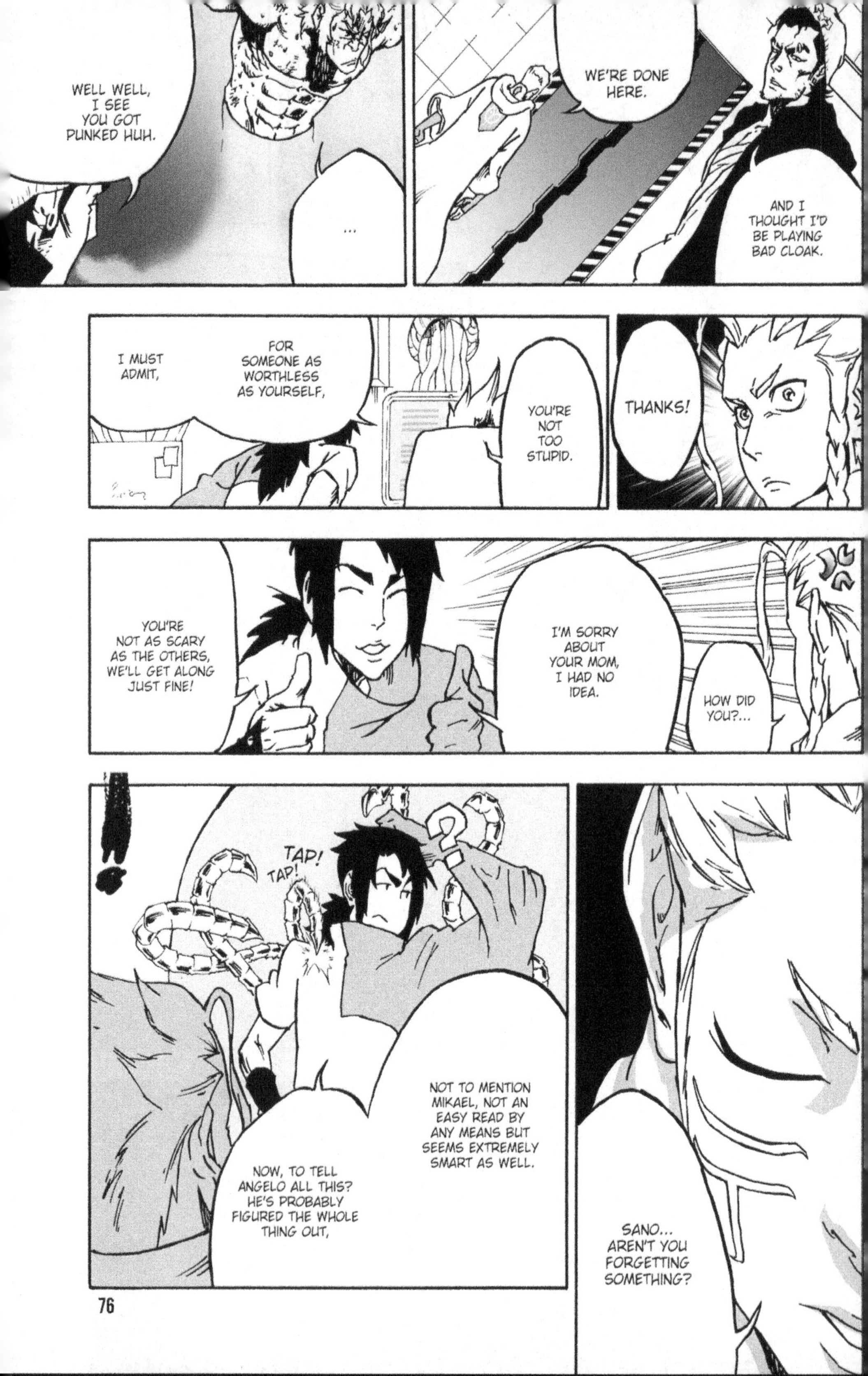
WELL WELL, I SEE YOU GOT PUNKED HUH.
...
WE'RE DONE HERE.
AND I THOUGHT I'D BE PLAYING BAD CLOAK.
I MUST ADMIT,
FOR SOMEONE AS WORTHLESS AS YOURSELF,
YOU'RE NOT TOO STUPID.
THANKS!
YOU'RE NOT AS SCARY AS THE OTHERS, WE'LL GET ALONG JUST FINE!
I'M SORRY ABOUT YOUR MOM, I HAD NO IDEA.
HOW DID YOU?...
TAP!
TAP!
NOW, TO TELL ANGELO ALL THIS? HE'S PROBABLY FIGURED THE WHOLE THING OUT,
NOT TO MENTION MIKAEL, NOT AN EASY READ BY ANY MEANS BUT SEEMS EXTREMELY SMART AS WELL.
SANO... AREN'T YOU FORGETTING SOMETHING?

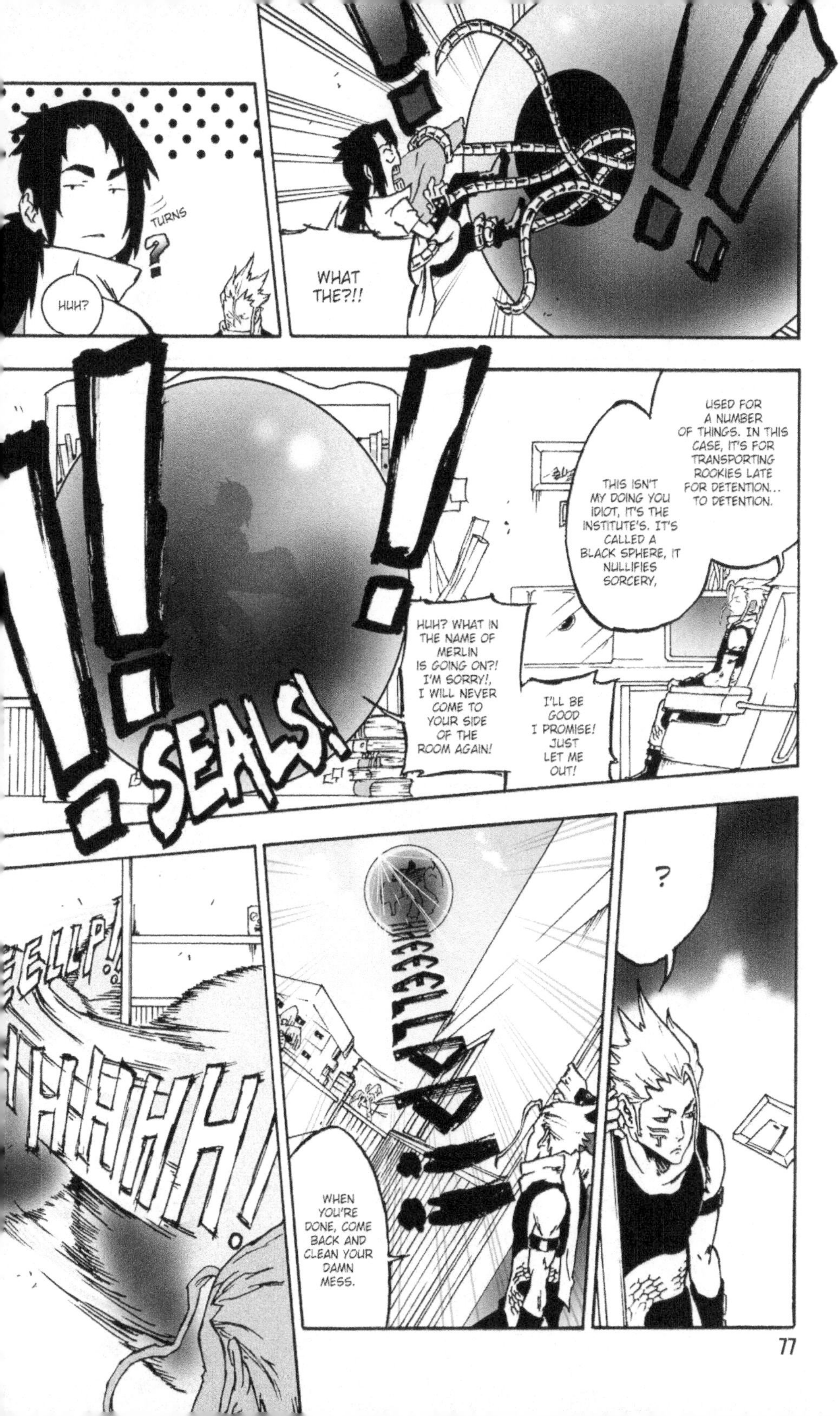
TURNS
?
HUH?
WHAT THE?!!
SEALS!
HUH? WHAT IN THE NAME OF MERLIN IS GOING ON?! I'M SORRY!, I WILL NEVER COME TO YOUR SIDE OF THE ROOM AGAIN!
I'LL BE GOOD I PROMISE! JUST LET ME OUT!
THIS ISN'T MY DOING YOU IDIOT, IT'S THE INSTITUTE'S. IT'S CALLED A BLACK SPHERE, IT NULLIFIES SORCERY,
USED FOR A NUMBER OF THINGS. IN THIS CASE, IT'S FOR TRANSPORTING ROOKIES LATE FOR DETENTION... TO DETENTION.
WHEN YOU'RE DONE, COME BACK AND CLEAN YOUR DAMN MESS.
?

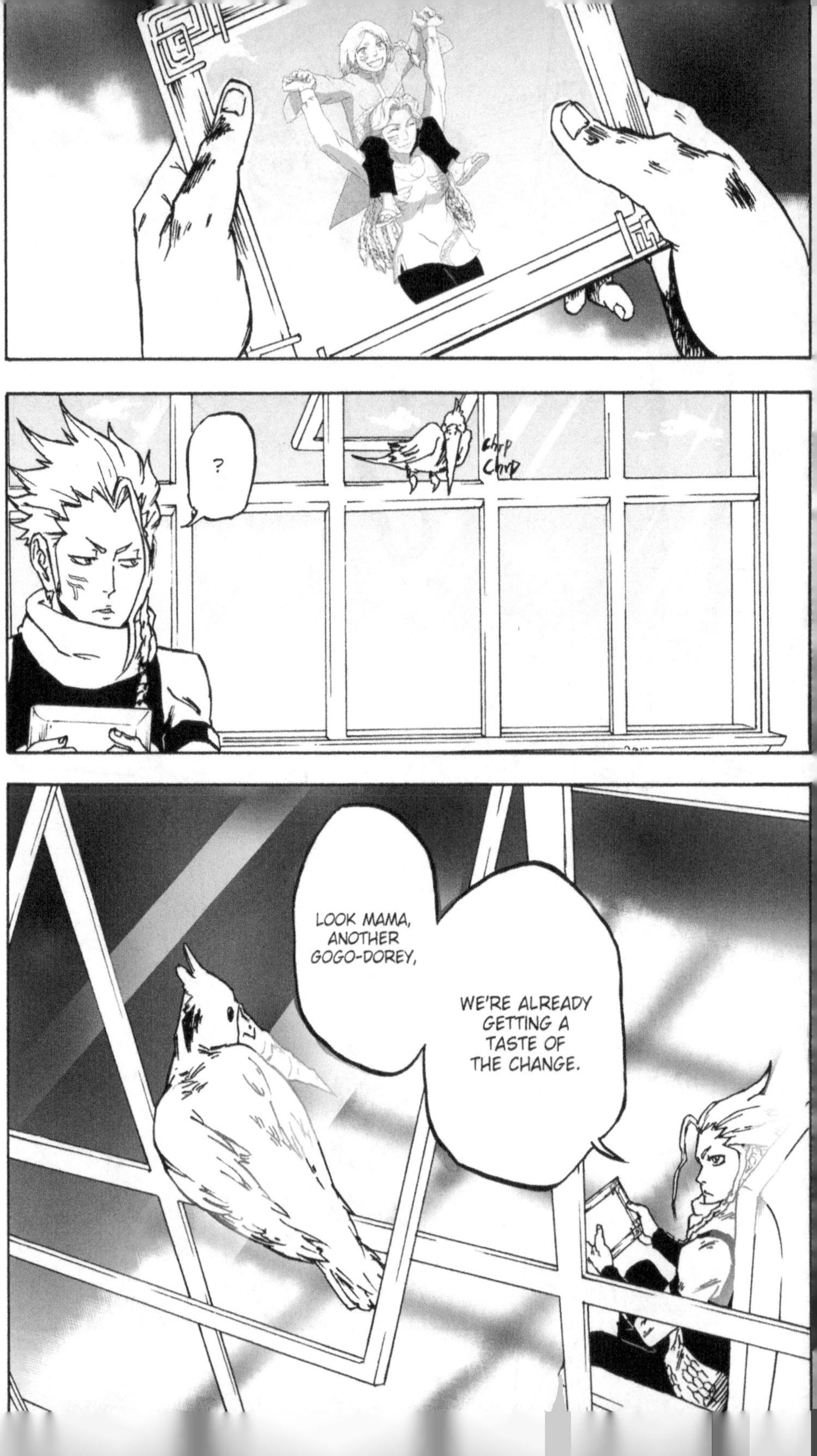
?
Chirp Chirp
LOOK MAMA, ANOTHER GOGO-DOREY,
WE'RE ALREADY GETTING A TASTE OF THE CHANGE.

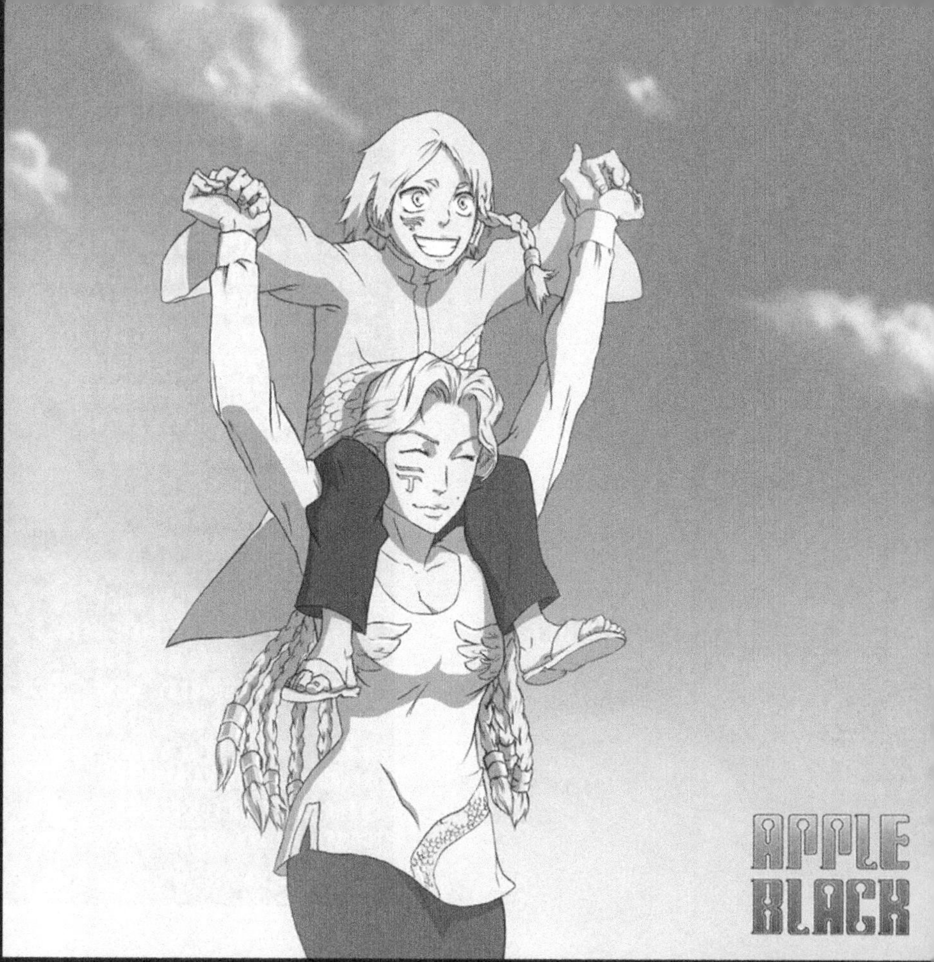
APPLE
BLACK

HANE SHIMOJIGOKU

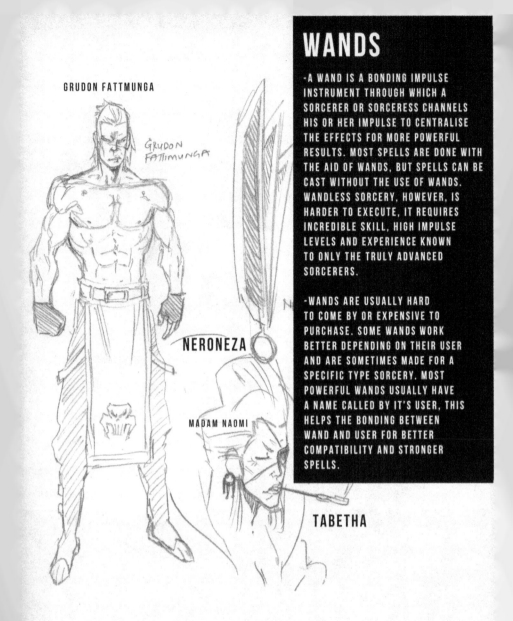

GRUDON FATTMUNGA

GRUDON FATTIMUNGA

NERONEZA

MADAM NAOMI

TABETHA

WANDS

-A WAND IS A BONDING IMPULSE INSTRUMENT THROUGH WHICH A SORCERER OR SORCERESS CHANNELS HIS OR HER IMPULSE TO CENTRALISE THE EFFECTS FOR MORE POWERFUL RESULTS. MOST SPELLS ARE DONE WITH THE AID OF WANDS, BUT SPELLS CAN BE CAST WITHOUT THE USE OF WANDS. WANDLESS SORCERY, HOWEVER, IS HARDER TO EXECUTE, IT REQUIRES INCREDIBLE SKILL, HIGH IMPULSE LEVELS AND EXPERIENCE KNOWN TO ONLY THE TRULY ADVANCED SORCERERS.

-WANDS ARE USUALLY HARD TO COME BY OR EXPENSIVE TO PURCHASE. SOME WANDS WORK BETTER DEPENDING ON THEIR USER AND ARE SOMETIMES MADE FOR A SPECIFIC TYPE SORCERY. MOST POWERFUL WANDS USUALLY HAVE A NAME CALLED BY IT'S USER, THIS HELPS THE BONDING BETWEEN WAND AND USER FOR BETTER COMPATIBILITY AND STRONGER SPELLS.

THE TYPICAL WAND IS USUALLY DEPICTED IN OTHER WORKS AS A THIN RODS OF WOOD OR IRON BUT IN THIS COMIC, A WAND COULD BE A THIN ROD OR A BROOM STICK, A BLADE, A SWORD, A HAND FAN, A PAIR OF GLASSES, A STAFF, GUNS, A PAIR OF WEAPONS, GLOVES, A LIGHTER OR EVEN A CIGARETTE, THE LIST GOES ON. ALMOST ANYTHING COULD BE A WAND AS LONG AS IT GOES THROUGH THE NECESSARY RITUALS TO BECOME ONE.

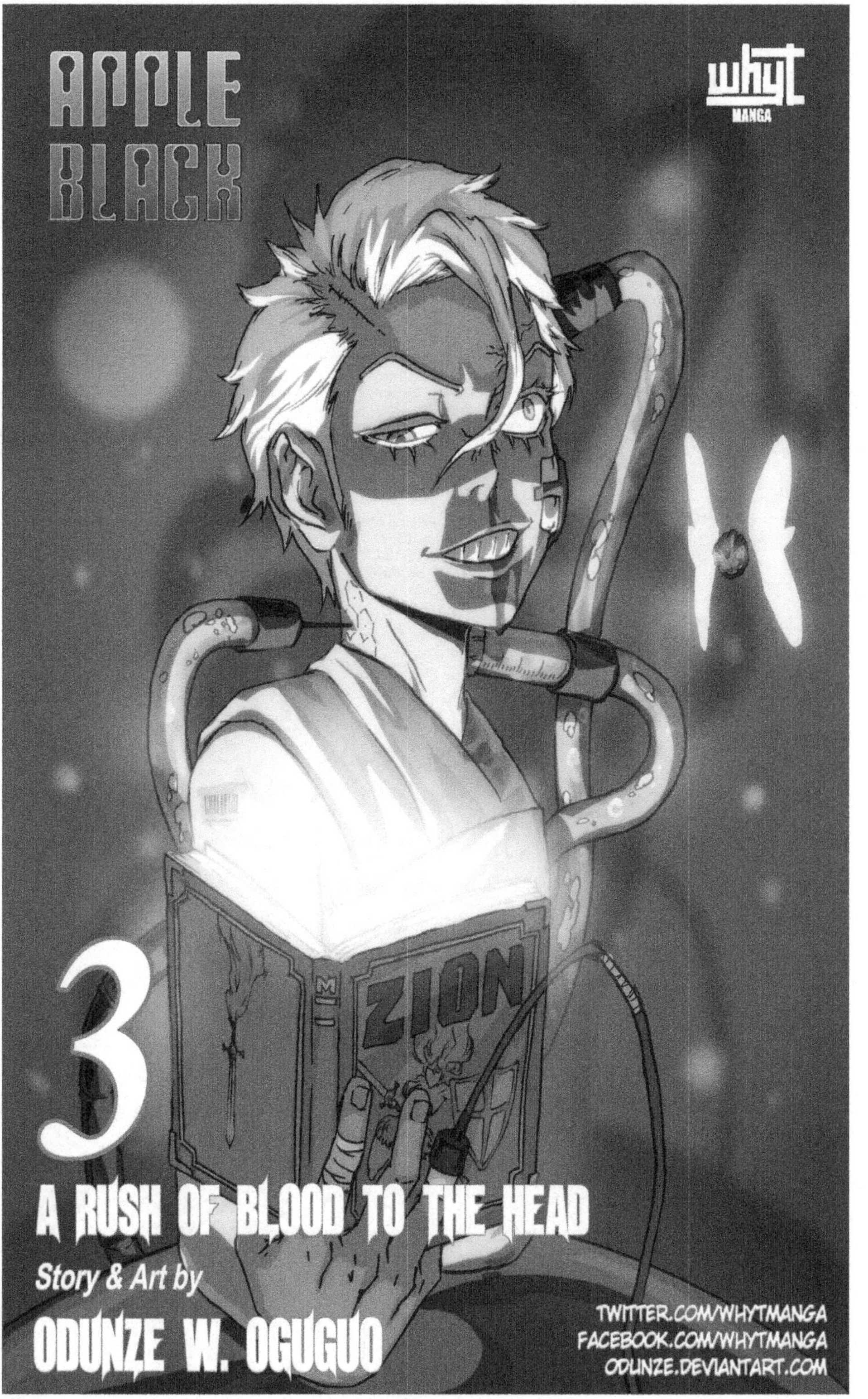
APPLE
BLACK
whyt
MANGA
ZION
3
A RUSH OF BLOOD TO THE HEAD
Story & Art by
ODUNZE W. OGUGUO
TWITTER.COM/WHYTMANGA
FACEBOOK.COM/WHYTMANGA
ODUNZE.DEVIANTART.COM

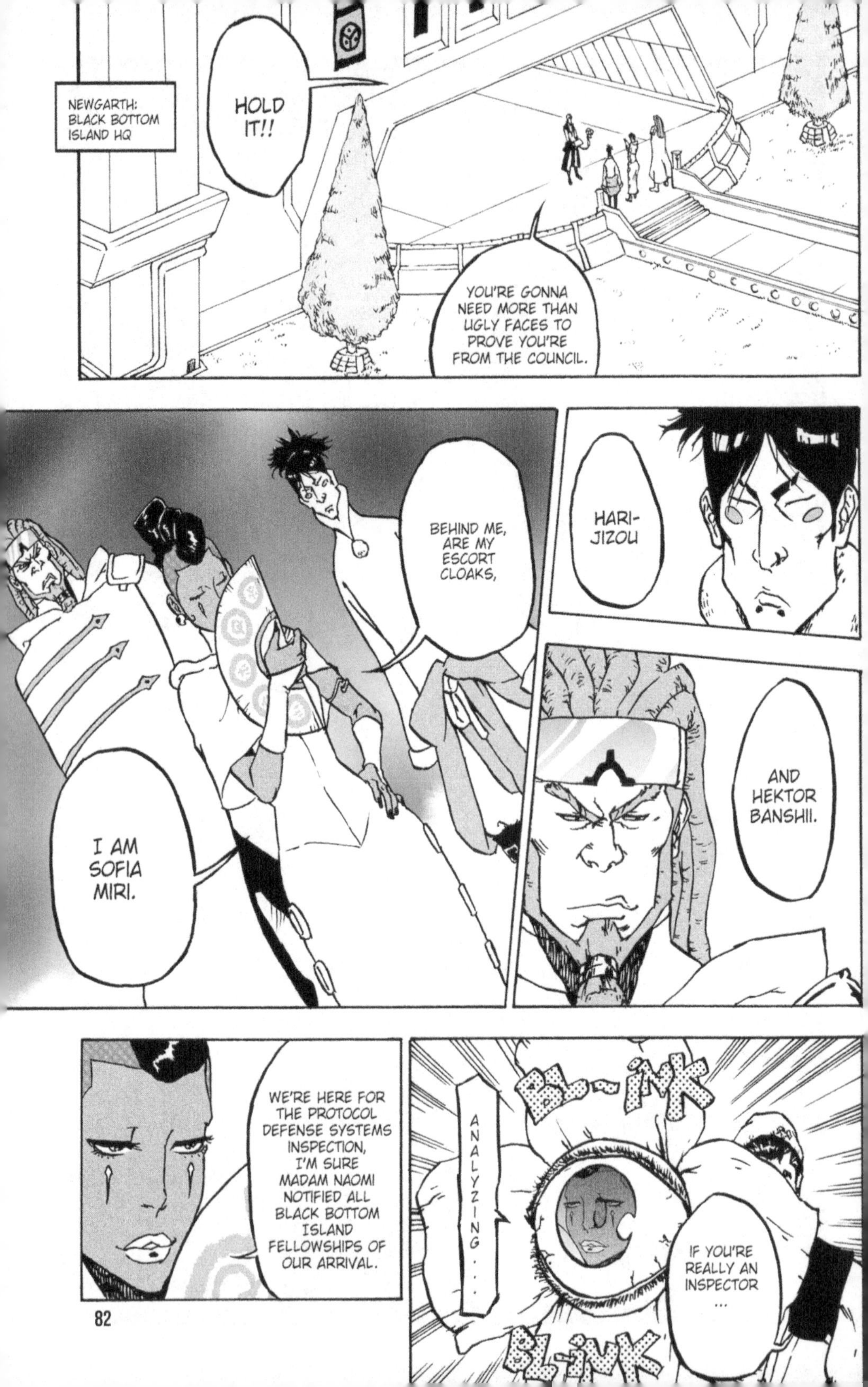
NEWGARTH: BLACK BOTTOM ISLAND HQ
HOLD IT!!
YOU'RE GONNA NEED MORE THAN UGLY FACES TO PROVE YOU'RE FROM THE COUNCIL.
I AM SOFIA MIRI.
BEHIND ME, ARE MY ESCORT CLOAKS,
HARI-JIZOU
AND HEKTOR BANSHII.
WE'RE HERE FOR THE PROTOCOL DEFENSE SYSTEMS INSPECTION, I'M SURE MADAM NAOMI NOTIFIED ALL BLACK BOTTOM ISLAND FELLOWSHIPS OF OUR ARRIVAL.
BL-INK
ANALYZING...
IF YOU'RE REALLY AN INSPECTOR ...
BL-INK

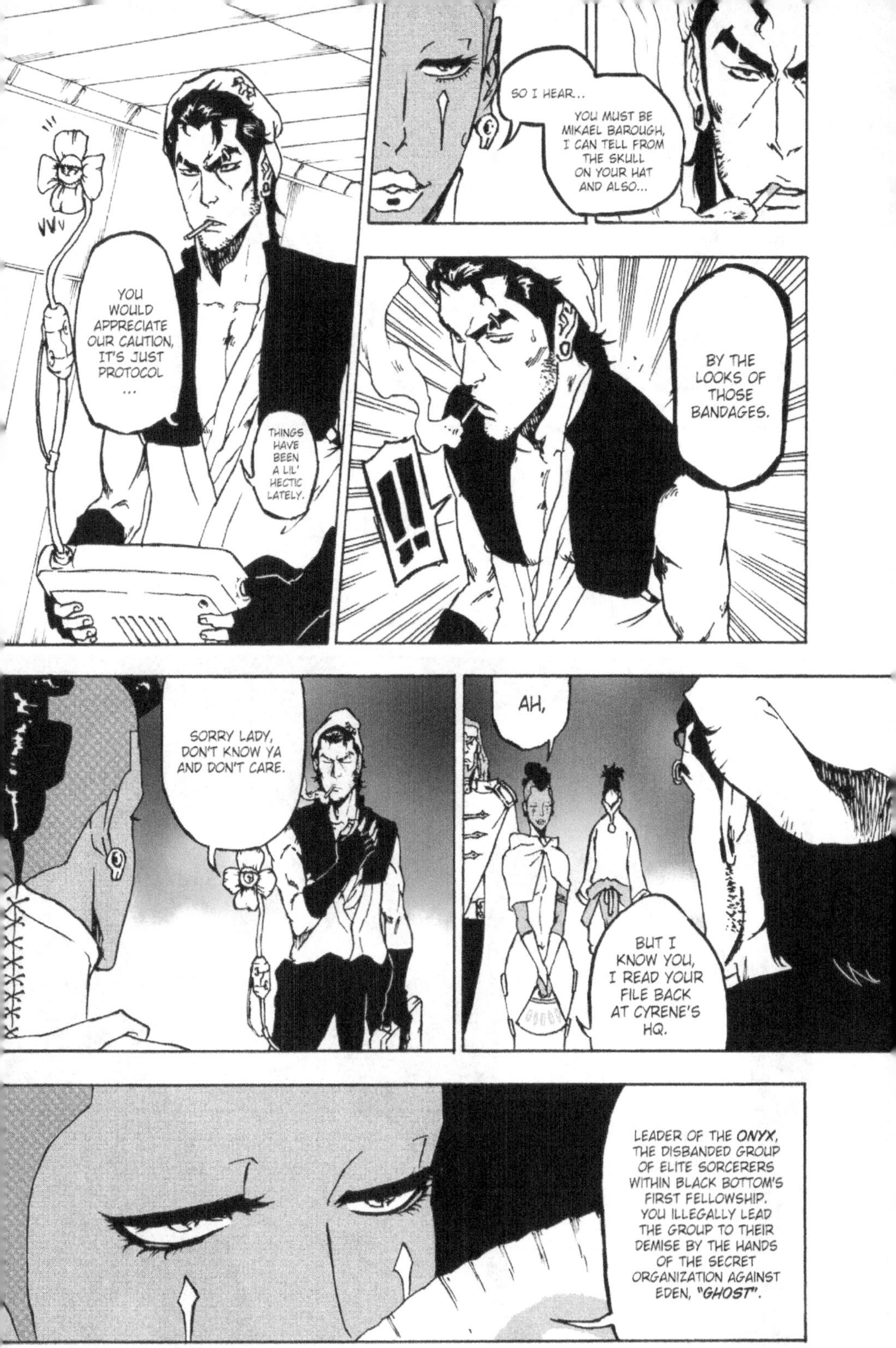
YOU WOULD APPRECIATE OUR CAUTION, IT'S JUST PROTOCOL ...
THINGS HAVE BEEN A LIL' HECTIC LATELY.
SO I HEAR..
YOU MUST BE MIKAEL BAROUGH, I CAN TELL FROM THE SKULL ON YOUR HAT AND ALSO...
BY THE LOOKS OF THOSE BANDAGES.
!!
SORRY LADY, DON'T KNOW YA AND DON'T CARE.
AH,
BUT I KNOW YOU, I READ YOUR FILE BACK AT CYRENE'S HQ.
LEADER OF THE ONYX, THE DISBANDED GROUP OF ELITE SORCERERS WITHIN BLACK BOTTOM'S FIRST FELLOWSHIP. YOU ILLEGALLY LEAD THE GROUP TO THEIR DEMISE BY THE HANDS OF THE SECRET ORGANIZATION AGAINST EDEN, "GHOST".

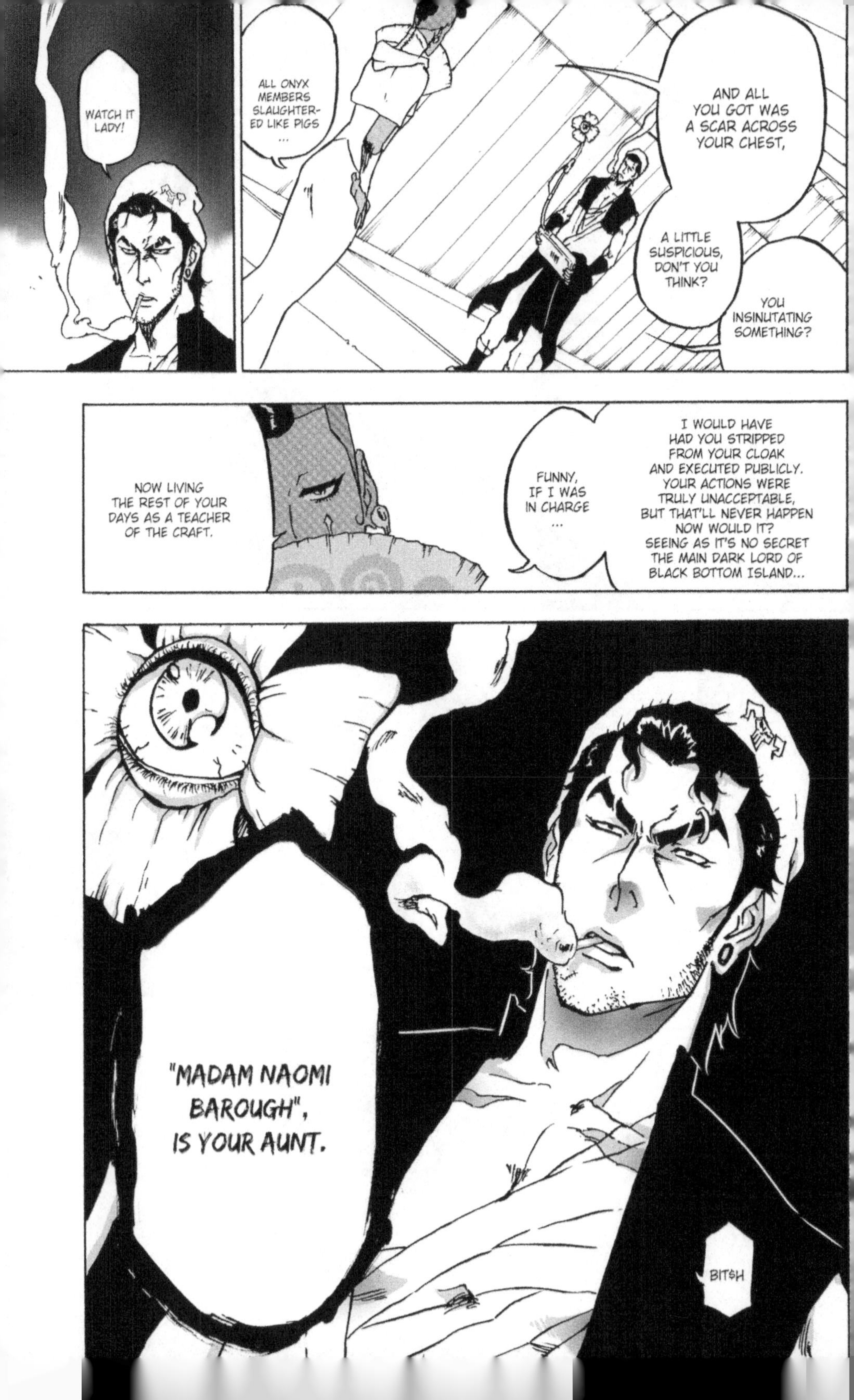
WATCH IT LADY!
ALL ONYX MEMBERS SLAUGHTERED LIKE PIGS ...
AND ALL YOU GOT WAS A SCAR ACROSS YOUR CHEST,
A LITTLE SUSPICIOUS, DON'T YOU THINK?
YOU INSINUTATING SOMETHING?
NOW LIVING THE REST OF YOUR DAYS AS A TEACHER OF THE CRAFT.
FUNNY, IF I WAS IN CHARGE ...
I WOULD HAVE HAD YOU STRIPPED FROM YOUR CLOAK AND EXECUTED PUBLICLY. YOUR ACTIONS WERE TRULY UNACCEPTABLE, BUT THAT'LL NEVER HAPPEN NOW WOULD IT? SEEING AS IT'S NO SECRET THE MAIN DARK LORD OF BLACK BOTTOM ISLAND...
"MADAM NAOMI BAROUGH", IS YOUR AUNT.
BIT$H

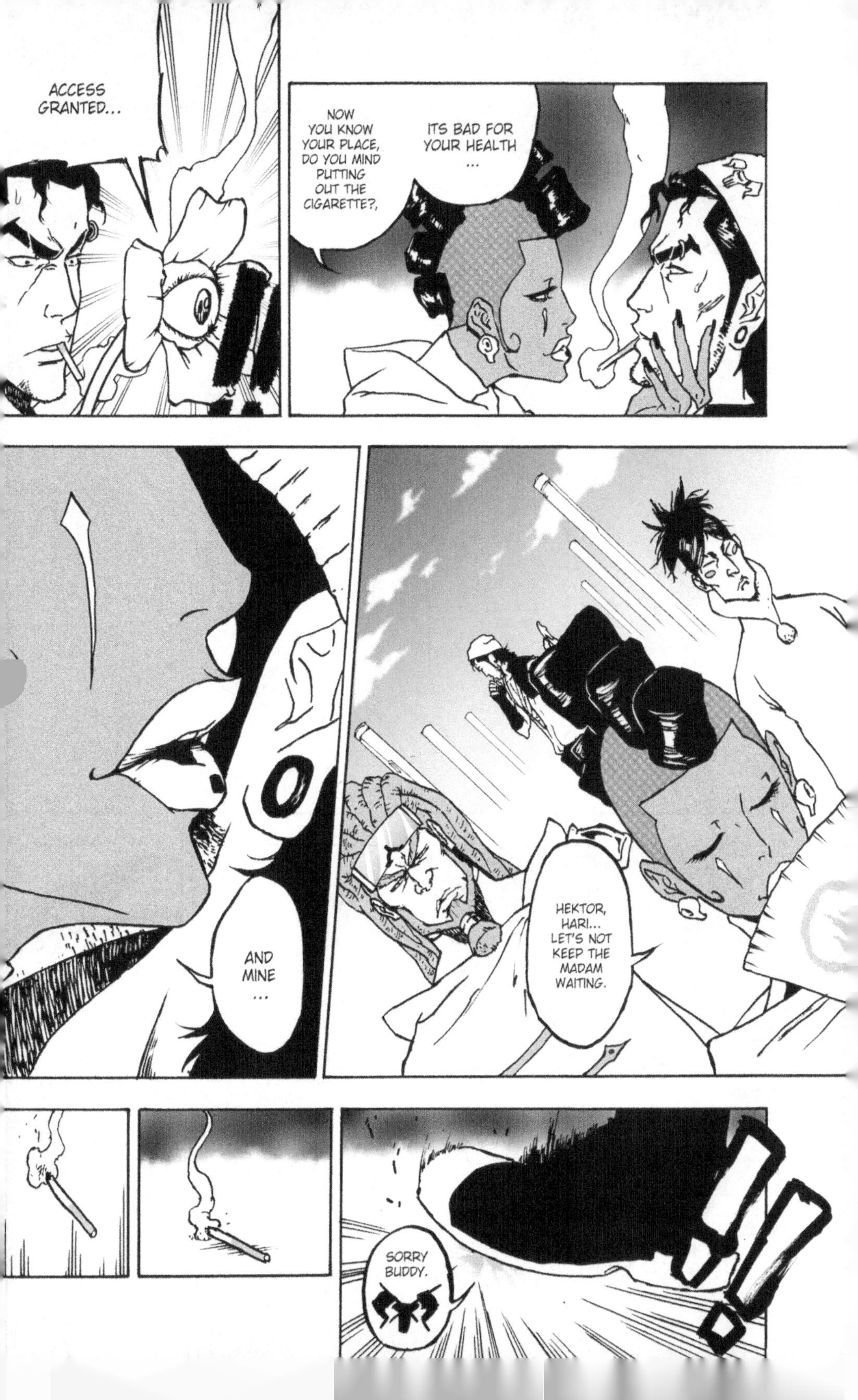
ACCESS GRANTED...
NOW YOU KNOW YOUR PLACE, DO YOU MIND PUTTING OUT THE CIGARETTE?,
ITS BAD FOR YOUR HEALTH ...
AND MINE ...
HEKTOR, HARI... LET'S NOT KEEP THE MADAM WAITING.
SORRY BUDDY.

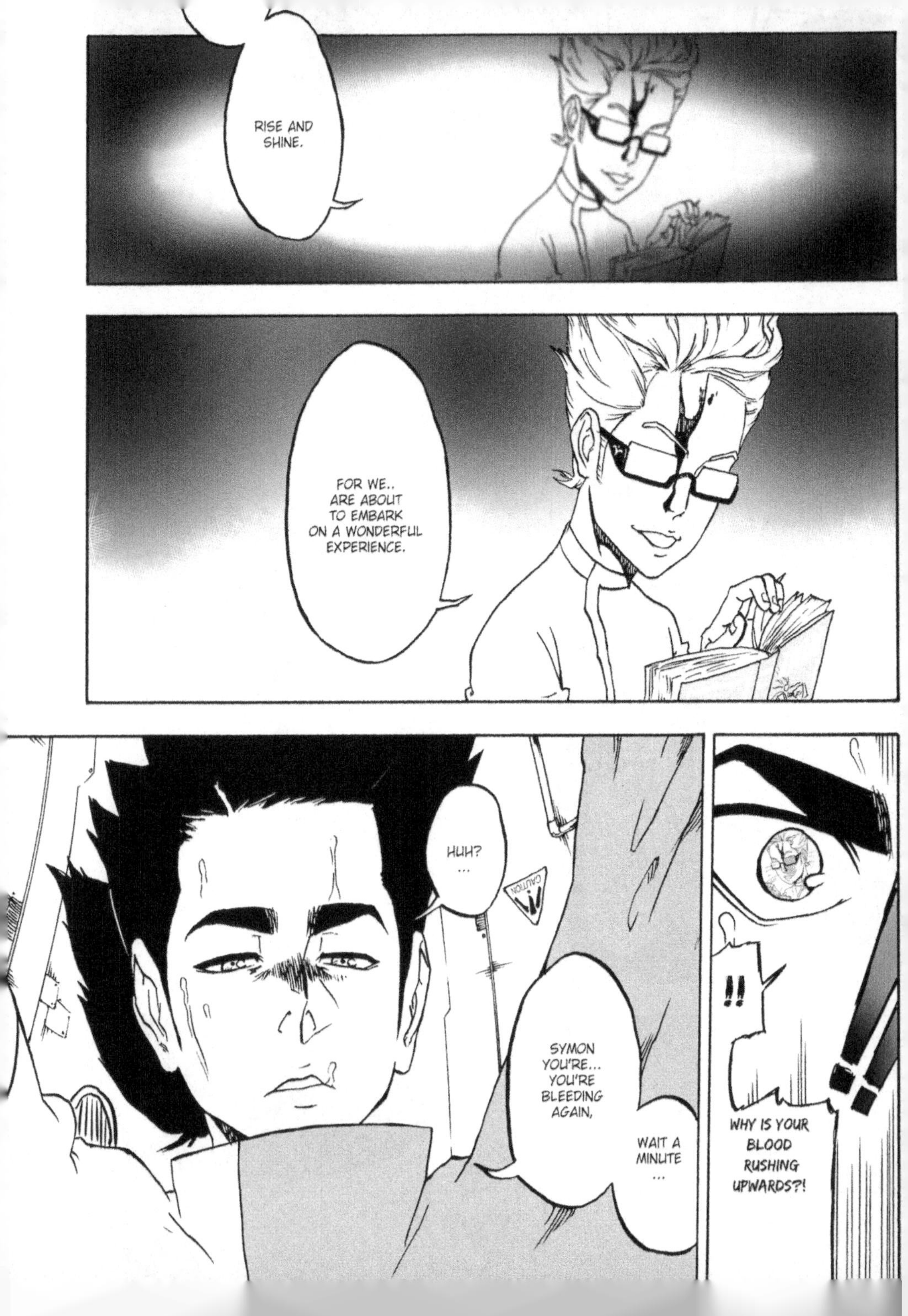
RISE AND SHINE.
FOR WE.. ARE ABOUT TO EMBARK ON A WONDERFUL EXPERIENCE.
HUH? ...
SYMON YOU'RE... YOU'RE BLEEDING AGAIN,
WAIT A MINUTE ...
!!
WHY IS YOUR BLOOD RUSHING UPWARDS?!

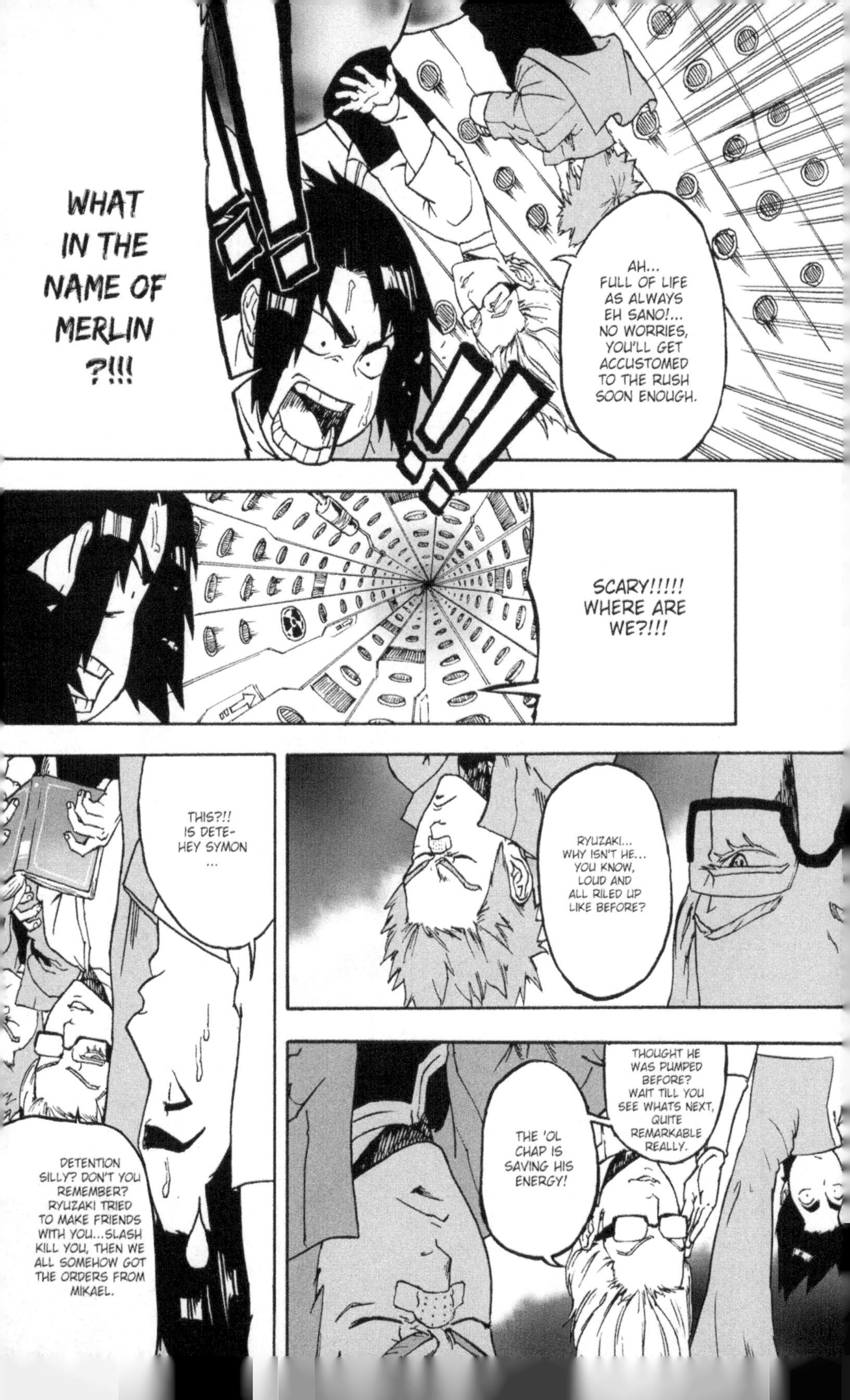
WHAT IN THE NAME OF MERLIN ?!!!
AH... FULL OF LIFE AS ALWAYS EH SANO!... NO WORRIES, YOU'LL GET ACCUSTOMED TO THE RUSH SOON ENOUGH.
SCARY!!!!! WHERE ARE WE?!!!
THIS?!! IS DETE- HEY SYMON ...
DETENTION SILLY? DON'T YOU REMEMBER? RYUZAKI TRIED TO MAKE FRIENDS WITH YOU...SLASH KILL YOU, THEN WE ALL SOMEHOW GOT THE ORDERS FROM MIKAEL.
RYUZAKI... WHY ISN'T HE... YOU KNOW, LOUD AND ALL RILED UP LIKE BEFORE?
THE 'OL CHAP IS SAVING HIS ENERGY!
THOUGHT HE WAS PUMPED BEFORE? WAIT TILL YOU SEE WHATS NEXT, QUITE REMARKABLE REALLY.

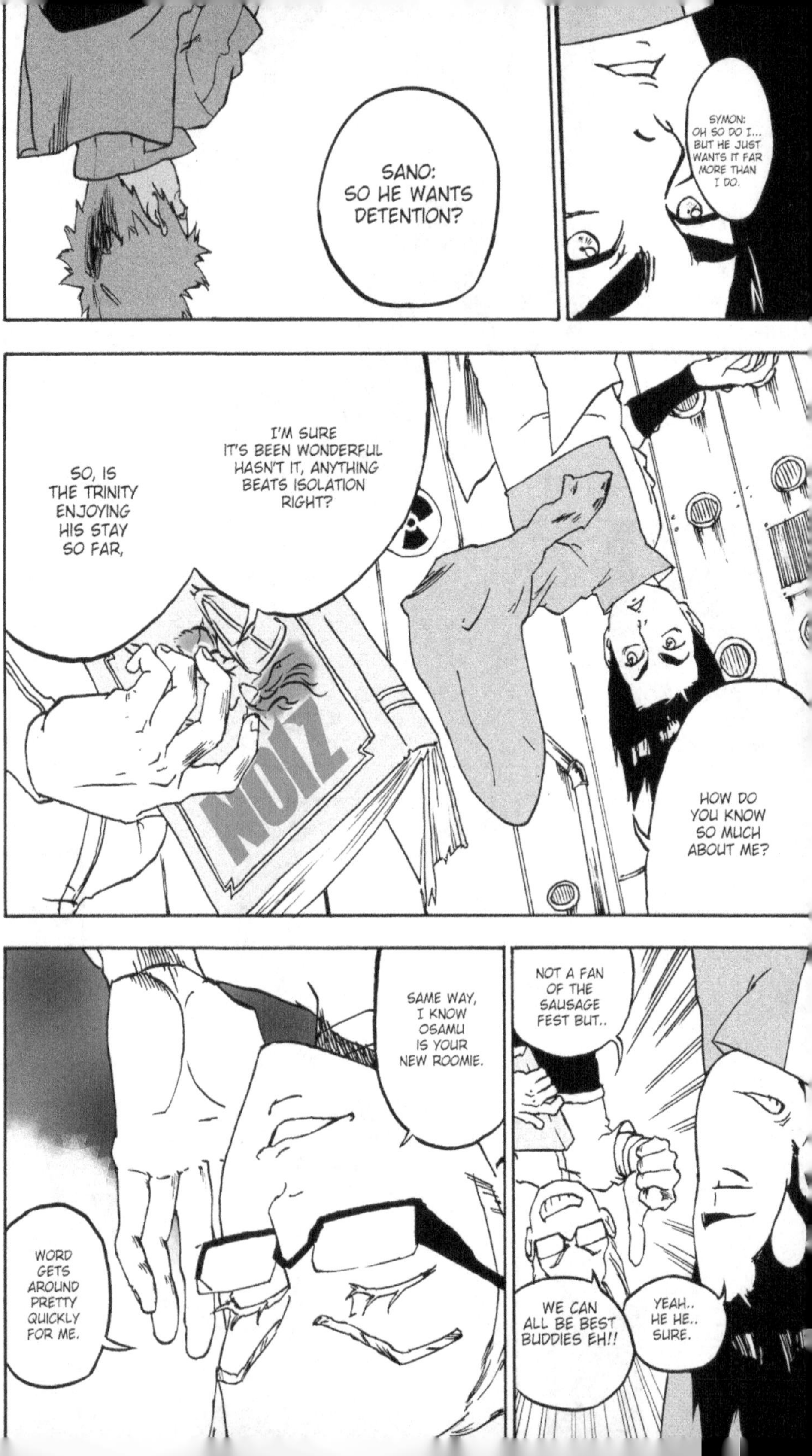
SANO: SO HE WANTS DETENTION?
SYMON: OH SO DO I... BUT HE JUST WANTS IT FAR MORE THAN I DO.
SO, IS THE TRINITY ENJOYING HIS STAY SO FAR,
I'M SURE IT'S BEEN WONDERFUL HASN'T IT, ANYTHING BEATS ISOLATION RIGHT?
NOIZ
HOW DO YOU KNOW SO MUCH ABOUT ME?
SAME WAY, I KNOW OSAMU IS YOUR NEW ROOMIE.
WORD GETS AROUND PRETTY QUICKLY FOR ME.
NOT A FAN OF THE SAUSAGE FEST BUT..
WE CAN ALL BE BEST BUDDIES EH!!
YEAH.. HE HE.. SURE.

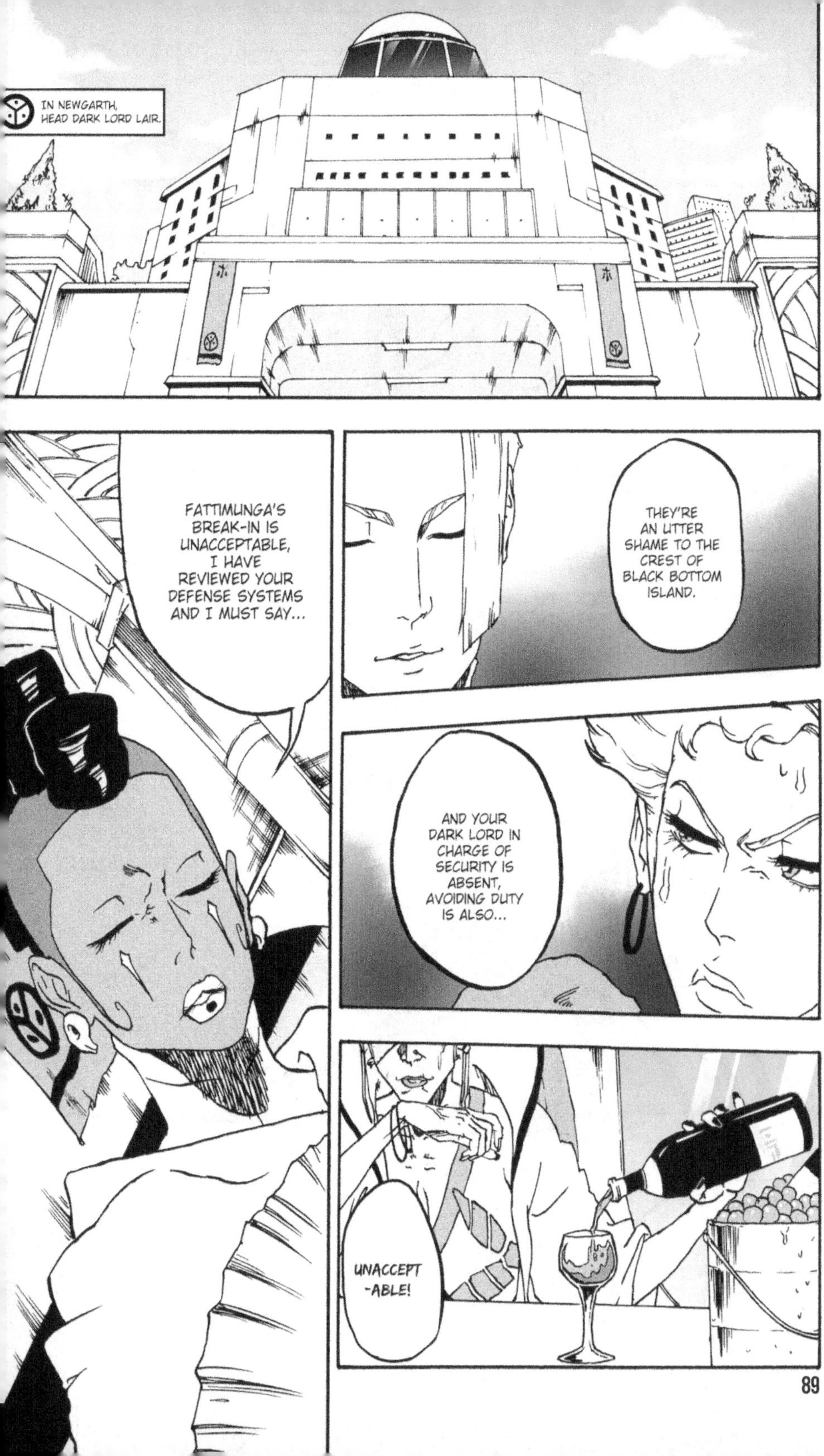
IN NEWGARTH, HEAD DARK LORD LAIR.
FATTIMUNGA'S BREAK-IN IS UNACCEPTABLE, I HAVE REVIEWED YOUR DEFENSE SYSTEMS AND I MUST SAY...
THEY'RE AN UTTER SHAME TO THE CREST OF BLACK BOTTOM ISLAND.
AND YOUR DARK LORD IN CHARGE OF SECURITY IS ABSENT, AVOIDING DUTY IS ALSO...
UNACCEPT -ABLE!

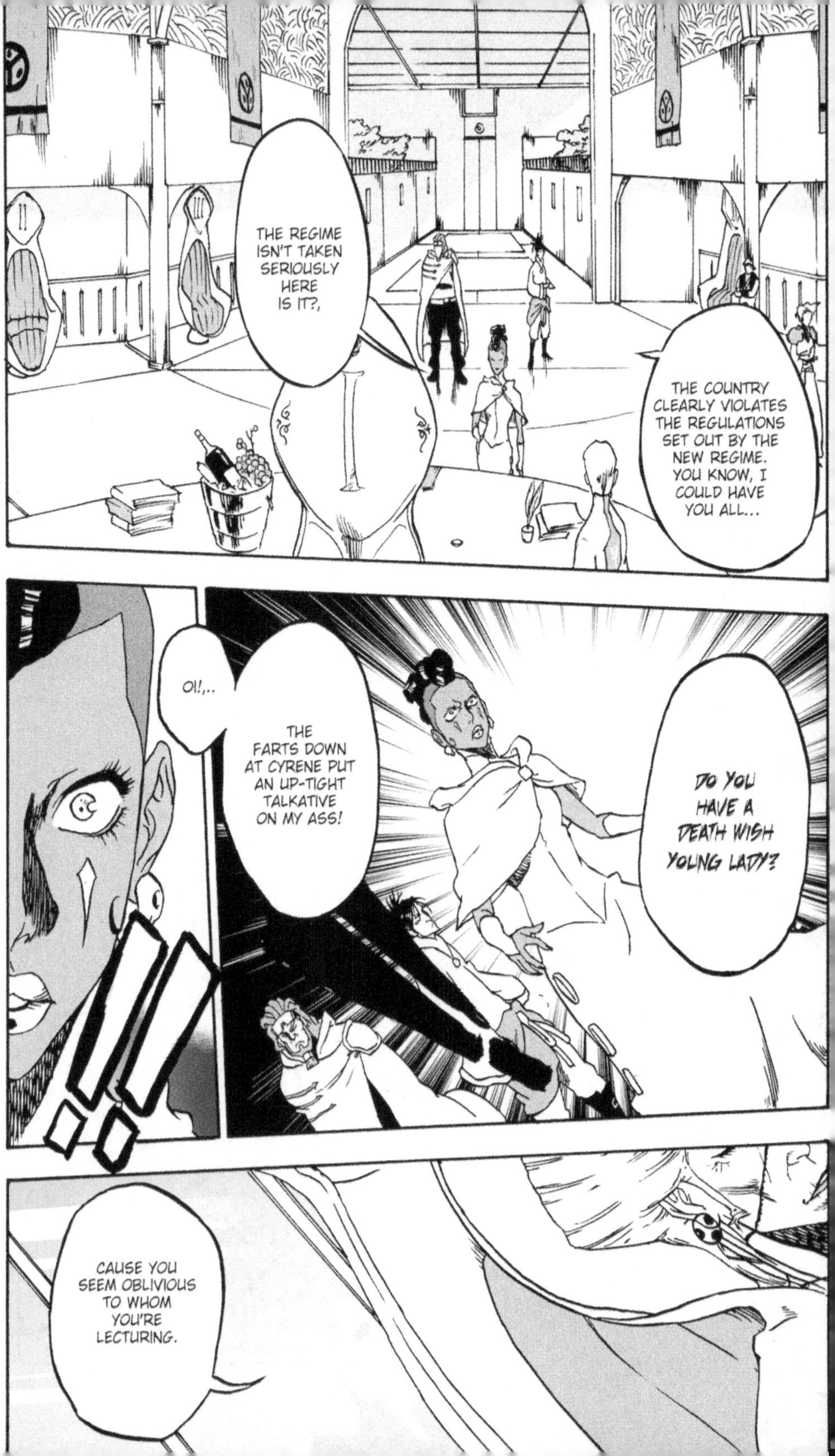
THE REGIME ISN'T TAKEN SERIOUSLY HERE IS IT?,
THE COUNTRY CLEARLY VIOLATES THE REGULATIONS SET OUT BY THE NEW REGIME. YOU KNOW, I COULD HAVE YOU ALL...
OI!,..
THE FARTS DOWN AT CYRENE PUT AN UP-TIGHT TALKATIVE ON MY ASS!
DO YOU HAVE A DEATH WISH YOUNG LADY?
CAUSE YOU SEEM OBLIVIOUS TO WHOM YOU'RE LECTURING.

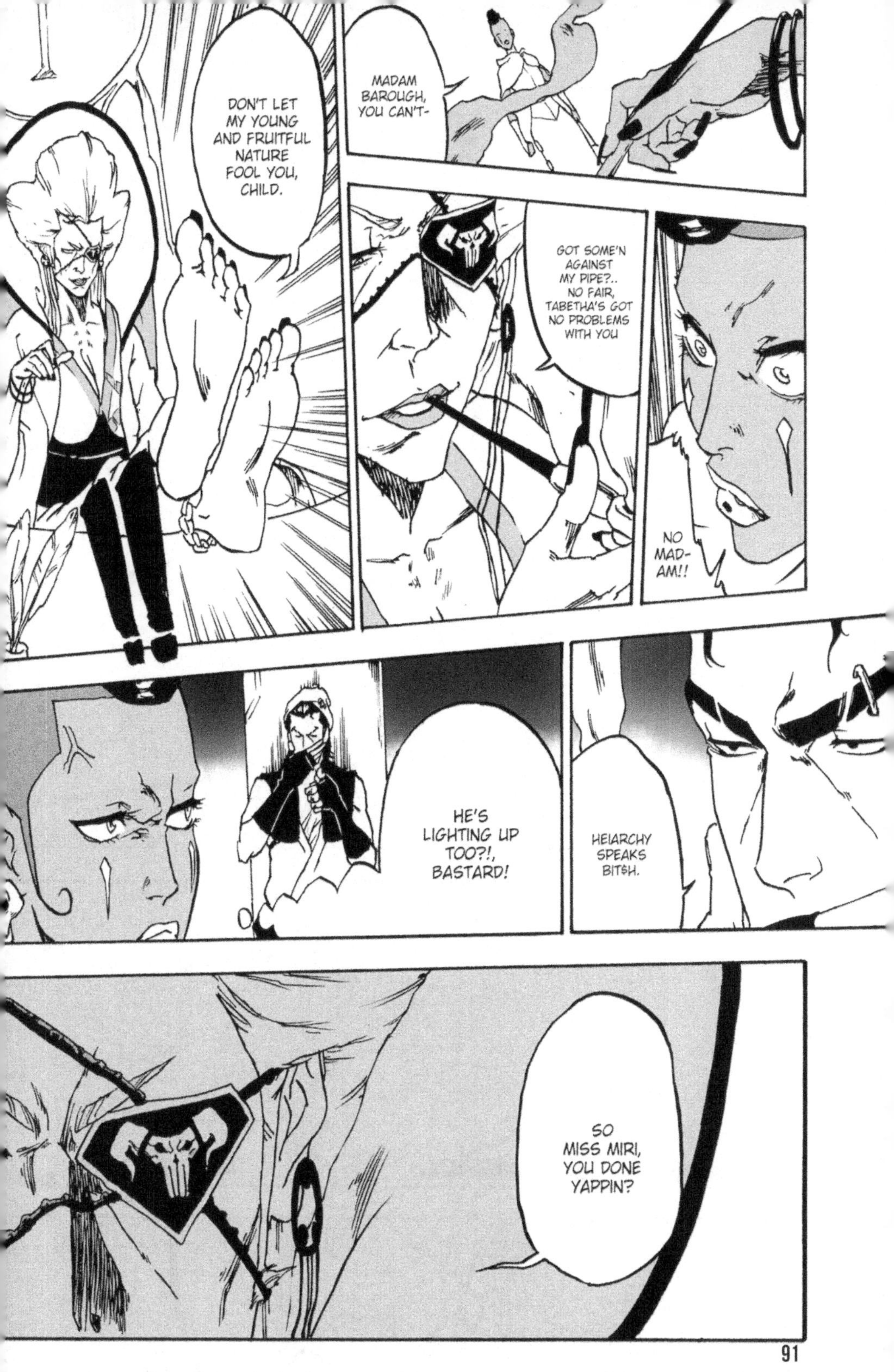
DON'T LET MY YOUNG AND FRUITFUL NATURE FOOL YOU, CHILD.
MADAM BAROUGH, YOU CAN'T-
GOT SOME'N AGAINST MY PIPE?.. NO FAIR, TABETHA'S GOT NO PROBLEMS WITH YOU
NO MAD-AM!!
HE'S LIGHTING UP TOO?!, BASTARD!
HEIARCHY SPEAKS BIT$H.
SO MISS MIRI, YOU DONE YAPPIN?

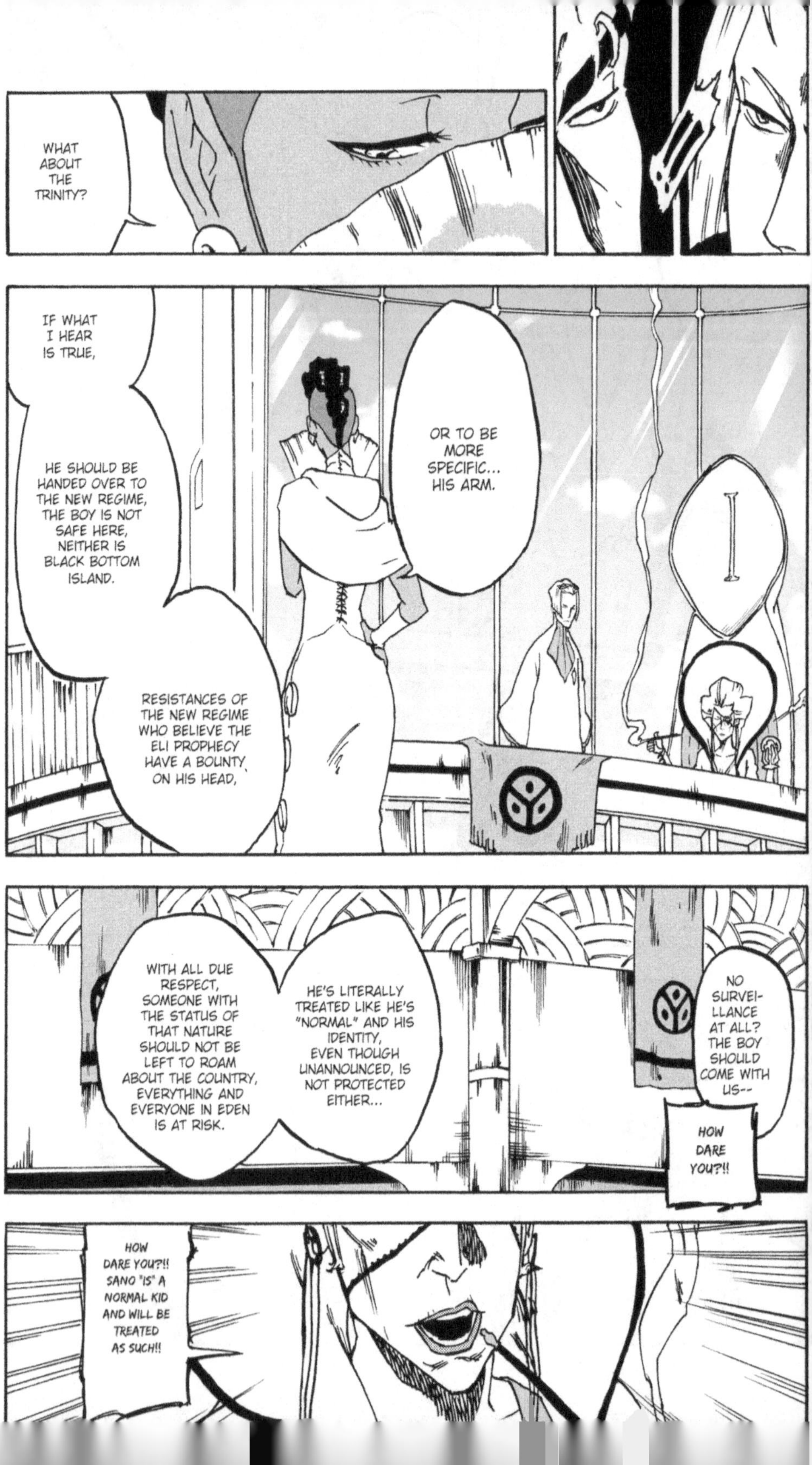
WHAT ABOUT THE TRINITY?
IF WHAT I HEAR IS TRUE,
HE SHOULD BE HANDED OVER TO THE NEW REGIME, THE BOY IS NOT SAFE HERE, NEITHER IS BLACK BOTTOM ISLAND.
RESISTANCES OF THE NEW REGIME WHO BELIEVE THE ELI PROPHECY HAVE A BOUNTY ON HIS HEAD,
OR TO BE MORE SPECIFIC... HIS ARM.
I
WITH ALL DUE RESPECT, SOMEONE WITH THE STATUS OF THAT NATURE SHOULD NOT BE LEFT TO ROAM ABOUT THE COUNTRY, EVERYTHING AND EVERYONE IN EDEN IS AT RISK.
HE'S LITERALLY TREATED LIKE HE'S "NORMAL" AND HIS IDENTITY, EVEN THOUGH UNANNOUNCED, IS NOT PROTECTED EITHER...
NO SURVEI-LLANCE AT ALL? THE BOY SHOULD COME WITH US--
HOW DARE YOU?!!
HOW DARE YOU?!! SANO "IS" A NORMAL KID AND WILL BE TREATED AS SUCH!!

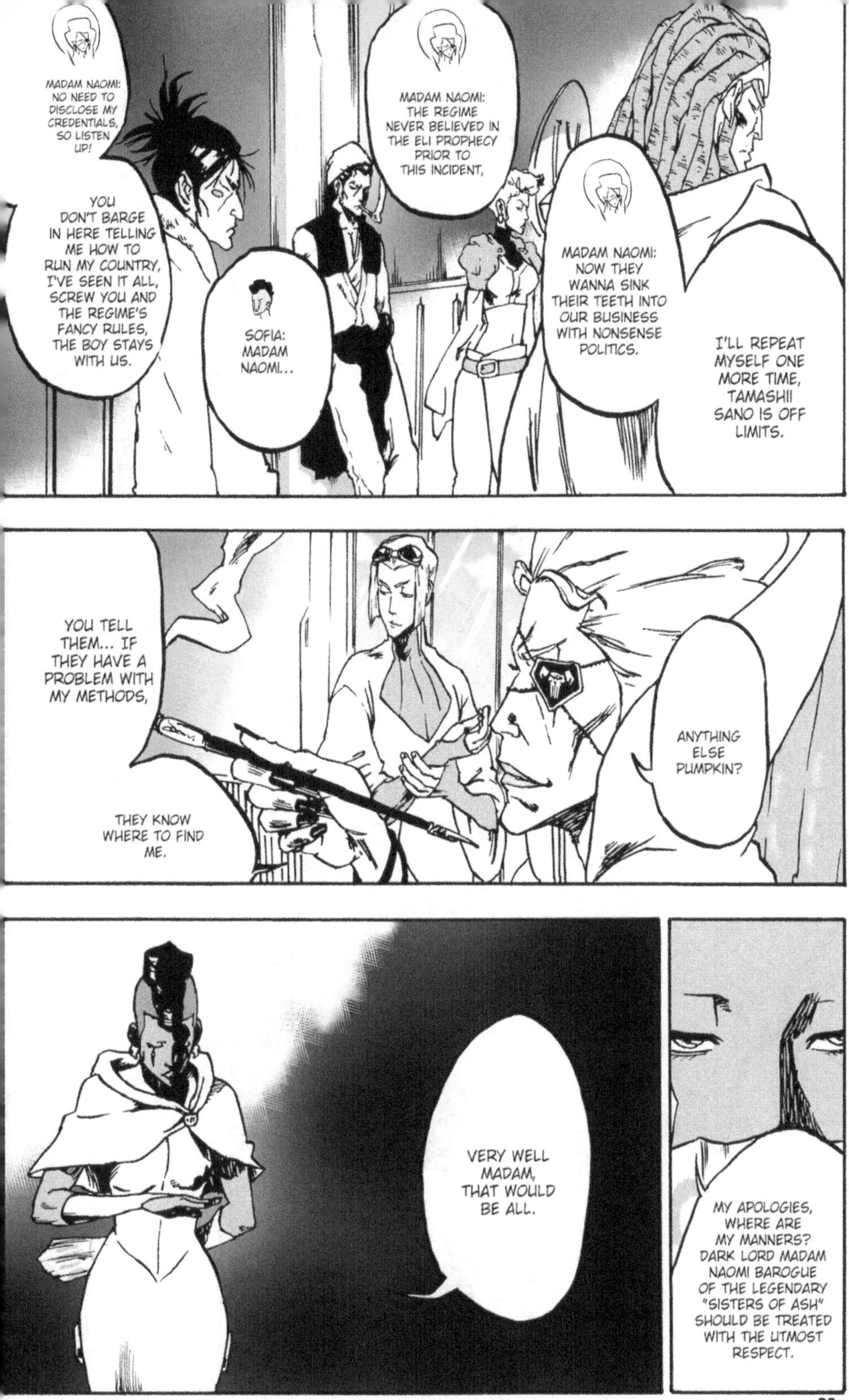

MADAM NAOMI: NO NEED TO DISCLOSE MY CREDENTIALS, SO LISTEN UP!
YOU DON'T BARGE IN HERE TELLING ME HOW TO RUN MY COUNTRY, I'VE SEEN IT ALL, SCREW YOU AND THE REGIME'S FANCY RULES, THE BOY STAYS WITH US.
SOFIA: MADAM NAOMI...
MADAM NAOMI: THE REGIME NEVER BELIEVED IN THE ELI PROPHECY PRIOR TO THIS INCIDENT,
MADAM NAOMI: NOW THEY WANNA SINK THEIR TEETH INTO OUR BUSINESS WITH NONSENSE POLITICS.
I'LL REPEAT MYSELF ONE MORE TIME, TAMASHII SANO IS OFF LIMITS.
YOU TELL THEM... IF THEY HAVE A PROBLEM WITH MY METHODS,
THEY KNOW WHERE TO FIND ME.
ANYTHING ELSE PUMPKIN?
VERY WELL MADAM, THAT WOULD BE ALL.
MY APOLOGIES, WHERE ARE MY MANNERS? DARK LORD MADAM NAOMI BAROGUE OF THE LEGENDARY "SISTERS OF ASH" SHOULD BE TREATED WITH THE UTMOST RESPECT.

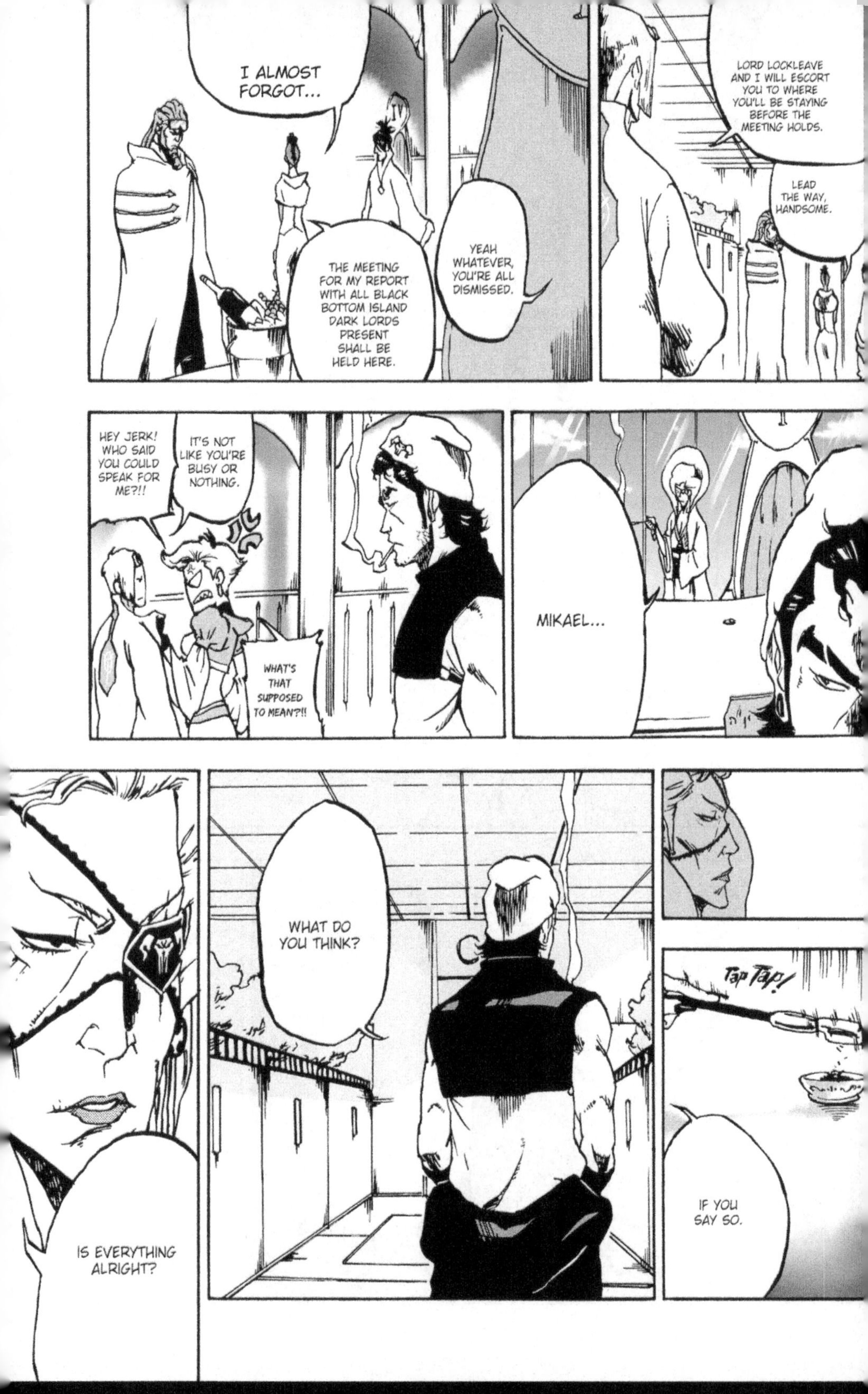
I ALMOST FORGOT...
THE MEETING FOR MY REPORT WITH ALL BLACK BOTTOM ISLAND DARK LORDS PRESENT SHALL BE HELD HERE.
YEAH WHATEVER, YOU'RE ALL DISMISSED.
LORD LOCKLEAVE AND I WILL ESCORT YOU TO WHERE YOU'LL BE STAYING BEFORE THE MEETING HOLDS.
LEAD THE WAY, HANDSOME.
HEY JERK! WHO SAID YOU COULD SPEAK FOR ME?!!
IT'S NOT LIKE YOU'RE BUSY OR NOTHING.
WHAT'S THAT SUPPOSED TO MEAN?!!
MIKAEL...
IS EVERYTHING ALRIGHT?
WHAT DO YOU THINK?
Tap Tap!
IF YOU SAY SO.

NOOOO!!!!
AND JUST WHEN I WAS GETTING ATTACHED TO THE CHARACTER.

UH.. I'M A LITTLE FRIGHTENED TO ASK BUT

WHAT EXACTLY ARE YOU READING?

THOUGHT YOU'D NEVER ASK!!

OH BLOAK, HE'S BLEEDING AGAIN.

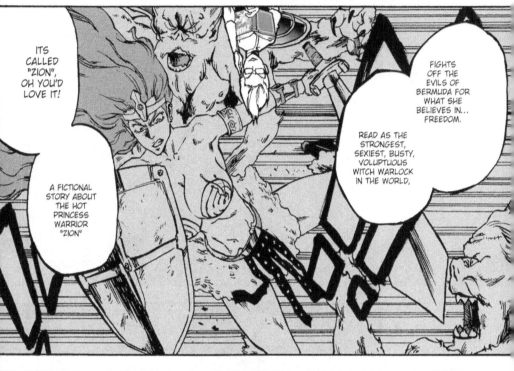

ITS CALLED "ZION", OH YOU'D LOVE IT!

A FICTIONAL STORY ABOUT THE HOT PRINCESS WARRIOR "ZION"

READ AS THE STRONGEST, SEXIEST, BUSTY, VOLUPTUOUS WITCH WARLOCK IN THE WORLD,

FIGHTS OFF THE EVILS OF BERMUDA FOR WHAT SHE BELIEVES IN... FREEDOM.

THAT'S THE BASIC GIST OF IT BUT ITS SO MUCH MORE, YOU SHOULD TRY IT, I GUARANTEE AMAZEMENT!

PROBABLY NOT, I'M MORE INTO MERLIN BOOKS, EVER HEARD OF THEM? I HAVE A LOT, USED TO BE MY FATHER'S.

95

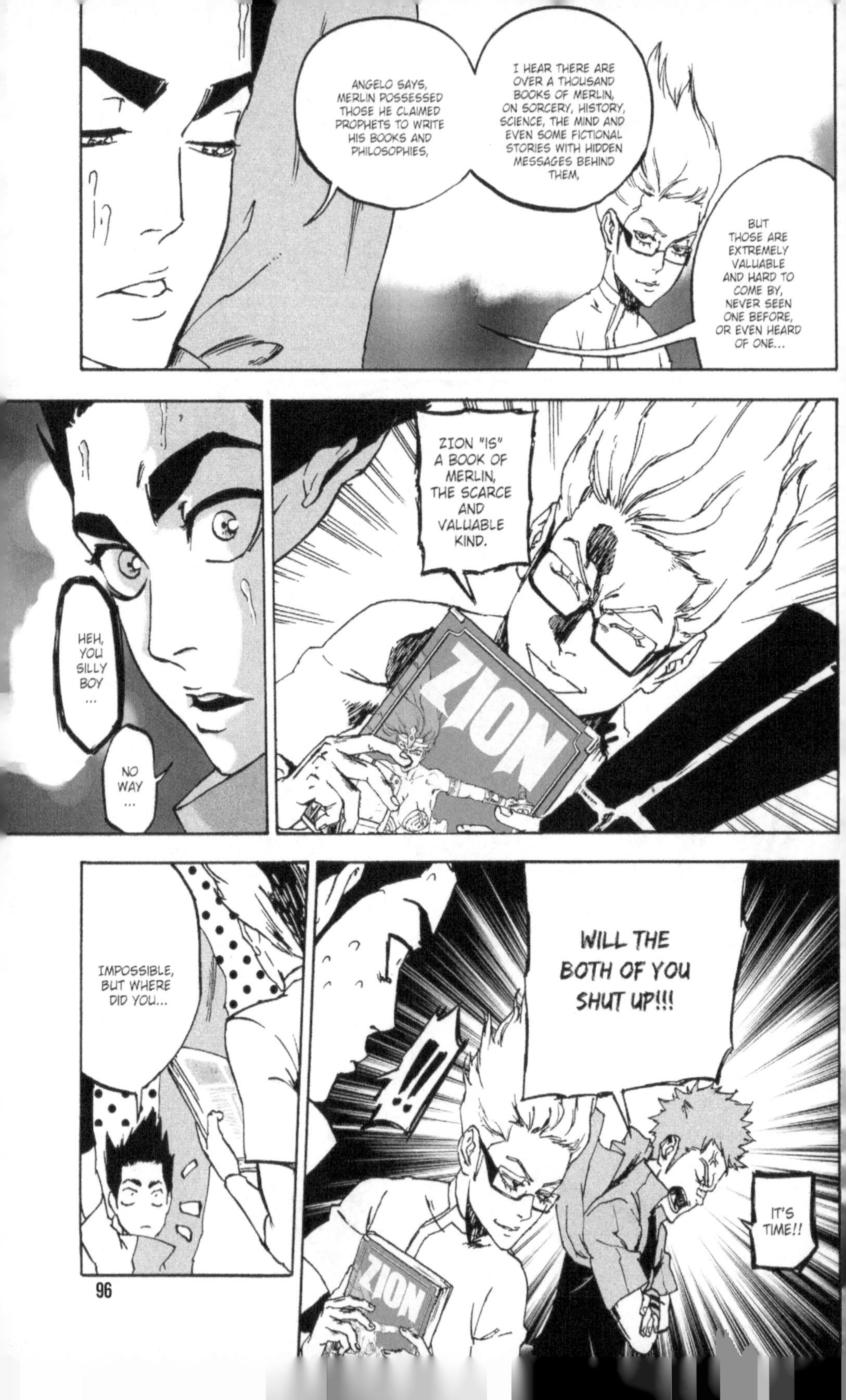

ANGELO SAYS, MERLIN POSSESSED THOSE HE CLAIMED PROPHETS TO WRITE HIS BOOKS AND PHILOSOPHIES,
I HEAR THERE ARE OVER A THOUSAND BOOKS OF MERLIN, ON SORCERY, HISTORY, SCIENCE, THE MIND AND EVEN SOME FICTIONAL STORIES WITH HIDDEN MESSAGES BEHIND THEM,
BUT THOSE ARE EXTREMELY VALUABLE AND HARD TO COME BY, NEVER SEEN ONE BEFORE, OR EVEN HEARD OF ONE...
HEH, YOU SILLY BOY ...
NO WAY ...
ZION "IS" A BOOK OF MERLIN, THE SCARCE AND VALUABLE KIND.
ZION
IMPOSSIBLE, BUT WHERE DID YOU...
WILL THE BOTH OF YOU SHUT UP!!!
!!
IT'S TIME!!
ZION

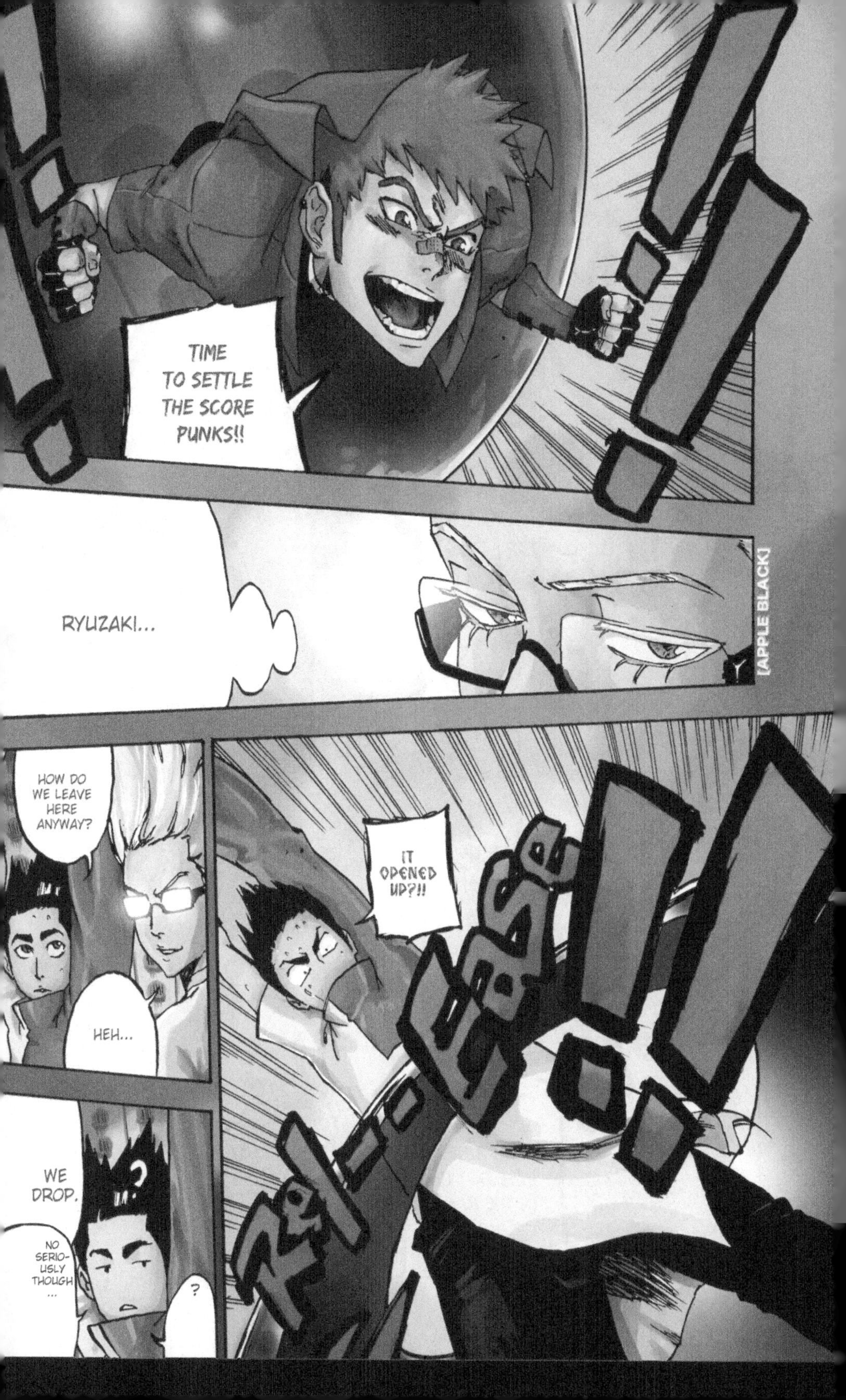
TIME TO SETTLE THE SCORE PUNKS!!
RYUZAKI...
[APPLE BLACK]
HOW DO WE LEAVE HERE ANYWAY?
HEH...
WE DROP.
?
NO SERIOUSLY THOUGH...
?
IT OPENED UP?!!

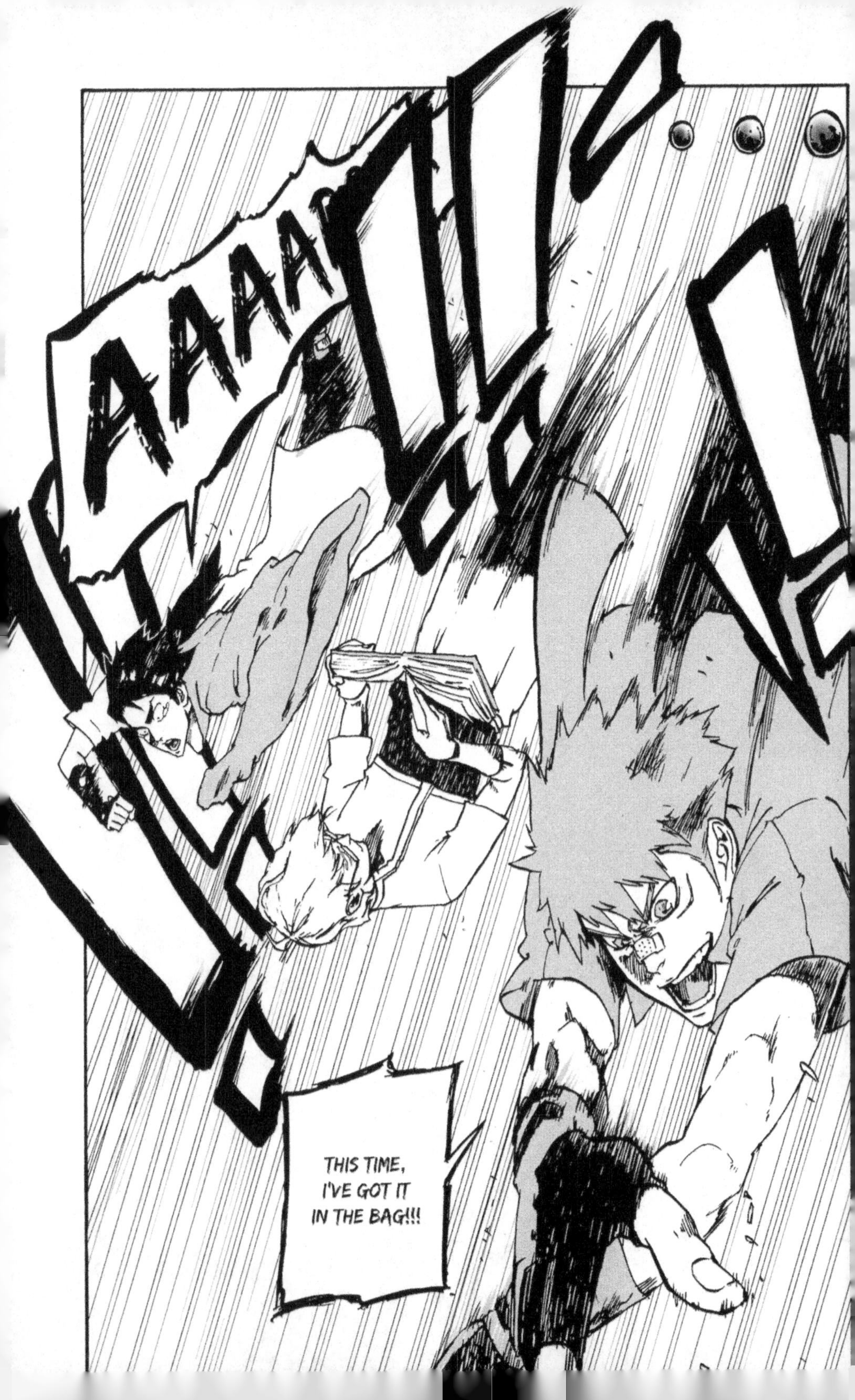
THIS TIME, I'VE GOT IT IN THE BAG!!!

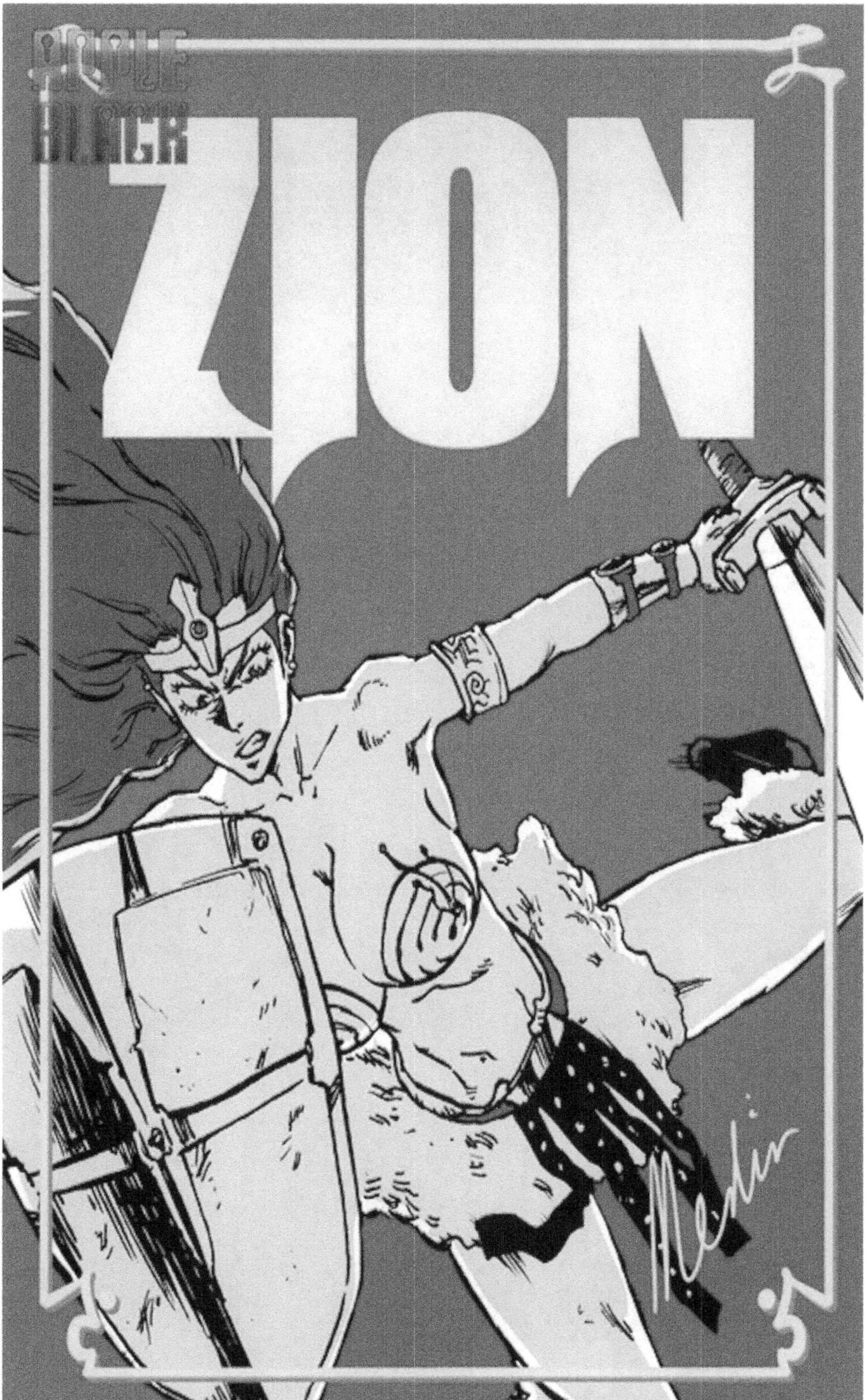

ZION

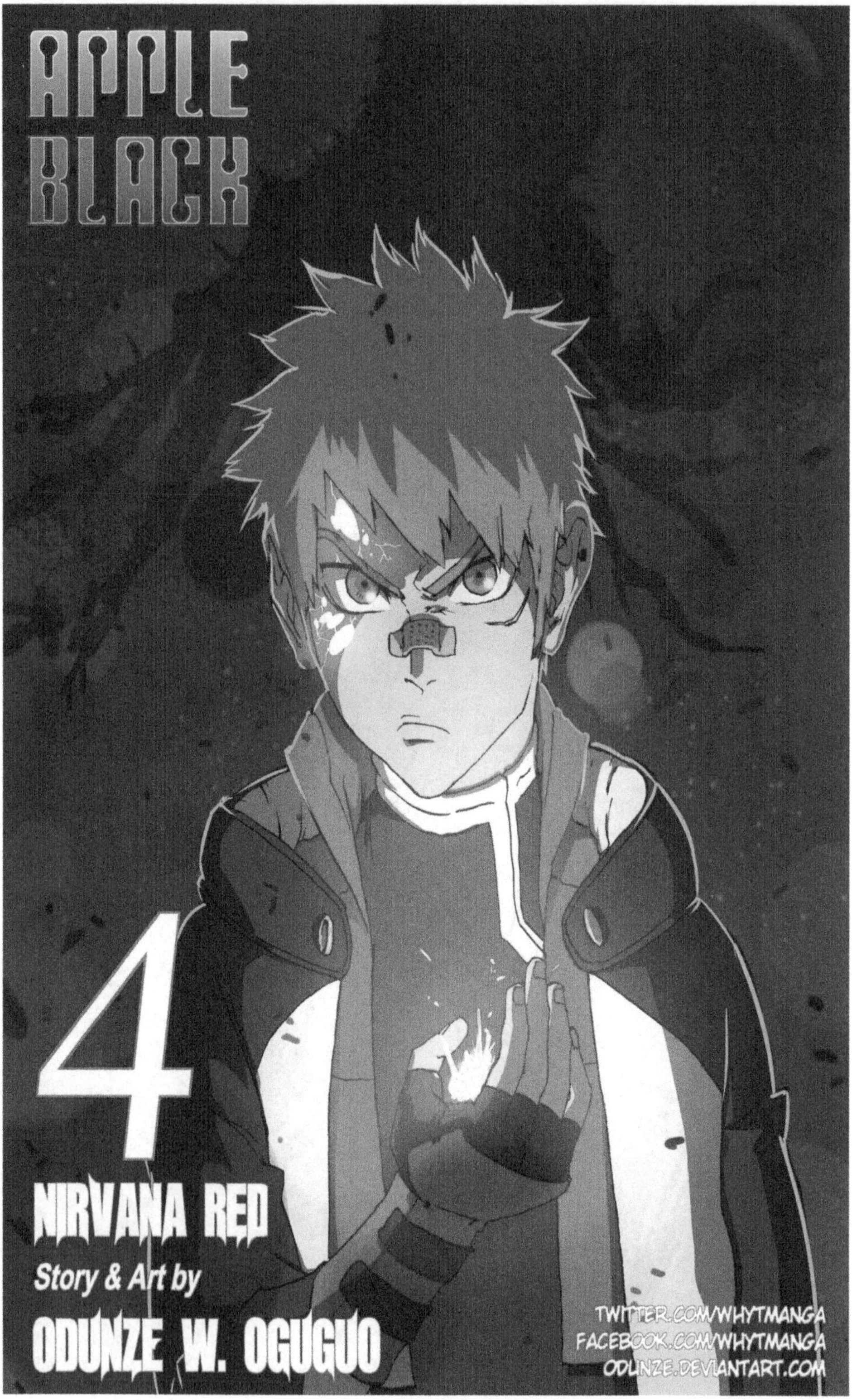
APPLE BLACK
4
NIRVANA RED
Story & Art by
ODUNZE W. OGUGUO
TWITTER.COM/WHYTMANGA
FACEBOOK.COM/WHYTMANGA
ODUNZE.DEVIANTART.COM

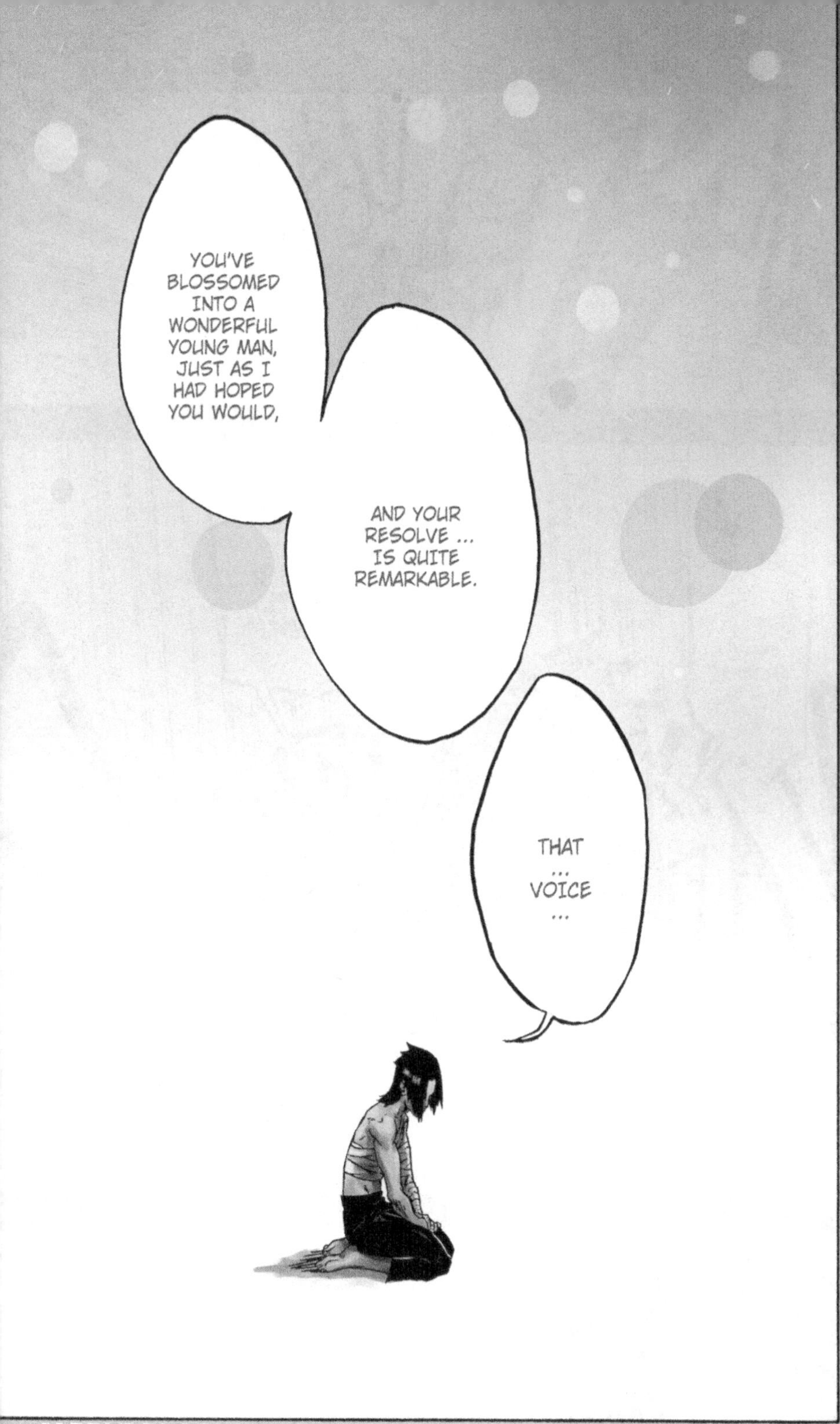
YOU'VE BLOSSOMED INTO A WONDERFUL YOUNG MAN, JUST AS I HAD HOPED YOU WOULD,
AND YOUR RESOLVE ... IS QUITE REMARKABLE.
THAT ... VOICE ...

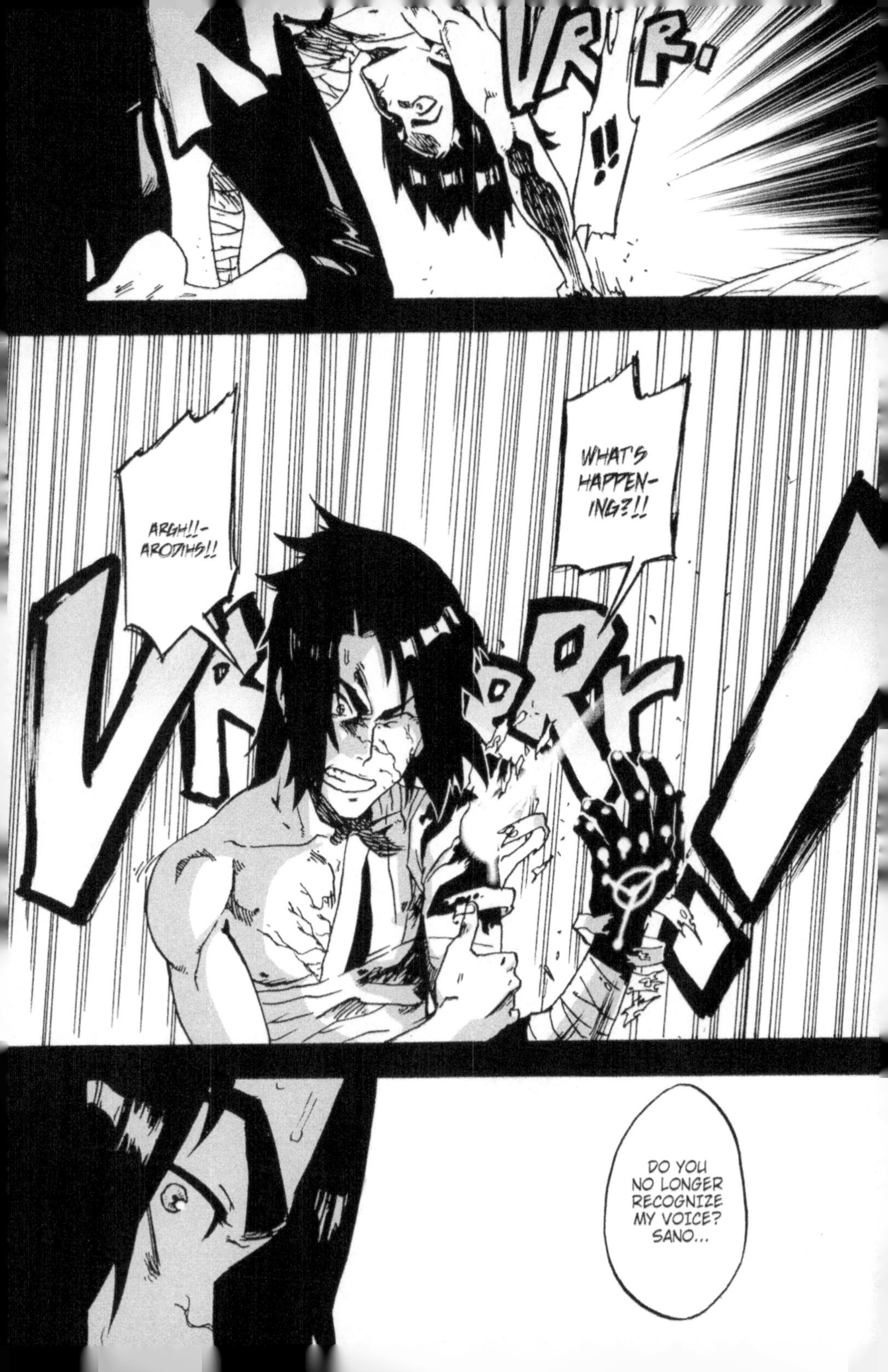
!!
ARGH!!- ARODIHS!!
WHAT'S HAPPEN-ING?!!
DO YOU NO LONGER RECOGNIZE MY VOICE? SANO...

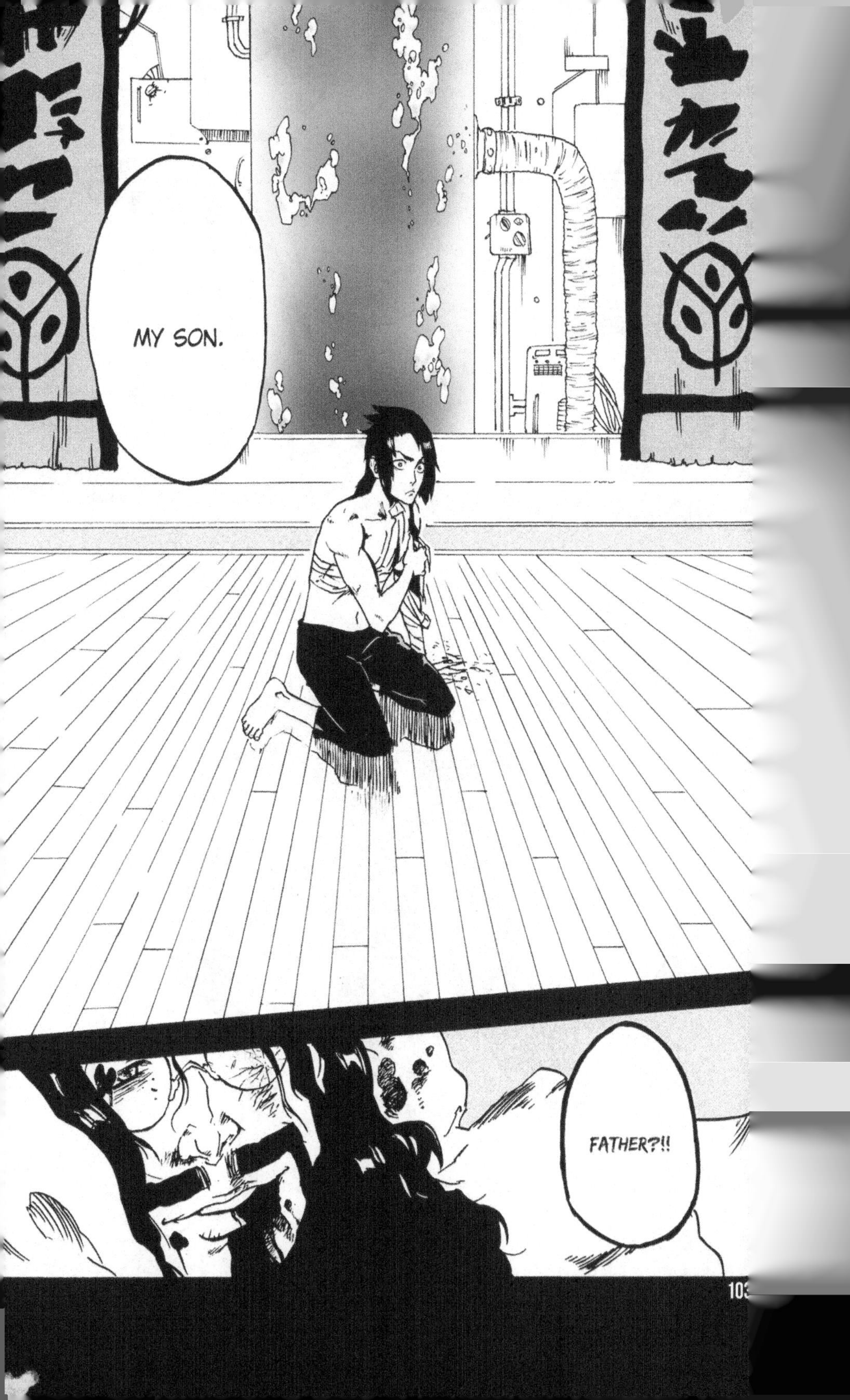
MY SON.
FATHER?!!

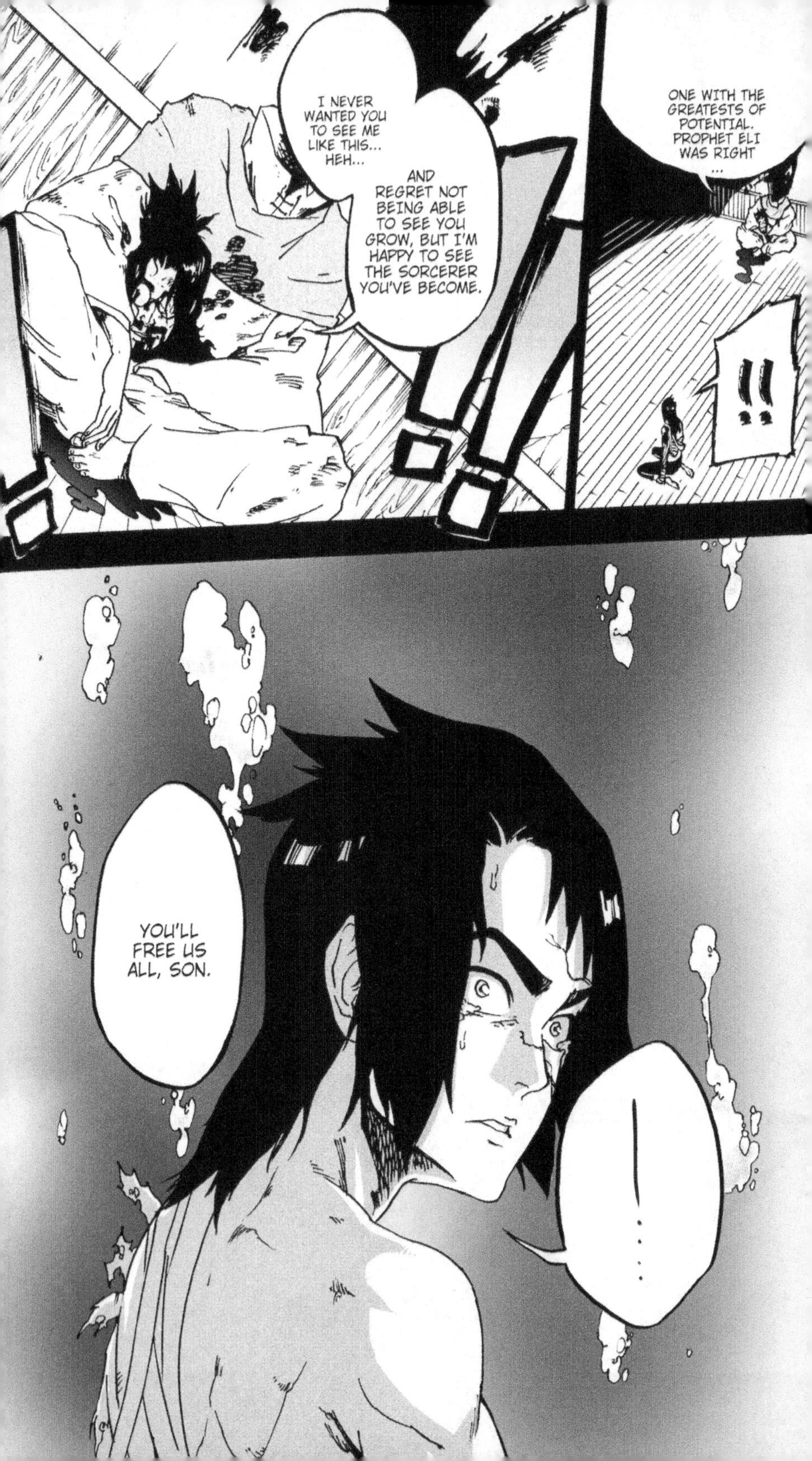
I NEVER WANTED YOU TO SEE ME LIKE THIS... HEH...
AND REGRET NOT BEING ABLE TO SEE YOU GROW, BUT I'M HAPPY TO SEE THE SORCERER YOU'VE BECOME.
ONE WITH THE GREATESTS OF POTENTIAL. PROPHET ELI WAS RIGHT ...
!!
YOU'LL FREE US ALL, SON.
!....

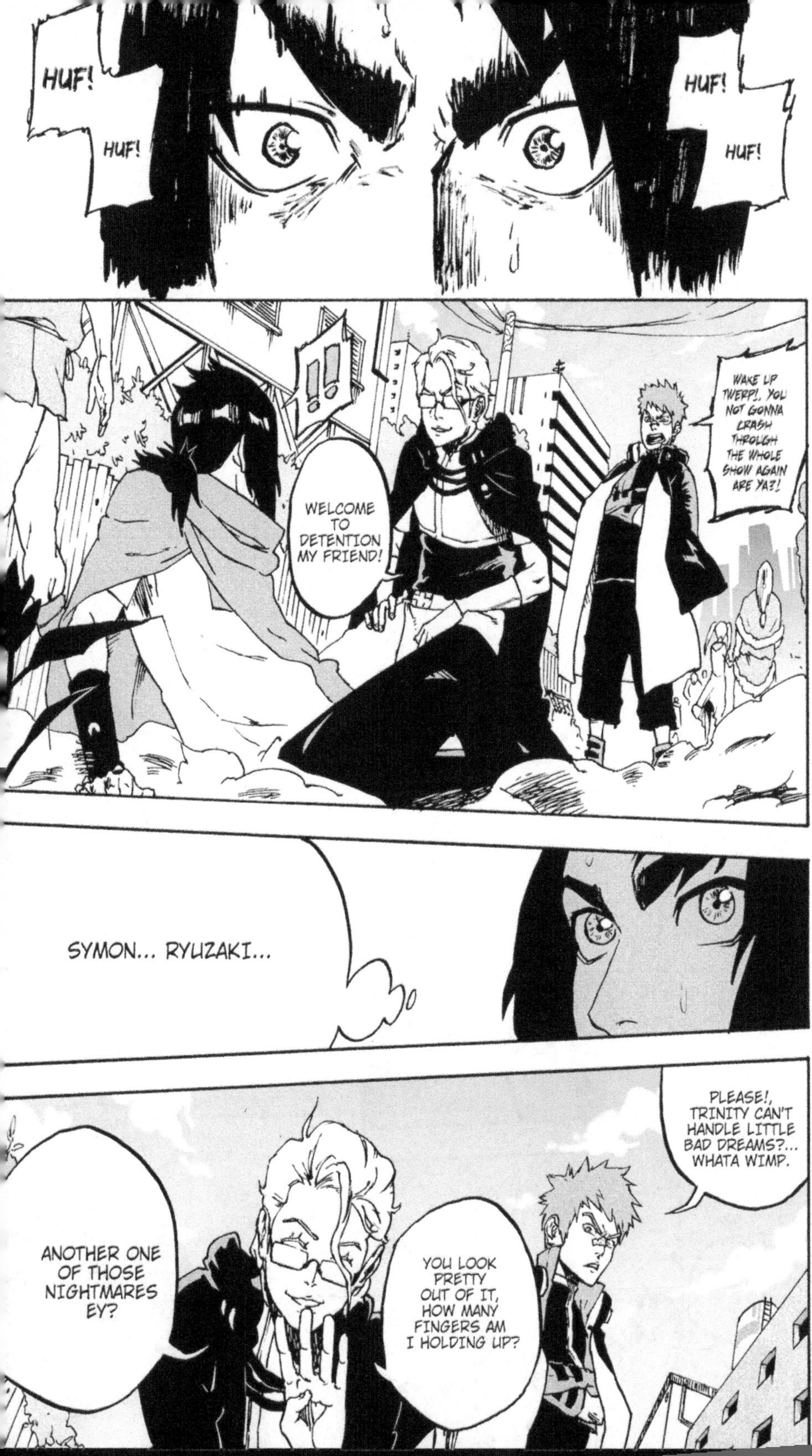
HUF!
HUF!
HUF!
HUF!
!!
WELCOME TO DETENTION MY FRIEND!
WAKE UP TWERP!. YOU NOT GONNA CRASH THROUGH THE WHOLE SHOW AGAIN ARE YA?!
SYMON... RYUZAKI...
ANOTHER ONE OF THOSE NIGHTMARES EY?
YOU LOOK PRETTY OUT OF IT, HOW MANY FINGERS AM I HOLDING UP?
PLEASE!, TRINITY CAN'T HANDLE LITTLE BAD DREAMS?... WHATA WIMP.

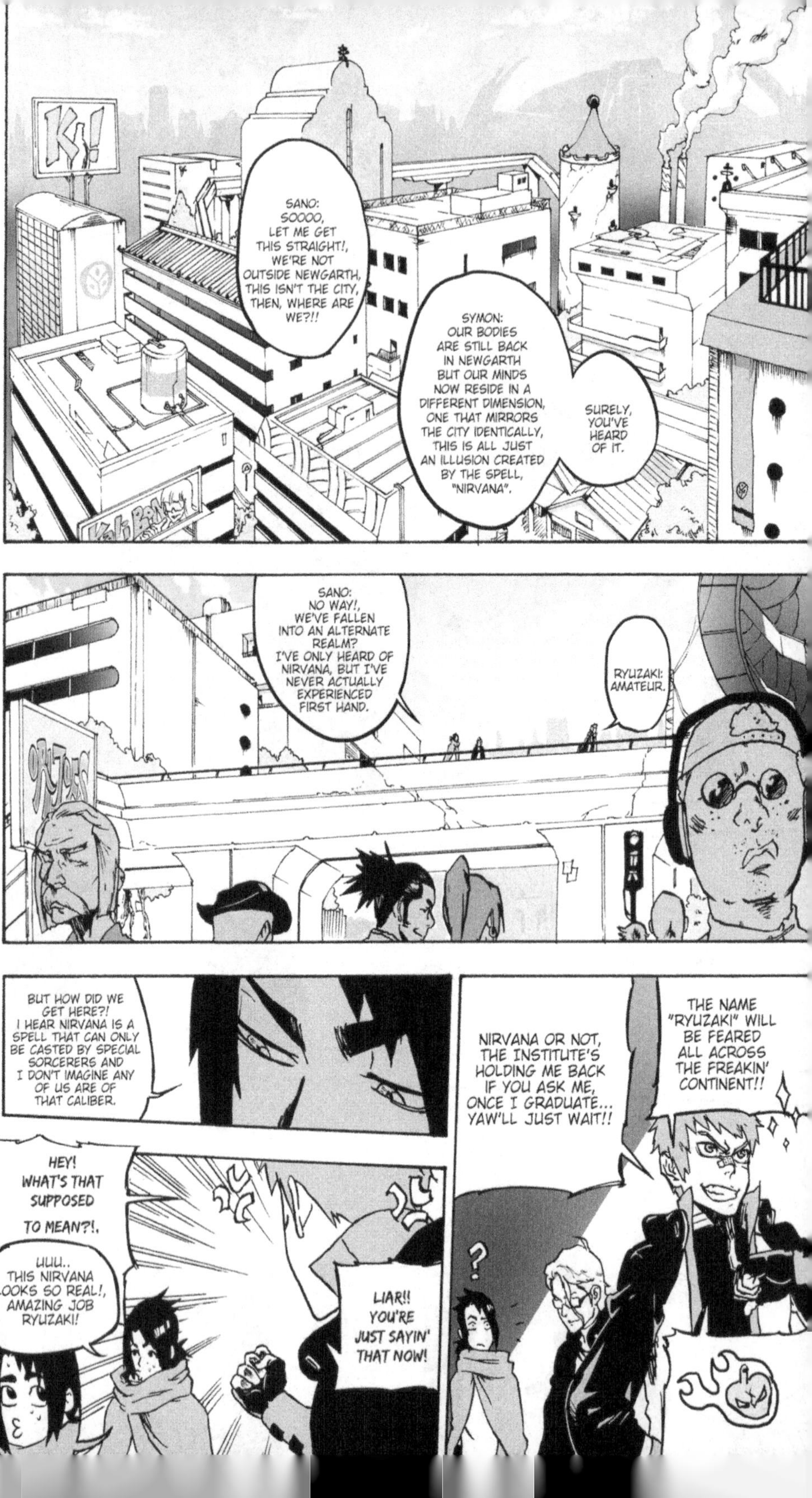
SANO: SOOOO, LET ME GET THIS STRAIGHT!, WE'RE NOT OUTSIDE NEWGARTH, THIS ISN'T THE CITY, THEN, WHERE ARE WE?!!
SYMON: OUR BODIES ARE STILL BACK IN NEWGARTH BUT OUR MINDS NOW RESIDE IN A DIFFERENT DIMENSION, ONE THAT MIRRORS THE CITY IDENTICALLY, THIS IS ALL JUST AN ILLUSION CREATED BY THE SPELL, "NIRVANA".
SURELY, YOU'VE HEARD OF IT.
SANO: NO WAY!, WE'VE FALLEN INTO AN ALTERNATE REALM? I'VE ONLY HEARD OF NIRVANA, BUT I'VE NEVER ACTUALLY EXPERIENCED FIRST HAND.
RYUZAKI: AMATEUR.
BUT HOW DID WE GET HERE?! I HEAR NIRVANA IS A SPELL THAT CAN ONLY BE CASTED BY SPECIAL SORCERERS AND I DON'T IMAGINE ANY OF US ARE OF THAT CALIBER.
HEY! WHAT'S THAT SUPPOSED TO MEAN?!.
UUU.. THIS NIRVANA LOOKS SO REAL!, AMAZING JOB RYUZAKI!
LIAR!! YOU'RE JUST SAYIN' THAT NOW!
NIRVANA OR NOT, THE INSTITUTE'S HOLDING ME BACK IF YOU ASK ME, ONCE I GRADUATE... YAW'LL JUST WAIT!!
THE NAME "RYUZAKI" WILL BE FEARED ALL ACROSS THE FREAKIN' CONTINENT!!

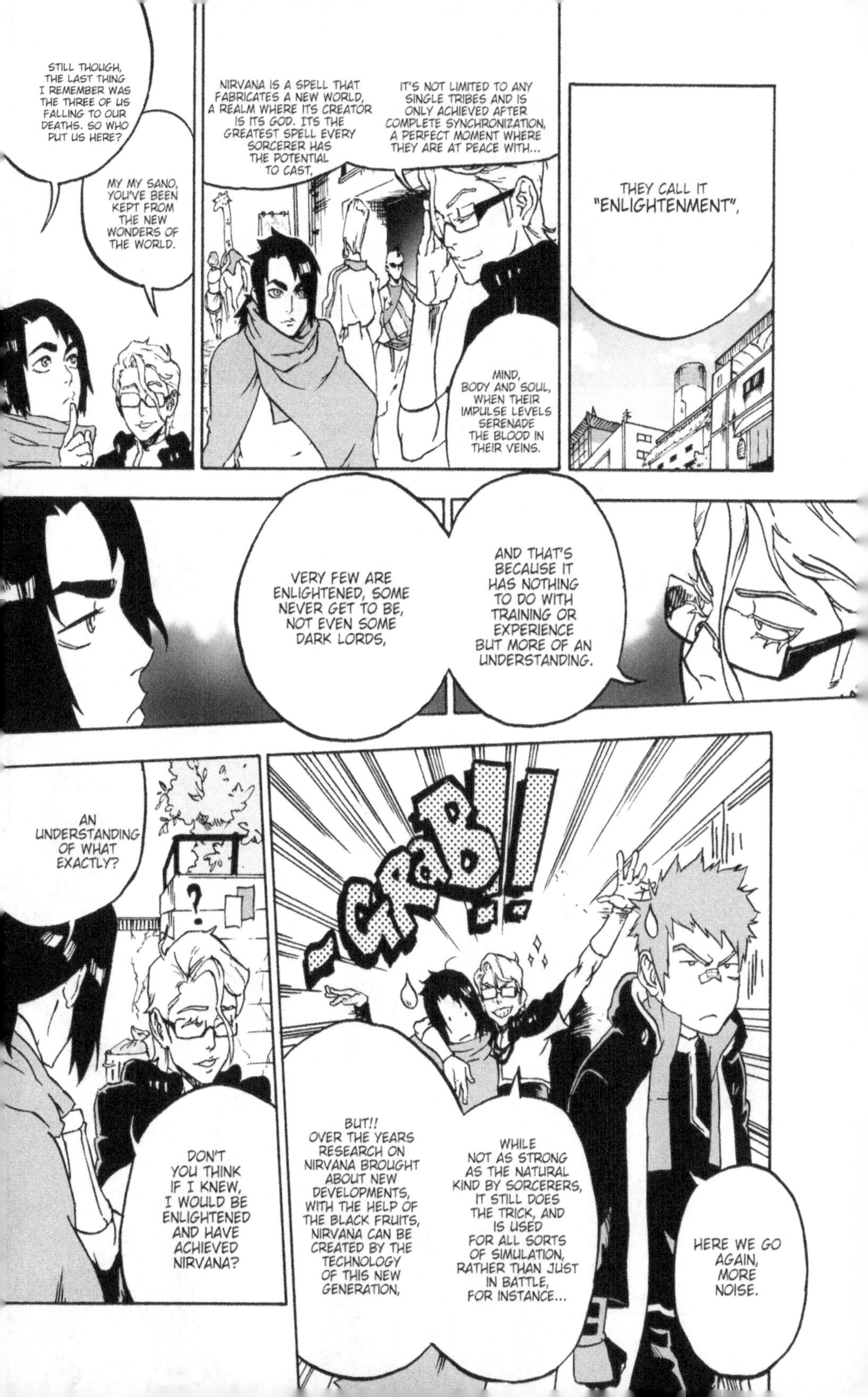
STILL THOUGH, THE LAST THING I REMEMBER WAS THE THREE OF US FALLING TO OUR DEATHS. SO WHO PUT US HERE?
MY MY SANO, YOU'VE BEEN KEPT FROM THE NEW WONDERS OF THE WORLD.
NIRVANA IS A SPELL THAT FABRICATES A NEW WORLD, A REALM WHERE ITS CREATOR IS ITS GOD. ITS THE GREATEST SPELL EVERY SORCERER HAS THE POTENTIAL TO CAST,
IT'S NOT LIMITED TO ANY SINGLE TRIBES AND IS ONLY ACHIEVED AFTER COMPLETE SYNCHRONIZATION, A PERFECT MOMENT WHERE THEY ARE AT PEACE WITH...
MIND, BODY AND SOUL, WHEN THEIR IMPULSE LEVELS SERENADE THE BLOOD IN THEIR VEINS.
THEY CALL IT "ENLIGHTENMENT",
VERY FEW ARE ENLIGHTENED, SOME NEVER GET TO BE, NOT EVEN SOME DARK LORDS,
AND THAT'S BECAUSE IT HAS NOTHING TO DO WITH TRAINING OR EXPERIENCE BUT MORE OF AN UNDERSTANDING.
AN UNDERSTANDING OF WHAT EXACTLY?
DON'T YOU THINK IF I KNEW, I WOULD BE ENLIGHTENED AND HAVE ACHIEVED NIRVANA?
GRAB!!
BUT!! OVER THE YEARS RESEARCH ON NIRVANA BROUGHT ABOUT NEW DEVELOPMENTS, WITH THE HELP OF THE BLACK FRUITS, NIRVANA CAN BE CREATED BY THE TECHNOLOGY OF THIS NEW GENERATION,
WHILE NOT AS STRONG AS THE NATURAL KIND BY SORCERERS, IT STILL DOES THE TRICK, AND IS USED FOR ALL SORTS OF SIMULATION, RATHER THAN JUST IN BATTLE, FOR INSTANCE...
HERE WE GO AGAIN, MORE NOISE.

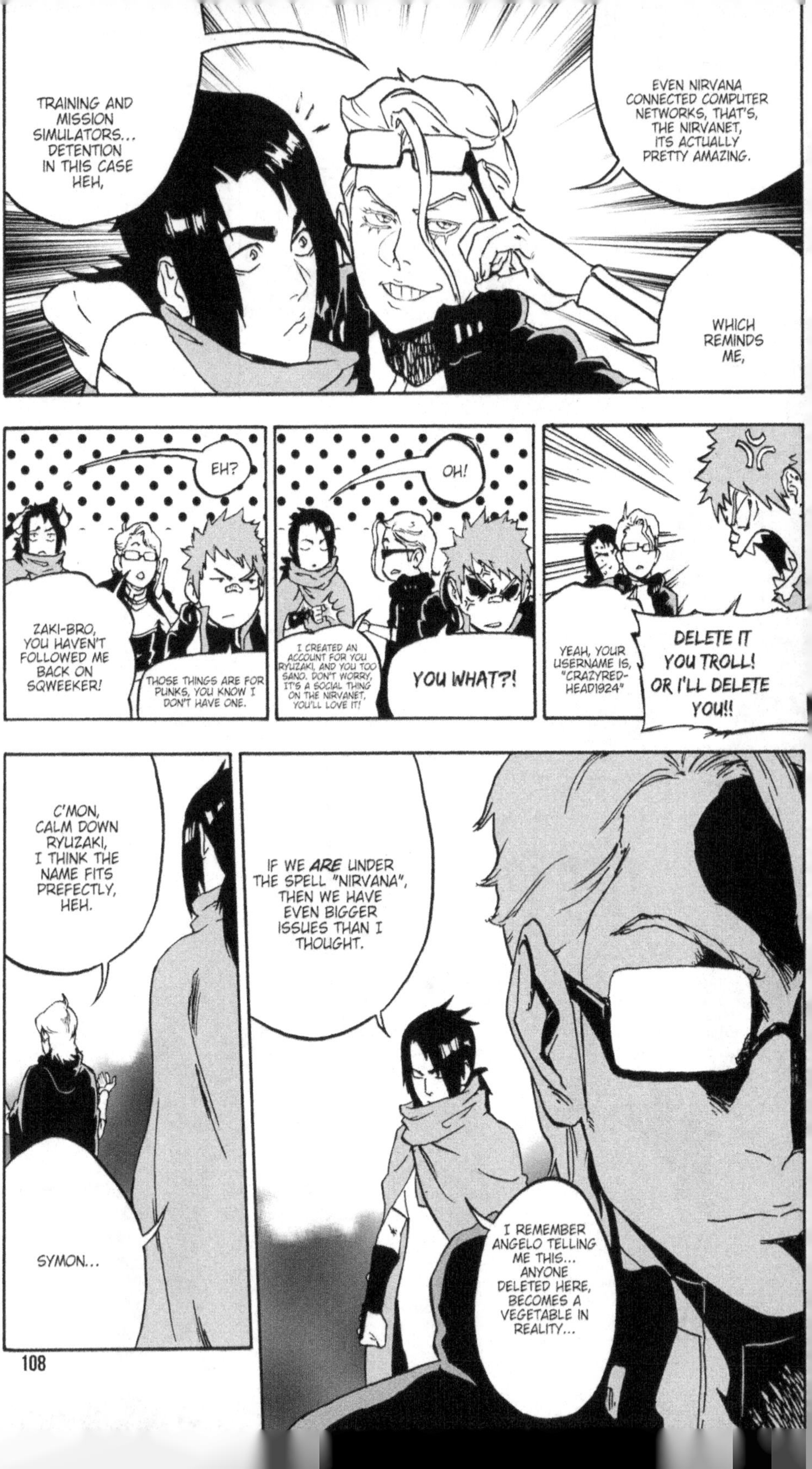
TRAINING AND MISSION SIMULATORS... DETENTION IN THIS CASE HEH,
EVEN NIRVANA CONNECTED COMPUTER NETWORKS, THAT'S, THE NIRVANET, ITS ACTUALLY PRETTY AMAZING.
WHICH REMINDS ME,
EH?
ZAKI-BRO, YOU HAVEN'T FOLLOWED ME BACK ON SQWEEKER!
THOSE THINGS ARE FOR PUNKS, YOU KNOW I DON'T HAVE ONE.
OH!
I CREATED AN ACCOUNT FOR YOU RYUZAKI, AND YOU TOO SANO. DON'T WORRY, IT'S A SOCIAL THING ON THE NIRVANET, YOU'LL LOVE IT!
YOU WHAT?!
YEAH, YOUR USERNAME IS, "CRAZYRED-HEAD1924"
DELETE IT YOU TROLL! OR I'LL DELETE YOU!!
C'MON, CALM DOWN RYUZAKI, I THINK THE NAME FITS PREFECTLY, HEH.
SYMON...
IF WE ***ARE*** UNDER THE SPELL "NIRVANA", THEN WE HAVE EVEN BIGGER ISSUES THAN I THOUGHT.
I REMEMBER ANGELO TELLING ME THIS... ANYONE DELETED HERE, BECOMES A VEGETABLE IN REALITY...

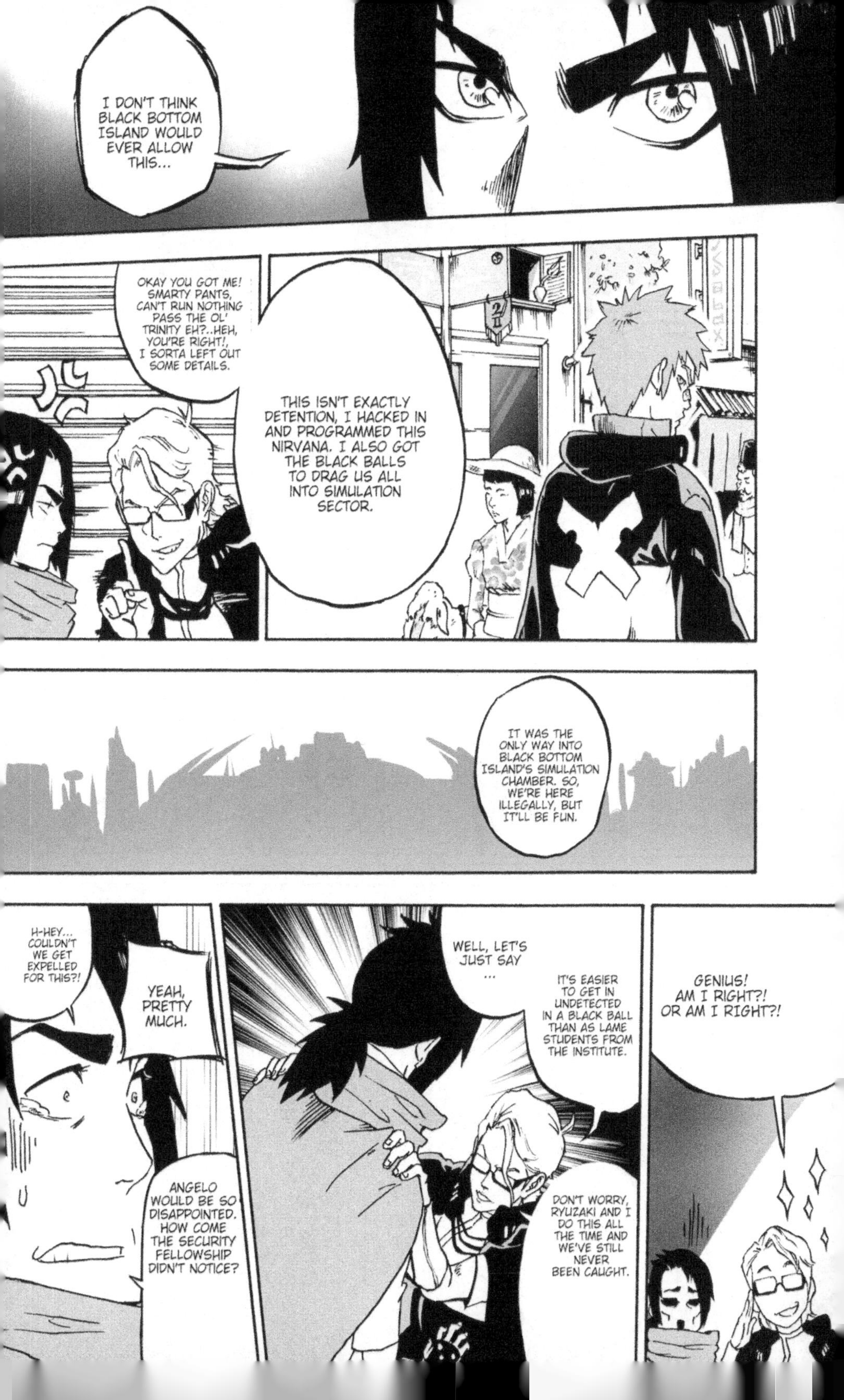
I DON'T THINK BLACK BOTTOM ISLAND WOULD EVER ALLOW THIS...
OKAY YOU GOT ME! SMARTY PANTS, CAN'T RUN NOTHING PASS THE OL' TRINITY EH?..HEH, YOU'RE RIGHT!, I SORTA LEFT OUT SOME DETAILS.
THIS ISN'T EXACTLY DETENTION, I HACKED IN AND PROGRAMMED THIS NIRVANA. I ALSO GOT THE BLACK BALLS TO DRAG US ALL INTO SIMULATION SECTOR.
IT WAS THE ONLY WAY INTO BLACK BOTTOM ISLAND'S SIMULATION CHAMBER. SO, WE'RE HERE ILLEGALLY, BUT IT'LL BE FUN.
H-HEY... COULDN'T WE GET EXPELLED FOR THIS?!
YEAH, PRETTY MUCH.
ANGELO WOULD BE SO DISAPPOINTED. HOW COME THE SECURITY FELLOWSHIP DIDN'T NOTICE?
WELL, LET'S JUST SAY ...
IT'S EASIER TO GET IN UNDETECTED IN A BLACK BALL THAN AS LAME STUDENTS FROM THE INSTITUTE.
DON'T WORRY, RYUZAKI AND I DO THIS ALL THE TIME AND WE'VE STILL NEVER BEEN CAUGHT.
GENIUS! AM I RIGHT?! OR AM I RIGHT?!

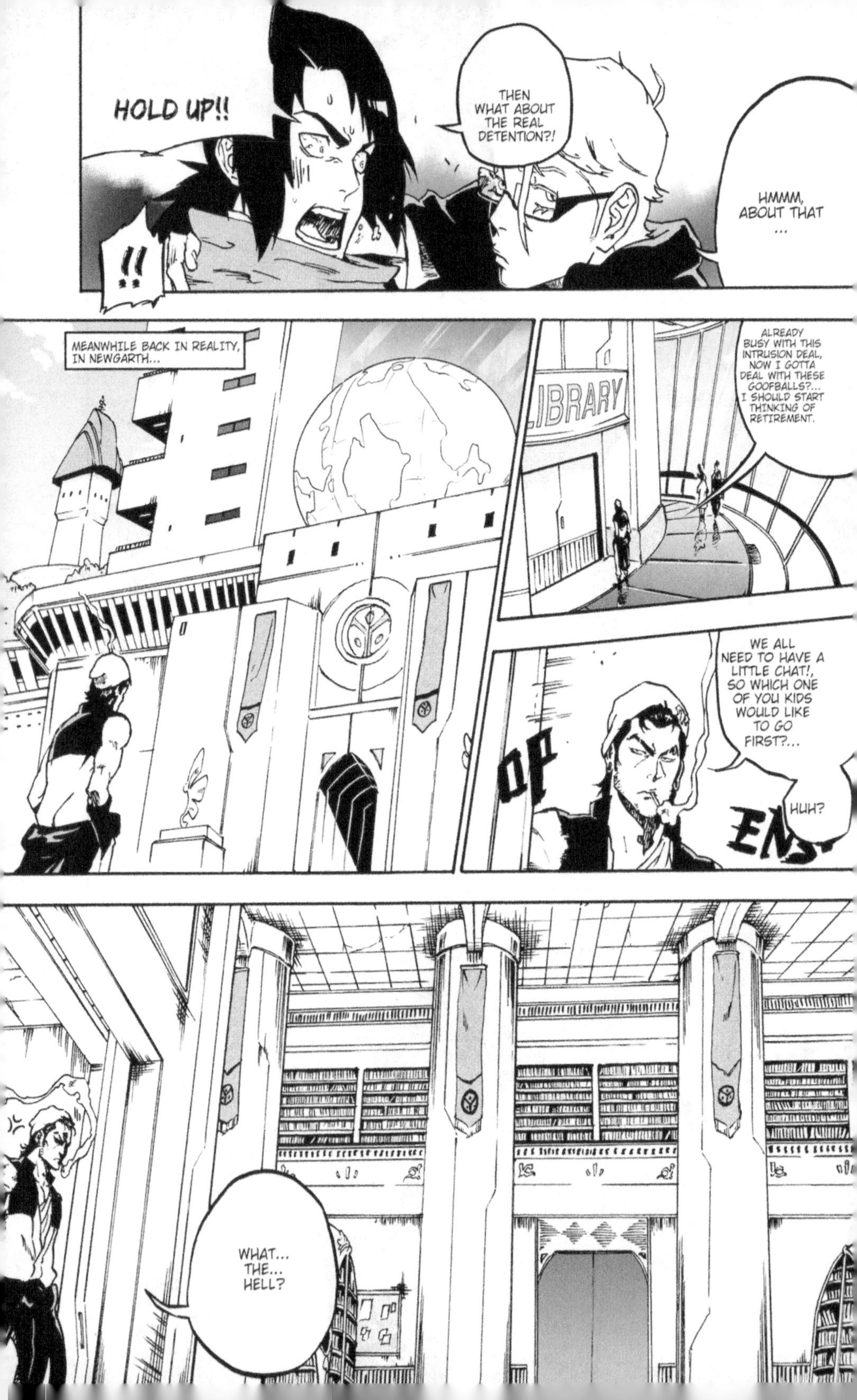
HOLD UP!!
!!
THEN WHAT ABOUT THE REAL DETENTION?!
HMMM, ABOUT THAT ...
MEANWHILE BACK IN REALITY, IN NEWGARTH...
LIBRARY
ALREADY BUSY WITH THIS INTRUSION DEAL, NOW I GOTTA DEAL WITH THESE GOOFBALLS?... I SHOULD START THINKING OF RETIREMENT.
OP
WE ALL NEED TO HAVE A LITTLE CHAT!, SO WHICH ONE OF YOU KIDS WOULD LIKE TO GO FIRST?...
ENS
HUH?
WHAT... THE... HELL?

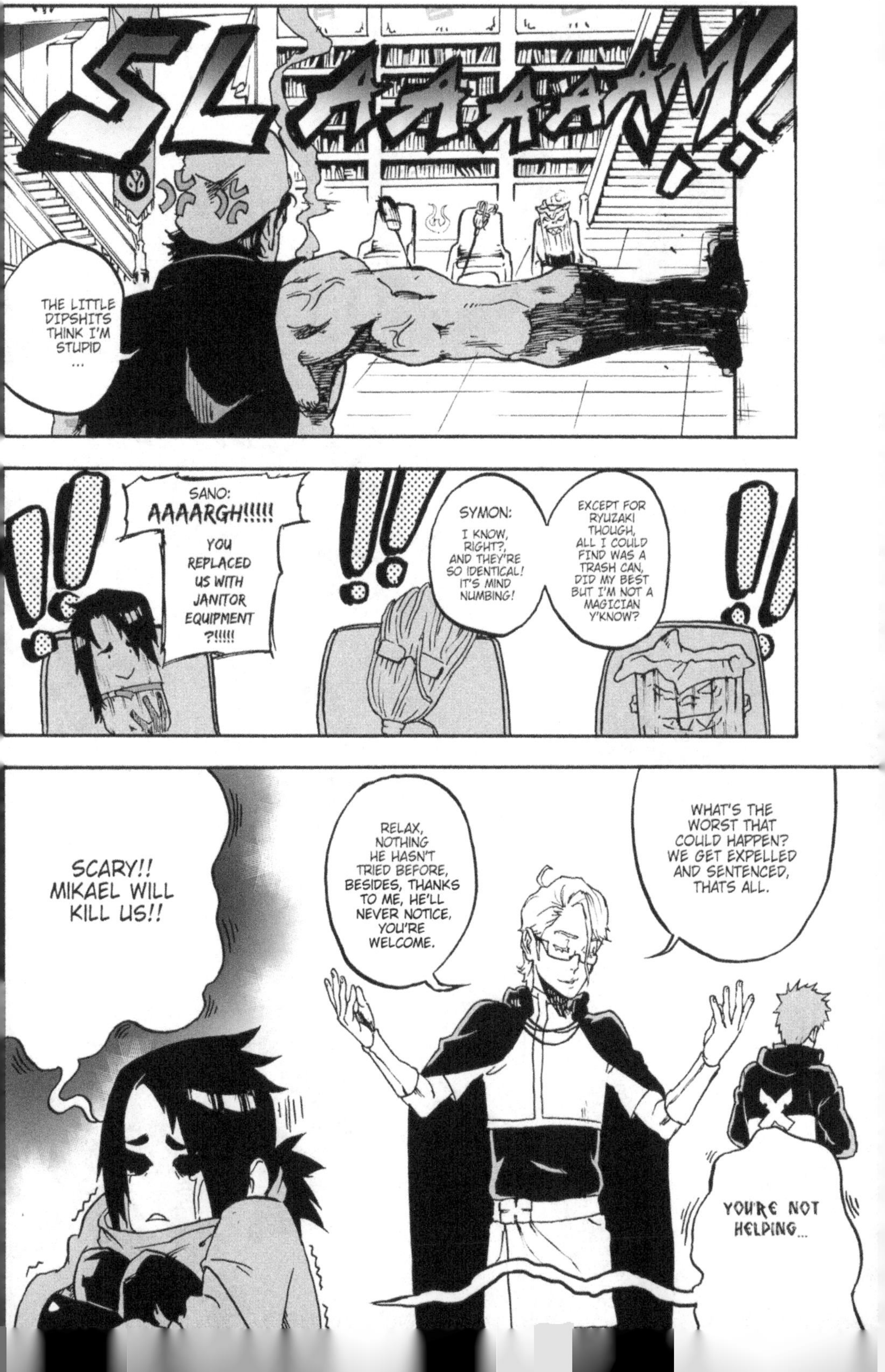
SLAAAAAM!!
THE LITTLE DIPSHITS THINK I'M STUPID ...
SANO: AAAARGH!!!!! YOU REPLACED US WITH JANITOR EQUIPMENT ?!!!!!
SYMON: I KNOW, RIGHT?, AND THEY'RE SO IDENTICAL! IT'S MIND NUMBING!
EXCEPT FOR RYUZAKI THOUGH, ALL I COULD FIND WAS A TRASH CAN, DID MY BEST BUT I'M NOT A MAGICIAN Y'KNOW?
SCARY!! MIKAEL WILL KILL US!!
RELAX, NOTHING HE HASN'T TRIED BEFORE, BESIDES, THANKS TO ME, HE'LL NEVER NOTICE, YOU'RE WELCOME.
WHAT'S THE WORST THAT COULD HAPPEN? WE GET EXPELLED AND SENTENCED, THATS ALL.
YOU'RE NOT HELPING...

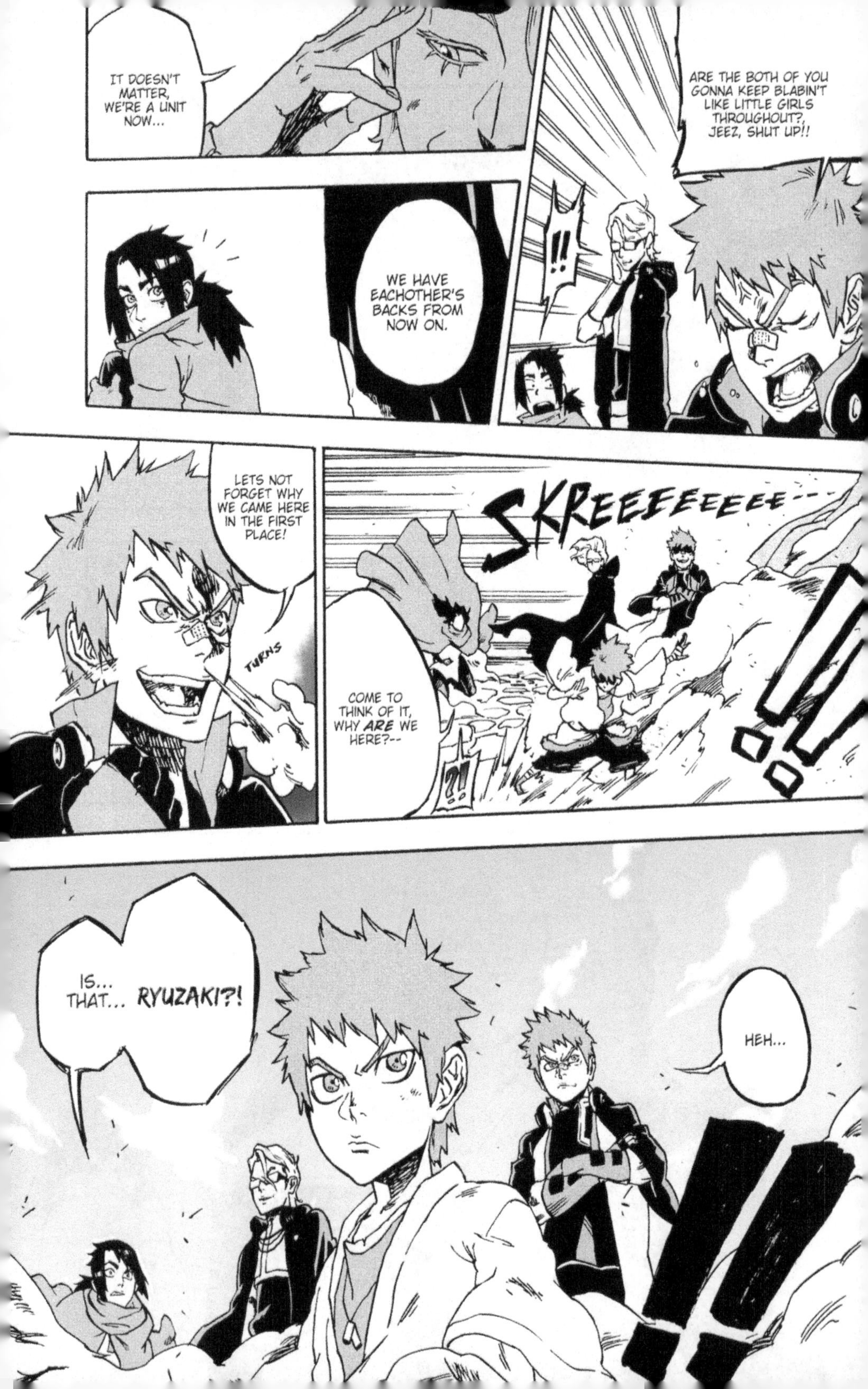
IT DOESN'T MATTER, WE'RE A UNIT NOW...
WE HAVE EACHOTHER'S BACKS FROM NOW ON.
ARE THE BOTH OF YOU GONNA KEEP BLABIN'T LIKE LITTLE GIRLS THROUGHOUT?, JEEZ, SHUT UP!!
!!
LETS NOT FORGET WHY WE CAME HERE IN THE FIRST PLACE!
TURNS
SKREEEEEEEEE---
COME TO THINK OF IT, WHY ARE WE HERE?--
?!
!!
IS... THAT... RYUZAKI?!
HEH...
!!

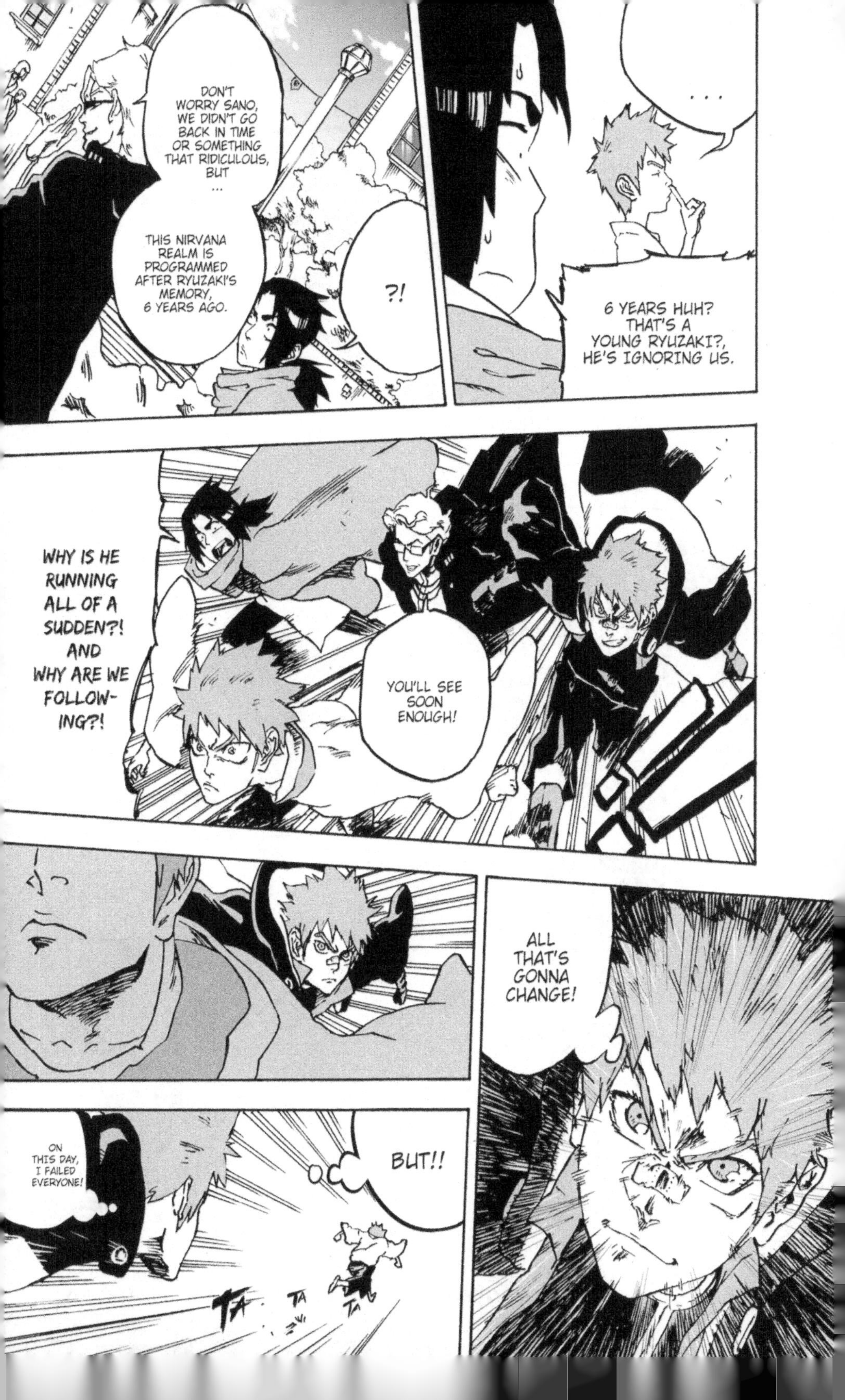
DON'T WORRY SANO, WE DIDN'T GO BACK IN TIME OR SOMETHING THAT RIDICULOUS, BUT ...
THIS NIRVANA REALM IS PROGRAMMED AFTER RYUZAKI'S MEMORY, 6 YEARS AGO.
?!
...
6 YEARS HUH? THAT'S A YOUNG RYUZAKI?, HE'S IGNORING US.
WHY IS HE RUNNING ALL OF A SUDDEN?! AND WHY ARE WE FOLLOW-ING?!
YOU'LL SEE SOON ENOUGH!
ON THIS DAY, I FAILED EVERYONE!
BUT!!
TA TA TA
ALL THAT'S GONNA CHANGE!

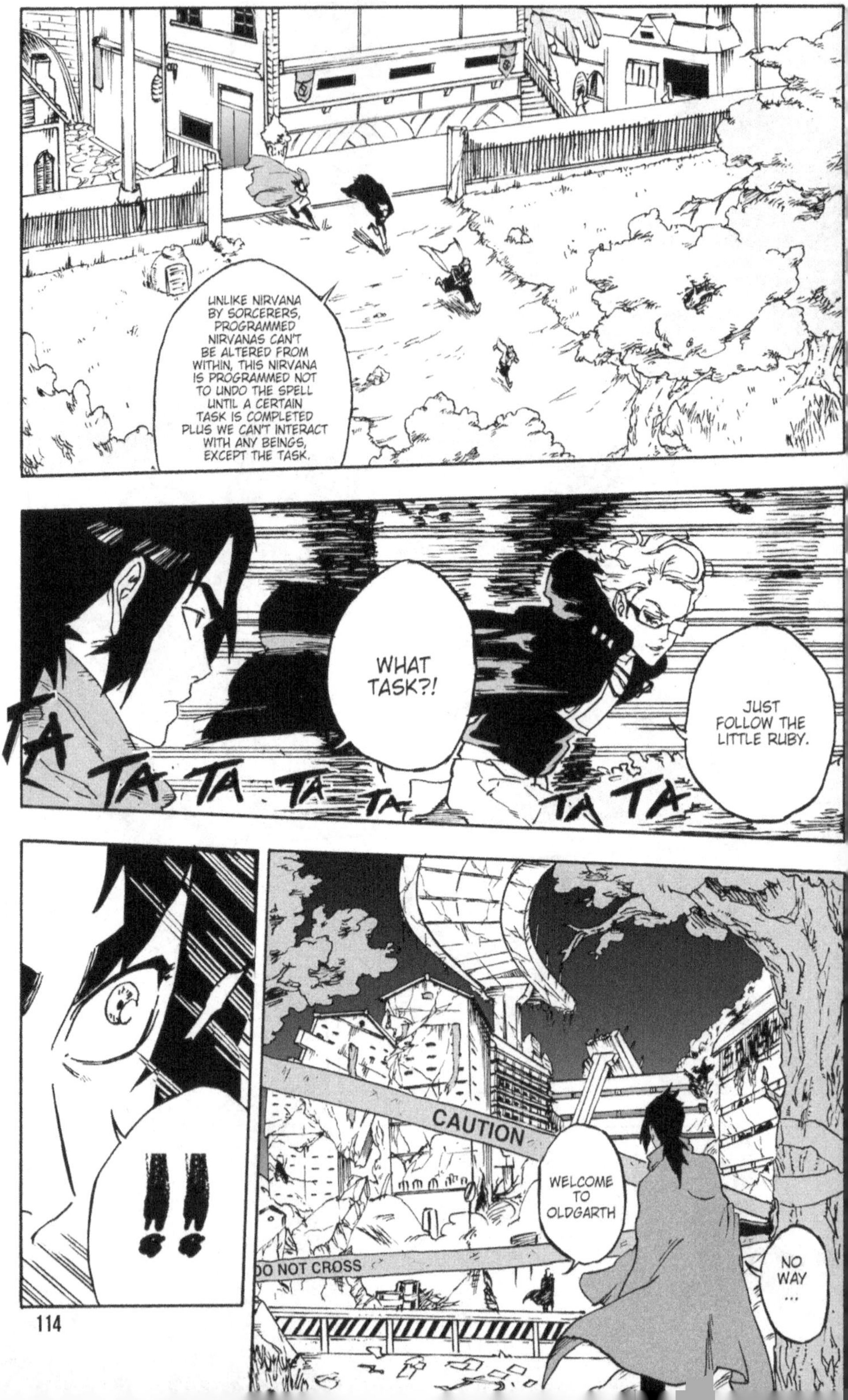

UNLIKE NIRVANA BY SORCERERS, PROGRAMMED NIRVANAS CAN'T BE ALTERED FROM WITHIN, THIS NIRVANA IS PROGRAMMED NOT TO UNDO THE SPELL UNTIL A CERTAIN TASK IS COMPLETED PLUS WE CAN'T INTERACT WITH ANY BEINGS, EXCEPT THE TASK.
TA TA TA TA TA TA TA
WHAT TASK?!
JUST FOLLOW THE LITTLE RUBY.
!!
CAUTION
WELCOME TO OLDGARTH
DO NOT CROSS
NO WAY ...

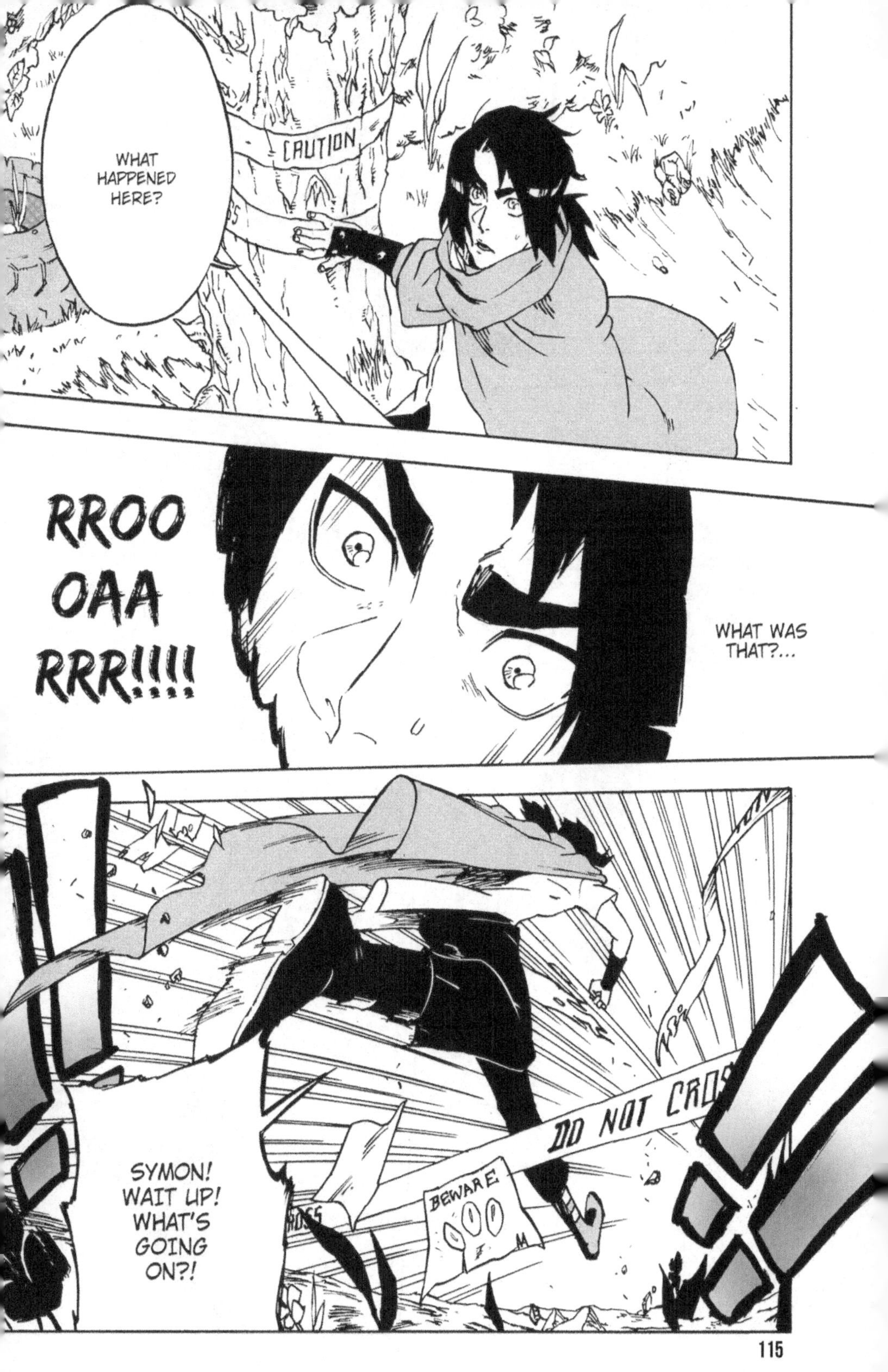
CAUTION
WHAT HAPPENED HERE?
RROO OAA RRR!!!!
WHAT WAS THAT?...
DO NOT CROS
BEWARE
SYMON! WAIT UP! WHAT'S GOING ON?!

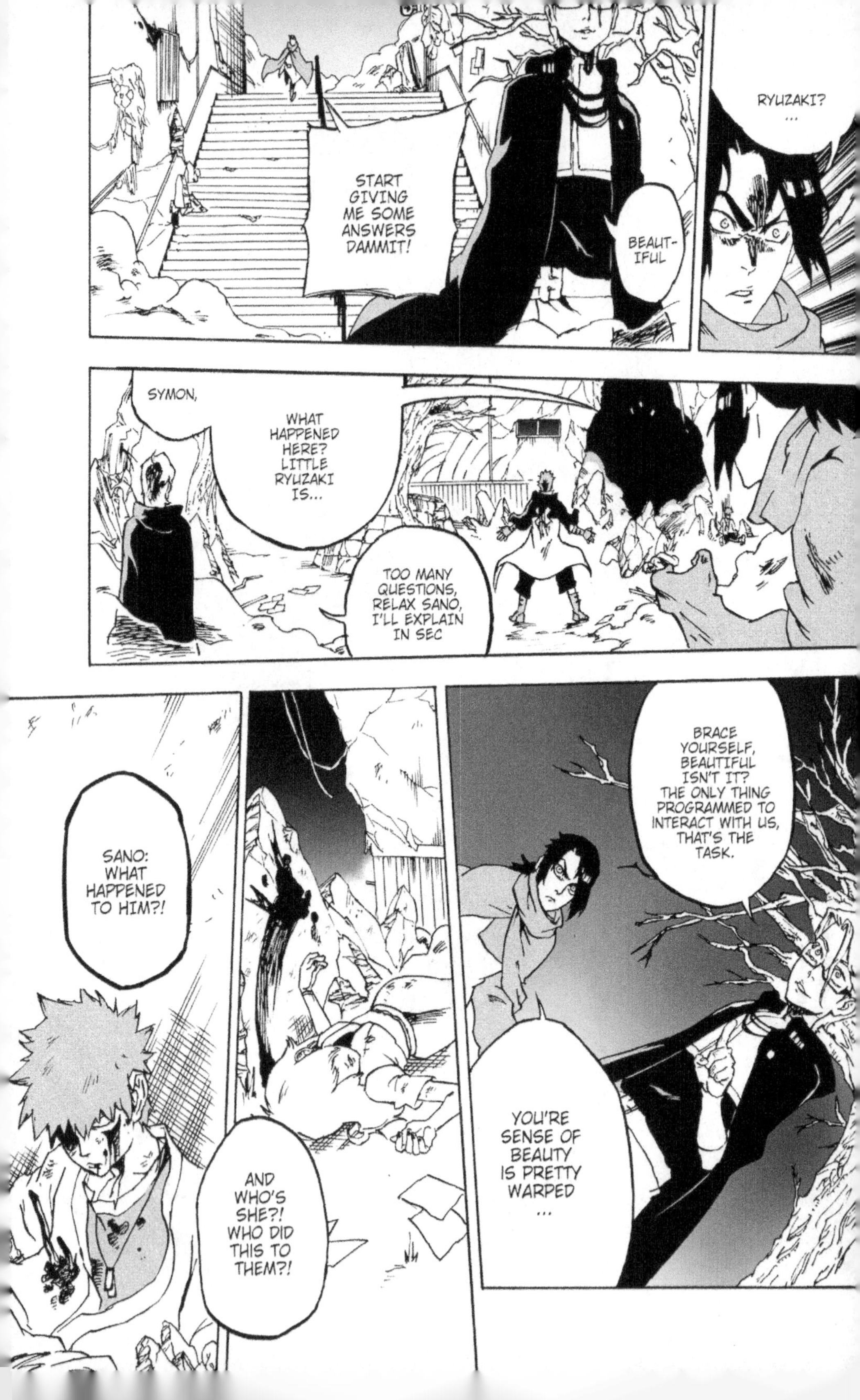
START GIVING ME SOME ANSWERS DAMMIT!
BEAUTIFUL
RYUZAKI? ...
SYMON,
WHAT HAPPENED HERE? LITTLE RYUZAKI IS...
TOO MANY QUESTIONS, RELAX SANO, I'LL EXPLAIN IN SEC
SANO: WHAT HAPPENED TO HIM?!
AND WHO'S SHE?! WHO DID THIS TO THEM?!
BRACE YOURSELF, BEAUTIFUL ISN'T IT? THE ONLY THING PROGRAMMED TO INTERACT WITH US, THAT'S THE TASK.
YOU'RE SENSE OF BEAUTY IS PRETTY WARPED ...

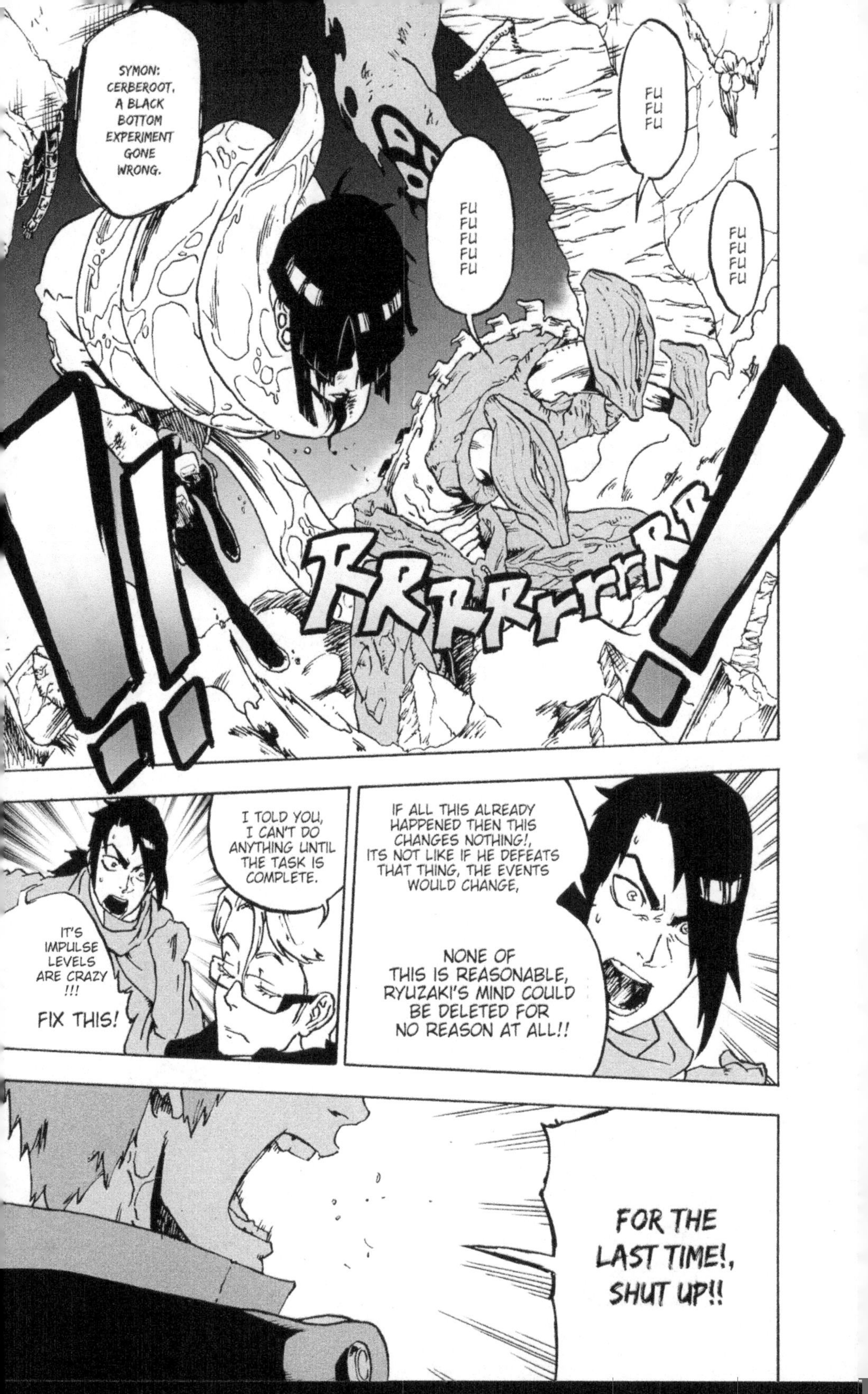
SYMON: CERBEROOT, A BLACK BOTTOM EXPERIMENT GONE WRONG.
FU FU FU FU FU
FU FU FU
FU FU FU FU
RRRRrrrRR
!!
!
I TOLD YOU, I CAN'T DO ANYTHING UNTIL THE TASK IS COMPLETE.
IT'S IMPULSE LEVELS ARE CRAZY !!!
FIX THIS!
IF ALL THIS ALREADY HAPPENED THEN THIS CHANGES NOTHING!, ITS NOT LIKE IF HE DEFEATS THAT THING, THE EVENTS WOULD CHANGE,
NONE OF THIS IS REASONABLE, RYUZAKI'S MIND COULD BE DELETED FOR NO REASON AT ALL!!
FOR THE LAST TIME!, SHUT UP!!

NO ONE SHOULD INTERFERE, HE'S ALL MINE!!

SUMMON! RED X BATONS!

YOU'RE NOT GONNA HELP?

OH MERLIN'S NO! YOU HEARD THE MAN! HE'LL HAVE MY HEAD ON A PLATE, I'D LAY OFF AS WELL AND LET HIM HAVE HIS FUN.

YOU COULD BE HIS LUCKY CHARM, RYUZAKI HAS NEVER DEFEATED THE MUTANT BEFORE.

WAIT A MINUTE! HOW DO YOU GUYS GET OUT OF NIRVANA IF HE NEVER WINS?! AND A MUTANT?

I SAID, RYUZAKI NEVER DEFEATS CERBEROOT, I NEVER SAID ANYTHING ABOUT THE TASK NOT GETTING COMPLETED.

AND YES, MUTANT. MOST ANIMALS AND PLANTS HAVE BEEN AFFECTED BY BLACK JUST AS HUMANS, TURNING THEM INTO TOOLS OF SORCERY AS WELL,

SOME SIDE EFFECTS ARE ANATOMY ALTERATIONS BECOMING MUTANTS, EVEN SOME VERY INTERESTING HUMANS UNDERGO THESE ALTERATIONS.

IN THIS CASE, WE HAVE THIS BEAUTY OF A BEAST FOR A MUTANT.

SANO: I'M STILL CONFUSED ...

118

ROO
OO
AAAA
AARR
RRR!!
!!

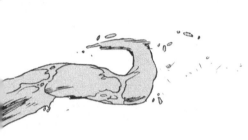

FLOU...

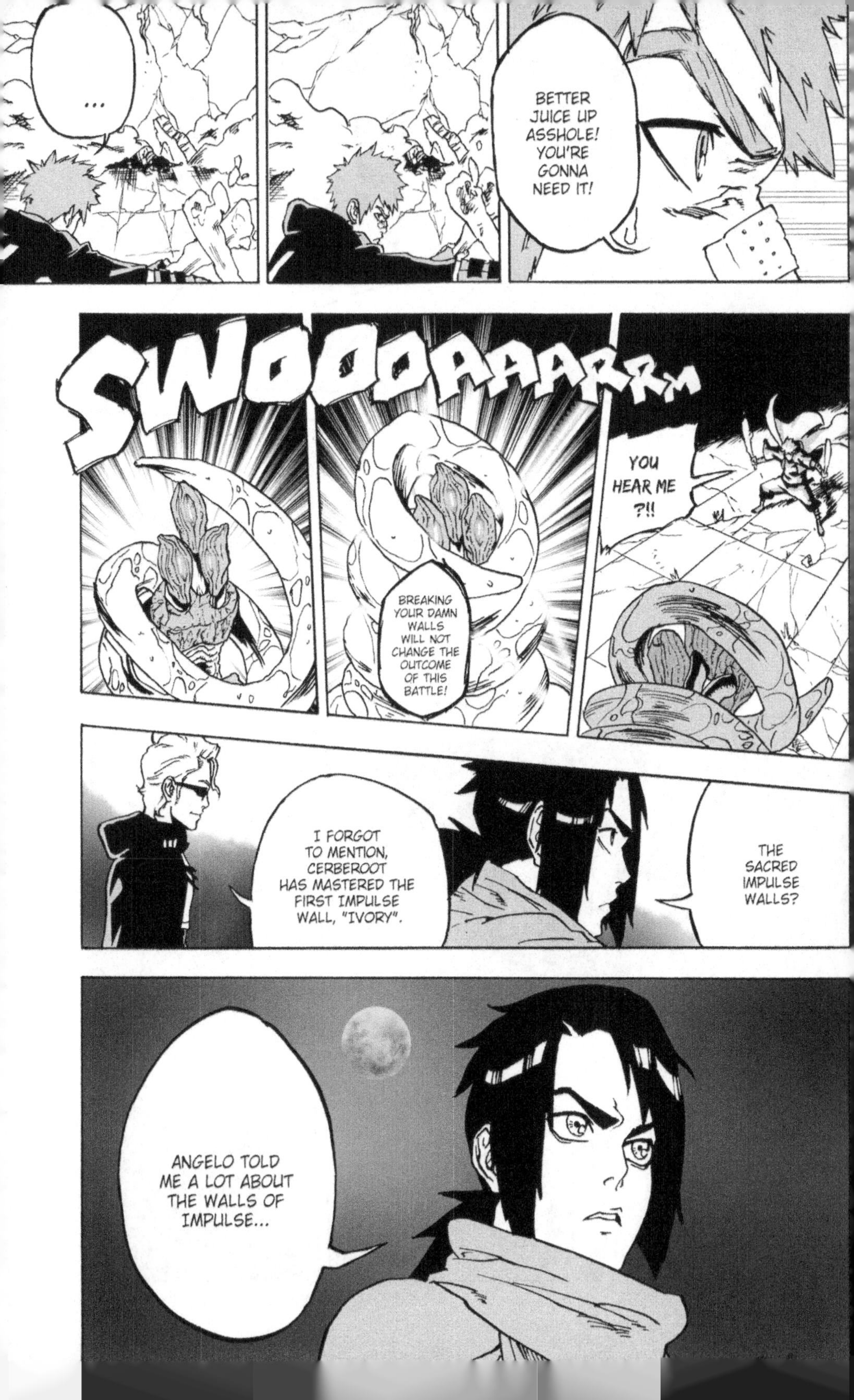
...
BETTER JUICE UP ASSHOLE! YOU'RE GONNA NEED IT!
SWOOOAAARRM
BREAKING YOUR DAMN WALLS WILL NOT CHANGE THE OUTCOME OF THIS BATTLE!
YOU HEAR ME ?!!
I FORGOT TO MENTION, CERBEROOT HAS MASTERED THE FIRST IMPULSE WALL, "IVORY".
THE SACRED IMPULSE WALLS?
ANGELO TOLD ME A LOT ABOUT THE WALLS OF IMPULSE...

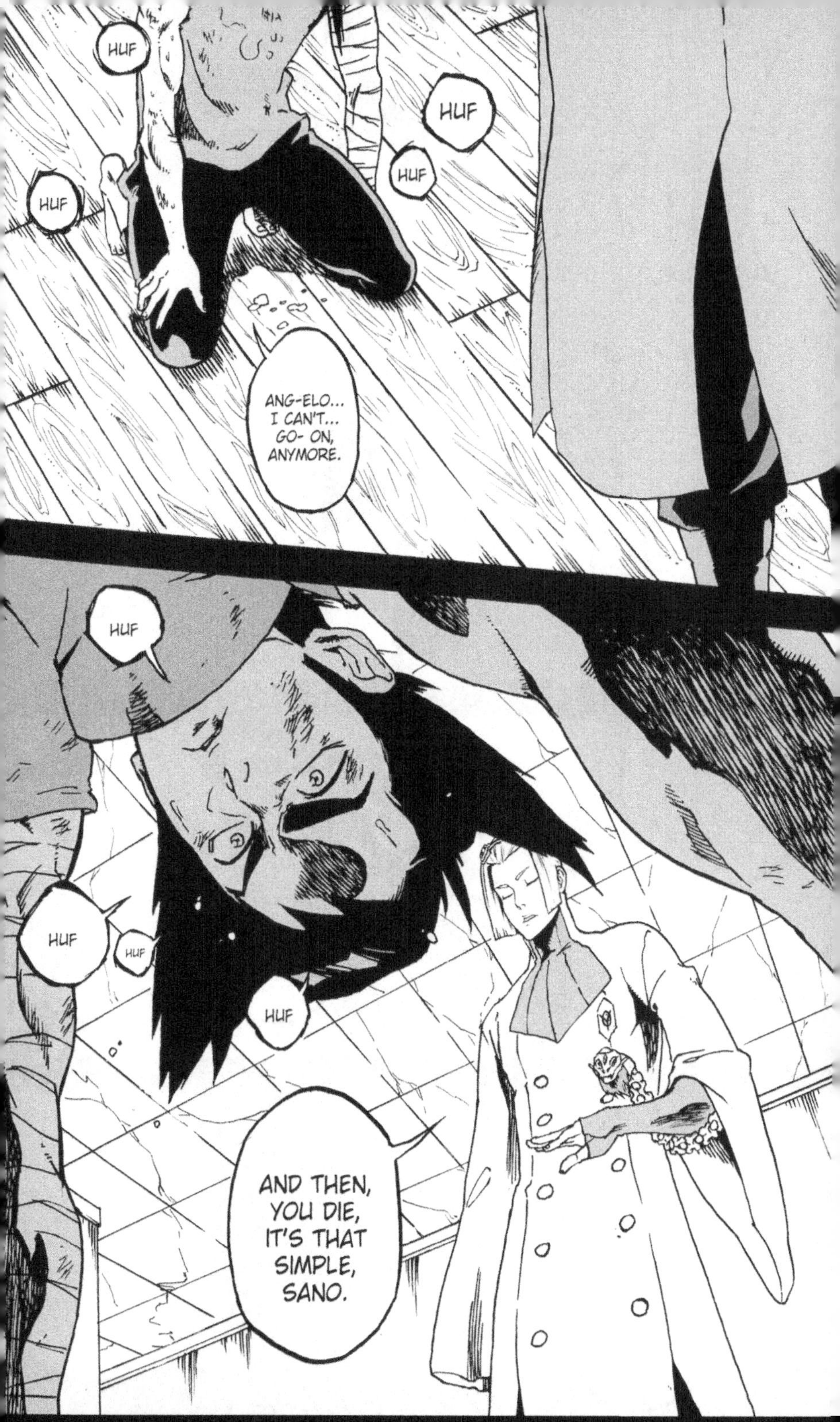
HUF
HUF
HUF
HUF
ANG-ELO... I CAN'T... GO- ON, ANYMORE.
HUF
HUF
HUF
HUF
AND THEN, YOU DIE, IT'S THAT SIMPLE, SANO.

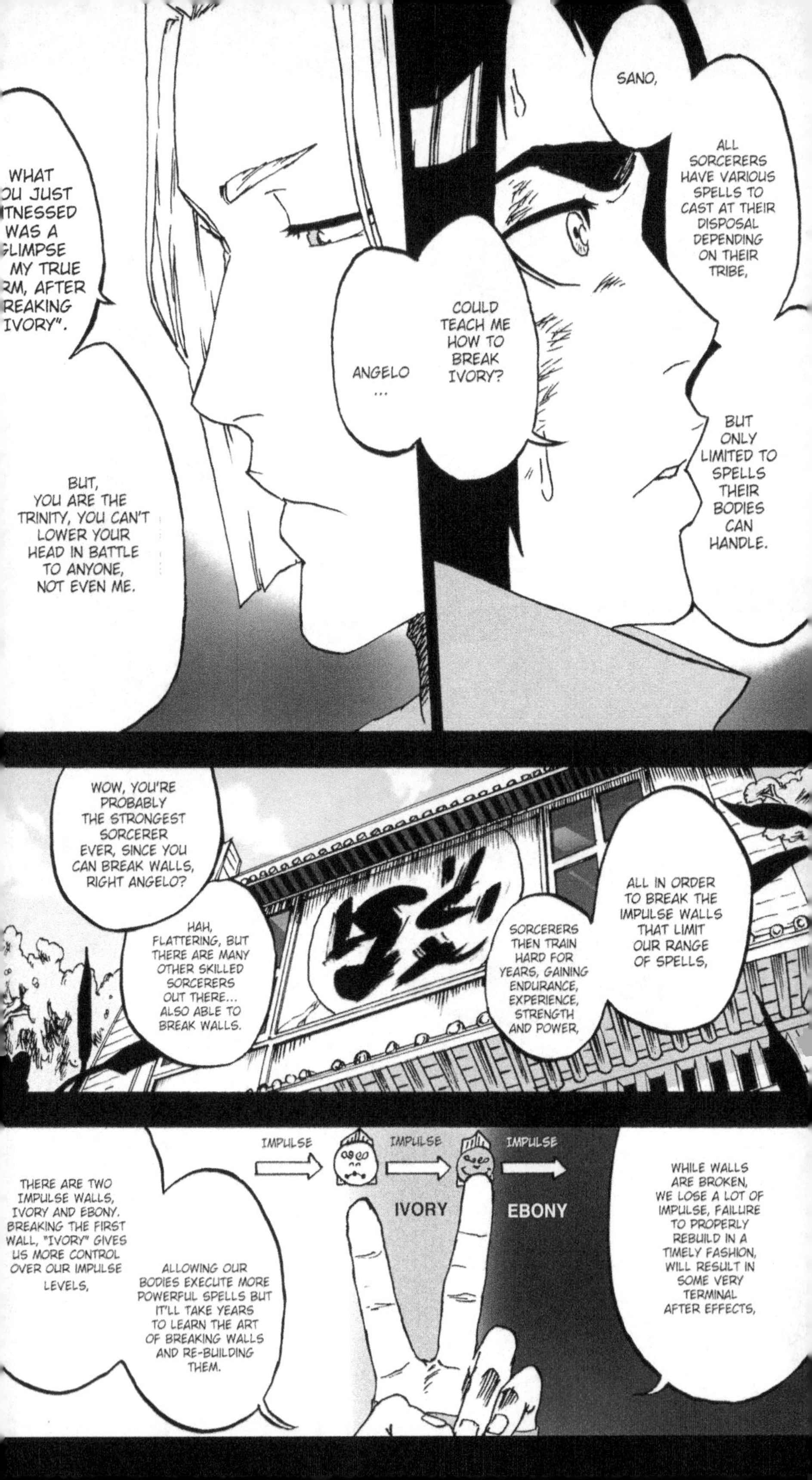
WHAT OU JUST ITNESSED WAS A GLIMPSE MY TRUE RM, AFTER REAKING IVORY".
BUT, YOU ARE THE TRINITY, YOU CAN'T LOWER YOUR HEAD IN BATTLE TO ANYONE, NOT EVEN ME.
SANO,
ALL SORCERERS HAVE VARIOUS SPELLS TO CAST AT THEIR DISPOSAL DEPENDING ON THEIR TRIBE,
ANGELO ...
COULD TEACH ME HOW TO BREAK IVORY?
BUT ONLY LIMITED TO SPELLS THEIR BODIES CAN HANDLE.
WOW, YOU'RE PROBABLY THE STRONGEST SORCERER EVER, SINCE YOU CAN BREAK WALLS, RIGHT ANGELO?
HAH, FLATTERING, BUT THERE ARE MANY OTHER SKILLED SORCERERS OUT THERE... ALSO ABLE TO BREAK WALLS.
SORCERERS THEN TRAIN HARD FOR YEARS, GAINING ENDURANCE, EXPERIENCE, STRENGTH AND POWER,
ALL IN ORDER TO BREAK THE IMPULSE WALLS THAT LIMIT OUR RANGE OF SPELLS,
THERE ARE TWO IMPULSE WALLS, IVORY AND EBONY. BREAKING THE FIRST WALL, "IVORY" GIVES US MORE CONTROL OVER OUR IMPULSE LEVELS,
ALLOWING OUR BODIES EXECUTE MORE POWERFUL SPELLS BUT IT'LL TAKE YEARS TO LEARN THE ART OF BREAKING WALLS AND RE-BUILDING THEM.
IMPULSE
IMPULSE
IMPULSE
IVORY
EBONY
WHILE WALLS ARE BROKEN, WE LOSE A LOT OF IMPULSE, FAILURE TO PROPERLY REBUILD IN A TIMELY FASHION, WILL RESULT IN SOME VERY TERMINAL AFTER EFFECTS,

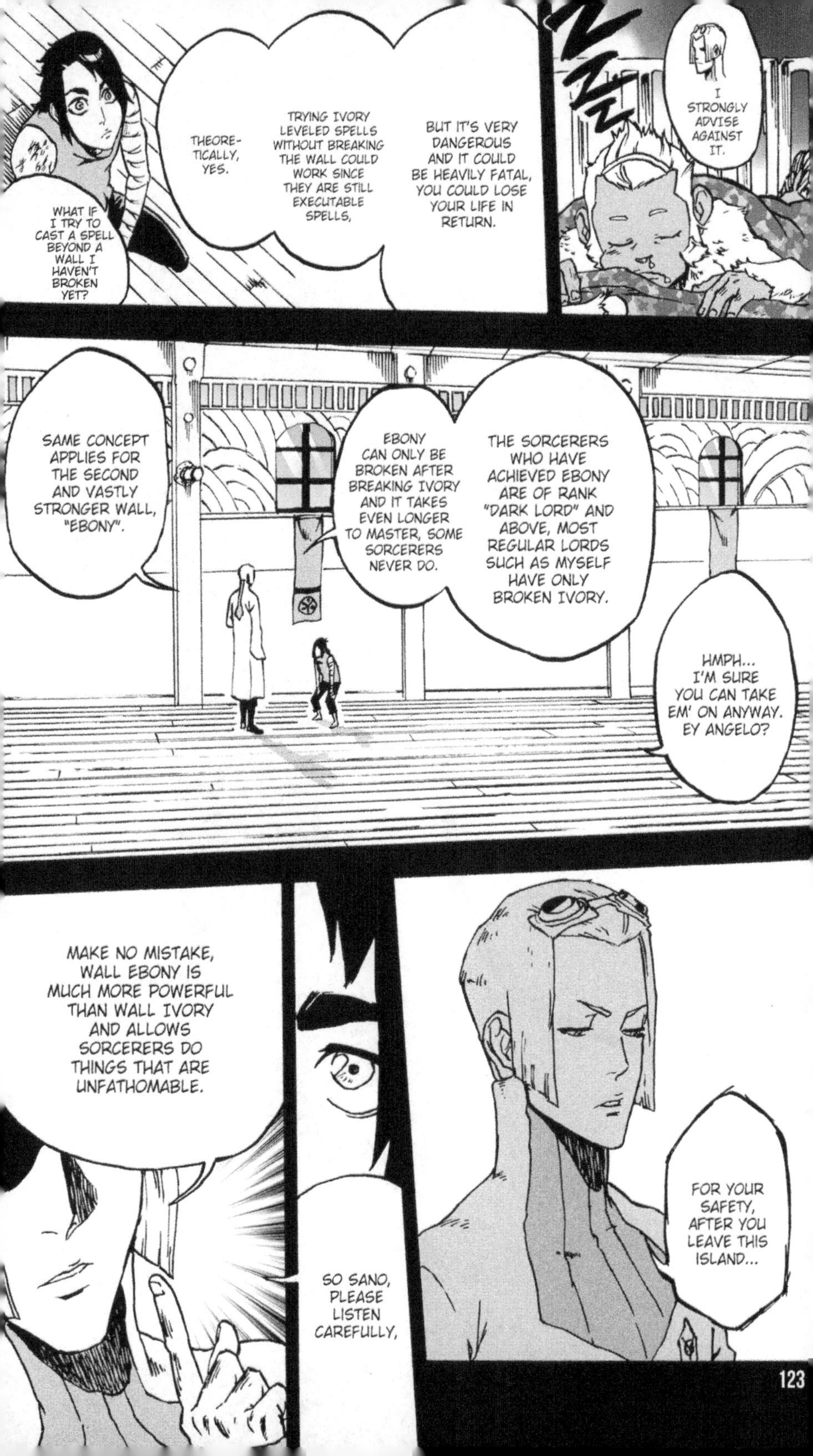
WHAT IF I TRY TO CAST A SPELL BEYOND A WALL I HAVEN'T BROKEN YET?
THEORE-TICALLY, YES.
TRYING IVORY LEVELED SPELLS WITHOUT BREAKING THE WALL COULD WORK SINCE THEY ARE STILL EXECUTABLE SPELLS,
BUT IT'S VERY DANGEROUS AND IT COULD BE HEAVILY FATAL, YOU COULD LOSE YOUR LIFE IN RETURN.
I STRONGLY ADVISE AGAINST IT.
SAME CONCEPT APPLIES FOR THE SECOND AND VASTLY STRONGER WALL, "EBONY".
EBONY CAN ONLY BE BROKEN AFTER BREAKING IVORY AND IT TAKES EVEN LONGER TO MASTER, SOME SORCERERS NEVER DO.
THE SORCERERS WHO HAVE ACHIEVED EBONY ARE OF RANK "DARK LORD" AND ABOVE, MOST REGULAR LORDS SUCH AS MYSELF HAVE ONLY BROKEN IVORY.
HMPH... I'M SURE YOU CAN TAKE EM' ON ANYWAY. EY ANGELO?
MAKE NO MISTAKE, WALL EBONY IS MUCH MORE POWERFUL THAN WALL IVORY AND ALLOWS SORCERERS DO THINGS THAT ARE UNFATHOMABLE.
SO SANO, PLEASE LISTEN CAREFULLY,
FOR YOUR SAFETY, AFTER YOU LEAVE THIS ISLAND...

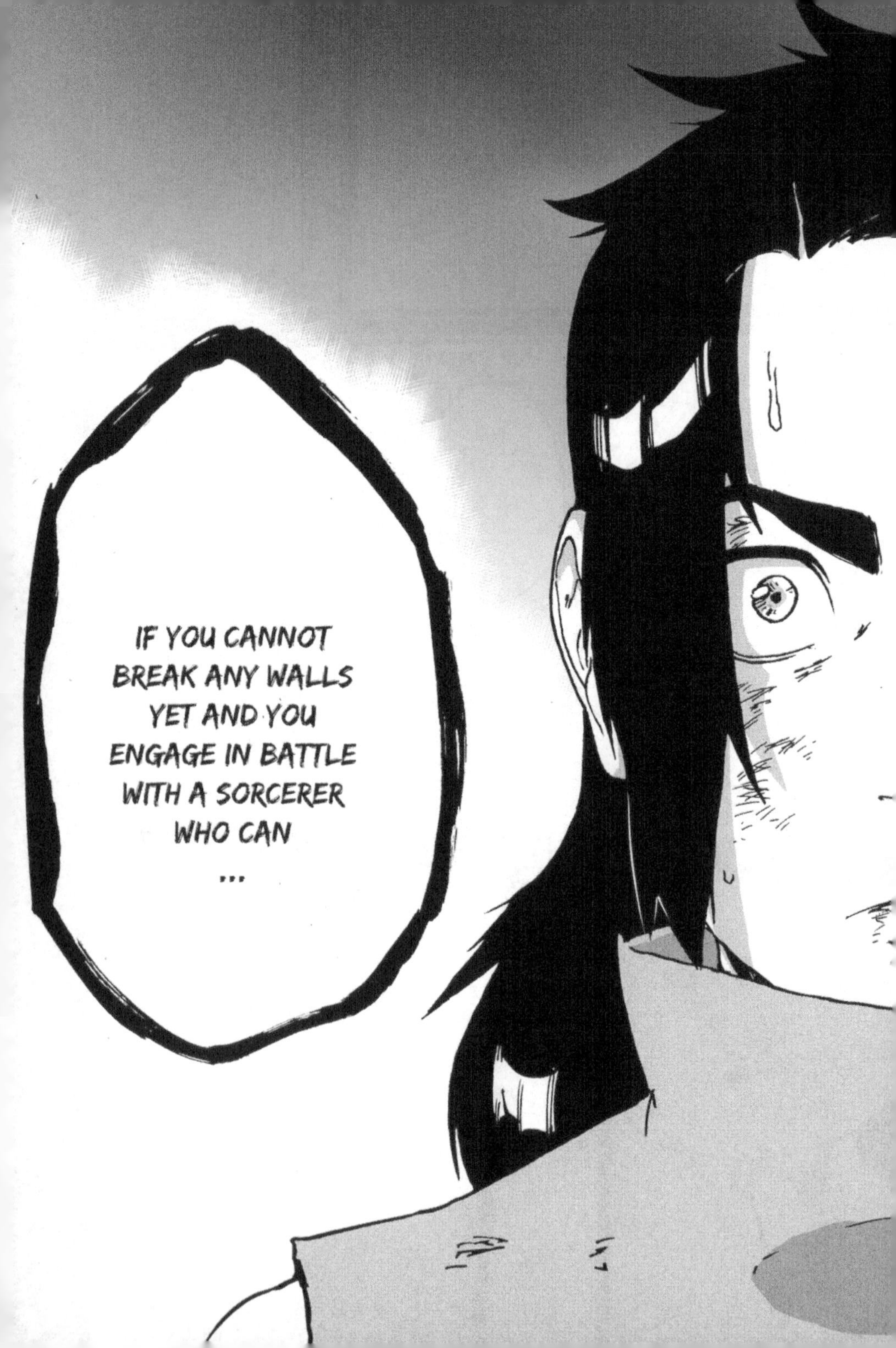
IF YOU CANNOT BREAK ANY WALLS YET AND YOU ENGAGE IN BATTLE WITH A SORCERER WHO CAN ...

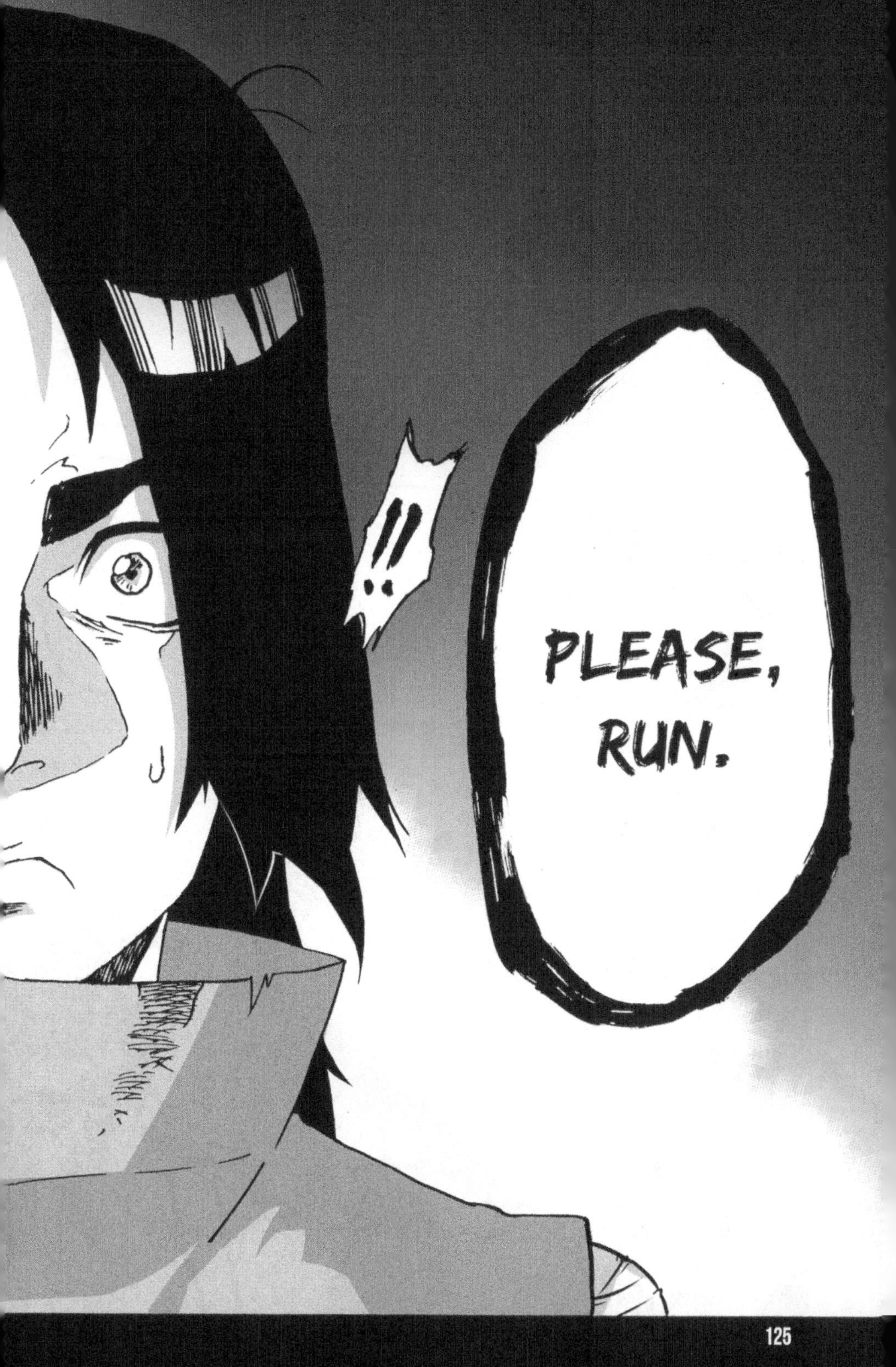
!!
PLEASE,
RUN.

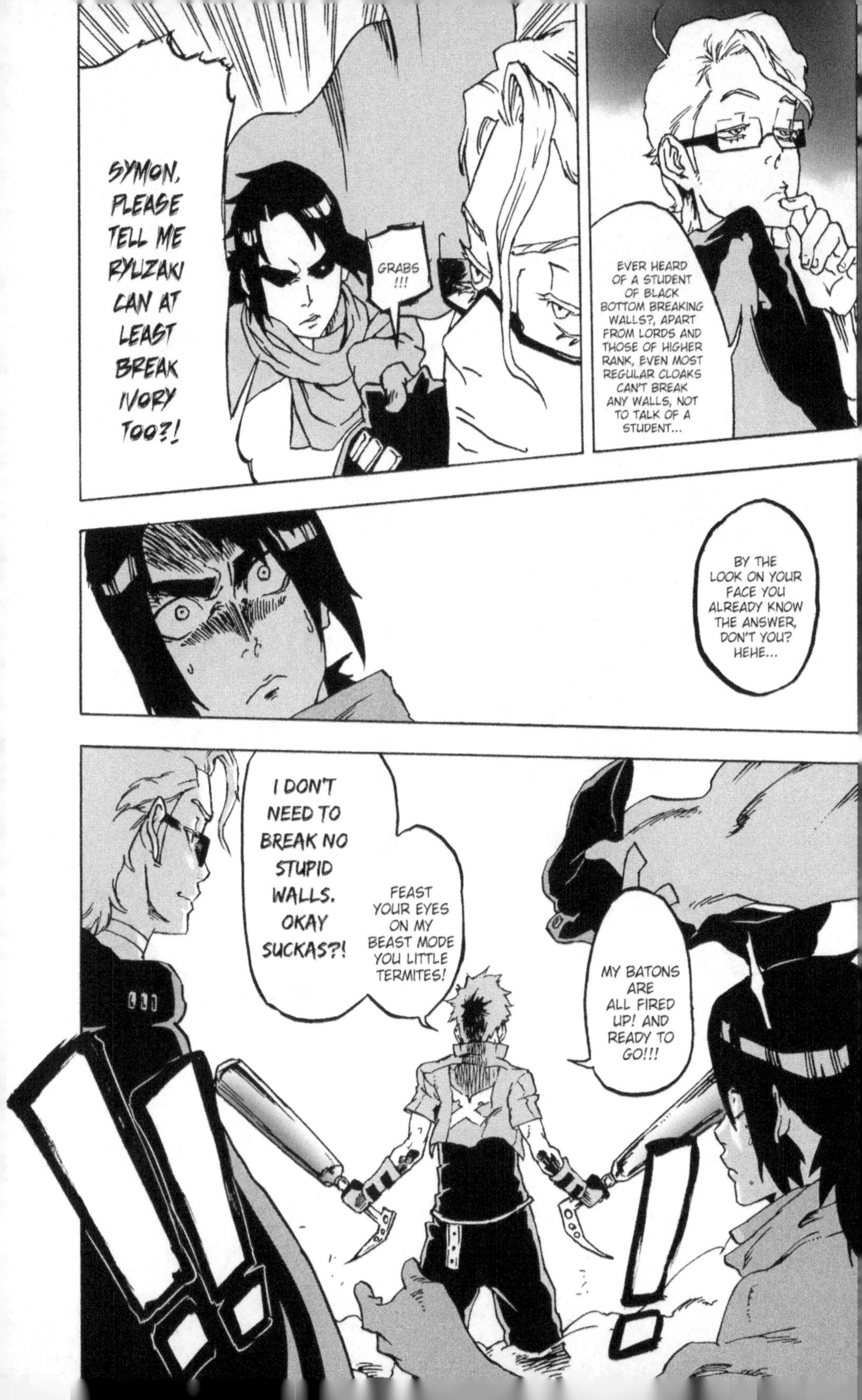
SYMON, PLEASE TELL ME RYUZAKI CAN AT LEAST BREAK IVORY TOO?!
GRABS !!!
EVER HEARD OF A STUDENT OF BLACK BOTTOM BREAKING WALLS?, APART FROM LORDS AND THOSE OF HIGHER RANK, EVEN MOST REGULAR CLOAKS CAN'T BREAK ANY WALLS, NOT TO TALK OF A STUDENT...
BY THE LOOK ON YOUR FACE YOU ALREADY KNOW THE ANSWER, DON'T YOU? HEHE...
I DON'T NEED TO BREAK NO STUPID WALLS. OKAY SUCKAS?!
FEAST YOUR EYES ON MY BEAST MODE YOU LITTLE TERMITES!
MY BATONS ARE ALL FIRED UP! AND READY TO GO!!!

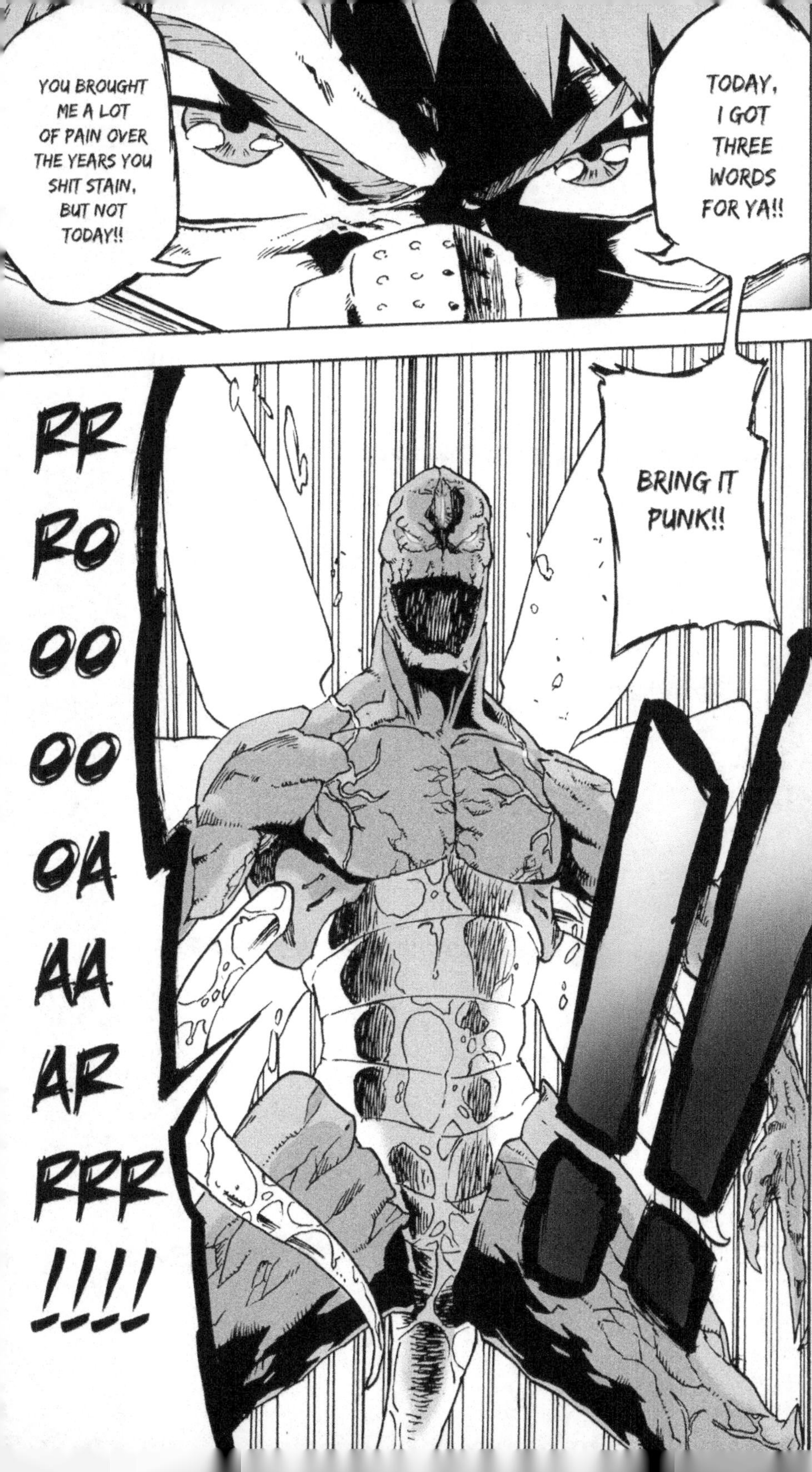
YOU BROUGHT ME A LOT OF PAIN OVER THE YEARS YOU SHIT STAIN, BUT NOT TODAY!!
TODAY, I GOT THREE WORDS FOR YA!!
RRROOOOOOAAAARRRR!!!!
BRING IT PUNK!!
!!

CERBEROOT BREAKS "IVORY"!!!

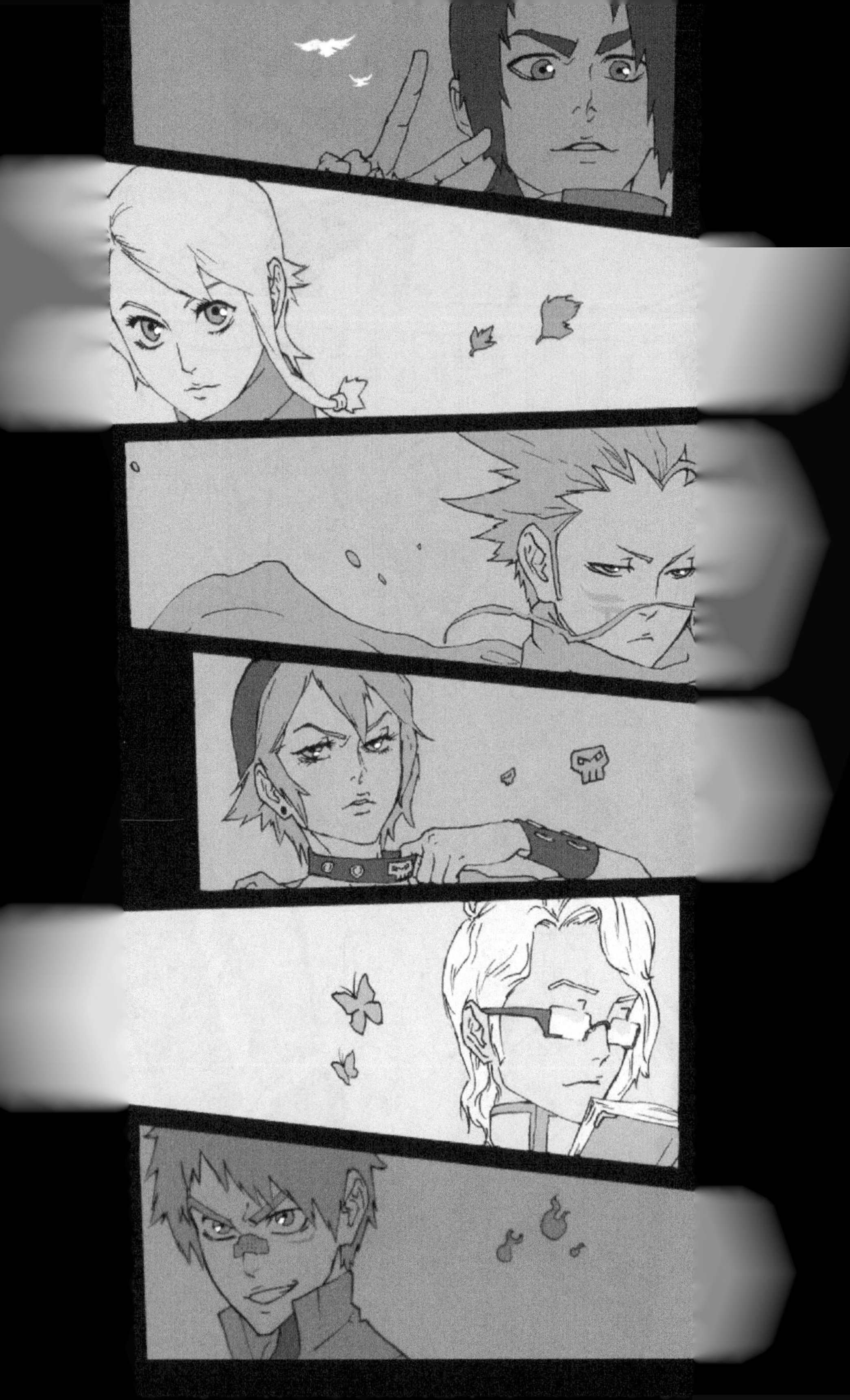

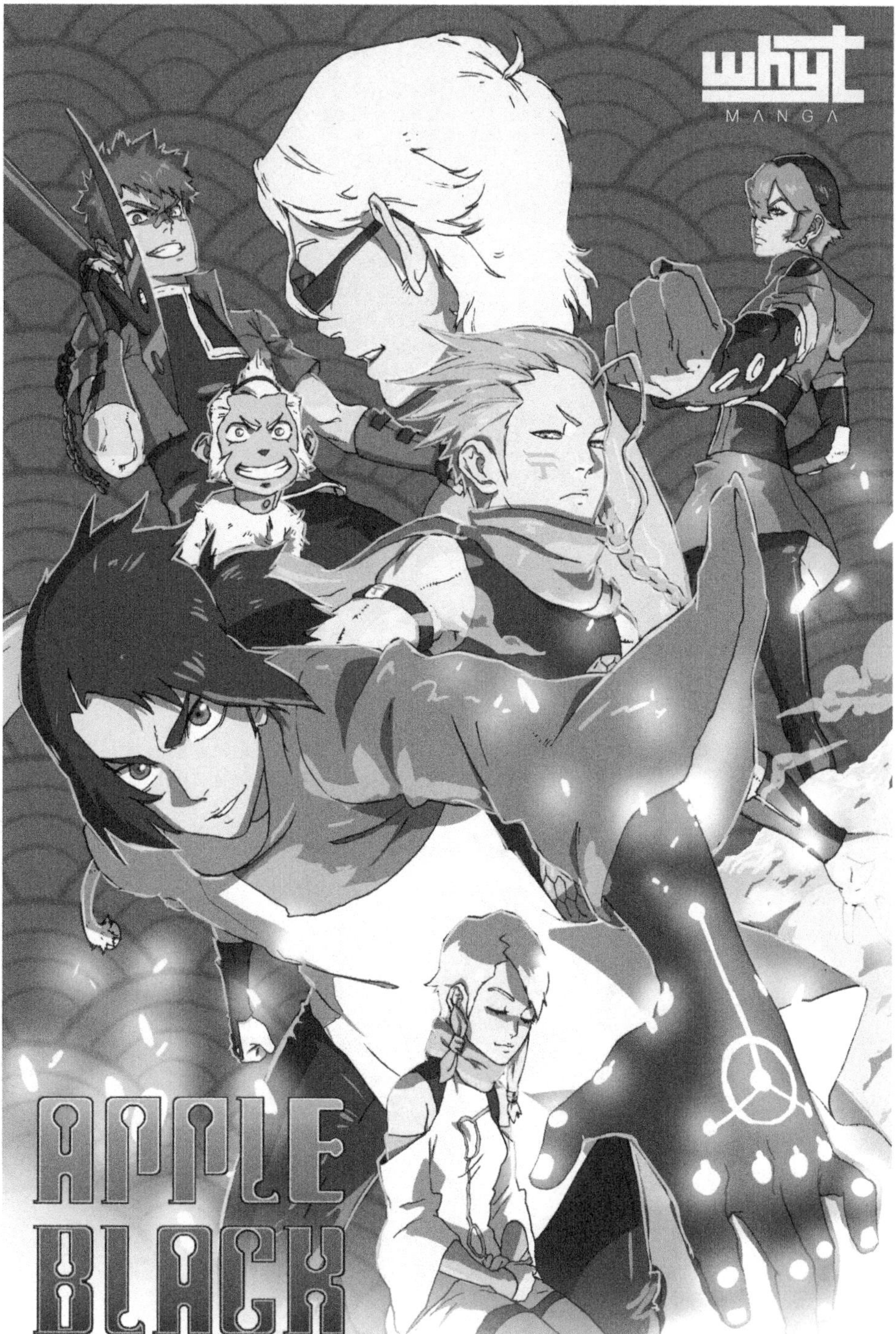
whyt
MANGA
APPLE
BLACK

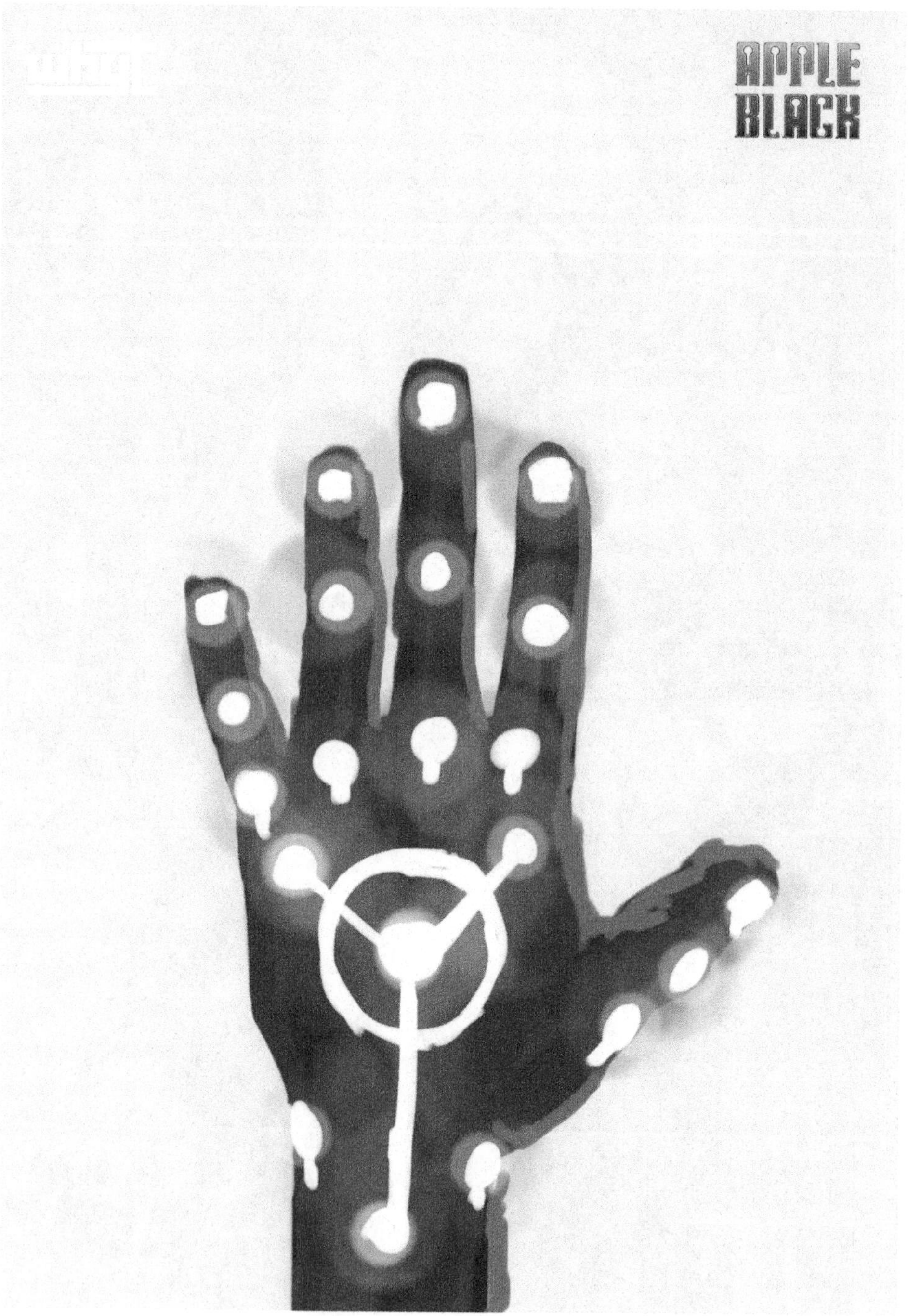
APPLE
BLACK

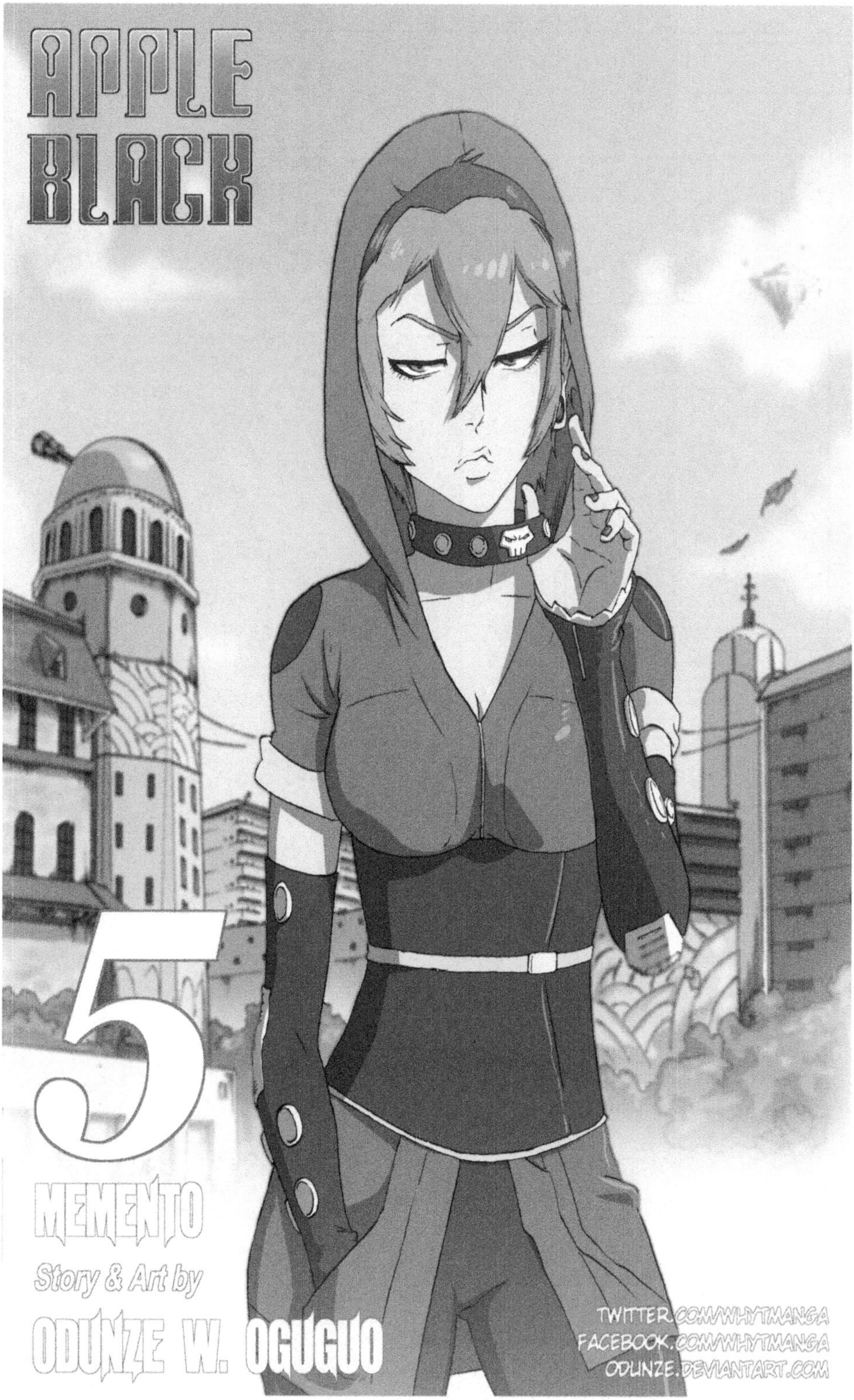
APPLE BLACK
5
MEMENTO
Story & Art by
ODUNZE W. OGUGUO
TWITTER.COM/WHYTMANGA
FACEBOOK.COM/WHYTMANGA
ODUNZE.DEVIANTART.COM

THE REAL WORLD.
NEWGARTH

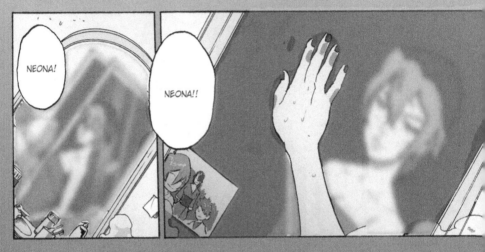

NEONA!

NEONA!!

NEON!!!

HURRY UP, WILL YA?!

[APPLE BLACK]

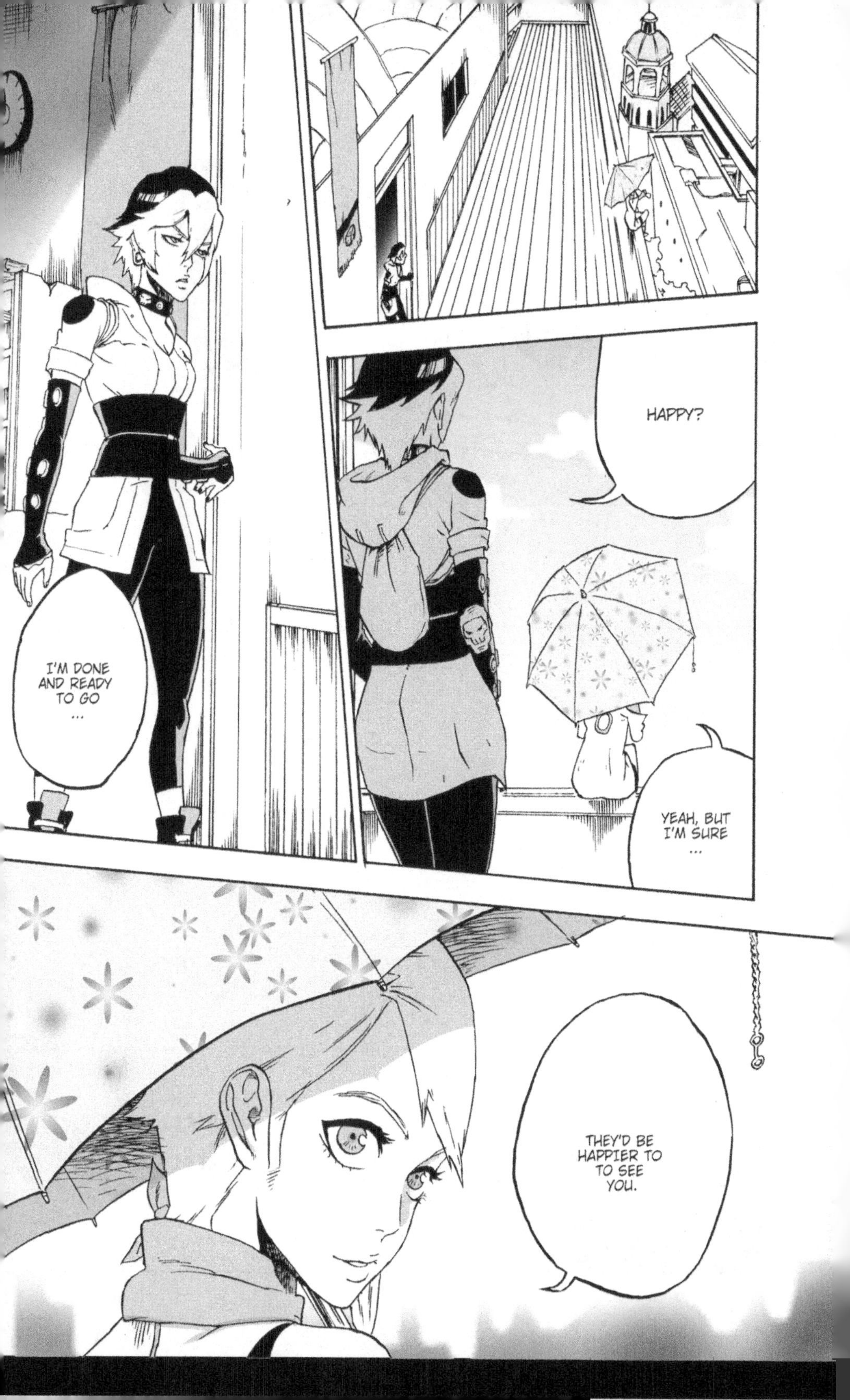
I'M DONE AND READY TO GO ...
HAPPY?
YEAH, BUT I'M SURE ...
THEY'D BE HAPPIER TO TO SEE YOU.

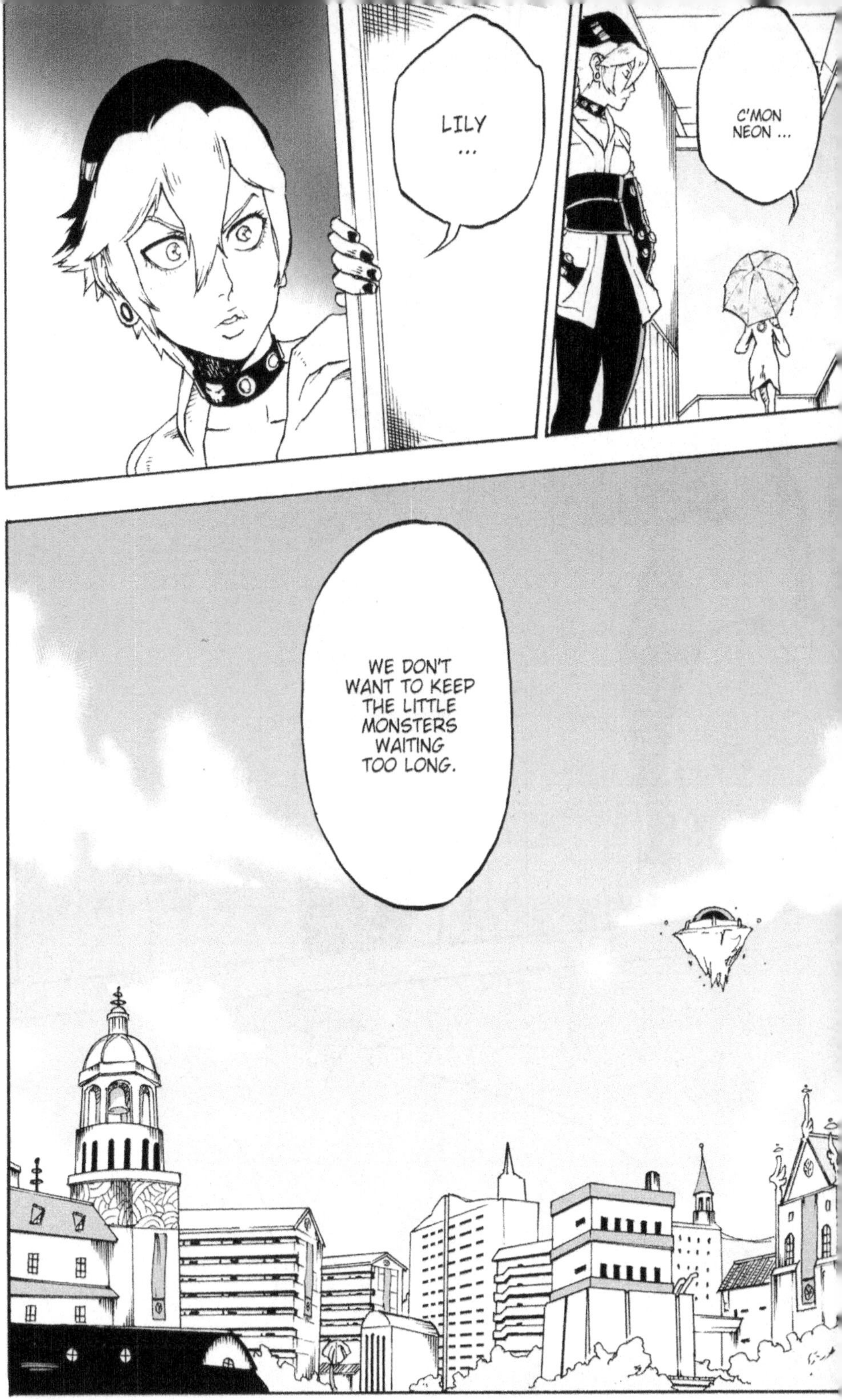
LILY ...
C'MON NEON ...
WE DON'T WANT TO KEEP THE LITTLE MONSTERS WAITING TOO LONG.

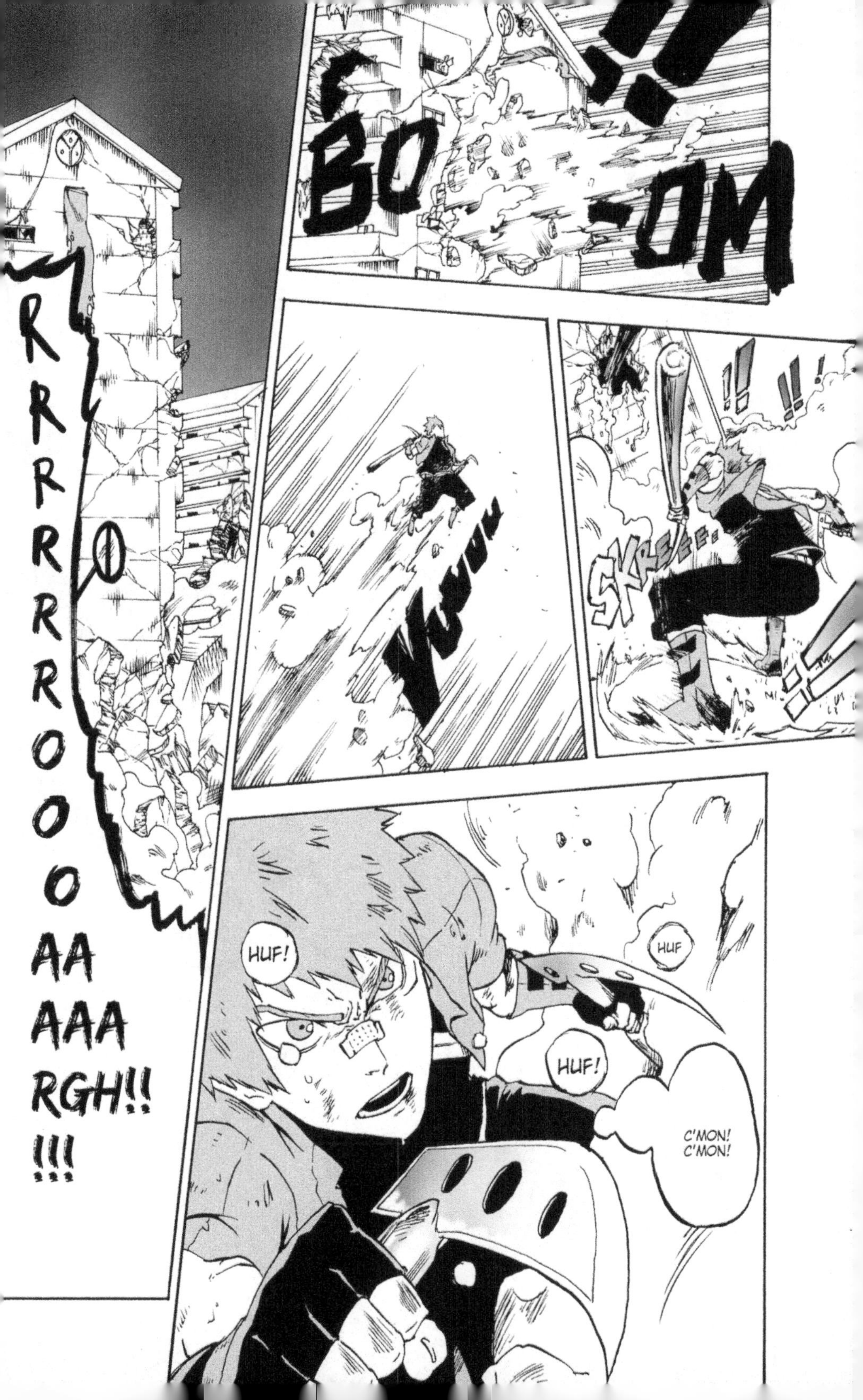
RRRRRROOOAAAAARGH!!!!!
BO-OM!!
!! !!
HUF!
HUF
HUF!
C'MON! C'MON!

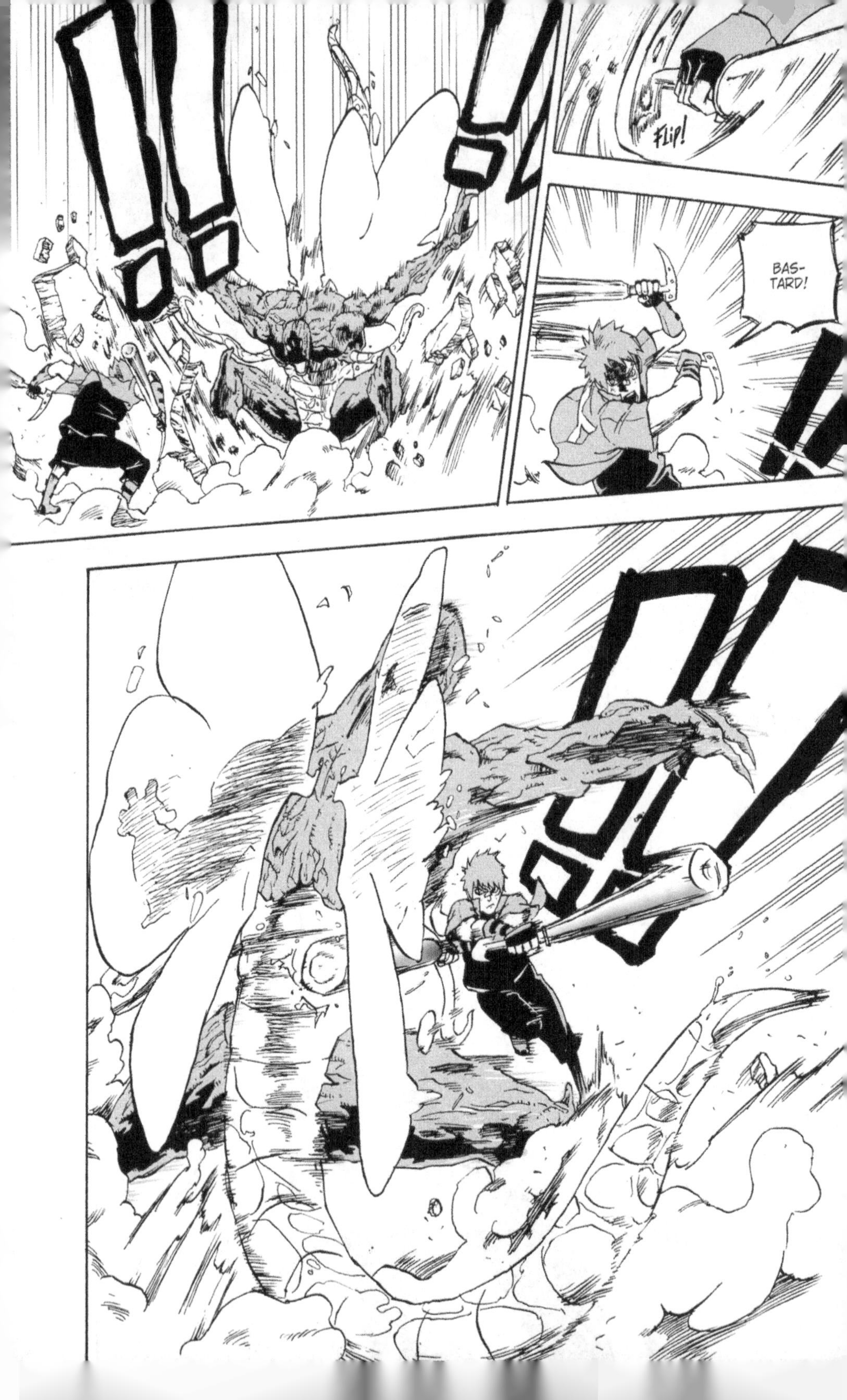
FLIP!
BAS-
TARD!

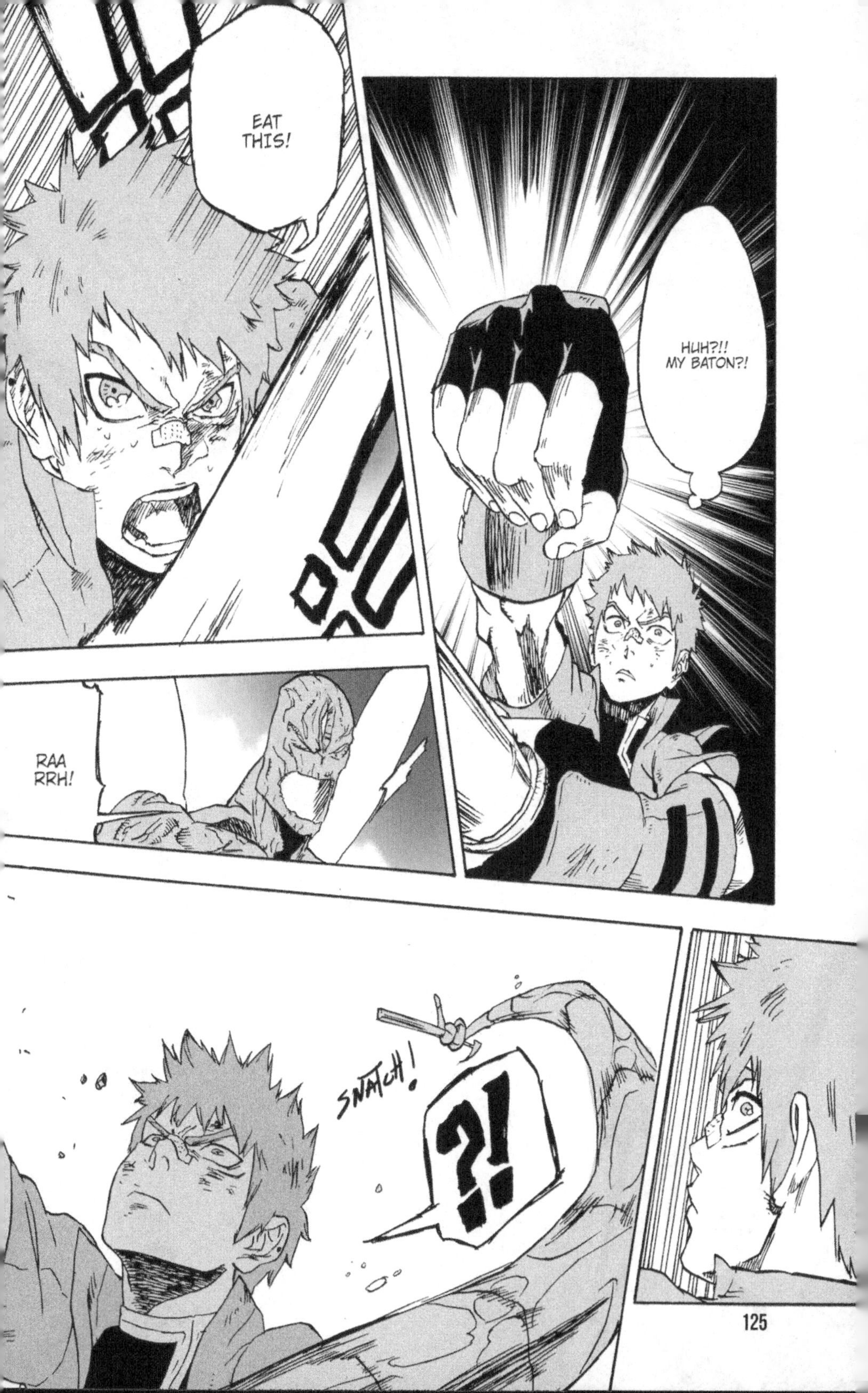

EAT THIS!
HUH?!! MY BATON?!
RAA RRH!
SNATCH!
?!

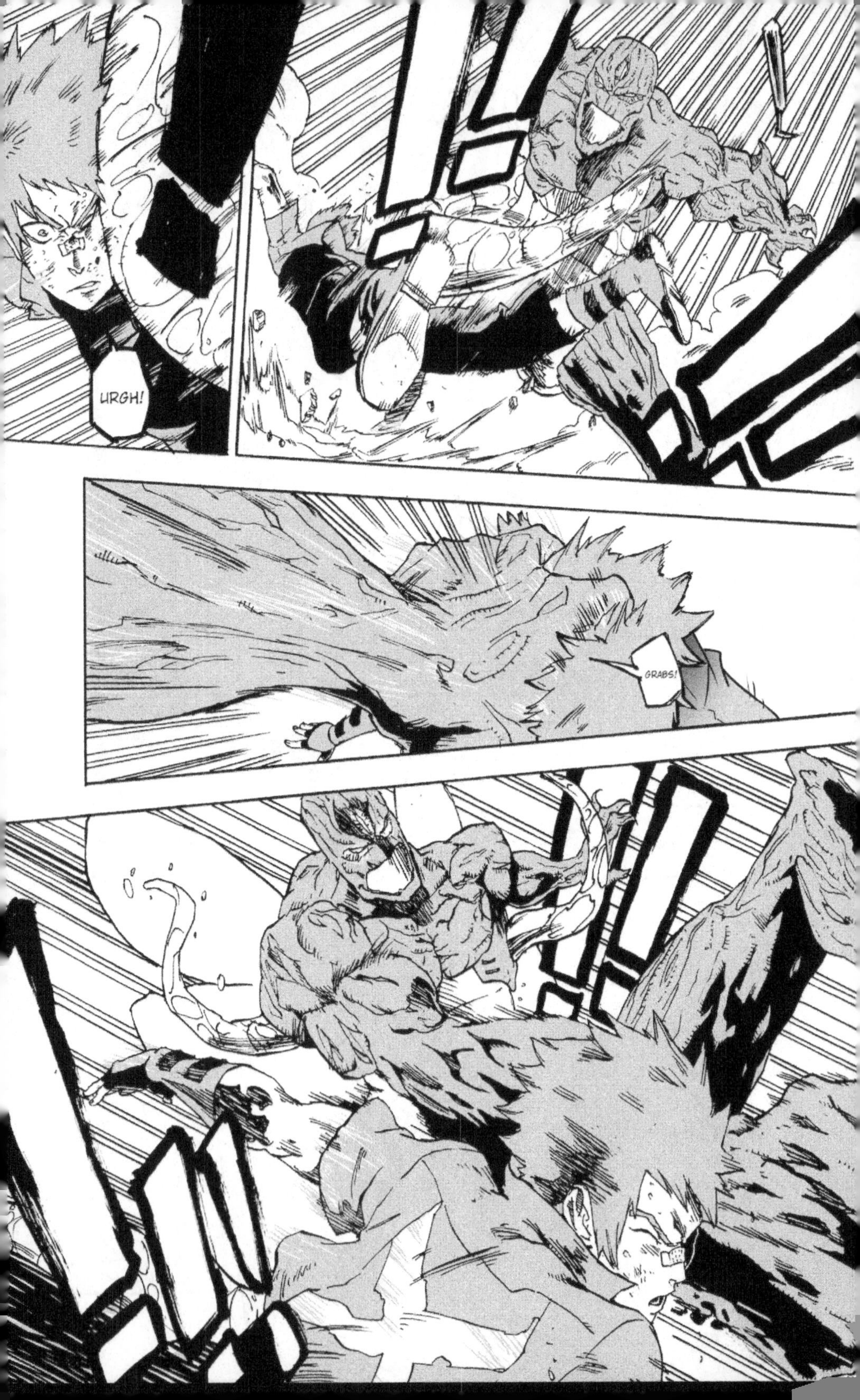
URGH!
GRABS!

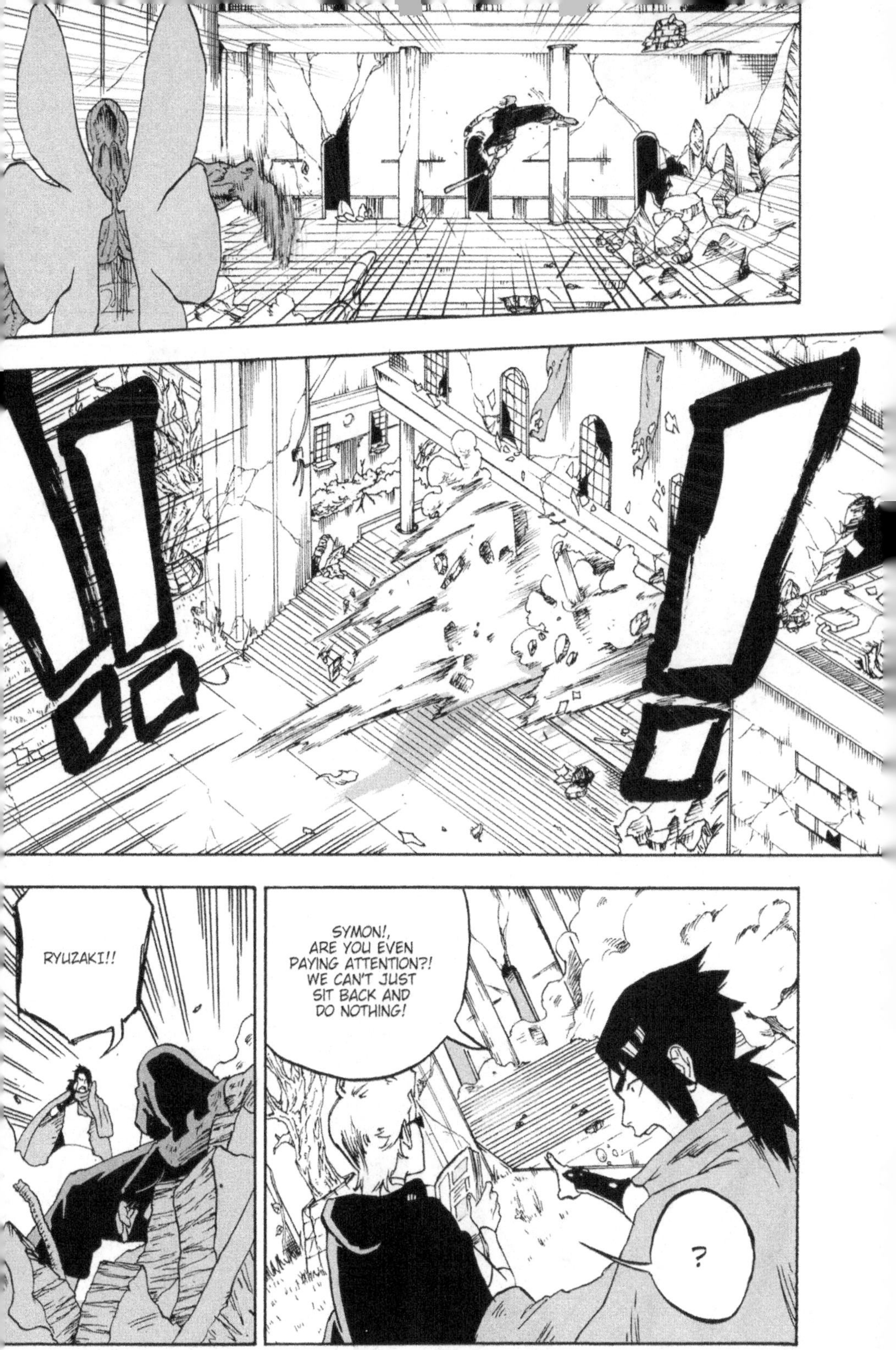
RYUZAKI!!
SYMON!, ARE YOU EVEN PAYING ATTENTION?! WE CAN'T JUST SIT BACK AND DO NOTHING!
?

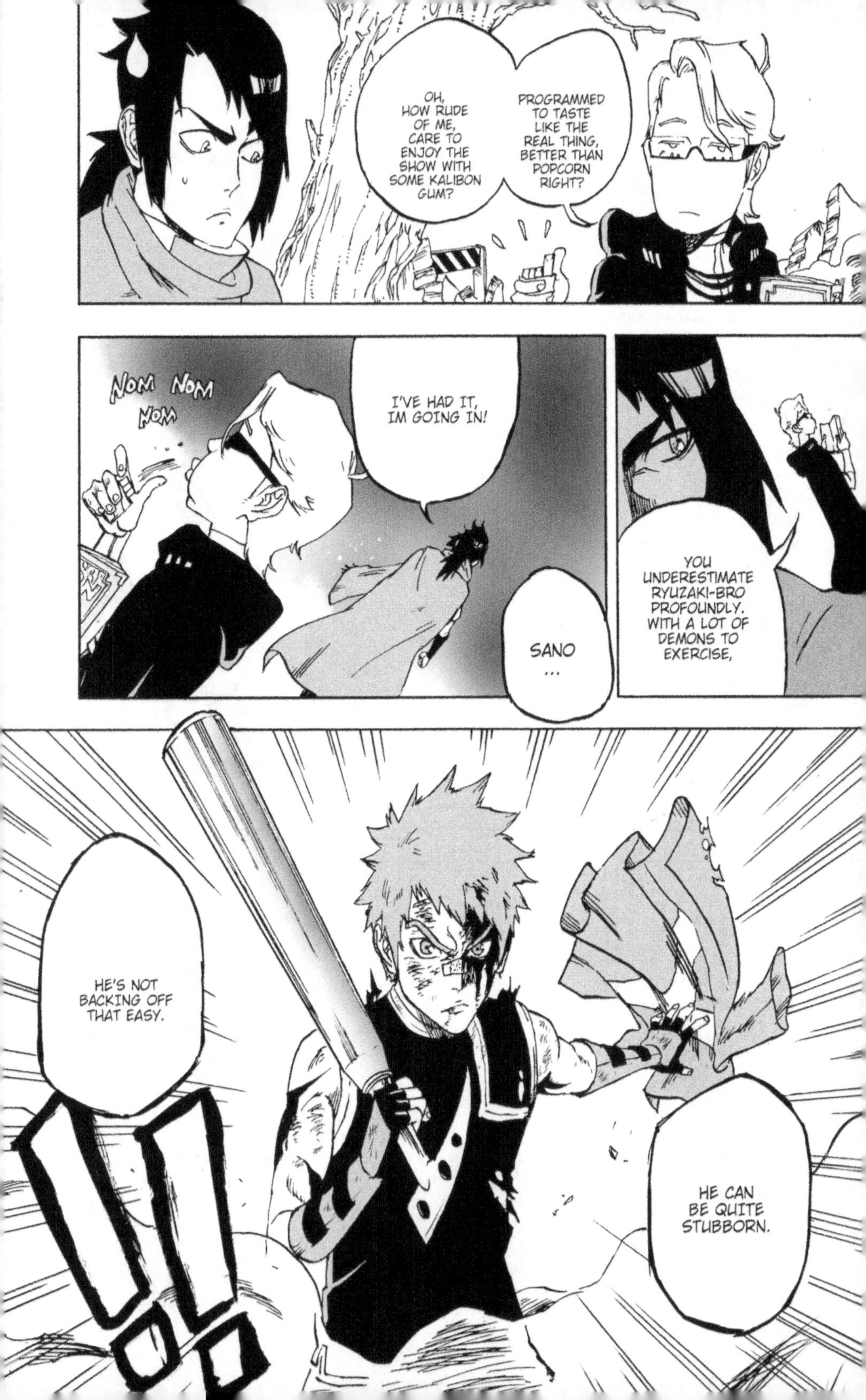
OH, HOW RUDE OF ME, CARE TO ENJOY THE SHOW WITH SOME KALIBON GUM?
PROGRAMMED TO TASTE LIKE THE REAL THING, BETTER THAN POPCORN RIGHT?
NOM NOM NOM
I'VE HAD IT, IM GOING IN!
SANO ...
YOU UNDERESTIMATE RYUZAKI-BRO PROFOUNDLY. WITH A LOT OF DEMONS TO EXERCISE,
HE'S NOT BACKING OFF THAT EASY.
HE CAN BE QUITE STUBBORN.

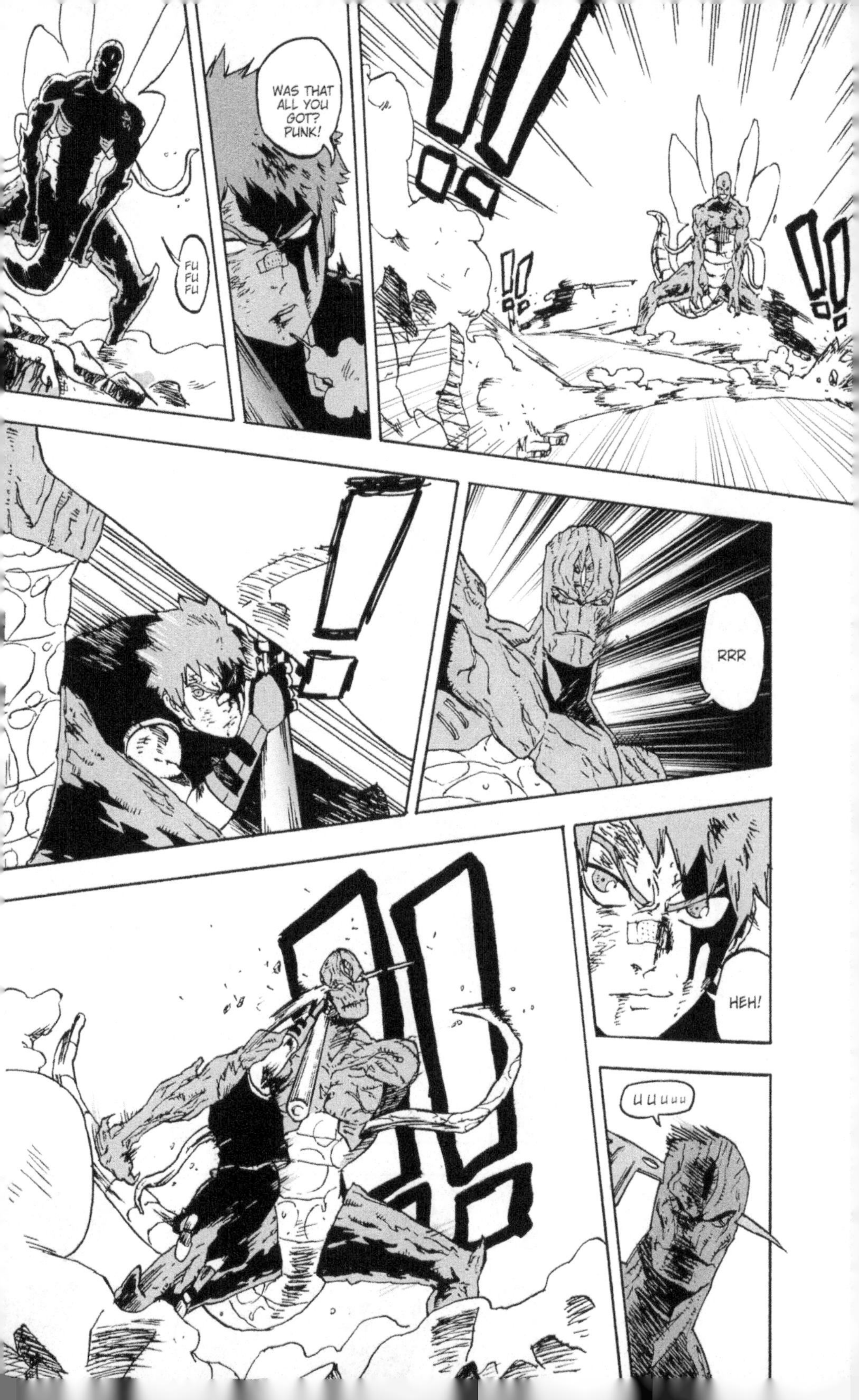
WAS THAT ALL YOU GOT? PUNK!
FU FU FU
RRR
HEH!
UUUUU

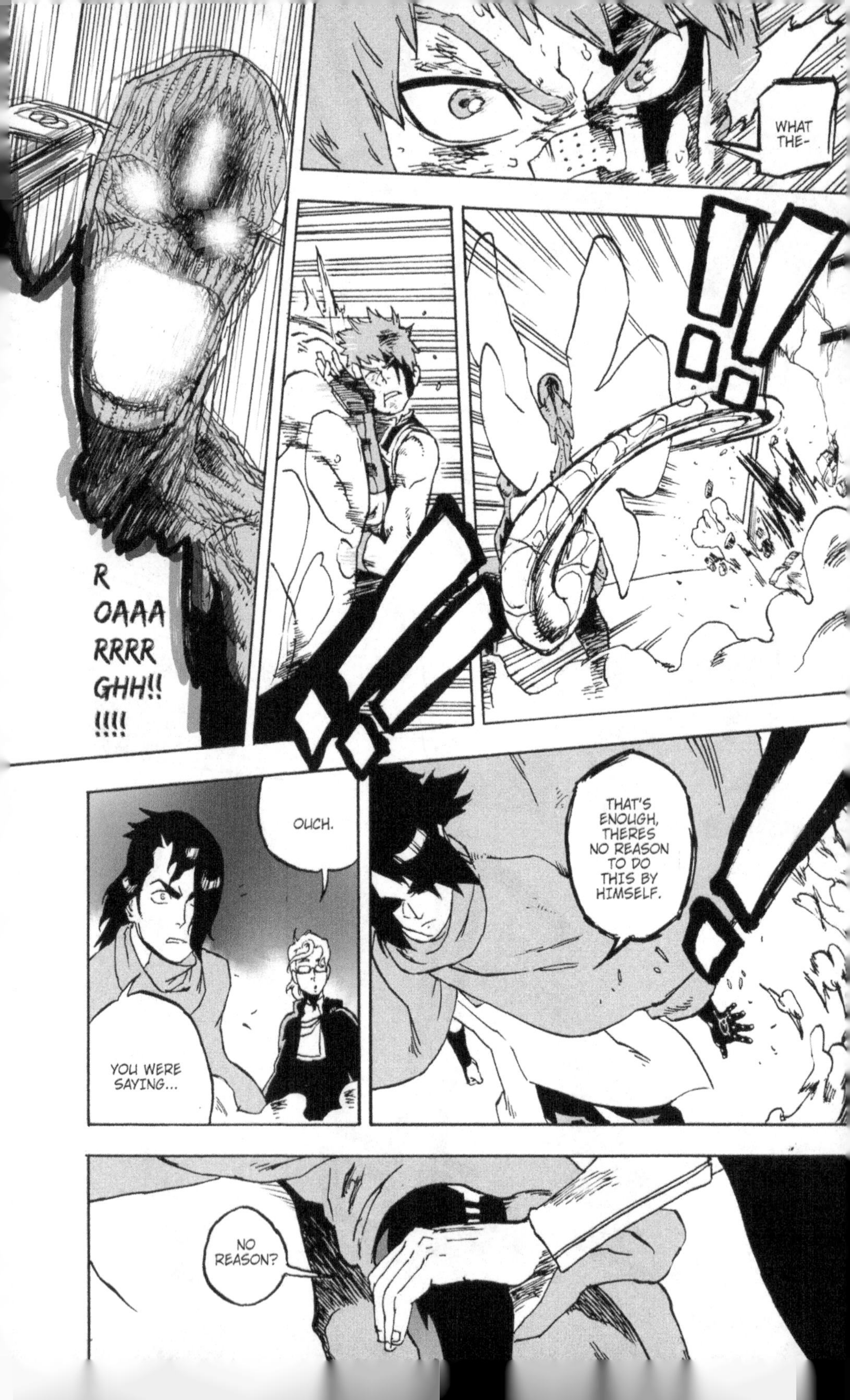
WHAT THE-
R OAAA RRRR GHH!! !!!!
YOU WERE SAYING...
OUCH.
THAT'S ENOUGH, THERES NO REASON TO DO THIS BY HIMSELF.
NO REASON?

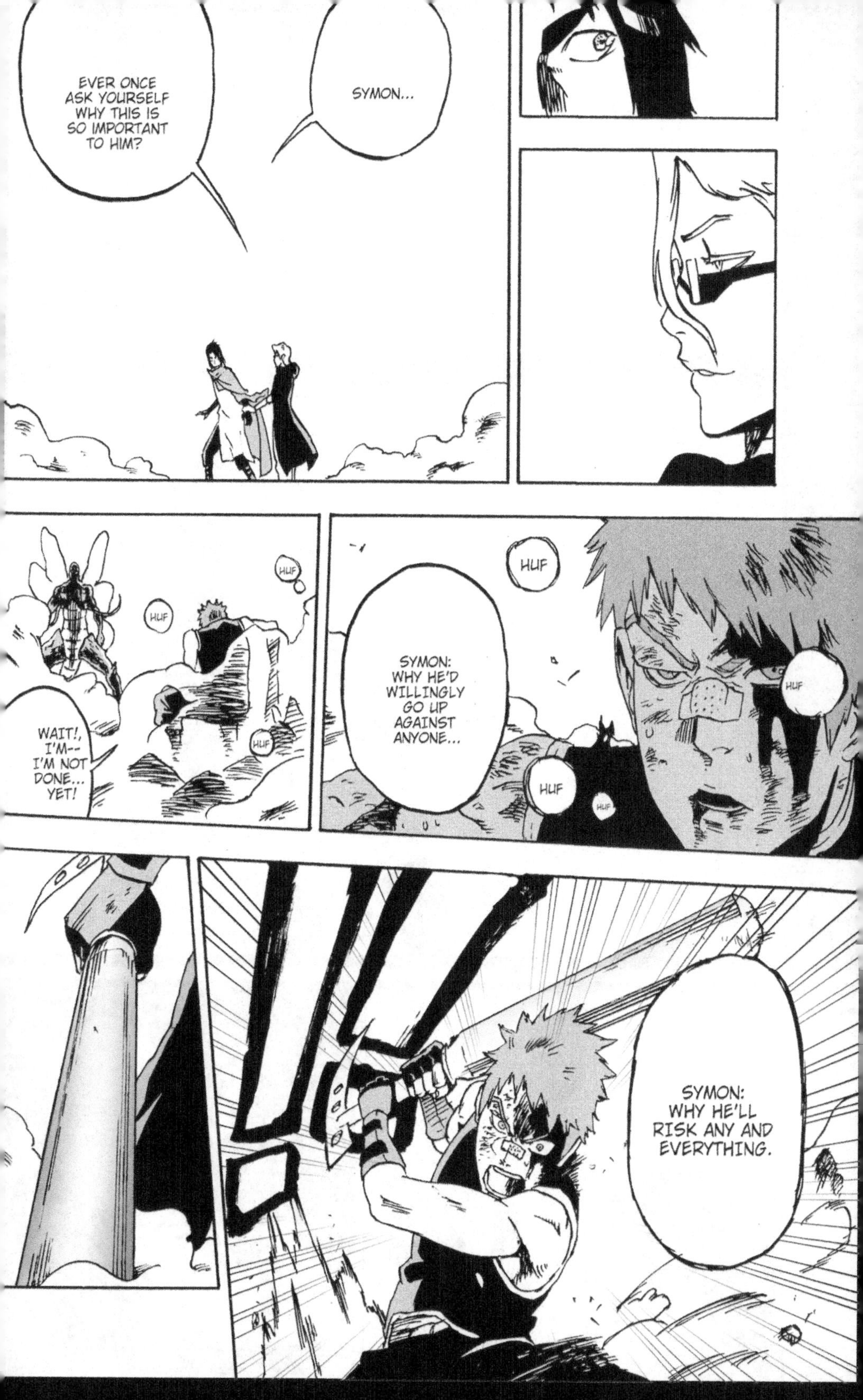
EVER ONCE ASK YOURSELF WHY THIS IS SO IMPORTANT TO HIM?
SYMON...
HUF
HUF
WAIT!, I'M-- I'M NOT DONE... YET!
HUF
HUF
SYMON: WHY HE'D WILLINGLY GO UP AGAINST ANYONE...
HUF
HUF
HUF
SYMON: WHY HE'LL RISK ANY AND EVERYTHING.

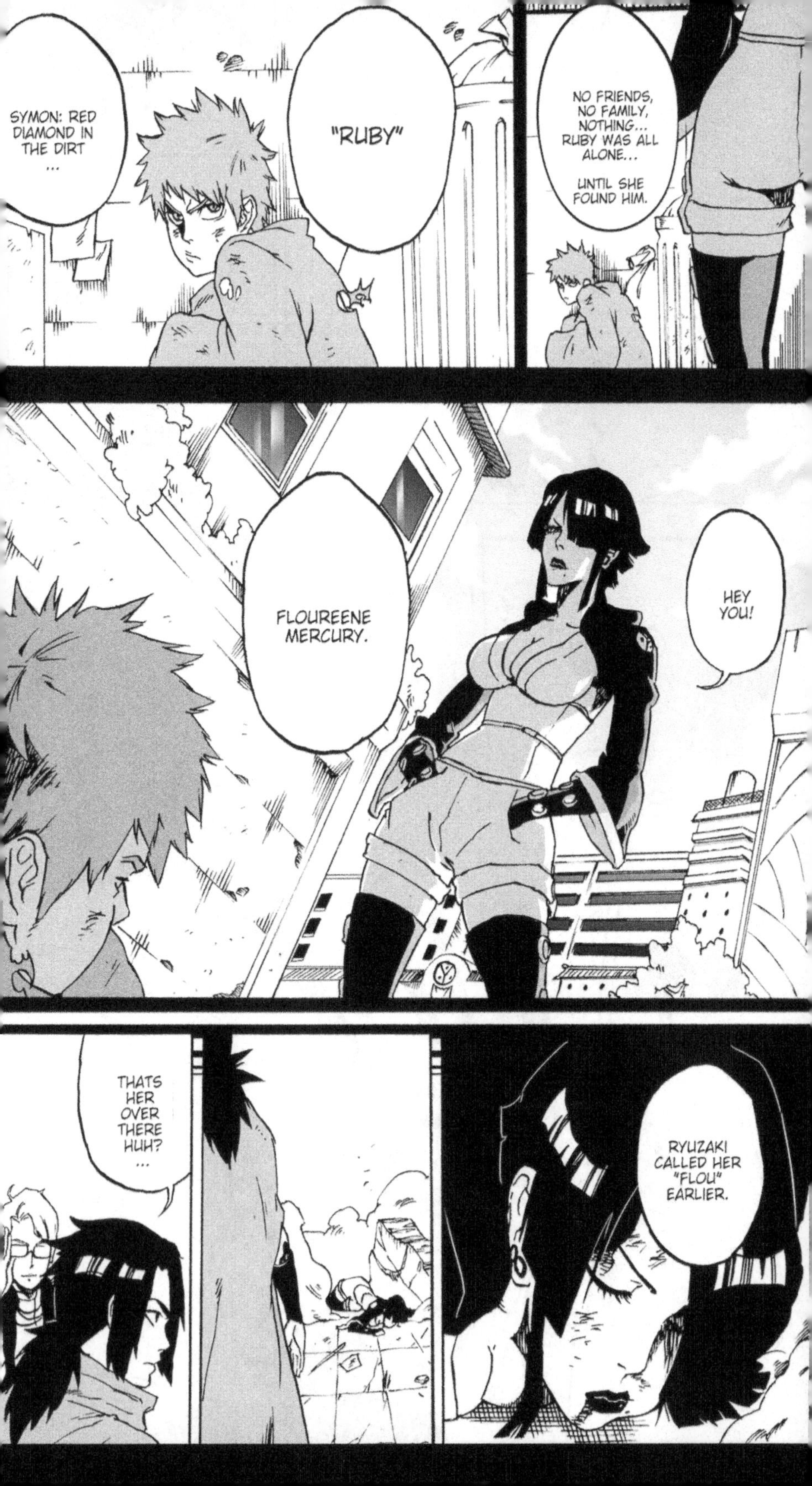
SYMON: RED DIAMOND IN THE DIRT ...
"RUBY"
NO FRIENDS, NO FAMILY, NOTHING... RUBY WAS ALL ALONE...
UNTIL SHE FOUND HIM.
FLOUREENE MERCURY.
HEY YOU!
THATS HER OVER THERE HUH? ...
RYUZAKI CALLED HER "FLOU" EARLIER.

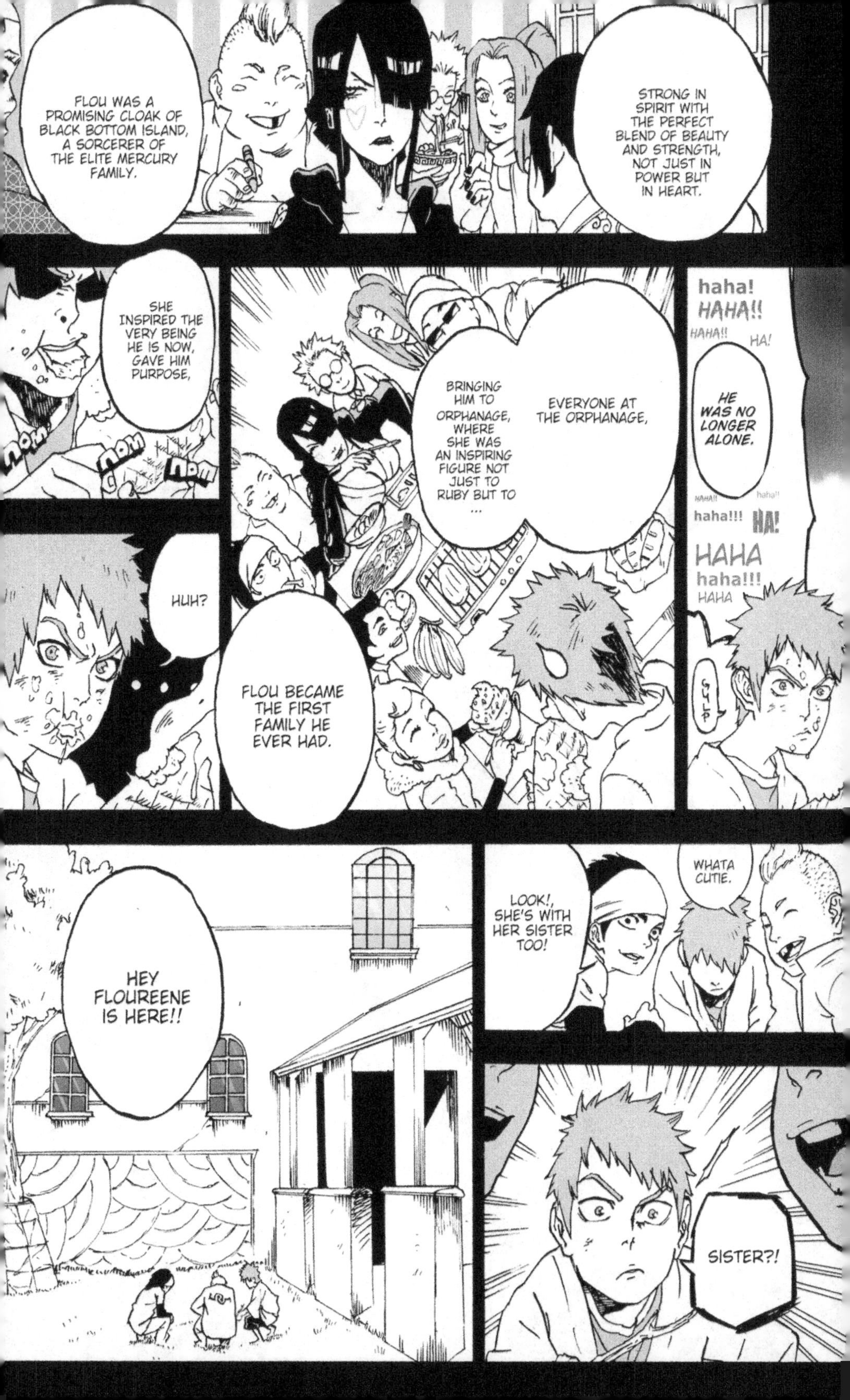
FLOU WAS A PROMISING CLOAK OF BLACK BOTTOM ISLAND, A SORCERER OF THE ELITE MERCURY FAMILY.
SIP
STRONG IN SPIRIT WITH THE PERFECT BLEND OF BEAUTY AND STRENGTH, NOT JUST IN POWER BUT IN HEART.
SHE INSPIRED THE VERY BEING HE IS NOW, GAVE HIM PURPOSE,
nom nom nom
HUH?
BRINGING HIM TO ORPHANAGE, WHERE SHE WAS AN INSPIRING FIGURE NOT JUST TO RUBY BUT TO ...
EVERYONE AT THE ORPHANAGE,
FLOU BECAME THE FIRST FAMILY HE EVER HAD.
haha! HAHA!! HAHA!! HA!
HE WAS NO LONGER ALONE.
HAHA!! haha!! haha!!! HA! HAHA haha!!! HAHA
GULP
HEY FLOUREENE IS HERE!!
LOOK!, SHE'S WITH HER SISTER TOO!
WHATA CUTIE.
SISTER?!

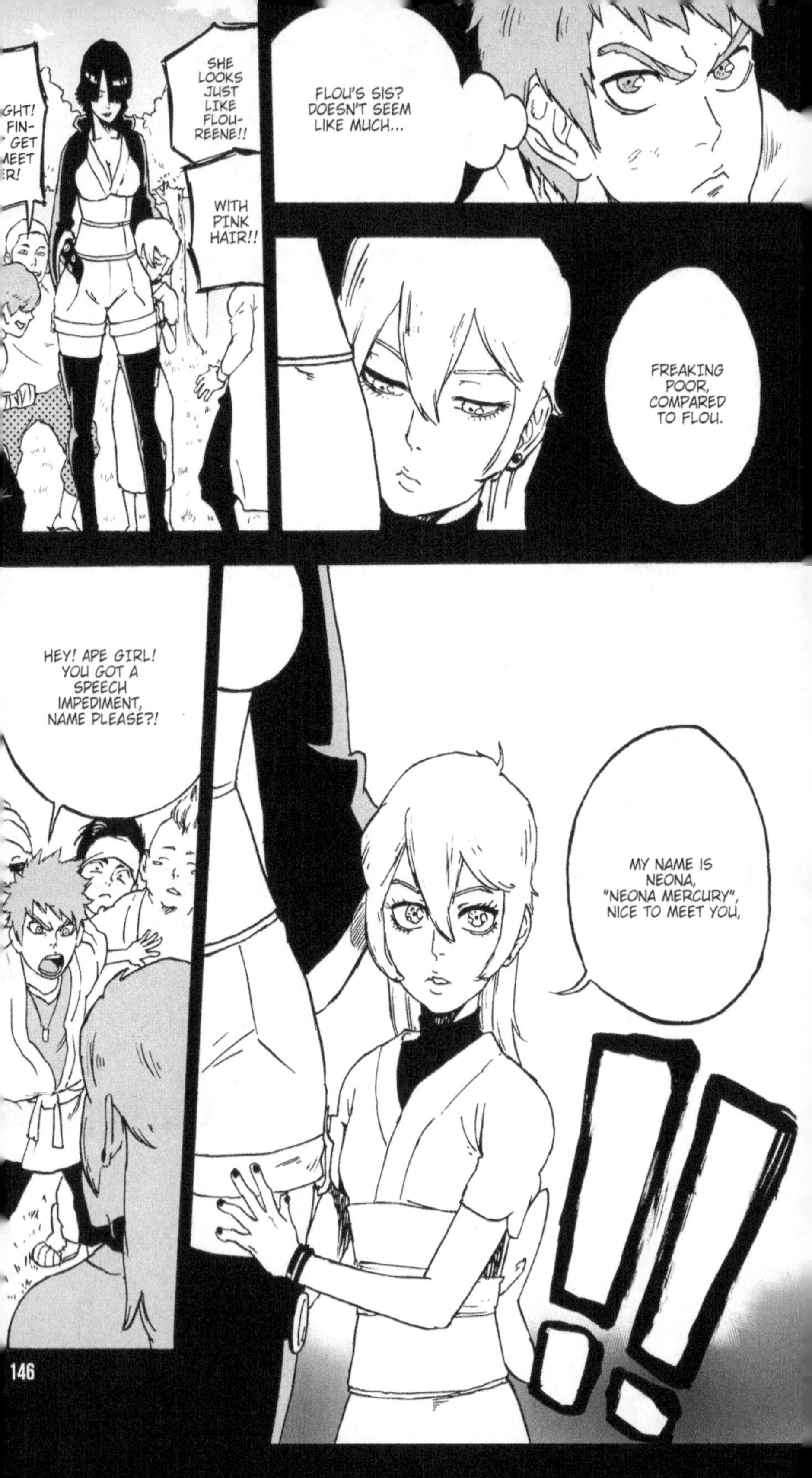
SHE LOOKS JUST LIKE FLOU-REENE!!
WITH PINK HAIR!!
FLOU'S SIS? DOESN'T SEEM LIKE MUCH...
FREAKING POOR, COMPARED TO FLOU.
HEY! APE GIRL! YOU GOT A SPEECH IMPEDIMENT, NAME PLEASE?!
MY NAME IS NEONA, "NEONA MERCURY", NICE TO MEET YOU,

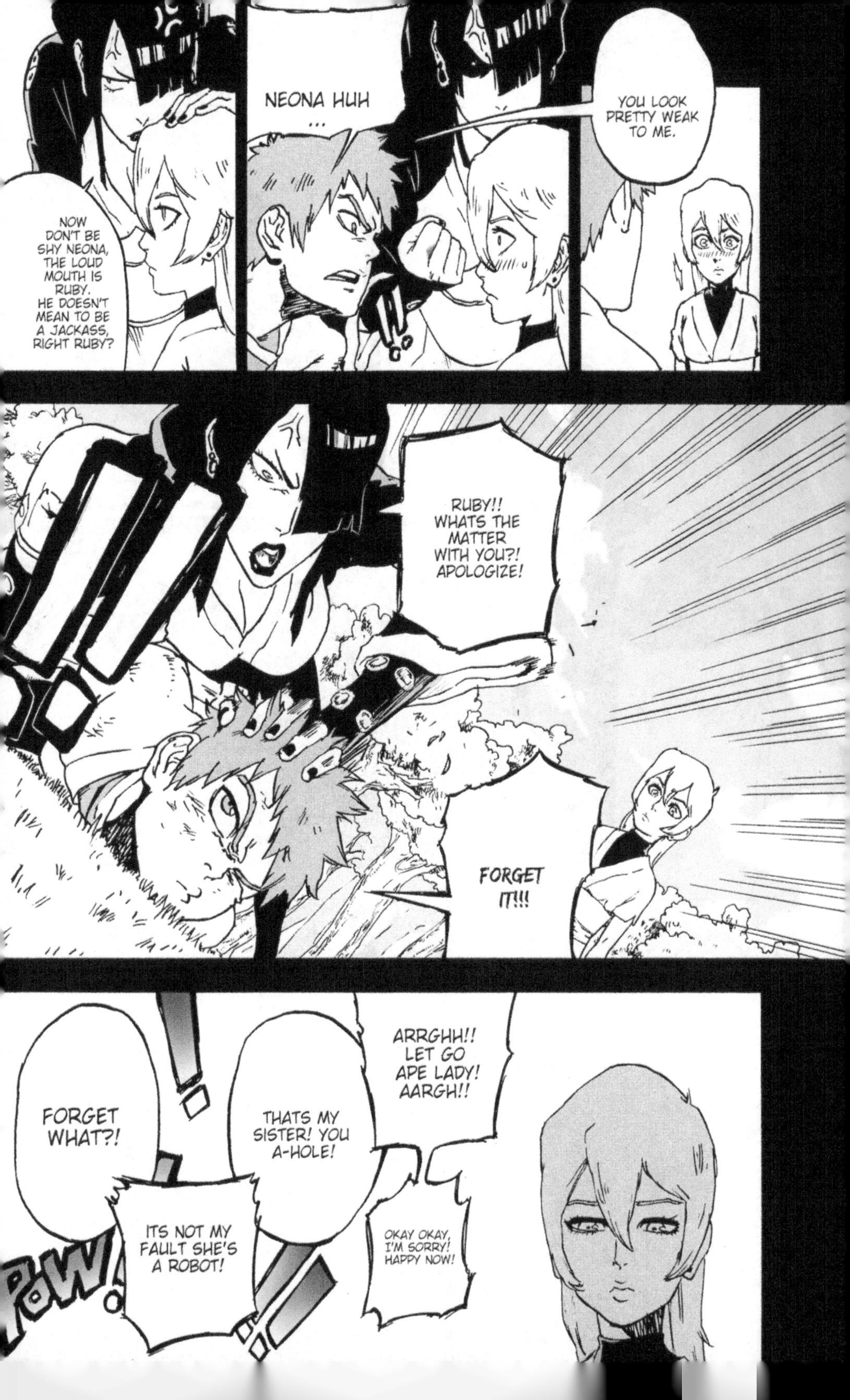
NOW DON'T BE SHY NEONA, THE LOUD MOUTH IS RUBY. HE DOESN'T MEAN TO BE A JACKASS, RIGHT RUBY?
NEONA HUH ...
YOU LOOK PRETTY WEAK TO ME.
RUBY!! WHATS THE MATTER WITH YOU?! APOLOGIZE!
FORGET IT!!!
FORGET WHAT?!
THATS MY SISTER! YOU A-HOLE!
ARRGHH!! LET GO APE LADY! AARGH!!
ITS NOT MY FAULT SHE'S A ROBOT!
POW
OKAY OKAY, I'M SORRY! HAPPY NOW!

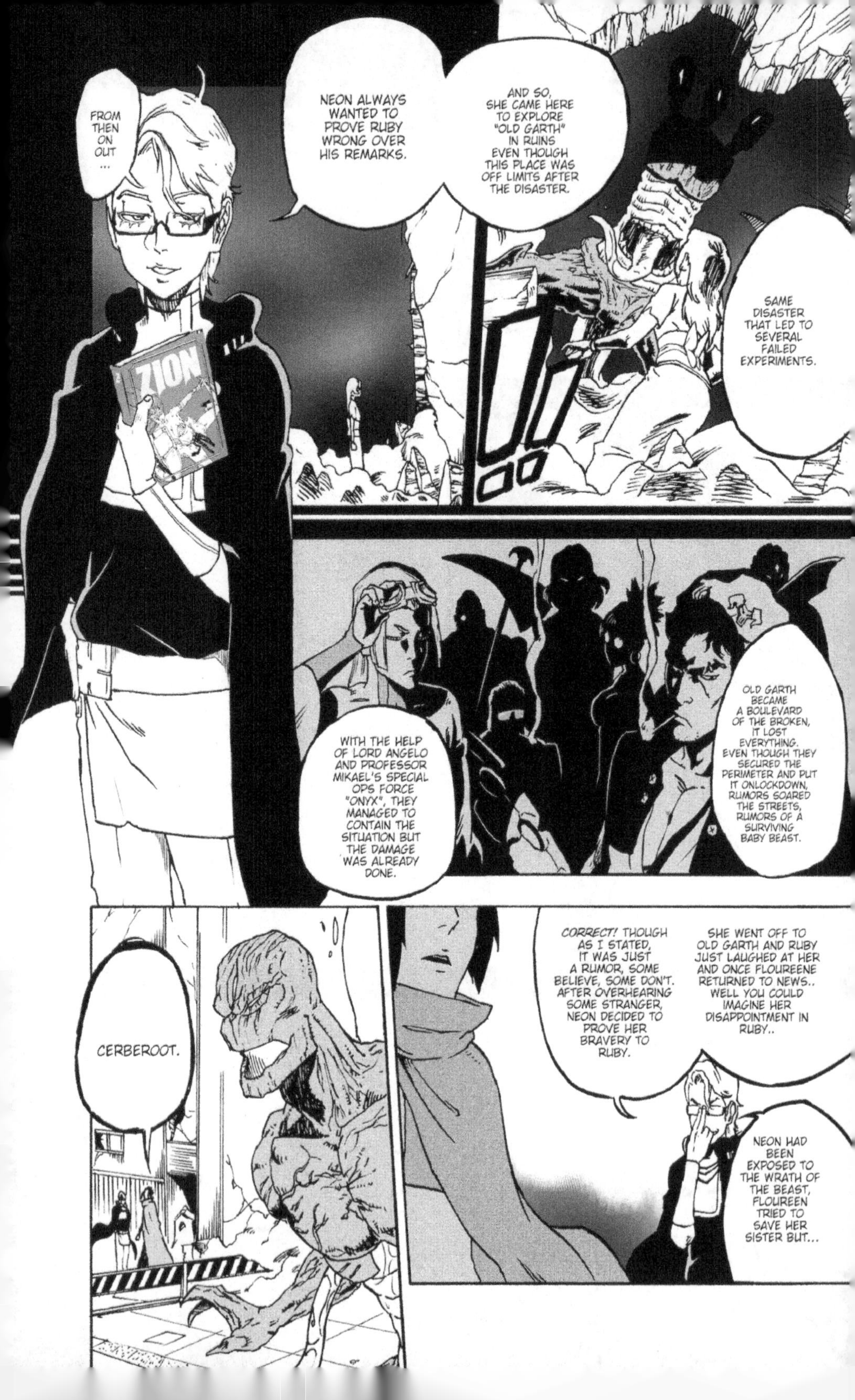
FROM THEN ON OUT ...
NEON ALWAYS WANTED TO PROVE RUBY WRONG OVER HIS REMARKS.
AND SO, SHE CAME HERE TO EXPLORE "OLD GARTH" IN RUINS EVEN THOUGH THIS PLACE WAS OFF LIMITS AFTER THE DISASTER.
SAME DISASTER THAT LED TO SEVERAL FAILED EXPERIMENTS.
WITH THE HELP OF LORD ANGELO AND PROFESSOR MIKAEL'S SPECIAL OPS FORCE "ONYX", THEY MANAGED TO CONTAIN THE SITUATION BUT THE DAMAGE WAS ALREADY DONE.
OLD GARTH BECAME A BOULEVARD OF THE BROKEN, IT LOST EVERYTHING. EVEN THOUGH THEY SECURED THE PERIMETER AND PUT IT ONLOCKDOWN, RUMORS SOARED THE STREETS, RUMORS OF A SURVIVING BABY BEAST.
CERBEROOT.
CORRECT! THOUGH AS I STATED, IT WAS JUST A RUMOR, SOME BELIEVE, SOME DON'T. AFTER OVERHEARING SOME STRANGER, NEON DECIDED TO PROVE HER BRAVERY TO RUBY.
SHE WENT OFF TO OLD GARTH AND RUBY JUST LAUGHED AT HER AND ONCE FLOUREENE RETURNED TO NEWS.. WELL YOU COULD IMAGINE HER DISAPPOINTMENT IN RUBY..
NEON HAD BEEN EXPOSED TO THE WRATH OF THE BEAST, FLOUREEN TRIED TO SAVE HER SISTER BUT...

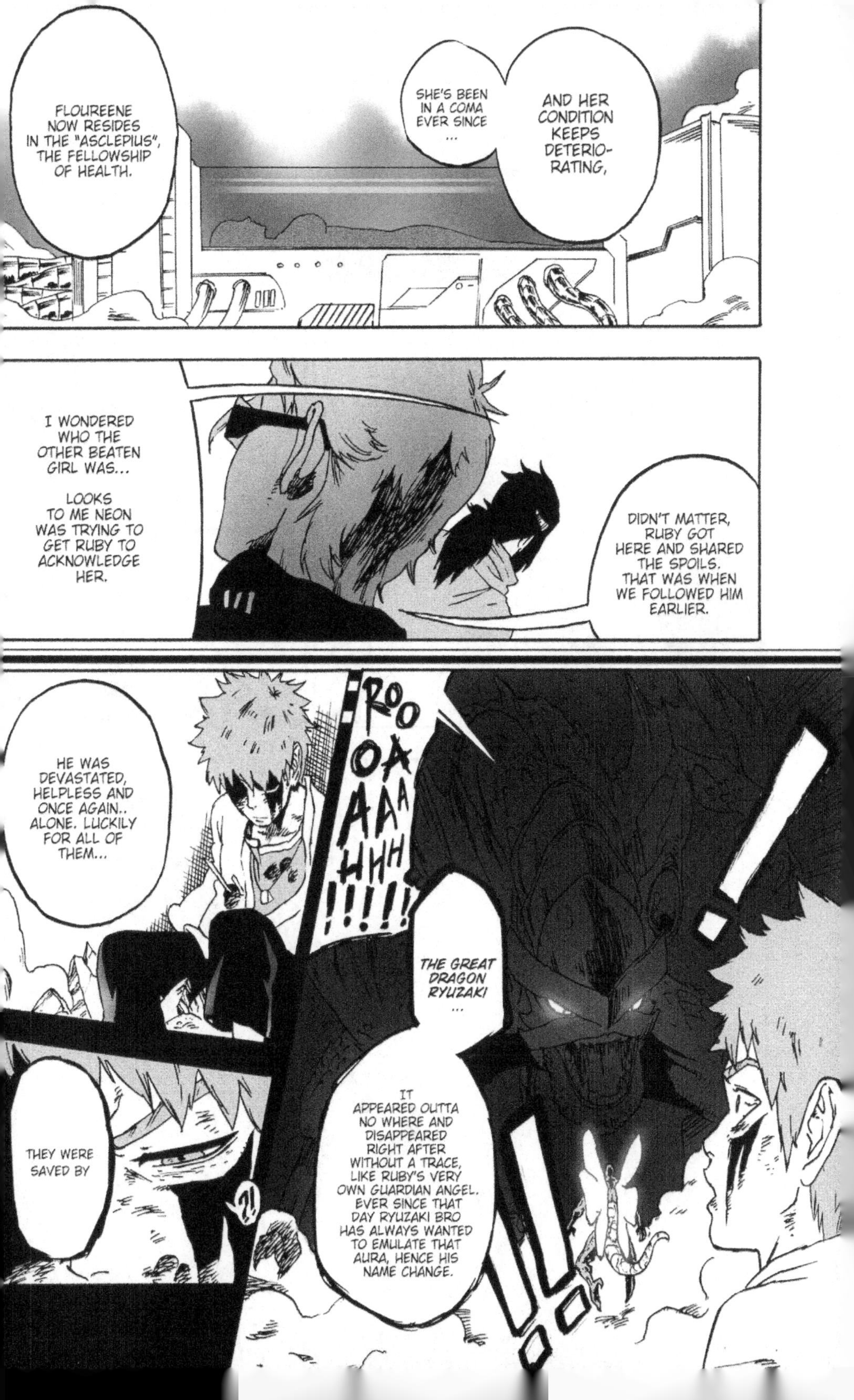
FLOUREENE NOW RESIDES IN THE "ASCLEPIUS", THE FELLOWSHIP OF HEALTH.
SHE'S BEEN IN A COMA EVER SINCE ...
AND HER CONDITION KEEPS DETERIO-RATING,
I WONDERED WHO THE OTHER BEATEN GIRL WAS...
LOOKS TO ME NEON WAS TRYING TO GET RUBY TO ACKNOWLEDGE HER.
DIDN'T MATTER, RUBY GOT HERE AND SHARED THE SPOILS. THAT WAS WHEN WE FOLLOWED HIM EARLIER.
HE WAS DEVASTATED, HELPLESS AND ONCE AGAIN.. ALONE. LUCKILY FOR ALL OF THEM...
ROOOAAAAHHH!!!!!
THEY WERE SAVED BY
?!
THE GREAT DRAGON RYUZAKI ...
IT APPEARED OUTTA NO WHERE AND DISAPPEARED RIGHT AFTER WITHOUT A TRACE, LIKE RUBY'S VERY OWN GUARDIAN ANGEL. EVER SINCE THAT DAY RYUZAKI BRO HAS ALWAYS WANTED TO EMULATE THAT AURA, HENCE HIS NAME CHANGE.
!!

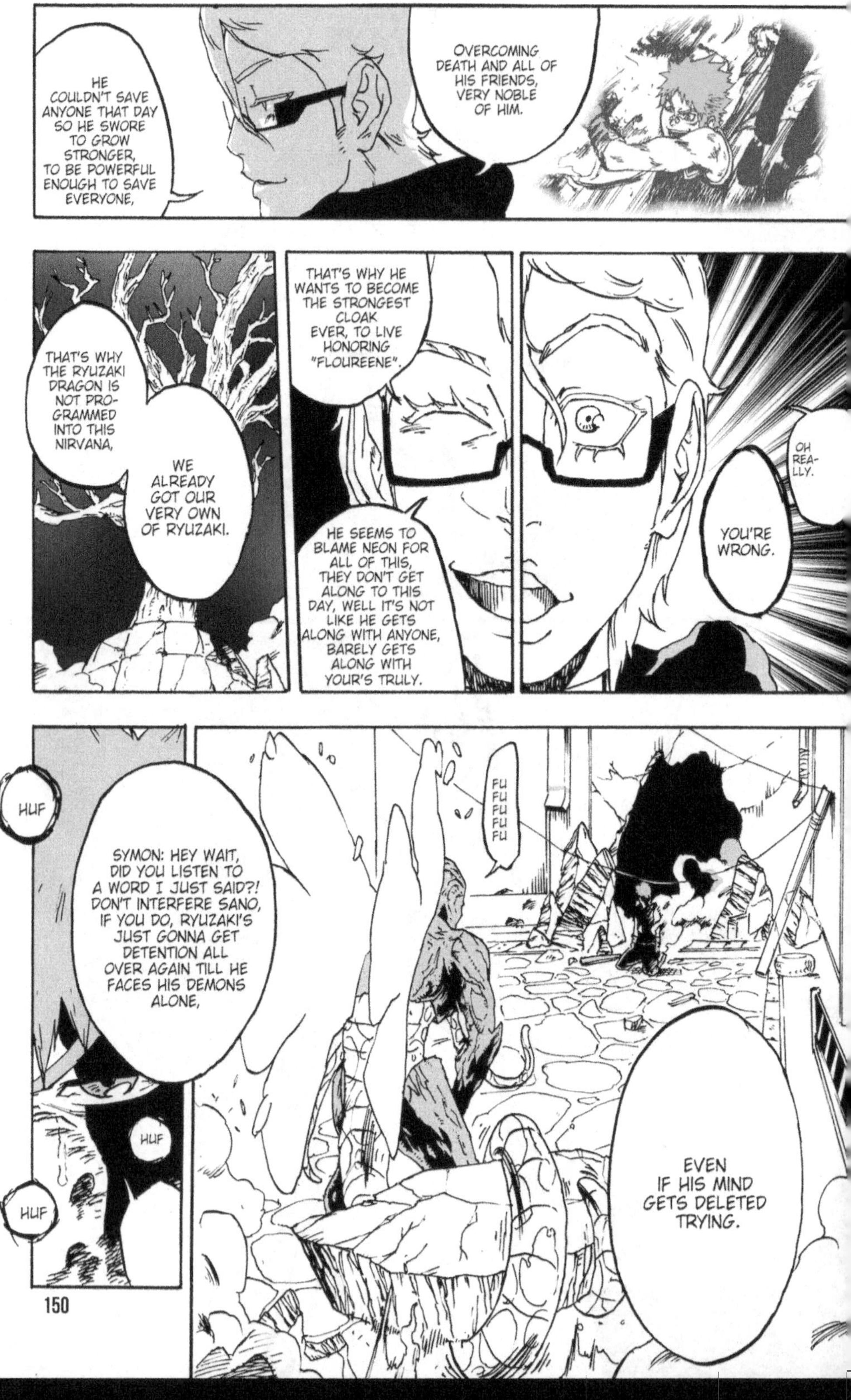

HE COULDN'T SAVE ANYONE THAT DAY SO HE SWORE TO GROW STRONGER, TO BE POWERFUL ENOUGH TO SAVE EVERYONE,
OVERCOMING DEATH AND ALL OF HIS FRIENDS, VERY NOBLE OF HIM.
THAT'S WHY THE RYUZAKI DRAGON IS NOT PRO-GRAMMED INTO THIS NIRVANA,
WE ALREADY GOT OUR VERY OWN OF RYUZAKI.
THAT'S WHY HE WANTS TO BECOME THE STRONGEST CLOAK EVER, TO LIVE HONORING "FLOUREENE".
HE SEEMS TO BLAME NEON FOR ALL OF THIS, THEY DON'T GET ALONG TO THIS DAY, WELL IT'S NOT LIKE HE GETS ALONG WITH ANYONE, BARELY GETS ALONG WITH YOUR'S TRULY.
YOU'RE WRONG.
OH REA-LLY.
HUF
SYMON: HEY WAIT, DID YOU LISTEN TO A WORD I JUST SAID?! DON'T INTERFERE SANO, IF YOU DO, RYUZAKI'S JUST GONNA GET DETENTION ALL OVER AGAIN TILL HE FACES HIS DEMONS ALONE,
HUF
HUF
FU FU FU FU FU
EVEN IF HIS MIND GETS DELETED TRYING.

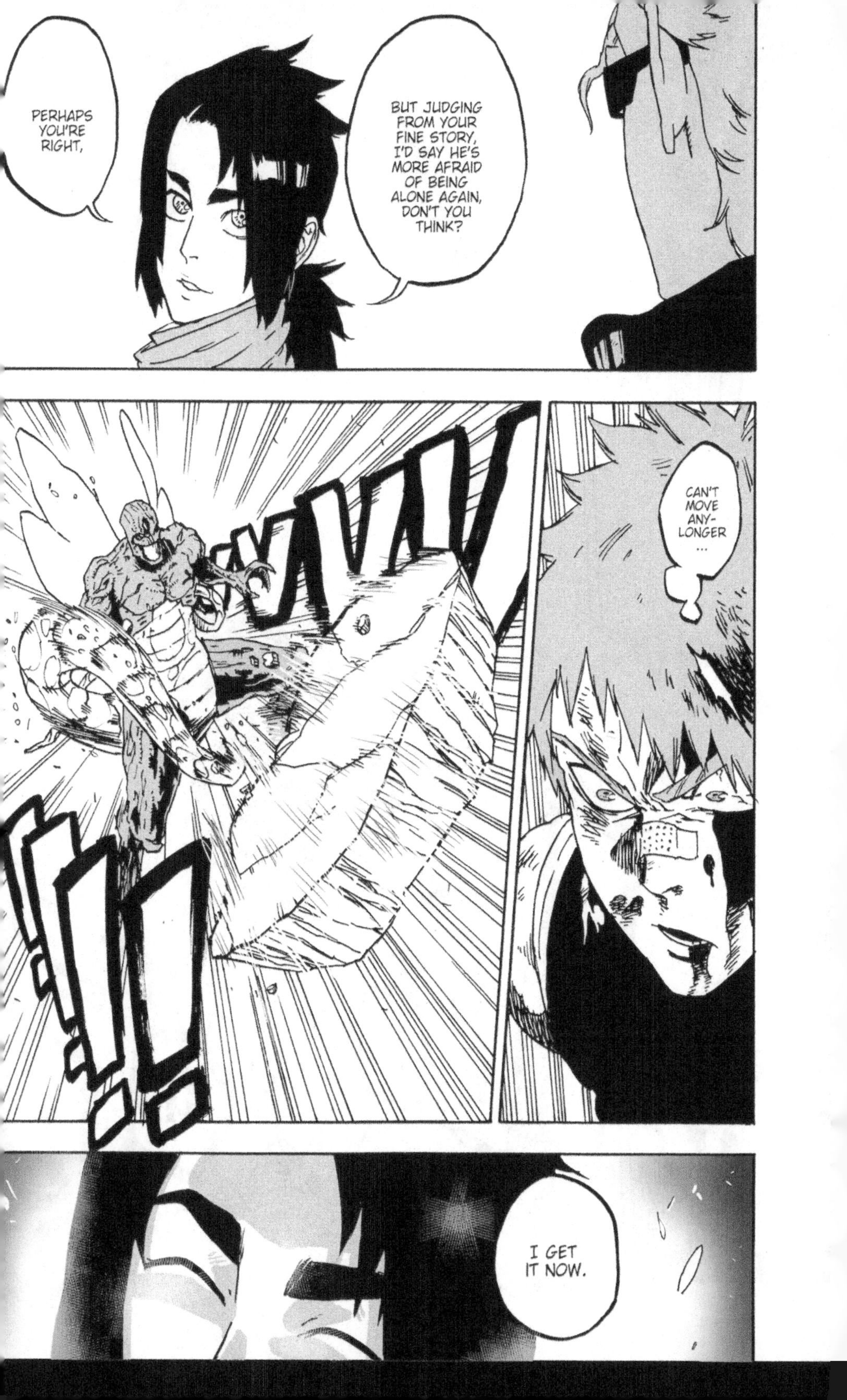
PERHAPS YOU'RE RIGHT,
BUT JUDGING FROM YOUR FINE STORY, I'D SAY HE'S MORE AFRAID OF BEING ALONE AGAIN, DON'T YOU THINK?
CAN'T MOVE ANY-LONGER ...
I GET IT NOW.

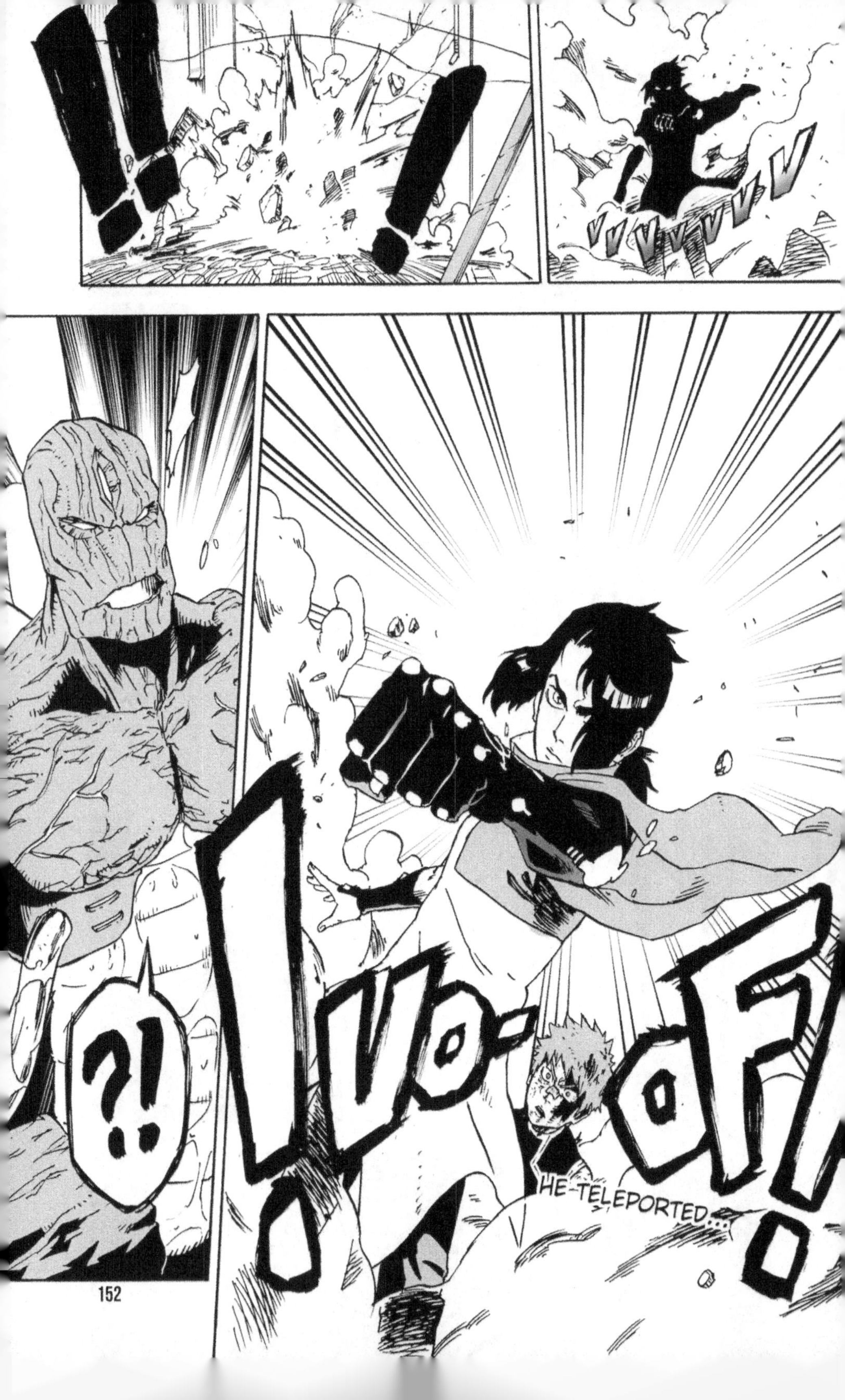
!!
!
?!
WO-OF!
HE-TELEPORTED...

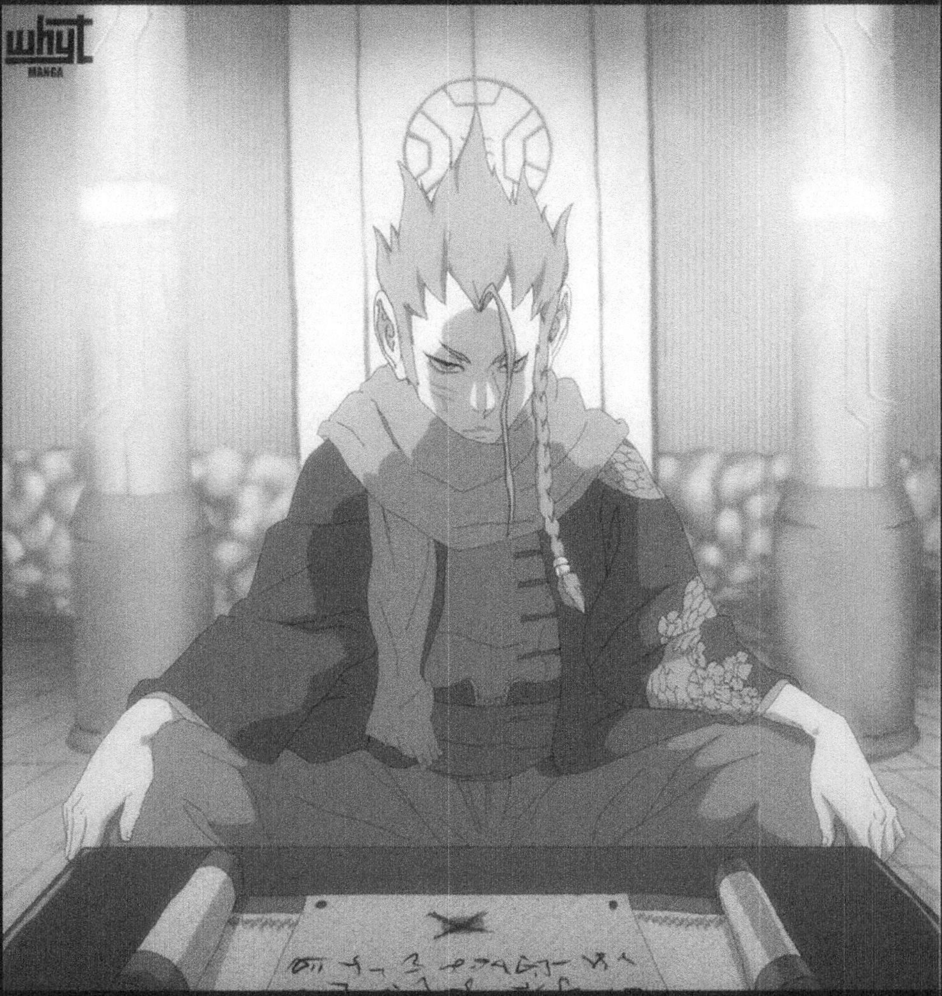

you are hereby Banished!

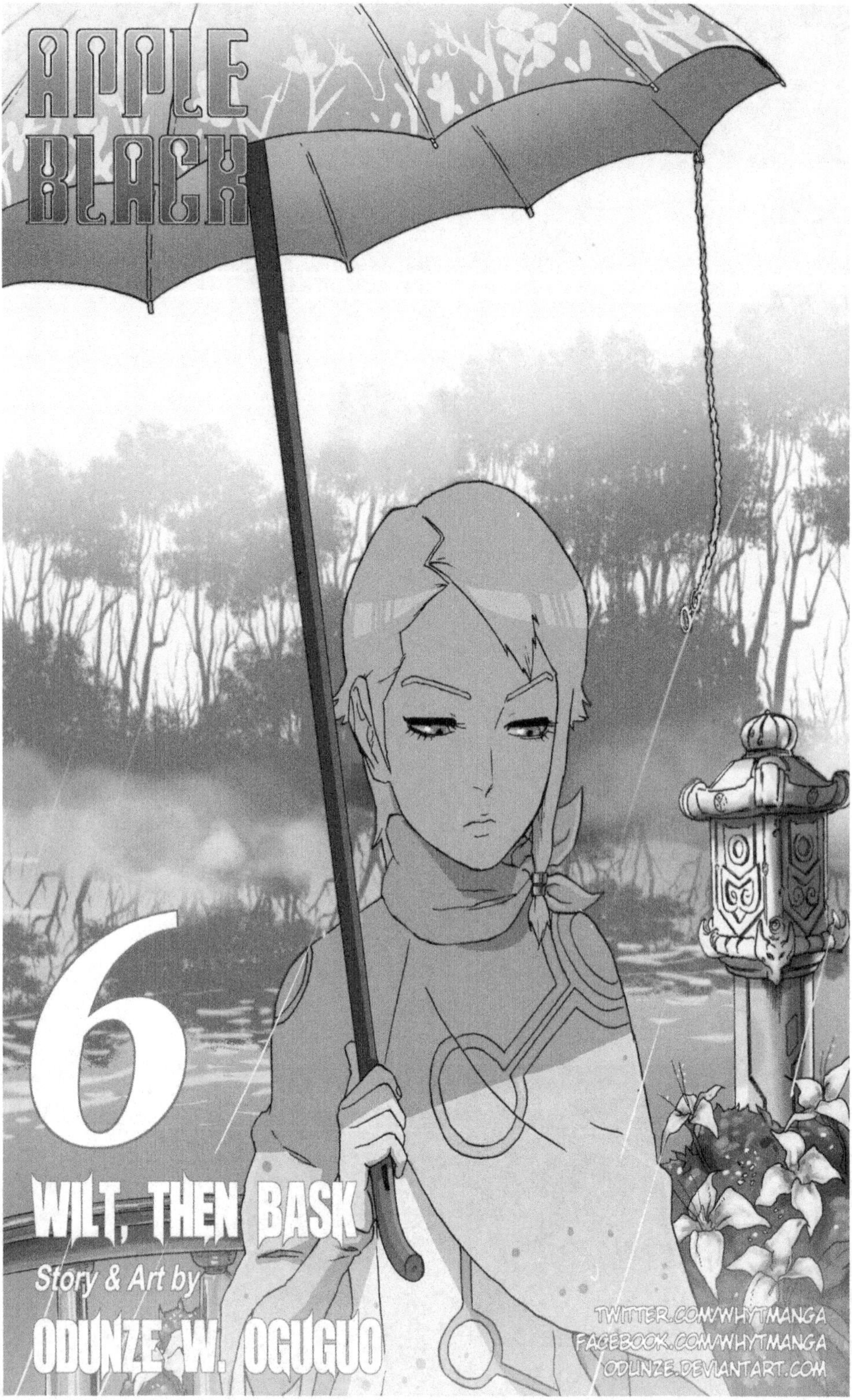

APPLE BLACK
6
WILT, THEN BASK
Story & Art by
ODUNZE W. OGUGUO
TWITTER.COM/WHYTMANGA
FACEBOOK.COM/WHYTMANGA
ODUNZE.DEVIANTART.COM

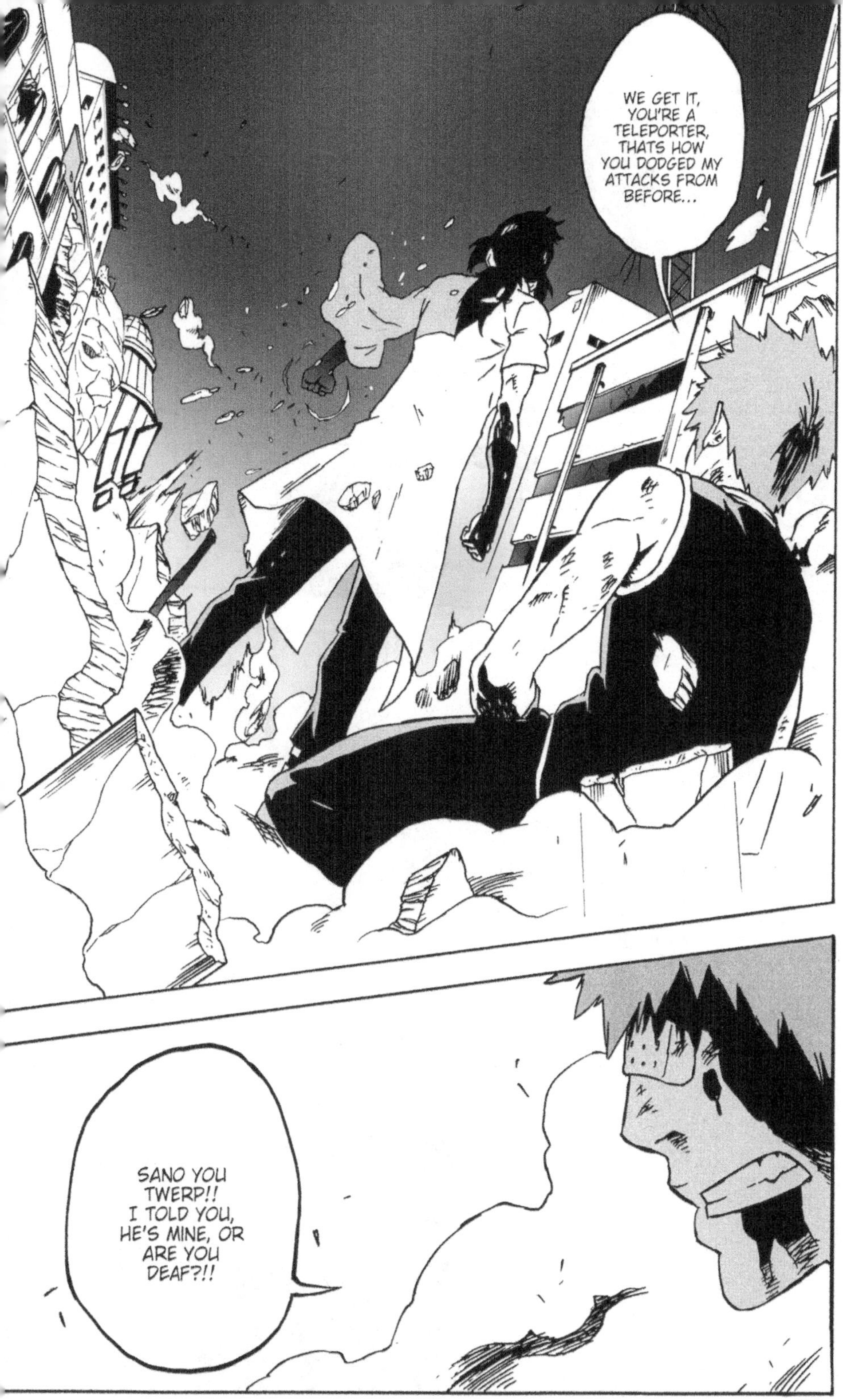
WE GET IT, YOU'RE A TELEPORTER, THATS HOW YOU DODGED MY ATTACKS FROM BEFORE...
SANO YOU TWERP!! I TOLD YOU, HE'S MINE, OR ARE YOU DEAF?!!

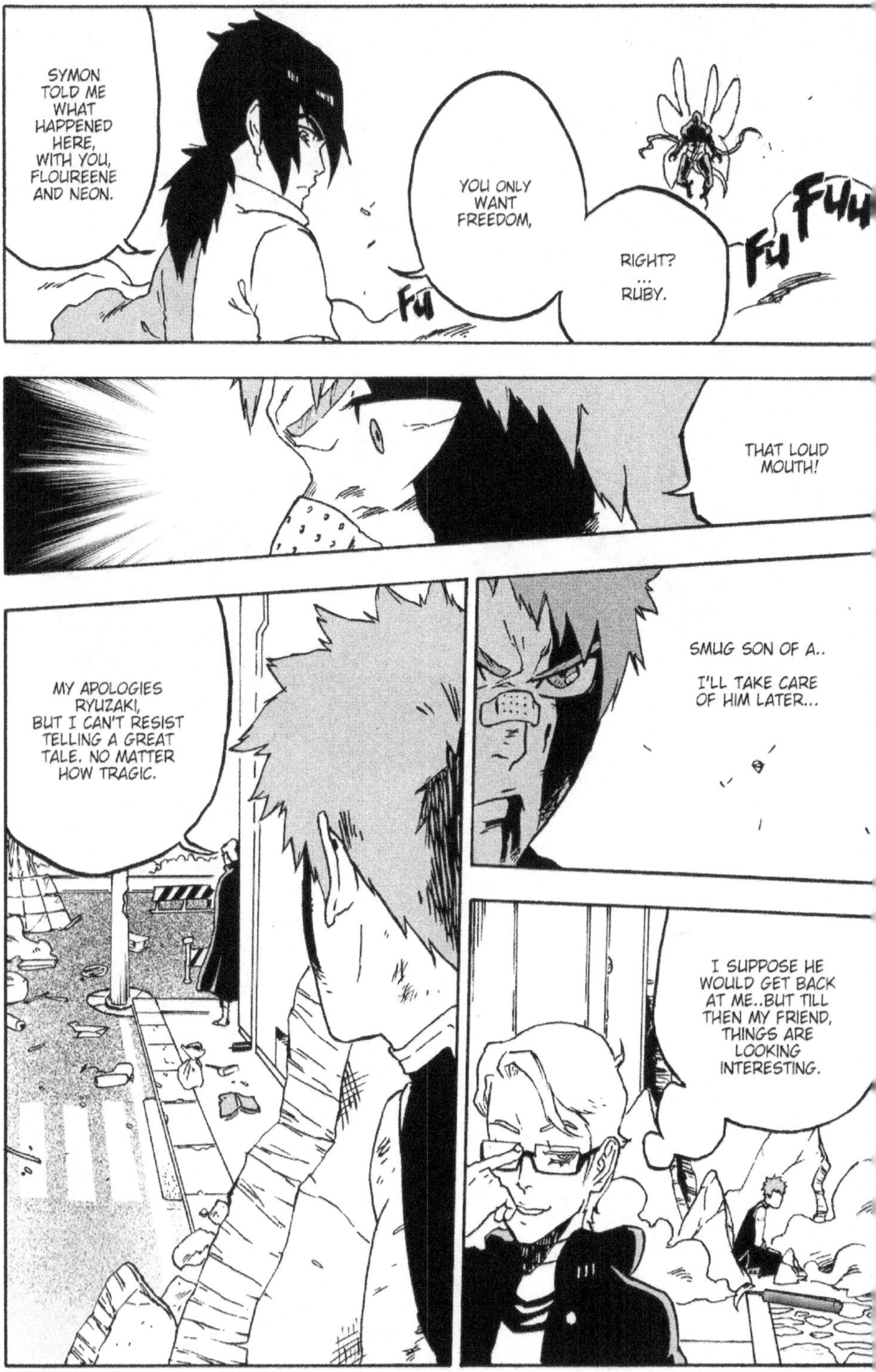
SYMON TOLD ME WHAT HAPPENED HERE, WITH YOU, FLOUREENE AND NEON.
YOU ONLY WANT FREEDOM,
RIGHT? ... RUBY.
FU
FU FUU
THAT LOUD MOUTH!
MY APOLOGIES RYUZAKI, BUT I CAN'T RESIST TELLING A GREAT TALE. NO MATTER HOW TRAGIC.
SMUG SON OF A..
I'LL TAKE CARE OF HIM LATER...
I SUPPOSE HE WOULD GET BACK AT ME..BUT TILL THEN MY FRIEND, THINGS ARE LOOKING INTERESTING.

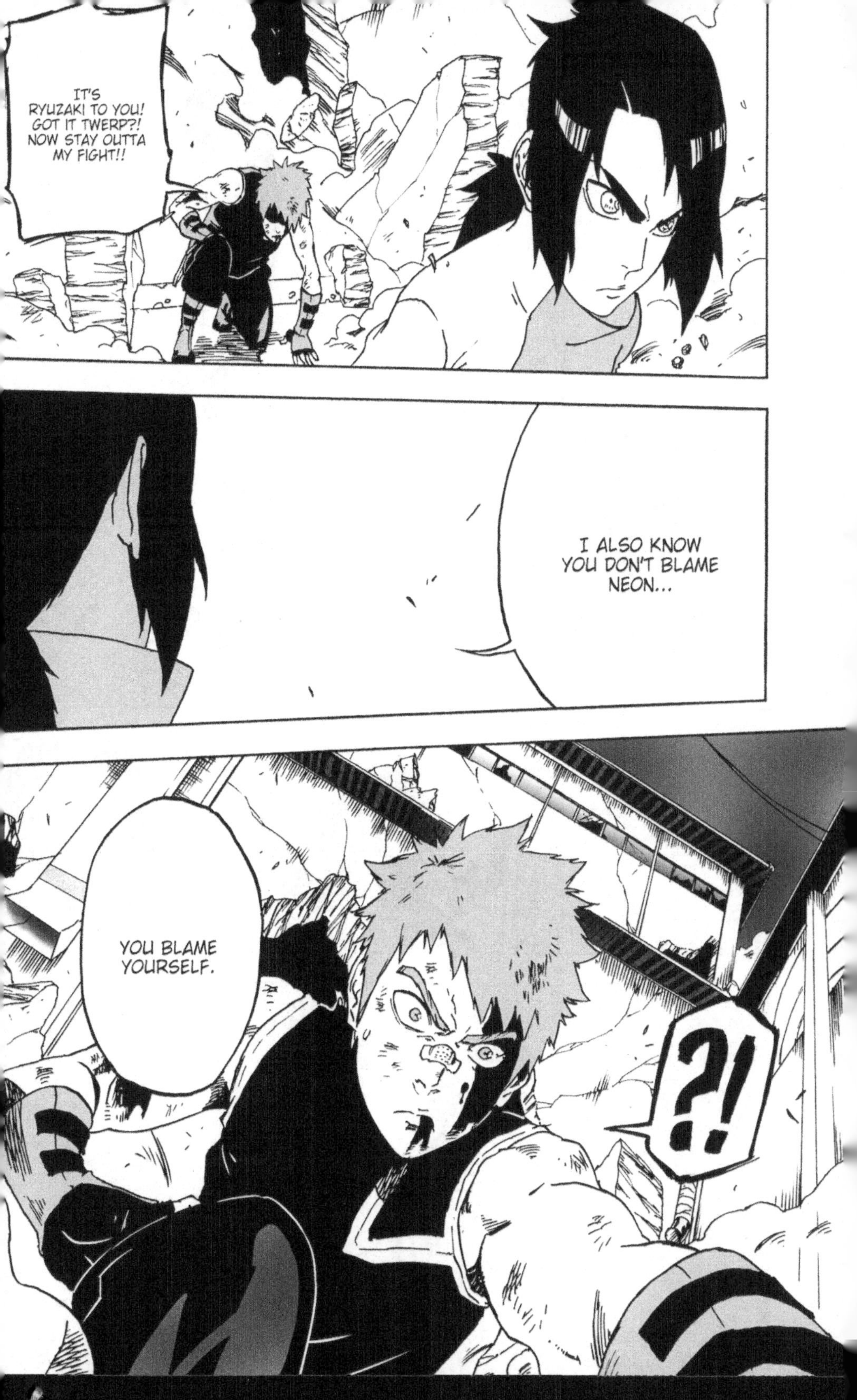
IT'S RYUZAKI TO YOU! GOT IT TWERP?! NOW STAY OUTTA MY FIGHT!!
I ALSO KNOW YOU DON'T BLAME NEON...
YOU BLAME YOURSELF.
?!

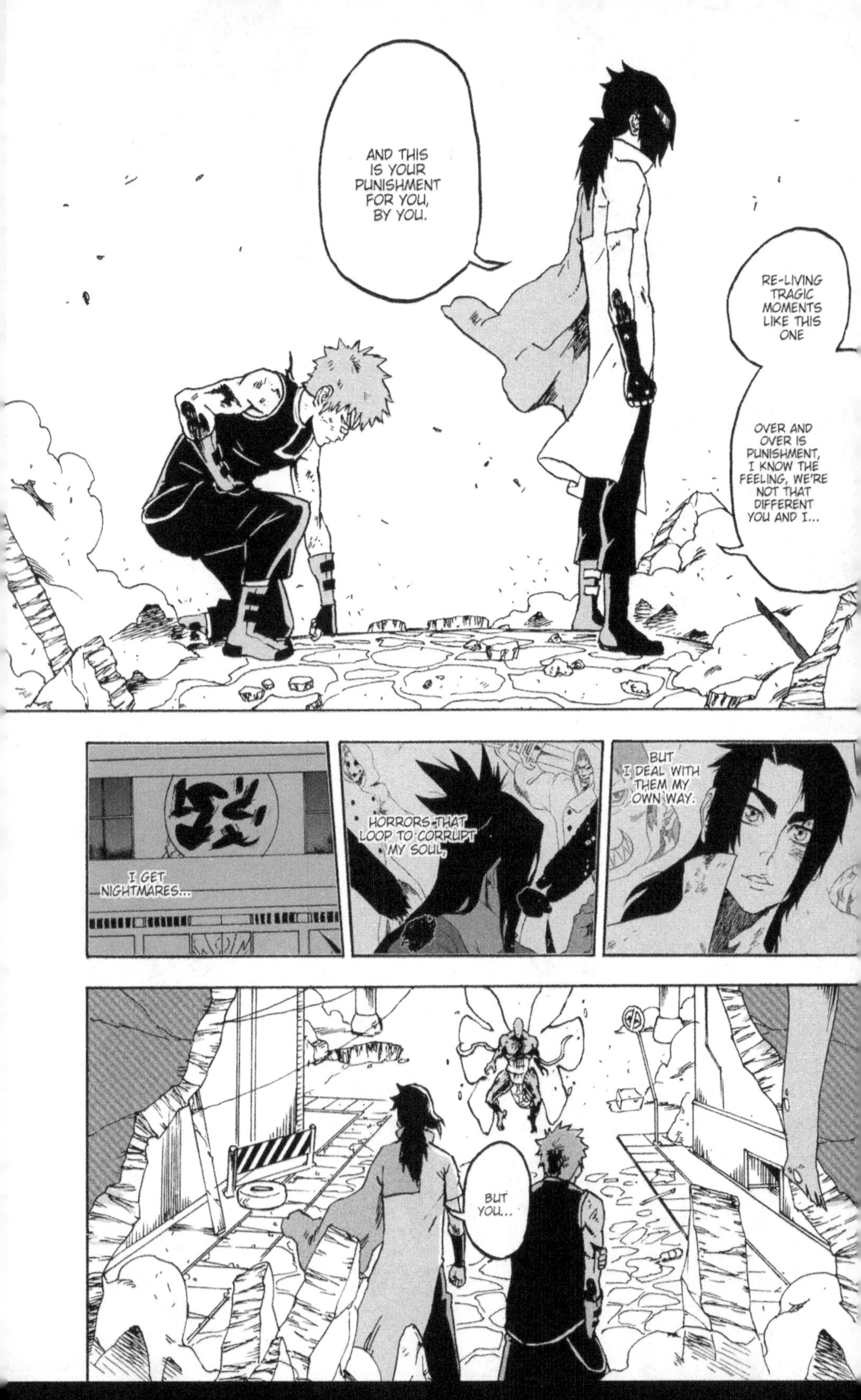
AND THIS IS YOUR PUNISHMENT FOR YOU, BY YOU.
RE-LIVING TRAGIC MOMENTS LIKE THIS ONE
OVER AND OVER IS PUNISHMENT, I KNOW THE FEELING, WE'RE NOT THAT DIFFERENT YOU AND I...
I GET NIGHTMARES...
HORRORS THAT LOOP TO CORRUPT MY SOUL,
BUT I DEAL WITH THEM MY OWN WAY.
BUT YOU...

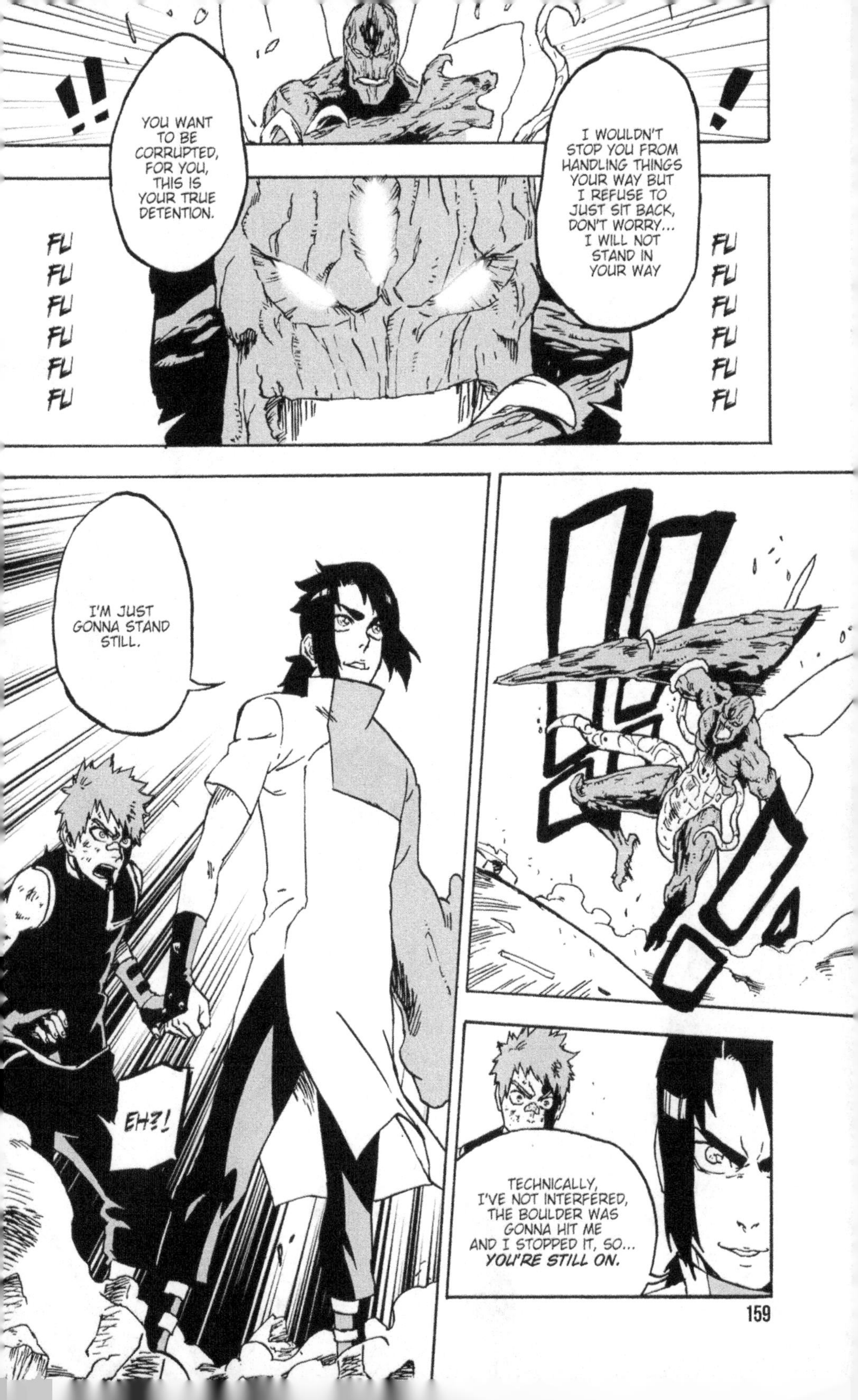
!!
YOU WANT TO BE CORRUPTED, FOR YOU, THIS IS YOUR TRUE DETENTION.
I WOULDN'T STOP YOU FROM HANDLING THINGS YOUR WAY BUT I REFUSE TO JUST SIT BACK, DON'T WORRY... I WILL NOT STAND IN YOUR WAY
!
FU FU FU FU FU FU
FU FU FU FU FU FU
I'M JUST GONNA STAND STILL.
EH?!
TECHNICALLY, I'VE NOT INTERFERED, THE BOULDER WAS GONNA HIT ME AND I STOPPED IT, SO... ***YOU'RE STILL ON.***

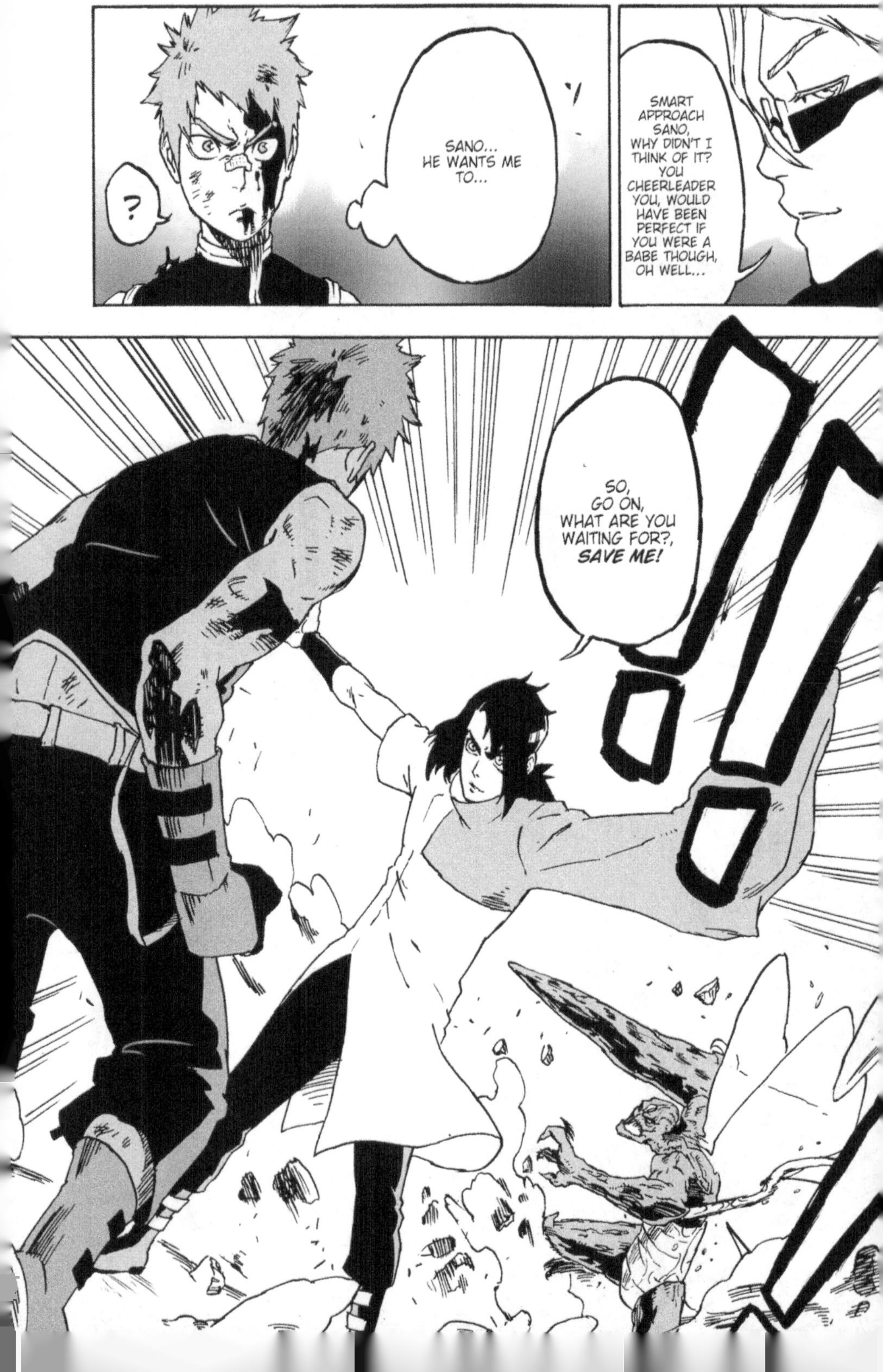
?
SANO... HE WANTS ME TO...
SMART APPROACH SANO, WHY DIDN'T I THINK OF IT? YOU CHEERLEADER YOU, WOULD HAVE BEEN PERFECT IF YOU WERE A BABE THOUGH, OH WELL...
SO, GO ON, WHAT ARE YOU WAITING FOR?, **SAVE ME!**

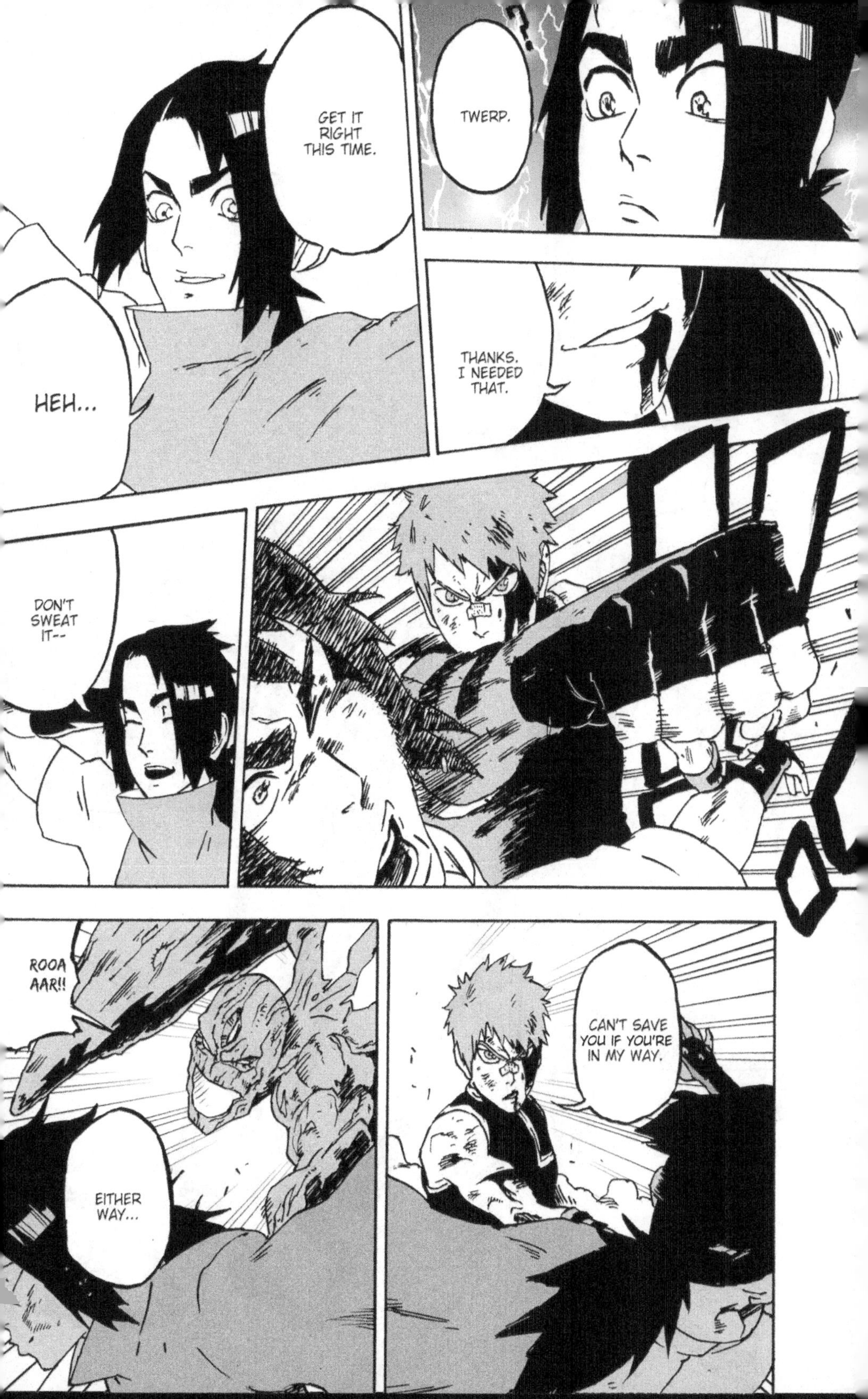
GET IT RIGHT THIS TIME.
TWERP.
HEH...
THANKS. I NEEDED THAT.
DON'T SWEAT IT--
ROOA AAR!!
EITHER WAY...
CAN'T SAVE YOU IF YOU'RE IN MY WAY.

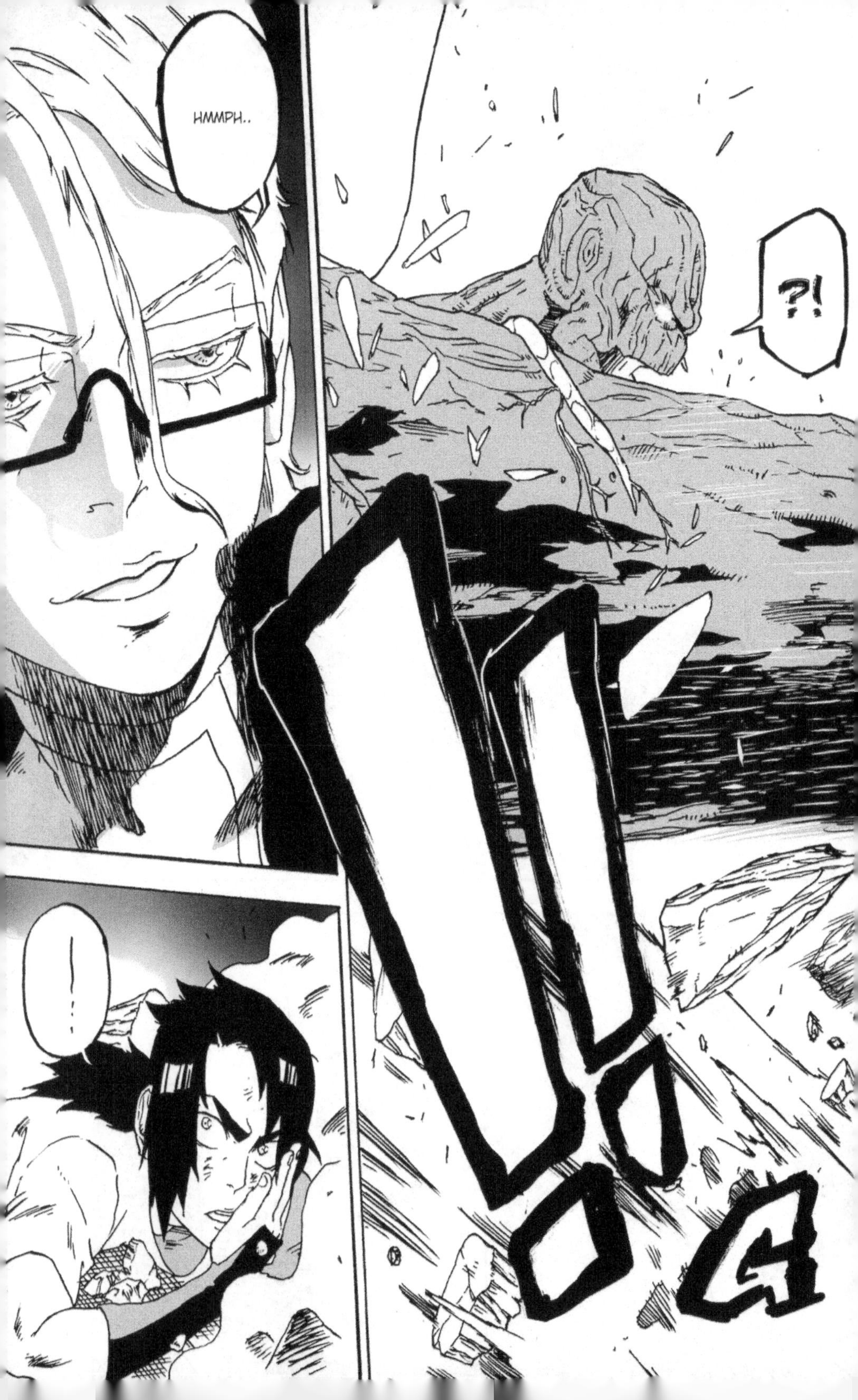
HMMPH..
?!
...!
!!

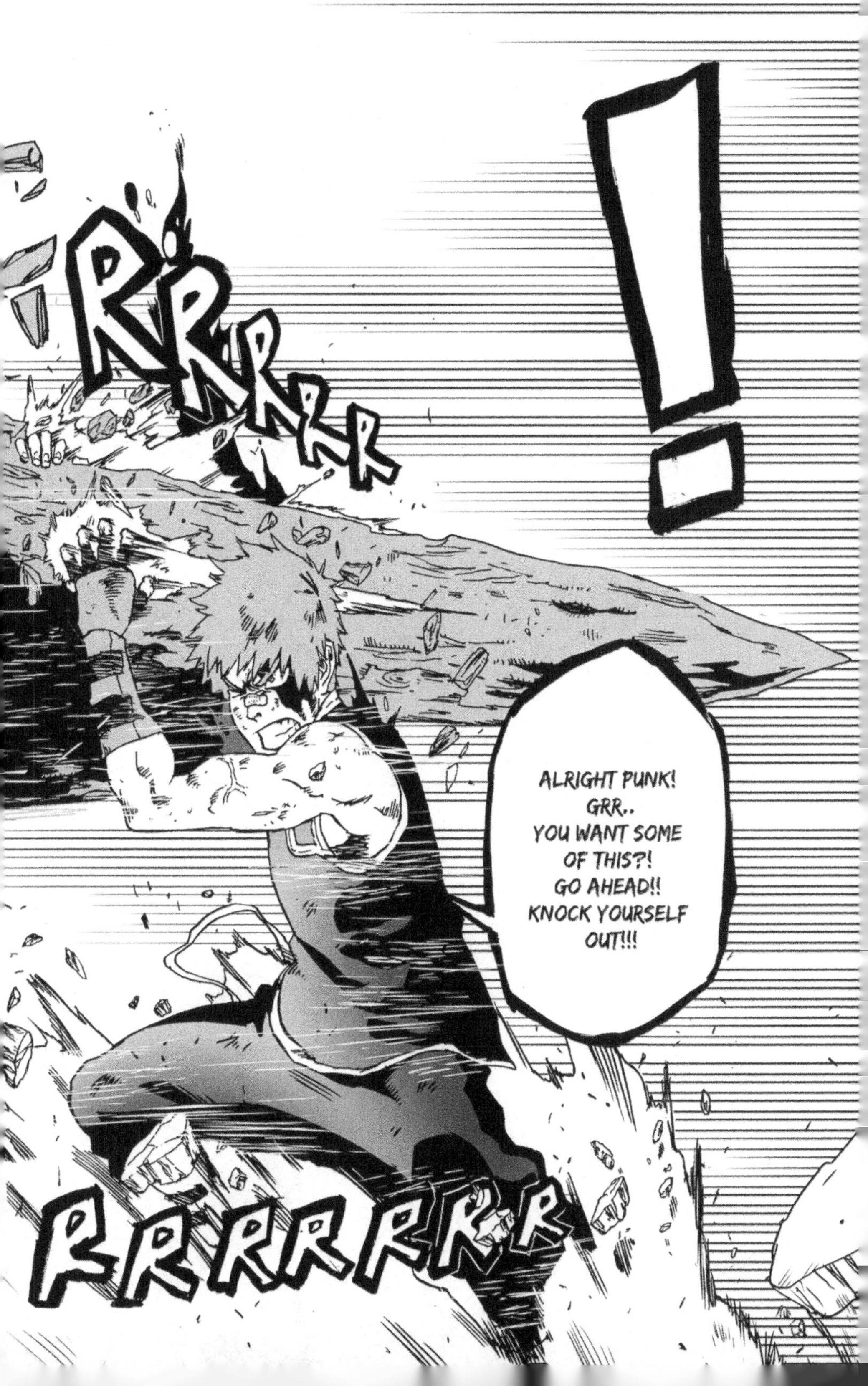
RRRRRR
!
ALRIGHT PUNK! GRR.. YOU WANT SOME OF THIS?! GO AHEAD!! KNOCK YOURSELF OUT!!!
RRRRRRRR

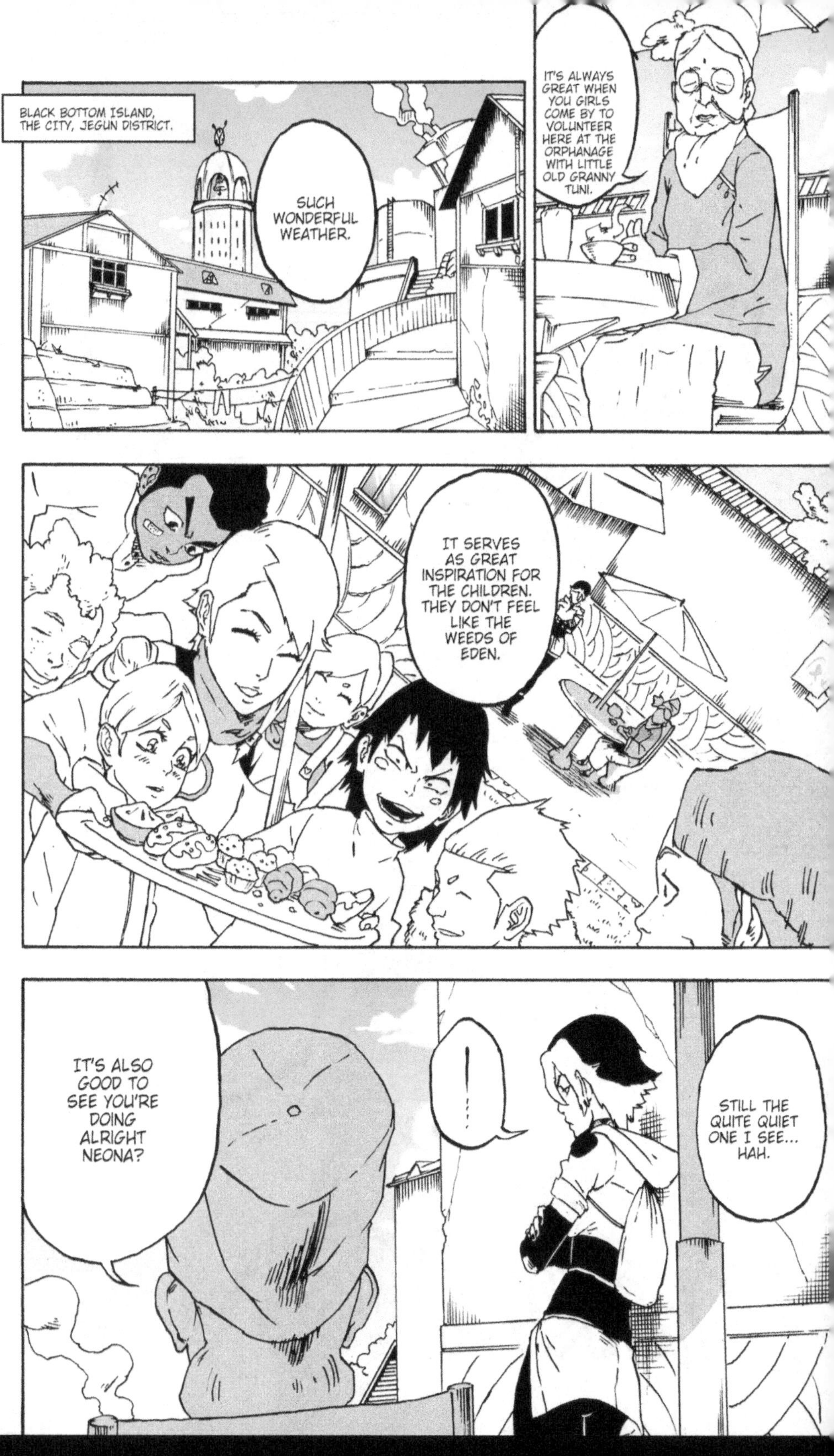
BLACK BOTTOM ISLAND, THE CITY, JEGUN DISTRICT.
SUCH WONDERFUL WEATHER.
IT'S ALWAYS GREAT WHEN YOU GIRLS COME BY TO VOLUNTEER HERE AT THE ORPHANAGE WITH LITTLE OLD GRANNY TUNI.
IT SERVES AS GREAT INSPIRATION FOR THE CHILDREN. THEY DON'T FEEL LIKE THE WEEDS OF EDEN.
IT'S ALSO GOOD TO SEE YOU'RE DOING ALRIGHT NEONA?
!
STILL THE QUITE QUIET ONE I SEE... HAH.

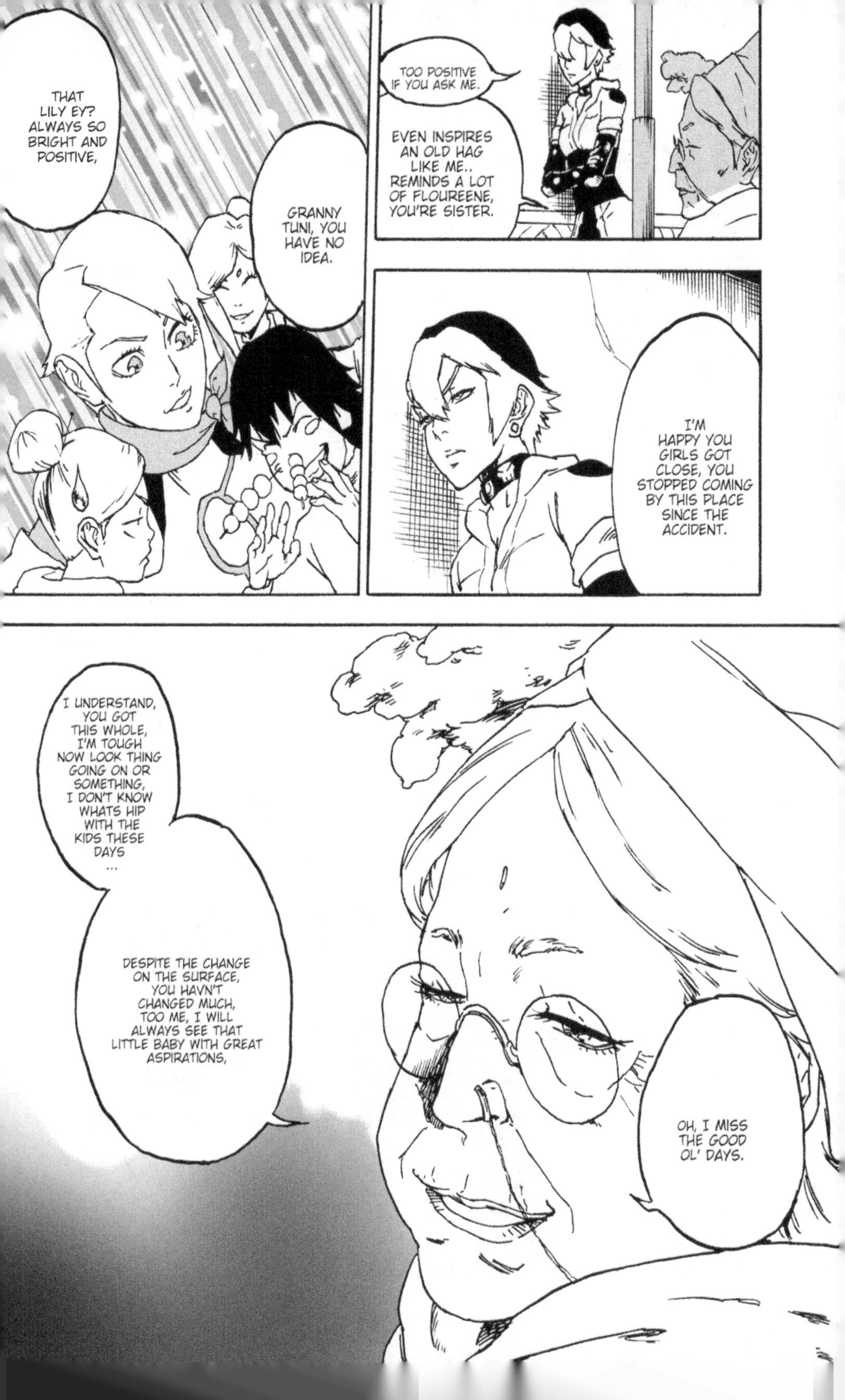
THAT LILY EY? ALWAYS SO BRIGHT AND POSITIVE,
GRANNY TUNI, YOU HAVE NO IDEA.
TOO POSITIVE IF YOU ASK ME.
EVEN INSPIRES AN OLD HAG LIKE ME.. REMINDS A LOT OF FLOUREENE, YOU'RE SISTER.
I'M HAPPY YOU GIRLS GOT CLOSE, YOU STOPPED COMING BY THIS PLACE SINCE THE ACCIDENT.
I UNDERSTAND, YOU GOT THIS WHOLE, I'M TOUGH NOW LOOK THING GOING ON OR SOMETHING, I DON'T KNOW WHATS HIP WITH THE KIDS THESE DAYS ...
DESPITE THE CHANGE ON THE SURFACE, YOU HAVN'T CHANGED MUCH, TOO ME, I WILL ALWAYS SEE THAT LITTLE BABY WITH GREAT ASPIRATIONS,
OH, I MISS THE GOOD OL' DAYS.

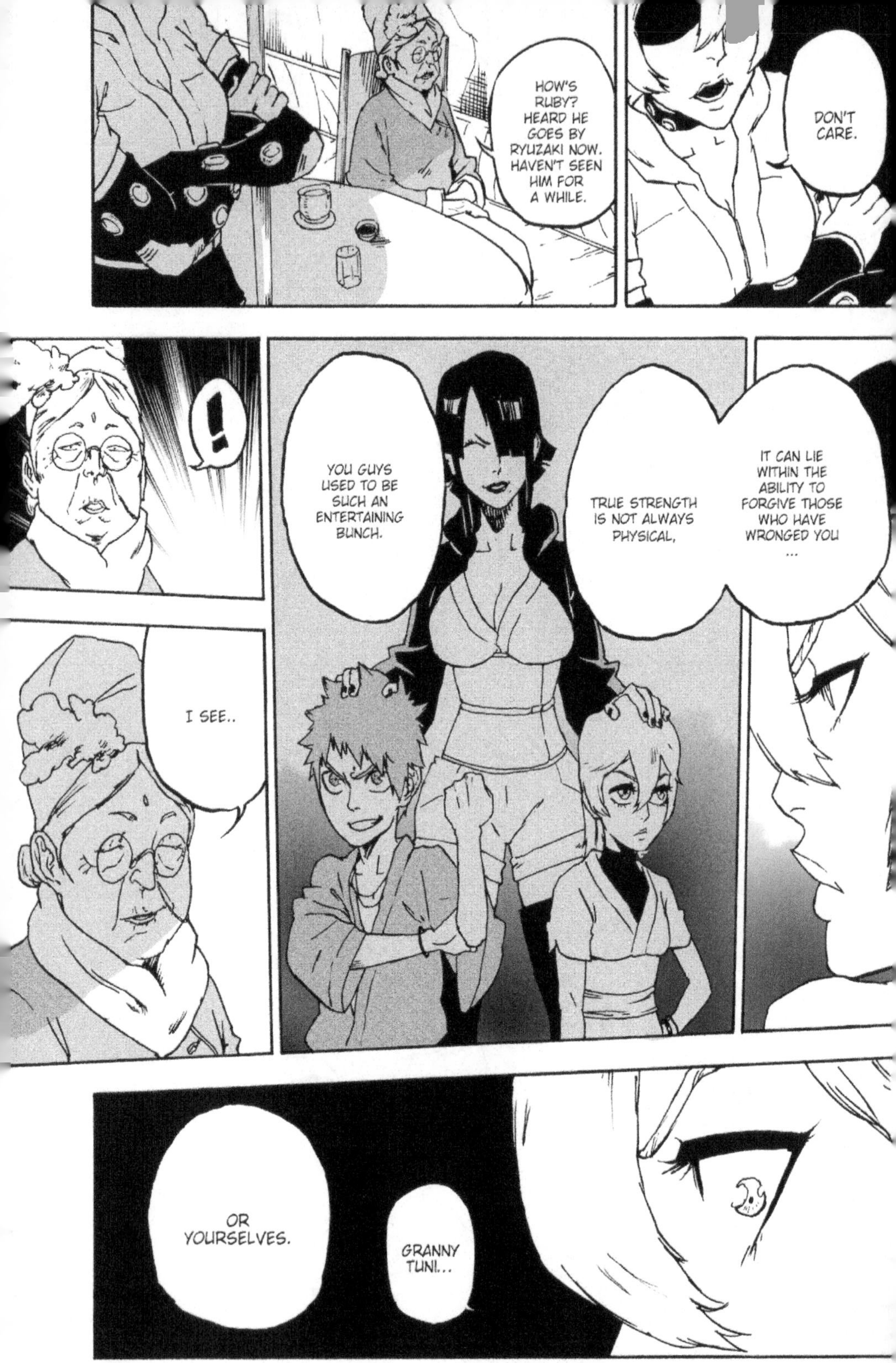
HOW'S RUBY? HEARD HE GOES BY RYUZAKI NOW. HAVEN'T SEEN HIM FOR A WHILE.
DON'T CARE.
!
YOU GUYS USED TO BE SUCH AN ENTERTAINING BUNCH.
TRUE STRENGTH IS NOT ALWAYS PHYSICAL,
IT CAN LIE WITHIN THE ABILITY TO FORGIVE THOSE WHO HAVE WRONGED YOU ...
I SEE..
OR YOURSELVES.
GRANNY TUNI...

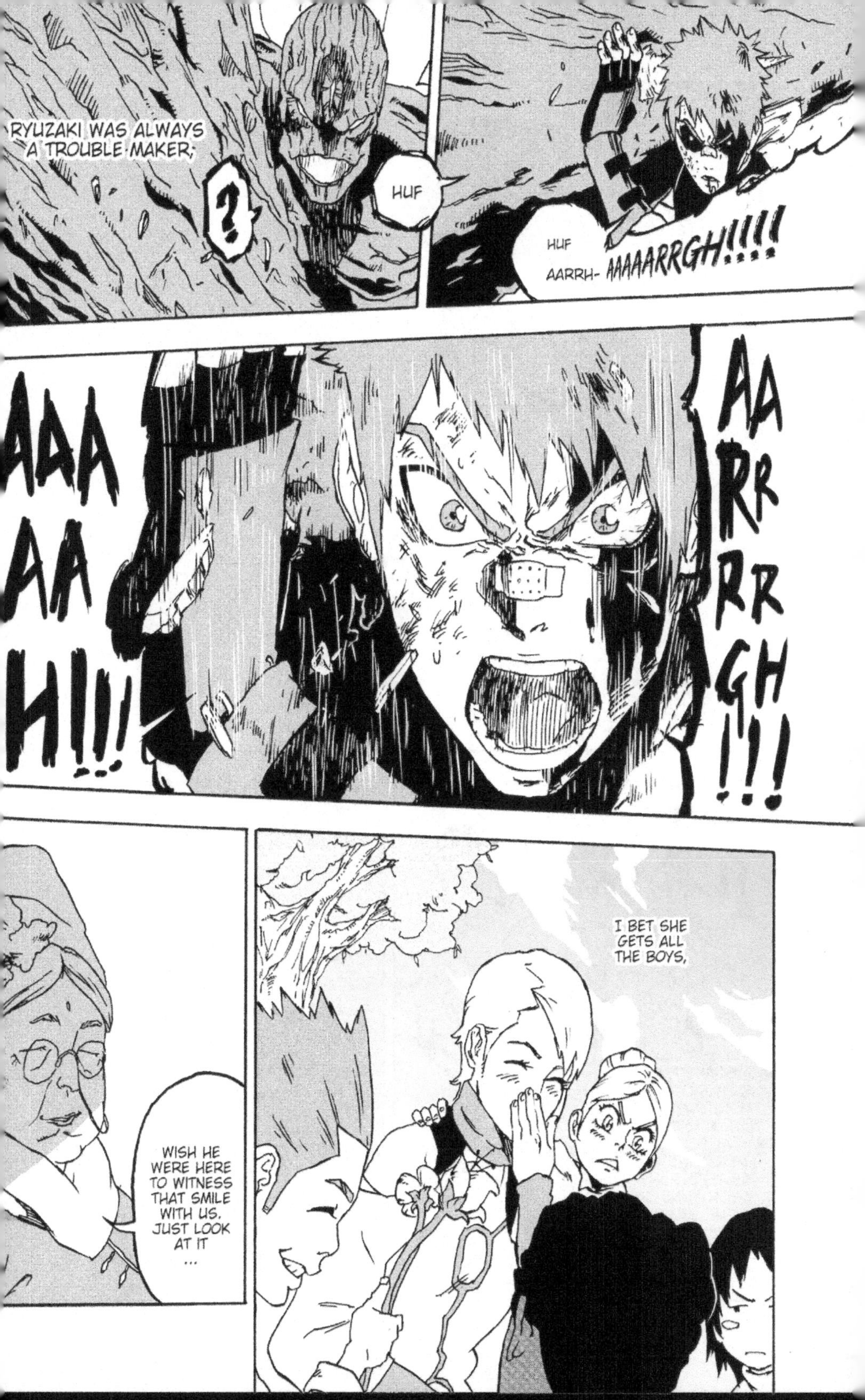
RYUZAKI WAS ALWAYS A TROUBLE MAKER;
?
HUF
HUF
AARRH- AAAAARRGH!!!!
AAAAAH!!!
AARRRRGH!!!
WISH HE WERE HERE TO WITNESS THAT SMILE WITH US. JUST LOOK AT IT ...
I BET SHE GETS ALL THE BOYS,

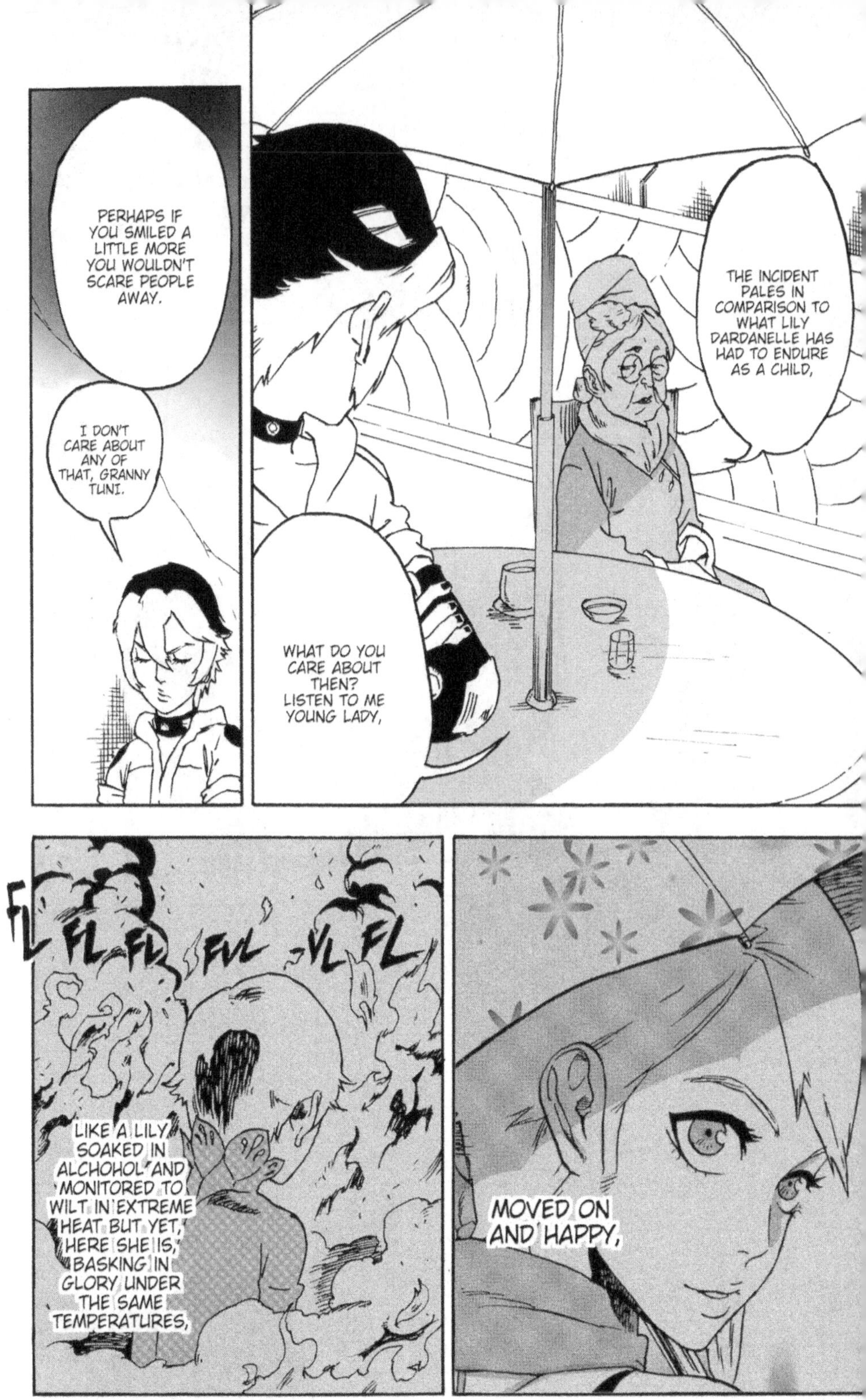

PERHAPS IF YOU SMILED A LITTLE MORE YOU WOULDN'T SCARE PEOPLE AWAY.
I DON'T CARE ABOUT ANY OF THAT, GRANNY TUNI.
WHAT DO YOU CARE ABOUT THEN? LISTEN TO ME YOUNG LADY,
THE INCIDENT PALES IN COMPARISON TO WHAT LILY DARDANELLE HAS HAD TO ENDURE AS A CHILD,
FL FL FL FVL -VL FL
LIKE A LILY SOAKED IN ALCHOHOL AND MONITORED TO WILT IN EXTREME HEAT BUT YET, HERE SHE IS, BASKING IN GLORY UNDER THE SAME TEMPERATURES,
MOVED ON AND HAPPY,

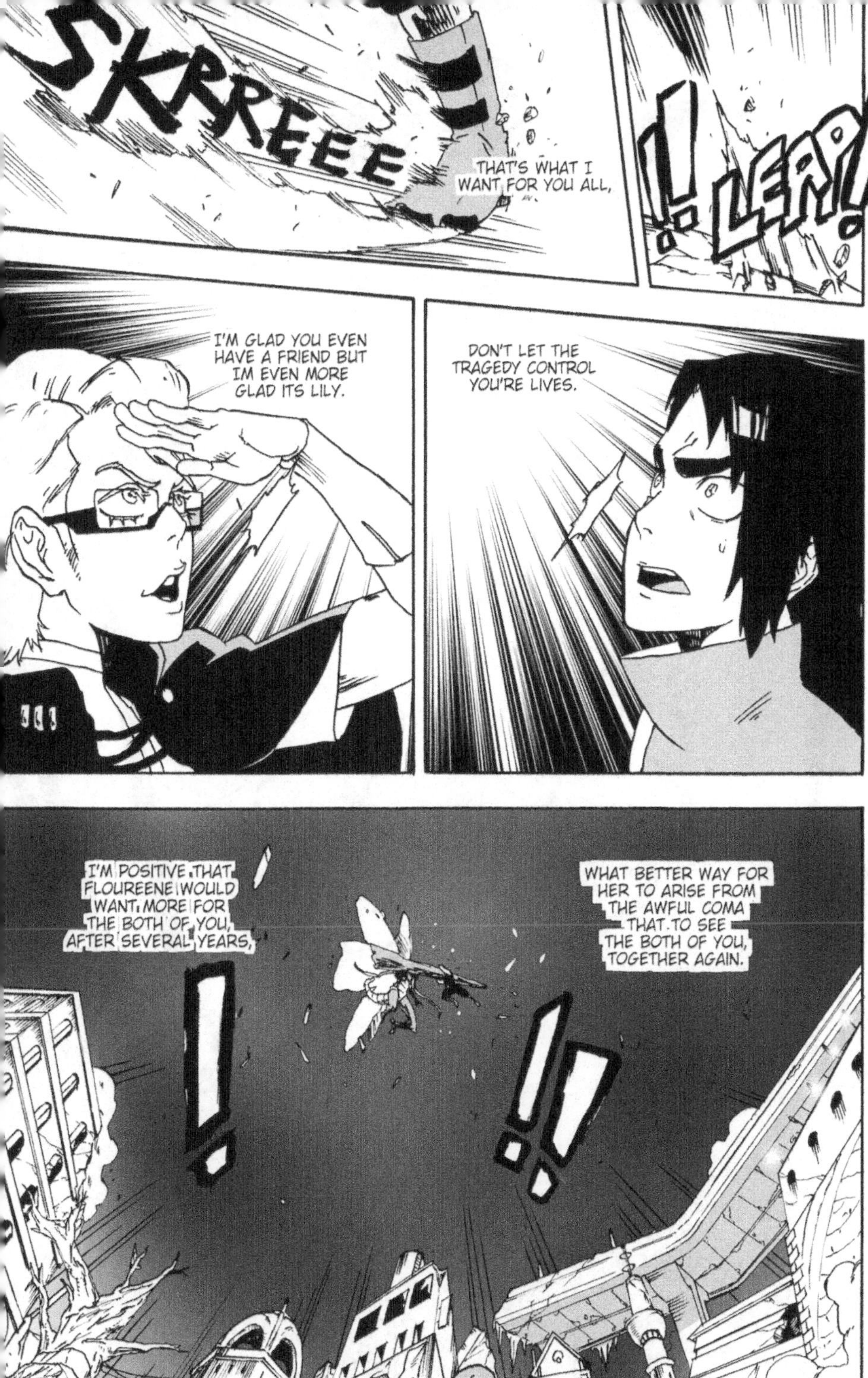
SKRREEEE
THAT'S WHAT I WANT FOR YOU ALL,
!! LEAP!
I'M GLAD YOU EVEN HAVE A FRIEND BUT IM EVEN MORE GLAD ITS LILY.
DON'T LET THE TRAGEDY CONTROL YOU'RE LIVES.
I'M POSITIVE THAT FLOUREENE WOULD WANT MORE FOR THE BOTH OF YOU, AFTER SEVERAL YEARS,
WHAT BETTER WAY FOR HER TO ARISE FROM THE AWFUL COMA THAT TO SEE THE BOTH OF YOU, TOGETHER AGAIN.
!
!!

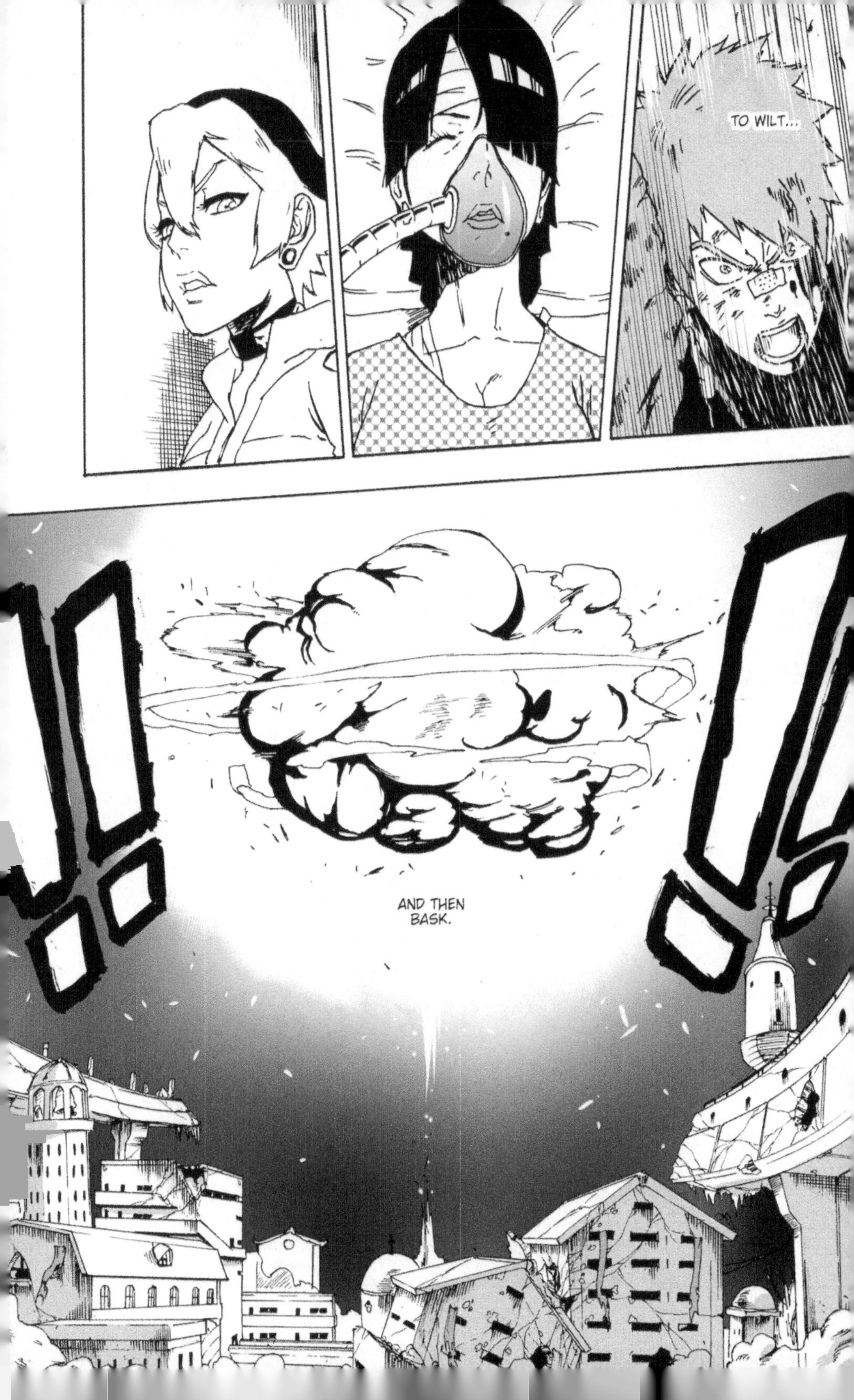
TO WILT...
!!
AND THEN
BASK.
!!

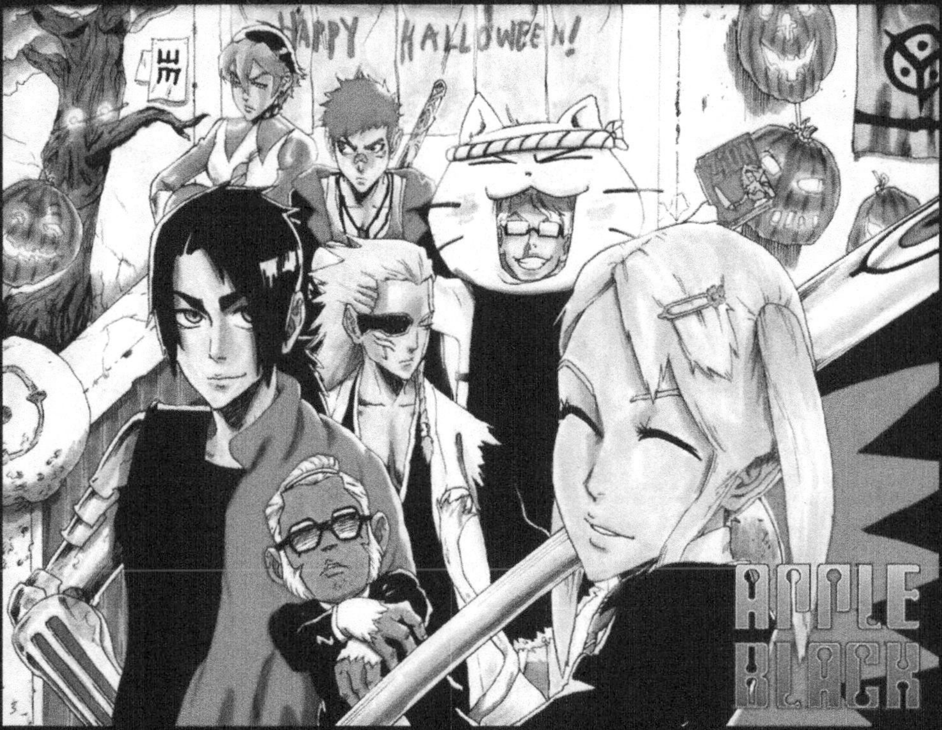
HAPPY HALLOWEEN!
APPLE BLACK

I USUALLY DRAW AN APPLE BLACK HALLOWEEN DRAWING EVERY YEAR AT THE APPROPRIATE TIME.
THIS PIECE OF ARTWORK HAD MY CHARACTER DRESS UP AS OTHER CHARACTERS FROM POP CULTURE.
DONE IN 2012.

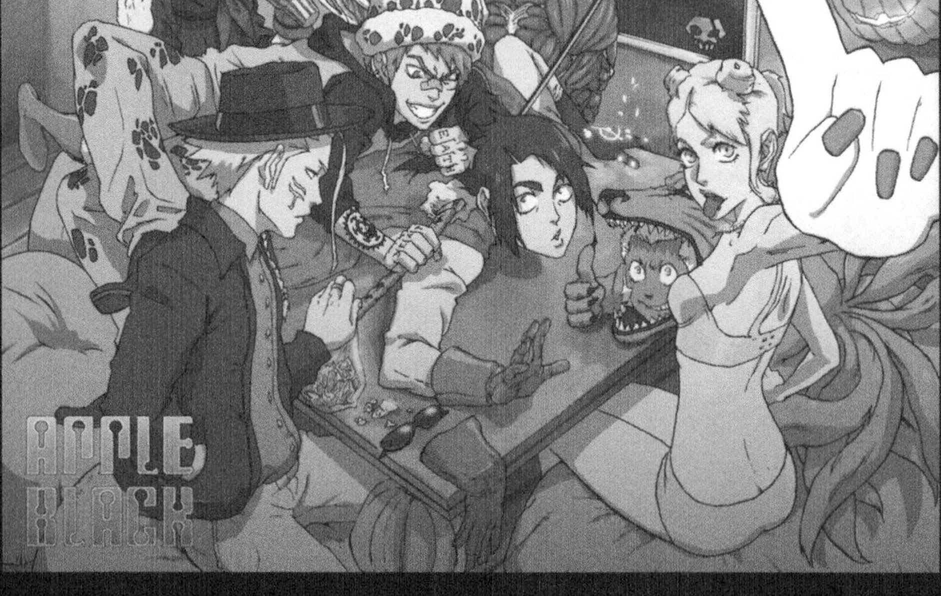
KALI BON!
APPLE BLACK

THIS WAS DONE IN 2013, CAN YOU NAME ALL THE CHARACTERS SANO AND THE REST OF THE GANG ARE DRESSED UP AS?

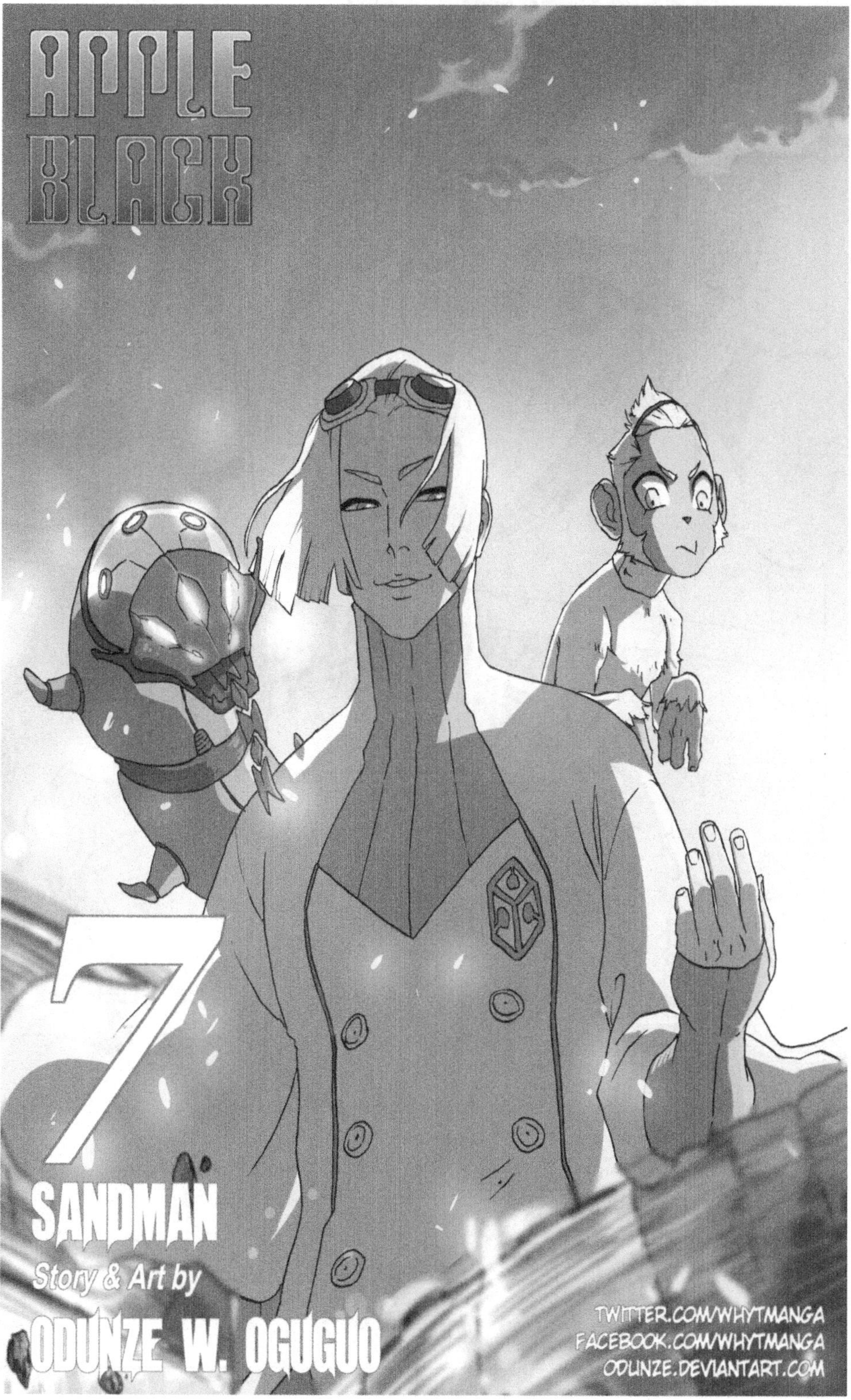
APPLE BLACK
7
SANDMAN
Story & Art by
ODUNZE W. OGUGUO
TWITTER.COM/WHYTMANGA
FACEBOOK.COM/WHYTMANGA
ODUNZE.DEVIANTART.COM

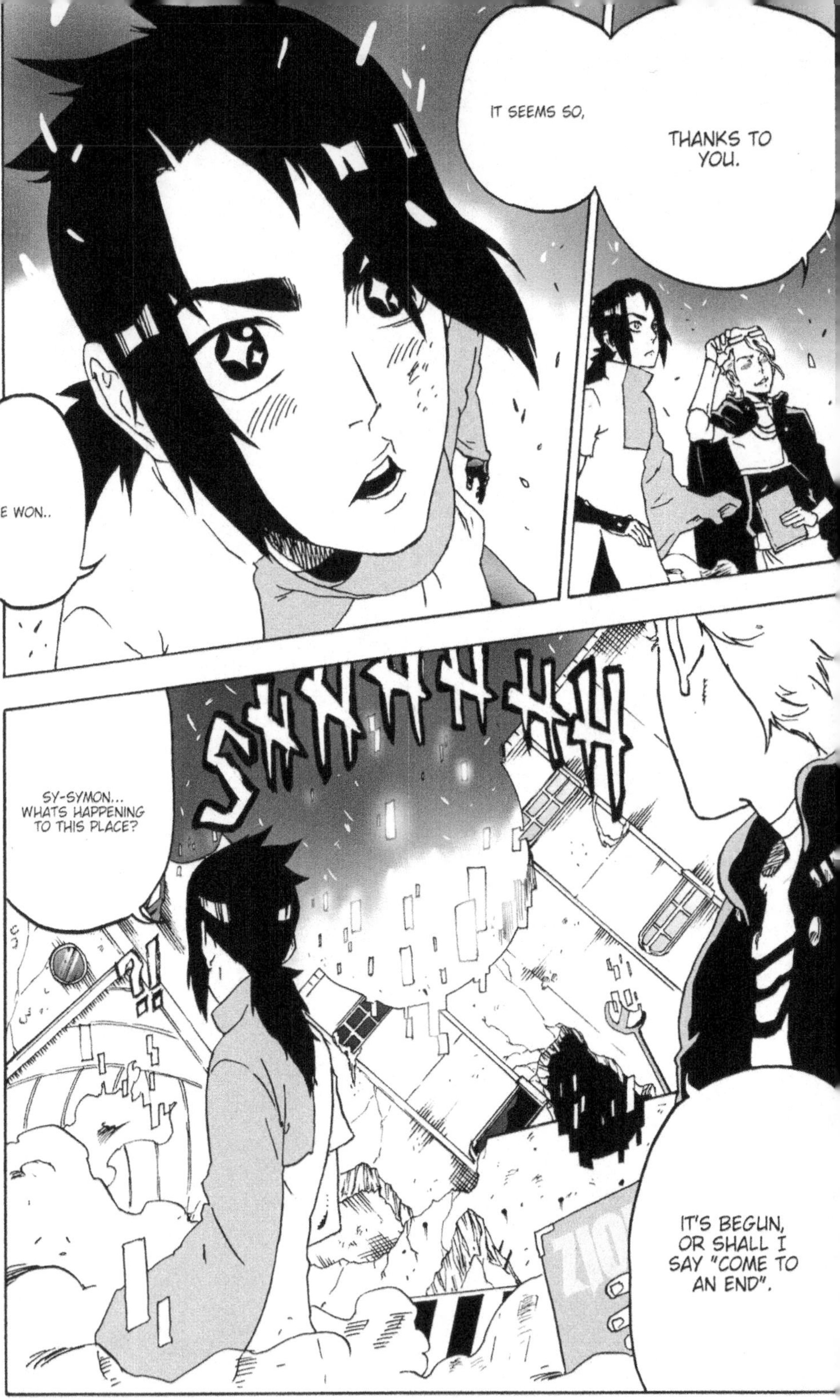
HE WON..
IT SEEMS SO,
THANKS TO YOU.
SY-SYMON... WHATS HAPPENING TO THIS PLACE?
IT'S BEGUN, OR SHALL I SAY "COME TO AN END".

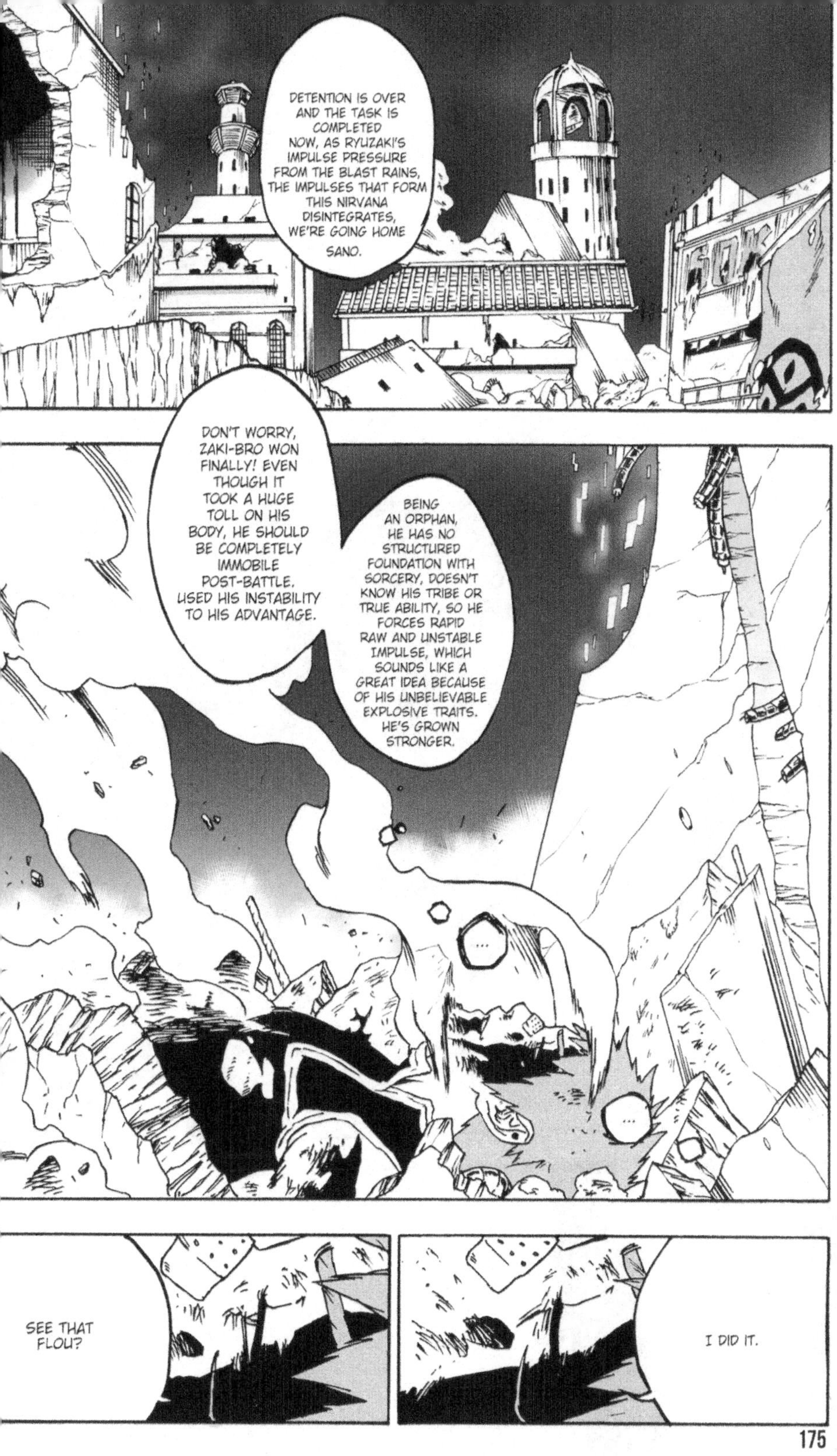
DETENTION IS OVER AND THE TASK IS COMPLETED NOW, AS RYUZAKI'S IMPULSE PRESSURE FROM THE BLAST RAINS, THE IMPULSES THAT FORM THIS NIRVANA DISINTEGRATES, WE'RE GOING HOME SANO.
DON'T WORRY, ZAKI-BRO WON FINALLY! EVEN THOUGH IT TOOK A HUGE TOLL ON HIS BODY, HE SHOULD BE COMPLETELY IMMOBILE POST-BATTLE. USED HIS INSTABILITY TO HIS ADVANTAGE.
BEING AN ORPHAN, HE HAS NO STRUCTURED FOUNDATION WITH SORCERY, DOESN'T KNOW HIS TRIBE OR TRUE ABILITY, SO HE FORCES RAPID RAW AND UNSTABLE IMPULSE, WHICH SOUNDS LIKE A GREAT IDEA BECAUSE OF HIS UNBELIEVABLE EXPLOSIVE TRAITS. HE'S GROWN STRONGER.
...
...
SEE THAT FLOU?
I DID IT.

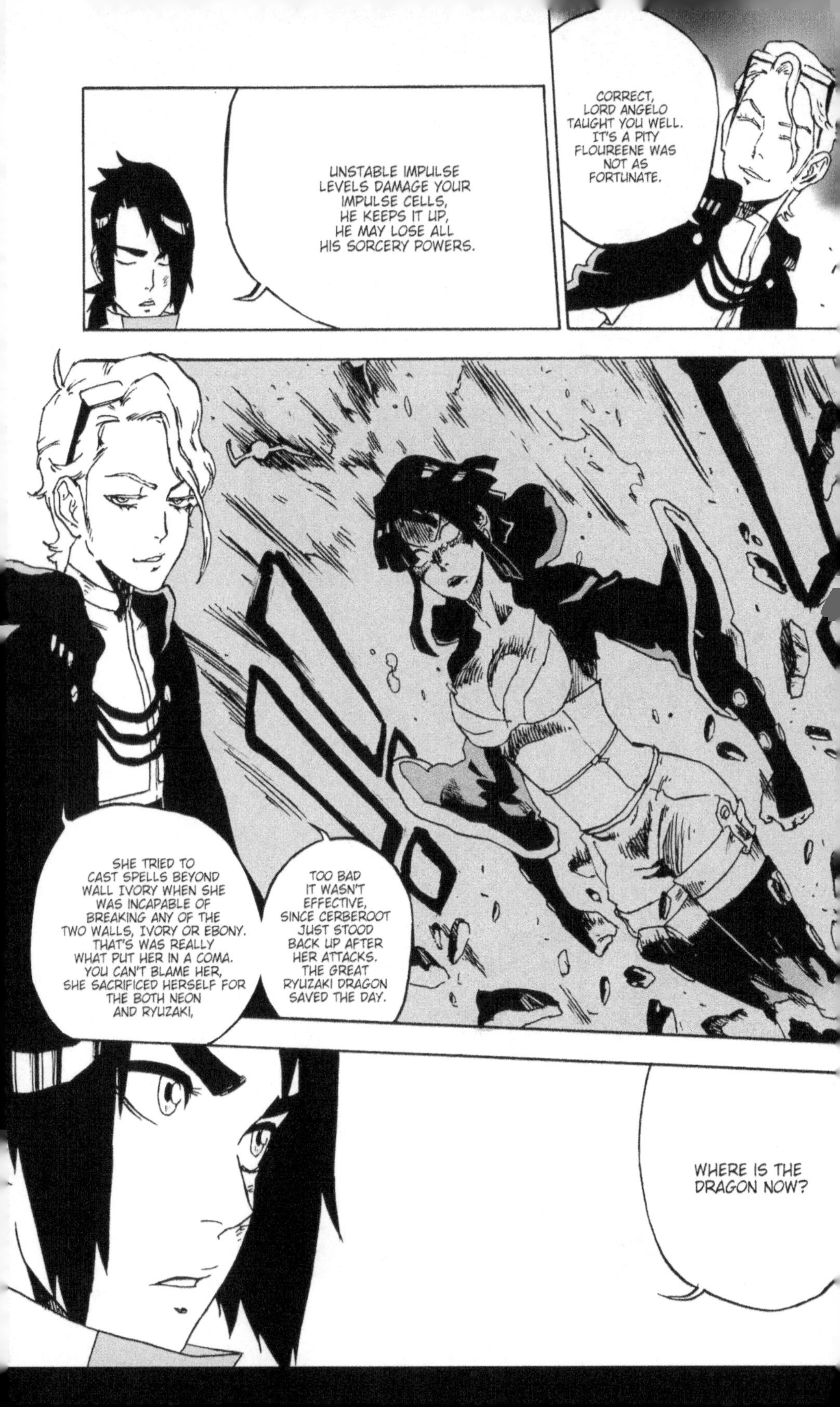
UNSTABLE IMPULSE LEVELS DAMAGE YOUR IMPULSE CELLS, HE KEEPS IT UP, HE MAY LOSE ALL HIS SORCERY POWERS.
CORRECT, LORD ANGELO TAUGHT YOU WELL. IT'S A PITY FLOUREENE WAS NOT AS FORTUNATE.
SHE TRIED TO CAST SPELLS BEYOND WALL IVORY WHEN SHE WAS INCAPABLE OF BREAKING ANY OF THE TWO WALLS, IVORY OR EBONY. THAT'S WAS REALLY WHAT PUT HER IN A COMA. YOU CAN'T BLAME HER, SHE SACRIFICED HERSELF FOR THE BOTH NEON AND RYUZAKI,
TOO BAD IT WASN'T EFFECTIVE, SINCE CERBEROOT JUST STOOD BACK UP AFTER HER ATTACKS. THE GREAT RYUZAKI DRAGON SAVED THE DAY.
WHERE IS THE DRAGON NOW?

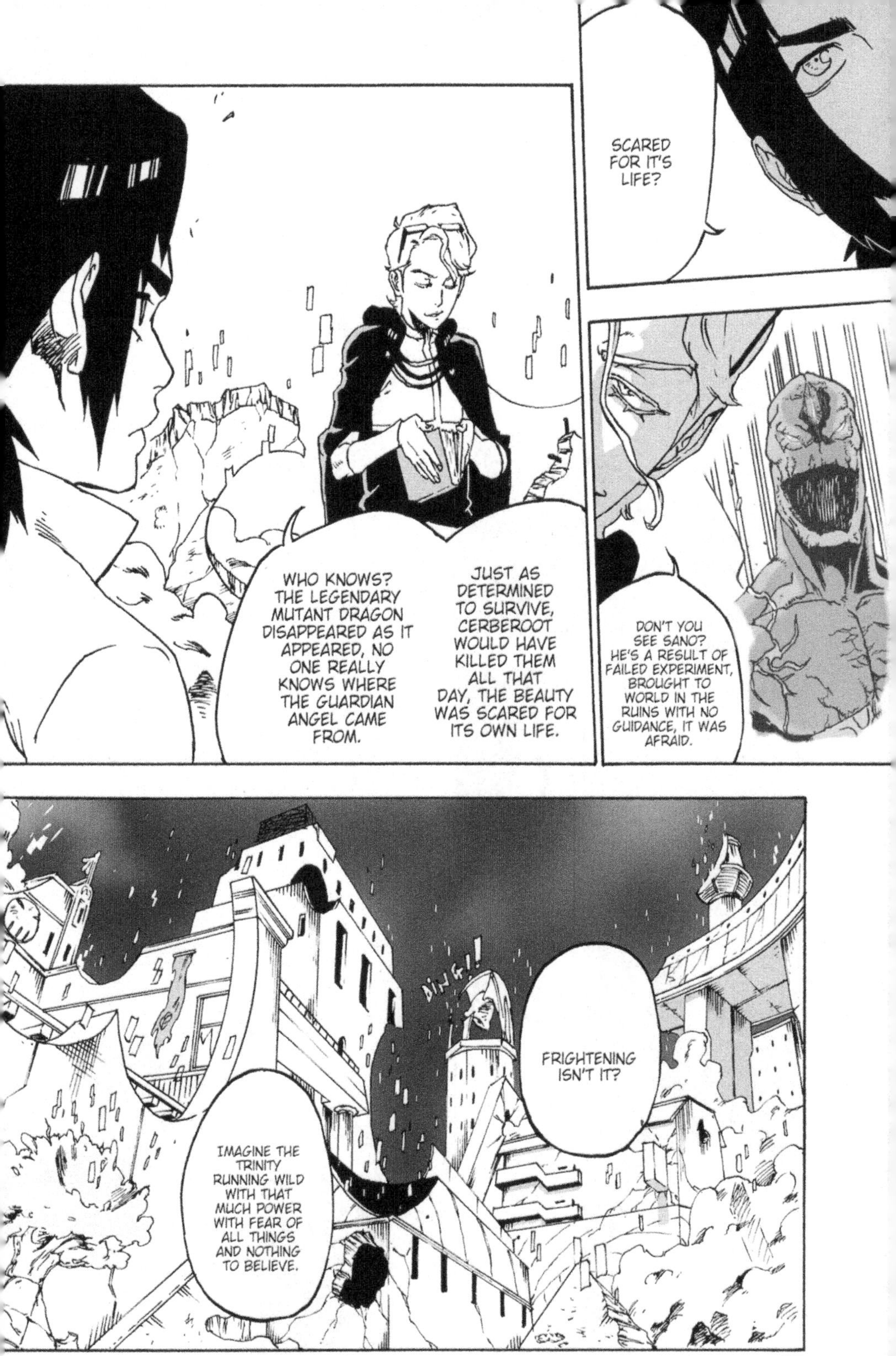
WHO KNOWS? THE LEGENDARY MUTANT DRAGON DISAPPEARED AS IT APPEARED, NO ONE REALLY KNOWS WHERE THE GUARDIAN ANGEL CAME FROM.
JUST AS DETERMINED TO SURVIVE, CERBEROOT WOULD HAVE KILLED THEM ALL THAT DAY, THE BEAUTY WAS SCARED FOR ITS OWN LIFE.
SCARED FOR IT'S LIFE?
DON'T YOU SEE SANO? HE'S A RESULT OF FAILED EXPERIMENT, BROUGHT TO WORLD IN THE RUINS WITH NO GUIDANCE, IT WAS AFRAID.
DING!!
FRIGHTENING ISN'T IT?
IMAGINE THE TRINITY RUNNING WILD WITH THAT MUCH POWER WITH FEAR OF ALL THINGS AND NOTHING TO BELIEVE.

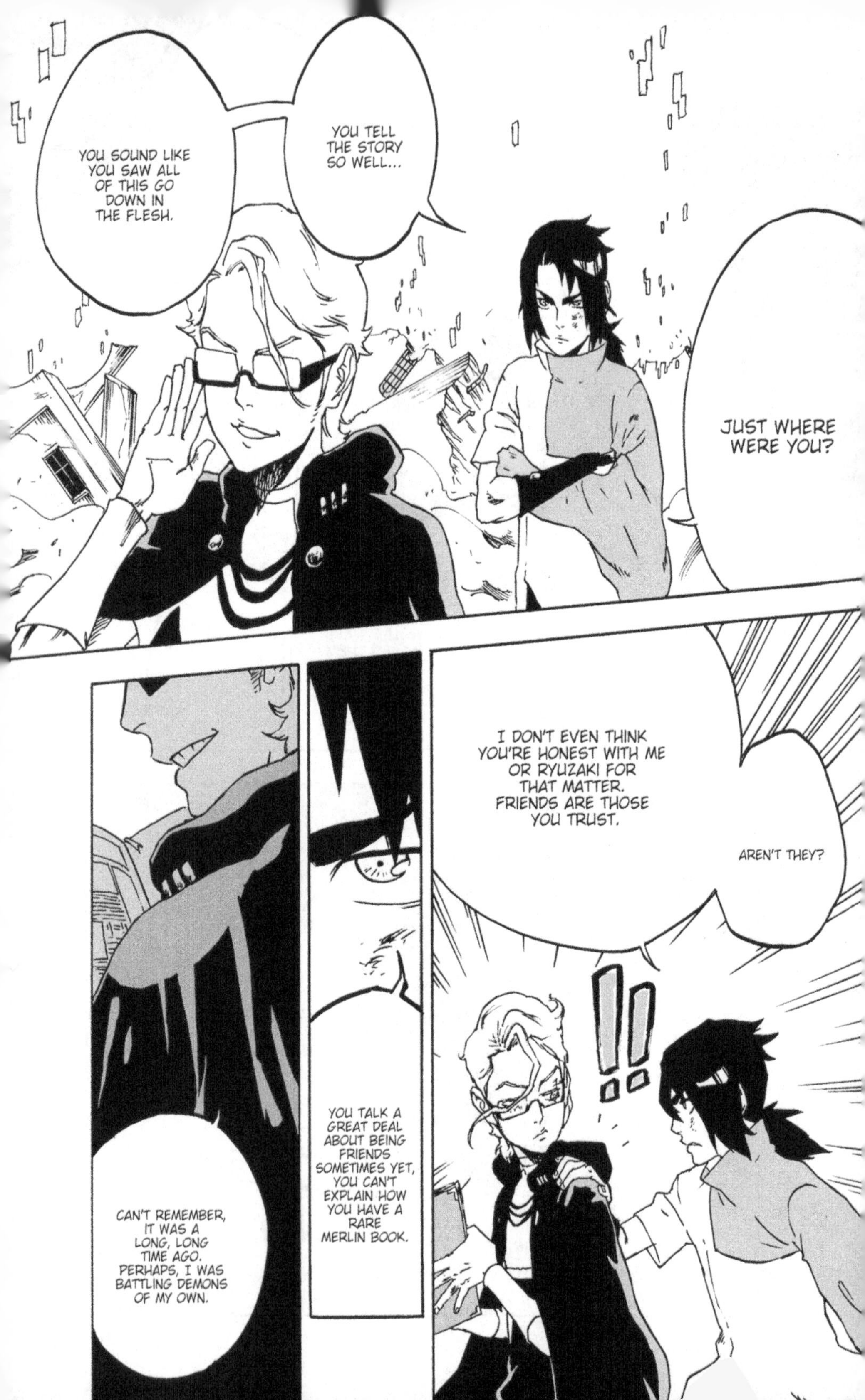
YOU SOUND LIKE YOU SAW ALL OF THIS GO DOWN IN THE FLESH.
YOU TELL THE STORY SO WELL...
JUST WHERE WERE YOU?
CAN'T REMEMBER, IT WAS A LONG, LONG TIME AGO. PERHAPS, I WAS BATTLING DEMONS OF MY OWN.
YOU TALK A GREAT DEAL ABOUT BEING FRIENDS SOMETIMES YET, YOU CAN'T EXPLAIN HOW YOU HAVE A RARE MERLIN BOOK.
I DON'T EVEN THINK YOU'RE HONEST WITH ME OR RYUZAKI FOR THAT MATTER. FRIENDS ARE THOSE YOU TRUST.
AREN'T THEY?
!!

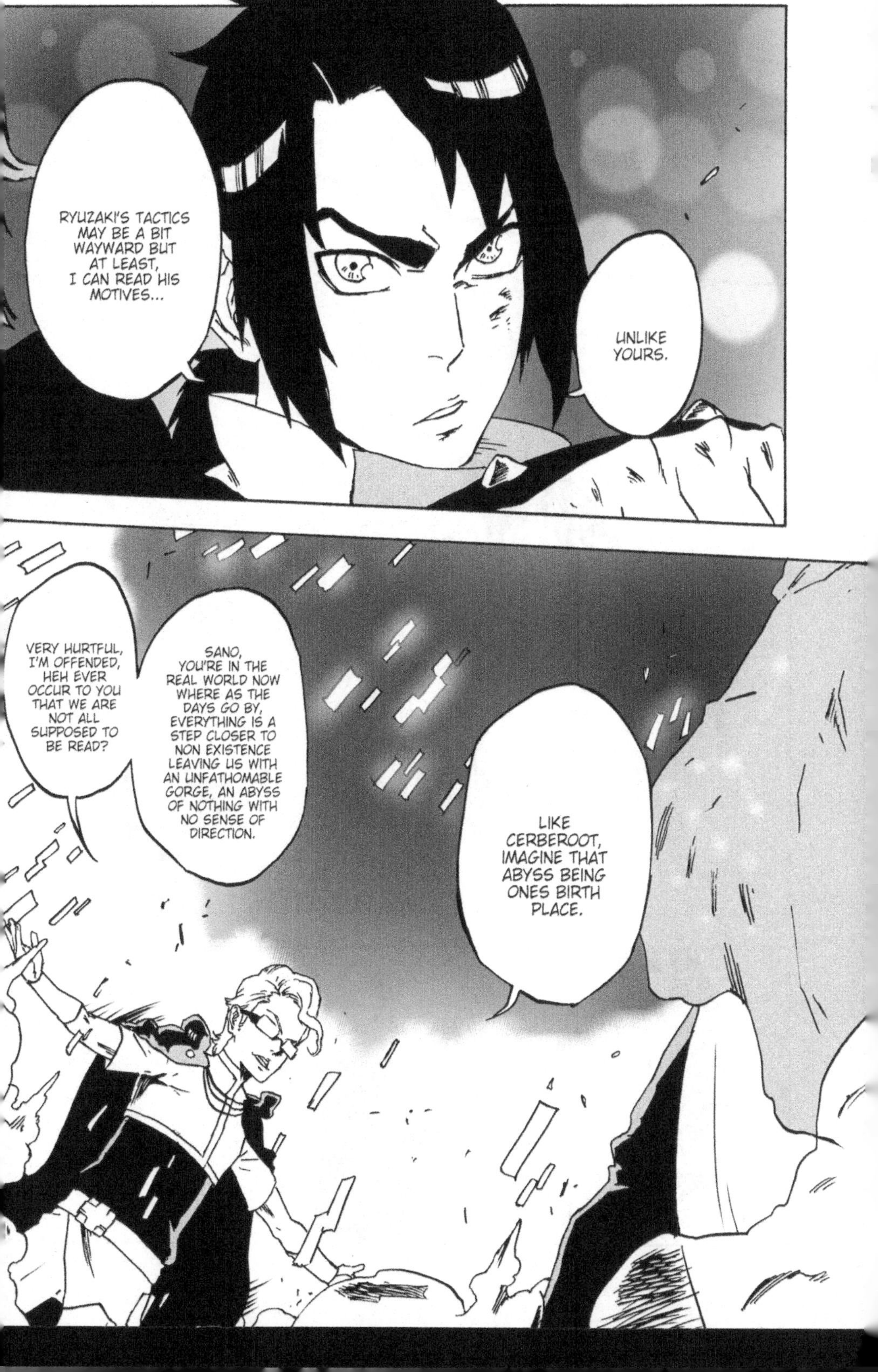
RYUZAKI'S TACTICS MAY BE A BIT WAYWARD BUT AT LEAST, I CAN READ HIS MOTIVES...
UNLIKE YOURS.
VERY HURTFUL, I'M OFFENDED, HEH EVER OCCUR TO YOU THAT WE ARE NOT ALL SUPPOSED TO BE READ?
SANO, YOU'RE IN THE REAL WORLD NOW WHERE AS THE DAYS GO BY, EVERYTHING IS A STEP CLOSER TO NON EXISTENCE LEAVING US WITH AN UNFATHOMABLE GORGE, AN ABYSS OF NOTHING WITH NO SENSE OF DIRECTION.
LIKE CERBEROOT, IMAGINE THAT ABYSS BEING ONES BIRTH PLACE.

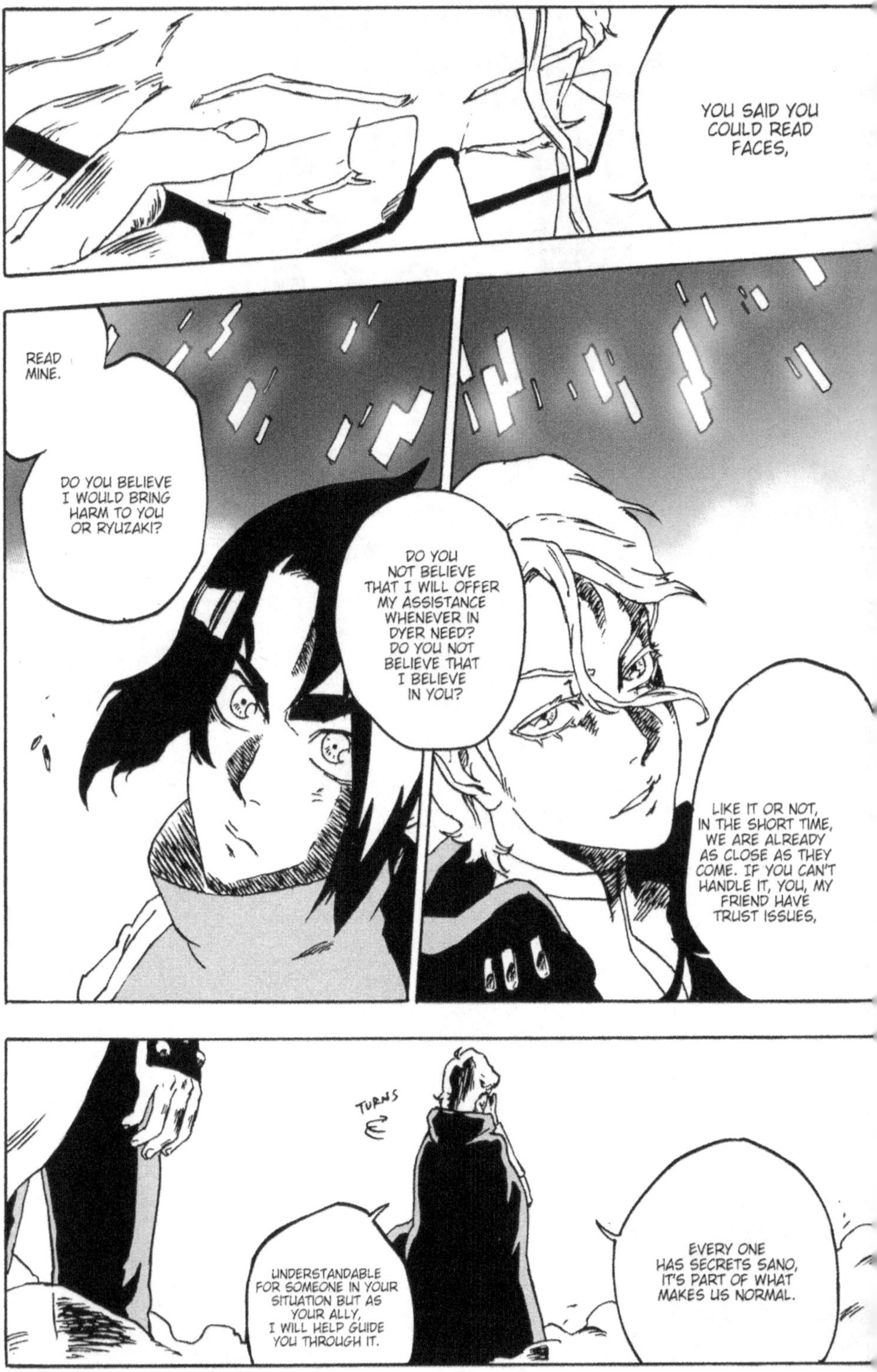
YOU SAID YOU COULD READ FACES,
READ MINE.
DO YOU BELIEVE I WOULD BRING HARM TO YOU OR RYUZAKI?
DO YOU NOT BELIEVE THAT I WILL OFFER MY ASSISTANCE WHENEVER IN DYER NEED? DO YOU NOT BELIEVE THAT I BELIEVE IN YOU?
LIKE IT OR NOT, IN THE SHORT TIME, WE ARE ALREADY AS CLOSE AS THEY COME. IF YOU CAN'T HANDLE IT, YOU, MY FRIEND HAVE TRUST ISSUES,
TURNS
UNDERSTANDABLE FOR SOMEONE IN YOUR SITUATION BUT AS YOUR ALLY, I WILL HELP GUIDE YOU THROUGH IT.
EVERY ONE HAS SECRETS SANO, IT'S PART OF WHAT MAKES US NORMAL.

I DON'T

OF COURSE YOU DO, YOU JUST DON'T KNOW IT YET. WHY DON'T YOU ASK THOSE CLOSEST TO YOU IF THEY HAVE NO SKELETONS IN THE CLOSET AND PUT YOUR FACE ANALYZING SKILLS TO GOOD USE.

WAIT! WHAT DO YOU—

TOO LATE BUDDY,

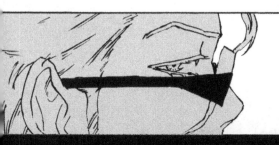

DETENTION'S OVER.

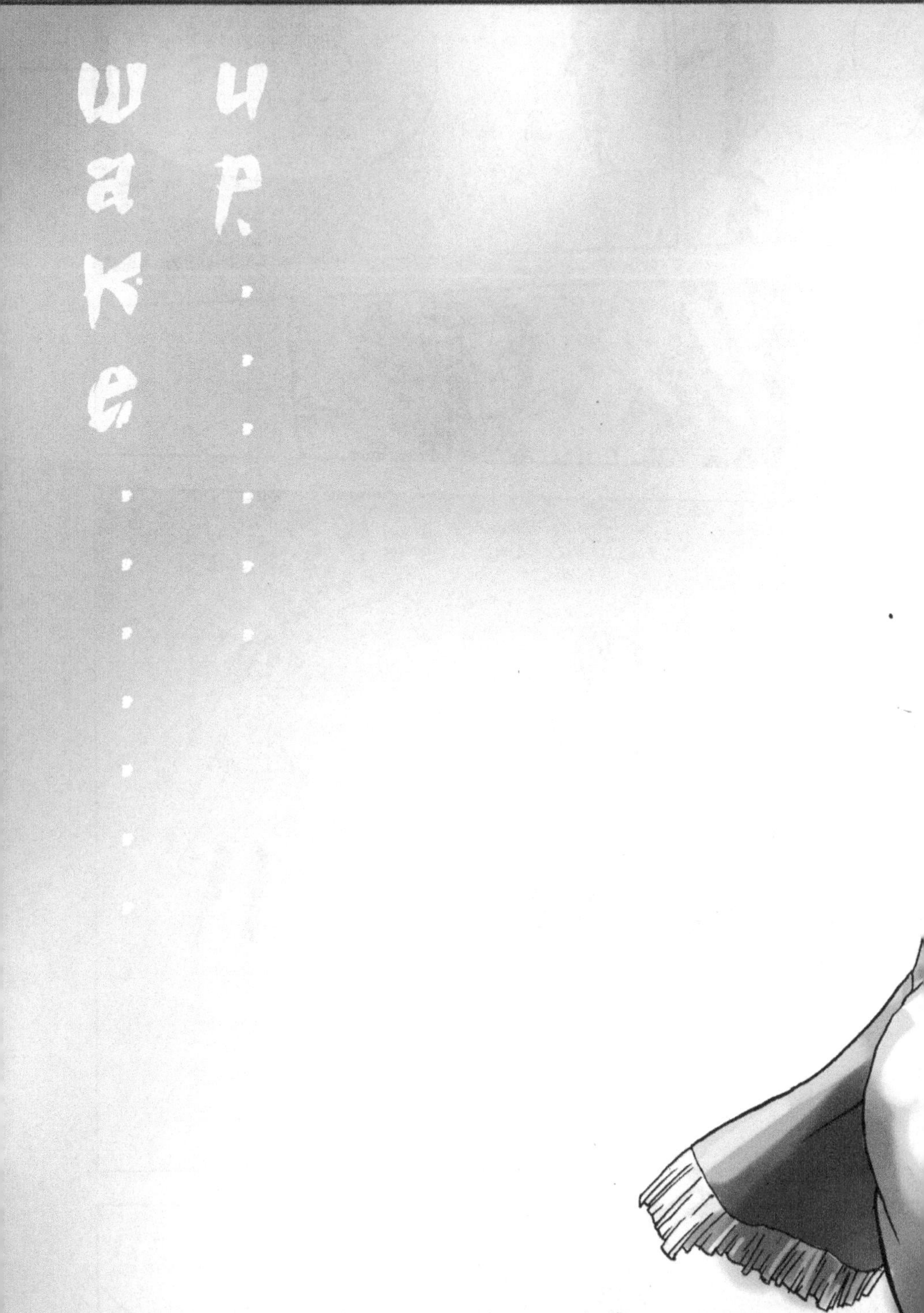
wake.......
up......

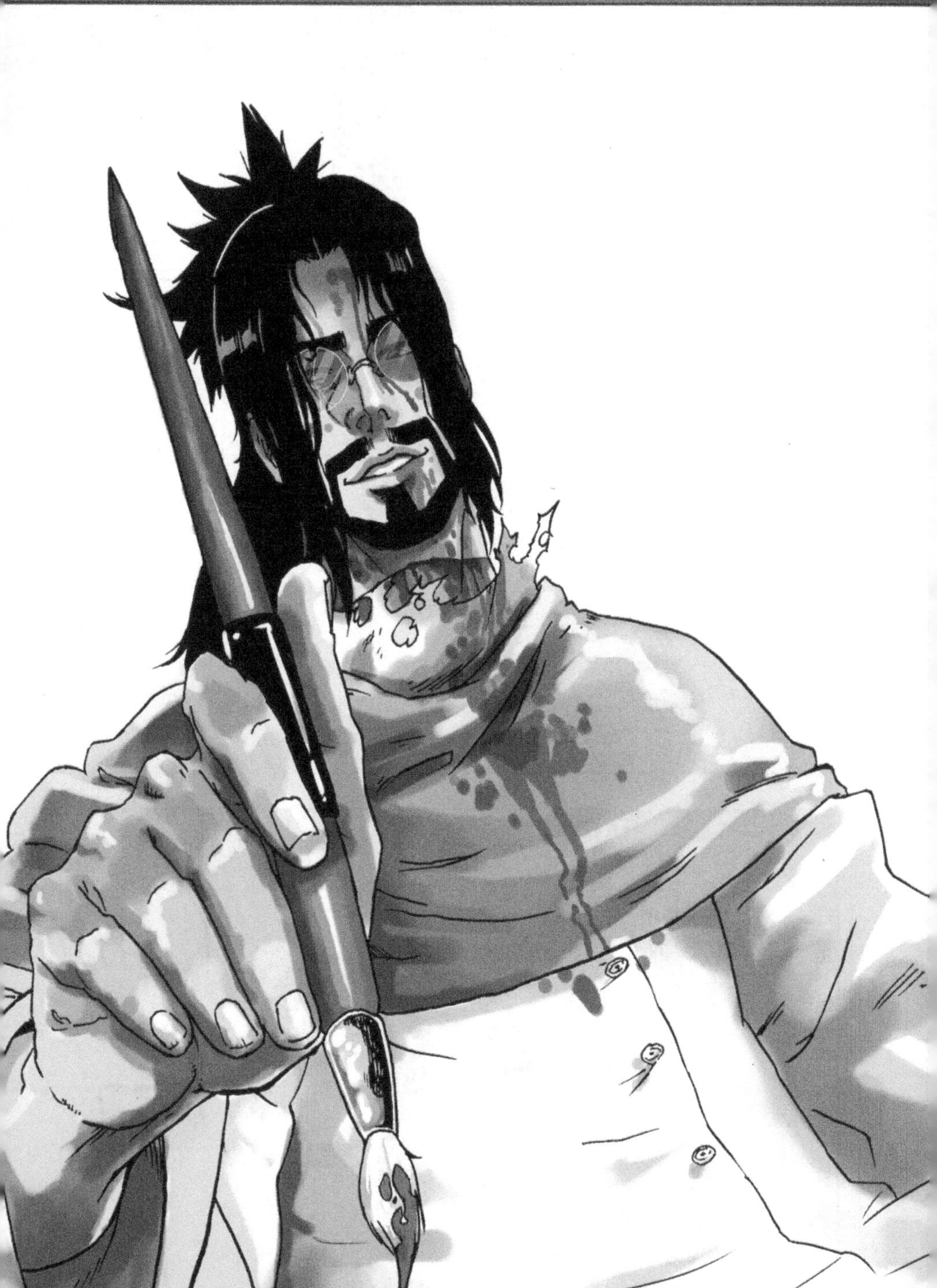

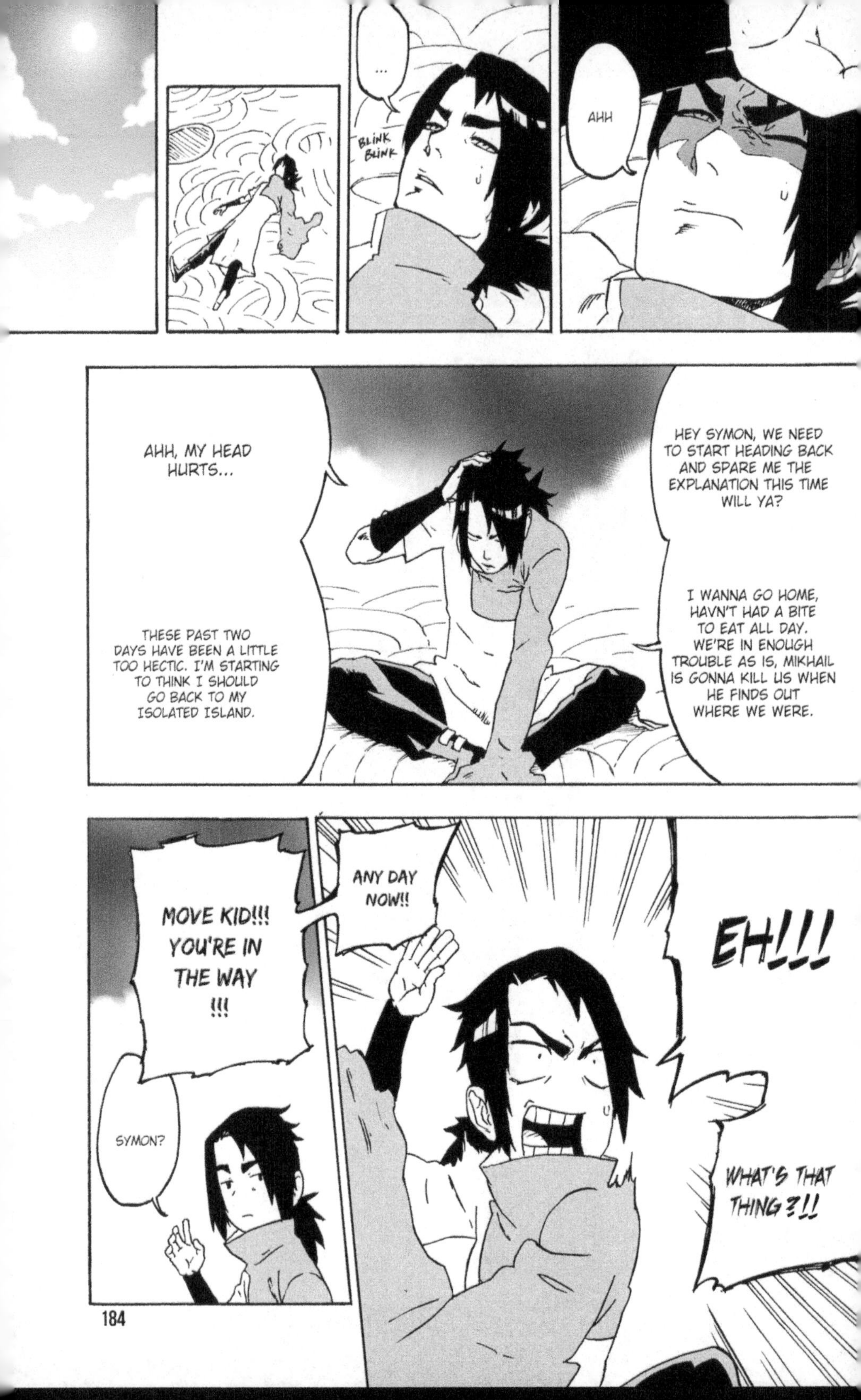
...
BLINK BLINK
AHH
AHH, MY HEAD HURTS...
THESE PAST TWO DAYS HAVE BEEN A LITTLE TOO HECTIC. I'M STARTING TO THINK I SHOULD GO BACK TO MY ISOLATED ISLAND.
HEY SYMON, WE NEED TO START HEADING BACK AND SPARE ME THE EXPLANATION THIS TIME WILL YA?
I WANNA GO HOME, HAVN'T HAD A BITE TO EAT ALL DAY. WE'RE IN ENOUGH TROUBLE AS IS, MIKHAIL IS GONNA KILL US WHEN HE FINDS OUT WHERE WE WERE.
MOVE KID!!! YOU'RE IN THE WAY !!!
SYMON?
ANY DAY NOW!!
EH!!!
WHAT'S THAT THING?!!

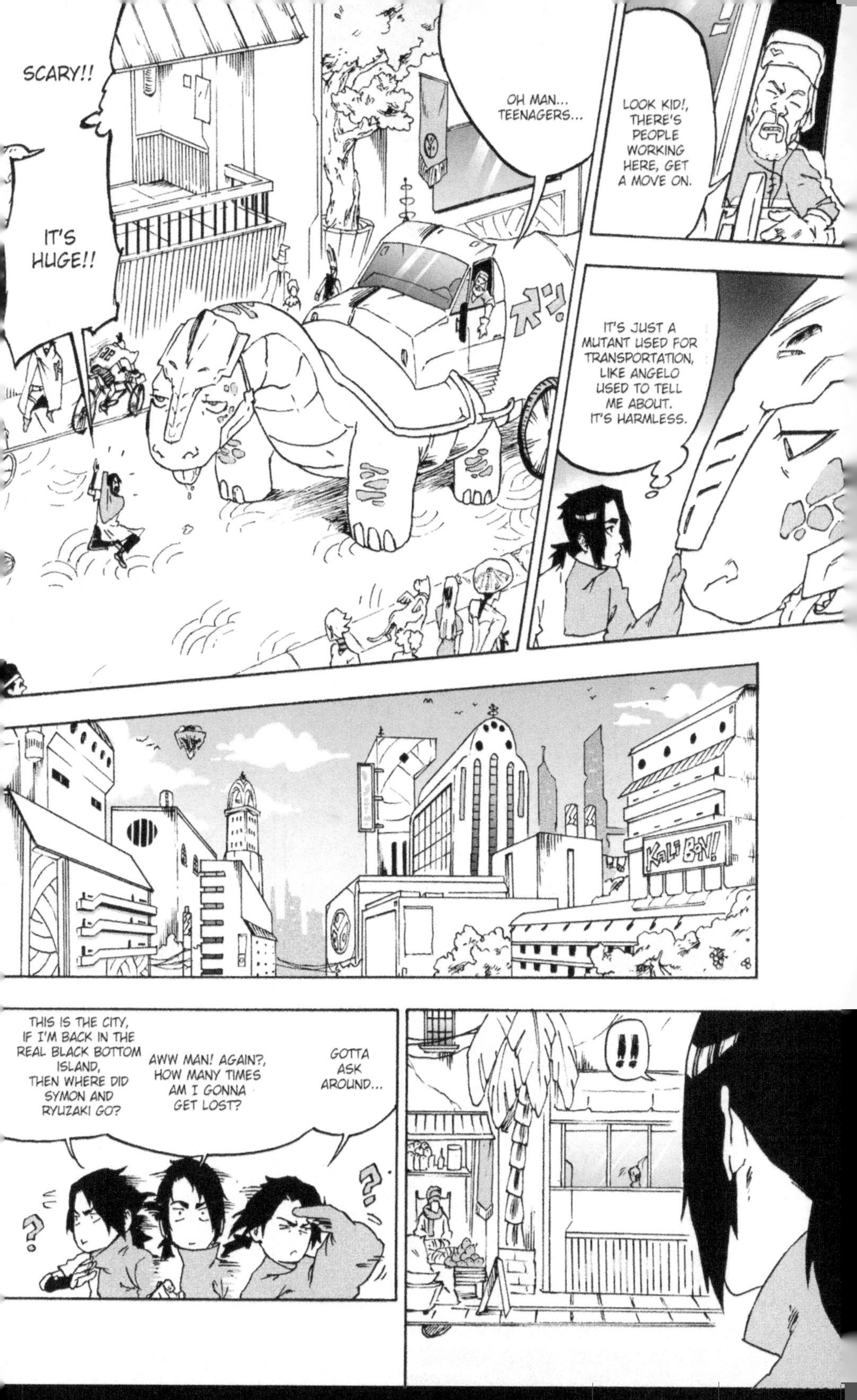
SCARY!!
IT'S HUGE!!
OH MAN... TEENAGERS...
LOOK KID!, THERE'S PEOPLE WORKING HERE, GET A MOVE ON.
IT'S JUST A MUTANT USED FOR TRANSPORTATION, LIKE ANGELO USED TO TELL ME ABOUT. IT'S HARMLESS.
KALI BAN!
THIS IS THE CITY, IF I'M BACK IN THE REAL BLACK BOTTOM ISLAND, THEN WHERE DID SYMON AND RYUZAKI GO?
AWW MAN! AGAIN?, HOW MANY TIMES AM I GONNA GET LOST?
GOTTA ASK AROUND...
!!

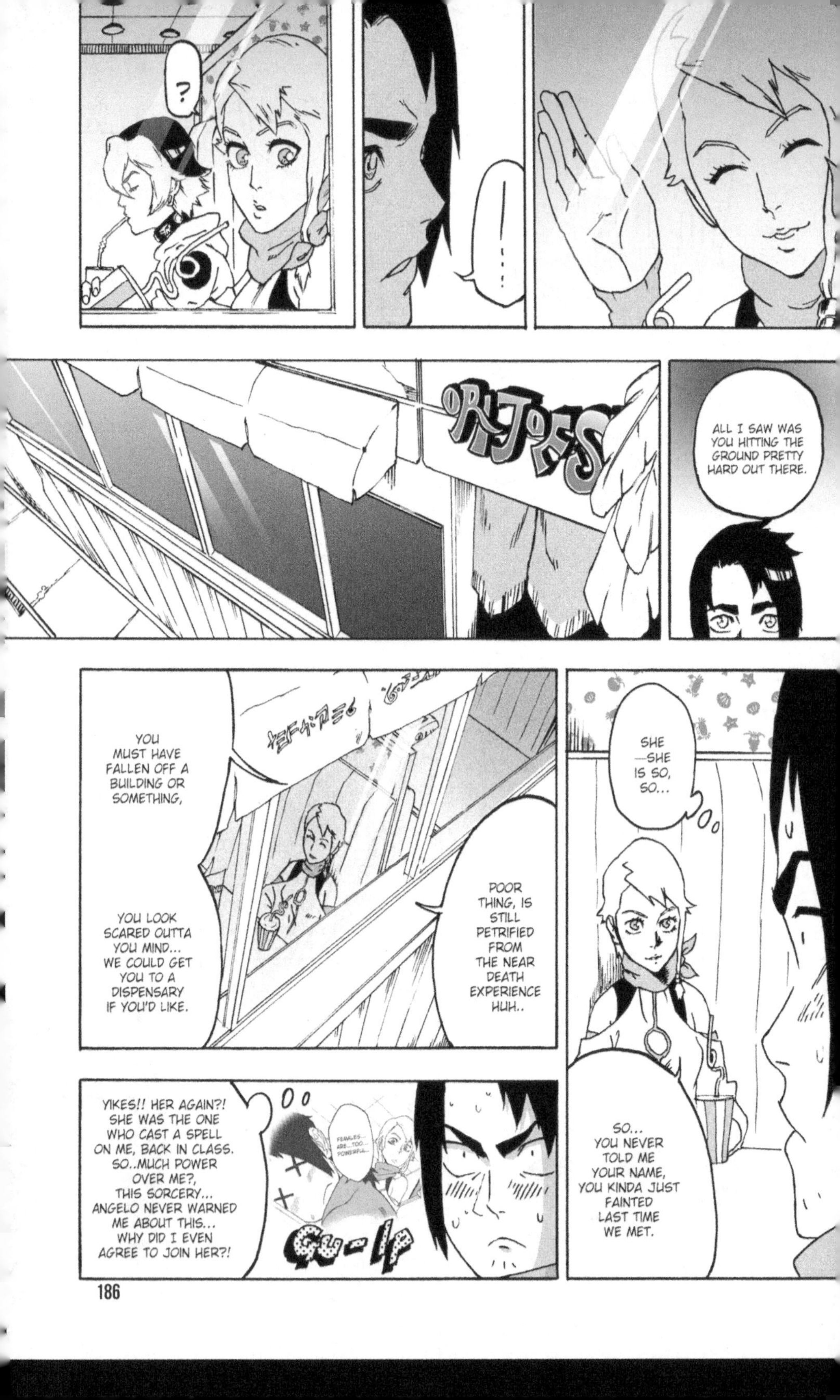
?
!
...
ALL I SAW WAS YOU HITTING THE GROUND PRETTY HARD OUT THERE.
YOU MUST HAVE FALLEN OFF A BUILDING OR SOMETHING,
YOU LOOK SCARED OUTTA YOU MIND... WE COULD GET YOU TO A DISPENSARY IF YOU'D LIKE.
POOR THING, IS STILL PETRIFIED FROM THE NEAR DEATH EXPERIENCE HUH..
YIKES!! HER AGAIN?! SHE WAS THE ONE WHO CAST A SPELL ON ME, BACK IN CLASS. SO..MUCH POWER OVER ME?, THIS SORCERY... ANGELO NEVER WARNED ME ABOUT THIS... WHY DID I EVEN AGREE TO JOIN HER?!
FEMALES... ARE... TOO... POWERFUL
GU-LP
SHE —SHE IS SO, SO...
SO... YOU NEVER TOLD ME YOUR NAME, YOU KINDA JUST FAINTED LAST TIME WE MET.

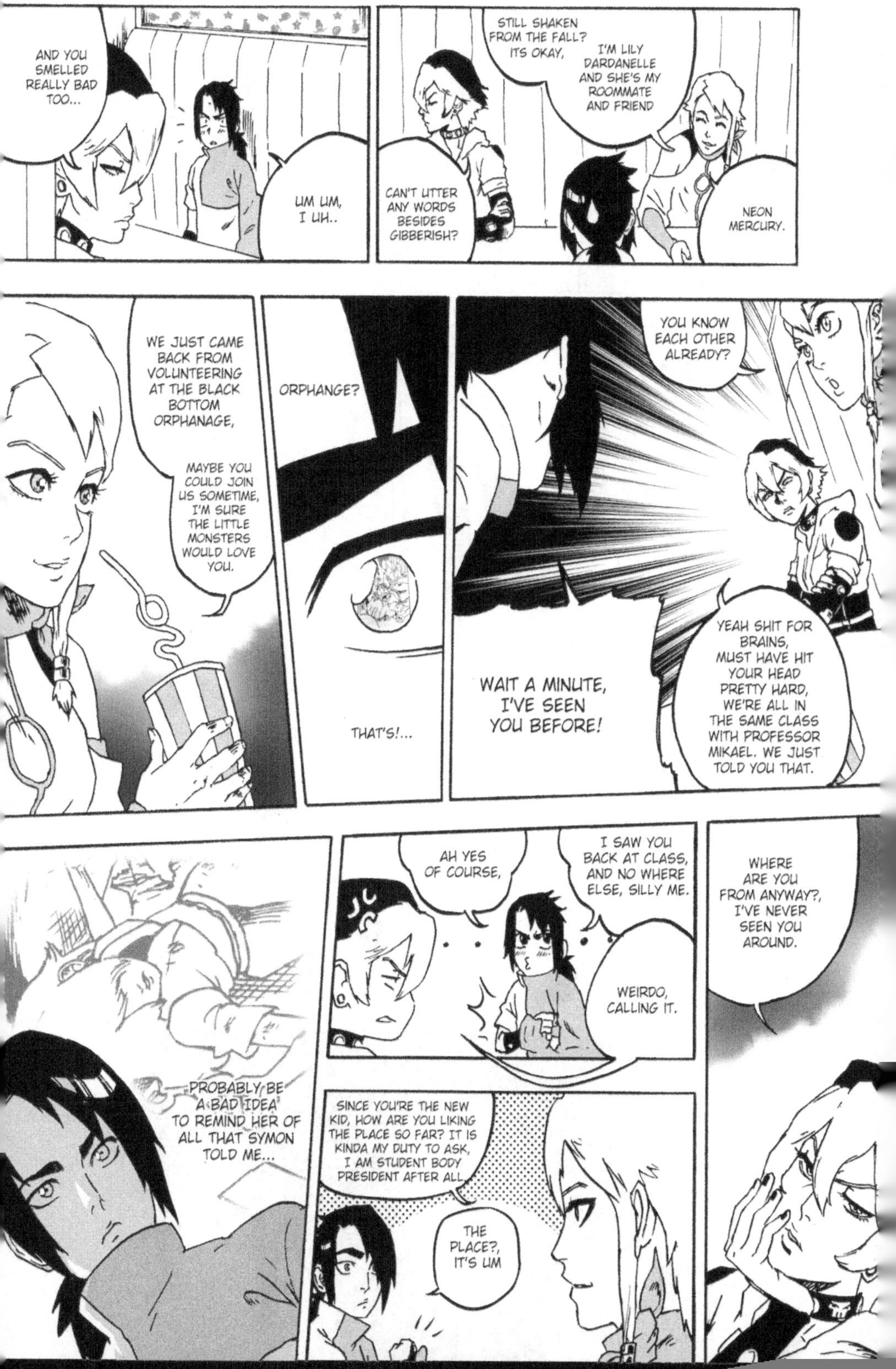
AND YOU SMELLED REALLY BAD TOO...
UM UM, I UH..
STILL SHAKEN FROM THE FALL? ITS OKAY,
CAN'T UTTER ANY WORDS BESIDES GIBBERISH?
I'M LILY DARDANELLE AND SHE'S MY ROOMMATE AND FRIEND
NEON MERCURY.
WE JUST CAME BACK FROM VOLUNTEERING AT THE BLACK BOTTOM ORPHANAGE,
MAYBE YOU COULD JOIN US SOMETIME, I'M SURE THE LITTLE MONSTERS WOULD LOVE YOU.
ORPHANGE?
THAT'S!...
YOU KNOW EACH OTHER ALREADY?
WAIT A MINUTE, I'VE SEEN YOU BEFORE!
YEAH SHIT FOR BRAINS, MUST HAVE HIT YOUR HEAD PRETTY HARD, WE'RE ALL IN THE SAME CLASS WITH PROFESSOR MIKAEL. WE JUST TOLD YOU THAT.
PROBABLY BE A BAD IDEA TO REMIND HER OF ALL THAT SYMON TOLD ME...
AH YES OF COURSE,
I SAW YOU BACK AT CLASS, AND NO WHERE ELSE, SILLY ME.
WEIRDO, CALLING IT.
WHERE ARE YOU FROM ANYWAY?, I'VE NEVER SEEN YOU AROUND.
SINCE YOU'RE THE NEW KID, HOW ARE YOU LIKING THE PLACE SO FAR? IT IS KINDA MY DUTY TO ASK, I AM STUDENT BODY PRESIDENT AFTER ALL.
THE PLACE?, IT'S UM

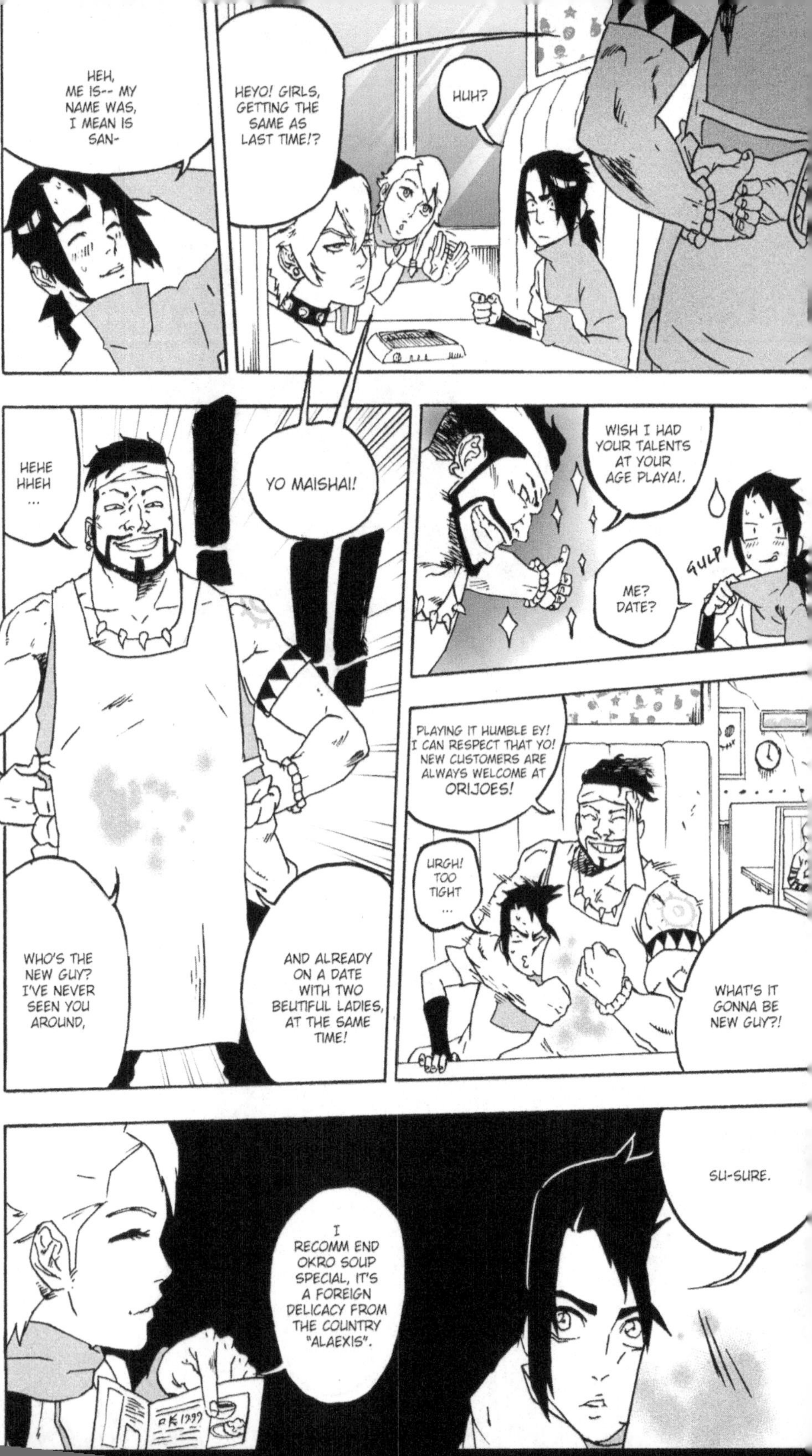
HEH,
ME IS-- MY NAME WAS, I MEAN IS SAN-
HEYO! GIRLS, GETTING THE SAME AS LAST TIME!?
HUH?
HEHE HHEH ...
YO MAISHAI!
WHO'S THE NEW GUY? I'VE NEVER SEEN YOU AROUND,
AND ALREADY ON A DATE WITH TWO BEUTIFUL LADIES, AT THE SAME TIME!
WISH I HAD YOUR TALENTS AT YOUR AGE PLAYA!.
ME? DATE?
GULP
PLAYING IT HUMBLE EY! I CAN RESPECT THAT YO! NEW CUSTOMERS ARE ALWAYS WELCOME AT ORIJOES!
URGH! TOO TIGHT ...
WHAT'S IT GONNA BE NEW GUY?!
I RECOMM END OKRO SOUP SPECIAL, IT'S A FOREIGN DELICACY FROM THE COUNTRY "ALAEXIS".
SU-SURE.

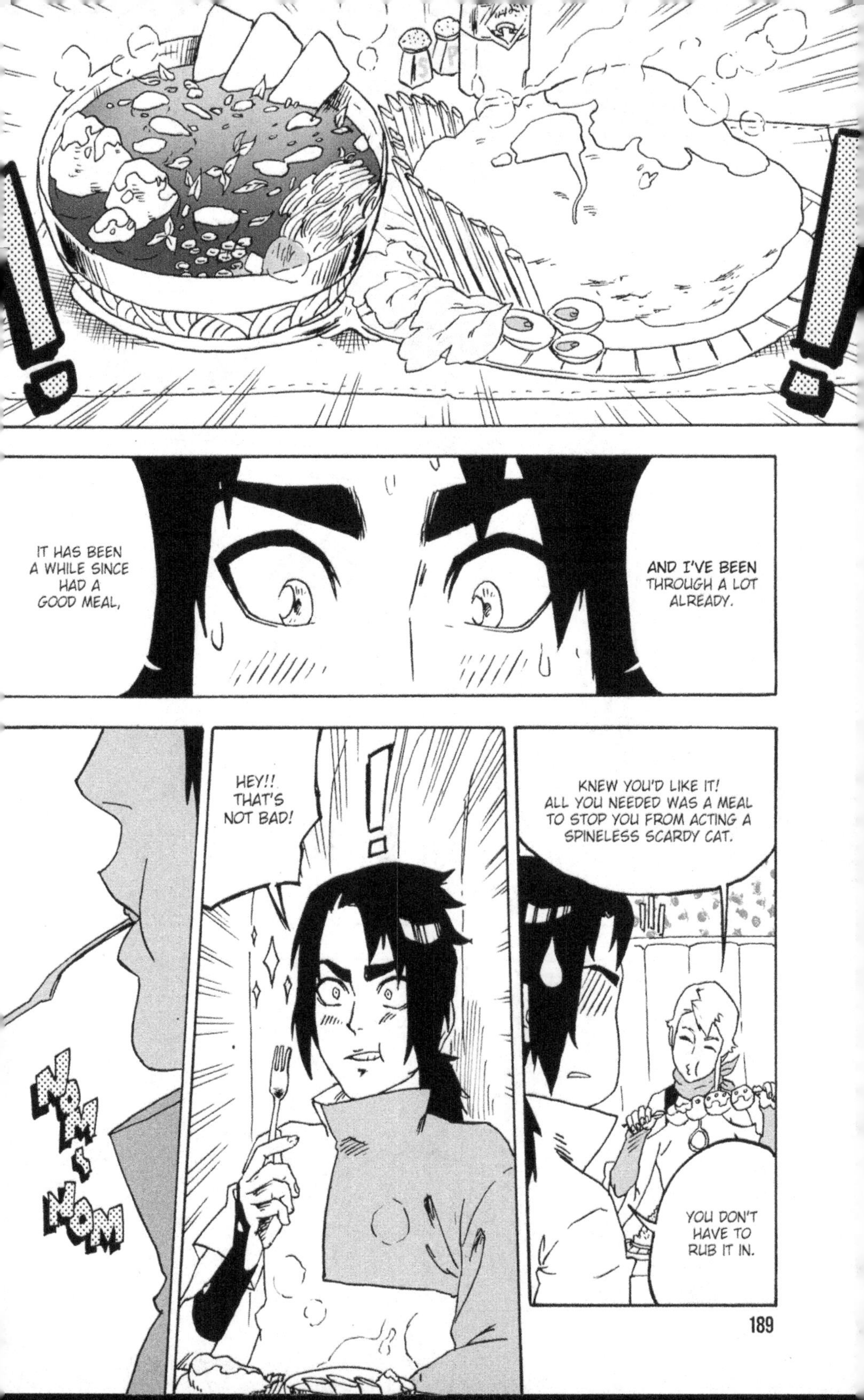
IT HAS BEEN A WHILE SINCE HAD A GOOD MEAL,
AND I'VE BEEN THROUGH A LOT ALREADY.
NOM NOM
HEY!! THAT'S NOT BAD!
KNEW YOU'D LIKE IT! ALL YOU NEEDED WAS A MEAL TO STOP YOU FROM ACTING A SPINELESS SCARDY CAT.
YOU DON'T HAVE TO RUB IT IN.

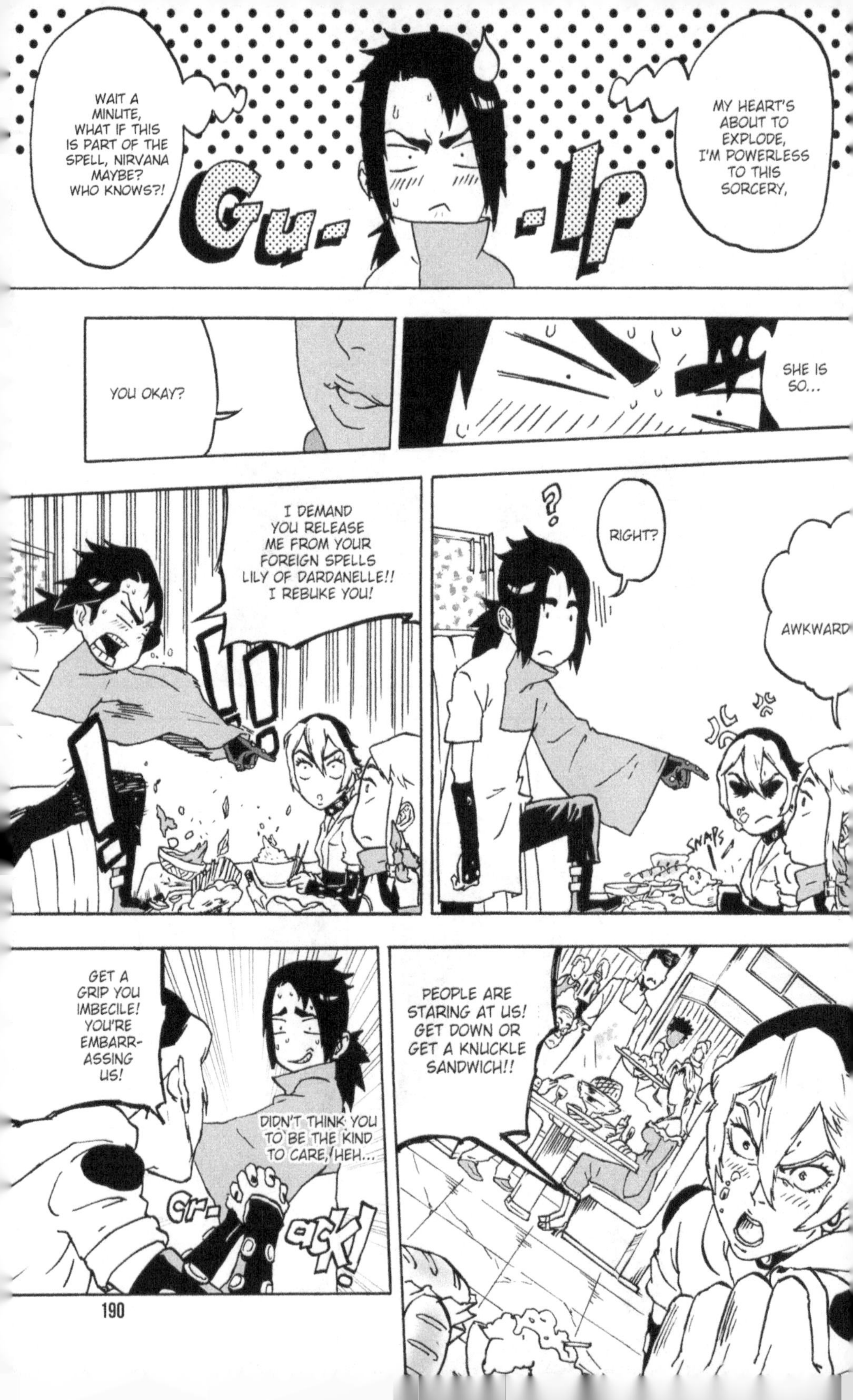
WAIT A MINUTE, WHAT IF THIS IS PART OF THE SPELL, NIRVANA MAYBE? WHO KNOWS?!
Gu- -lp
MY HEART'S ABOUT TO EXPLODE, I'M POWERLESS TO THIS SORCERY,
YOU OKAY?
SHE IS SO...
I DEMAND YOU RELEASE ME FROM YOUR FOREIGN SPELLS LILY OF DARDANELLE!! I REBUKE YOU!
RIGHT?
AWKWARD
SNAPS
GET A GRIP YOU IMBECILE! YOU'RE EMBARR-ASSING US!
DIDN'T THINK YOU TO BE THE KIND TO CARE, HEH...
Cr- ack!
PEOPLE ARE STARING AT US! GET DOWN OR GET A KNUCKLE SANDWICH!!

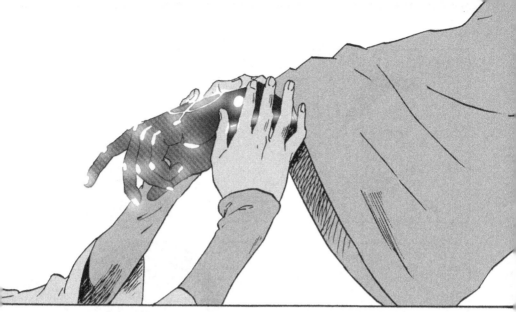

WHAT IS IT?

AMAZING. I WAS WONDERING WHAT YOU HAD UNDERNEATH YOUR PURPLE GARMENT.

UH- MY ARM?

IT'S CALLED ARODIHS, LEFT ARM OF MERLIN, THE GOD OF SORCERY,.

YOU'RE THE SON OF SERGO TAMASHII AREN'T YOU?,

YOU'RE DAD HAS A STATUE MADE AFTER HIM ON THE OUTSKIRTS, "THE STATUE OF PEACE". YOU'RE THE TRINITY?

CAN'T BELIEVE THIS WEIRDO IS OUR SAVIOR? JUST SWELL,

WHAT DOES THE SYMBOL MEAN?, I'VE READ A LOT ABUIOT THE PROPEHCY,

YOU WERE BORN WITH THIS ATTACHED TO YOU, WHAT DOES IT DO?

IT...UM...YOU'D THINK, I KNOW ALL THERE IS TO KNOW ABOUT THE ELI PROPHECY, MY FATHER, HIS RESEARCH, THIS ARM, I'M NOT EVEN SURE WHAT I'M SUPPOSED TO SAVE...

SITS

191

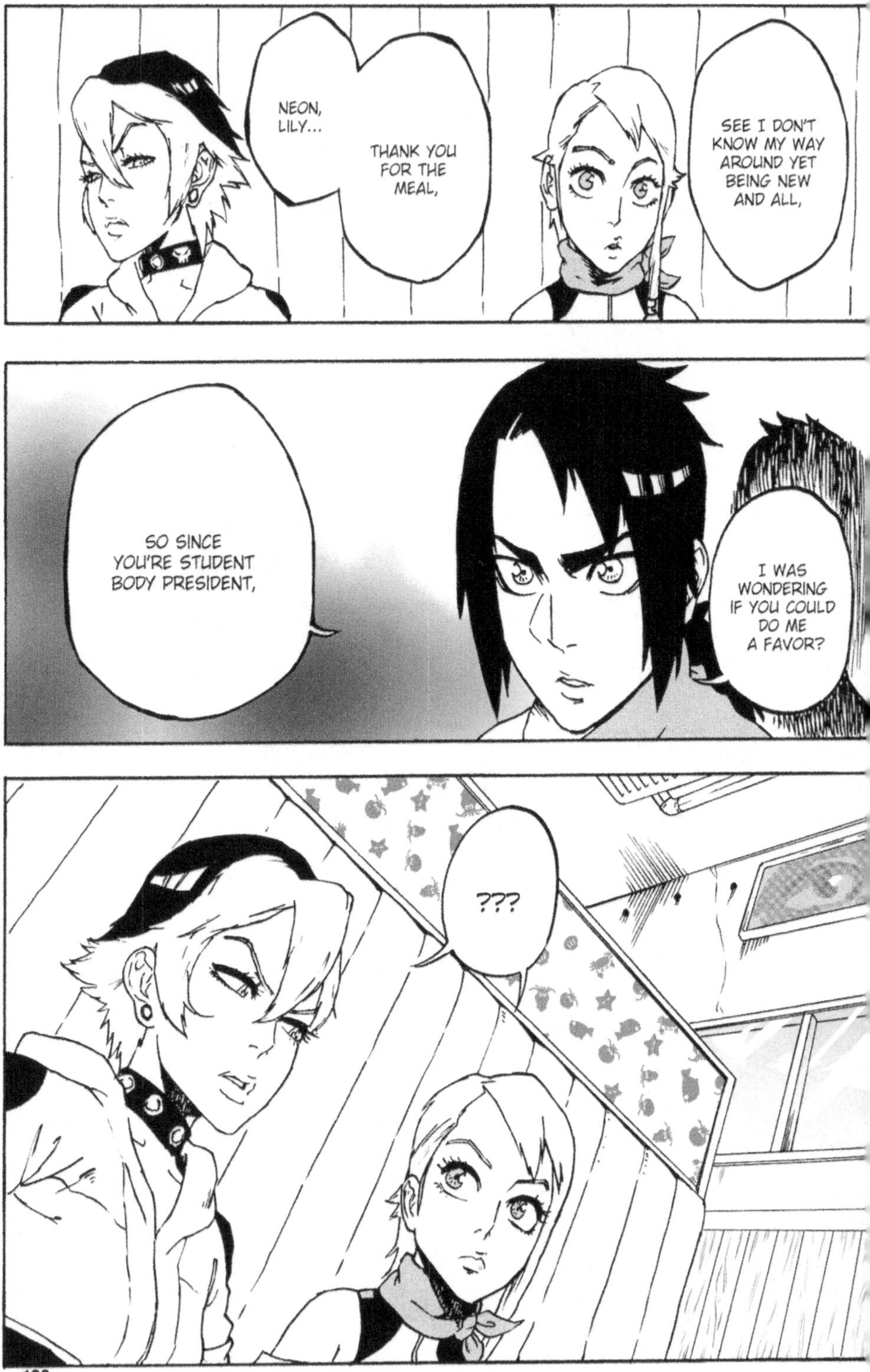
NEON, LILY...
THANK YOU FOR THE MEAL,
SEE I DON'T KNOW MY WAY AROUND YET BEING NEW AND ALL,
SO SINCE YOU'RE STUDENT BODY PRESIDENT,
I WAS WONDERING IF YOU COULD DO ME A FAVOR?
???

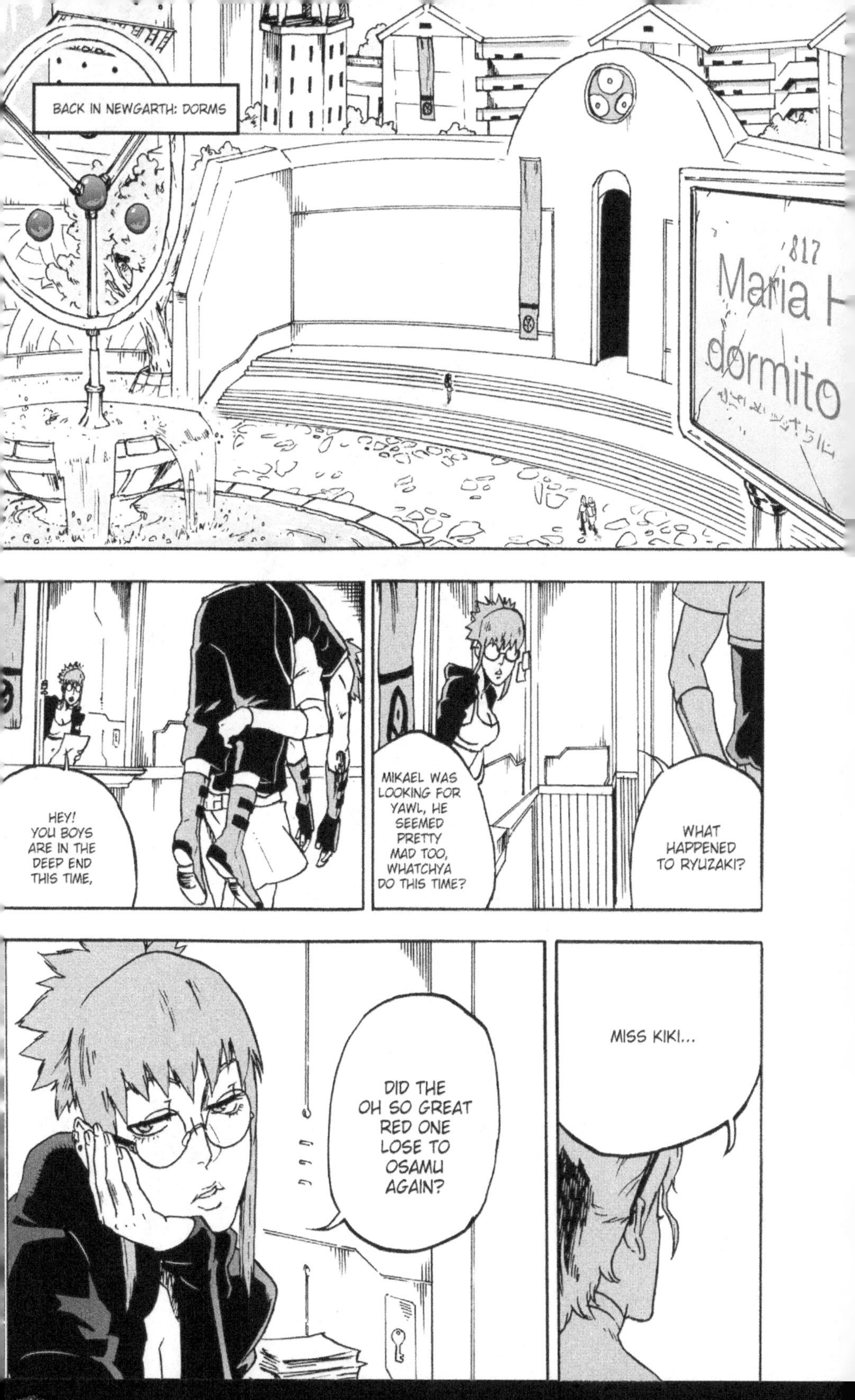
BACK IN NEWGARTH: DORMS
817
Maria H
dormito
HEY! YOU BOYS ARE IN THE DEEP END THIS TIME,
MIKAEL WAS LOOKING FOR YAWL, HE SEEMED PRETTY MAD TOO, WHATCHYA DO THIS TIME?
WHAT HAPPENED TO RYUZAKI?
DID THE OH SO GREAT RED ONE LOSE TO OSAMU AGAIN?
MISS KIKI...

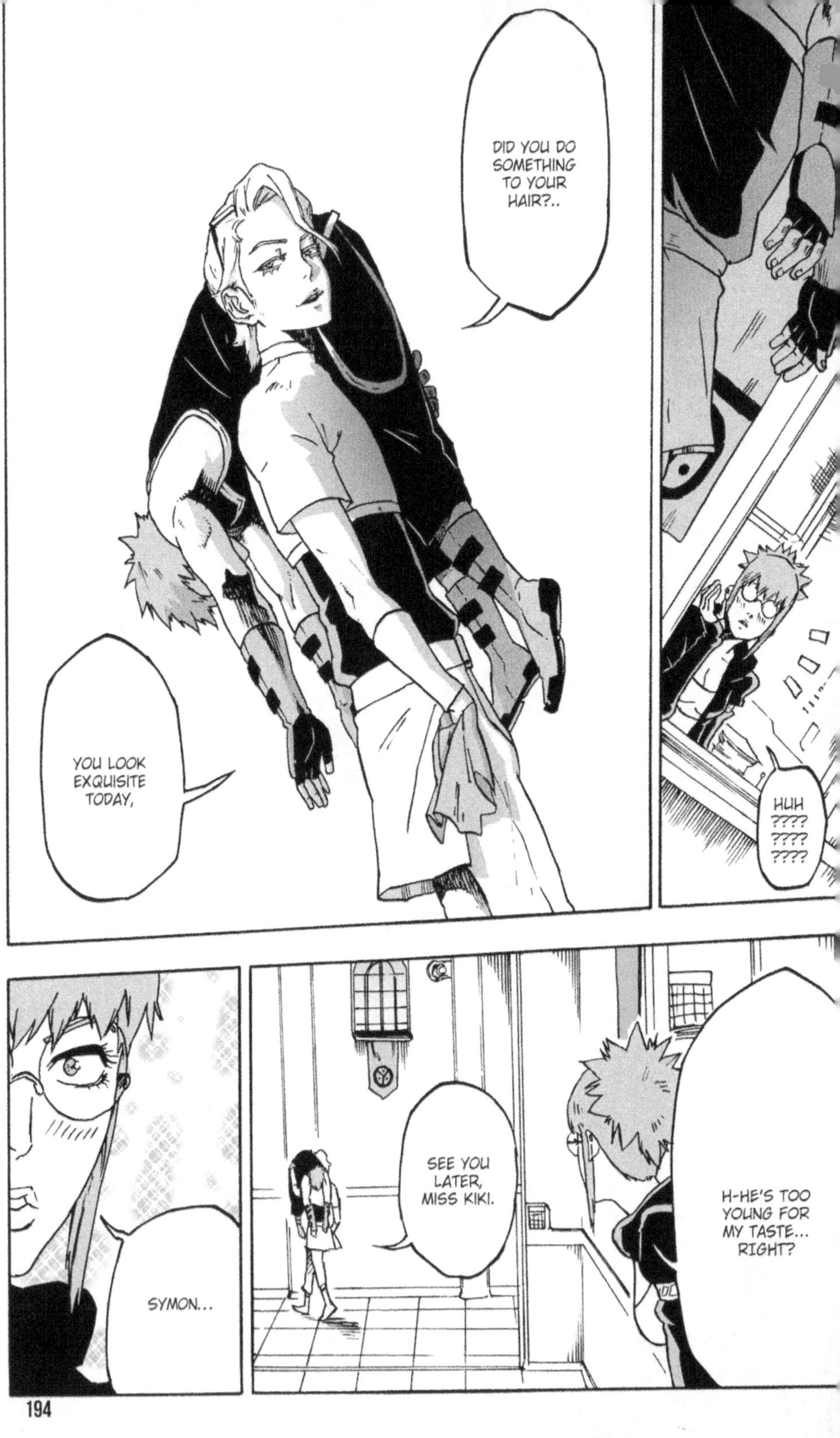
DID YOU DO SOMETHING TO YOUR HAIR?..
YOU LOOK EXQUISITE TODAY,
HUH ???? ???? ????
SYMON...
SEE YOU LATER, MISS KIKI.
H-HE'S TOO YOUNG FOR MY TASTE... RIGHT?

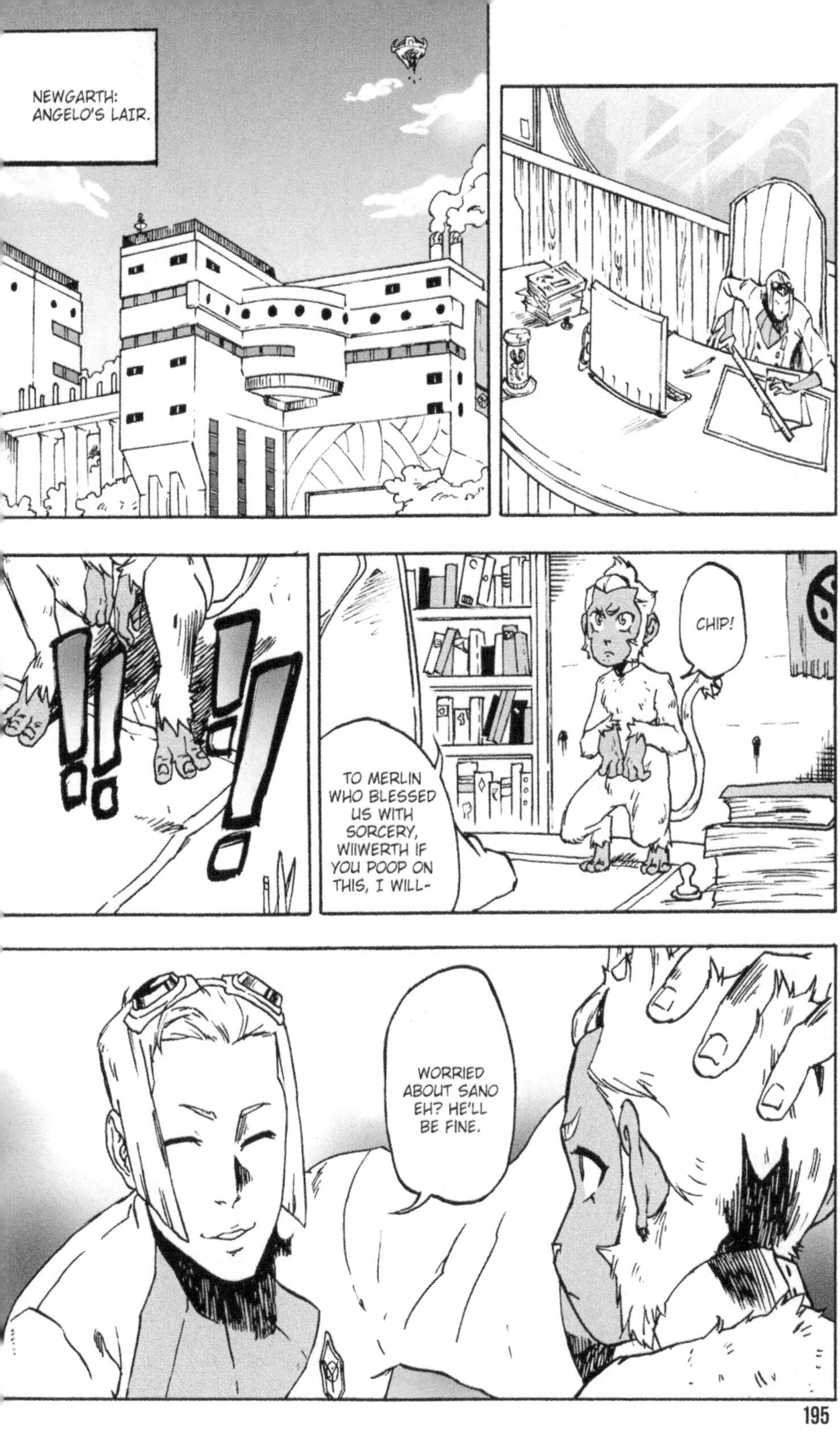
NEWGARTH: ANGELO'S LAIR.
TO MERLIN WHO BLESSED US WITH SORCERY, WIIWERTH IF YOU POOP ON THIS, I WILL-
CHIP!
WORRIED ABOUT SANO EH? HE'LL BE FINE.

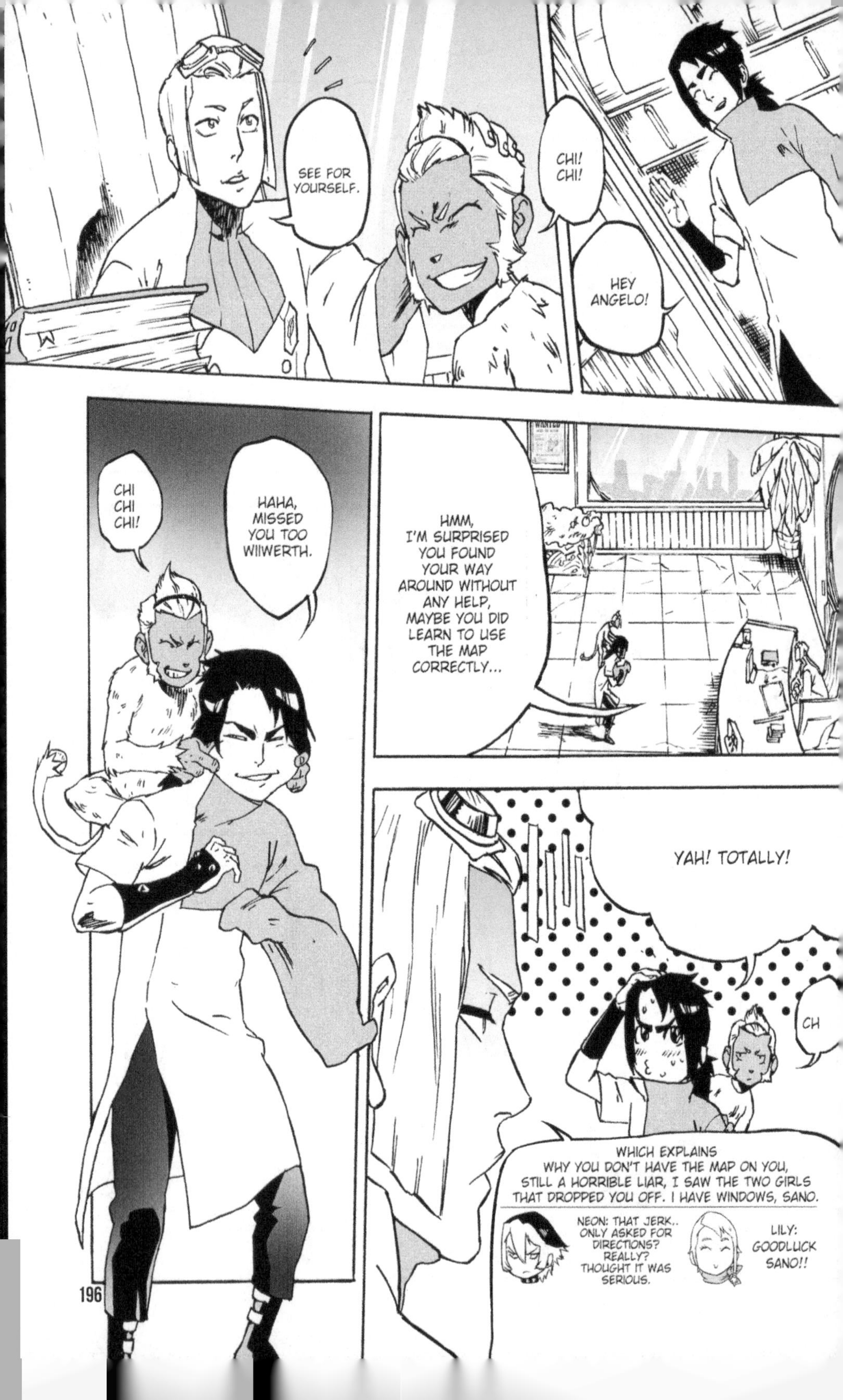
SEE FOR YOURSELF.
CHI! CHI!
HEY ANGELO!
CHI CHI CHI!
HAHA, MISSED YOU TOO WIIWERTH.
HMM, I'M SURPRISED YOU FOUND YOUR WAY AROUND WITHOUT ANY HELP, MAYBE YOU DID LEARN TO USE THE MAP CORRECTLY...
YAH! TOTALLY!
CH
WHICH EXPLAINS WHY YOU DON'T HAVE THE MAP ON YOU, STILL A HORRIBLE LIAR, I SAW THE TWO GIRLS THAT DROPPED YOU OFF. I HAVE WINDOWS, SANO.
NEON: THAT JERK.. ONLY ASKED FOR DIRECTIONS? REALLY? THOUGHT IT WAS SERIOUS.
LILY: GOODLUCK SANO!!

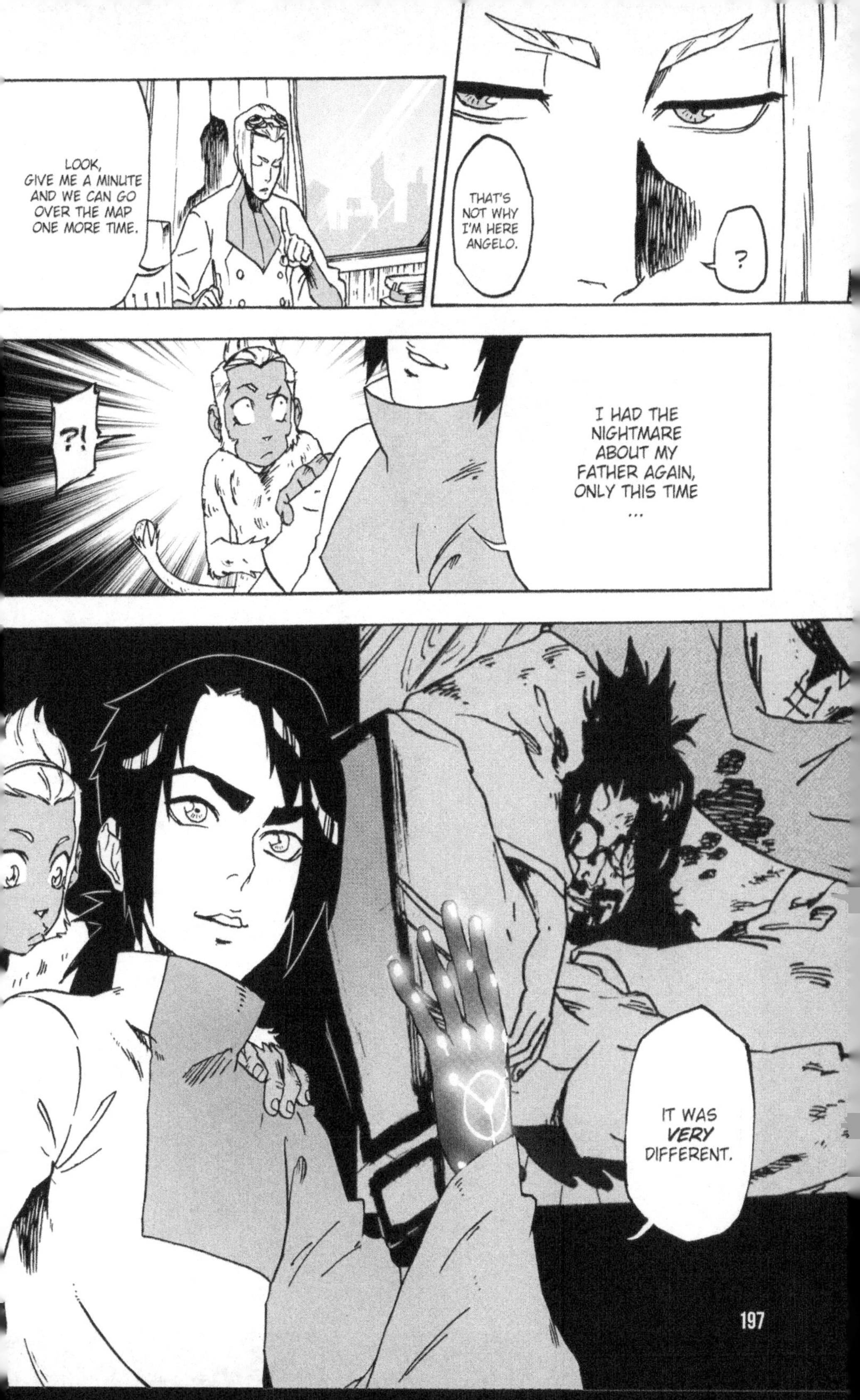
LOOK, GIVE ME A MINUTE AND WE CAN GO OVER THE MAP ONE MORE TIME.
THAT'S NOT WHY I'M HERE ANGELO.
?
?!
I HAD THE NIGHTMARE ABOUT MY FATHER AGAIN, ONLY THIS TIME ...
IT WAS *VERY* DIFFERENT.

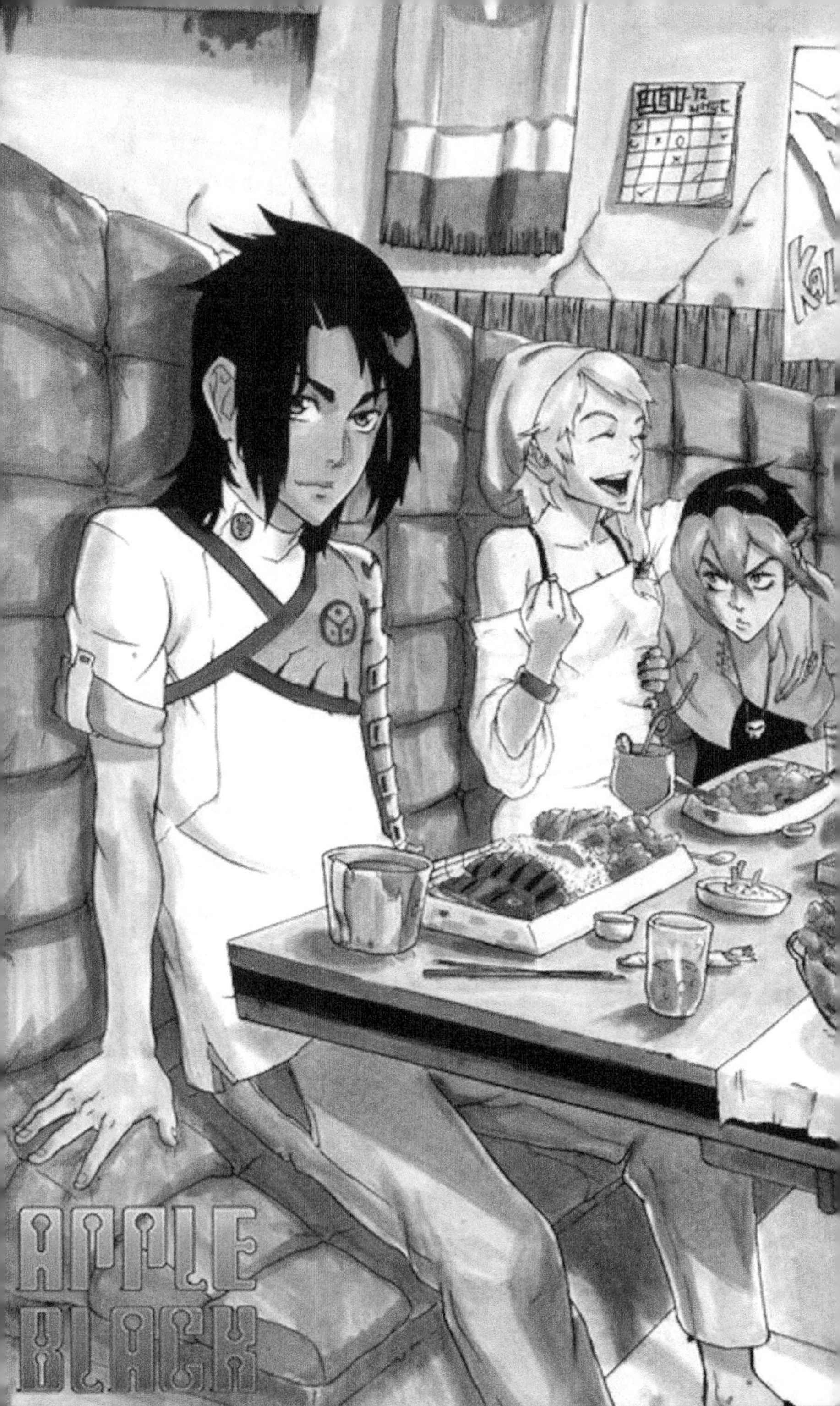
APPLE
BLACK

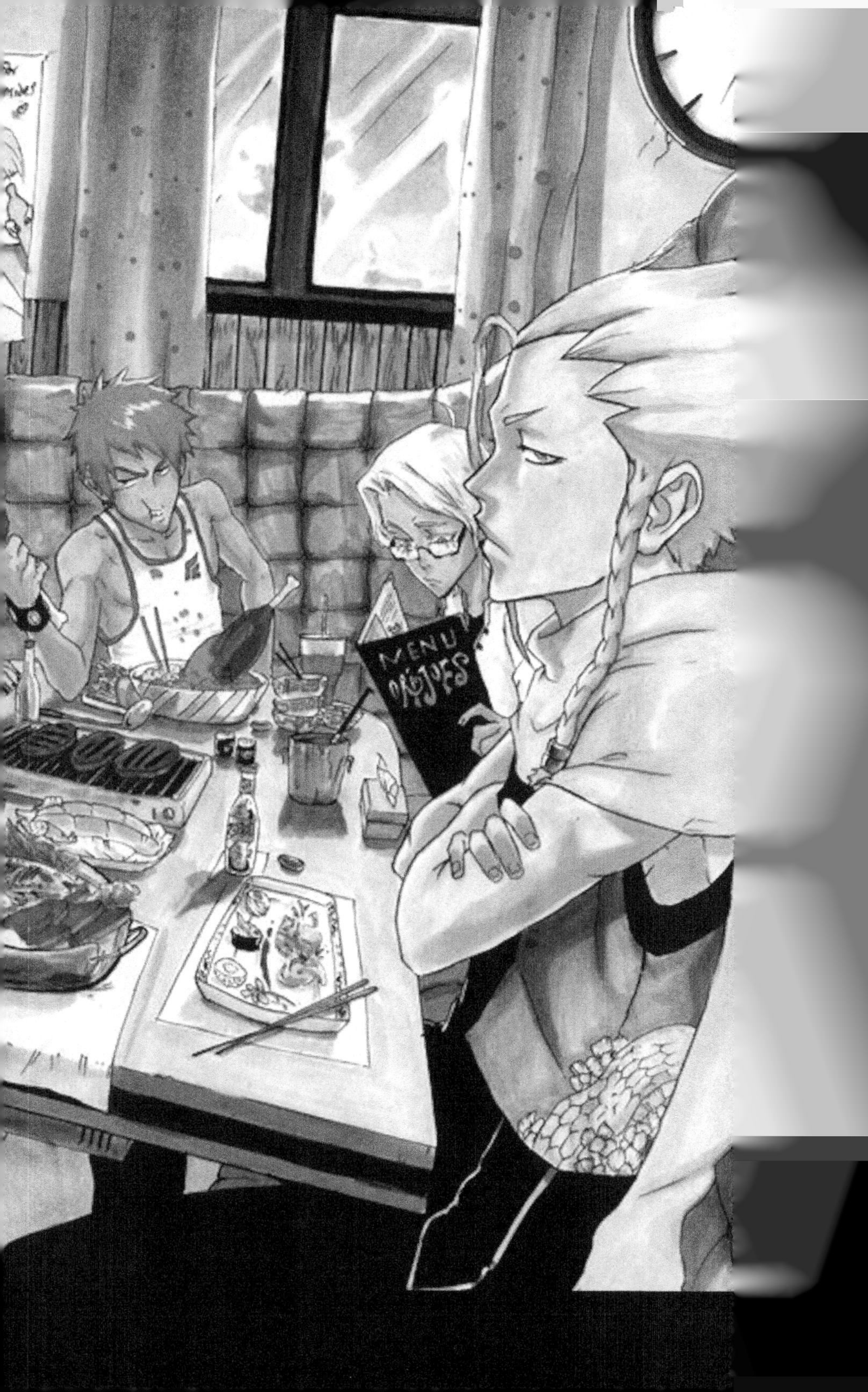
MENU

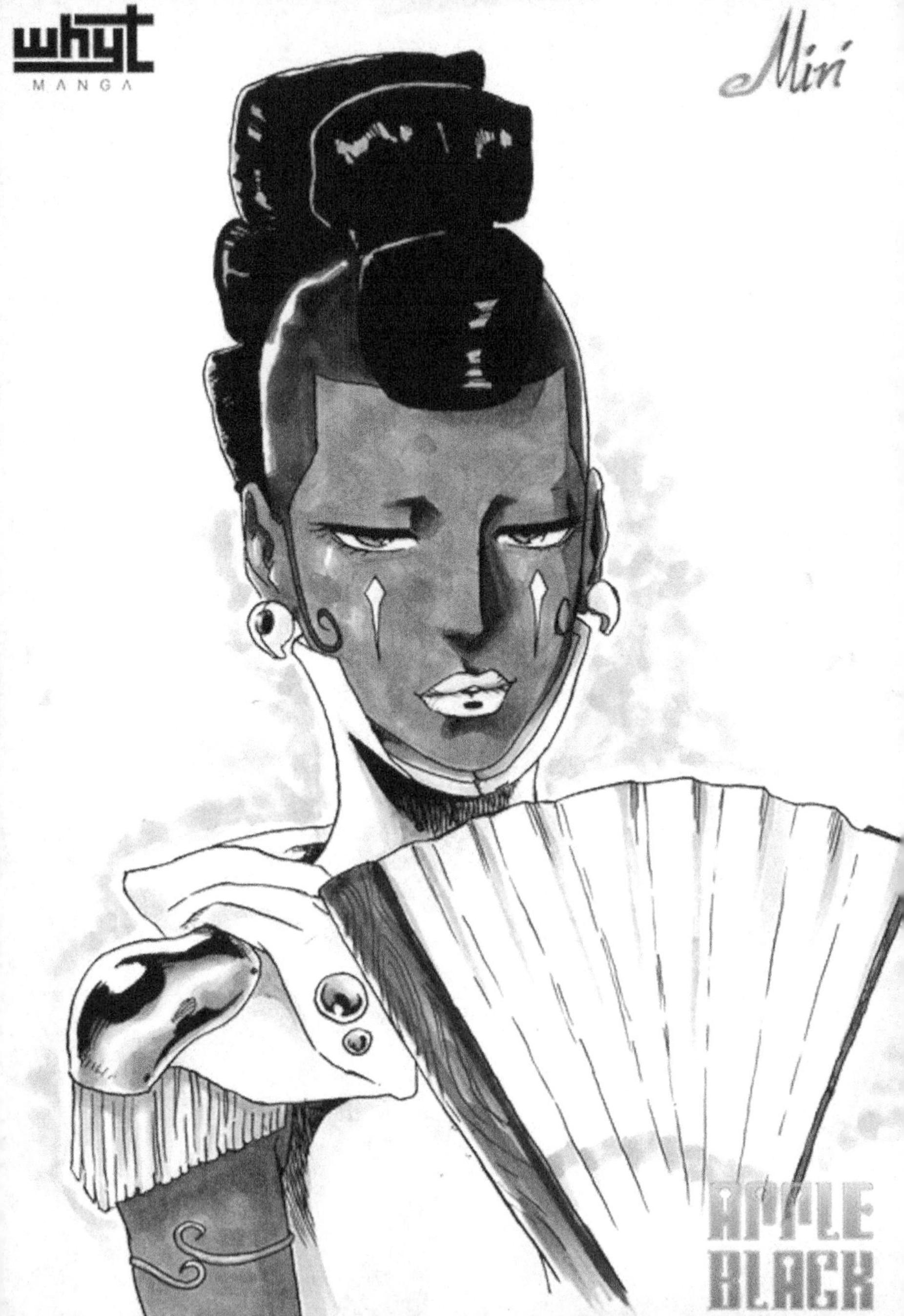
whyt
MANGA
Miri
APPLE
BLACK

SOFIA MIRI

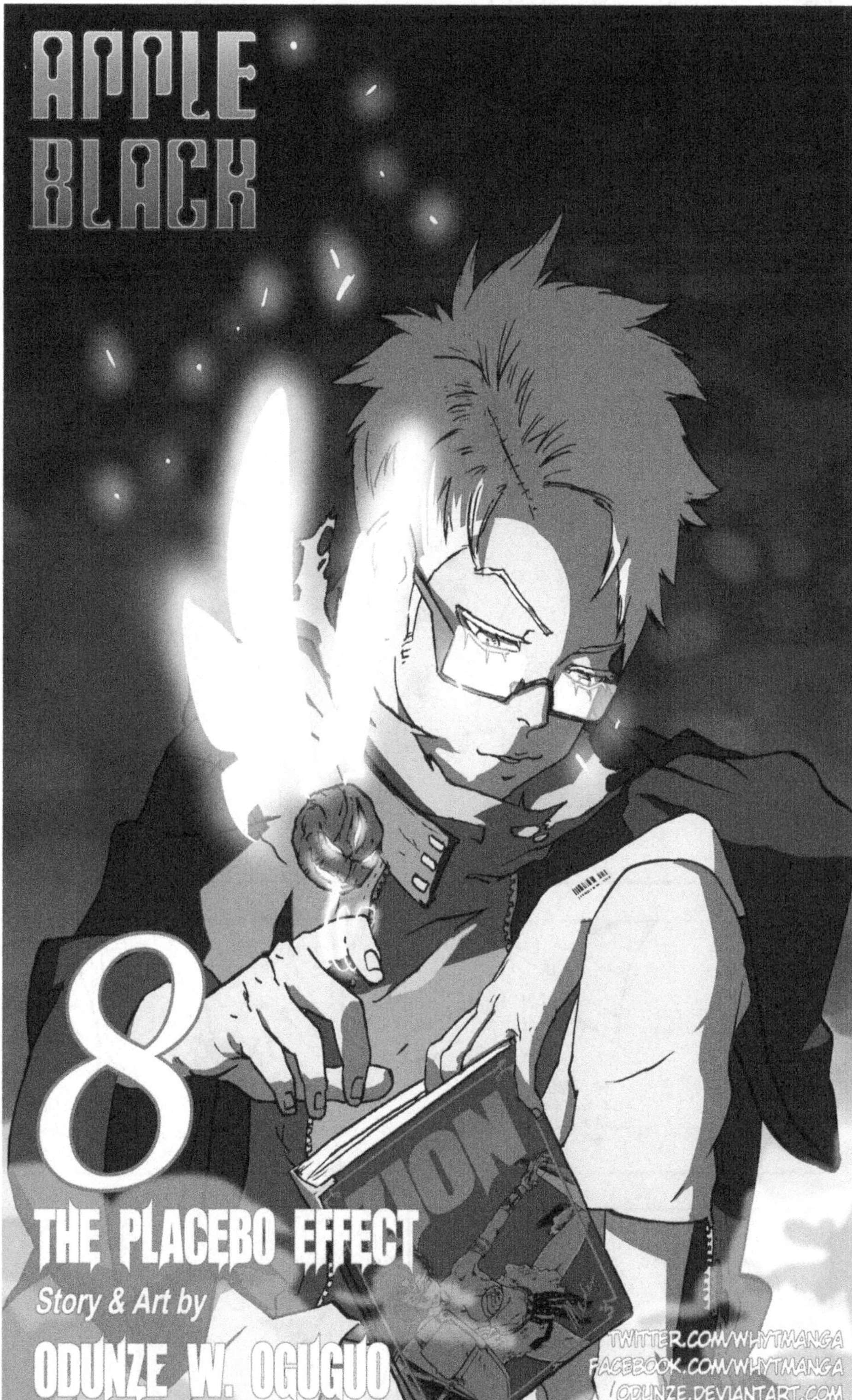
APPLE BLACK
8
THE PLACEBO EFFECT
Story & Art by
ODUNZE W. OGUGUO
TWITTER.COM/WHYTMANGA
FACEBOOK.COM/WHYTMANGA
ODUNZE.DEVIANTART.COM

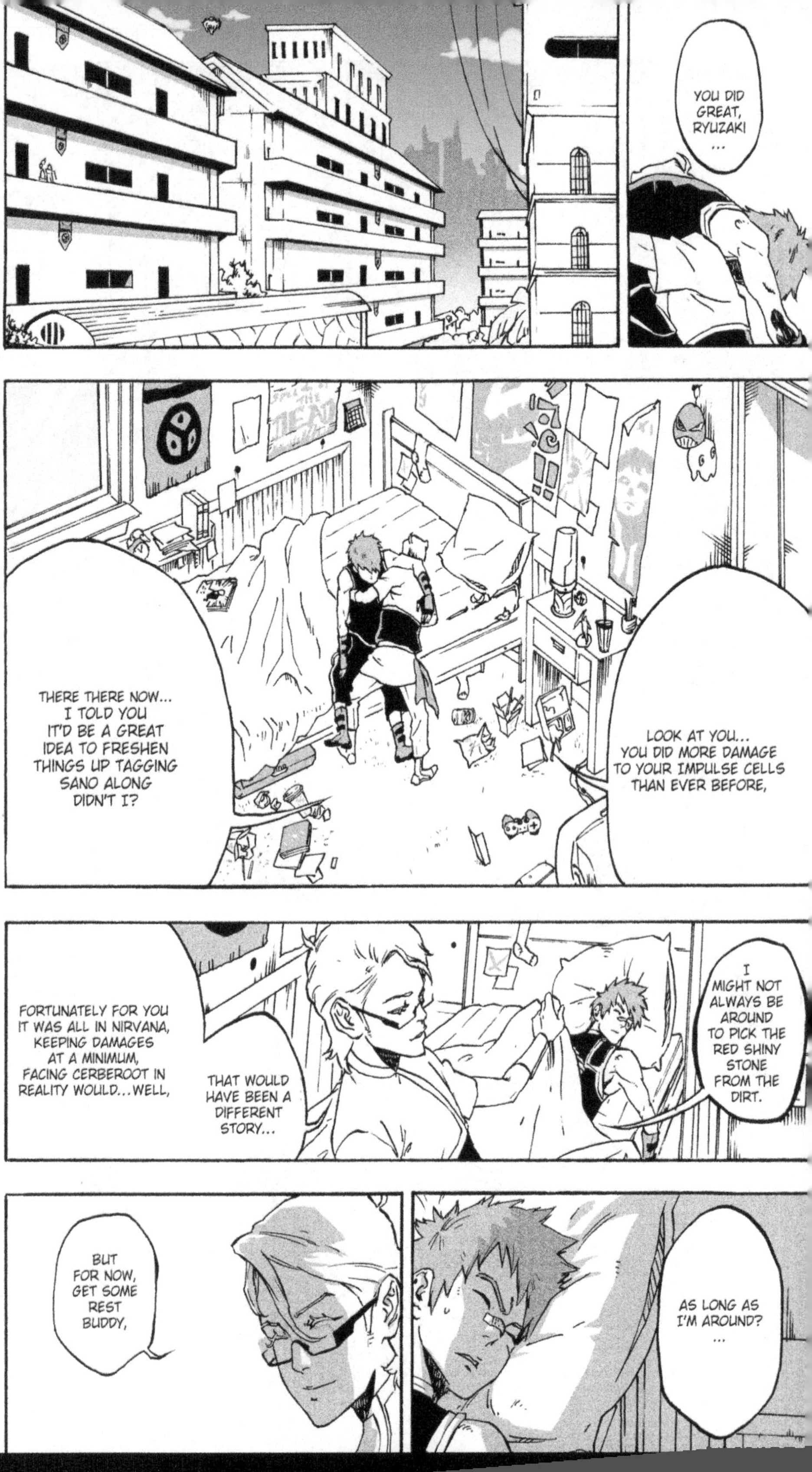
YOU DID GREAT, RYUZAKI ...
THERE THERE NOW... I TOLD YOU IT'D BE A GREAT IDEA TO FRESHEN THINGS UP TAGGING SANO ALONG DIDN'T I?
LOOK AT YOU... YOU DID MORE DAMAGE TO YOUR IMPULSE CELLS THAN EVER BEFORE,
FORTUNATELY FOR YOU IT WAS ALL IN NIRVANA, KEEPING DAMAGES AT A MINIMUM, FACING CERBEROOT IN REALITY WOULD...WELL,
THAT WOULD HAVE BEEN A DIFFERENT STORY...
I MIGHT NOT ALWAYS BE AROUND TO PICK THE RED SHINY STONE FROM THE DIRT.
BUT FOR NOW, GET SOME REST BUDDY,
AS LONG AS I'M AROUND? ...

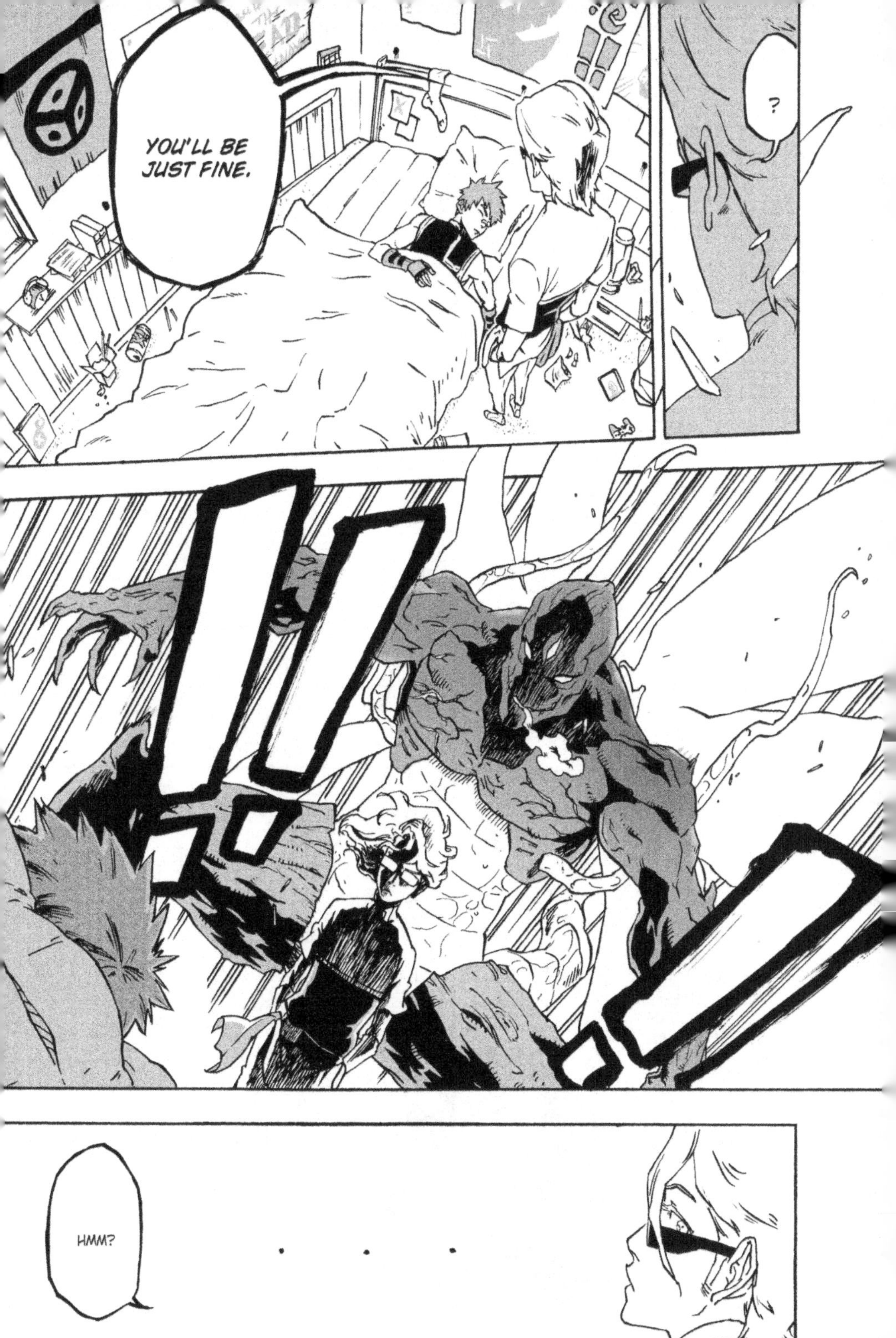
YOU'LL BE JUST FINE.
?
HMM?
. . .

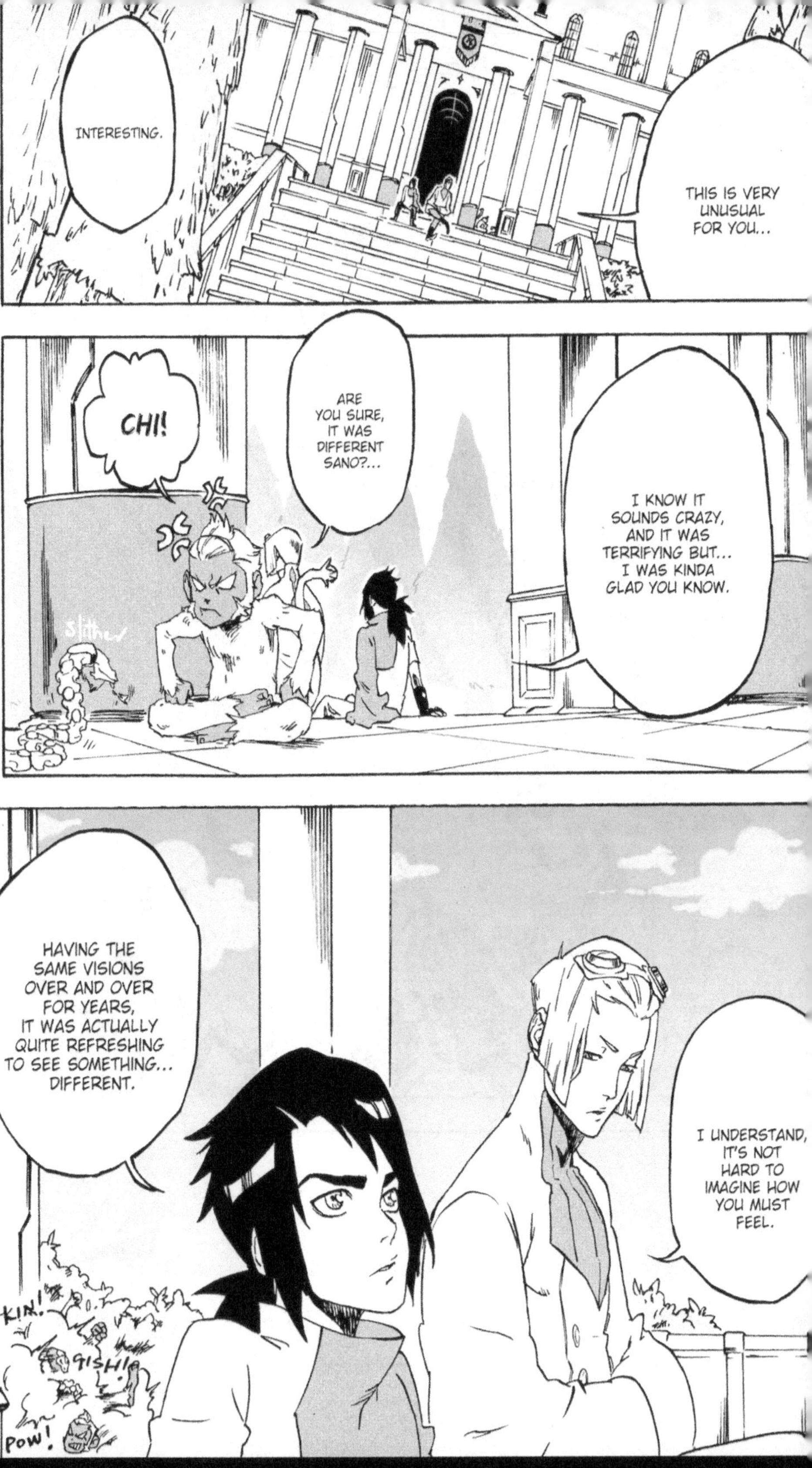
INTERESTING.
THIS IS VERY UNUSUAL FOR YOU...
CHI!
ARE YOU SURE, IT WAS DIFFERENT SANO?...
I KNOW IT SOUNDS CRAZY, AND IT WAS TERRIFYING BUT... I WAS KINDA GLAD YOU KNOW.
slither
HAVING THE SAME VISIONS OVER AND OVER FOR YEARS, IT WAS ACTUALLY QUITE REFRESHING TO SEE SOMETHING... DIFFERENT.
I UNDERSTAND, IT'S NOT HARD TO IMAGINE HOW YOU MUST FEEL.
KIN!
GISHI
POW!

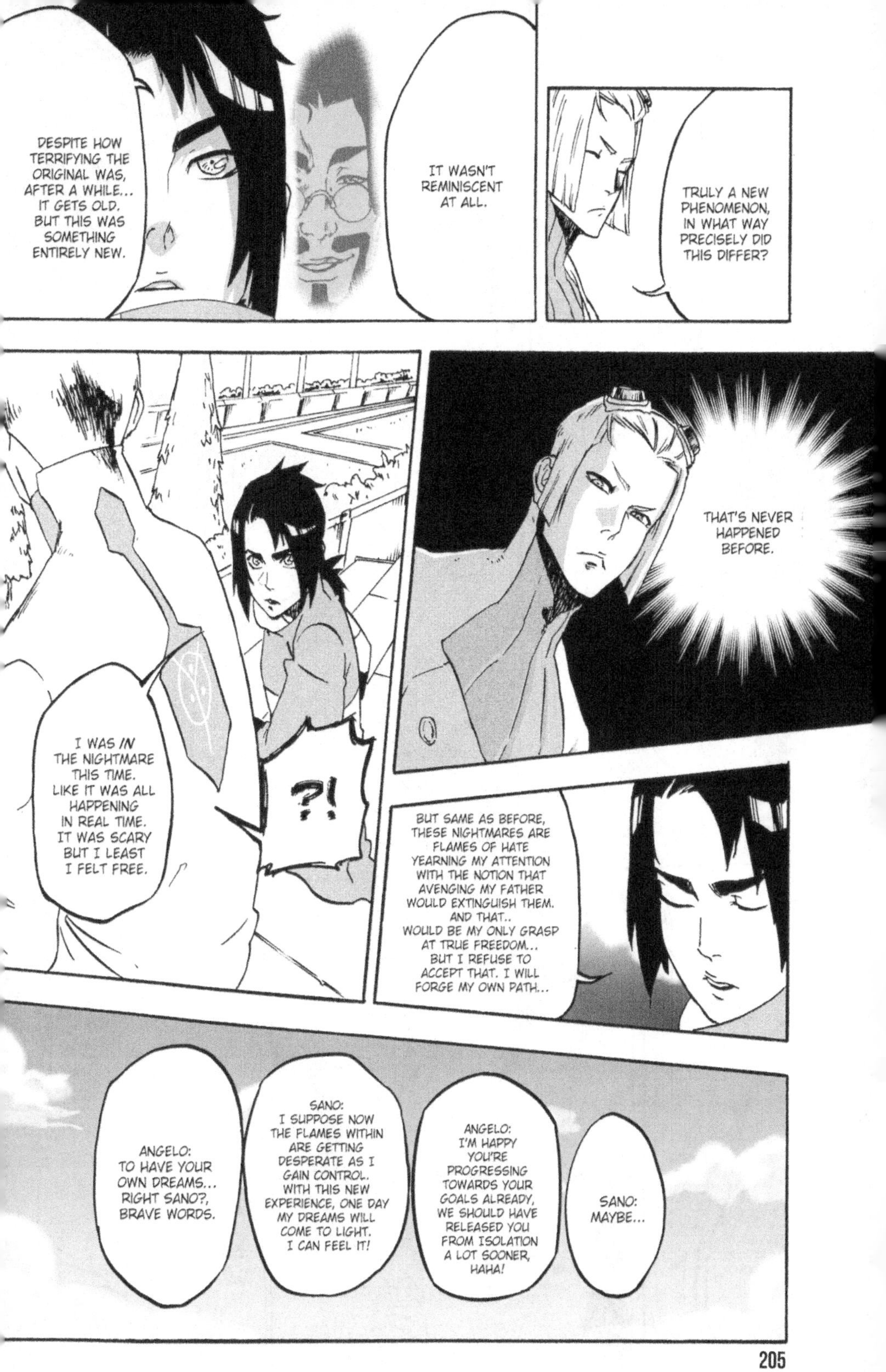
DESPITE HOW TERRIFYING THE ORIGINAL WAS, AFTER A WHILE... IT GETS OLD. BUT THIS WAS SOMETHING ENTIRELY NEW.
IT WASN'T REMINISCENT AT ALL.
TRULY A NEW PHENOMENON, IN WHAT WAY PRECISELY DID THIS DIFFER?
I WAS *IN* THE NIGHTMARE THIS TIME. LIKE IT WAS ALL HAPPENING IN REAL TIME. IT WAS SCARY BUT I LEAST I FELT FREE.
?!
THAT'S NEVER HAPPENED BEFORE.
BUT SAME AS BEFORE, THESE NIGHTMARES ARE FLAMES OF HATE YEARNING MY ATTENTION WITH THE NOTION THAT AVENGING MY FATHER WOULD EXTINGUISH THEM. AND THAT.. WOULD BE MY ONLY GRASP AT TRUE FREEDOM... BUT I REFUSE TO ACCEPT THAT. I WILL FORGE MY OWN PATH...
ANGELO: TO HAVE YOUR OWN DREAMS... RIGHT SANO?, BRAVE WORDS.
SANO: I SUPPOSE NOW THE FLAMES WITHIN ARE GETTING DESPERATE AS I GAIN CONTROL. WITH THIS NEW EXPERIENCE, ONE DAY MY DREAMS WILL COME TO LIGHT. I CAN FEEL IT!
ANGELO: I'M HAPPY YOU'RE PROGRESSING TOWARDS YOUR GOALS ALREADY, WE SHOULD HAVE RELEASED YOU FROM ISOLATION A LOT SOONER, HAHA!
SANO: MAYBE...

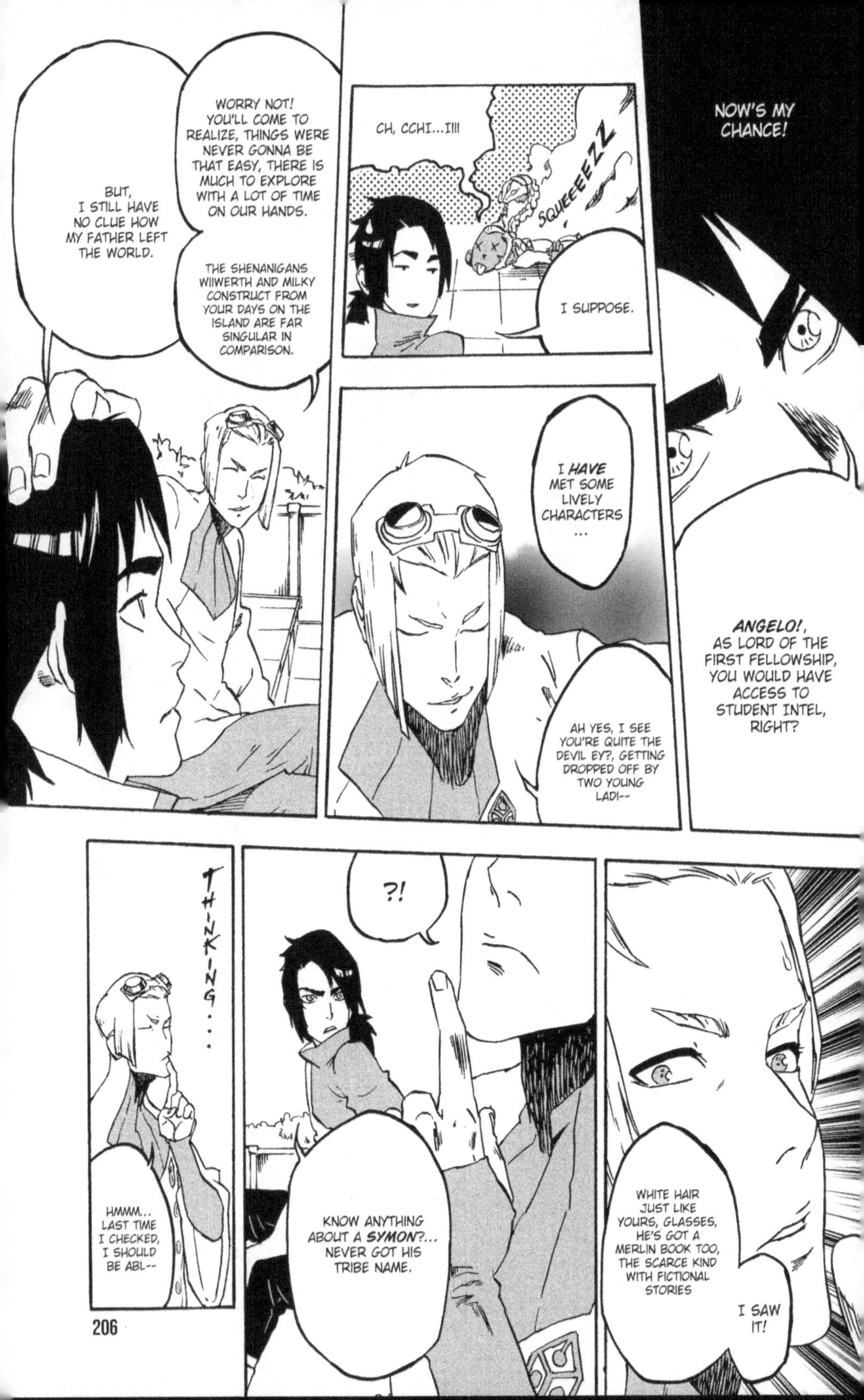
BUT, I STILL HAVE NO CLUE HOW MY FATHER LEFT THE WORLD.
WORRY NOT! YOU'LL COME TO REALIZE, THINGS WERE NEVER GONNA BE THAT EASY, THERE IS MUCH TO EXPLORE WITH A LOT OF TIME ON OUR HANDS.
THE SHENANIGANS WIIWERTH AND MILKY CONSTRUCT FROM YOUR DAYS ON THE ISLAND ARE FAR SINGULAR IN COMPARISON.
CH, CCHI...I!!!
SQUEEEEEZZ
I SUPPOSE.
I *HAVE* MET SOME LIVELY CHARACTERS ...
AH YES, I SEE YOU'RE QUITE THE DEVIL EY?, GETTING DROPPED OFF BY TWO YOUNG LADI--
NOW'S MY CHANCE!
ANGELO!, AS LORD OF THE FIRST FELLOWSHIP, YOU WOULD HAVE ACCESS TO STUDENT INTEL, RIGHT?
THINKING...
HMMM... LAST TIME I CHECKED, I SHOULD BE ABL--
?!
KNOW ANYTHING ABOUT A ***SYMON***?... NEVER GOT HIS TRIBE NAME.
WHITE HAIR JUST LIKE YOURS, GLASSES, HE'S GOT A MERLIN BOOK TOO, THE SCARCE KIND WITH FICTIONAL STORIES
I SAW IT!

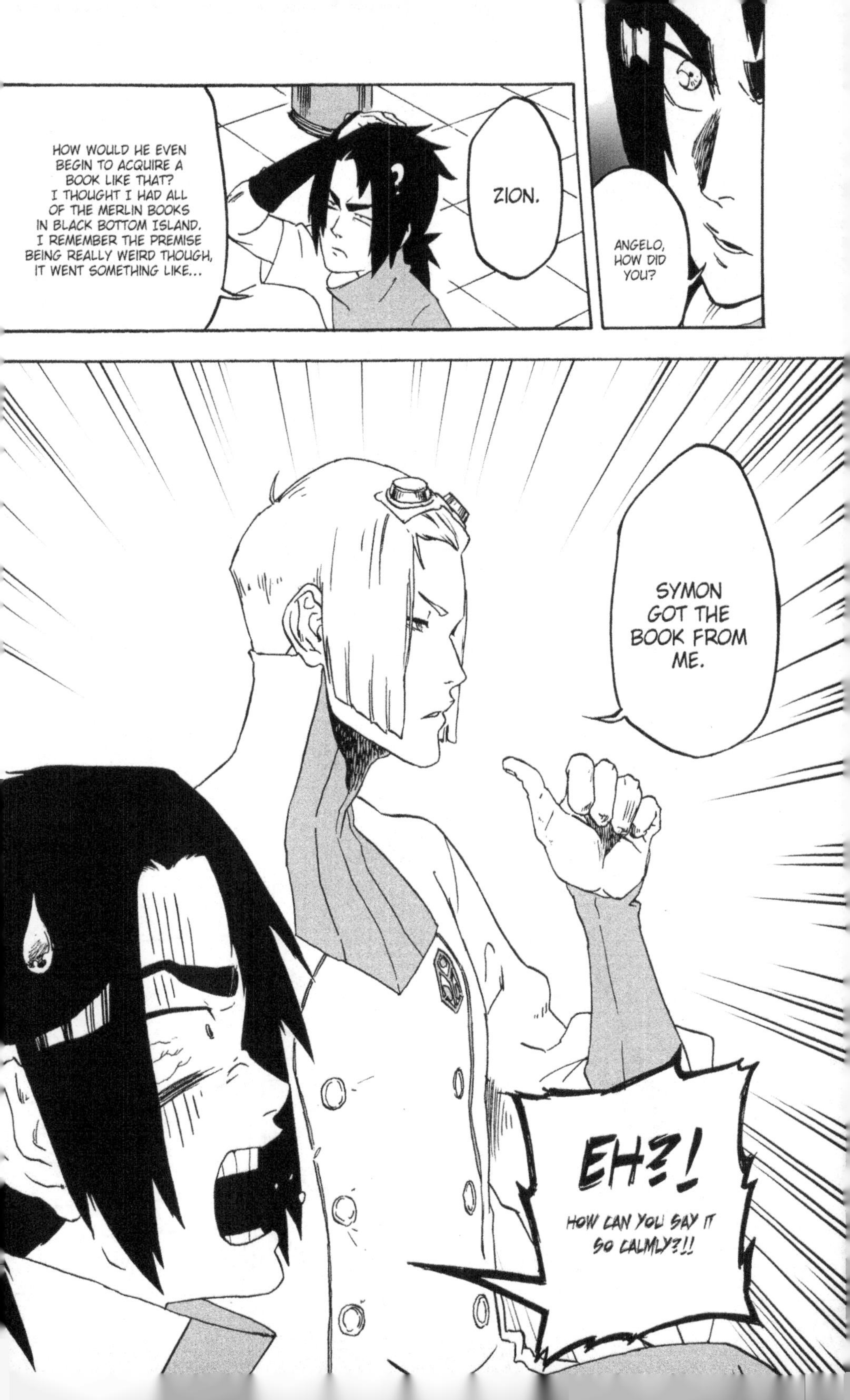
HOW WOULD HE EVEN BEGIN TO ACQUIRE A BOOK LIKE THAT? I THOUGHT I HAD ALL OF THE MERLIN BOOKS IN BLACK BOTTOM ISLAND. I REMEMBER THE PREMISE BEING REALLY WEIRD THOUGH, IT WENT SOMETHING LIKE...
?
ZION.
ANGELO, HOW DID YOU?
SYMON GOT THE BOOK FROM ME.
EH?!
HOW CAN YOU SAY IT SO CALMLY?!!

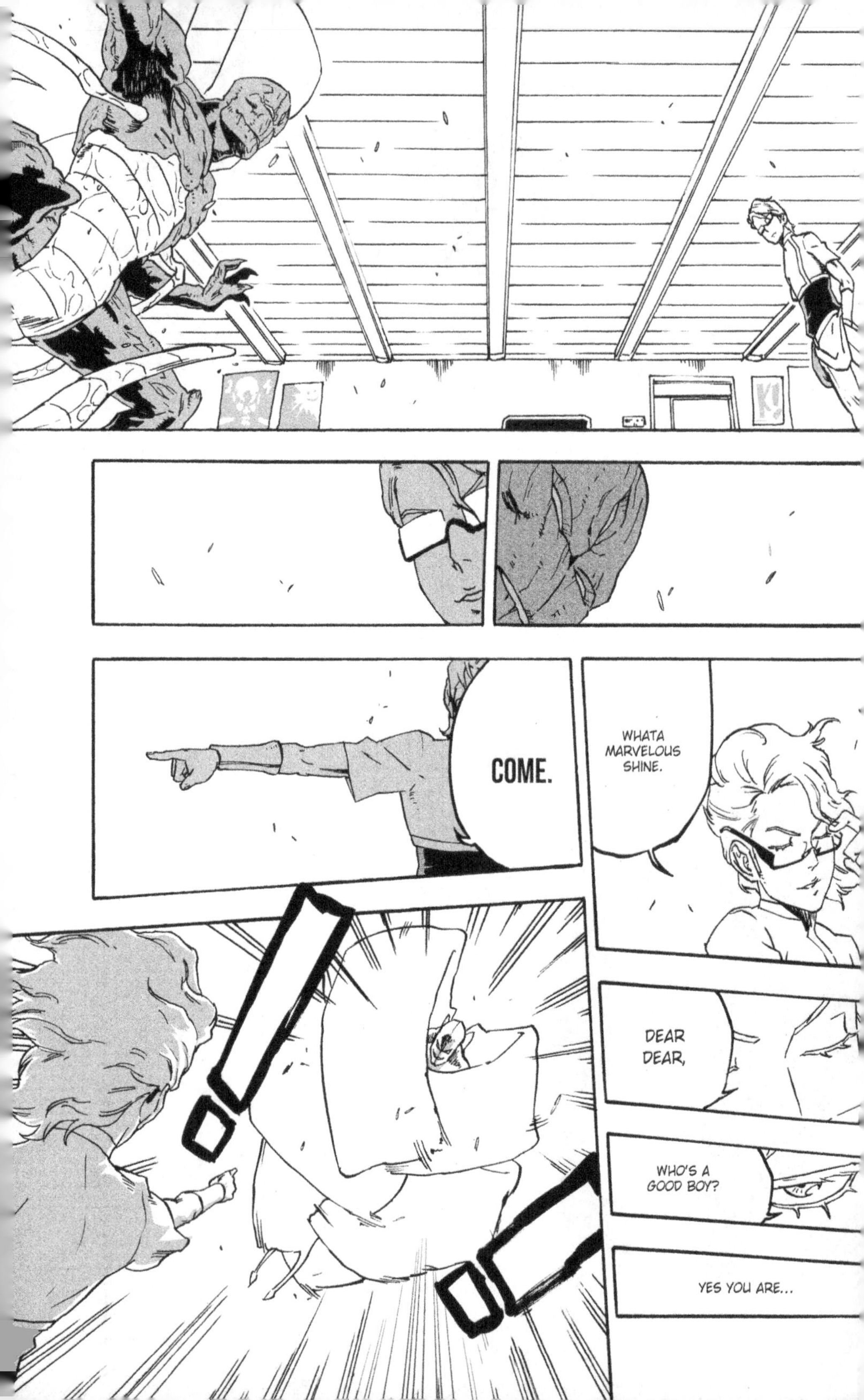
COME.
WHATA MARVELOUS SHINE.
DEAR DEAR,
WHO'S A GOOD BOY?
YES YOU ARE...

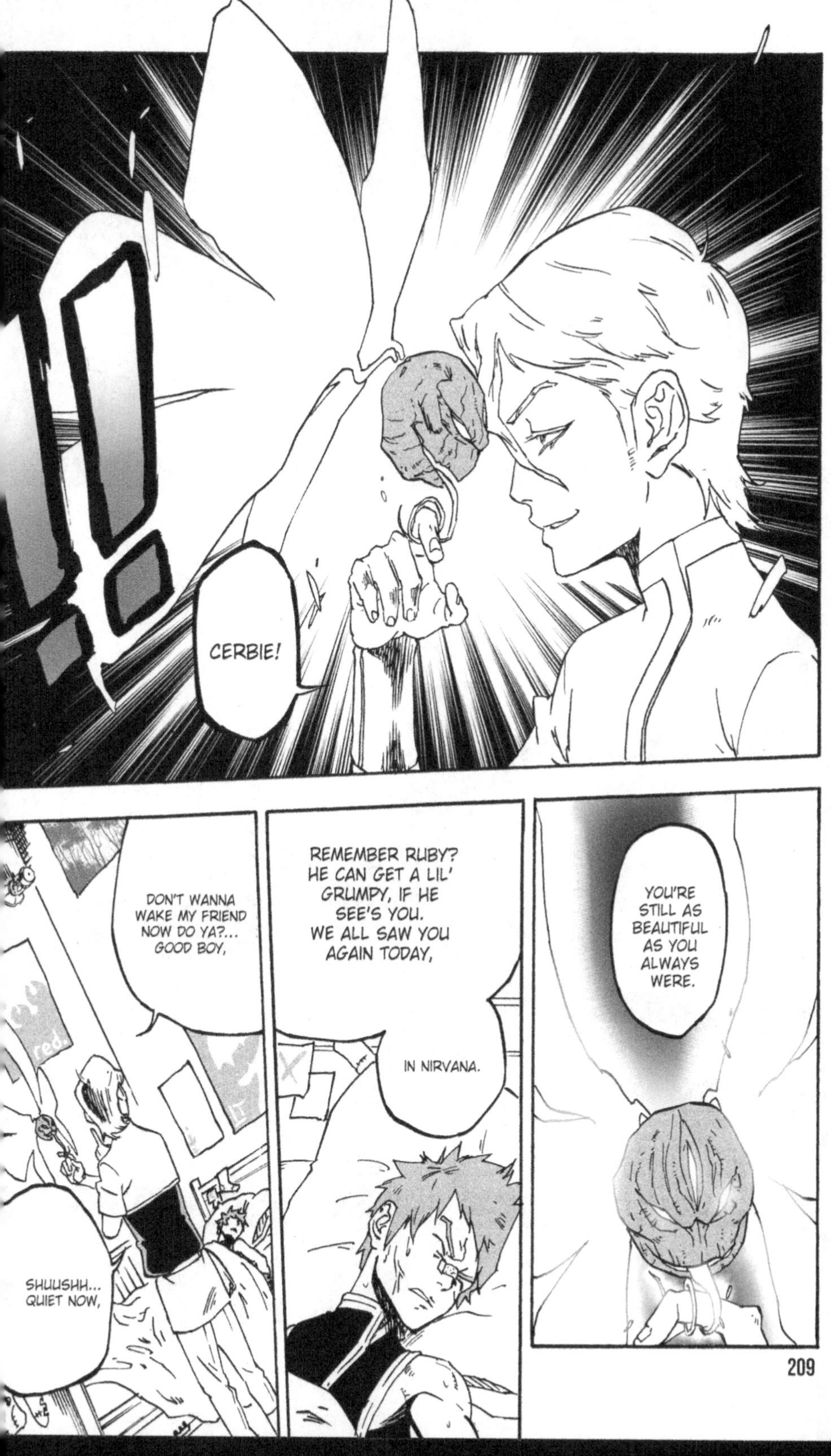
CERBIE!
DON'T WANNA WAKE MY FRIEND NOW DO YA?... GOOD BOY,
SHUUSHH... QUIET NOW,
REMEMBER RUBY? HE CAN GET A LIL' GRUMPY, IF HE SEE'S YOU. WE ALL SAW YOU AGAIN TODAY,
IN NIRVANA.
YOU'RE STILL AS BEAUTIFUL AS YOU ALWAYS WERE.

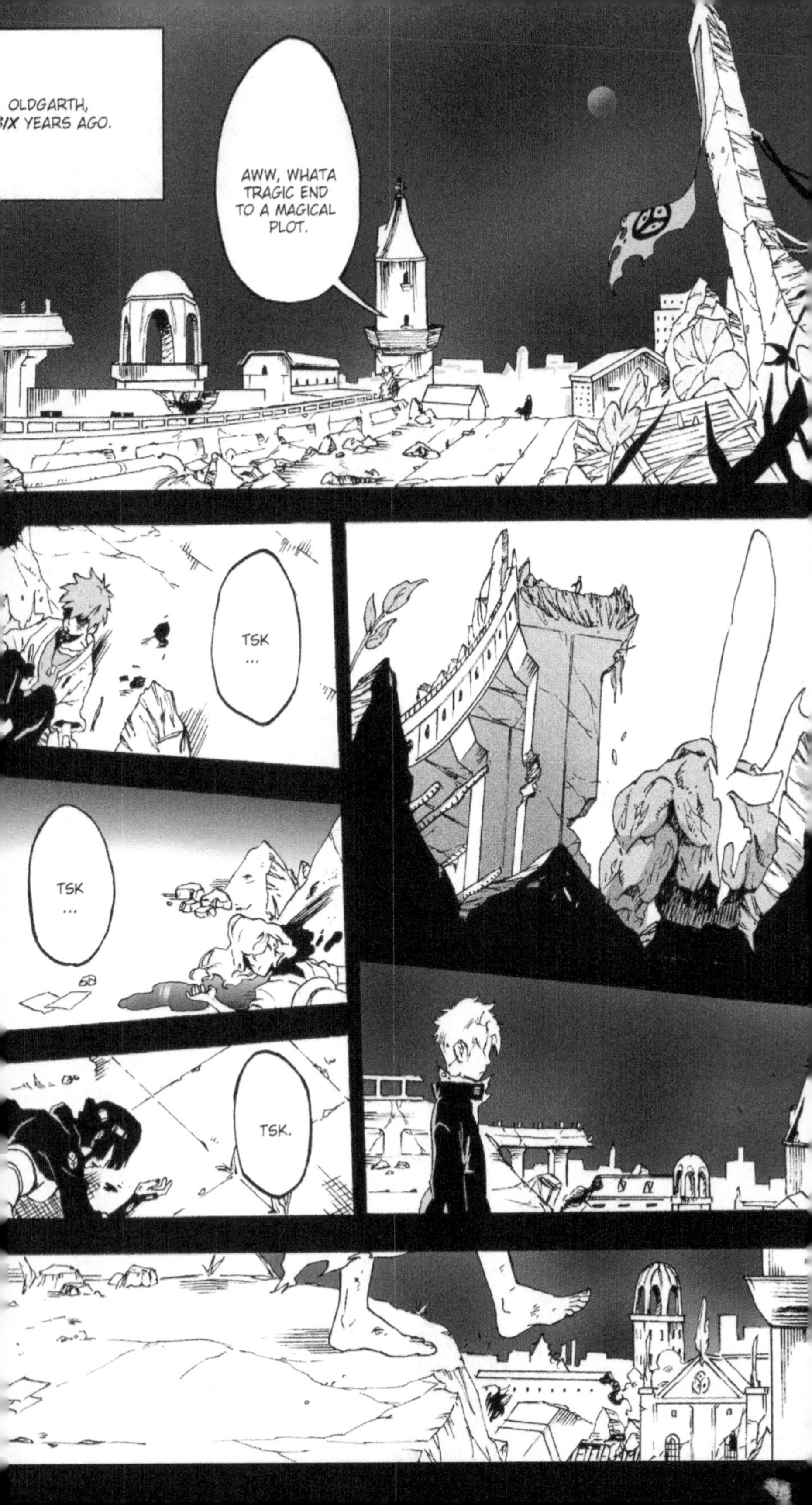
OLDGARTH, SIX YEARS AGO.
AWW, WHATA TRAGIC END TO A MAGICAL PLOT.
TSK ...
TSK ...
TSK.

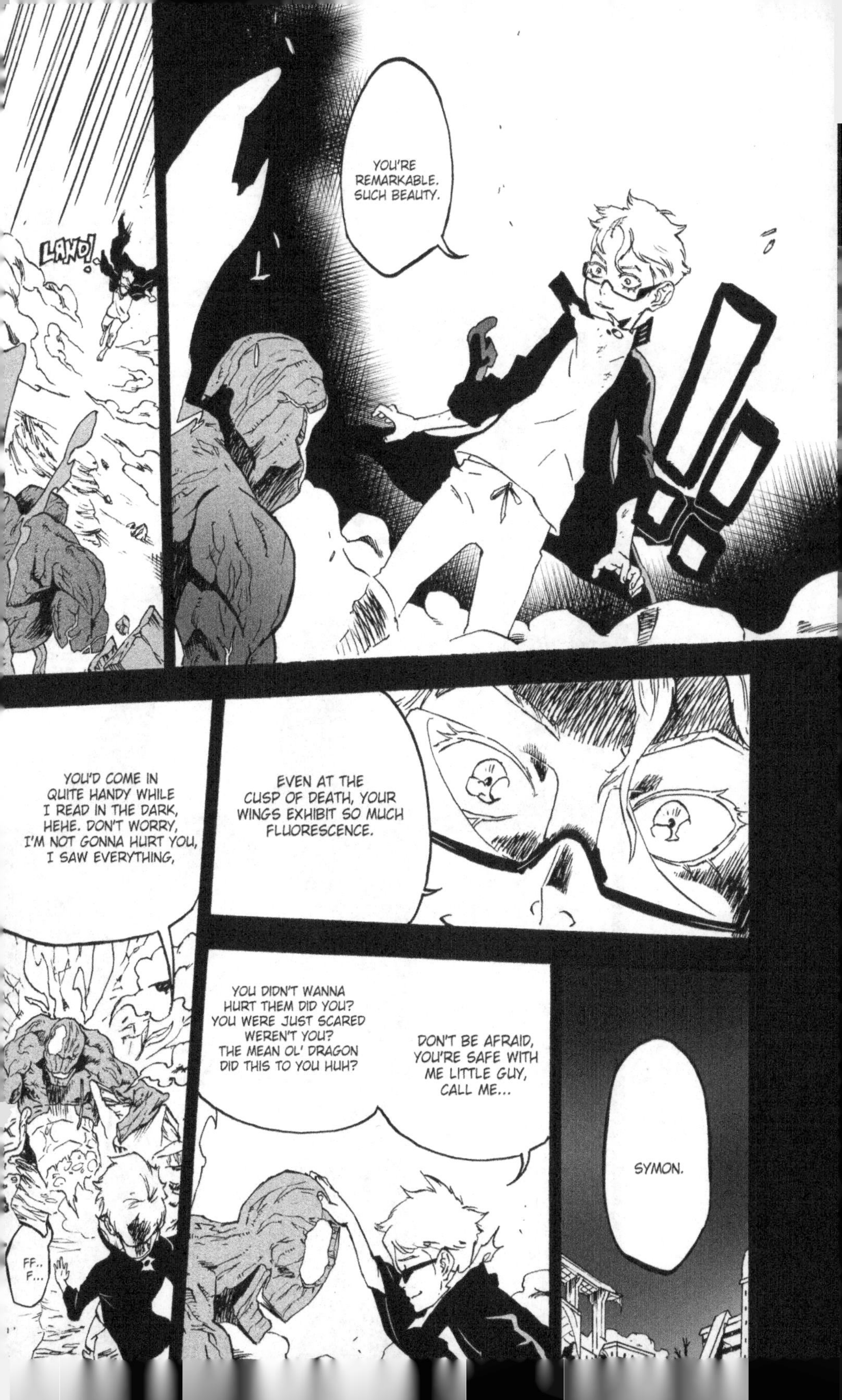
LAND!
YOU'RE REMARKABLE. SUCH BEAUTY.
YOU'D COME IN QUITE HANDY WHILE I READ IN THE DARK, HEHE. DON'T WORRY, I'M NOT GONNA HURT YOU, I SAW EVERYTHING,
FF.. F...
EVEN AT THE CUSP OF DEATH, YOUR WINGS EXHIBIT SO MUCH FLUORESCENCE.
YOU DIDN'T WANNA HURT THEM DID YOU? YOU WERE JUST SCARED WEREN'T YOU? THE MEAN OL' DRAGON DID THIS TO YOU HUH?
DON'T BE AFRAID, YOU'RE SAFE WITH ME LITTLE GUY, CALL ME...
SYMON.

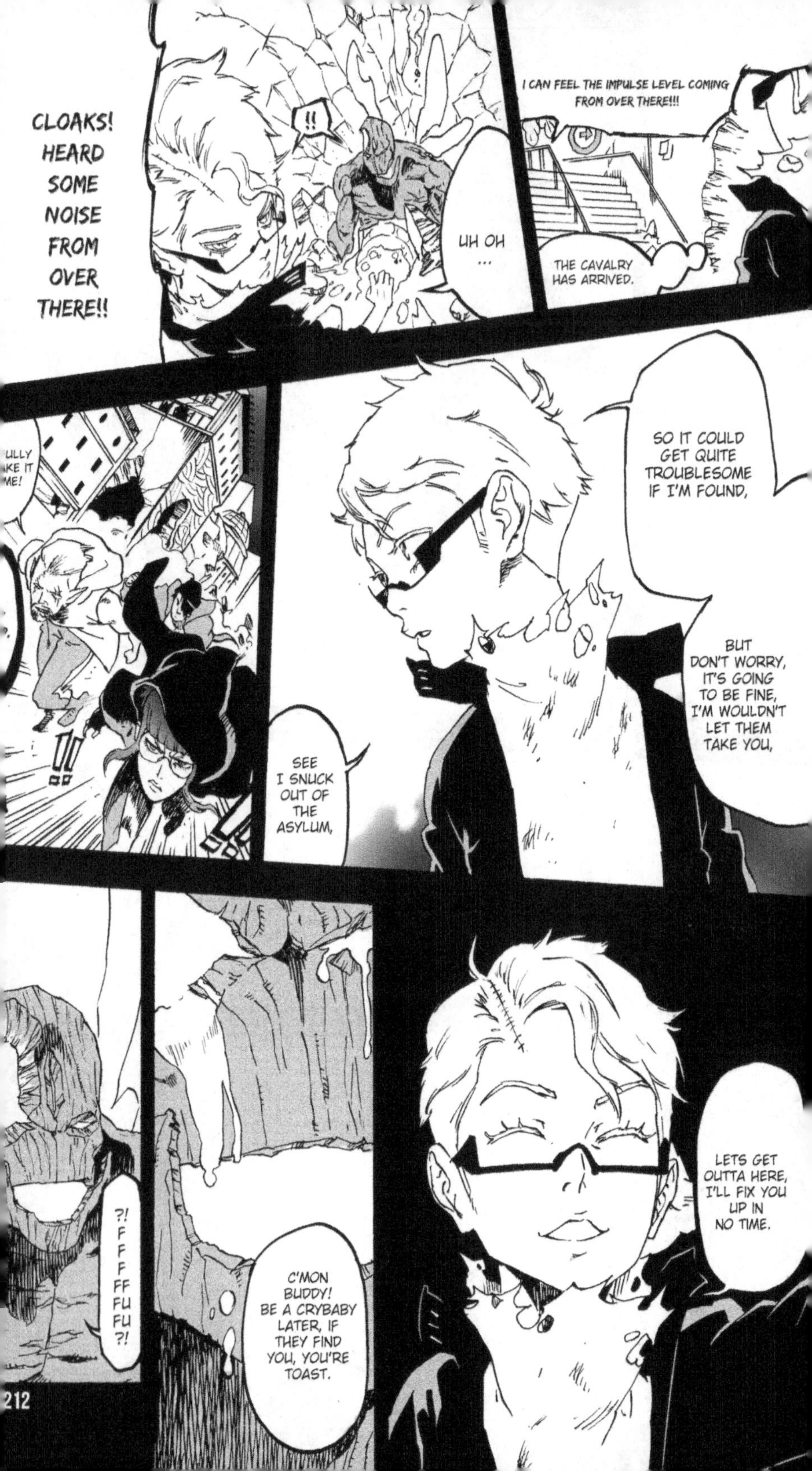
CLOAKS! HEARD SOME NOISE FROM OVER THERE!!
!!
UH OH ...
I CAN FEEL THE IMPULSE LEVEL COMING FROM OVER THERE!!!
THE CAVALRY HAS ARRIVED.
!!
SEE I SNUCK OUT OF THE ASYLUM,
SO IT COULD GET QUITE TROUBLESOME IF I'M FOUND,
BUT DON'T WORRY, IT'S GOING TO BE FINE, I'M WOULDN'T LET THEM TAKE YOU,
?! FFFFFFUFU ?!
C'MON BUDDY! BE A CRYBABY LATER, IF THEY FIND YOU, YOU'RE TOAST.
LETS GET OUTTA HERE, I'LL FIX YOU UP IN NO TIME.

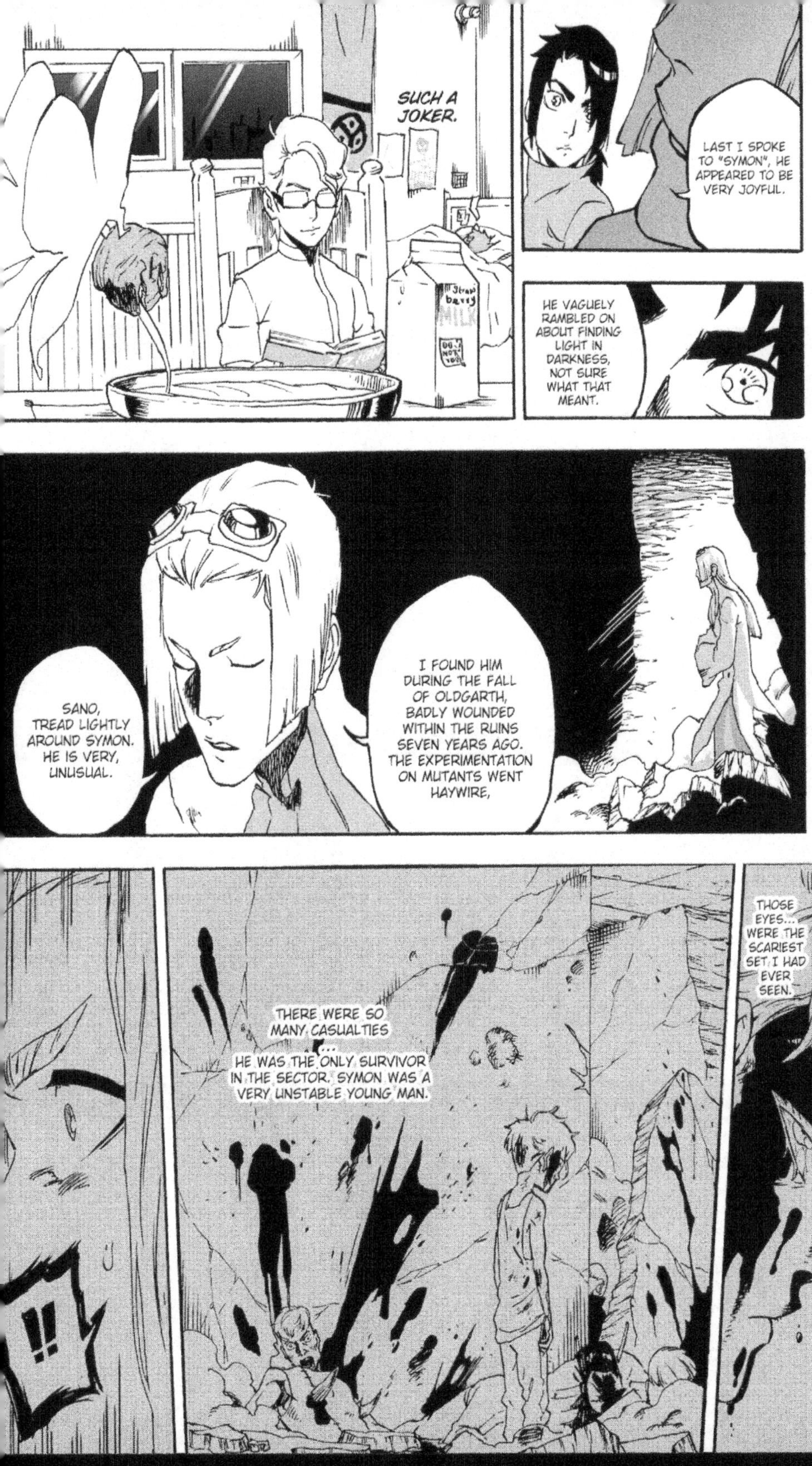
SUCH A JOKER.
MILK
LAST I SPOKE TO "SYMON", HE APPEARED TO BE VERY JOYFUL.
HE VAGUELY RAMBLED ON ABOUT FINDING LIGHT IN DARKNESS, NOT SURE WHAT THAT MEANT.
SANO, TREAD LIGHTLY AROUND SYMON. HE IS VERY, UNUSUAL.
I FOUND HIM DURING THE FALL OF OLDGARTH, BADLY WOUNDED WITHIN THE RUINS SEVEN YEARS AGO. THE EXPERIMENTATION ON MUTANTS WENT HAYWIRE,
!!
THERE WERE SO MANY CASUALTIES ...
HE WAS THE ONLY SURVIVOR IN THE SECTOR. SYMON WAS A VERY UNSTABLE YOUNG MAN.
THOSE EYES... WERE THE SCARIEST SET I HAD EVER SEEN.

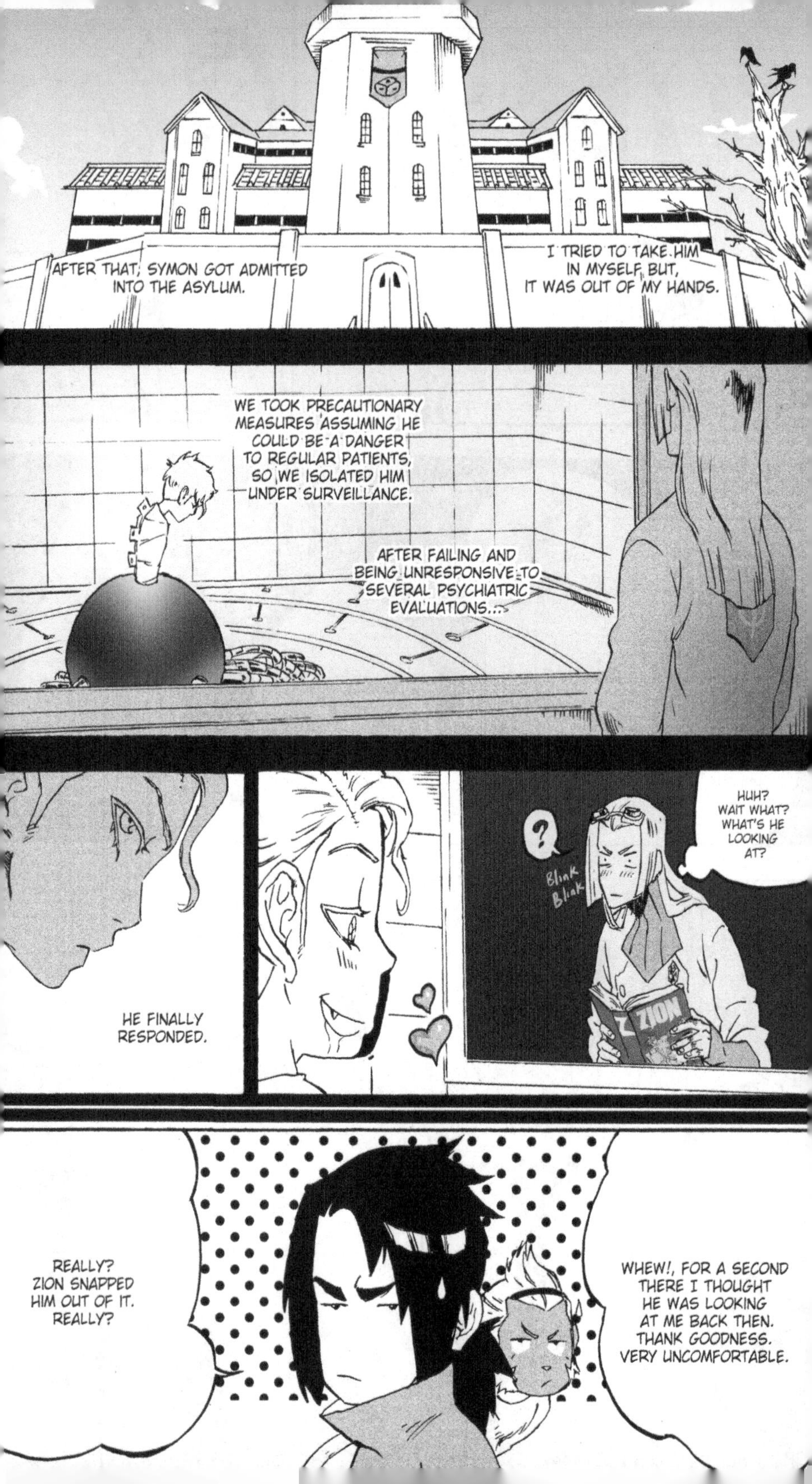
AFTER THAT, SYMON GOT ADMITTED INTO THE ASYLUM.
I TRIED TO TAKE HIM IN MYSELF BUT, IT WAS OUT OF MY HANDS.
WE TOOK PRECAUTIONARY MEASURES ASSUMING HE COULD BE A DANGER TO REGULAR PATIENTS, SO WE ISOLATED HIM UNDER SURVEILLANCE.
AFTER FAILING AND BEING UNRESPONSIVE TO SEVERAL PSYCHIATRIC EVALUATIONS...
HE FINALLY RESPONDED.
?
Blink Blink
HUH? WAIT WHAT? WHAT'S HE LOOKING AT?
ZION
REALLY? ZION SNAPPED HIM OUT OF IT. REALLY?
WHEW!, FOR A SECOND THERE I THOUGHT HE WAS LOOKING AT ME BACK THEN. THANK GOODNESS. VERY UNCOMFORTABLE.

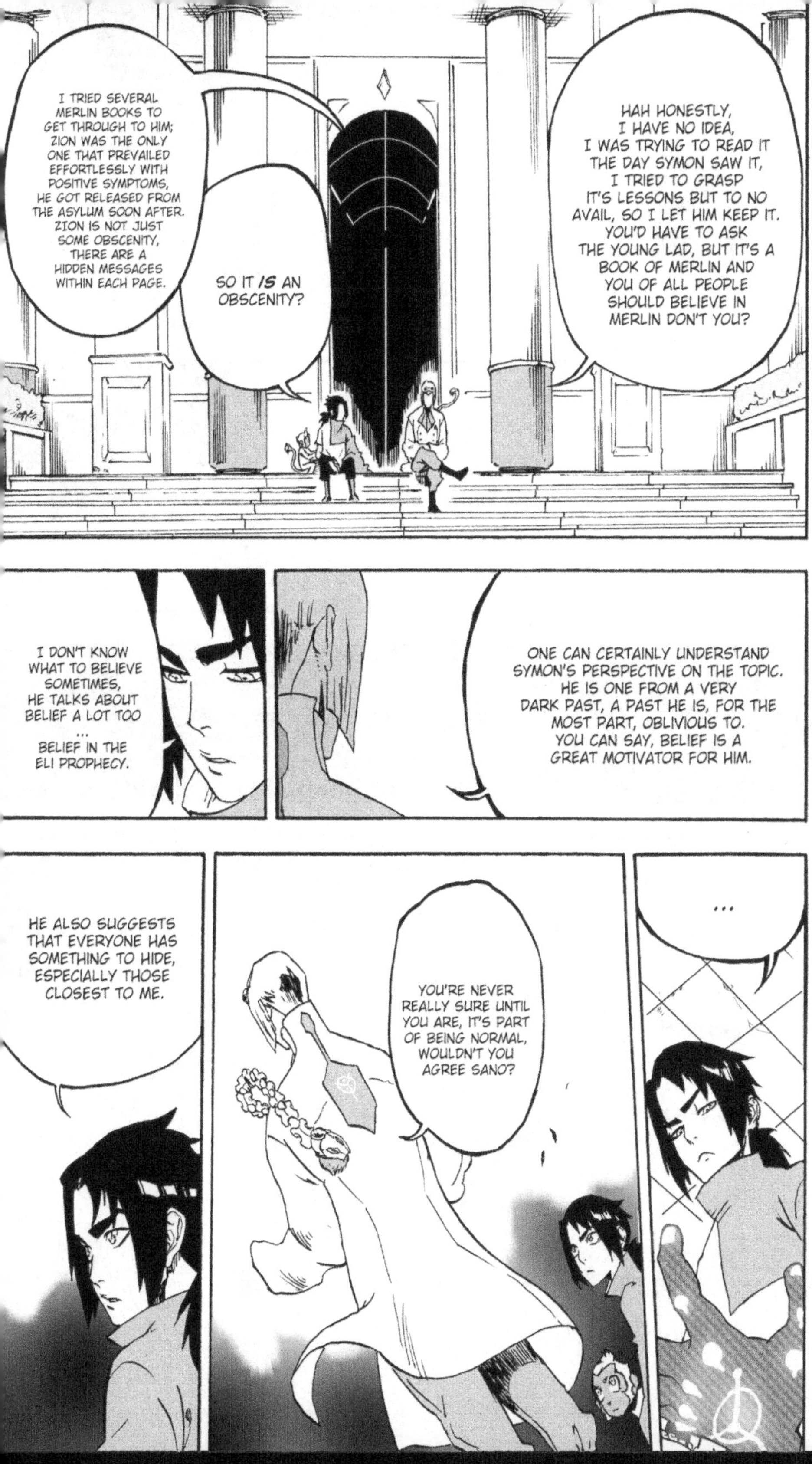
I TRIED SEVERAL MERLIN BOOKS TO GET THROUGH TO HIM; ZION WAS THE ONLY ONE THAT PREVAILED EFFORTLESSLY WITH POSITIVE SYMPTOMS, HE GOT RELEASED FROM THE ASYLUM SOON AFTER. ZION IS NOT JUST SOME OBSCENITY, THERE ARE A HIDDEN MESSAGES WITHIN EACH PAGE.
SO IT *IS* AN OBSCENITY?
HAH HONESTLY, I HAVE NO IDEA, I WAS TRYING TO READ IT THE DAY SYMON SAW IT, I TRIED TO GRASP IT'S LESSONS BUT TO NO AVAIL, SO I LET HIM KEEP IT. YOU'D HAVE TO ASK THE YOUNG LAD, BUT IT'S A BOOK OF MERLIN AND YOU OF ALL PEOPLE SHOULD BELIEVE IN MERLIN DON'T YOU?
I DON'T KNOW WHAT TO BELIEVE SOMETIMES, HE TALKS ABOUT BELIEF A LOT TOO ... BELIEF IN THE ELI PROPHECY.
ONE CAN CERTAINLY UNDERSTAND SYMON'S PERSPECTIVE ON THE TOPIC. HE IS ONE FROM A VERY DARK PAST, A PAST HE IS, FOR THE MOST PART, OBLIVIOUS TO. YOU CAN SAY, BELIEF IS A GREAT MOTIVATOR FOR HIM.
HE ALSO SUGGESTS THAT EVERYONE HAS SOMETHING TO HIDE, ESPECIALLY THOSE CLOSEST TO ME.
YOU'RE NEVER REALLY SURE UNTIL YOU ARE, IT'S PART OF BEING NORMAL, WOULDN'T YOU AGREE SANO?
...

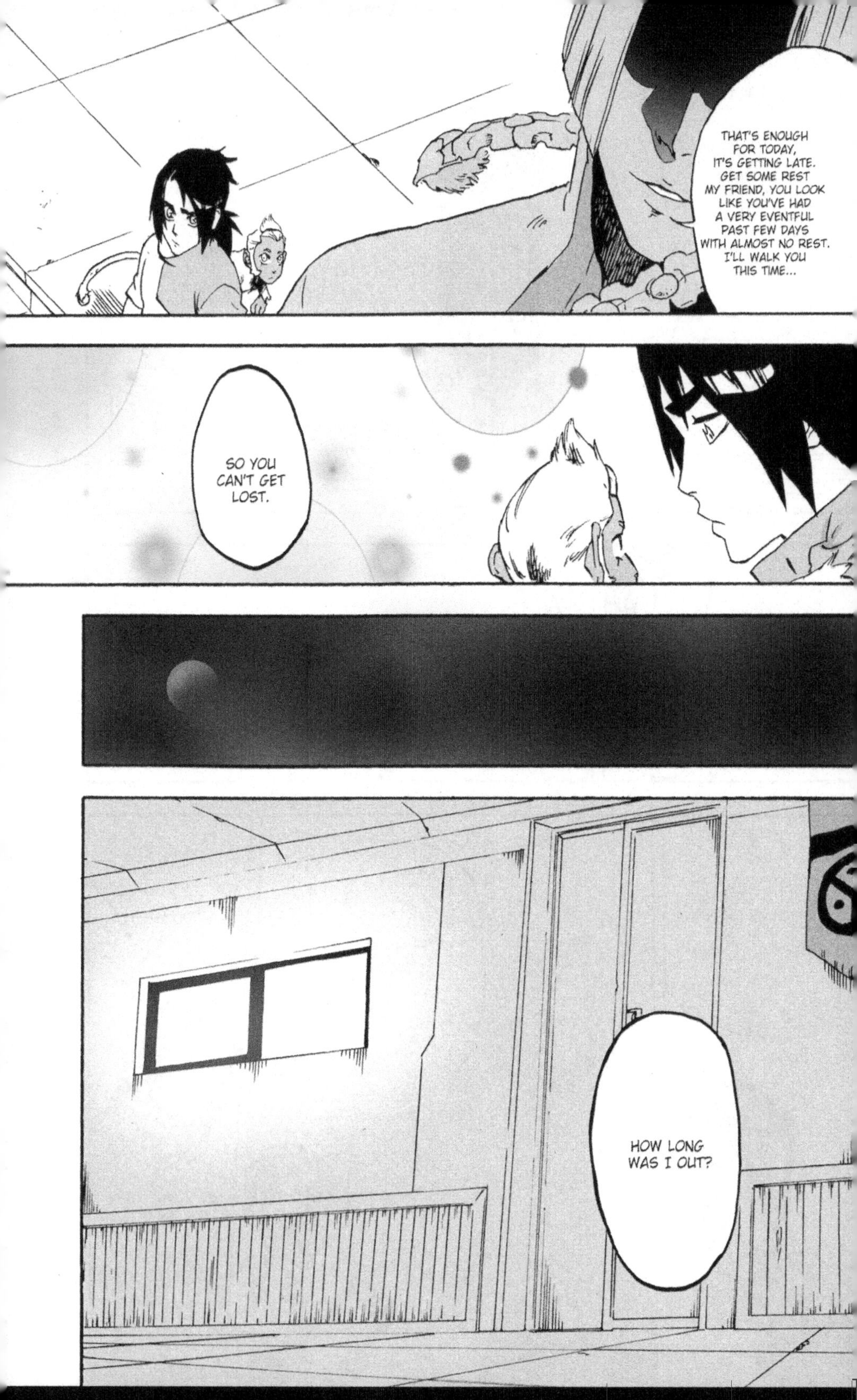
THAT'S ENOUGH FOR TODAY, IT'S GETTING LATE. GET SOME REST MY FRIEND, YOU LOOK LIKE YOU'VE HAD A VERY EVENTFUL PAST FEW DAYS WITH ALMOST NO REST. I'LL WALK YOU THIS TIME...
SO YOU CAN'T GET LOST.
HOW LONG WAS I OUT?

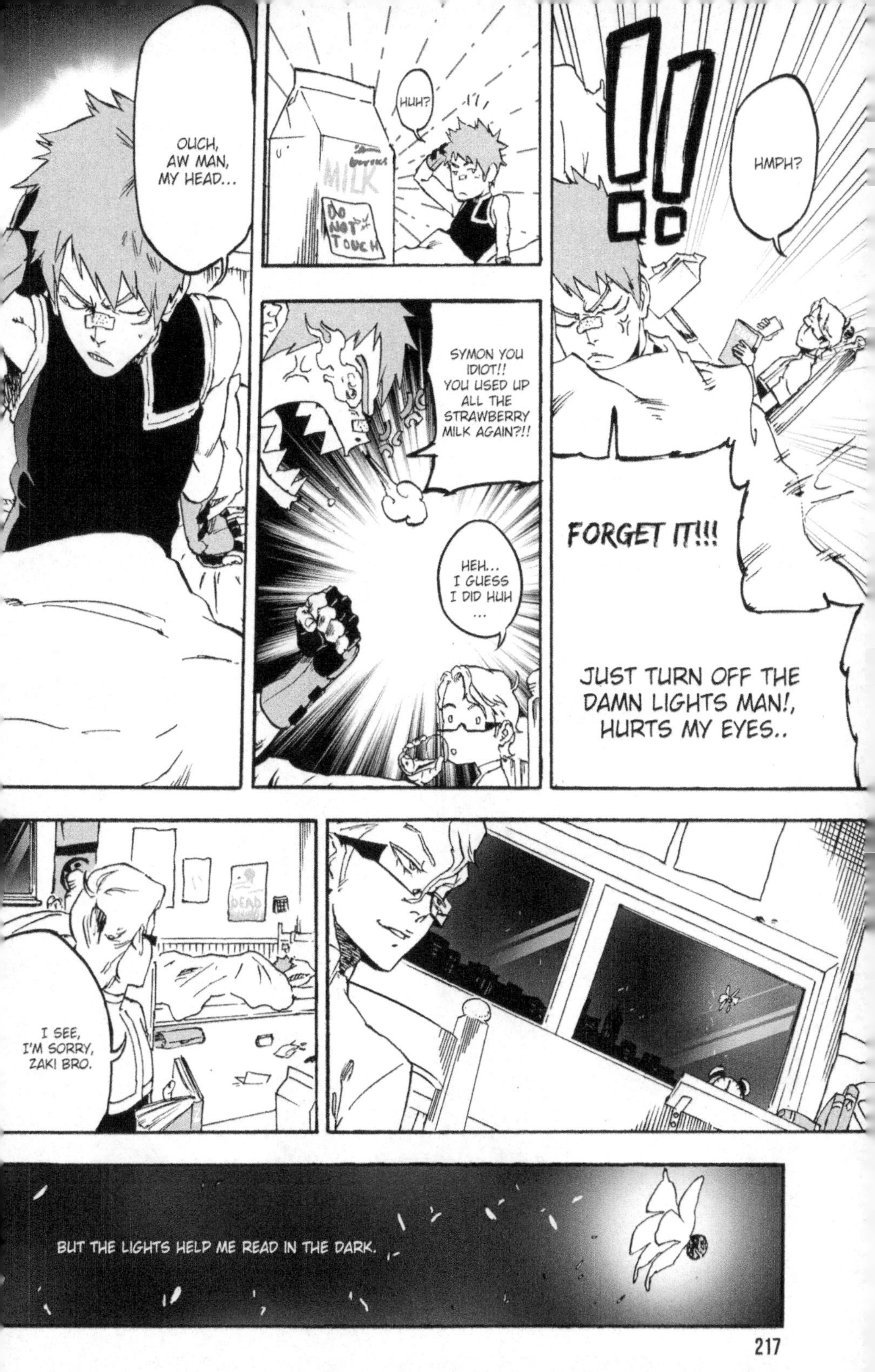
OUCH, AW MAN, MY HEAD...
MILK
DO NOT TOUCH
HUH?
SYMON YOU IDIOT!! YOU USED UP ALL THE STRAWBERRY MILK AGAIN?!!
HEH... I GUESS I DID HUH ...
HMPH?
FORGET IT!!!
JUST TURN OFF THE DAMN LIGHTS MAN!, HURTS MY EYES..
DEAD
I SEE, I'M SORRY, ZAKI BRO.
BUT THE LIGHTS HELP ME READ IN THE DARK.

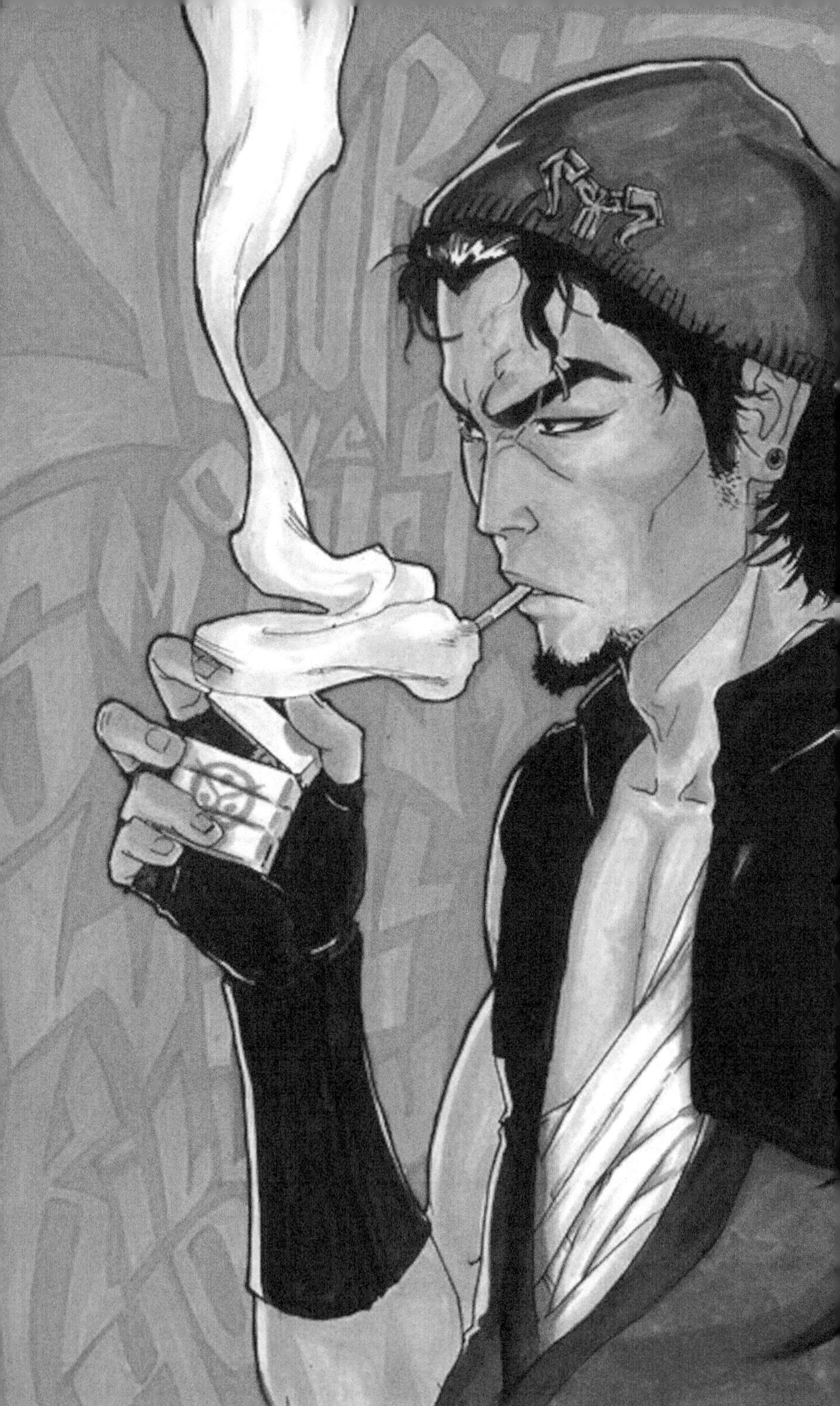

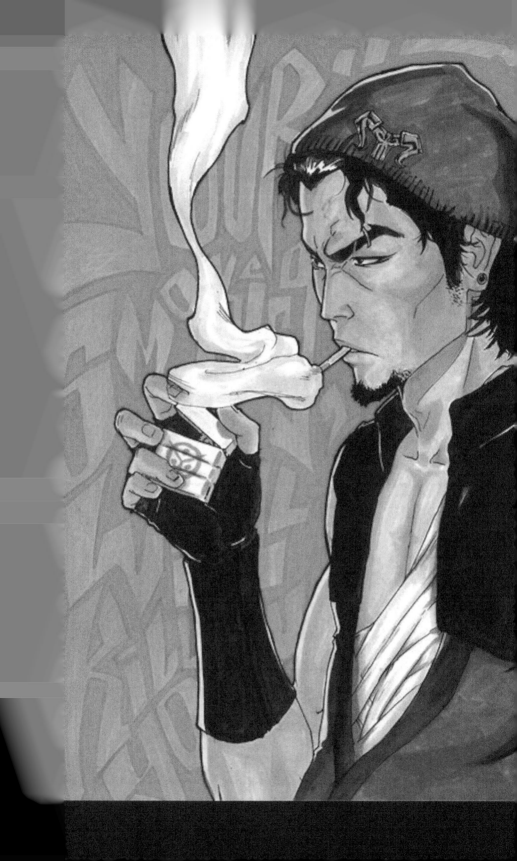

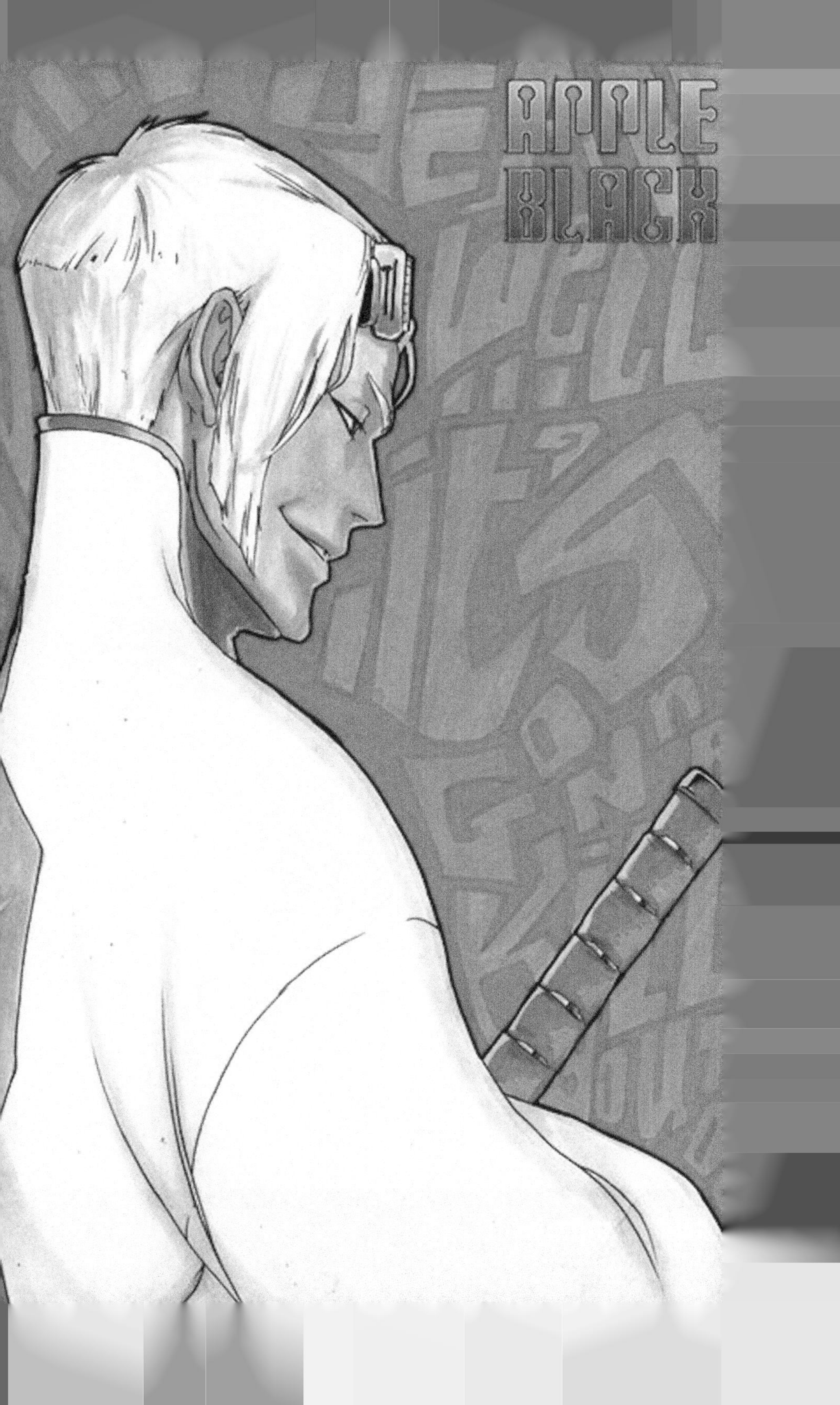
APPLE
BLACK

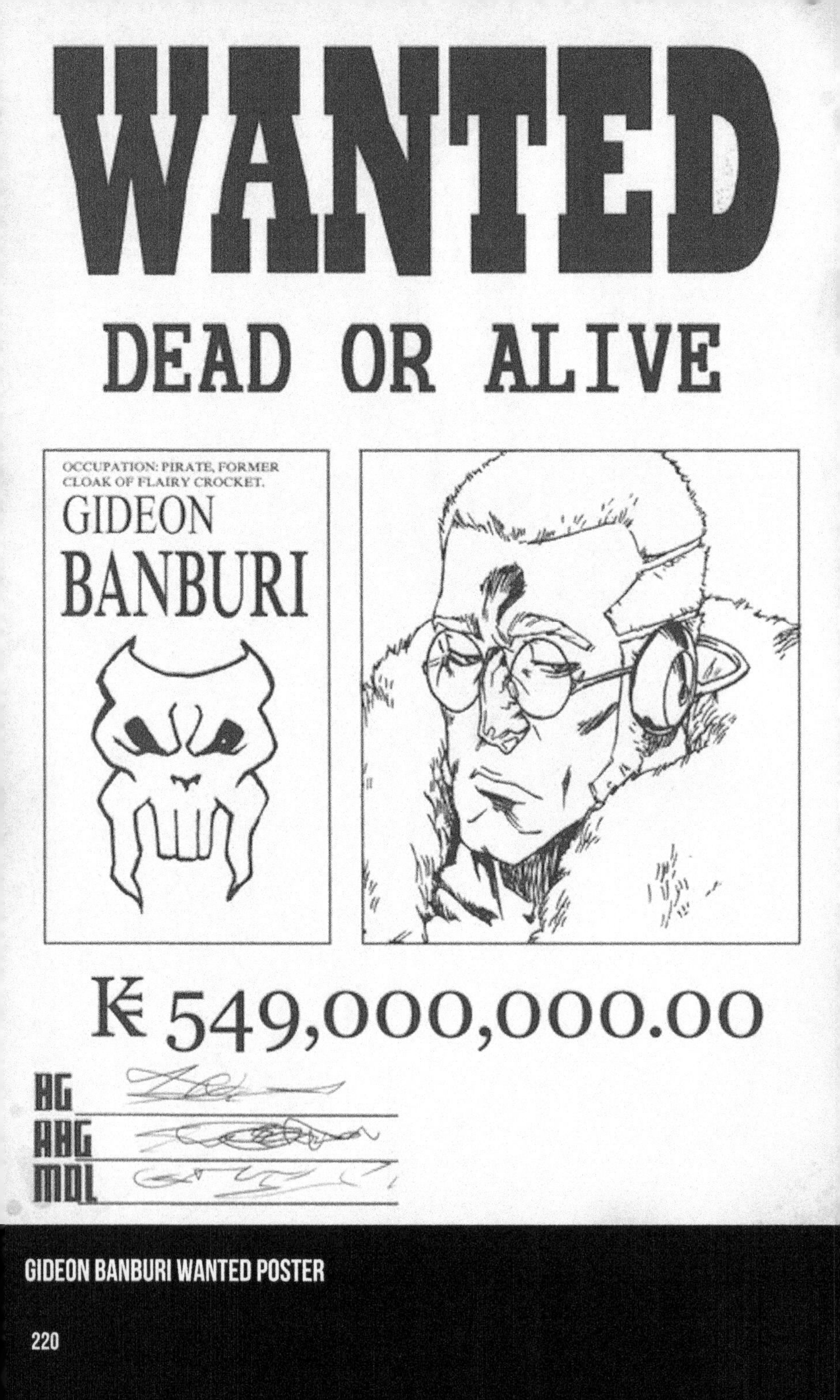
WANTED
DEAD OR ALIVE
OCCUPATION: PIRATE, FORMER CLOAK OF FLAIRY CROCKET.
GIDEON
BANBURI
₭ 549,000,000.00
HG
AHG
MQL

GIDEON BANBURI WANTED POSTER

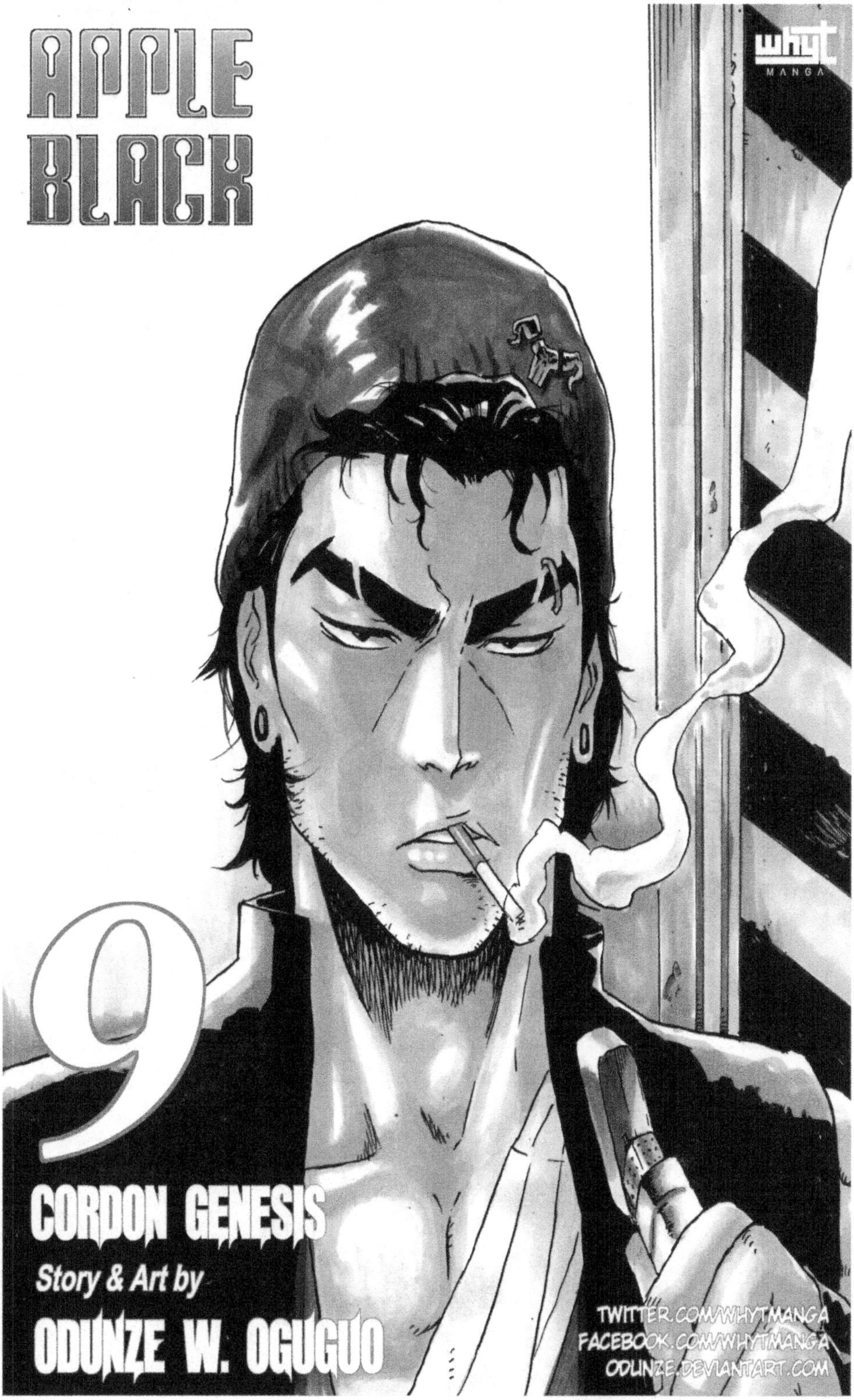
APPLE BLACK
whyt MANGA
9
CORDON GENESIS
Story & Art by
ODUNZE W. OGUGUO
TWITTER.COM/WHYTMANGA
FACEBOOK.COM/WHYTMANGA
ODUNZE.DEVIANTART.COM

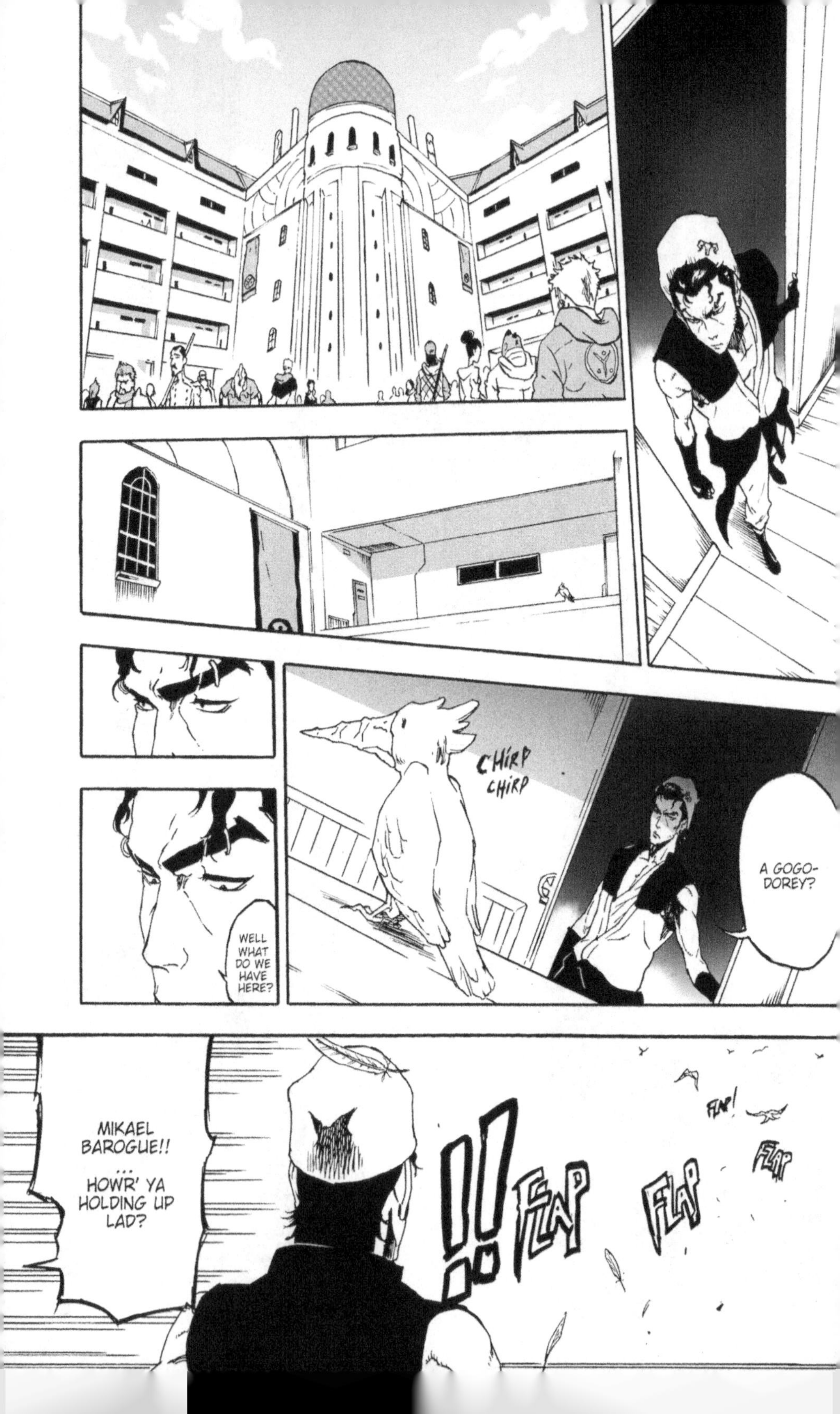

WELL WHAT DO WE HAVE HERE?
CHIRP CHIRP
A GOGO-DOREY?
MIKAEL BAROGUE!! ... HOWR' YA HOLDING UP LAD?
!!
FLAP
FLAP
FLAP!
FLAP

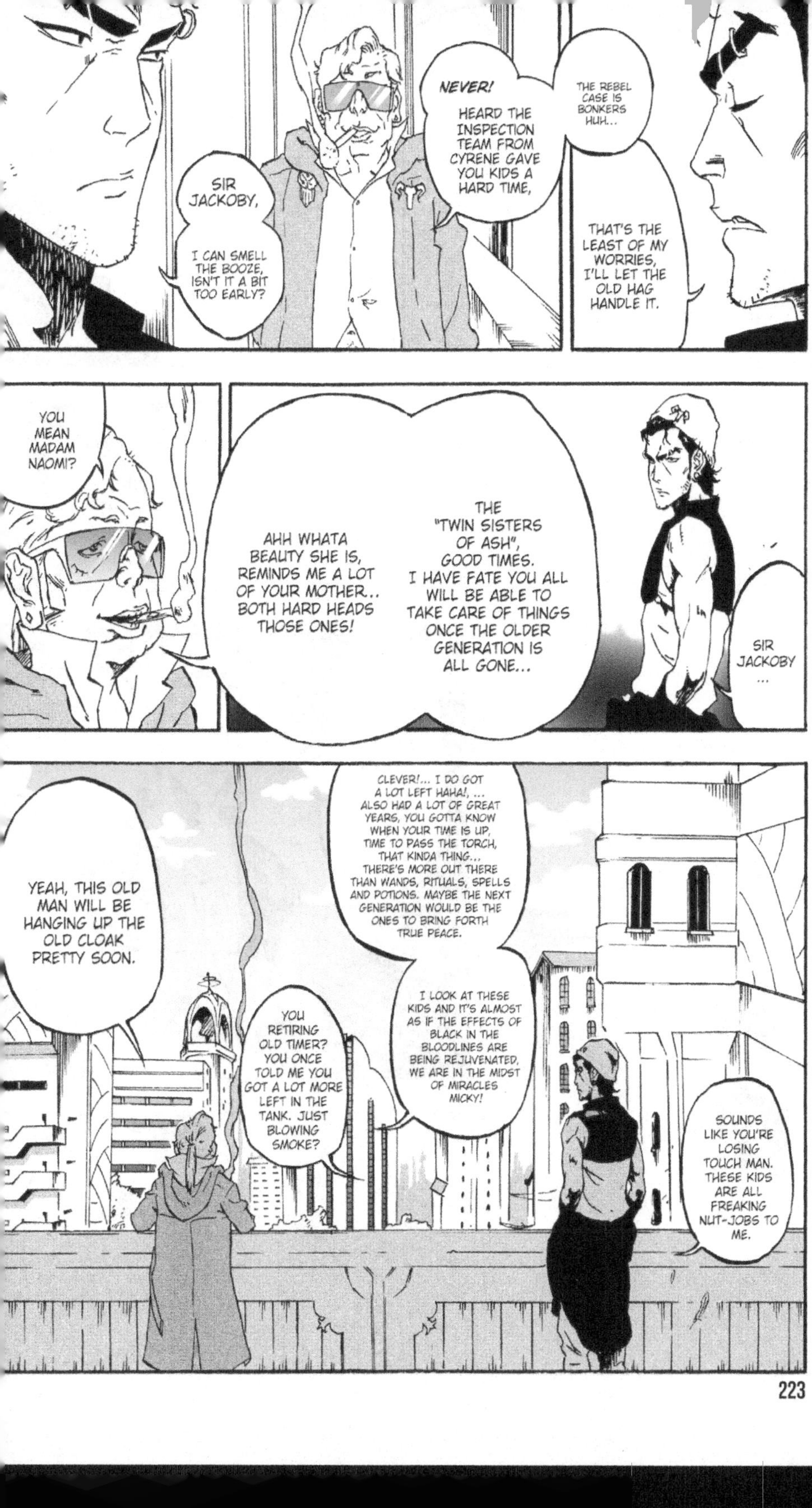
SIR JACKOBY,
I CAN SMELL THE BOOZE, ISN'T IT A BIT TOO EARLY?
NEVER!
HEARD THE INSPECTION TEAM FROM CYRENE GAVE YOU KIDS A HARD TIME,
THE REBEL CASE IS BONKERS HUH...
THAT'S THE LEAST OF MY WORRIES, I'LL LET THE OLD HAG HANDLE IT.
YOU MEAN MADAM NAOMI?
AHH WHATA BEAUTY SHE IS, REMINDS ME A LOT OF YOUR MOTHER... BOTH HARD HEADS THOSE ONES!
THE "TWIN SISTERS OF ASH", GOOD TIMES. I HAVE FATE YOU ALL WILL BE ABLE TO TAKE CARE OF THINGS ONCE THE OLDER GENERATION IS ALL GONE...
SIR JACKOBY ...
YEAH, THIS OLD MAN WILL BE HANGING UP THE OLD CLOAK PRETTY SOON.
YOU RETIRING OLD TIMER? YOU ONCE TOLD ME YOU GOT A LOT MORE LEFT IN THE TANK. JUST BLOWING SMOKE?
CLEVER!... I DO GOT A LOT LEFT HAHA!, ... ALSO HAD A LOT OF GREAT YEARS, YOU GOTTA KNOW WHEN YOUR TIME IS UP, TIME TO PASS THE TORCH, THAT KINDA THING... THERE'S MORE OUT THERE THAN WANDS, RITUALS, SPELLS AND POTIONS. MAYBE THE NEXT GENERATION WOULD BE THE ONES TO BRING FORTH TRUE PEACE.
I LOOK AT THESE KIDS AND IT'S ALMOST AS IF THE EFFECTS OF BLACK IN THE BLOODLINES ARE BEING REJUVENATED, WE ARE IN THE MIDST OF MIRACLES MICKY!
SOUNDS LIKE YOU'RE LOSING TOUCH MAN. THESE KIDS ARE ALL FREAKING NUT-JOBS TO ME.

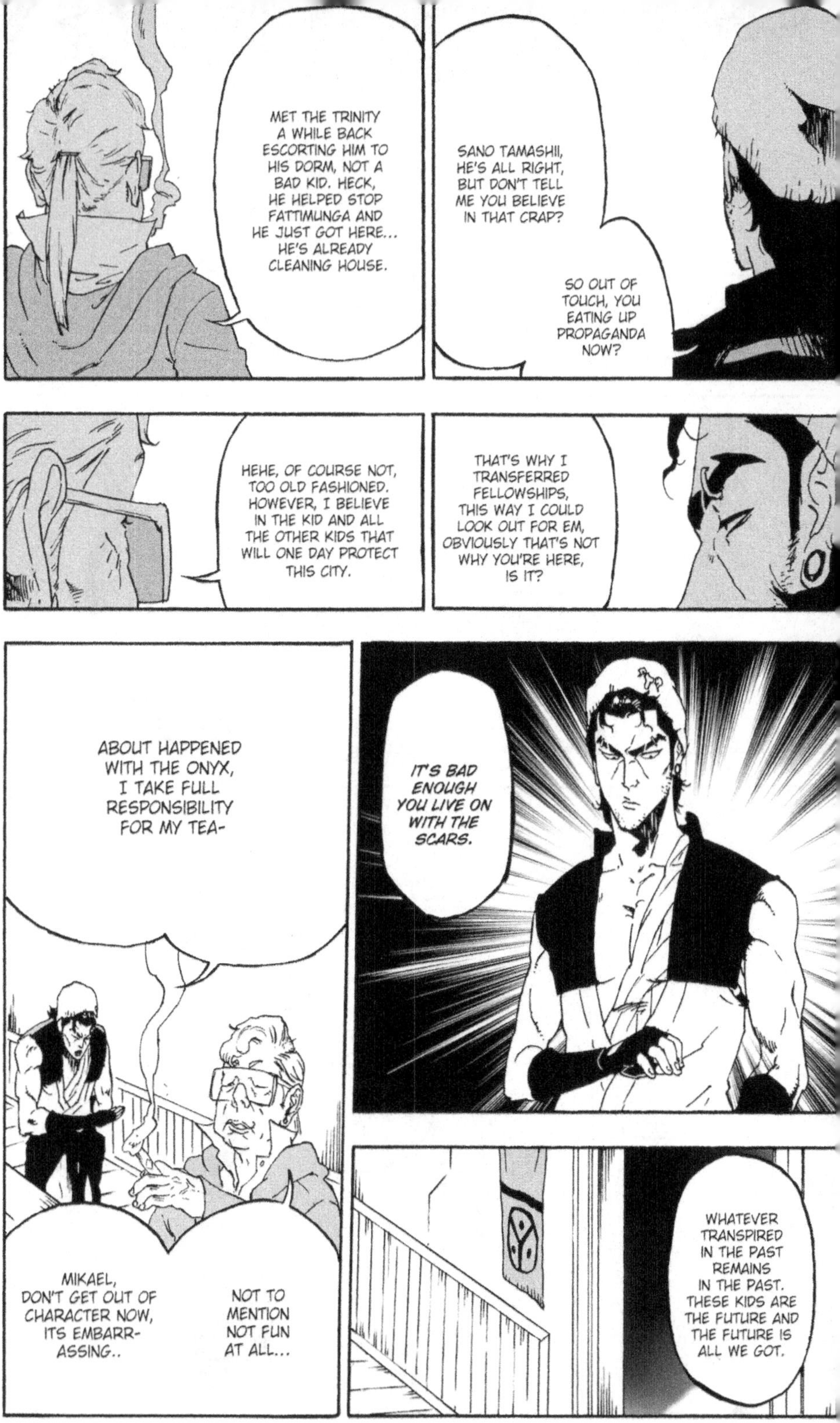
MET THE TRINITY A WHILE BACK ESCORTING HIM TO HIS DORM, NOT A BAD KID. HECK, HE HELPED STOP FATTIMUNGA AND HE JUST GOT HERE... HE'S ALREADY CLEANING HOUSE.
SANO TAMASHII, HE'S ALL RIGHT, BUT DON'T TELL ME YOU BELIEVE IN THAT CRAP?
SO OUT OF TOUCH, YOU EATING UP PROPAGANDA NOW?
HEHE, OF COURSE NOT, TOO OLD FASHIONED. HOWEVER, I BELIEVE IN THE KID AND ALL THE OTHER KIDS THAT WILL ONE DAY PROTECT THIS CITY.
THAT'S WHY I TRANSFERRED FELLOWSHIPS, THIS WAY I COULD LOOK OUT FOR EM, OBVIOUSLY THAT'S NOT WHY YOU'RE HERE, IS IT?
ABOUT HAPPENED WITH THE ONYX, I TAKE FULL RESPONSIBILITY FOR MY TEA-
MIKAEL, DON'T GET OUT OF CHARACTER NOW, ITS EMBARR-ASSING..
NOT TO MENTION NOT FUN AT ALL...
IT'S BAD ENOUGH YOU LIVE ON WITH THE SCARS.
WHATEVER TRANSPIRED IN THE PAST REMAINS IN THE PAST. THESE KIDS ARE THE FUTURE AND THE FUTURE IS ALL WE GOT.

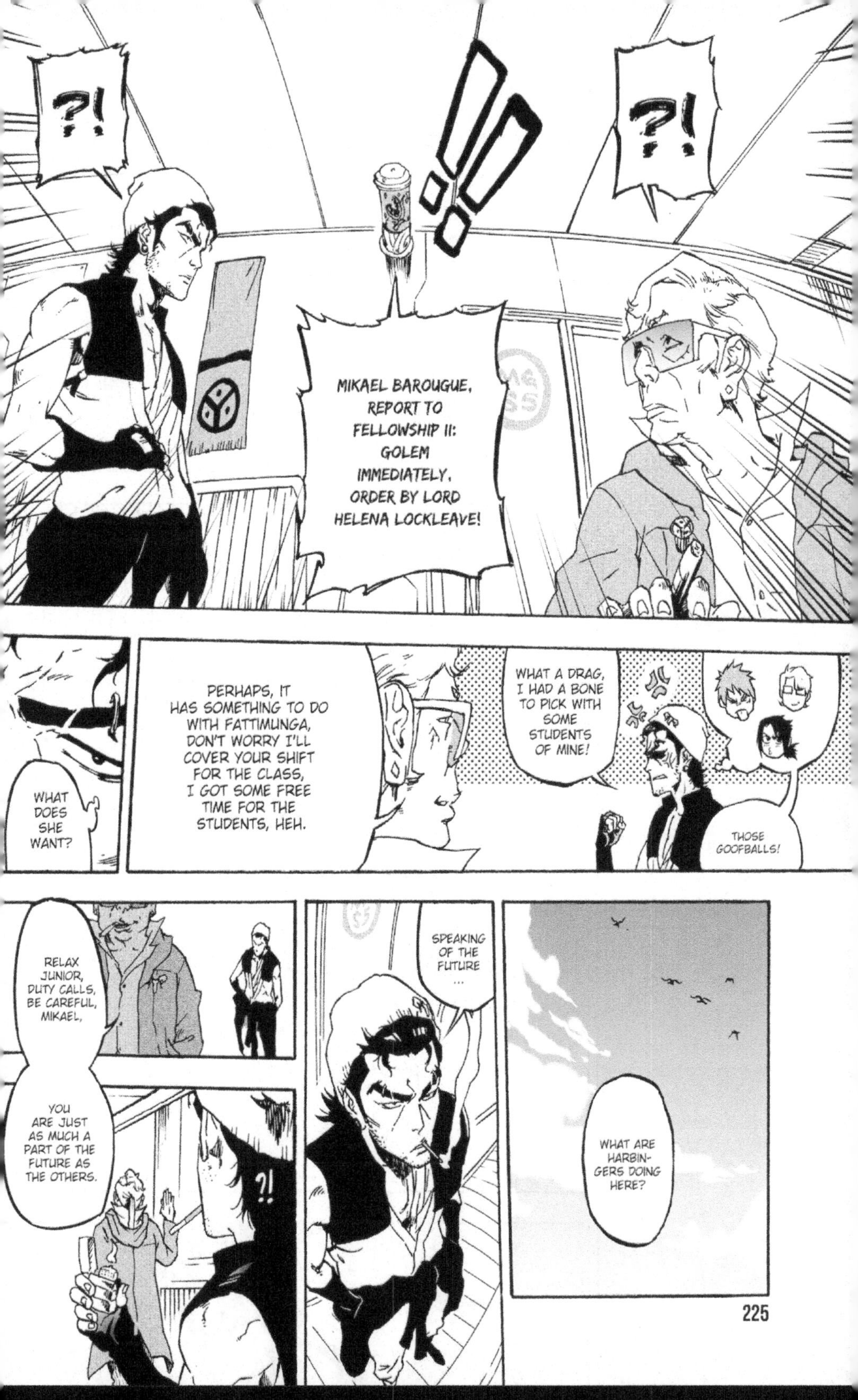
?!
!!
?!
MIKAEL BAROUGUE, REPORT TO FELLOWSHIP II: GOLEM IMMEDIATELY, ORDER BY LORD HELENA LOCKLEAVE!
WHAT DOES SHE WANT?
PERHAPS, IT HAS SOMETHING TO DO WITH FATTIMUNGA, DON'T WORRY I'LL COVER YOUR SHIFT FOR THE CLASS, I GOT SOME FREE TIME FOR THE STUDENTS, HEH.
WHAT A DRAG, I HAD A BONE TO PICK WITH SOME STUDENTS OF MINE!
THOSE GOOFBALLS!
RELAX JUNIOR, DUTY CALLS, BE CAREFUL, MIKAEL,
YOU ARE JUST AS MUCH A PART OF THE FUTURE AS THE OTHERS.
?!
SPEAKING OF THE FUTURE ...
WHAT ARE HARBIN-GERS DOING HERE?

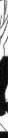

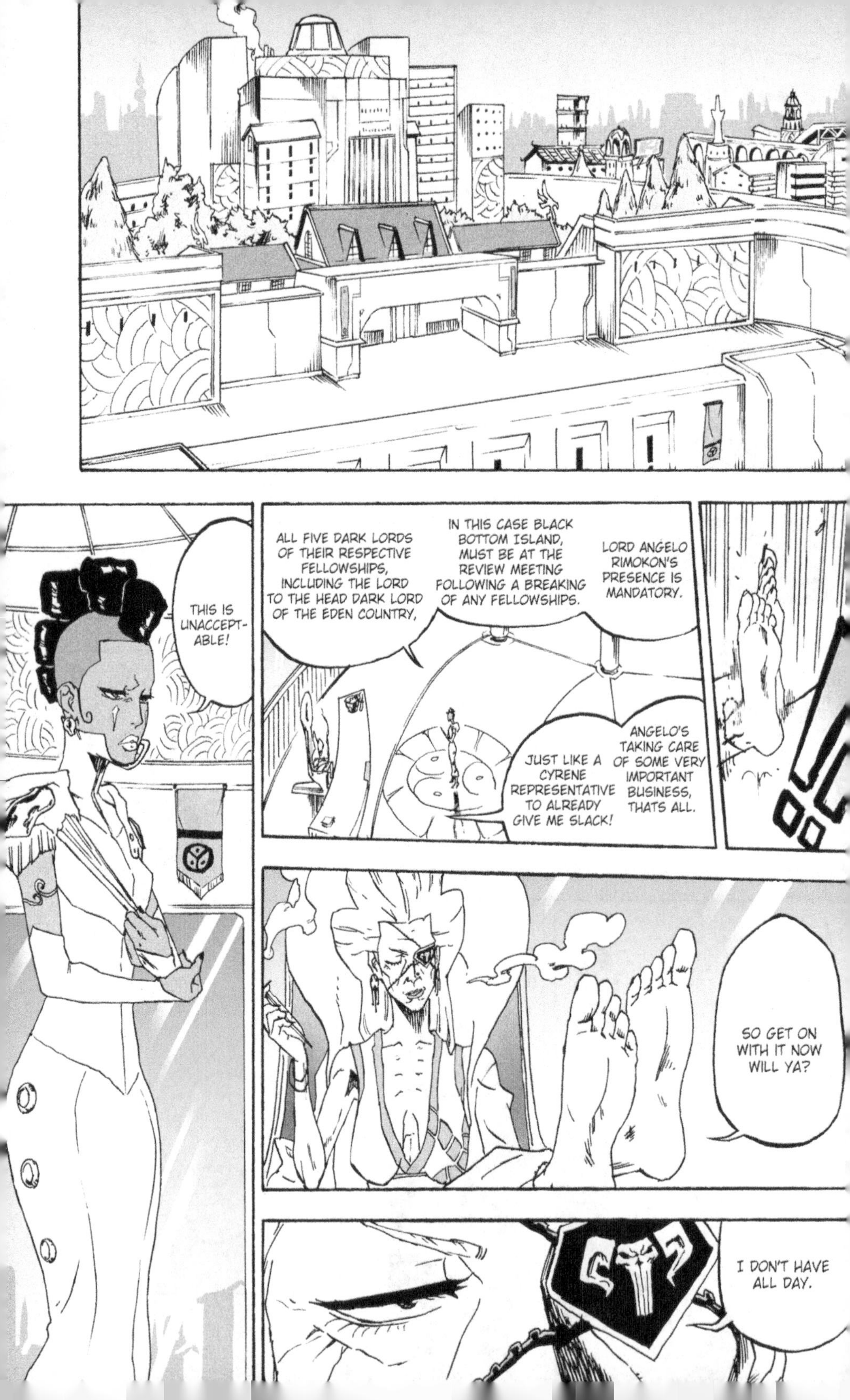
THIS IS UNACCEPTABLE!
ALL FIVE DARK LORDS OF THEIR RESPECTIVE FELLOWSHIPS, INCLUDING THE LORD TO THE HEAD DARK LORD OF THE EDEN COUNTRY,
IN THIS CASE BLACK BOTTOM ISLAND, MUST BE AT THE REVIEW MEETING FOLLOWING A BREAKING OF ANY FELLOWSHIPS.
LORD ANGELO RIMOKON'S PRESENCE IS MANDATORY.
ANGELO'S TAKING CARE OF SOME VERY IMPORTANT BUSINESS, THATS ALL.
JUST LIKE A CYRENE REPRESENTATIVE TO ALREADY GIVE ME SLACK!
SO GET ON WITH IT NOW WILL YA?
I DON'T HAVE ALL DAY.

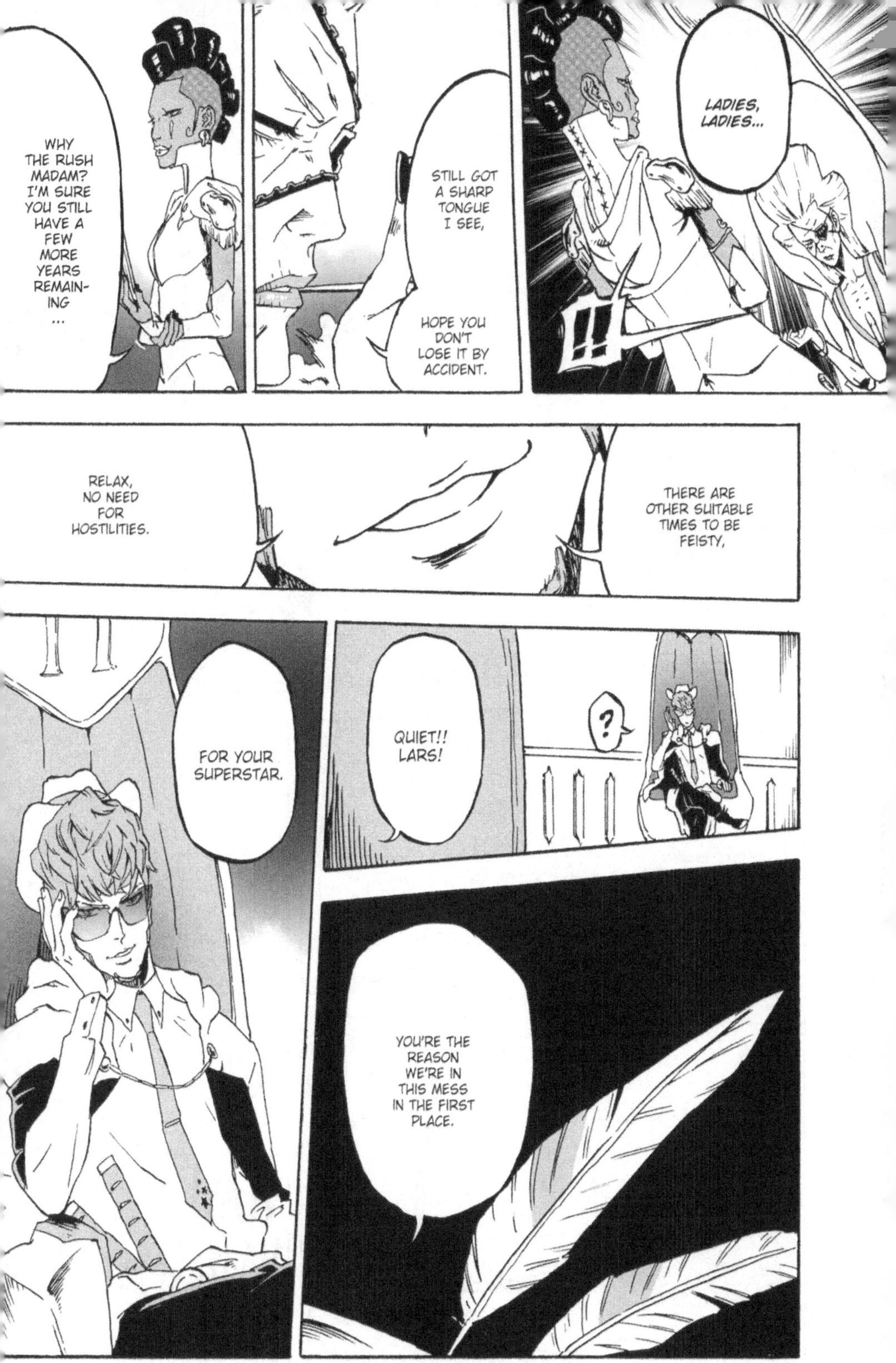
WHY THE RUSH MADAM? I'M SURE YOU STILL HAVE A FEW MORE YEARS REMAINING...
STILL GOT A SHARP TONGUE I SEE,
HOPE YOU DON'T LOSE IT BY ACCIDENT.
LADIES, LADIES...
!!
RELAX, NO NEED FOR HOSTILITIES.
THERE ARE OTHER SUITABLE TIMES TO BE FEISTY,
FOR YOUR SUPERSTAR.
QUIET!! LARS!
?
YOU'RE THE REASON WE'RE IN THIS MESS IN THE FIRST PLACE.

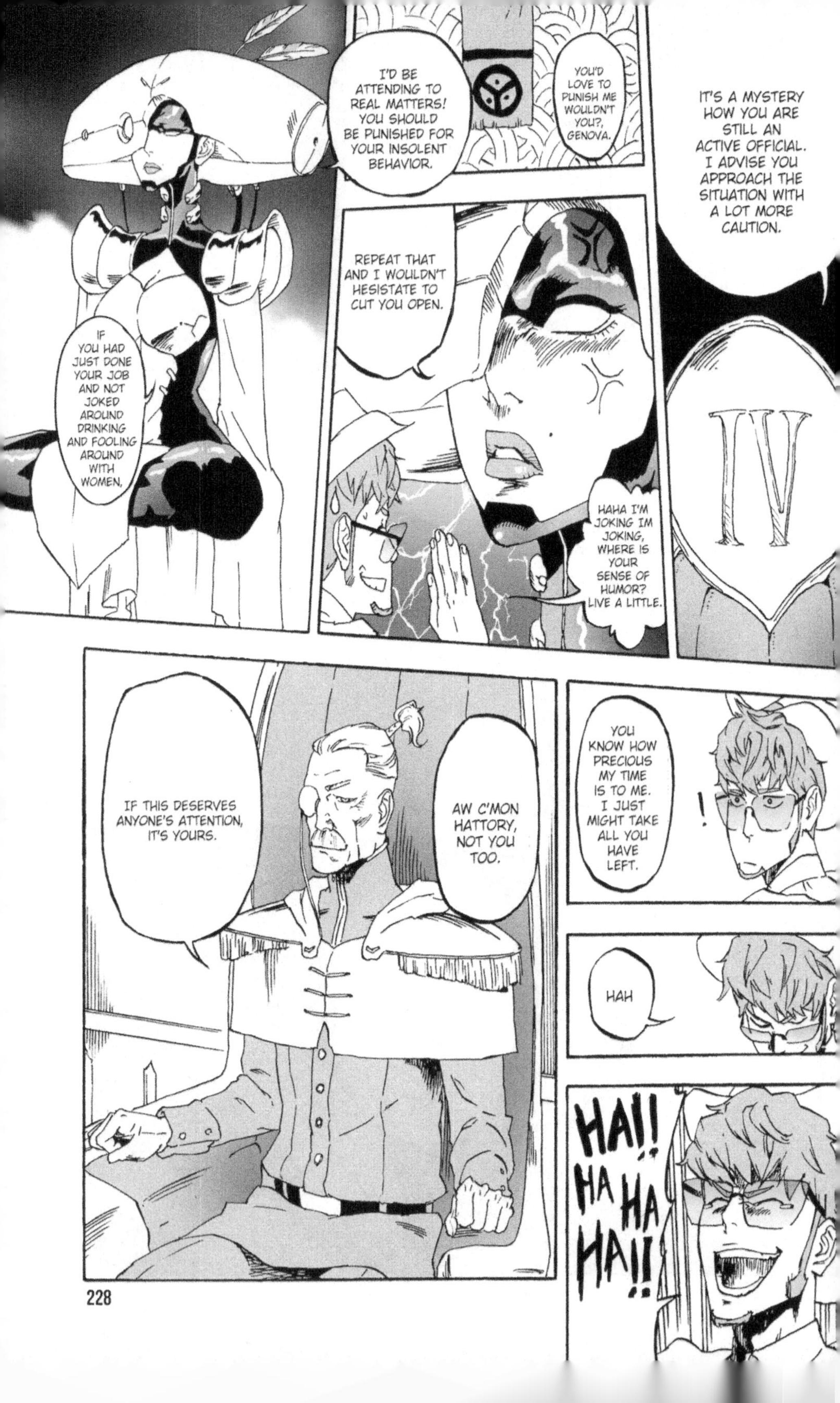
IF YOU HAD JUST DONE YOUR JOB AND NOT JOKED AROUND DRINKING AND FOOLING AROUND WITH WOMEN,
I'D BE ATTENDING TO REAL MATTERS! YOU SHOULD BE PUNISHED FOR YOUR INSOLENT BEHAVIOR.
YOU'D LOVE TO PUNISH ME WOULDN'T YOU?, GENOVA.
REPEAT THAT AND I WOULDN'T HESISTATE TO CUT YOU OPEN.
HAHA I'M JOKING IM JOKING, WHERE IS YOUR SENSE OF HUMOR? LIVE A LITTLE.
IT'S A MYSTERY HOW YOU ARE STILL AN ACTIVE OFFICIAL. I ADVISE YOU APPROACH THE SITUATION WITH A LOT MORE CAUTION.
IV
IF THIS DESERVES ANYONE'S ATTENTION, IT'S YOURS.
AW C'MON HATTORY, NOT YOU TOO.
YOU KNOW HOW PRECIOUS MY TIME IS TO ME. I JUST MIGHT TAKE ALL YOU HAVE LEFT.
!
HAH
HA!! HA HA HA!!

HAHA! HAHA HAH AHA! HA!! ...

HAH! OH-MY! TIME!

HAH HAH! HA!

I'M SORY. I'M SORRY HAH!

MORON.

YOU'RE LUCKY I FIND YOU QUITE THE CATCH.

THE DEFENSE OF BLACK BOTTOM ISLAND, IS SADLY YOUR RESPON-SIBILITY.

WELL, THE SHOW CAN'T POSSIBLY GO ON WITHOUT ME...

AFTERALL, I'M THE *STAR* OF THE SHOW.

WHAT ABOUT YOU DARK LORD OF THE THIRD FELLOWSHIP? DO YOU SHARE THE SAME SENTIMENTS?

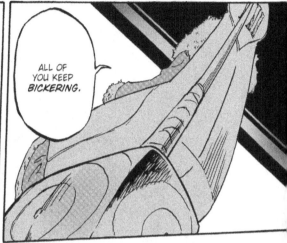

ALL OF YOU KEEP *BICKERING.*

WHO CARES IF WE GET INTRUDERS?, I WELCOME THEM ALL, JUST SO I CAN PUMMEL THEM ALL ONE BY ONE.

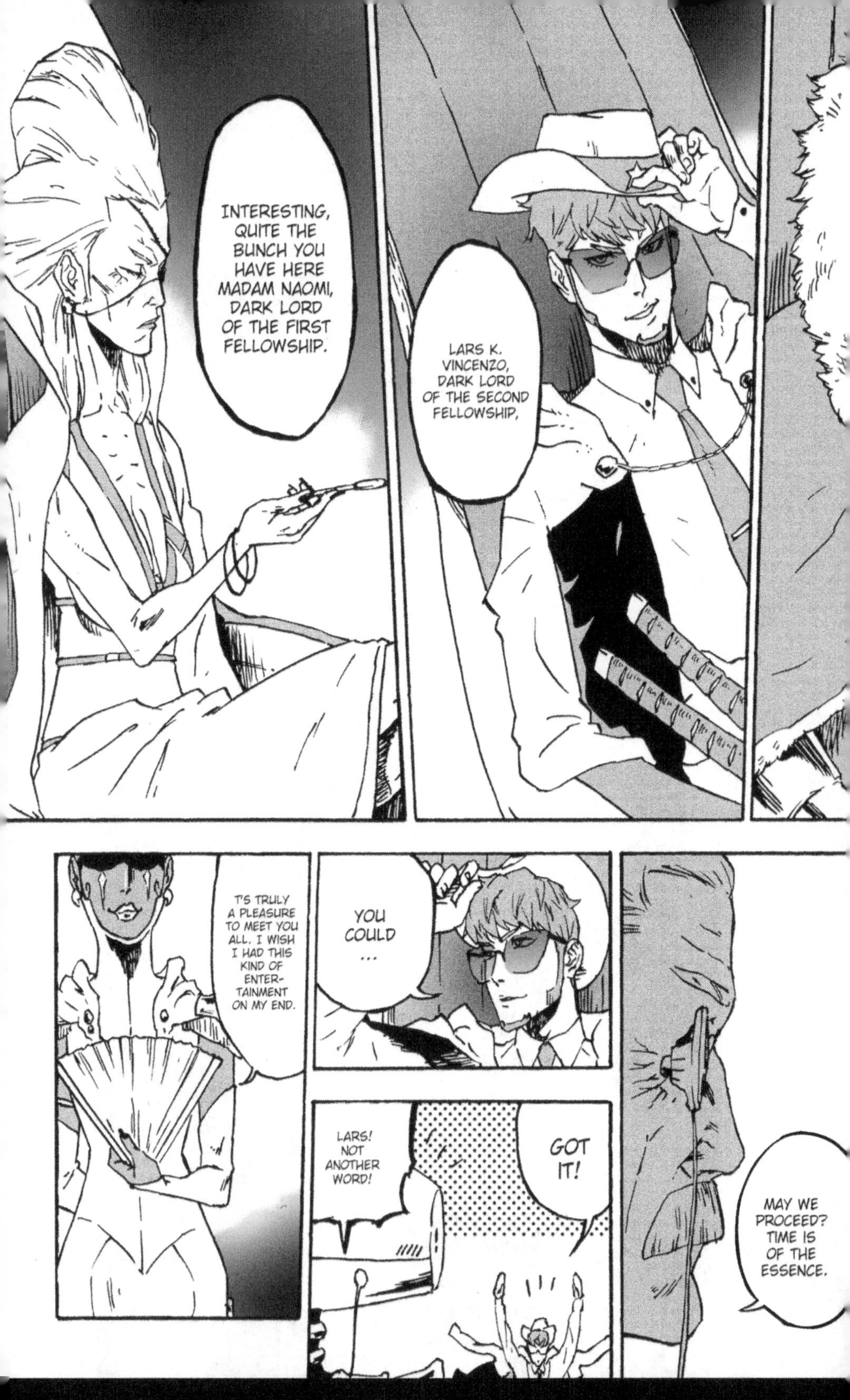
INTERESTING, QUITE THE BUNCH YOU HAVE HERE MADAM NAOMI, DARK LORD OF THE FIRST FELLOWSHIP.
LARS K. VINCENZO, DARK LORD OF THE SECOND FELLOWSHIP,
T'S TRULY A PLEASURE TO MEET YOU ALL. I WISH I HAD THIS KIND OF ENTER-TAINMENT ON MY END.
YOU COULD ...
LARS! NOT ANOTHER WORD!
GOT IT!
MAY WE PROCEED? TIME IS OF THE ESSENCE.

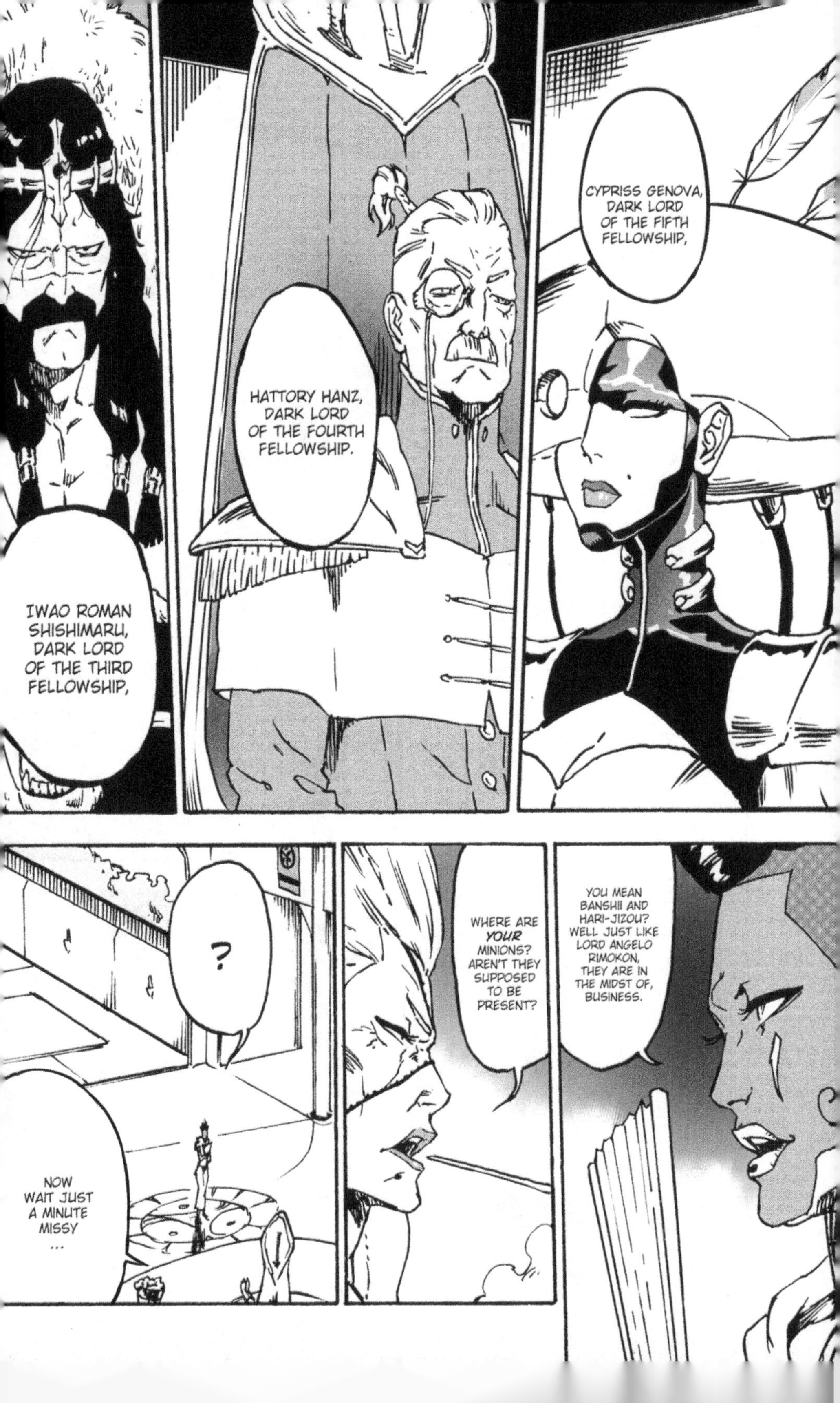
IWAO ROMAN SHISHIMARU, DARK LORD OF THE THIRD FELLOWSHIP,
HATTORY HANZ, DARK LORD OF THE FOURTH FELLOWSHIP.
CYPRISS GENOVA, DARK LORD OF THE FIFTH FELLOWSHIP,
?
NOW WAIT JUST A MINUTE MISSY ...
WHERE ARE *YOUR* MINIONS? AREN'T THEY SUPPOSED TO BE PRESENT?
YOU MEAN BANSHII AND HARI-JIZOU? WELL JUST LIKE LORD ANGELO RIMOKON, THEY ARE IN THE MIDST OF, BUSINESS.

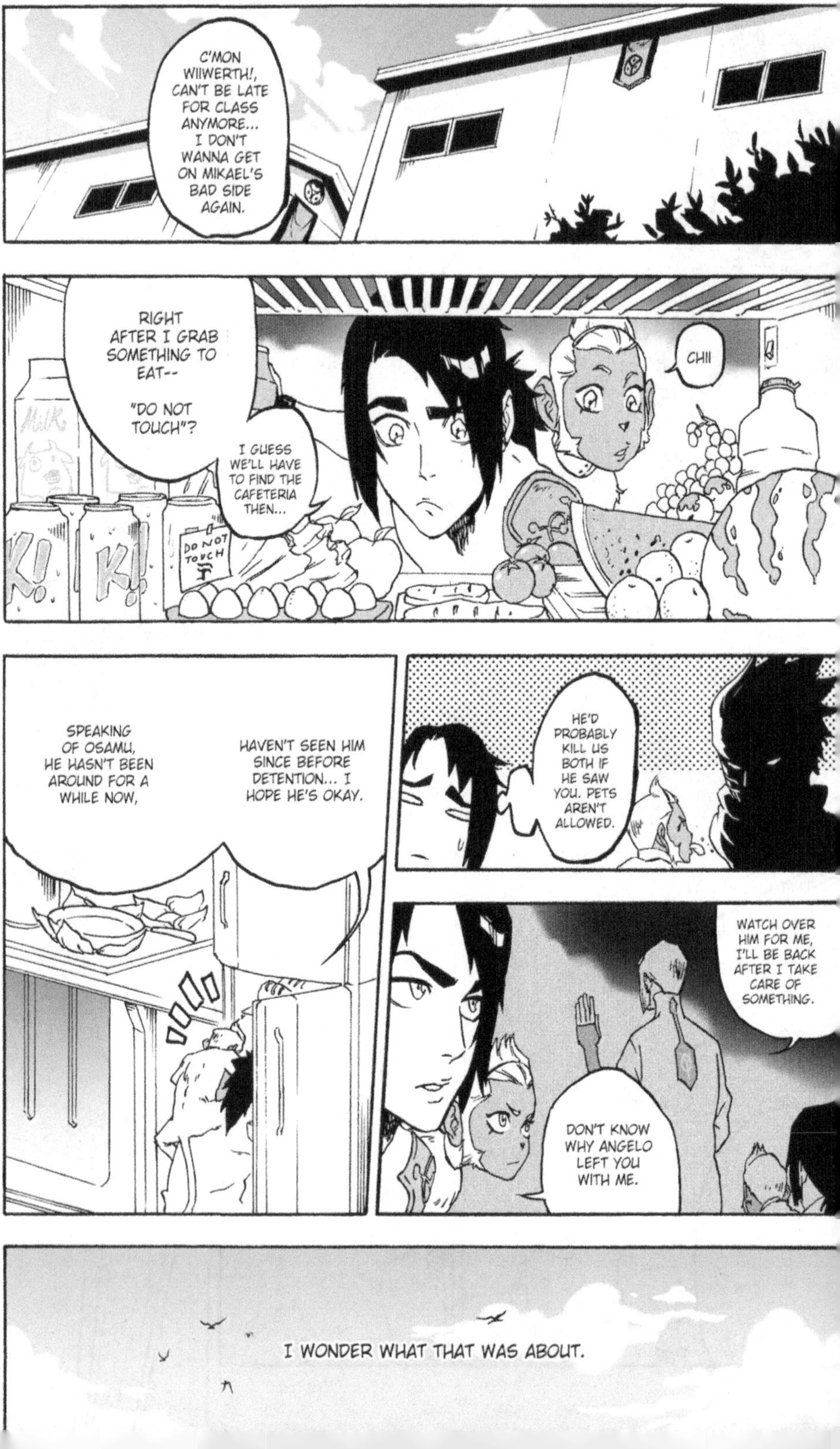
C'MON WIIWERTH!, CAN'T BE LATE FOR CLASS ANYMORE... I DON'T WANNA GET ON MIKAEL'S BAD SIDE AGAIN.
RIGHT AFTER I GRAB SOMETHING TO EAT-- "DO NOT TOUCH"?
MILK
DO NOT TOUCH
KI!
KI!
I GUESS WE'LL HAVE TO FIND THE CAFETERIA THEN...
CHII
SPEAKING OF OSAMU, HE HASN'T BEEN AROUND FOR A WHILE NOW,
HAVEN'T SEEN HIM SINCE BEFORE DETENTION... I HOPE HE'S OKAY.
HE'D PROBABLY KILL US BOTH IF HE SAW YOU. PETS AREN'T ALLOWED.
WATCH OVER HIM FOR ME, I'LL BE BACK AFTER I TAKE CARE OF SOMETHING.
DON'T KNOW WHY ANGELO LEFT YOU WITH ME.
I WONDER WHAT THAT WAS ABOUT.

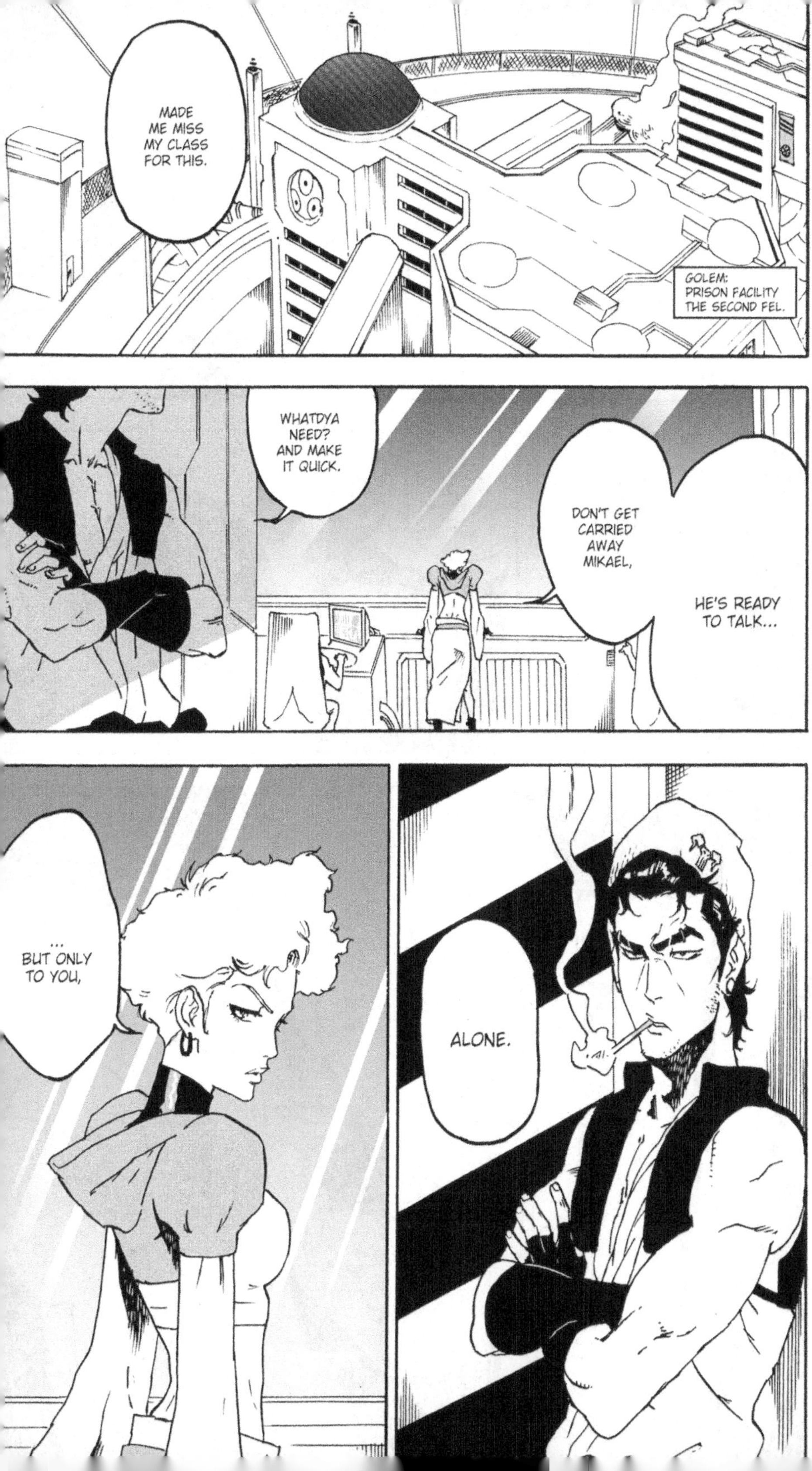
MADE ME MISS MY CLASS FOR THIS.
GOLEM: PRISON FACILITY THE SECOND FEL.
WHATDYA NEED? AND MAKE IT QUICK.
DON'T GET CARRIED AWAY MIKAEL,
HE'S READY TO TALK...
... BUT ONLY TO YOU,
ALONE.

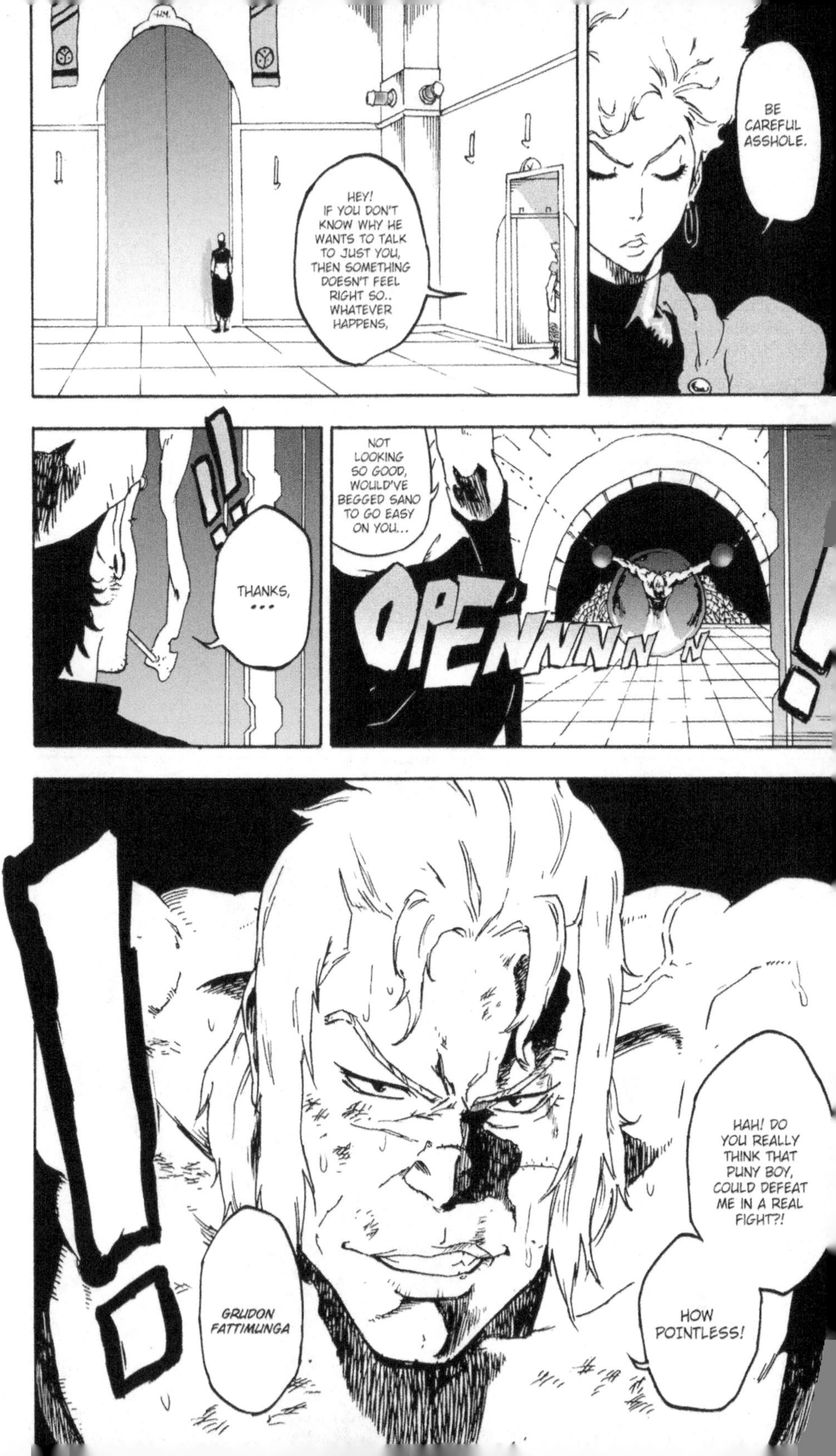
HEY! IF YOU DON'T KNOW WHY HE WANTS TO TALK TO JUST YOU, THEN SOMETHING DOESN'T FEEL RIGHT SO.. WHATEVER HAPPENS,
BE CAREFUL ASSHOLE.
THANKS, ...
NOT LOOKING SO GOOD, WOULD'VE BEGGED SANO TO GO EASY ON YOU...
OPENNNNNNN
HAH! DO YOU REALLY THINK THAT PUNY BOY, COULD DEFEAT ME IN A REAL FIGHT?!
GRUDON FATTIMUNGA
HOW POINTLESS!

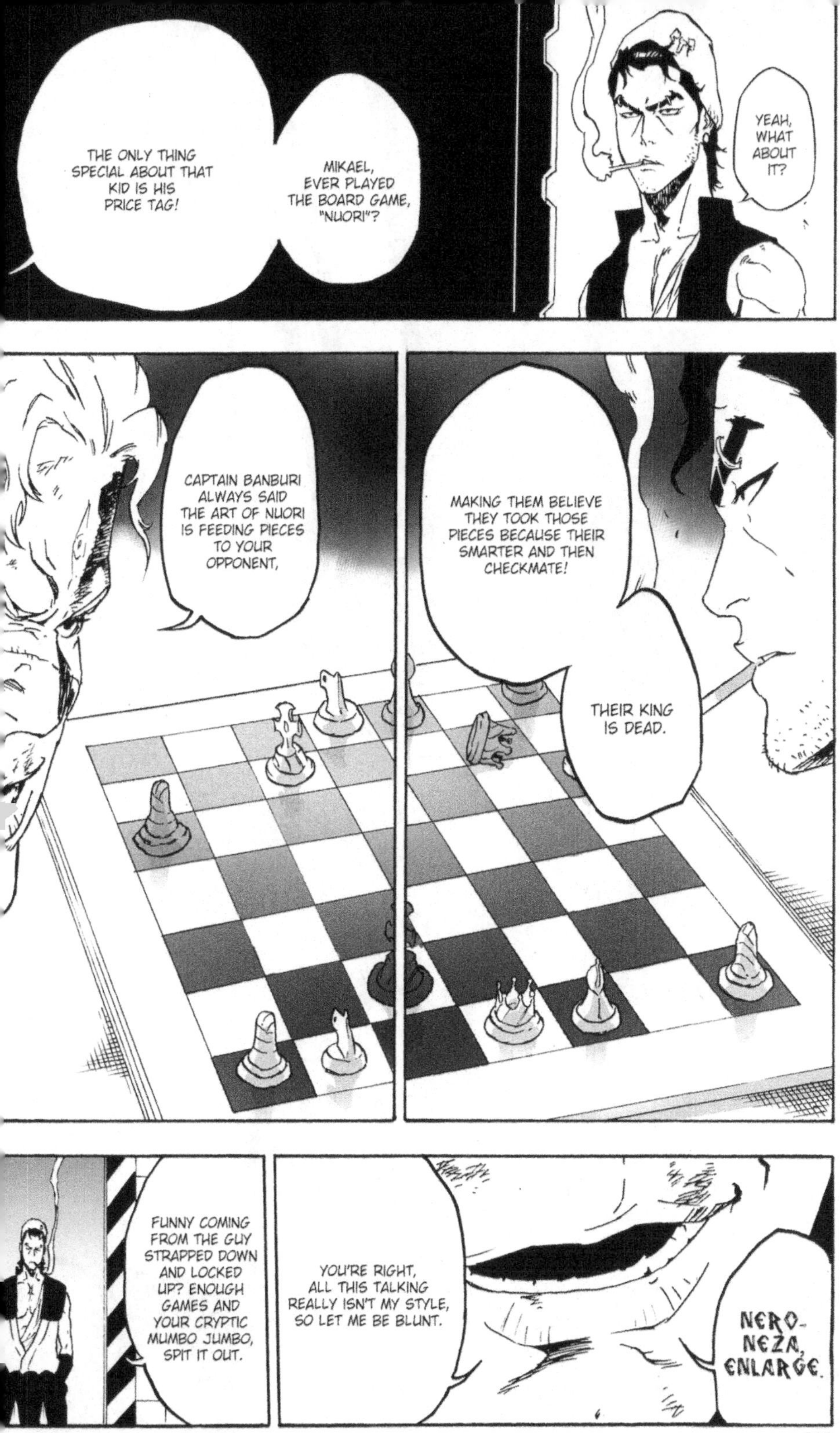
THE ONLY THING SPECIAL ABOUT THAT KID IS HIS PRICE TAG!
MIKAEL, EVER PLAYED THE BOARD GAME, "NUORI"?
YEAH, WHAT ABOUT IT?
CAPTAIN BANBURI ALWAYS SAID THE ART OF NUORI IS FEEDING PIECES TO YOUR OPPONENT,
MAKING THEM BELIEVE THEY TOOK THOSE PIECES BECAUSE THEIR SMARTER AND THEN CHECKMATE!
THEIR KING IS DEAD.
FUNNY COMING FROM THE GUY STRAPPED DOWN AND LOCKED UP? ENOUGH GAMES AND YOUR CRYPTIC MUMBO JUMBO, SPIT IT OUT.
YOU'RE RIGHT, ALL THIS TALKING REALLY ISN'T MY STYLE, SO LET ME BE BLUNT.
NERO-NEZA, ENLARGE.

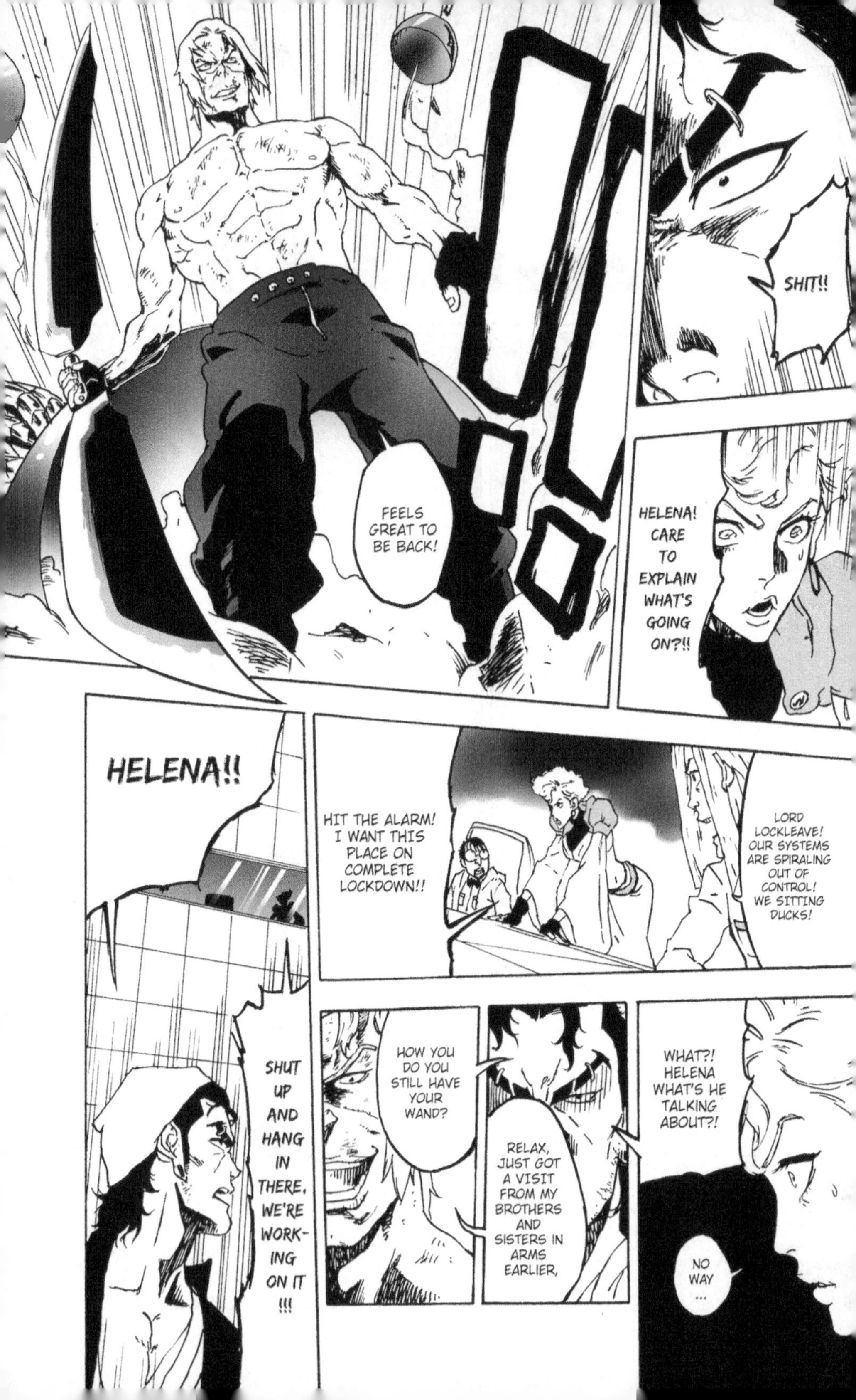
FEELS GREAT TO BE BACK!
SHIT!!
HELENA! CARE TO EXPLAIN WHAT'S GOING ON?!!
HELENA!!
SHUT UP AND HANG IN THERE, WE'RE WORK-ING ON IT !!!
HIT THE ALARM! I WANT THIS PLACE ON COMPLETE LOCKDOWN!!
LORD LOCKLEAVE! OUR SYSTEMS ARE SPIRALING OUT OF CONTROL! WE SITTING DUCKS!
HOW YOU DO YOU STILL HAVE YOUR WAND?
RELAX, JUST GOT A VISIT FROM MY BROTHERS AND SISTERS IN ARMS EARLIER,
WHAT?! HELENA WHAT'S HE TALKING ABOUT?!
NO WAY ...

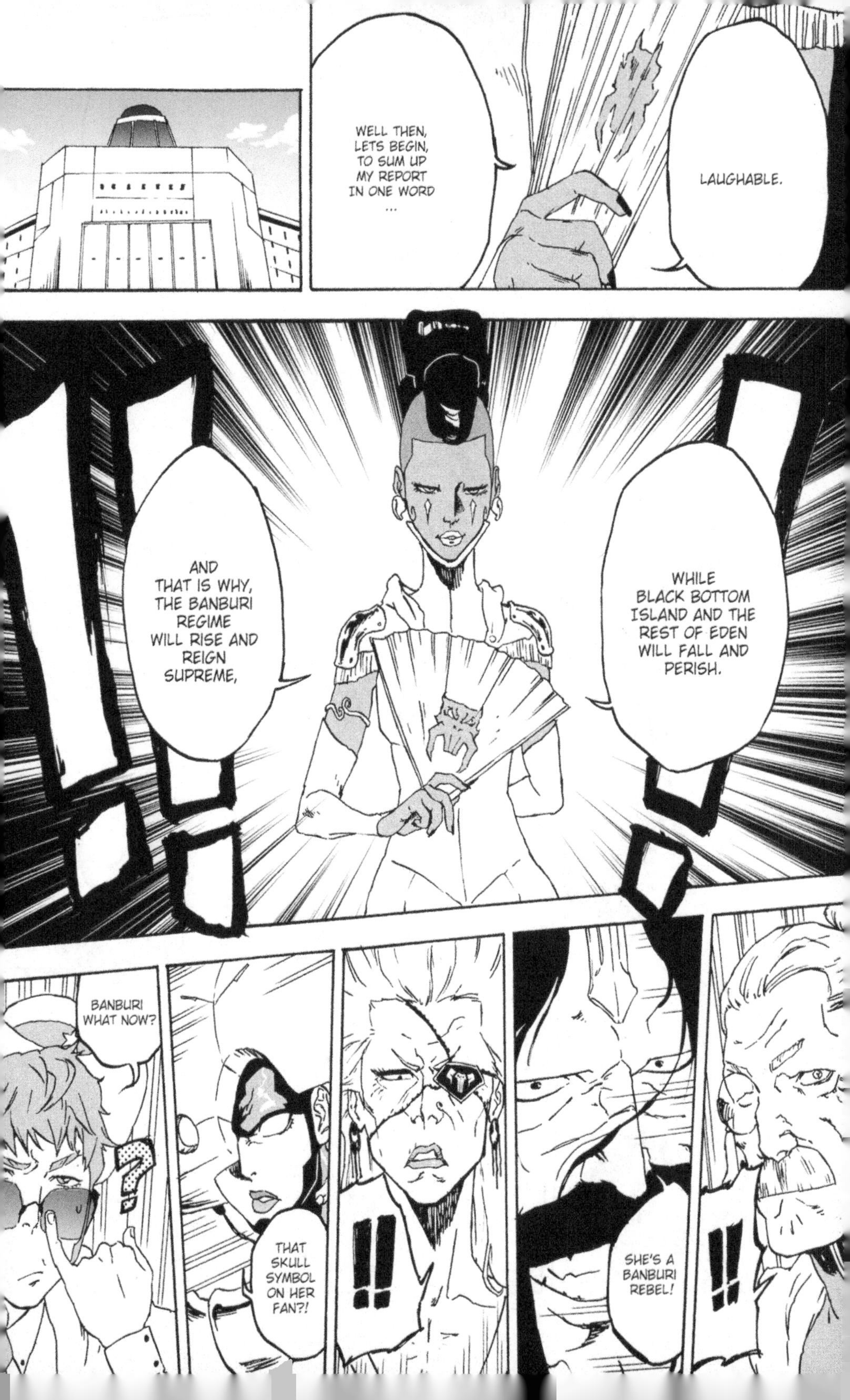
WELL THEN, LETS BEGIN, TO SUM UP MY REPORT IN ONE WORD ...
LAUGHABLE.
AND THAT IS WHY, THE BANBURI REGIME WILL RISE AND REIGN SUPREME,
WHILE BLACK BOTTOM ISLAND AND THE REST OF EDEN WILL FALL AND PERISH.
BANBURI WHAT NOW?
THAT SKULL SYMBOL ON HER FAN?!
SHE'S A BANBURI REBEL!

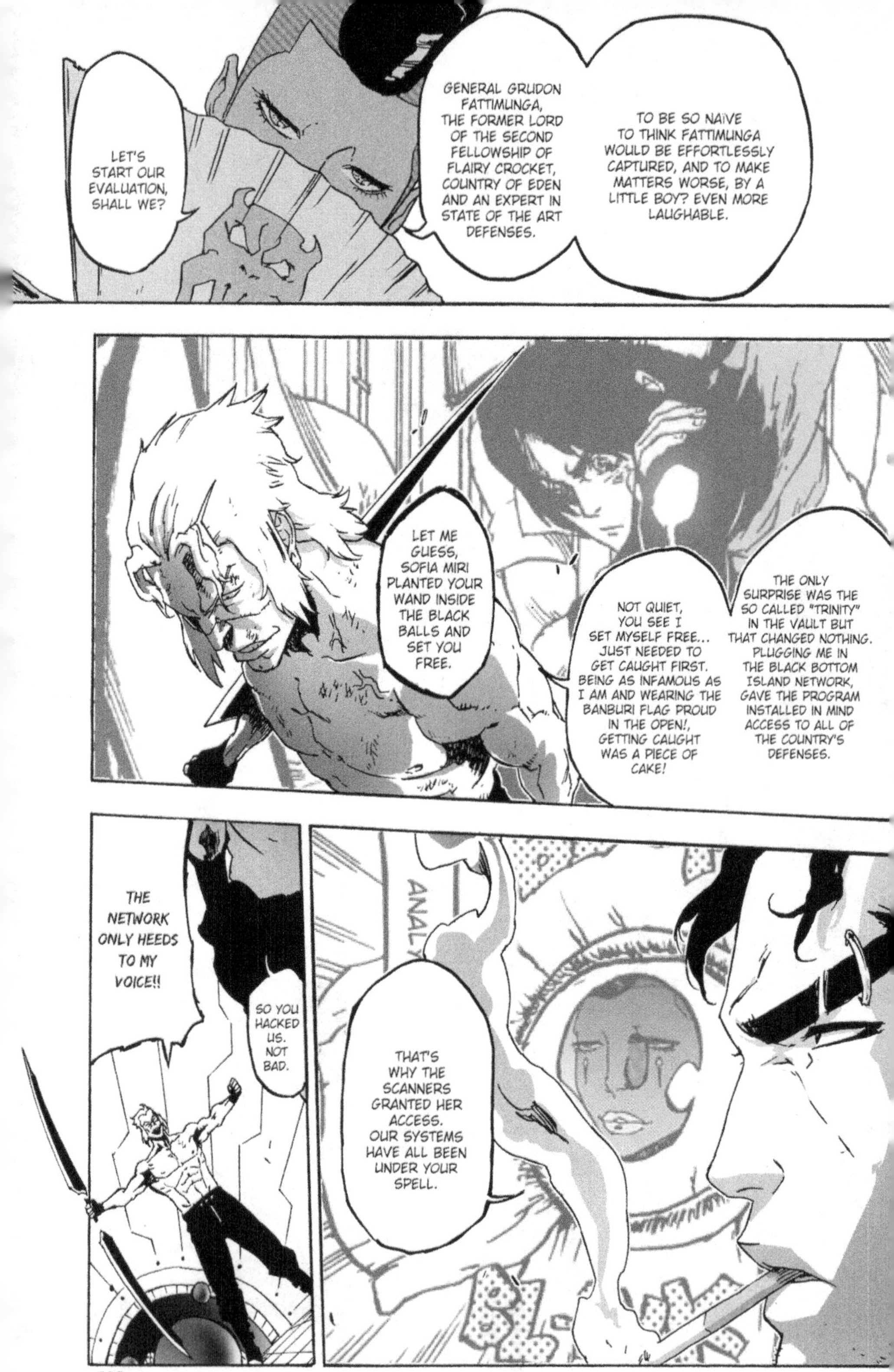
LET'S START OUR EVALUATION, SHALL WE?
GENERAL GRUDON FATTIMUNGA, THE FORMER LORD OF THE SECOND FELLOWSHIP OF FLAIRY CROCKET, COUNTRY OF EDEN AND AN EXPERT IN STATE OF THE ART DEFENSES.
TO BE SO NAIVE TO THINK FATTIMUNGA WOULD BE EFFORTLESSLY CAPTURED, AND TO MAKE MATTERS WORSE, BY A LITTLE BOY? EVEN MORE LAUGHABLE.
LET ME GUESS, SOFIA MIRI PLANTED YOUR WAND INSIDE THE BLACK BALLS AND SET YOU FREE.
NOT QUIET, YOU SEE I SET MYSELF FREE... JUST NEEDED TO GET CAUGHT FIRST. BEING AS INFAMOUS AS I AM AND WEARING THE BANBURI FLAG PROUD IN THE OPEN!, GETTING CAUGHT WAS A PIECE OF CAKE!
THE ONLY SURPRISE WAS THE SO CALLED "TRINITY" IN THE VAULT BUT THAT CHANGED NOTHING. PLUGGING ME IN THE BLACK BOTTOM ISLAND NETWORK, GAVE THE PROGRAM INSTALLED IN MIND ACCESS TO ALL OF THE COUNTRY'S DEFENSES.
THE NETWORK ONLY HEEDS TO MY VOICE!!
SO YOU HACKED US. NOT BAD.
THAT'S WHY THE SCANNERS GRANTED HER ACCESS. OUR SYSTEMS HAVE ALL BEEN UNDER YOUR SPELL.

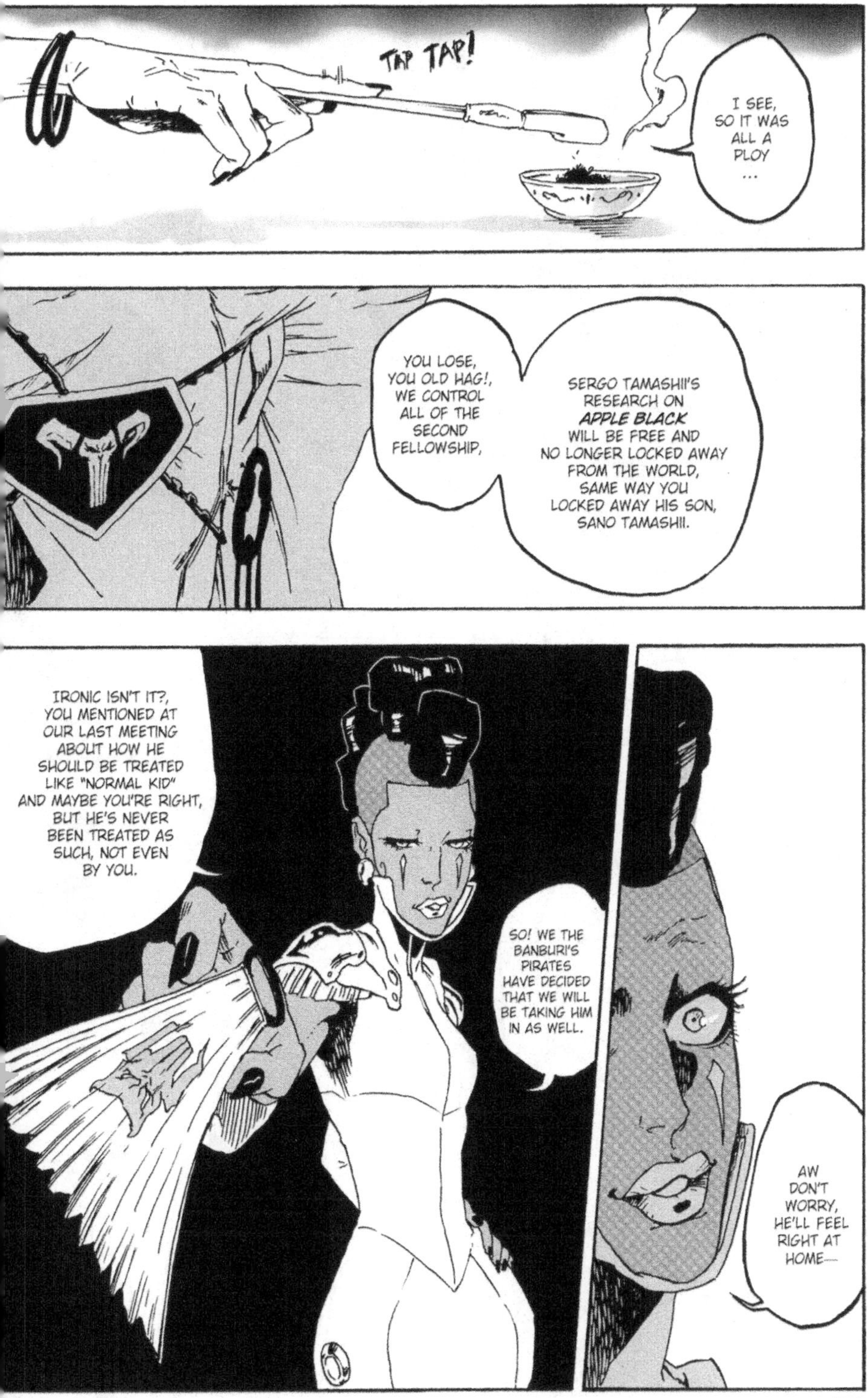
TAP TAP!
I SEE, SO IT WAS ALL A PLOY ...
YOU LOSE, YOU OLD HAG!, WE CONTROL ALL OF THE SECOND FELLOWSHIP,
SERGO TAMASHII'S RESEARCH ON APPLE BLACK WILL BE FREE AND NO LONGER LOCKED AWAY FROM THE WORLD, SAME WAY YOU LOCKED AWAY HIS SON, SANO TAMASHII.
IRONIC ISN'T IT?, YOU MENTIONED AT OUR LAST MEETING ABOUT HOW HE SHOULD BE TREATED LIKE "NORMAL KID" AND MAYBE YOU'RE RIGHT, BUT HE'S NEVER BEEN TREATED AS SUCH, NOT EVEN BY YOU.
SO! WE THE BANBURI'S PIRATES HAVE DECIDED THAT WE WILL BE TAKING HIM IN AS WELL.
AW DON'T WORRY, HE'LL FEEL RIGHT AT HOME—

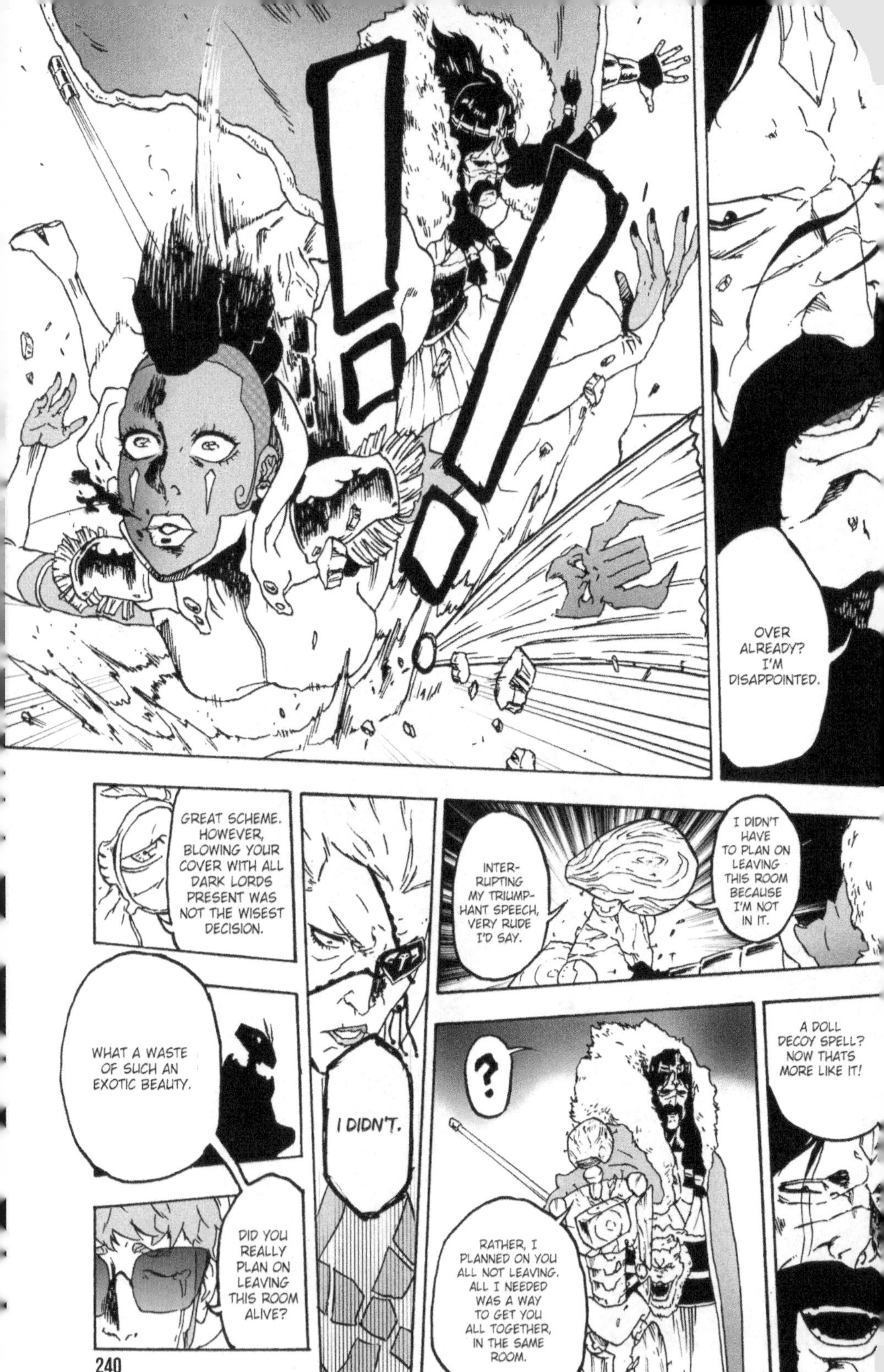

!!
OVER ALREADY? I'M DISAPPOINTED.
GREAT SCHEME. HOWEVER, BLOWING YOUR COVER WITH ALL DARK LORDS PRESENT WAS NOT THE WISEST DECISION.
WHAT A WASTE OF SUCH AN EXOTIC BEAUTY.
DID YOU REALLY PLAN ON LEAVING THIS ROOM ALIVE?
I DIDN'T.
INTER-RUPTING MY TRIUMPH-HANT SPEECH, VERY RUDE I'D SAY.
I DIDN'T HAVE TO PLAN ON LEAVING THIS ROOM BECAUSE I'M NOT IN IT.
?
RATHER, I PLANNED ON YOU ALL NOT LEAVING. ALL I NEEDED WAS A WAY TO GET YOU ALL TOGETHER, IN THE SAME ROOM.
A DOLL DECOY SPELL? NOW THATS MORE LIKE IT!

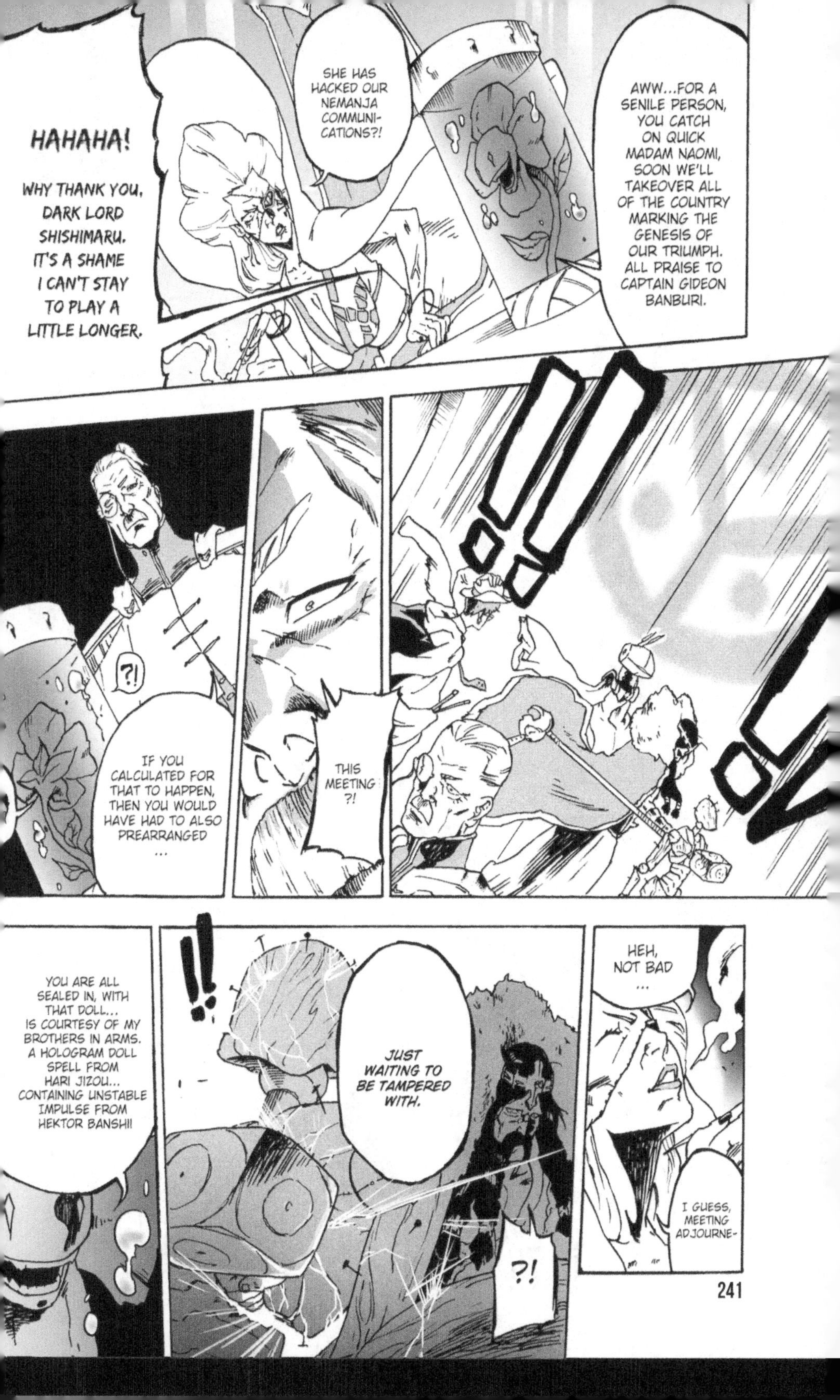
HAHAHA!
WHY THANK YOU, DARK LORD SHISHIMARU. IT'S A SHAME I CAN'T STAY TO PLAY A LITTLE LONGER.
SHE HAS HACKED OUR NEMANJA COMMUNI- CATIONS?!
AWW...FOR A SENILE PERSON, YOU CATCH ON QUICK MADAM NAOMI, SOON WE'LL TAKEOVER ALL OF THE COUNTRY MARKING THE GENESIS OF OUR TRIUMPH. ALL PRAISE TO CAPTAIN GIDEON BANBURI.
?!
IF YOU CALCULATED FOR THAT TO HAPPEN, THEN YOU WOULD HAVE HAD TO ALSO PREARRANGED ...
THIS MEETING ?!
!!
YOU ARE ALL SEALED IN, WITH THAT DOLL... IS COURTESY OF MY BROTHERS IN ARMS. A HOLOGRAM DOLL SPELL FROM HARI JIZOU... CONTAINING UNSTABLE IMPULSE FROM HEKTOR BANSHI!
!!
JUST WAITING TO BE TAMPERED WITH.
?!
HEH, NOT BAD ...
I GUESS, MEETING ADJOURNE-

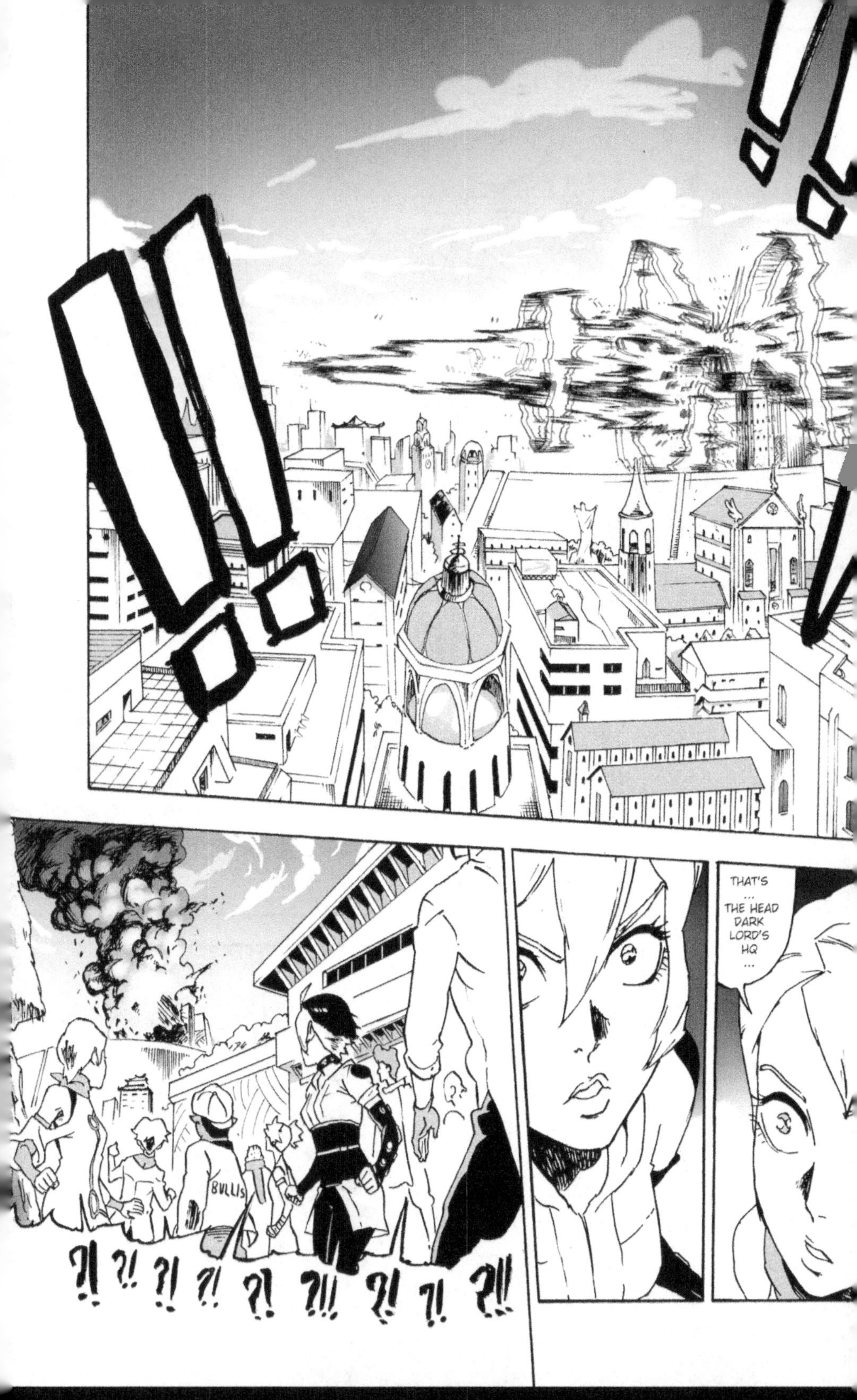
!!
!!
BULLIS
?! ?! ?! ?! ?! ?!! ?! ?! ?!!
THAT'S ... THE HEAD DARK LORD'S HQ ...

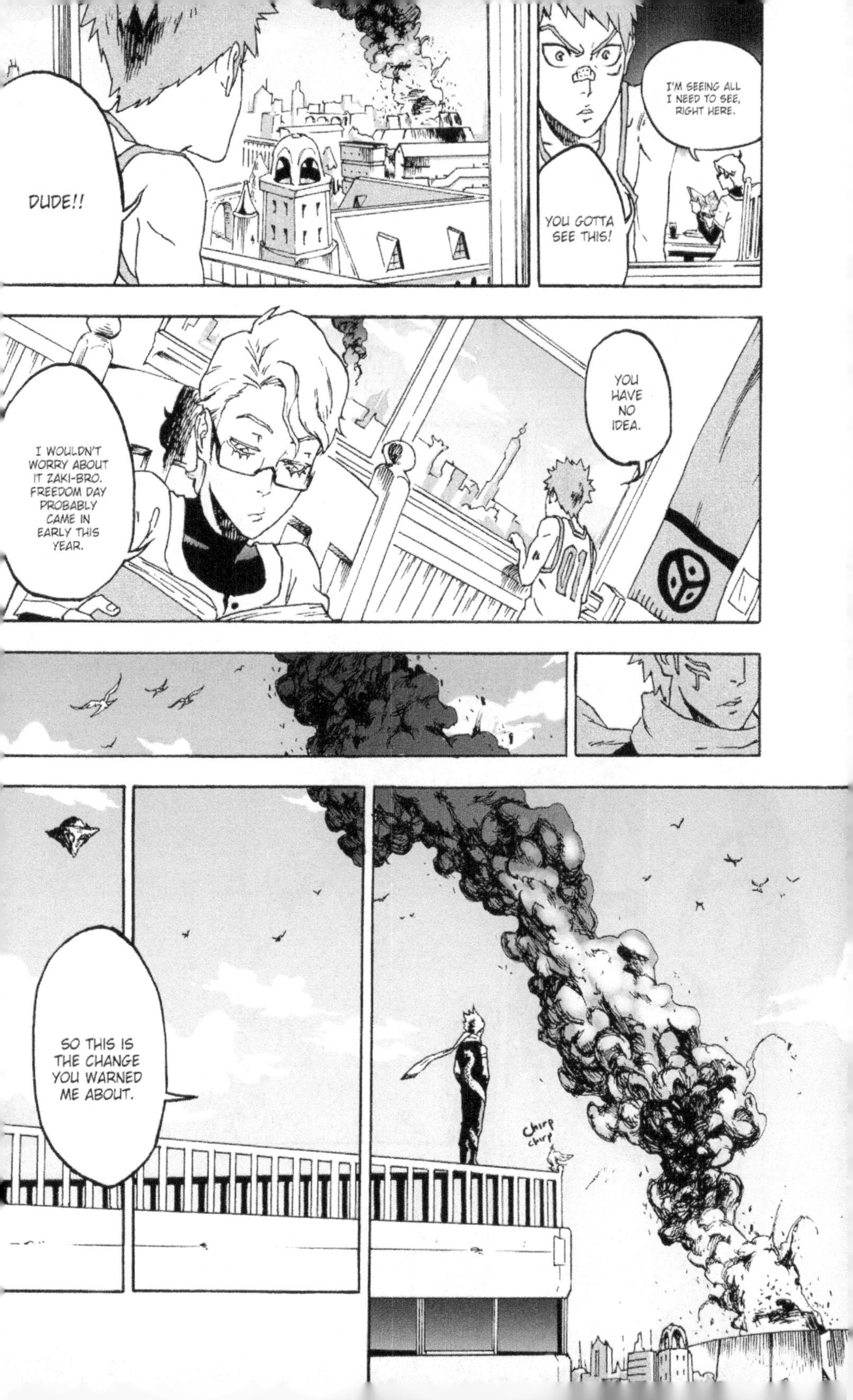
DUDE!!
I'M SEEING ALL I NEED TO SEE, RIGHT HERE.
YOU GOTTA SEE THIS!
I WOULDN'T WORRY ABOUT IT ZAKI-BRO. FREEDOM DAY PROBABLY CAME IN EARLY THIS YEAR.
YOU HAVE NO IDEA.
SO THIS IS THE CHANGE YOU WARNED ME ABOUT.
Chirp chirp

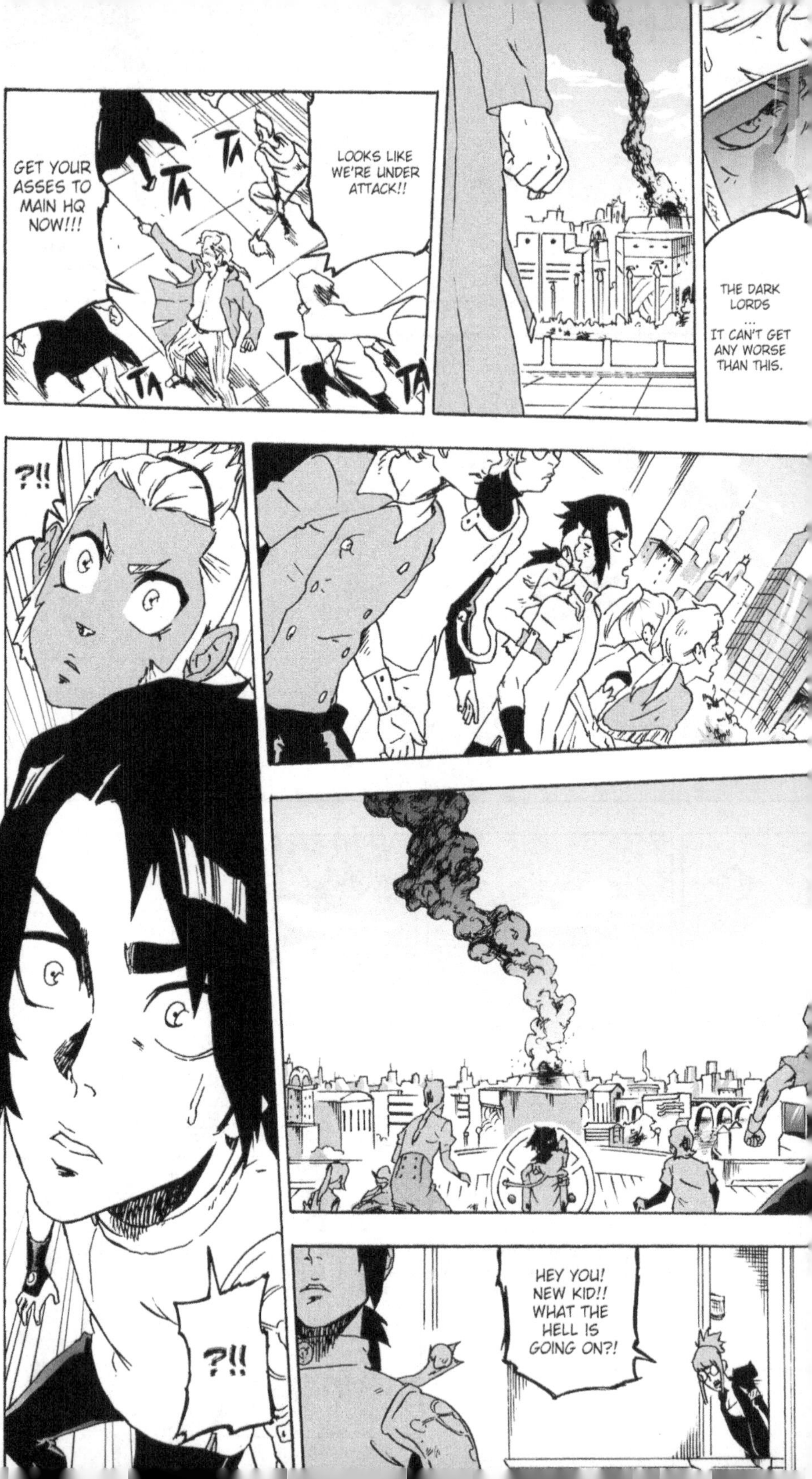
GET YOUR ASSES TO MAIN HQ NOW!!!
TA
TA
TA
T
TA
TA
LOOKS LIKE WE'RE UNDER ATTACK!!
THE DARK LORDS ... IT CAN'T GET ANY WORSE THAN THIS.
?!!
?!!
HEY YOU! NEW KID!! WHAT THE HELL IS GOING ON?!

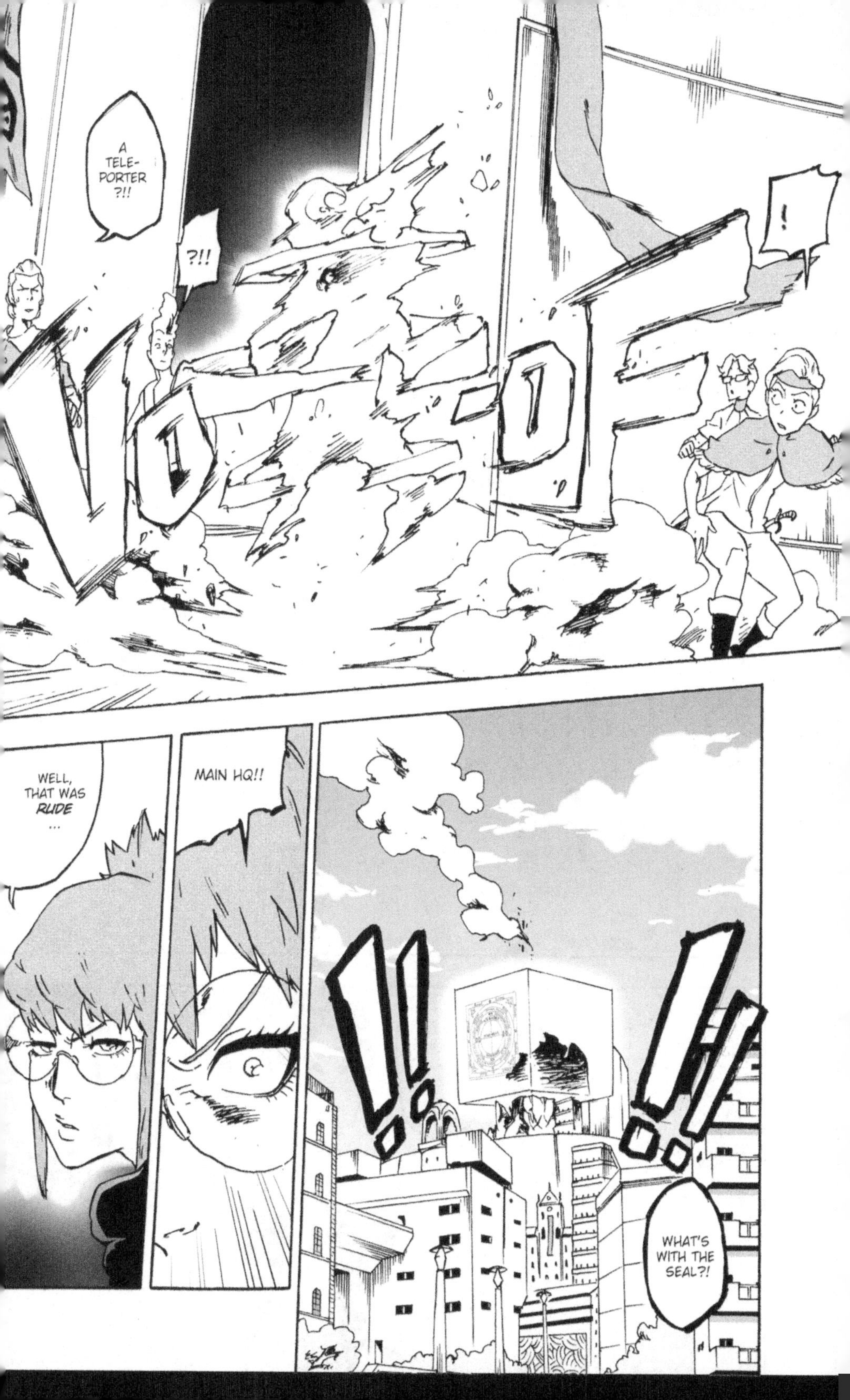
A TELE-PORTER?!!
?!!
!
WELL, THAT WAS RUDE ...
MAIN HQ!!
!!
!!
WHAT'S WITH THE SEAL?!

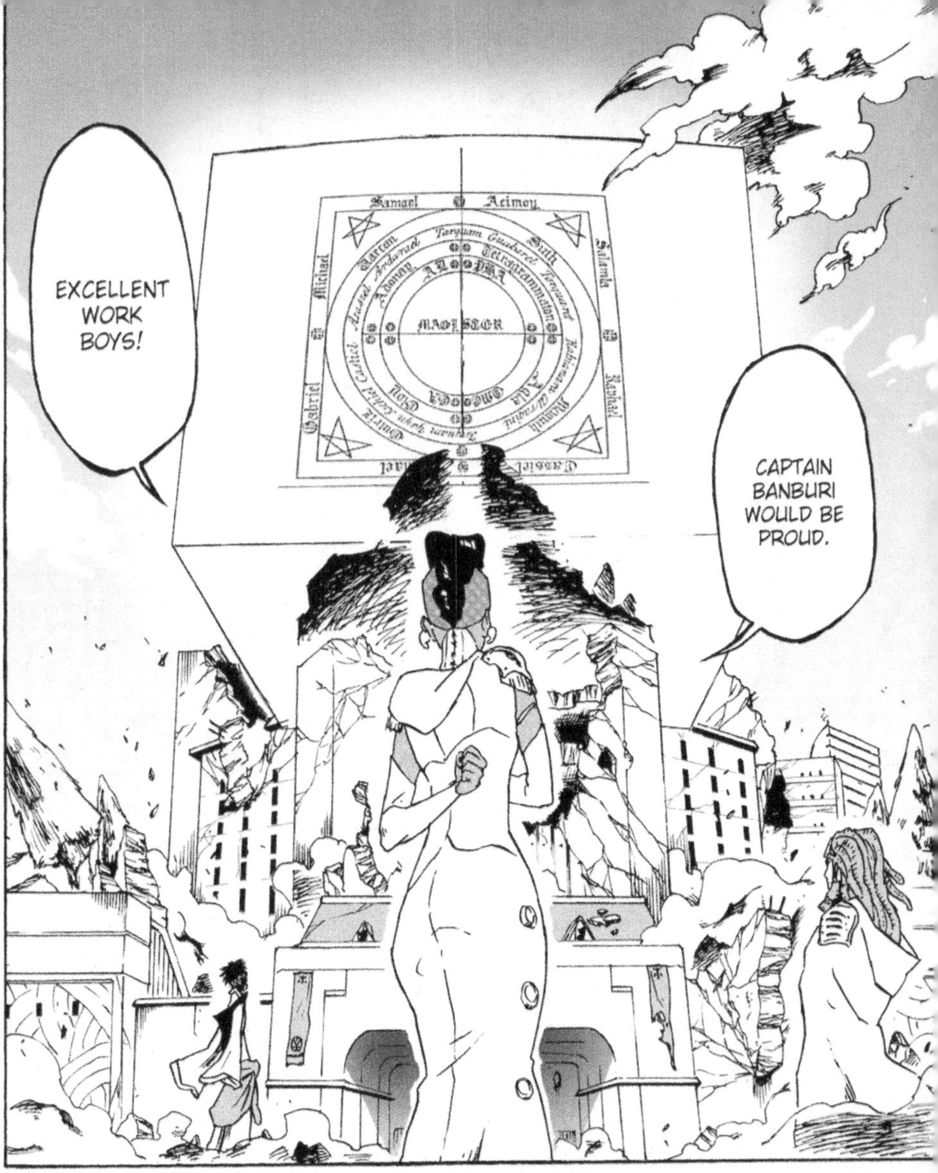
EXCELLENT WORK BOYS!
CAPTAIN BANBURI WOULD BE PROUD.

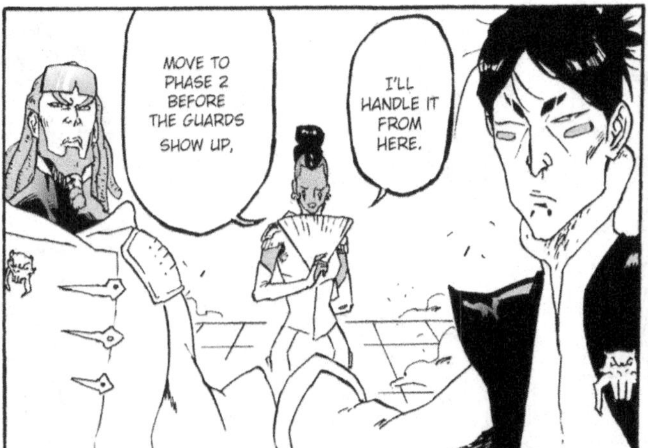
MOVE TO PHASE 2 BEFORE THE GUARDS SHOW UP,
I'LL HANDLE IT FROM HERE.

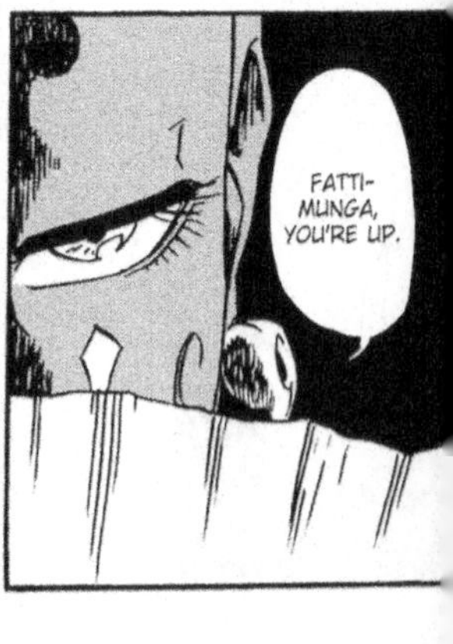
FATTI-MUNGA, YOU'RE UP.

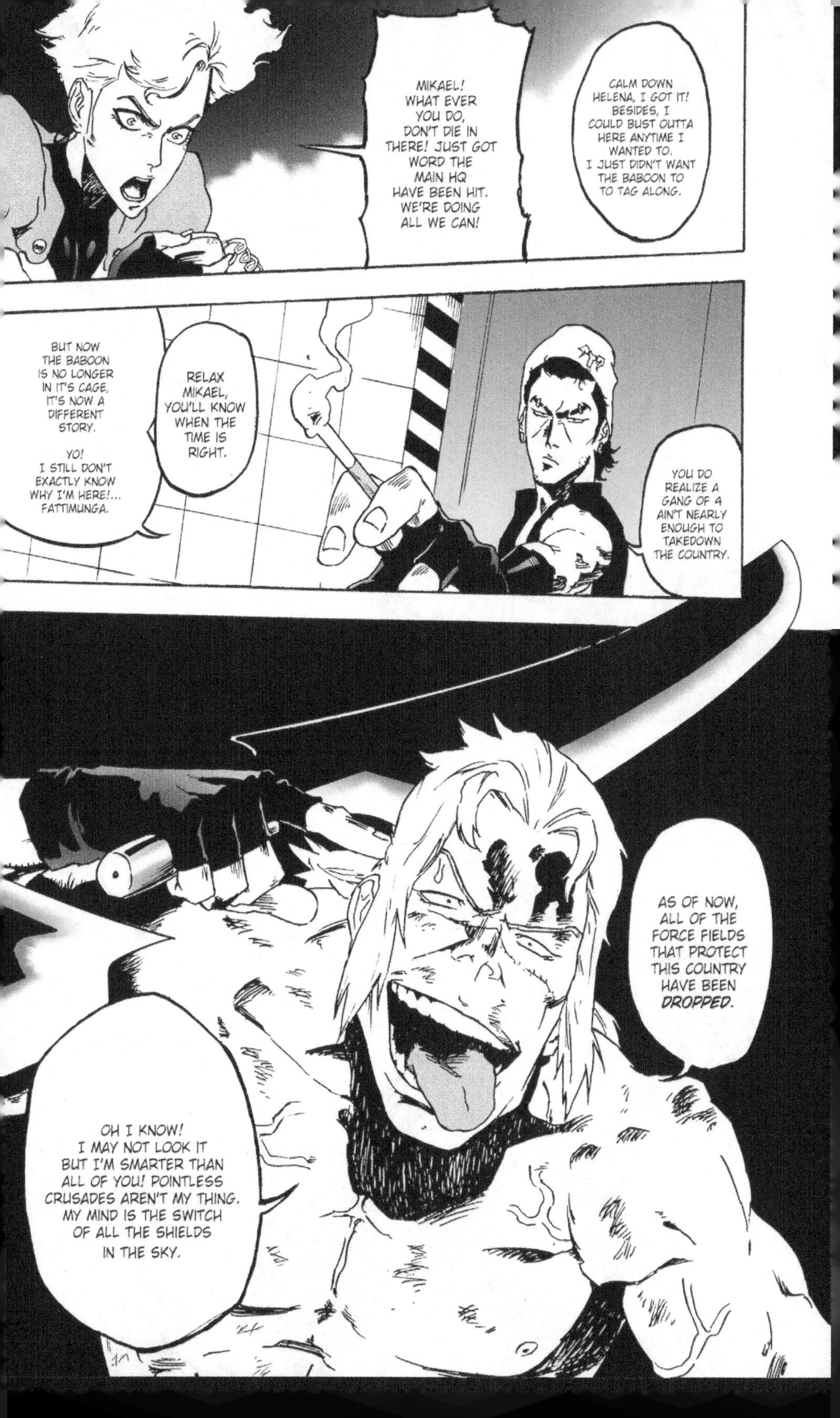
MIKAEL! WHAT EVER YOU DO, DON'T DIE IN THERE! JUST GOT WORD THE MAIN HQ HAVE BEEN HIT. WE'RE DOING ALL WE CAN!
CALM DOWN HELENA, I GOT IT! BESIDES, I COULD BUST OUTTA HERE ANYTIME I WANTED TO. I JUST DIDN'T WANT THE BABOON TO TO TAG ALONG.
BUT NOW THE BABOON IS NO LONGER IN IT'S CAGE, IT'S NOW A DIFFERENT STORY.
YO! I STILL DON'T EXACTLY KNOW WHY I'M HERE!... FATTIMUNGA.
RELAX MIKAEL, YOU'LL KNOW WHEN THE TIME IS RIGHT.
YOU DO REALIZE A GANG OF 4 AIN'T NEARLY ENOUGH TO TAKEDOWN THE COUNTRY.
AS OF NOW, ALL OF THE FORCE FIELDS THAT PROTECT THIS COUNTRY HAVE BEEN ***DROPPED.***
OH I KNOW! I MAY NOT LOOK IT BUT I'M SMARTER THAN ALL OF YOU! POINTLESS CRUSADES AREN'T MY THING. MY MIND IS THE SWITCH OF ALL THE SHIELDS IN THE SKY.

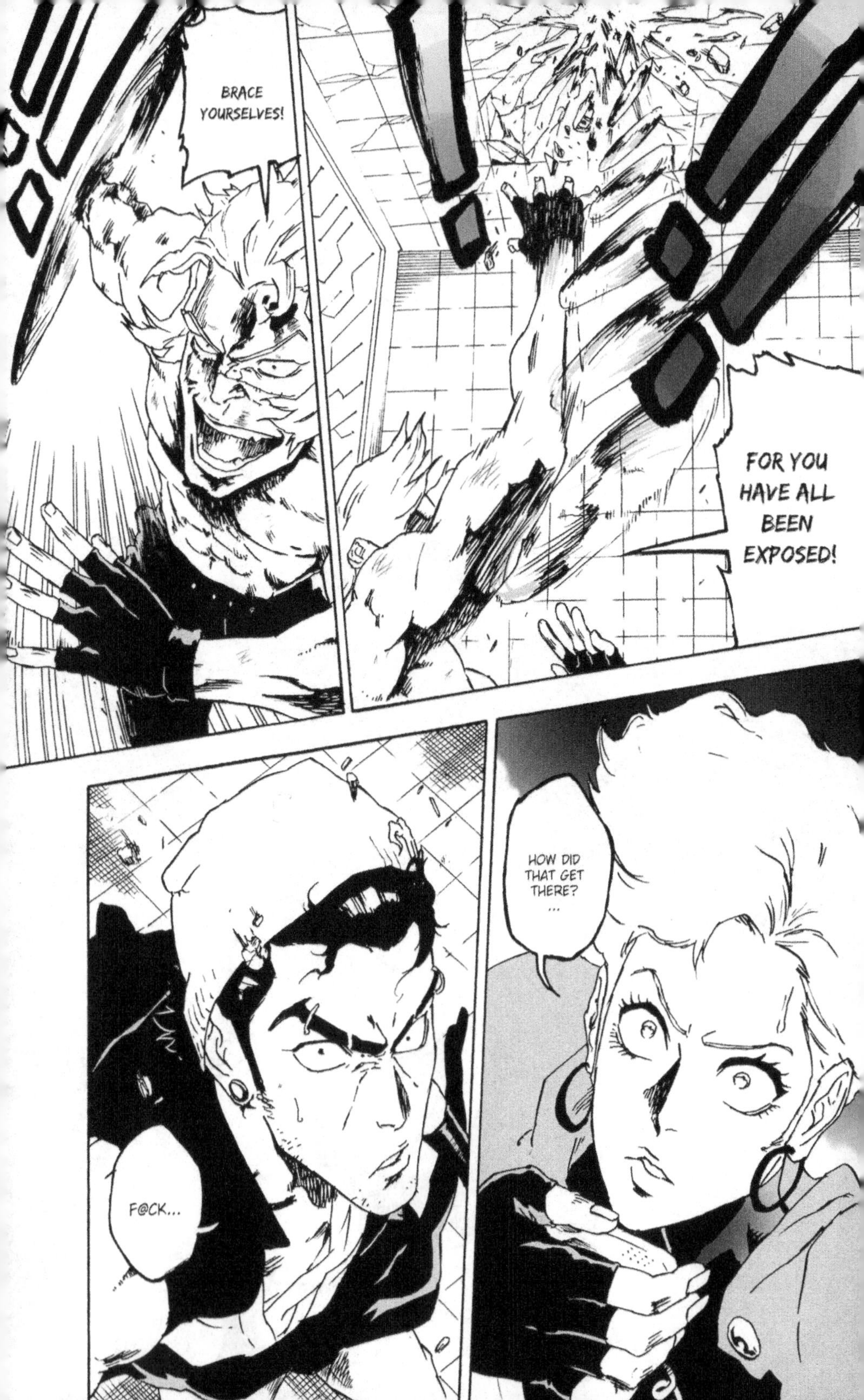
BRACE YOURSELVES!
FOR YOU HAVE ALL BEEN EXPOSED!
F@CK...
HOW DID THAT GET THERE? ...

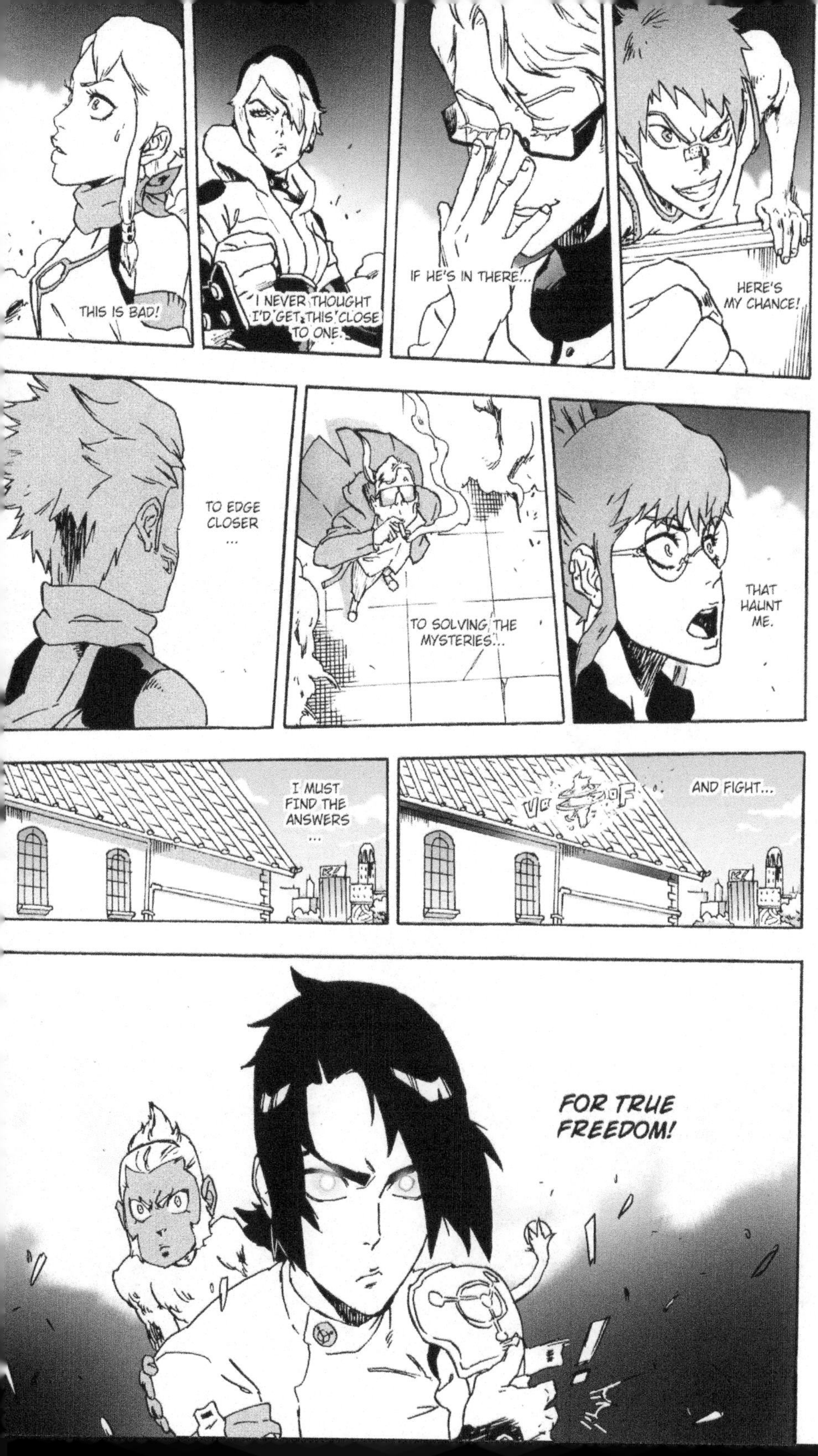
THIS IS BAD!
I NEVER THOUGHT I'D GET THIS CLOSE TO ONE.
IF HE'S IN THERE...
HERE'S MY CHANCE!
TO EDGE CLOSER ...
TO SOLVING THE MYSTERIES...
THAT HAUNT ME.
I MUST FIND THE ANSWERS ...
AND FIGHT...
FOR TRUE FREEDOM!

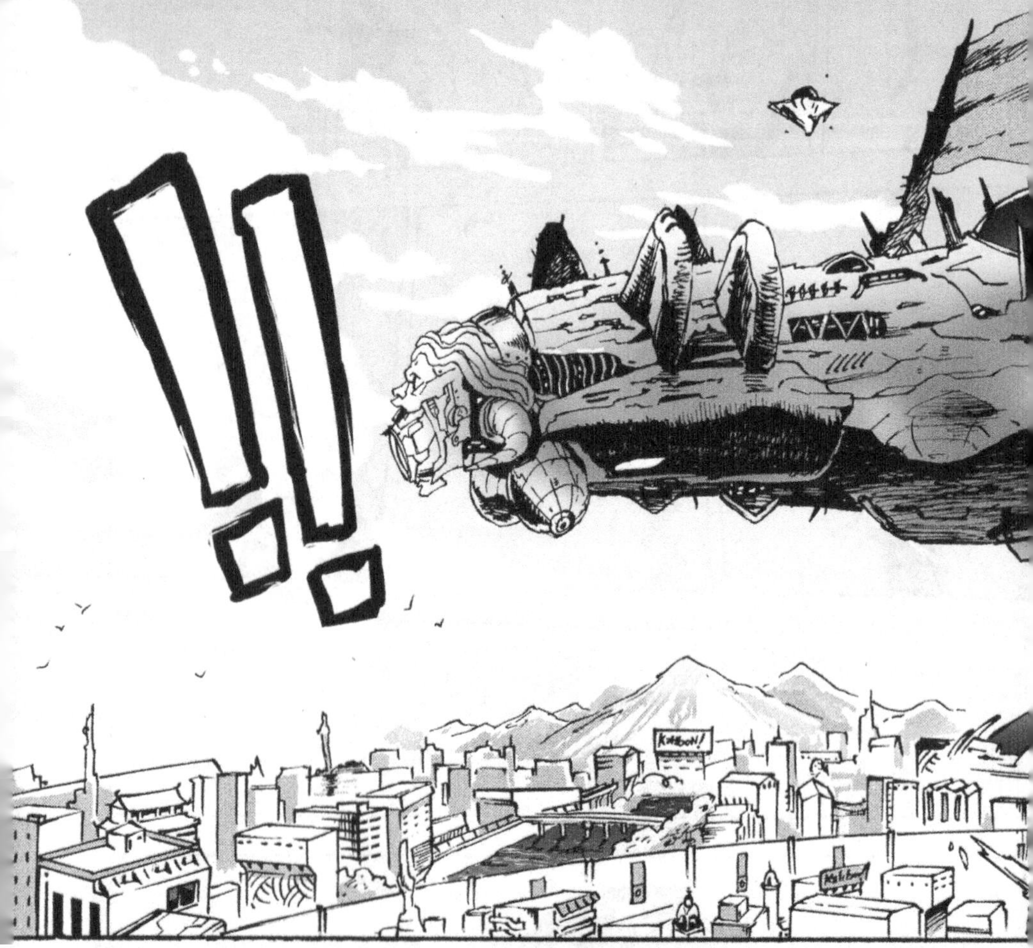
!!
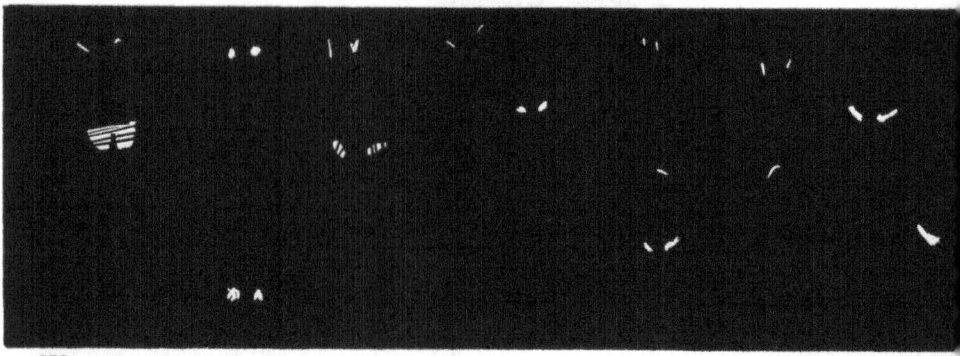

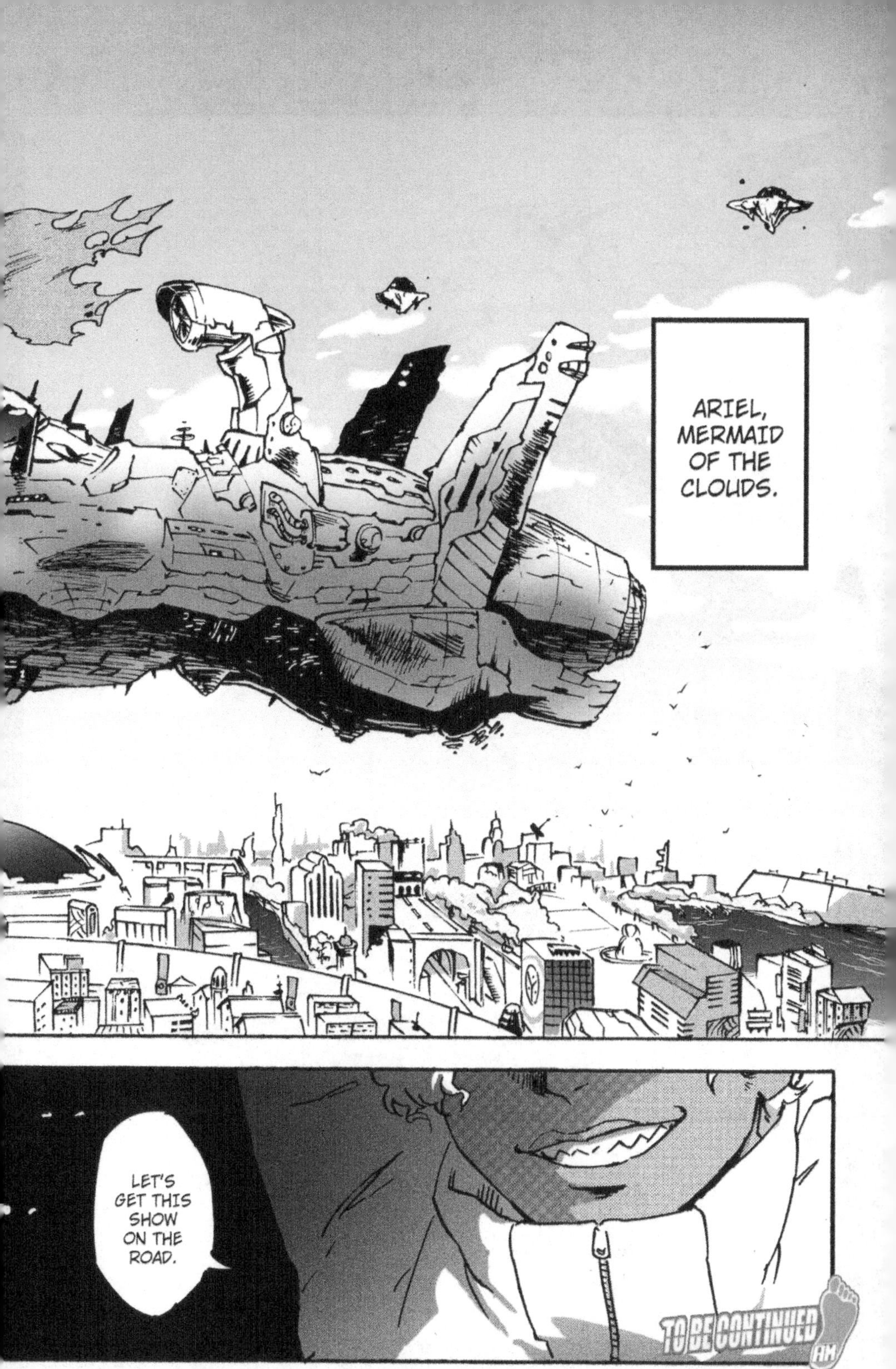
ARIEL, MERMAID OF THE CLOUDS.
LET'S GET THIS SHOW ON THE ROAD.
TO BE CONTINUED

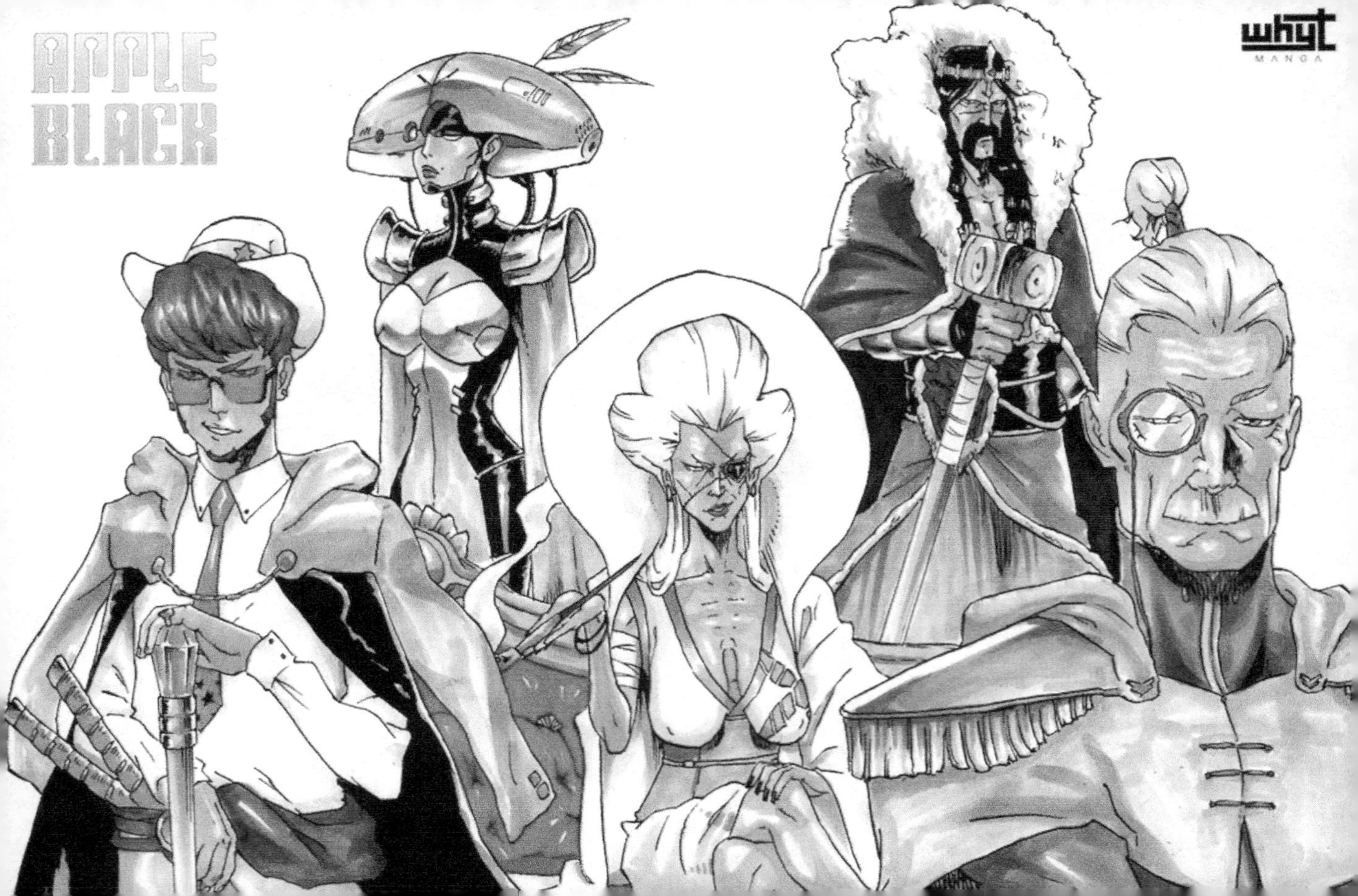
APPLE
BLACK
whyt
MANGA

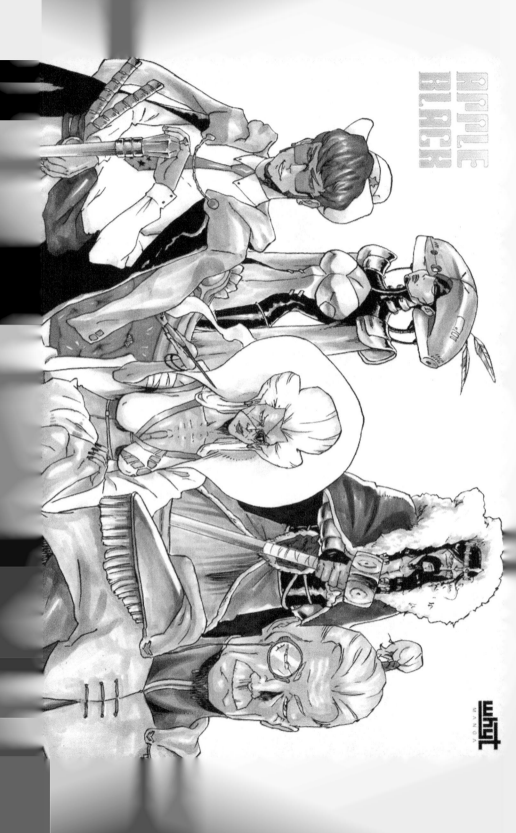

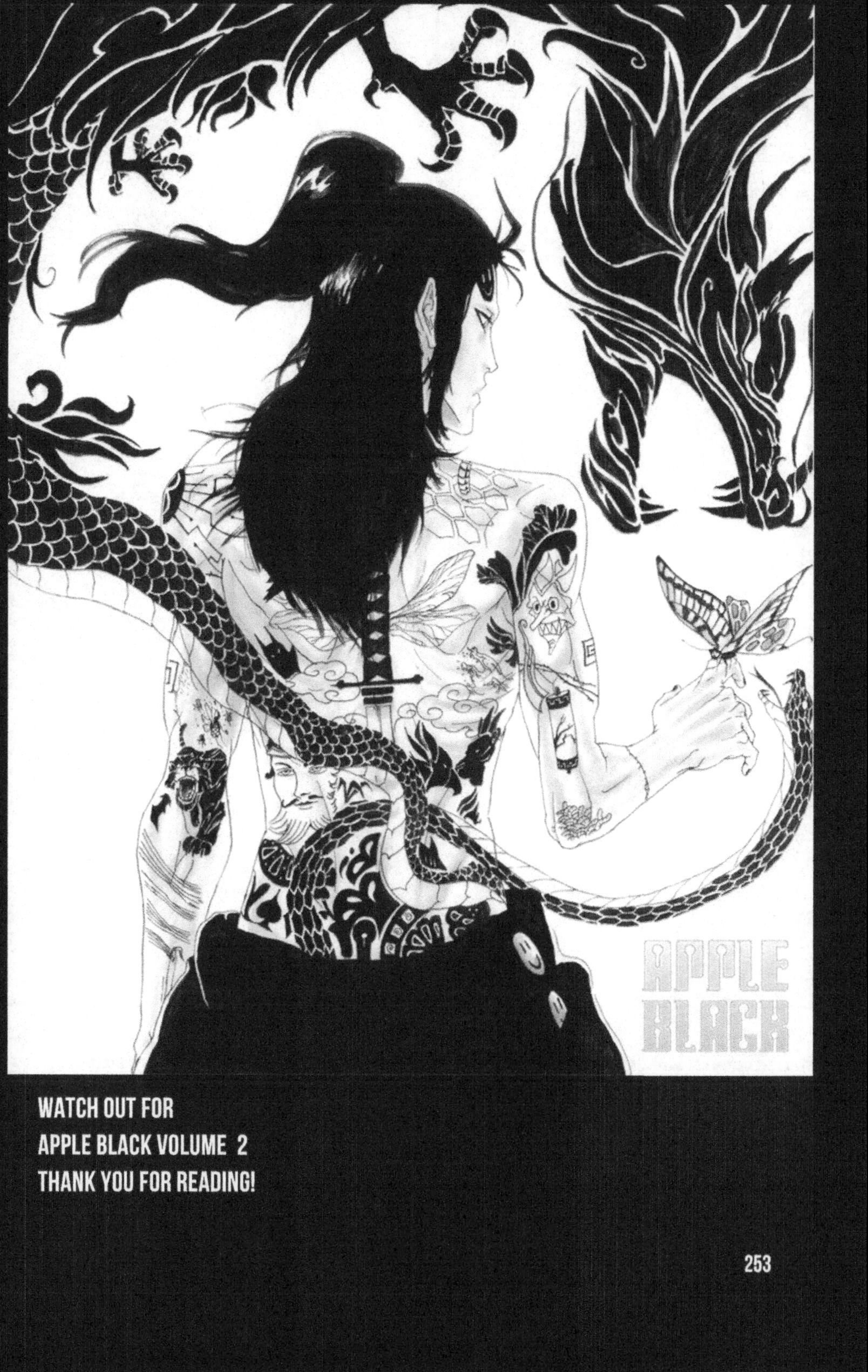
APPLE
BLACK

WATCH OUT FOR

APPLE BLACK VOLUME 2

THANK YOU FOR READING!

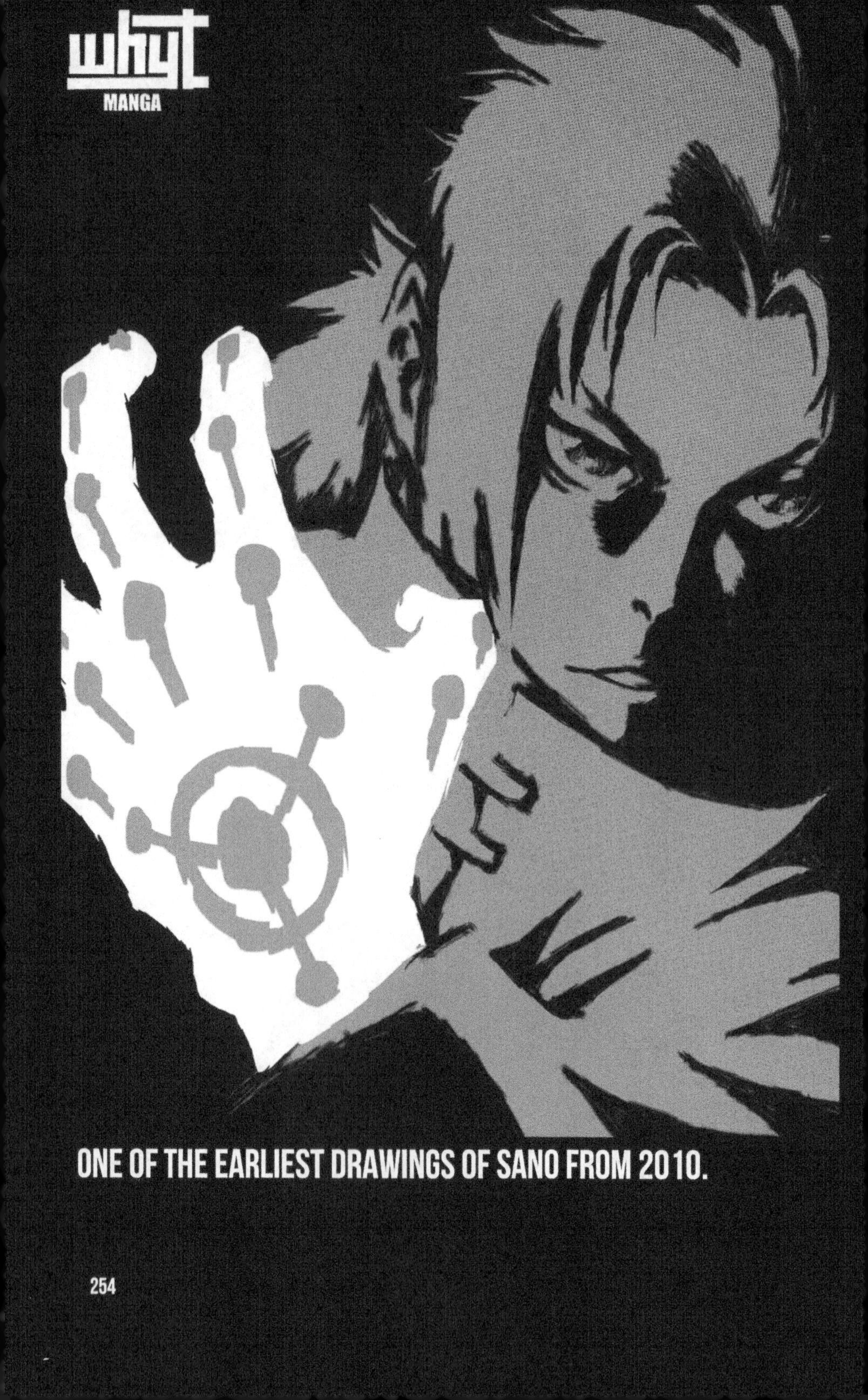

ONE OF THE EARLIEST DRAWINGS OF SANO FROM 2010.

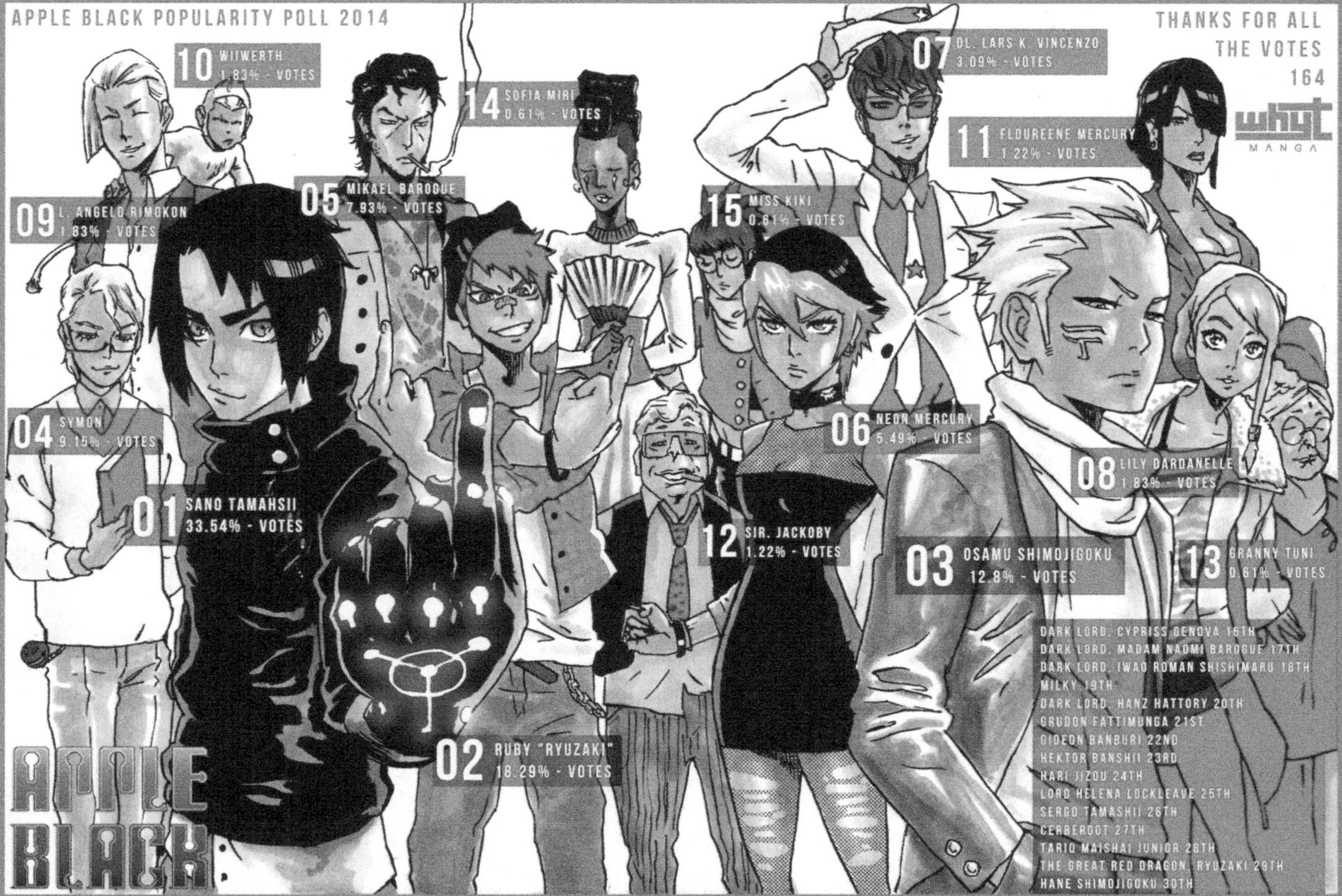
APPLE BLACK POPULARITY POLL 2014
THANKS FOR ALL THE VOTES 164
WHYT MANGA
10 WIIWERTH 1.83% - VOTES
14 SOFIA MIRI 0.61% - VOTES
07 DL. LARS K. VINCENZO 3.09% - VOTES
11 FLOUREENE MERCURY 1.22% - VOTES
05 MIKAEL BAROGUE 7.93% - VOTES
09 L. ANGELO RIMOKON 1.83% - VOTES
15 MISS KIKI 0.61% - VOTES
04 SYMON 9.15% - VOTES
06 NEON MERCURY 5.49% - VOTES
08 LILY DARDANELLE 1.83% - VOTES
01 SANO TAMAHSII 33.54% - VOTES
12 SIR. JACKOBY 1.22% - VOTES
03 OSAMU SHIMOJIGOKU 12.8% - VOTES
13 GRANNY TUNI 0.61% - VOTES
DARK LORD, CYPRISS GENOVA 16TH
DARK LORD, MADAM NAOMI BAROGUE 17TH
DARK LORD, IWAO ROMAN SHISHIMARU 18TH
MILKY 19TH
DARK LORD, HANZ HATTORY 20TH
GRUDON FATTIMUNGA 21ST
GIDEON BANBURI 22ND
HEKTOR BANSHII 23RD
HARI JIZOU 24TH
LORD HELENA LOCKLEAVE 25TH
SERGO TAMASHII 26TH
CERBEROOT 27TH
TARIQ MAISHAI JUNIOR 28TH
THE GREAT RED DRAGON, RYUZAKI 29TH
HANE SHIMOJIGOKU 30TH
02 RUBY "RYUZAKI" 18.29% - VOTES
APPLE BLACK

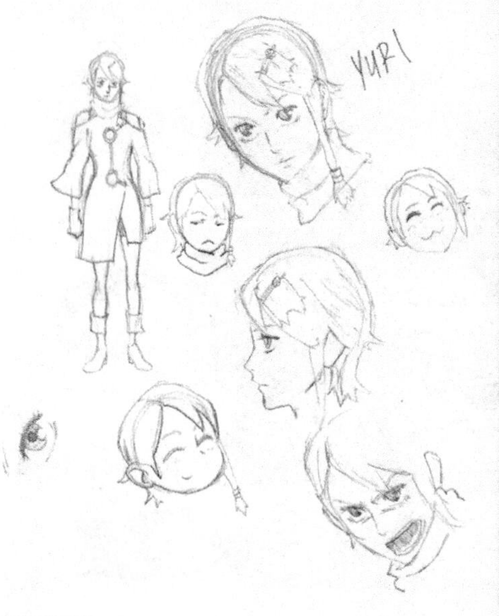
YURI

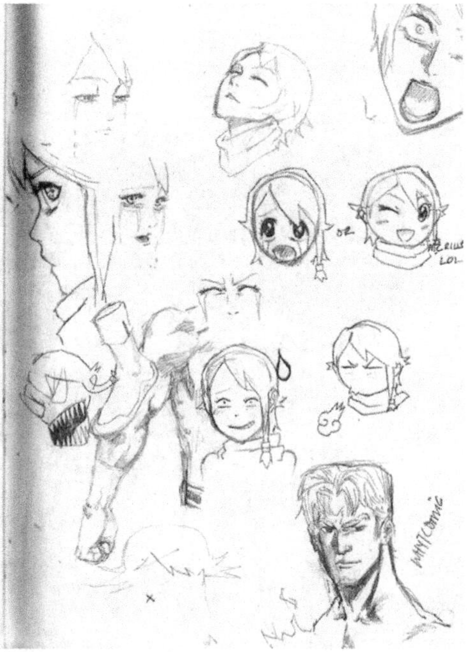
OR
LOL

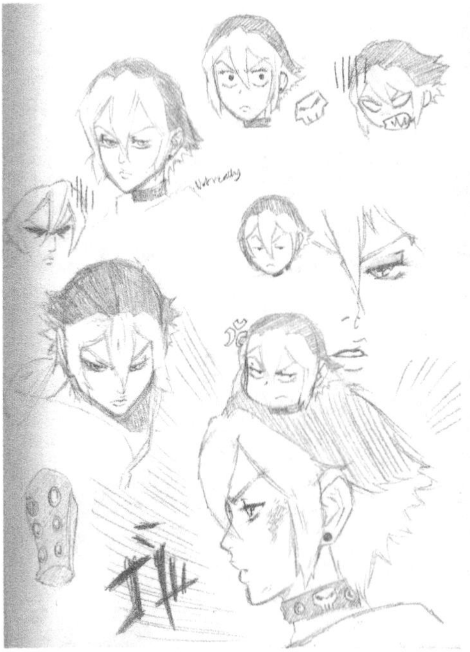
Not really

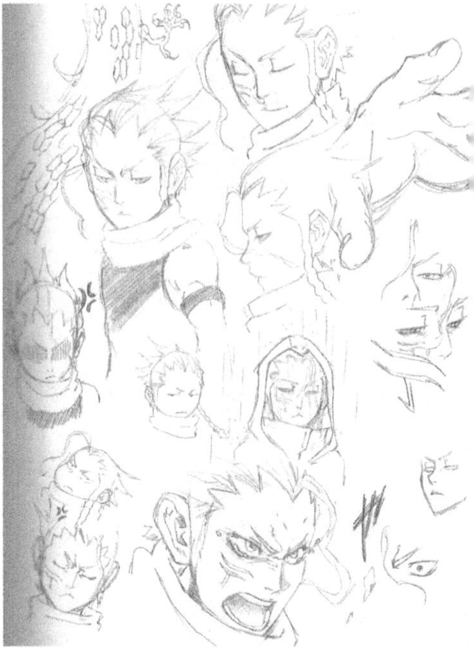

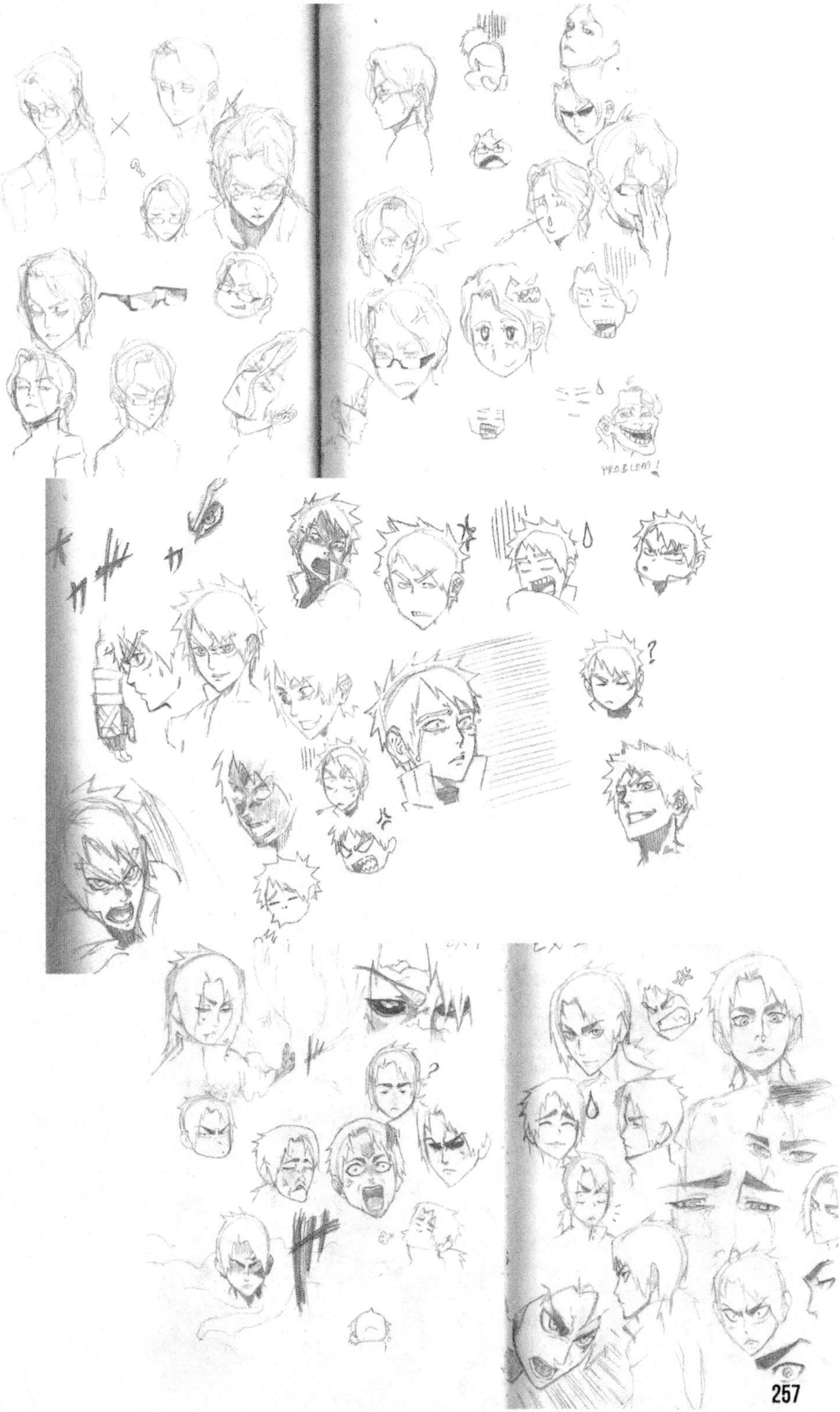
PROBLEM!

APPLE BLACK
whyt MANGA
www.youtube.com/WhytMangaTV
APPLE BLACK
SATURDAY

APPLE BLACK

APPLE BLACK VOL. 1
FREEDOM DAYS
GRAPHIC NOVEL

SATURDAY TANK EDITION.

STORY AND ART BY
ODUNZE OGUGUO

whyt MANGA

TOUCH UP ART & LETTERING | ODUNZE OGUGUO
DESIGN | WALLY NGUYEN & ODUNZE OGUGUO
PRODUCTION GUIDANCE | RAYMOND BROWN
PUBLISHER | FREDERICK L. JONES

Special Thanks to contributors, creators and fans who have supported APPLE BLACK and Saturday AM. Finally, a huge appreciation is due to those friends and family who have stood by the creators of MyFutprint Entertainment--this book is the first fruit of our hard-fought efforts and we will make you all proud!.

Printed in the U.S.A.

Published by MyFutprint Entertainment, LLC
P.O. Box 1454
Morrisville, NC 27560

9780692351376
First Printing, December 2014

MYFUTPRINT

SATURDAY AM TANKS

SATURDAY AM
www.saturday-am.com

NOTE: This Saturday Tank is perfect for TEENS and is recommended for ages 13 and up. This volume contains fantasy violence, realistic harm and mild swearing.

Made in the USA
Middletown, DE
10 November 2018